Main Currents in Caribbean Thought

The Historical Evolution of Caribbean Society in Its Ideological Aspects, 1492–1900

GORDON K. LEWIS

Introduction by Anthony P. Maingot

UNIVERSITY OF NEBRASKA PRESS
LINCOLN AND LONDON

First Nebraska paperback printing: 2004

Library of Congress Cataloging-in-Publication Data
Lewis, Gordon K.
Main currents in Caribbean thought: the historical evolution of Caribbean society in its
ideological aspects, 1492–1900 / Gordon K. Lewis; introduction by Anthony P.
Maingot.
    p.   cm.
Originally published: Baltimore: John Hopkins University Press, 1983. With new
introd.
Includes bibliographical references and index.
ISBN 0-8032-8029-7 (pbk.: alk. paper)
1. Caribbean Area—Civilization.   I. Title.
F2169.L48   2004
972.9—dc22   2004000618

Introduction

Anthony P. Maingot

Gordon K. Lewis was born in Wales, Great Britain, in 1919. What both the date and place of birth meant to Lewis's later intellectual career was succinctly put by the writer of the announcement of his receipt of a *doctor honoris causa* from the University of the West Indies in Trinidad in 1984: "[Lewis's] was the Wales of the industrial south, its hills bare and brooding, plundered by the ruthless wheels of industry. . . . Torn and ravaged by the General Strike of 1926, the economic crisis of 1929 and the Depression of the 1930s, South Wales left a lasting impression of deep social injustice wrought by the still unbridled capitalism of the day."

With degrees from University College, Balliol College, and Cardiff, Oxford, and Harvard universities, Lewis was a fully trained and published scholar by the time he arrived in Puerto Rico in 1951. He came as assistant to Harvard's Carl Friedrich, who had been contracted as a special consultant to the constitutional assembly of the island. By the time he passed away in Puerto Rico in 1991 Lewis had produced a truly impressive list of books on the Caribbean, many today considered classics. Not the least of these classics was his monumental work *Puerto Rico: Freedom and Power in the Caribbean*, which appeared in 1963. A story that says as much about the scholarship and policy relevance of that book as it does about the democratic spirit of one of the main targets of the book—then-governor of Puerto Rico Luis Muñoz Marín—is that the governor ordered his entire cabinet to read and discuss it. With Jamaica and Trinidad and Tobago having just moved to full independence with leaders like Norman Manley and Eric Williams, both of whom were great admirers of Governor Muñoz and his political party, Lewis's book captured a Caribbean-wide audience because it had pan-Caribbean relevance. By 1983, when his *Main Currents in Caribbean Thought* appeared, Lewis's stature and reputation as an insightful and penetrating—and invariably acerbic—political analyst had no peer in Caribbean studies.

In the present volume Lewis delivers what he had often promised in previous works: an interpretation of the Caribbean as a whole, from European discovery to the present. He brings the story to 1900, clearly intimating in it a second volume (which was written but has yet to be published).

Aside from the broad sweep of intellectual history and penetrating philosophical points of analysis this book contains, the reader will also find reiterated here all the methodological strictures about doing Caribbean studies laid down by Lewis as early as the 1960s. First and foremost was Lewis's insistence that the region could be fully understood only when studied in its entirety. He was an adamant critic of both the "sterile" (his word), survey-based scholarship of the American positivist school and the "parochialism" and "insularity" (again, his own words) of studies limited to one linguistic part of the region. "No one," Lewis wrote, "could really claim to be a full practitioner in Caribbean Studies until he came to write ultimately, on the Caribbean as a whole." Keep in mind that this meant dealing with "fifty or more" island societies. To Lewis, only celebrated Jamaican historian Elsa Goveia had come close to meeting that high standard and even she had limited herself to the historiography of the British West Indies. Additionally, Goveia had dealt with the history of ideas. Lewis is dealing much more extensively with ideology, defined as "the total complex of ideas, sentiments, outlooks, attitudes, and values" of a given society. This ideology, let it be understood, was traced as a seamless thread over four hundred years. Following logically from this was his insistence that Caribbean studies had to be broadly comparative and profoundly historical.

Lewis's study hews remarkably close to these strictures and as a result reveals Lewis at the height of his scholarly and intellectual creativity. It is impossible not to be impressed with the erudition, the passion, and the style displayed here, which together make this the study Lewis had so long promised. Indeed, his major ideological and intellectual thrusts had already been evident in two books that preceded this one: *The Virgin Islands: A Caribbean Lilliput* (1972) and *Notes on the Puerto Rican Revolution* (1974). To be more precise, the subtitle of the Puerto Rico book—*An Essay on American Dominance and Caribbean Resistance*—give us an inkling of how Lewis's own political positions were evolving. It is patently clear that by 1983 Lewis was in full, even radical, ideological evolution. Between 1975, when he began writing *Main Currents*, and 1983, when the manuscript was finished and published, Lewis had transited from firmly adhering to his original Fabianism or Christian Socialism to a more radical, more strictly Marxist position. It should be said that Lewis had always argued, and argues here, that no such thing as value-free scholarship exists, that ideas and political positions are an integral part of the research enterprise, and that the validity of ideas and positions can be established by the rigor of the scholarship. Here, however, his political rhetoric is clearly ratcheted up quite a few notches. While Lewis's widely recognized confrontational and acerbic style remained the same, his new ideological edge made his style appear even more so. He had come to believe that only a Marxist revolution *á la* Cuba could change the domination by what he termed the "obstinate aristocracies" of the region as well as U.S. "imperial" domination. Thus in a very crucial way this book was Lewis's call on the intellectuals of the region to leave their ivory towers, to engage, and to contribute to the birth of a different—a more just and egalitarian—Caribbean. Breaking through the historical materialist orthodoxy showed Lewis the voluntarist romantic and utopian.

How close, then, does Lewis come to meeting an intellectual, scholarly, and ideological bar that is set so high? The unvarnished answer can be contained in one word: magnificently! In 329 pages Lewis carries the story—and that is what it is—of four centuries of Spanish, British, Dutch, French, and Danish political, religious, and ideological imposition, and the response to them by the region's residents. In order to understand the origins of the cultural and linguistic balkanization of the region, the answers are here. If curious about the variety of approaches to race and race mixing, Lewis will enlighten and educate. On the other hand, if reared on the multiple legends, myths, and lyrically adulatory biographies of figures such as the Puerto Rican Betances, the Dominican Luperón, or the Cuban Jose Martí, you will quite surely be jolted by Lewis's opinions. And that jolting is his explicit intellectual and political purpose, not just a turn of phrase. As he put it elsewhere much earlier on, "the scholar has the obligation to be hospitable to all ideas, to congratulate his adversary on his convictions even while trying to detach him from them."

Quite evidently, any introduction to a book such as this can hope to do no less. It is impossible to fail to pick up the gauntlet or to shy from the thrust and parry of the intellectual debate Lewis relished and called for throughout his life. Political correctness was a posture for which he had nothing but disdain. A debate, then, is the challenge that needs to be taken up.

FUNDAMENTAL IDEAS

The terms of the debate are set from the very beginning with the outlining of his two fundamental theses about Caribbean history. First is the intrinsic and recurring violence at all levels of Caribbean society. The region's "seminal moments," he tells us, "have been moments of violent upheaval, of widespread social and cultural shock." And, as he does throughout the text, he extrapolates and projects to the contemporary Caribbean milieu. Thus the modern Caribbean "still carries the imprint of that heritage." Lewis's second thesis is certainly no less controversial: contributing fundamentally to that foundation of violence is the fact that the dominant economic system introduced by the Europeans was capitalism. Nothing benign can be found in Lewis's use of the word; he consistently uses it as synonymous with exploitation. "Like capitalism everywhere," he says, "Caribbean sugar capitalism was no respecter of persons." Within the parameters set by both violence and exploitative capitalism, racial and cultural intermingling—themselves the result of exploitation—evolved into what he calls the "creole nature" of Caribbean society. It was, he tells us repeatedly throughout the text, a "philistine, brutalized society."

The process of creolization started with the contact between the Spaniards and the Indo-Antillean peoples, the Siboney, Taino-Arawak, and Carib. The love these natives held for their island homes, says Lewis, was the true genesis of Caribbean nationalism, a clash between the myths and folklore of the natives (an implicit form of ideology) with the explicitly materialistic Spanish ideology of the cross, the sword, and greed. The cross only rarely produced a humanist, yet such was the person of Fray Bartolome de Las Casas, who to Lewis was the first

Caribbean historian and bibliographer. Las Casas originally harmonized the doctrine of Old World Christian liberty with New World rational thought. While Lewis does not reveal anything new about the history of Las Casas (not furthering Lewis Hanke's scholarship, for instance), it is his interpretation that intrigues. Las Casas's ideas, Lewis says, "anticipated the concept of a Commonwealth of Nations as it was instituted, centuries later, in the British colonial empire." As is his wont, Lewis makes enormous analogical stretches, sometimes across several centuries. Are they always plausible? Perhaps not. Yet they are invariably entertaining and thought provoking. To Lewis, Las Casas's contribution was seminal; by arguing right against might Las Casas set the parameters for the great "Caribbean debate." Again, Lewis reaches across the centuries to identify a nineteenth-century figure, the Puerto Rican Luis Muñoz Rivera, as continuing in that tradition.

Despite its controversial interpretations, the story of great historical figures such as Las Casas and many others proceeds smoothly until chapter 3, where Lewis goes from merely lamenting capitalism to theorizing about it in orthodox Marxian terms. "Ideas," he says, "realize themselves in the form of social institutions only when forms of production make it possible." The "planter ideology" that he had described with vivid details becomes nothing more than "the ideological superstructure" of slavery as a mode of production. Thus, in the final analysis it was never a debate between people with a "proslavery" ideology and those with an "antislavery" or abolitionist ideology, but rather a debate between one economic system and the other. This interpretation certainly merits a response since it contains several sticky theoretical issues.

If ideology can never rise above the parameters set by material conditions or modes of production, as classical Marxist theory states, why then does Lewis repeatedly celebrate certain figures who, on Lewis's own telling, clearly not only rose above and against the existing system but indeed also against their own social class? There are the Labats and DuTetres with their "astonishing achievements"; there is the Martinican abolitionist Victor Schoelcher, who is so brilliantly, even heroically, portrayed in the text. Equally brilliant is Lewis's description of the English-born but long-term Jamaica resident Edward Long. Lewis describes Long as a "self-conscious Jamaican" who advanced a Whig conception of liberty "in the best Lockean manner."

In fact, how to interpret what Lewis himself, albeit only occasionally, describes as the early development of the charming "picaroon" nature of Caribbean creole society, its *joie de vivre* and the "famous *magie antillaise*" shared apparently by all social classes? Are social styles and aesthetics totally divorced from a material base? How could such philistine and brutalized societies produce such charming personal traits and this vibrant social milieu?

Additionally, and similarly counterintuitive, are the role, propriety, and relevance of moral condemnation in historical materialist ontologies. One may recall Marx asking, in *The Jewish Question*, why anyone who understood the laws of history would bother condemning religion. Was not religion a mere superstructural phenomenon already condemned by history? Lewis repeatedly departs from contextual analysis to mete out some severe rhetorical blows on individuals and groups, indeed on whole island societies, regardless of reigning economic system. "If the Mediterranean was the cradle of European civilization," he tells us, "the Caribbean was in very truth its graveyard." There is only occasionally some amelioration of the harsh, condemnatory tone that runs throughout the story. But why, if (theoretically at least) the system allowed no moral options and men only *thought* they were making history? Why, for instance, belabor the Haitians Ardouin and Madiou for seeing their national reality through the eyes of Lamartine and Hugo rather than of Marx? Why regard Martí's justly celebrated ideological eclecticism as a "fatal imprecision" that ignored the "historically inevitable" clash of Cuban classes rooted in existing property relations? Ah, because even though Lewis is loathe to admit it, in his heart of hearts he does believe that moral options exist, and this is why he describes the proslavery-antislavery confrontation as "a mortal cultural struggle." His erstwhile Fabian and Methodist origins occasionally betray his more recent Marxism, as can be seen in his admission that, "The important truth to emphasize, surely is the nature of Christianity as a general civilizing idea. 'A general idea,' Whitehead has written, 'is always a danger to the existing order.' "

Nowhere is Lewis's theoretical conundrum more evident than in his patently clear and evident admiration throughout the book for Edmund Burke. Surely no one needs to be reminded that Marx, and Marxists generally, felt nothing but contempt for Burke. Indeed, in *Capital* Marx slurs Burke as that "celebrated sophist and sycophant" in the pay of the English oligarchy and the American colonial elite. Burke was, said Marx, nothing more than "an out-and-out vulgar bourgeois." Well, Lewis dissents and dissents often. "Burke," he tells us early on, "clearly was the first English statesman to comprehend the moral import of the problem of subject races . . . his doctrine of trusteeship became the operative ideal of the best of the English colonial administrative class . . . and the leading idea in all of the reforming West Indian forces." Burke's idea of trusteeship and the universal Christian ideal of liberty were two of Lewis's most cherished concepts. Not far behind, however, was another tenet of Whig democratic thinking and practice that persists in Lewis's writing and occasionally but critically creeps through: the Lockean principle of contractualism, that is, the contract or common sanction that binds government and citizen together. Quite evidently ignoring Marx's dismissal of Locke as "the advocate of the bourgeoisie against the working class," Lewis expresses great admiration for those men who acted in Lockean terms. And he does mention a few. Alas, when Lewis moves from biography to broad sweeps of social and political philosophy he appears to forget the role of ideas, of men and women making history, even of Edmund Burke and John Locke.

HARSH CONCLUSIONS

There is no softening of the tone as Lewis concludes this work, and the theme of "cultural philistinism" returns with a vengeance. By the end of the nineteenth century, Lewis writes that the Caribbean islands were still "the slums of empire." The old colonial mentality still persisted, as did an even more pervasive sense of cultural inferiority and dependence. Few islands come in for more vitriolic condemnation than those that are still not independent. Again, one feels a need to respond to this obvious challenge. If one is to follow both the Burkean idea of trusteeship and the Lockean natural rights doctrine of government by the consent of the people, why should we consider as perverse, as he does, the situation of Puerto Rico and the French West Indies? Don't the people of these islands repeatedly have the opportunity to freely decide their futures? To Lewis, political independence and national sovereignty respond to something akin to a natural law. Throughout the book Lewis pays the highest compliments to those leaders whose actions sought "to hold intact the national patrimony," such as the Haitian Jean Jacques Dessalines or the Dominican Luperón. Similarly, the most celebrated Cuban leaders were those whose nationalism was geared toward the island's absolute independence and sovereignty. The emphasis on national state sovereignty, separate from the wishes of the people, is neither Burkean nor Lockean. And it can be considered classical Marxism only if one believes that the millions of people in Puerto Rico, Martinique, Curacao, and so forth, are all suffering from some form of political false consciousness (hardly a tenable thesis post-perestroika or glasnost). Equally untenable, if not more so, is the thesis that in what he calls "the more radical" post-1959 Cuban literature will the Caribbean find true "psychological decolonization." Of course, Lewis finished writing in 1983 before the collapse of the Soviet system and the end of the extraordinarily generous subsidies provided to Cuba. One can only wonder how the second volume deals with those phenomenal changes.

    It is a truism of literary criticism that any narrative driven under the impetus of contemporary controversies will invite equally heated dissenting opinions. The great intellectual contribution of Gordon Lewis's scholarship, so evident in this book, is that he welcomed, indeed invited, dissent. Beyond the dazzling breadth of his knowledge of the Greater Caribbean and his scintillating style a fire burned in Lewis's belly, a fire born of the moral indignation of one who is never jaded or cynical. Paradoxically, Lewis's own moral and ideological proclivities are the truest testament to the continued import of ideas, and of men and women of ideas, leading to social change.

with love and devotion for
Sybil
and our children
Jonathan
Kathryn
Diana
David
Jacqueline

Contents

	Preface	*xv*
1.	The Sociohistorical Setting	1
2.	The Sixteenth and Seventeenth Centuries: The Beginnings of Caribbean Thought	29
3.	The Eighteenth and Nineteenth Centuries: The Proslavery Ideology	94
4.	The Eighteenth and Nineteenth Centuries: The Antislavery Ideology	171
5.	The Growth of Nationalist Thought to 1900	239
6.	Conclusion	321
	Notes	331
	Index	365

Preface

In a sense this book has been a generation in the making; for when I first began to teach at the University of Puerto Rico in the 1950s I realized that, as a European, I had entered into an experience entirely different in character from anything I had encountered earlier, either as a student in Britain or as a teacher in various universities of the United States. I undertook my apprenticeship in Caribbean studies by writing, variously, on Puerto Rico, the Virgin Islands, and the British West Indies. But I saw, from the start, that no one could really claim to be a full practitioner in Caribbean studies until he came to write, ultimately, on the Caribbean as a whole. This book, I venture to hope, is the fulfillment of that imperative.

The book seeks to fill a gap in Caribbean studies in a very special sense. For all of the academic disciplines that have contributed to writing on the region have, by their nature, been concerned only in a marginal sense with ideas or idea systems. They have not addressed themselves, as a primary concern, to the ideologies that have shaped the evolution of Caribbean society. The book, then, is not meant to be a history of the region nor, indeed, a study of its leading institutions, but rather a descriptive and critical analysis of the total complex of ideas, sentiments, outlooks, attitudes, and values that, in the fullest sense of the word, constitute the ideology of the groups that have figured in the Caribbean story. In this sense, the book attempts to do for the region as a whole what the late Elsa Goveia did for the English-speaking segment of the region in her pioneering volume of 1956, *A Study on the Historiography of the British West Indies*. Furthermore, to the degree that this book draws upon resources in Caribbean languages other than English, it attempts to surmount the linguistic fragmentation that has characterized Caribbean scholarship as well as Caribbean history.

The Caribbean, of course, like any other society, means individual Caribbean persons. It would be impossible for me to mention all of them who, throughout my residency of some twenty-five years, have helped me so much to understand their history and their society. I trust that they will all accept my thanks. Likewise, the book owes much to the accumulated scholarship of other writers on the region. For the Caribbean, composed as it is of some fifty or more separate and different island societies, is of such a variety and complexity that no one single scholar can hope by himself or herself to encompass it all. My collective debt to them, I hope, is apparent both in references throughout the text and in the notes.

As always, I am indebted to the University of Puerto Rico for help, mainly in the form of reduced teaching loads and sundry secretarial services; successive deans of the College of Social Sciences and successive directors of the Institute of Caribbean Studies have been particularly helpful. Dr. Vernon Esteves, Dean of Studies, helped in the financing of the typing of the manuscript, a task which was splendidly performed by Asunción Pérez de Fuentes. I further express my thanks to Vera Rubin of the Research Institute for the Study of Man for an initial financial grant which made it possible for me to begin the actual composition of the book in 1975; also to the National Endowment for the Humanities for a very modest travel grant at the same time. I am also grateful to Richard Price for his continuing encouragement, and to Mr. J. G. Goellner of The Johns Hopkins University Press for his understanding and patience.

But it would be dreadfully remiss of me if I failed, finally, to mention three particular friends who have helped in very special ways to bring this book to fruition. First, I thank Richard Morse for his early reading of the manuscript, which, typically, was at once generously enthusiastic and properly critical, so that any deficiencies in the book as it now appears are certainly mine and not his. Second, I am grateful to Dr. Jorge Montilla Negrón for his professional skill, personal understanding, and guidance, at once gentle but firm, as he took care of a somewhat serious illness in my family, which, more than any other single factor, has delayed the publication of the book. Third, I am likewise grateful to Dr. Fernando Monserrate, an early friend of my wife when she first came to Puerto Rico, and who throughout the same family crisis has been a friend and counselor to us. Both of them have helped to guide us through our ordeal. Every family in distress must pray for the presence of such physicians.

I add as a final comment that the dedication of this book means far more than its words convey. There are love and devotion, and gratitude for those gifts, too intimate even to search for proper expression.

Chapter One

The Sociohistorical
Setting

From the very beginnings of its history in the late fifteenth century there has been vexatious confusion concerning the definition, both geographical and cultural, of the Caribbean region. The confusion started early, with the mistaken belief of Columbus that he had landed, in his first historic voyage of 1492, on the island outskirts of the legendary Cathay. The delusion was perpetuated in the wondrous tales, *voyages imaginaires*, and travelers' reports of the sixteenth century. Columbus himself died believing in the myth. It is true that very early the European cartographers more or less adequately drew the contours of the islands, as the maps by Juan de la Cosa and Baldessare Castiglione show. But the maps still assumed the Columbian misconception. It was only the discovery of the Pacific that finally convinced men that the vast expanses of a new ocean separated the newly discovered lands from the Indies proper; and even then the old legend was replaced with the new legend of a North West passage to the Orient.

Furthermore, even when the geographical puzzle had been solved, a new cultural puzzle continued, in the sense that the peoples and cultures of the Caribbean archipelago were indiscriminately mixed up with the romantic idea of the New World of the Americas as a whole. Thus, for the period that it lasted, the European literature of the extraordinary voyage—of which the most famous example was Defoe's *Robinson Crusoe*, set by repute in the southern Caribbean island of Tobago—portrayed the Caribbean in fabulous terms of Carib cannibals, El Dorado golden cities, heroic pirates, and the rest. The distortions wrought by that tradition of legend, moreover, did not altogether die in the eighteenth century, for they have been reproduced in our own day in a new advertising literature for tourists that portrays the Caribbean as a tourist paradise, a set of islands in the sun full of sun, sand, and sex.

The confusion about Caribbean identity—what it is and what it ought to be—can again be seen in a somewhat more sophisticated manner in the scholarly literature on the region. Conventional-minded writers from the imperial centers have seen the region as a backward area requiring guidance from outside to modernize it, which really means to westernize it—which in turn means to shape it into yet another capitalist-industrial society beholden to the foreign investor; Sir Harold Mitchell's *Caribbean Patterns* is a representative example of the genre.[1] By contrast, a whole school of black nationalist writers, following Herskovits, have seen the region as part of the African Diaspora, thus tending to overlook its European, Asian, and Arab ethnic components.[2] The revived debate in our own day on the place of slavery in Western civilization, to take another example, has been tempted to see the area as merely a part of the vast middle district of the Americas, *America Meridionalis*, stretching from the southern United States to northeastern Brazil, which became the locale of the slave-based plantation system. But that particular interpretation, in its own turn, is questionable, since it overlooks the fact that the hard core of the slavery and plantation systems was the Antillean sugar island like Jamaica and Saint Domingue while, by contrast, the late-blooming cotton plantations of the southern United States were at best a pale reflection of the systems in their most perfected form. The argument also overlooks the fact that the historical evolution of both early colonial Brazil and the antebellum American South was away from the Caribbean heartland, the one moving into the South American general system, the other moving forward to its ultimate assimilation into the North American industrial system. It was the Caribbean that remained behind in terms of "progress," to become the most completely colonized region of the entire hemisphere. So, notwithstanding the curious fact that the most famous of all novels on American slavery, Mrs. Stowe's crude and sanctimonious *Uncle Tom's Cabin*, dealt with slavery in the American South, and notwithstanding, too—although on a different level—the fact that when Marx himself came to write on slavery he concentrated on cotton slavery rather than sugar slavery, it still remains the truth that it was in the Caribbean "sugar islands" that the agrosocial system of slavery developed into its fullest and most harsh form.

CARIBBEAN CHARACTERISTICS

Against these various myths and misconceptions, the truth is, rather, that both in geographical and sociocultural terms the Caribbean has possessed and still possesses its own distinctive and idiosyncratic characteristics. Geographically, it is to be understood as a set of tropical island societies situated within the archipelago that curves from the Greater Antilles and the Bahamas in the north to Trinidad and the Dutch Leeward Islands off the Venezuelan coast in the south, along with the continental coastal strip of the Guianas, which have always been islands in everything except the strictly physical sense. Culturally, the region possesses its own social forms, ethnic formations, political institutions, and normative values—all of a marked singularity and distinguishing it from the neighboring mainland societies. All of its member societies, notwithstanding their own special individuality—the obvious fact, for example, that the English left their mark on Barbados, the French on Martinique, the Dutch on Surinam, the Spanish on Cuba, the Danes on the Virgin Islands—have been shaped throughout by the same architectonic forces of conquest, colonization, slavery, sugar monoculture, colonialism, and racial and ethnic admixture. All of their characteristic problems, lasting into the period of the present day—poverty, persistent unemployment, underdevelopment, economic dependency, social rivalries and ethnic animosities, weak personal and social identity, political fragmentation, and the rest—have their roots in that very background.

The history of the region has already been covered by an extensive literature, written, of course, from different ideological viewpoints by, variously, the early planter historians, the school of metropolitan scholars, the local nationalist historians, and, more recently, the more radically oriented Black Power and Marxist groups. The literature is immense, covering a historical time span of nearly five centuries. Its contributors obviously cannot be placed into a single category. For if, in the beginning, there is the Dominican bishop-historian Las Casas, composing his vast *Historia de las Indias* in the convent cells of both the Old World and the New as at once a massive indictment of Spanish cruelty and an early religio-anthropological defense of the aboriginal Indian cultures, at the end there is the nationalist scholar-politician Eric Williams putting together in his *History of the People of Trinidad and Tobago* a textbook for his people at the same moment that he takes his place as first Prime Minister of the newly independent nation. In between, there is a veritable host of writers and authors from every nation involved in the Caribbean colonial adventure, as well as the slowly developing Creole schools of the local intelligentsia. All of them, for all of their differences of view, have shown clearly that despite the contrasts between one island-society and another—and despite the different identifying names that the region has acquired throughout its momentous history (the Spanish Main, the West Indies, the Antilles, the Caribbean)—the area is characterized by a distinctive communalty of leading features that justify the concept of a collective sociocultural character, setting it apart from its neighbors.[3]

The first of those features, and that from which everything else flows, is the fact that the European colonial powers created Caribbean colonies *de novo*, practically virgin territories—once, of course, the original Taino-Arawak-Carib Indian stocks had been reduced by exploitative practices—peopled by means of the slave trade and, after slavery abolition, by means of various indenture schemes, by uprooted and decultured immigrant groups.

That is to say, every person in the Caribbean cast of dramatis personae has been a newcomer: the colonizer, the African slave, the sugar planter, the merchant, the overseer, the Asiatic estate worker, the colonial official. They came to be members of overseas communities that were culturally naked, devoid of inherited tradition and accumulated custom; or rather, to be more exact, communities that were seen to be naked through the prejudiced vision of the newcomers, cavalierly overlooking the existence, before they arrived, of the pre-Columbian tradition and custom. The New World thus became, as it were, a *tabula rasa* on which the European colonizers, as the new master class, put their imprint as they wished. The Spanish conquistadores, the first of such groups, used the islands mainly as stepping-stones to conquest and settlement in what were to become the mainland viceroyalties, with the result that it was more likely to be in Peru and Mexico, rather than in Cuba and Puerto Rico, that they left behind them settled families and properties as the basis, later on, for the growth of a new and indigenous Creole nobility. The English, French, and Dutch, coming after them, also came as birds of passage, seeking quick profits in the lucrative slave trade and slavery systems, but also leaving their cultural imprint behind them. Then after 1898, the Americans, seeking new raw material resources and new markets for their capitalist industrial expansionism, imposed the twin vices of Manifest Destiny and Dollar Diplomacy on their newly acquired Caribbean possessions, and also brought with them their own brand of racial prejudice and discrimination.

All of the Caribbean societies, then, were not so much colonies in the ancient sense as truly modern colonies. Sidney Mintz has aptly summarized their character in a perceptive essay:

> The Caribbean colonies were not European imperial possessions erected upon massive indigenous bases in areas of declining great literate civilizations, as was true in India and Indonesia; they were not mere ports of trade, like Macao or Shanghai, where ancestral cultural hinterlands could remain surprisingly unaffected in spite of the exercise of considerable European power; they were not "tribal" mosaics, within which European colonizers carried on their exploitation accompanied by some curious vision of the "civilizing" function, as in the Congo, or New Guinea; nor were they areas of intense European settlement, when new forms of European culture provided an acculturation "anchor" for other newcomers, as in the United States or Australia. They were, in fact, the oldest "industrial" colonies of the West outside Europe, manned almost entirely with introduced populations, and fitted to European needs with peculiar intensity and permissiveness.[4]

They were, in brief (and among other things) frontier societies, so it is surprising that in all of the scholarship written on the area, only one author, the Dutch Caribbeanist R.A.J. van Lier, in his 1949 book on Dutch Surinam, *Frontier Society: A Social Analysis of the History of Surinam*, has utilized the famous Frederick Jackson Turner thesis on the American West to illuminate this important aspect of Caribbean development.[5] The analogy, indeed, is appropriate, although van Lier did not pursue its implications. But if a future historian does so, he will have to ask himself why Turner's eulogy of frontier democracy as an antidote to Atlantic-seaboard industrial capitalism did not bear any fruit, and thus why, pressing the analogy, the eighteenth-century dream of the Caribbean as a tropical New World paradise did not, in its own turn, bear fruit.

The answer to that question, of course, would have to concern itself with the second leading feature of Caribbean society: the fact that until the abolitionist movement finally succeeded in the nineteenth century, it was a slave society. Its institutional base was the production unit of the sugar estate; its driving motive, the profit incentive so much at the heart of the capitalist spirit. It needed at once heavy capital investment and cheap labor. The first was provided by the West Indian planter and the metropolitan merchant. The second was provided by the imported African slave. It is true that black slave labor was preceded, historically, by unfree white servant labor and followed, after Emancipation, by contract indentured labor; as a result, the socioeconomic history of the region for the best part of the sixteenth-century and some of the seventeenth century was that of the "poor white," the "Redleg," the transported felon, the deported political prisoner—all of them constituting a form of white servitude—while the socioeconomic history of a large part of the nineteenth century was that of the contracted Asian immigrant, the Chinese worker and trader, and the small, independent white farmer and worker like the Cuban *campesino* and the Puerto Rican *jibaro*. But in between those two periods, for some three centuries or more, it was the history of the plantation economy with its black-slave labor force, and with its social relations shaped by the white master–black worker nexus. The slave person was recruited by means of what its defenders euphemistically termed the African trade. The horrors of the Middle Passage are well enough known, and need no repeating. But it is worth noting the statistical extent of the phenomenon. Philip Curtin's carefully researched book of 1969, *The Atlantic Slave Trade: A Census*, estimates that for the full period in which the trade flourished, 1450-1888, some ten million Africans were forcibly captured and transshipped to the New World, with a possible mortality loss on the slavers of between 13 and 33 percent. The figures are all the more telling since, as the author points out, they are based on a deliberately conservative estimate.[6] Thus, after an early unsuccessful experiment with white peasant settlement labor, the Caribbean economy became identified with the black person, and both economy and person shared the stigmata of despised occupation.

Caribbean society thus became a society of masters and slaves. It constituted open and systematic exploitation of chattel labor, characteristically exemplified in the typical plantation estate run on the military lines of an armed camp, and based, in the final resort, on the psychology of terror. The history alone of slave revolts, from which no sugar island was exempt, is enough to show how omnipresent was the danger of rebellion; and it is enough to read a document like Lady Nugent's Jane Austen-like journal, written during her stay as Governor's wife in Jamaica during the period of the Napoleonic Wars, to be made aware of how that danger was ever present in the mind of the planter class, requiring the almost constant presence of a friendly naval squadron or of reliable "home" regiments to allay its terrible pressure. It was a society, as one early West Indian historian concerned, on the whole, to defend it, termed a society that was based on fear, and fear supersedes right. The master was such not by earned affection or inherited custom—as in societies based on traditional feudalism—but by power of ownership alone. The slave, in turn, was legally an item of capital equipment only, not a laborer with personal status arising out of contract. In the phrase used by Edmund Burke in that statesman's great speech of 1789 in the House of Commons debate on the trade, he was dead as to all voluntary agency.[7]

In such a society, any sense of effective community based on shared values was, of course, impossible. That was seen clearly by Moreau de Saint-Méry in his description of Saint Domingue, on the very eve of the great upheaval of 1789. In his *Description . . .de la partie française de l'Isle Saint-Domingue*, he wrote:

> But in colonial establishments recently created by successive emigrations, the signs of a general ensemble are not to be seen; instead, these societies are shapeless mixtures, and subject to diverse influences; and this lack of cohesion is especially marked when a great colony is made up of individuals who have come there in search of a clime distant and wholly different from their own, because then each person adheres to many usages of the country he has left behind, only slightly modified and adapted to the country he has come into. How much more is this the case when, in the newly adopted country where they find themselves thrown together by chance, the settlers are surrounded by slaves.[8]

That passage clearly illustrates how impossible it was for such a society to develop into a genuine community, with common interests binding all of its members into a coherent civic whole, with common values and common aspirations. The community ideal, then—which received its first noble expression in the work of Las Casas, writing as he did as the first of the Caribbean utopian visionaries—was frustrated from the very beginning. For slavery involved a dual inequality: one economic, the other racial. That was noted, in turn, by the French aristocrat writer Chastellux in his volume composed on the North American colonies in 1782, *Voyages dans l'Amérique septentrionale dans les années 1780, 1781, et 1782*. "It is not only the slave who is beneath the master," he wrote, "it is the negro who is beneath the white man."[9] The observation applied equally, if indeed not more so, to the islands.

The Caribbean society, in sum, was not only a mercantilist-based capitalist society. It was also a racist society. Racial insult was added to economic injury. That explains why a theory of economic exploitation alone—of which there is a substantial literature by Caribbean authors of the Marxist persuasion—is insufficient to explain the totality of Caribbean exploitation. The exploitation of the Caribbean masses was not simply one-dimensional. It was two-dimensional. And the racial exploitation left behind it deep psychic wounds quite different in character and quality from those derived from economic-class exploitation. Nor was that truth altered in any way by the fact that different European colonizing groups put their distinctive mark upon different Caribbean colonies: the English in Barbados, the French in Saint Domingue, the Spanish in Cuba, the Dutch in Surinam, the Danish in the Virgin Islands. For they all carried with them the same European conviction of racial superiority.

From almost the very beginning, then, and certainly once the slave-based sugar-plantation regime was established as the major motor force of the region's economic growth and development, the characteristic Caribbean correlation between color and class made itself evident. The dominant note of the society became that of a virulent Negrophobia. That is evident enough in the apologetic literature that the slavery vested interests spawned as slavery came under attack from metropolitan humanitarian and liberal forces sometime after 1750. The Jamaican planter-historians like Long and Edwards, the Saint Domingue colonist-historians like Dubuisson and Moreau de St.-Méry, the later Cuban writers like Saco, not to mention the innumerable European detractors of the nineteenth century who portrayed the new Haitian republic as a society ruled by an obscene and nameless black savagery—all combined to paint the negative stereotype of the Caribbean African person as lazy, irresponsible, mendacious, sexually aggressive, mentally inferior, and biologically retarded. To read that literature is to enter into the mindless labyrinth of the white racist psyche. It created the legend of black Sambo-Quashie, the Negro lazybones. It fashioned the "noble lie" of the white planter as a generous master and the black slave as an ungrateful ward. It justified both the slave trade and slavery by erecting a myth of an African hell from which the slave person had been mercifully rescued in order to enter the American heaven. It set up an ideology of racial purity that was belied by the racial-social realities of Caribbean society. Above all else, it institutionalized racial prejudice.[10] The French visitor Baron de Wimpffen noted it in a graphic passage of his book on Saint Domingue, written on the eve of the upheaval of 1789.

Race prejudice surpassed social prejudice, for it took the place of *distinctions de rang, mérite de la naissance, honneurs et même de la fortune*; in such a way that even if a black could prove his descent from the Negro king who came to adore Jesus Christ in his manger, even if he combined in his person the genius of a celestial intelligence with all the gold from the bowels of the earth, he would still be regarded as a vile slave, a *noir*, by the most cretinous, the most foolish, the poorest of whites.[11]

That general bias, it is worth adding, had two long-term consequences, even after the evil structure of slavery had itself disappeared. In the first place, it infected the social climate of the European colonizing powers themselves, since, following a general law of colonialism, the colonies became breeding grounds of racist ideas imported into the metropolitan centers. Second, it left behind in the general social psychology of the Caribbean peoples themselves feelings of dependency, inadequacy, and low self-esteem aggravated by poor national identity that continue to plague them even to the present day. And, suggestively, it is no accident that those Caribbean peoples least marked by that sociopsychological morbidity are those, like the Cuban and the Haitian, who have achieved their political independence by means of wars of armed struggle against their colonial oppressors.

The third feature of Caribbean society was its racial and ethnic admixture. The admixture was, of course, created by the compulsive pressures of the black-white dichotomy in the slavery period. The coexistence of sex and slavery—with white master meeting the woman slave on unequal terms—led to the sexual exploitation of the female slave person. The testimony of every observer—Père Labat, Lady Nugent, Bryan Edwards, Père du Tertre, Humboldt, "Monk" Lewis, Schomburgk, and many others—agreed in painting a portrait of the planter life-style full of drinking, dancing, insipid conversation, gargantuan eating, and sexual excess.[12] It is not necessary to think in terms of, as it were, a lurid and melodramatic novel by the Guianese novelist Edgar Mittelholzer to comprehend the extent and importance of the miscegenative process that took place. The planter-rake might abuse an estate girl. But far more generally he was likely to establish her as a mistress in her own household, as his wife in everything except name; and the descriptions of visitors indicate that the habit of interracial concubinage frequently produced remarkably stable unions. There was clearly tension between moral precept and sexual attraction, for the Puritan ethic from the beginning was under serious assault from the social conditions created by slavery, including the well-known numerical imbalance between the sexes.

Inevitably, the old moral standards lost out in that struggle. The very vehemence with which a planter-historian like Edward Long inveighed in his *History of Jamaica* against what he saw as the sexual irresponsibility of his fellow planters—so threatening to their authority, as he perceived it—indicates that the miscegenative practice was too widespread to be changed or modified. Even in the Danish West Indies of the time, where the spirit of Lutheran Protestantism was strong, the barrier of color was crossed, as is evident in the well-known idyll of Governor von Scholten and his colored mistress, Anna Heegaard. Another Jamaican historian—Bryan Edwards, in his *History of the British West Indies*—also had his share of fear of the slave person, yet even he tried his hand at writing on the theme of the Sable Venus, in the eighteenth-century manner of literary primitivism.[13] All in all, the European came to the Caribbean already deeply stained with the racist psyche of ancestral white attitudes, finding blackness repulsive and whiteness angelic.

But the conditions of island colonial life drove him inevitably, unless he were some sort of Saint Anthony, into the habit of interracial sexual liaison. We still await the historian who, using the Freudian insights into the psychosexual roots of human behavior, will tell us what that actually meant in terms of human suffering, both for black and for white, in the Caribbean setting.

In any case, the social, economic, and cultural consequences of the process are clear enough. It laid the ethnic foundations of the Caribbean peoples. In general terms, it created the multilayered pigmentocracy of the region's social and ethnic groups. As good an artistic portrayal as any of the end result can be seen in the series of copper mounted oil paintings by an unknown eighteenth century Mexican painter, graphically revealing the different grades and combinations of racial mixture, from *loba* and *barcino* to *mestizo* and *albarzado*, and in which the appealing beauty of the mixture fails to be diminished by the denigrating epithets that were attached to them.[14] In particular terms, the process of racial admixture facilitated the rise of the racially mixed group known, variously, as "free coloreds," *gens de couleur*, and *gente de color*—originally the mixed offspring of white father and black mother, and then, generation by generation, refurbished its ranks to become, in its own turn, the progenitor of the modern-day "black bourgeoisie." It became an urbanized town set of people, moving slowly into the professions, economically well-to-do, socially ambitious, and sometimes even themselves owners of slaves. Few things are more suggestive of their social status and new pride of special color—what Edward Long in an apt phrase termed "the pride of amended blood"—than the unanimity with which travelers to the islands, and especially in the nineteenth century, noted their existence and how they had managed to build up a flourishing subculture of wealth and fashion in the main towns, at times politically progressive in fighting for their rights but always the most creolized of groups in their social behavior patterns. Constituting what the Puerto Rican poet Luis Palés Matos has called the *mulata-antilla* (Antillean mulatto), they were perhaps the only social echelon fashioned whole and new out of the colonial environment.[15] The fruit of both biological crossing and cultural mixing, they testified to the truth—so important for an understanding of the modern Caribbean—that any claim to racial purity, even on the part of groups like white Creoles in Cuba or East Indians in Trinidad (who might appear on the face of things to be racially unsullied) was as socially inoperable as it was scientifically unsound.

The trajectory of race relations in the Caribbean, this is to say, proceeded along lines quite different from those of race relations, for example, in the United States. For whereas in the American republic there grew up an impassable barrier between the races that was buttressed by institutionalized structures of prejudice and discrimination, in the Caribbean there germinated an elaborate network of delicate nuances of "shade" and color that required a fine detective eye to recognize. The rough and unsophisticated brutality of American race attitudes was thus softened in the Caribbean by the concept of social color, whereby a person's particular classification in the total scheme was determined not so much objectively by skin color as by the other criteria of education, social position, and wealth. In American society, money "talks"; in Caribbean society, money "whitens." If racial democracy is to survive anywhere in the twentieth century, then, it probably stands its best chance in the Caribbean.

The evolution of Caribbean society and culture have really been the evolution of three major constituent elements:

1. The growth of colonialism, once the overseas colonies had been established by the European colonizing powers.

2. The initiation and expansion of the slave and slavery systems.

3. A distinctive Creole culture and Creole institutions based on the twin factors of race and class.

All three elements developed over the centuries as highly organized structures and with accompanying social values. They built up at one and the same time the design and the spirit of Caribbean society. They created in a thousand imperceptible ways the famous *magie antillaise*—the general mixture of popular religions, rich and inventive languages, island political forms, oral folklore, folkways—all of it set within the violent and magnificent natural beauty of the islands—which has evoked the astonished admiration of every generation of visitors.

The evolutionary process, of course, was unequal. The very nature of colonialism—the fact that each colonial power followed its own separate Caribbean policy, oftentimes in open conflict with those of its rivals—made for unequal development in every important field, from economic activity and political organization to social structure and race relations. This accounts for the enormous range and variation of present-day Caribbean societies. Not the least interesting of the different criteria that shaped them is the religious criterion, basically the difference between the Catholic colonizing powers and the Protestant. Columbus and his followers came to the New World with a baggage of religious intolerance rather than racial phobia, with the result that the early Spanish settlements set a pattern of racial mixing between Indian, Negro, and Spaniard not matched in the later English and Dutch settlements; with the further result that it is in Havana and Santo Domingo and San Juan rather than in any other capital city that the modern visitor will encounter the characteristic facial features of that mixture, so admirably depicted (if an example is needed) in Velazquez's portrait of his Moorish *ayudante*, Juan de Pareja. On the other hand, the tradition of religious tolerance in Protestant Holland and Denmark made possible the early settlement of Jewish refugees in both Dutch Curaçao and Danish St. Thomas, thus laying the foundations of the present-day Sephardic Jewish burgher-mercantile groups in both of those societies.

Indeed, the complex interplay between Catholicism, Protestantism, and capitalism that took place in European society after 1600 also had its special repercussions in the colonial world. Both religions facilitated sugar capitalism in the Caribbean, so that there was very little difference between Protestant sugar planters in Barbados and Catholic sugar planters in Cuba, both of whom were driven by the profit motive. Yet there were some differences. The Catholic missions were generally far more tolerant of the foibles of their island congregations, while the Protestant missions sought, mostly unsuccessfully, to impose a harsh puritanism upon their converts. Clerical celibacy was probably more honored in the breach than in the observance, as much in the colonies as in Catholic Europe itself, while all descriptions of the Protestant missions show them to be intractably puritanical. These differences left their mark. That helps to explain, among other things, why the centers of the tremendous bacchanal-fiesta of Carnival in the New World—New Orleans, Santiago de Cuba, Port-of-Spain, Rio de Janeiro—came to be located in territories shaped by Catholicism and not in those shaped by Puritanism. It also helps to explain, even today, the difference, say, between the self-conscious solemnity of Virgin Islanders and the vivacious *joie de vivre* of Haitians. To spend a week in St. Croix is to experience a sort of colonial version of a tortured Ibsen play; while, by contrast, to spend a week in Haiti or Martinique is to feel the enchantment of Lafcadio Hearn with the *brio* with which their inhabitants avail themselves of the slightest pretext for enjoyment and celebration—and which Patrick Leigh-Fermor has beautifully described in his *The Violins of Saint-Jacques*.[16]

There were differences, too, in the nature of the impact of slavery. Everywhere, it is true, it created a melting pot society forcing each newcomer, whether he wanted to or not, to work and live with others whom he found culturally or ethnically distasteful; it is worth noting that East Indian immigrants in Trinidad and the Guianas lost their old caste structure much more readily than they surrendered their antipathy to Black people. At the same time, the impact of the general slavery system was unequal. Sometimes it was merely a matter of longevity. Thus, whereas Barbados was a fully developed sugar-slave economy for more than 250 years, the period of slavery lasted only a bare fifty years in Trinidad, and there are historians who have suggested that that difference is a key to understanding the contrast, today, between the stolid social respectability of Barbadians and the marked Byzantine anti-social individualism of Trinidadians. Sometimes, again, it was a matter of extent and scope. Thus, whereas slavery was the main pillar of Cuba's society almost to the end of the nineteenth century, in Puerto Rico, also Spanish, it was marginal to an economy of highland peasants and small-scale coffee *hacendados*; and again, there are observers who have argued that that difference helps explain the difference between the patriotic bellicosity of the Cuban character and the social docility of the Puerto Rican, the latter trait giving rise as it has done to the legend of the *puertorriqueño docil* (the complaisant Puerto Rican).[17]

Even the manner of the abolition of slavery was another differentiating factor. In the French case it required the armed struggle of the national war of liberation of 1791–1804 against a purblind and reactionary planter class in Saint Domingue; in the British case it was, in part, the outcome of a fifty-year campaign on the part of the liberal-humanitarian forces in Westminster politics, aided by the declining profitability of the system and the consequent decline of the influence of the West India interest in metropolitan politics. Those different methods were bound to leave their mark on the respective colonial societies. So, whereas in the British islands abolition by parliamentary edict made possible the future development of a constitutionalist politics, in liberated Haiti the aftermath of fratricidal civil war and anticolonial rebellion was the growth of a "strong man" politics based on force—that being essentially the history of the Haitian presidency from Dessalines to the Duvaliers. The British Crown Colonies were governed by a metropolitan system in which, after 1689, a liberal bourgeoisie was in effective control of the state, whereas the French and Spanish colonies were under regimes, in Paris and Madrid, in which such a bourgeoisie was never really able to win out against the tradition-bound forces of army, church, territorial aristocracy, and semifeudal peasantry. No comparison could better illustrate how, in colonial systems, the character of the overseas dependency is shaped, for good or ill, by the character of the ruling class of the mother country.

Undoubtedly, much of Caribbean history is to be understood in terms of this inequity of development, leading to the characteristic idiosyncrasy of each individual territory or group of territories. All of that has been exacerbated by the final idiosyncrasy of language. Each colonizing power imposed its language on its colonial subjects, thus leading to a disabling linguistic fragmentation in the region. It produced the well-known trait of *insularismo* (insularity). Each island, in David Lowenthal's well-chosen phrase, became "a museum in which archaic distinctions were carefully preserved."[18] The language barriers encouraged the condition. The condition explains why, even today, so many Caribbean-born scholars prefer to concern themselves with the island of their birth or, at best, with one group of islands. It also explains why academic research in the regional universities still remains insularist, with the University of Puerto Rico concentrating on matters Puerto Rican and the University of the West Indies concentrating on what is known as the Commonwealth Caribbean. It further explains why, in the sphere of government and politics, nothing in the way of a regional federal or confederal organization has yet succeeded, not to speak of a viable region-wide economic community. Nor has there yet grown up a sense of Caribbean consciousness in the regional communal psychology. Not surprisingly, there are Caribbean observers ready to argue pessimistic conclusions from all this.[19]

The pessimism is, perhaps, not altogether justified. Although a healthy antidote to much of the romantic nonsense that is uttered about Caribbean unity, it is necessary to point out that the insularity is an accident of history. It is not necessarily a permanent law of Caribbean society. Just as history, in the past, made it, so history, in the future, can unmake it. Be that as it may, it still remains the fact that all of the regional societies, however separated they are from each other, possess a common history. The leading fact of that history, in turn, has been an economic exploitation remarkably similar in all of its features. That truth has been obscured because too many pleasing myths, even in academic scholarship, have grown up about the regional history. There is the myth that the early Spanish conquistadores were heroic soldiers of fortune, bringing Spanish civilization with them. In fact, of course, they brought with them, rather, the beginning of a new colonial capitalism with its own overseas bureaucratic organization; and it is enough to read Zarate's account of the conquest of Peru to realize that within a brief generation after the overthrow of the Inca empire by the Pizarro brothers, the adventurers had been replaced by a new colonial governmental system of ecclesiastical officials, mayors, and royal appointees dedicated to the systematic exploitation of the conquered territories.[20] The process, of course, started with Columbus himself, for, as Hans Koning has shown in his lively book, *Columbus: His Enterprise*, the Admiral of the Ocean was not simply a single-minded visionary whose navigational skill led to the discovery of the Americas but much more—the leader of an ambitious commercial venture financed by the Spanish monarchs and their business allies.[21] There is the further myth, absorbed by generations of English schoolchildren, that the English Elizabethan seamen were fighting to bring Protestant liberty to a region dominated by Catholic tyranny or were daring heroes opening up the Atlantic passages; and it is enough to read Samuel Eliot Morison's last book, *The European Discovery of America: The Southern Voyages, A.D. 1492-1616*, to appreciate how bourgeois historians have managed to purvey that interpretation right into the present period.[22] The truth is, of course, that the Elizabethan adventurers, as piratical as their rivals, laid the ground for a colonialist regime as oppressive as that of the Spanish. The conquest and colonization of the Caribbean, in sum, can only be properly understood if it is seen as a chapter in the expansion of early capitalist society, leading to the massive slavery of transported Africans, the economic importance of sugar as a cash crop pregnant with immense profits, and the exploitative relationship between the tropical colony and the temperate metropolis.

The primacy of the economic factor is important. For modes of social relations, even forms of social thought, are shaped everywhere by modes of production. If the history of the Middle East has been oil and the history of the American Midwest corn, the history of the Caribbean has been sugar. "I do not know," wrote Bernardin de Saint-Pierre, "if coffee and sugar are necessary to the happiness of Europe, but I do know that those two crops have been the scourge of two parts of the world."[23] In the Caribbean at least that meant the sovereignty of King Sugar. All of the sugar islands felt its consequences. Even those islands that, like Saint Thomas, were only commercial entrepôts derived their prosperity from the sugar economy. And even the

smaller, lilliputian islets which themselves did not produce sugar, like An-
guilla or Barbuda or the Grenadines, were affected by it insofar as they were
dependent wards of larger sugar islands. It is true that some Caribbean territories were reserved for special purposes set apart from the sugar economy;
so, British Honduras in the Mosquito Bay area became a settlement of ma-
hogany cutters, Bermuda and the Bahamas specialized in the nefarious
"wrecking" trade, and French Guiana, to the eternal shame of the Third Republic, became a notorious penal colony. But these were exceptions that
proved the general rule.

Despite all the differentiating factors, then, all of the islands were shaped
by the economics and politics of slave-based sugar enterprise. The Caribbean
subject-peoples were scourged by the same disease, tarred by the same brush.
That is evident in a number of ways. There is the common pattern of expatriate
ownership, so that if in the British West Indian case the ostentatious luxury
and profligate spending of absentee planters became a byword in eighteenth-
century England (as they are portrayed in the pages of Sterne and Smollett) it
was the same story in the French and Spanish cases; as Paul Morand put it in
his 1928 book, *Hiver Caraïbe*, the *grand seigneurs* of the reign of Philip II,
once enriched, had no more bothered to attend in person to their New World
holdings than the court nobility of Louis XVI had visited their Saint Domingue
plantations.[24] There is the remarkable similarity in the various descriptions
of colonial conditions—the terms of work, the abuses, the codes of punishments—whether one reads the proceedings of the Council of the Indies, the
reports of English colonial governors to the Privy Council, or the information
collected by the functionaries of Colbert and Richelieu. There are the similarities of social structure, with its correlations between class and color, based
on the trinity of white planter, colored middle group, and black slave. Even
social values were similar: the whites of every island being obsessed with
sugar; the coloreds with social emancipation and civil rights; the slave masses,
deculturated and detribalized, building up their own secret, subterranean,
New World founded on a rich cultural amalgam of African and Caribbean
elements. That last point helps to explain why, up to the present time, the
vodun priest, the Rastafarian cultist, and the Shango acolyte all share a common view of the total relationships between man, nature, and society fundamentally different in its first principles from the tradition of Western
rationalism.

The sociocultural unity of the region, finally, is there in the way in which a
common experience of suffering and oppression gave birth to a common experience of resistance. It is no accident that when the West Indian historian
C.L.R. James came to write his pioneer study of 1938, *A History of Negro
Revolt*, he had little difficulty in starting with the Saint Domingue servile war
of 1791—itself preceded by so many unsuccessful slave revolts—and ending
with the Garveyite movement of the early twentieth century, for, as he perceived, they were all imbued with a common passion for black liberation—

diverse tributaries, as it were, of a common cause possessed of its own embracing logic.[25] And all of those similarities were located in a single world of time and place. Perhaps, indeed, the most striking testimony in support of the point being made here is the remarkable unanimity with which travelers to the region, almost from the very beginning, remarked on the stark contrast everywhere between the beauty of its natural habitat and the Gothic horrors of its social scene: where every prospect pleases and only man is vile.

This, all together, is the background to the contemporary Caribbean. It is important to understand what it really means, because, in the Caribbean, there is a very special sense in which the legacy of the past plays the role of a brooding omnipresence to the present. The various permutations of French Antillean and Haitian politics still follow the model of the various stages of the revolutionary period after 1789. Political ideologies, in Haiti, especially, are still set within the framework of traditional loyalty to the memory of Toussaint or Pétion or Boyer. Throughout the region *slavery* is still a word to conjure with, going back to the post-Emancipation period when popular feeling was preoccupied with the suspicion that the colonial powers were ready, at any given opportunity, to reintroduce the slavery system. The Haitian "revolution of 1946" was thus conceived as an attempt by the new class of black political leaders to remedy the damage that had been done by the American occupation forces and their mulatto allies, while in the British West Indies a reforming party like the People's National Movement in Trinidad could come to power in 1956 by deliberately invoking the "white Massa" tradition. Any effort to abridge freedom on the part of an overweening government is immediately denounced as an attempted return to "slave" conditions. For Caribbean history has been a violent history. Its midwife has been force, not persuasion. It has not been the sort of quiet, imperceptible change from generation to generation—with precedent broadening down to precedent, each successive change flowing naturally from the other—which explains the institutional continuity and social placidity, say, of English history. Its seminal moments have been moments of violent upheaval, of widespread social and cultural shock. It still carries the imprint of that heritage.

The three primary moments of that historical background are readily identifiable: the original Discovery, leading to the period of post-Conquest slavery; the period of slavery emancipation, leading to the period of post-Emancipation society; and national political independence in the twentieth century, leading to the period of postcolonial national sovereignty. Those three periods constitute, so to speak, moral earthquakes which destroy an existing order of things and are recorded on the seismograph of ideological systems. The first gave rise to the proslavery creed; the second to the antislavery creed; the third to the creed of nationalism. Put together, the one frequently running into the other, they add up to the accumulated moral deposit of Caribbean society and culture. Each period generated its own values, operational norms, and belief structures, contributing, all in all, to the ideological history of the region. The Caribbean of the modern period can only be fully understood in terms of that moral deposit and ideological content.

THE CARIBBEAN AND THE MEDITERRANEAN

The Caribbean has frequently been compared to the Mediterranean. It is an apt comparison and warrants examination. In both cases, civilizations arose as seaborne empires, enveloped in the brooding omnipresence of a vast mass of water: the Mediterranean an ancient lake enclosed in the land areas of Africa, Europe, and Asia Minor, and the Caribbean girt by the Central American and South American littoral areas and the circling archipelago of the islands. The geography of the sea in both cases, shaped, with inexorable force, the character of the social and economic structures that arose within them, so that just as Mediterranean trade and shipping was that of navigators hugging coastal waters and rarely venturing into the open sea, so Caribbean maritime life clung to the inner shores of the mainland and the leeward side of the islands. The turn of tide and wind, until the advent of steam power in the nineteenth century, determined everything, including the outcome of naval battles like Lepanto and the Battle of the Saints. There is, indeed, a sort of geographical determinism that has shaped the history of both areas. In the Mediterranean, it was a combination of the benign climate of Southern Europe and the harsher tropical climate of North Africa; in the Caribbean it was the overwhelming sun-drenched luminosity of a tropical atmosphere made tolerable by the ever-present trade winds. They have been climates at once beautiful and dangerous. The beauty—that of areas like French Provence or the Riviera, that of the famous *magie antillaise*—has throughout enraptured the peoples of the more temperate climates, converting both areas in the twentieth century into famous and lucrative tourist economies. The danger, correspondingly, always lurked beneath the beauty. A failure of rainfall could destroy a sugar crop in Barbados or Saint Domingue just as surely as a failure of the Nile to rise in its annual flow could destroy the Egyptian riverine agriculture. Both basins were erected, in part, on subterranean volcanic faults, so that Mount Pelée in Martinique could destroy the city of Saint Pierre in 1902 just as surely as Mount Vesuvius had earlier destroyed Pompeii in A.D. 79. It is no accident, then, that the Caribbean and the Mediterranean constitute today the richest fields in the new science of underwater archaeology. In the Caribbean particularly, that arose from the crucial fact that between 1555 and 1649 the area was the site of the first stage in the transatlantic voyage of the famed Spanish treasure fleets with their elaborate convoy systems to protect them against their Protestant enemies— leading to major disasters such as the Dutch capture in 1628 of the complete *Nueva España Flota* before it reached Havana, and the loss in 1715 of the

"Combined Armada of 1715" by shipwreck. Nor is it any accident, to press the point further, that if the history of the Mediterranean began with the mythic voyages of the Greek argonauts, that of the Caribbean began with the earthshaking voyage of Columbus and the intrepid voyages of all the European mariners who followed him.[26] Merely to notice the similarity between a trip taken today on a pleasure boat among the Grecian isles and one taken among the Caribbean ports is to immediately be aware of the way in which, in both regions, the imperatives of geography and climate shaped, in almost identical fashion, their social structures and their historical development.

And History has followed Geography. Alexander conquered the Eastern Mediterranean and, after that, the ancient Persian and Indian empires in much the same way that the Spanish bands of Cortes and Pizarro, starting out from the bases of Cuba and Panama, conquered the Aztec and Inca empires. To read the account of Cortes's expedition into the Valley of Mexico written by the soldier Bernal Díaz in his old age is like reading Xenophon's description in his *Anabasis* of how he led his force of Greek mercenaries against desperate odds out from the heart of ancient Mesopotamia to the sea. Both civilizations—this is to say, Mediterranean and Caribbean—were based, to a degree unknown to other civilizations, on the brutalizing right of conquest; the Caribbean aboriginal Indian and the African slave possessed no more rights, as persons, than did the *proles* of the ancient world. In both cases, moreover, the institutional expression of that class oppression was slavery, and Las Casas, in a pregnant sentence, compared the Spanish system of forced labor in the islands to the system of enslavement that the Romans, earlier, had imposed upon Spain itself, quoting as evidence grim passages from the account of the ancient Greek historian Diodori Sicula.[27]

Both civilizations, in that respect, were set apart from the Northern European societies, with their different tradition of feudal serfdom; for if the Mediterranean was as much, culturally and religiously, a prolongation of Africa and Arabia as of Eurasia, the Caribbean was as much a transatlantic extension of West Africa as it was of Elizabethan England. Even their pigmentations were different: The Northern European societies were Nordic-white, the Mediterranean was phenotypically more Moorish-Arabic, and the Caribbean, certainly after the middle of the seventeenth century, was overwhelmingly negroid. That explains why it is misleading to seek to understand the Caribbean in European terms, as so much of the traditional metropolitan scholarship has vainly attempted to do. The region's history is not just the overseas history of France or England or Holland; so to see it is to indulge in ethnocentric distortion. It is, rather—and here again the Mediterranean analogy is fruitful—a regional history characterized by:

1. the resistance of Creole cultures to external pressures initiated by the European colonialist expansionist movement,

2. the slow growth of racially and culturally hybrid societies made possible by the fact that no single colonizing power was able at any time to impose its

will upon the area as a whole.

So, while North America remained ineluctably Anglo-Saxon and Latin America intractably Catholic-Hispanic, the Caribbean, by comparison, emerged as a series of rich, fascinating, polyglot societies, eclectic, porous, absorptive, notwithstanding the formal national affiliation of each one of them to an overseas mother country. Those national boundaries—indeed, so artificial in the way that they violated the natural divisions of the region—constituted, in effect, not so much barriers as permeable membranes for a massive and constant flow and interflow of groups and individuals.

The twin lodestars of both of these two historic societies, indeed, are that, first, of perpetual motion, the vast cyclical movements of peoples as immigrants and emigrants, and, second, that of their racial and cultural intermingling. In the Caribbean, of course, the migratory mass movement was, first and foremost, that of the "African trade," followed, in later centuries, by Asiatic immigration and then by the movement of West Indian laborers to, variously, Cuba, Santo Domingo, the Panama Canal Zone, the Aruba oil refineries, the United States, Canada, and Britain. In a competitive society where traditional European norms went rapidly by the board, the various ethnic segments became easily mixed. The resultant mix was described early on in books like Du Tertre's *Histoire générale des Antilles Habitées par les Français* (1667-71) and Père Labat's *Voyage aux Isles d'Amérique* (1722), with their lively accounts of the cosmopolitan societies of the sugar islands and strange communities where colonists, indentured servants, freed Indians, slaves, buccaneers, Catholics, "heretics," Jews, transported political prisoners, felons, "poor whites," and "maroon" slaves, mingled in a fascinating exoticism under tropical skies. This was a *picaroon* world not unlike the polyglot, multilingual trading cities of the Mediterranean of the Hellenistic period. It is the world, transported to another time and place, of the period so vividly described in the *Acts of the Apostles* or the various letters of Paul of Tarsus written to the new Christian churches of Asia Minor.[28]

In the realm of ideology, it helped to break down old nationalistic and religious barriers, so that if it produced, in the Mediterranean, the Pauline doctrine of universalistic brotherhood between Jew and Gentile, in the Caribbean it produced an embryonic nationalism among the despised black-brown-yellow elements, based on the feeling that they were all oppressed by the same master class, all tarred by the same brush of white European racism. Just as Saint Paul, journeying in endless anxiety to communicate his good tidings, replaced the spirit of old formalistic Judaism with a new spirit of an all-embracing Christian liberty, so Las Casas devoted a lifetime of transatlantic journeyings to combatting the repressive temper of the Inquisition in the Indies with the creed of a common humanity. Even the conversions of these two men were similar; for if Saint Paul has his road to Damascus revelation, Las Casas has described in a famous passage in his *Historia de las Indias* how in Cuba in 1514 he came to realize the real character of Indian slavery through coming across a passage in Ecclesiasticus as he was preparing a sermon to preach to the Spaniards.[29] Neither of these two Christian evangelists, admittedly, went beyond a vague message of moral equality to a more radical doctrine of social equality; Pauline Christianity wanted only to humanize the master-servant relationship, while Las Casas retained the principle of private property in his numerous land-reform schemes. But both, in their different ways, by their teachings enlarged the horizons of human hope in their respective societies.

There is yet another point to be made in this excursus into the comparative analysis of the older Mediterranean and the more modern Caribbean historic systems. Both of them were erected upon the violent conflict between rival imperial entities: in the Mediterranean between Latin Christendom and Ottoman Islam; in the Caribbean between the first overseas empire of the Spanish Crown and its English, Dutch, and French rivals. That fact led to brutal consequences in both cases; for if the Crusades of the later medieval period constituted the effort of the European Christian powers to impose an alien religion by force upon non-Christian peoples, the record of the Caribbean is the effort of the same powers, later on, to transport the wars of religion of the sixteenth and seventeenth centuries to New World societies already possessed of their own elaborate and sophisticated religiometaphysical structures of thought and belief. In both cases, as a result, there emerged a deep abyss between the religion of the master classes and that of the subject masses, between, that is to say, the accepted state religion and the subterranean popular religions. Christianity itself, as the pioneering investigations of scholars like Strauss, Feuerbach, and Cumont have shown, owed its structures of dogma and myth in large part to the older cult-religions, like the Mithra cult, of the pre-Christian period.[30] In similar fashion, the real religions of the Caribbean poor have been syncretic belief-systems combining the imported Christian ideas with earlier ideas, mainly African—*Shango*, the secret Negro cults of the Americas, not to mention the Afro-Trinidadian Shango-obeah complex, *Bamboo-tamboo*, and *Camboulay*, the Afro-Jamaican Rastafarian and *Pocomania* following, Haitian *vodun* and its tremendous apocalyptic Afro-Haitian vision, Puerto Rican spiritualism, Cuban *santería* with its esoteric amalgam of Yoruba gods and Catholic saints. To speak at any length with a Rastafarian bearded cultist, with his vision of Jamaica as an oppressive Egyptian bondage, is to return to the world of the unknown author-mystic of the Book of Revelation, with its fierce denunciation of the hated Roman Empire. The sole qualification that has to be added to that analogy, of course, relates to the fact that, in the Caribbean, the wealthy and the powerful were also at the same time white and European, given the almost exact correlation that has existed in the society between class and race.

Or—to put all this in another way—if culture, generally, is understood in the anthropological sense rather than in the literary sense, it is the black

masses of Caribbean society who throughout have been its real custodian. Just
as early Christianity was essentially the movement of the disinherited masses
of the Mediterranean towns and cities, so the cult movements of the Caribbean have been identified with the slave and ex-slave masses. If Troeltsch's
famous distinction between church and sect is accepted, the churches belonged to the plantocracy and its allies, the sects to the oppressed majority.[31]
That was the case with the Protestant churches in the English islands, a situation only radically changed when, especially after slavery Emancipation, the
Baptist, Methodist, and Moravian persuasions were increasingly taken over
by the black converts. It was the case, again, with the French Catholic Church
in independent Haiti, which frequently collaborated with the mulatto state-
power in attempts to exterminate what was regarded as the "primitive" and
"barbaric" rituals of the vodun priest—who, in reality, conferred a sort of
theological rationalization upon the rich oral African tradition of the Haitian
peasantry. Just as the literature of the early Christian revelation saw the rich
man as one who can hardly hope for entrance into the Kingdom of Heaven,
so the nonliterary tradition of the Caribbean sects has seen him as a white op-
pressor belonging to a European tradition at once alien, expatriate, unreach-
able, and ultimately irremediable. It is in that sense that men like Garvey in
the twentieth century must be seen, not in secular, but in religious terms, a
direct descendant, as it were, of those Minor Prophets of the Old Testament
who saw the Babylonian Captivity of the Jews as a deserved punishment for
their treasonable surrender to wealth and corruption and power.

CARIBBEAN POPULAR CULTURE

The history, then, of Caribbean culture in its anthropological sense (and on
which, in the nature of things, much of its literary culture is based) is the history of forms created by the masses: in religion, music, dance, language, folklore, and entertainment. The common experience which infects any cultural
manifestation of genuine vitality has been the special creation of the common
folk, who have originated, and defended, their own art forms against the sterile and borrowed pseudo-European culture of the educated classes. As the
economic exploitative systems of colonialism and imperialism created tension,
antagonism, and violence, the masses invented their own mechanisms of survival, in part resistant, in part accommodating. That has been the case all
over. To begin with, of course, the survival process was the history of the popular, lower-class European culture brought by the European common man to
the region, reflecting, as it were, the rich folklore contained in the pages of
Cervantes as against the mandarin culture contained in the pages of Erasmus. It was the case, later on, with the popular religion brought in by the African slave tradition and then elaborated upon by the Americanizing process,
whether one thinks of Barbadian hymnology, or sects like the Shouters in Trin-

idad, or, as already noted, Haitian vodun. It is well known how, in that latter case, slave leaders like Makandal and Boukman manipulated the magico-religious power of vodun to accentuate slave revolutionary consciousness. Here, indeed, the Mediterranean analogy is again appropriate; for if the radical spirit of early Christianity was only finally quenched when its leaders, under Constantine, allowed their religion to become an official buttress of the Roman social order, so vodun became a conservative force when, under the later Duvalier regime, it became a collaborative agent of the state power. In the realm of language there are the rich, inventive Creole Patois idioms, stigmatized as "bad English" by their upper-class detractors but now belatedly recognized by the linguistic anthropologists as languages in their own right; and they have given rise, in the form of a West Indian literary renaissance of recent years, to a new West Indian fiction which, in novel, verse, and play, swings in its language with the response of all the senses to the vivid quality of the immediate Caribbean world.

Or again, there is the whole world of Caribbean entertainment. The song and dance tradition of the slave plantation surreptitiously survived to become the basis of the revived Afro-American nationalism of the present-day period, no better illustrated than in the case of Trinidadian Carnival, Calypso, and Steel band. The great pre-Lenten Carnival event, from the beginning, was the voice of the common Negro folk, despite the fact that its origins were French. The calypso art mode, in turn, arose out of social adversity, and the typical calypsonian, the *kaisonien extraordinaire*, sprang from the working class and became, in great practitioners like Attila the Hun, the Roaring Lion, Lord Executor, a weapon in an anti-English, anticolonial politics. The steel band, finally, of the post-1945 period emerged from the social recesses of the Laventille hill shantytowns to become, as it were, a new status symbol for its aspiring members. And in all of these instances the popular art form had to struggle against the hostility of both white colonial officialdom and middle-class Creole respectability—so much so that these art forms only became acceptable as legitimate expressions of Creole nationhood at the moment when the elements of polite Creole society decided to use them for their own class purposes or when, suggestively, they were "discovered" by the pacesetting art circles of the white metropolitan centers; as, indeed, has happened in recent years both with Trinidadian calypso and steel bands; and the *art primitif* of the Haitian painters.[32]

If, to conclude, any awareness of a Caribbean nationhood has developed in the region—that is to say, a felt differentiation of national identity—it has been, certainly, the end result of Creole values, norms, and modes of self-consciousness carried and defended by those groups, mostly of worker and peasant, that have the most easily identified themselves with their particular island society. And, once again, the analogy with early Mediterranean Christianity comes to mind: for just as the early tone of the Gospels—that the misery of the poor is to be laid at the door of the rich—was replaced by a new apologetic for poverty, as well as for slavery, once the church became a vast institutionalized power bloc, so, in the particular case of Trinidadian calypso, there is a world of difference between a calypsonian like Attila satirizing the foibles of British colonial governors and, some thirty years later, a calypsonian like the Mighty Sparrow eulogizing the People's National Movement, which, after independence in 1962, became the new governing elite of the Creole black bourgeoisie.

Yet when the popular sources of Caribbean ideology are being discussed, it is still too early to say that this is the end of the story. Seminal ideas have a way of transcending the bonds imposed upon them by class interest and national power. Christianity itself became a conservative force. But that has not prevented the survival of its pristine message of justice and equality, as is shown by the history of those minority forces that continued, despite persecution from the Princes of the Church, to uphold it: sects like the medieval Beguins and Waldenses, orders like that of Saint Francis, the later movements like Christian Socialism and Catholic Socialism in the nineteenth century and, in our own day, movements such as the revolutionary Christianity identified with figures like Camilo Torres. Correspondingly, it is still too early to say that Haitian vodun or Trinidadian calypso may not again become creative elements in the shaping of a new Caribbean revolutionary ideology, just as, indeed, *négritude* has found a new birth in the ideology of Black Power.

For the very essence of popular folk culture, everywhere, is its intrinsic plasticity, its capacity to incorporate new experience into its basic values and attitudes. In its Caribbean manifestations, then, there is a recognizable continuity in its various expressions throughout the entire historical period of its existence. Recent examples from Puerto Rico will suffice to prove that generalization. The recent work of investigators like Pedro and Elsa Escabí has shown how the old verse form of the *décima* (ten-line verse form) remains a living repository—especially in the rural areas, but even in the new urbanized areas—of popular attitudes towards society, religion, birth, life, and death; while as late as the 1960s yet another dedicated collector, Marcelino Canino Salgado, found that the oldest of all *coplas* (four-verse stanzas) mentioned by Manuel Alonso in his pioneer work of 1849 on the Puerto Rican mountain peoples, *El Gibaro*, was still known by the majority of young people interviewed in both town and countryside.[33] Both of these findings are all the more remarkable when it is remembered that contemporary Puerto Rico, more than any other modern Caribbean society, has been the helpless recipient, since 1898, of a truly massive process of forced Americanization. Cultural persistency is a potent force in the struggle of dependent peoples to retain their separate identity. That truth, in Caribbean studies, has been too frequently overlooked only because so much of the literature on the region has been written by a European and North American scholarship too much obsessed with the canons of "progress," "modernization," "westernization," and "industrialization."

Yet however fascinating and useful the comparison between Mediterranean and Caribbean history may be, there remains one final point which those historians who make it seldom mention. That is the stark, simple fact that when all is said and done, Caribbean society, from the beginning, was the creature, indeed the victim, of Mediterranean capitalist expansion as, towards the end of the fifteenth century, Spain—and after Spain the Protestant Northern European states—broke out of the siege to which it had been subjected by feudal social barriers, the Moorish invasion, and the Islamic roadblocks of the Mediterranean commercial routes. The key to that process was at once the new wealth of the New World and the new opportunities for profit opened up by sugar slavery and the slave trade; its agents were the growing mercantile houses of Seville, Bordeaux, Nantes, Bristol, and Liverpool, whose capital helped establish the Caribbean slave plantation—in alliance, of course, with their respective national states. The subsequent history of the Caribbean, as already noted, the so-called Enterprise of the Indies, was one (not to put too fine a point on it) of murder, genocide, exploitation, and savage plunder. Of all the forms of colonization carried out by the European maritime powers, this was, on any showing, the most depredatory of all.

For—if a glance is taken at other forms—the colonization of such countries as Canada, Australia, and New Zealand was one of large-scale settlement by Europeans in comparatively empty virgin spaces, while the colonization of ancient civilizations like India, Indonesia, and to a certain extent Africa was one in which European elites had to come to terms with entire indigenous populations already possessed of entrenched cultures that the conquerors could not easily destroy. The colonization of the Caribbean, on the contrary, witnessed the early decimation of what indigenous populations there were, to be followed by the massive forced importation of enslaved peoples to serve the interests of a transient metropolitan ruling class. It brutalized both master and slave. It uprooted religion and culture from their cosmic moorings, with all of the well-known consequences of that process. It created a Caribbean hell, in the form of slavery, which shocked even the European mind of the period, inured as it was to the cheapness of human life. Even Adam Smith, whose commonsensical, plangent prose rarely betrayed real feeling, was moved to indignant outburst at the spectacle; and in a frequently quoted passage of his *Theory of the Moral Sentiments* he compared the Spartan discipline and courage of the American native peoples with the effeminacy of European society. "These nations of heroes," he wrote, "have been subjected to the refuse of the jails of Europe." The sentence sums up a whole chapter of Caribbean social history. It is a note, let it be added, rarely struck in the more contemporary Anglo-American scholarly literature on the Caribbean, with its spurious objectivity learned from positivist philosophy. The modern reader must go to a French anthropologist like Lévi-Strauss, in his superb *Tristes Tropiques*, which is at once an autobiographical memoir and an essay on the decay of Western "civilization," for an enraged indictment—speaking particularly to the evil record of Luso-Brazilian society in its war against the South American Indian—of how the filth of that "civilization" has irrevocably contaminated the non-European peoples of the world. If, then, the Mediterranean was the cradle of European civilization, the Caribbean was in very truth its graveyard.[34]

CARIBBEAN THOUGHT

All this, then, constitutes the historical background to the growth of Caribbean thought, whether it be considered—following Mannheim's distinction—in terms of ideology or in terms of Utopia. It was a history of some five hundred years of colonialism, characterized by a rapidity, a completeness, and, above all else, an almost complete absence of social control that made it stand out as unique when compared to other colonial adventures. It was the hardcore area of slavery in the Americas; and its colonial status lasted longer than any comparable colonial situation in Asia, Latin America, or Africa. All that conferred upon it, despite linguistic and religious differences, a generality of common properties, so much so that it is possible to identify surprising similarities not only in the various political movements that sprang up in all of the colonies, English, French, Spanish, or Dutch, but also in the ideologies that they spawned. The uniformity of Caribbean life and thought, this is to say, is in the long run more significant, and of more lasting consequence, than its diversity.

It is urgent to insist upon the systems of thought, even more than upon the collective life-experience out of which they were born. For it has been the general attitude of writers on the region—metropolitan and, in some cases, local—that there is no history of ideas in the region worth speaking about. The attitude, undoubtedly, has its roots in the history of the region itself. The European liberal feeling of disgust for the "poor white" and the rich planter alike extended itself into a feeling of disdain for the region as a whole, and what London thought about Jamaica was only matched by what Paris thought about Saint Domingue and what Madrid thought about Cuba. It is suggestive that the trial of Warren Hastings had contributed the great speeches of Burke to the English anticolonial literature while, by comparison, the attempt, some eighty years later, to impeach Governor Eyre in the Jamaica scandal of Morant Bay dismally failed and raised little more than a ripple in English intellectual life, despite the fact that the younger Mill himself was involved in the impeachment move. Even Marx, when he came to write on slavery, was concerned solely with the southern United States and hardly noticed the Caribbean. That general attitude was fed, in turn, by colonial ennui, colonial self-contempt, and colonial feelings of dependency—the well-known colonial mentality—in West Indians themselves. Whether, in the Puerto Rican case—to take twentieth-century examples only—it is Pedreira writing, in his essay *Insularismo*, an argument of racial degeneracy and colonial despair among his own people or René Marqués composing, in his essay *El Puertorriqueño dócil*, a theory of Puerto Rican collective impotence, or whether, in the Trinidadian case, it is the novelist Vidia Naipaul asserting, in his *The Middle Passage*, that the West Indies have never created anything, metropolitan disdain was followed by colonial self-contempt.[35]

The anti-Caribbean animus has thus conspired to obscure the fact that from the very beginning there grew up a genuine Caribbean historiography, a Caribbean sociology, a Caribbean anthropology; in brief, a movement of ideas at once created by European ideologies concerned with the New World, by European residents in the islands, and, later, by a Caribbean intelligentsia itself. But it all had to struggle against the myth of cultural philistinism. In the British case, for example, it is well known how in the Empire as a whole the study of colonial societies was begun by serious-minded colonial officers fascinated by the outposts to which they had been appointed, long before the academic mandarinate took over. But that contribution was inhibited in the West Indian case by a hierarchy of status whereby the first-class–Oxford-honors man went to Africa or India, while the passman was turned over to a minor appointment in one of the West Indian islands. The prejudice lasted well into the modern period. Eric Williams has described, in his autobiographical volume *Inward Hunger*, how, as a colonial student at Oxford in the 1930s, he discovered that of all the Oxonian scholars concerned with colonial studies, only one, Vincent Harlow, had made himself knowledgeable about the West Indies.[36] At much the same time Lord Sydney Olivier, onetime Fabian Socialist governor of Jamaica, was complaining that his own authoritative books on Jamaica had been received in the London journals as if they were merely tourist guidebooks and not, as they were, a studied defense of the West Indian subjugated peoples against colonial capitalism.[37] For every pamphlet that the Fabian Colonial Research Bureau put out on the West Indies, it put out a dozen on India or Kenya. When, furthermore, the English writer Maurice Collis, as a colonial career officer, came to write his fascinating books on the historic encounter between the European and the non-European worlds, he chose, not the Caribbean, but the ancient civilizations of Southeast Asia to illuminate his theme.[38] This explains why, even today, the academic study of the Caribbean is even more sadly neglected in the British academic world than is that of Latin America. The situation, true, is somewhat better in the North American university world; scholars like Herskovits and Ragatz, after all, were not trailblazers in their respective fields of Caribbean anthropology and Caribbean history for nothing. But even there the present-day preoccupation with the region seems at times based on little more than a self-interested and career-oriented exercise within the labyrinthine world of the American doctoral dissertation.[39]

There is a brief passage in Philip Curtin's introduction to his book *Two Ja-maicas: The Role of Ideas in a Tropical Colony, 1830–1865* that aptly illus-trates how even a scholar sympathetic to the region and its peoples may fall into this kind of attitude. He writes:

> The sense in which this is a study of ideas should not be misunderstood. If intellec-tual history is taken to be the history of Great Ideas or Great Books, then the kind of history that follows must be called something else. Nineteenth-century Jamaican ideas are not often worthy of notice for their own sake, and the principal interest is not in the intellectual effort of the exceptional person.[40]

In one sense, of course, that is true. It is true to the degree that the history of ideas, in the classical manner, belongs to the Graeco-Roman, medieval European, and modern European periods. The Caribbean colonial society, by contrast, was an antiintellectual society. In Père Labat's lament, every-thing was imported into the West Indies except books. The Caribbean slav-ocracy never learned the lesson, as did the slave-owning classes of the ancient world, of combining slavery with the arts. It is enough to read the scathing accounts of the life of the rich Cuban plantation plutocracy during the golden age of that sugar society in the nineteenth century penned by North Ameri-can and European visitors—and conveniently collected in Roland Ely's 1963 study *Cuando reinaba su majestad el azúcar*—to realize how much of that life was one of flagrant ostentatiousness, Creole indolence, sexual dissolute-ness, corruption, idleness, extravagant entertainment, and a snobbish search for empty titles; they lived (in the words of one visitor) as if they were cour-tiers in the Versailles palace of *Le grand monarque*.[41] Intellectual life of any real quality could hardly be expected to emerge in such a decadent society.

But Curtin's observation hardly holds good if other considerations are taken into account. He himself was speaking to a one-generational experience in a single island-society. Visitors from abroad were usually restricted to the lavish hospitality of the planters' clubs and country mansions; so that it would be difficult to imagine, for example, from reading the visitors' accounts reported in Ely's study, that there existed in the Cuba of that same period a vigorous intellectual tradition of Cuban philosophy, history, and constitutional law. Again, one would hardly gather (to take another example) from reading *The English in the West Indies*—the English historian James Anthony Froude's account of his visit to the West Indies during the last quarter of the nine-teenth century, which repeated all of the reactionary views that its author had imbibed from his planter hosts—that there existed in both Trinidad and Ja-maica respectable schools of local historians. The truth is, of course, that if a wider Caribbean perspective is adopted, and if the totality of published works on the entire region is taken into account, the Caribbean is possessed of an intellectual history of no mean proportions.

That history, spanning the entire 500 years of the regional experience, was really born out of two major processes. The first was the influence upon the

region of European-metropolitan modes of thought and the manner in which
that influence was felt by the gradually emerging literary elites of the Caribbean urban centers. Those modes of thought encompassed the whole of
European intellectual history itself, in linear historical order: the late medieval humanism of the Hispanic Mediterranean; the rationalism of the French
Enlightenment, filtered through the influence of the American and French
Revolutions; English humanitarianism, most notably expressed in the campaigns for the abolition of the slave trade and slavery; nineteenth- and twentieth-century Socialist thought. The second process was that of a subtle
creolizing movement, whereby all of those modes of thought were absorbed
and assimilated and were then reshaped to fit the special and unique require-
ments of Caribbean society as they developed from one period to the next.
The moral and intellectual baggage of Europe, this is to say, once unloaded,
became indubitably Caribbean. The end result cannot simply be seen as, so
to speak, a provincial expression on the circumference of civilization of something that can be appreciated only at its center. It constituted, rather, an
effort—often groping and uncertain—after a culture to be regarded as genuinely Caribbean; in the course of which it borrowed, sometimes with almost
servile acknowledgment and sometimes with embarrassed shame, from the
achievements of the older world. Thus, these twin processes, side by side, ultimately gave birth to an indigenous collection of ideas and values that can
properly be termed Caribbean *sui generis*. There took place, that is to say, a
process, altogether, of intellectual and moral miscegenation matching the
other process of sexual, racial, and cultural miscegenation. Everything taken
or received from the Old World became different as it was adapted to its new
home. The "middle passage" of transported African slaves was accompanied
by a "middle passage" of ideologies.

In her pioneering study *A Study on the Historiography of the British West
Indies to the End of the Nineteenth Century*, the West Indian historian Elsa
Goveia has noted the general character of that process as it related to the
English-speaking sector of Caribbean life. In her concluding remarks, she
observes:

> A great diversity of subjects and methods have gone to the making of historical
> writings on the British West Indies. Narrative history, particularly narrative history
> of exclusively political events, is only one form, and hardly the dominant form, to
> be found among the West Indian histories. Within the covers of these works, there
> are examinations of the physical environment and of its influence on the life of
> men, studies in ethnology and social structure, economic analyses, technological
> discussions of navigation, agriculture, and manufacturing processes, and besides
> all these, historical enquiries into some of the most profound questions of morals,
> philosophy, and politics. The range of these writings is exceedingly wide, and this
> is one of the peculiar and most powerful fascinations of West Indian historiog-
> raphy. From the very beginning, the historians of the islands have tended to con-
> cern themselves with the description and analysis of a whole society. They have
> been students of institutions as well as of events.[42]

The same observations apply, on a larger scale, to Caribbean thought and ideology as a whole. It is only because the outside world has failed to see the region in those serious terms—the Europeans tending to see it as a collection of obscure and unimportant colonies, the Latin Americans as unnatural and marginal pockets of European influence, and the North Americans as simply a sphere of their own American influence—that this aspect of Caribbean life has been overlooked.

Chapter Two

The Sixteenth
and Seventeenth Centuries:
The Beginnings of
Caribbean Thought

The genesis of Caribbean thought goes back, it is clear, to the historic encounter between the Old World and the New. It is part and parcel of the expansion of the intellectual horizons of Renaissance Europe engineered by the opening up of new continents and their penetration by the European spirit: not only the New World proper but also the new knowledge garnered about Africa and Asia as a consequence of travel and discovery—a process that goes back historically to Marco Polo, and most particularly to the great Jesuit missionary-travelers who entered the hitherto mythical worlds of China, India, Japan, and Central Asia. It was the great age of discovery, when there were new worlds to conquer for the adventurous spirit tired of European life, and it lasted for some four hundred years or more; in one sense it ended perhaps with Sir Francis Younghusband's expedition into inner Tibet of 1904. It produced a new literature of travelers' tales, reports of mariners, and information relayed back to royal and aristocratic patrons by pioneering seamen. It laid the foundations of the new science of exact cartography. Not least of all, it revolutionized the world outlook of the European mind. Europe could no longer think of itself as the center of the universe, for it gradually became clear that there existed other, extra-European civilizations, cultures, and religions equal to, and sometimes superior to, the accepted European forms.

All this, of course, was intimately connected to the great evolutions of science and technology that marked the sixteenth century. The discoveries of Bruno, Galileo, Kepler, and Copernicus replaced medieval theology with the new science of rationalistic analysis. After the publication of the Copernican hypothesis, the shift of the new scientific spirit to secularism becomes more and more relentless. The old cosmology yields to the new. The medieval principle of homocentricity is replaced with the new principle of cosmic heterogeneity, out of which emerges at once a new picture of the universe and a new control of nature. At the same time, the literature of the extraordinary voyage—reaching its apogee in works like *Telemaque* and *Robinson Crusoe*—helps to dispel the old ideas of the superiority of European man and the moral primacy of European culture, replacing them with visions of non-European societies in which the splendor of nature is contrasted with the evils of civil society. Just as, then, the new discoveries of astronomy revealed non-terrestrial worlds challenging the old concepts of medieval religion and cosmology, so the great voyages of discovery revealed new, non-European cultures founded on moral and social principles unknown to the European experience.

There are three important aspects of these twin revolutions that deserve notice. In the first place, they were both closely related to new technological advances. Just as the discovery of the compound microscope and the achievements of Tycho Brahe in more accurate astronomical invention made possible the new study of the universe, so the great improvements in marine instruments, including the perfecting of the mariner's compass, accelerated the new intercontinental voyages to the degree that they released the seaman from the protective shroud of the coast and enabled him to venture into the oceanic waters. Second, neither revolution took place overnight, for they had to fight against the resistance of inherited prejudice. The scientific revolution did not deter Newton from a lifelong obsession with the conventional problems of dogmatic theology, while the revolution of exploration did not make Columbus, for example, into a modern man. The pen portrait, indeed, that Las Casas painted of the admiral in the first book of his *Historia de las Indias* showed Columbus to be a devout Catholic who believed that his discoveries had as their great mysterious purpose the conquest of the Indies for Catholic Christianity, as well as being a conventional mind of the sixteenth century that accepted uncritically all of the old ideas, including the ordained right of absolute kingship. In the third place, the new discoveries unleashed in European man a dual, indeed contradictory, response. On the one hand, as the accounts of the discoveries attest, there was a feeling of astonished wonder at newly revealed worlds so different in every way from Europe; on the other, there was a ready eagerness—springing from the fatal hubris of European man and reinforced by the new spirit of capitalist enterprise—to use and exploit them for both private and public enrichment. It was, of course, the latter response that won out in the long run, if only because the spirit of humility before new worlds belonged essentially to the historians and writers who remained at home, while the exploitative spirit belonged to those who actually undertook the conquests: the soldiers of fortune, the rapacious proconsuls, the motley crews, the scum of European society which Adam Smith noted in the passage quoted earlier.

That third point is important. The Dutch cultural historian Henri Baudet has elaborated upon it in his brilliant, short essay *Paradise on Earth: Some Thoughts on European Images of Non-European Man* (1965):

> Two relations, separate but indivisible, are always apparent in the European consciousness. One is in the realm of political life in its broadest sense, in the atmosphere...of concrete relations with concrete non-European countries, peoples, and worlds. This is the relationship that freely employs political, military, socioeconomic, and sometimes missionary terminology. It is this relationship that has also, in general, dominated the pens of the historians who have recorded the history of our Western resistance and of our expansion. The other relationship has reigned in the minds of men. Its domain is that of the imagination, of all sorts of images of non-Western people and worlds which have flourished in our culture—images derived not from observation, experience, and perceptible reality but from a psychological urge. That urge creates its own realities which are totally different from the political realities of the first category. But they are in no way subordinate in either strength or clarity since they have always possessed that absolute reality value so characteristic of the rule of the myth.[1]

The first category of response is summed up, of course, in the subsequent history of European capitalist-imperialist expansionism, which everywhere, and with depressing uniformity, destroyed or at the very least mutilated all native cultures in the name of progress: the Amerindian way of life in the Caribbean (that is, the aboriginal Indians, especially in the Guianas), the North American culture of the Plains Indians, the African tribal systems, the peasant structures of the Indian continent, the ancient feudal structures of mainland China. The second category can be seen, in one way, as the expression of the guilt complex created in the world of the European imagination by that grim record of mindless destruction, and summed up in a famous passage of ironical commentary in chapter 15 of Montesquieu's *L'Esprit des Lois*, in which he summarizes the conventional arguments in favor of slavery only to conclude that if Europeans allowed the Negroes to be men, it could only be at the price of admitting that they themselves were not Christians.[2] This European mental image was based, psychologically, on the truth that, in Johan Huizinga's phrase, a culture wishing to be free of itself experiences a perpetual longing for the uncivilized.

The American continent, and within it the Caribbean region, played a vital and strategic role in these developments. For America was a completely new, virgin, freshly discovered land. Ever since Plato and Herodotus, after all, the East and the Far East had been known to exist. By contrast, America, apart from a vague myth of Atlantis, was utterly unknown. Its discovery by Columbus—although probably predated by the Norsemen of an earlier period—seized the European mind of the time with utter astonishment. It was almost as if a new, unsuspected planet had been discovered by the astronomers. Everything was new: the islands, the aboriginal peoples, the fauna and flora, the Indian customs and religions, and, most especially, the tropical sensuality of the climate. This sense of utter wonder, indeed, is the very first note struck in the history of Caribbean literature, and it lasted well into the nineteenth century, as the account of each traveler, one following the other, sufficiently shows. Columbus thought that he had reached the coastal regions of the legendary Cathay. Cortes and his handful of soldiers, as their companion-historian Bernal Díaz described it in his account, could think of nothing but the legends of Amadis when the splendid magnificence of the Aztec Valley of Mexico unfolded before their unbelieving gaze. Ponce de León searched in vain for the Fountain of Youth in his Florida expedition. Raleigh, in his turn, imagined that he would find the fabled city of El Dorado in the wild region of the Orinoco Gulf.

In all of these figures the two elements mentioned by Baudet—the pragmatically political and the romantically imaginative—merged into each other; nowhere is this better illustrated than in the curious fact that, when Columbus came to write his first letter to his royal patrons reporting the findings of his first voyage, he could, at one and the same time, extol the native Indians for their innocence and timidity which, he claimed, would make them easily susceptible to conversion, and then proceed to add that they would make as many slaves for the Spanish navy as their Majesties would wish to command. A similar ambivalence of temper, between the practical and the romantic, is evident in the fact that, in the same letter, Columbus noted down with care matters concerning the etymology, sartorial habits, and life-styles of the natives, yet at the same time credulously believed their stories of fabled Amazons living to the south. He was, in brief, the first Caribbean naturalist, and at the same time the first chronicler of fictitious America.[3] His reports, including the journal of his first voyage—which was preserved for history only because Las Casas transcribed it for use in composing his *Historia*—reflected at once the new astronomy and cosmography of the age that he had picked up in his stay at Lisbon and his conviction that his great achievement was based, not on those new sciences, but on his reading of the prophets Isaiah and Esdras.[4] This ambivalence of attitude illustrates perfectly how at one and the same time the Columbian voyages helped to break down the provincial temper of medievalism which equated its own outlook with eternal principles and yet, despite that, also to bring to the New World much of the old prescientific spirit, including, it is worth noting, the institution of the Spanish Inquisition itself, which Bishop Alonso Manso brought to the Antilles some forty years after the Discovery.

To put all this in a slightly different way, what took place was a gradual fusion of the transported body of European ideas, both old and new, and the new societies of the New World. Much has been written by historians of *Caribbeana* of the Middle Passage, by means of the slave trade, of persons forcibly transported from Africa to the Indies. Little has been written on the Middle Passage of systems of values and thought. Yet the one is as important as the other for an understanding of the foundation of the resultant American societies. It was a process, of course, that took place on the continent as a whole, both in the island colonies and in the mainland colonies. As already noted, it had two constituent elements: one, the sea-passage of European-metropolitan systems of thought to the new lands, and, two, their creolization as they were absorbed and reshaped to express the special context and character of the American experience. The sea-passage generated a sea-change. The inherited baggage of myth, religion, and folk song that the African slave brought with him became transmuted into a new Afro-American culture system; similarly, the European immigrant, whether indentured servant or capitalist-planter, Catholic or Protestant, brought with him the inherited baggage of ideas prevalent in sixteenth- and seventeenth-century Europe, and they, in turn, became transmuted into a new Euro-American culture system. It was, in brief, an Americanizing process, the slow, gradual, and sometimes painful implantation of the American idea and the American spirit.

THE CARIBBEAN AND THE MAINLAND

It is instructive to glance briefly at this process as it developed during this early period on the mainland proper, that is, in the Spanish viceroyalties of Mexico and New Spain, since it constitutes a foretaste of what was to emerge also in the ocean colonies. It is a comparison also particularly illuminating since during this early period the lines of distinction between the mainland possessions and the island possessions were not as sharply drawn as they were to become later. The Spanish seaborne empire, after all, it has to be remembered, began in the island colonies of Cuba, Hispaniola, and Puerto Rico, and it was no accident that up to the last—the end of the nineteenth century— they remained the most loyal of all of the possessions of the Spanish New World. And it was in Havana, Santo Domingo, and San Juan that the first generation of Spanish officials put together the beginning of the legal and administrative machinery of the overseas bureaucracy that was later transferred to, and perfected in, the mainland capitals.

The emergence of a distinctive Indo-Iberian Creole civilization can already be seen in the sixteenth century. The note of *mestizo* autonomy can be seen as early as the *Comentarios Reales* written by the Inca Garcilaso de la Vega (1609), with its romantic nostalgia for the glory of the pre-Columbian highland culture, a note which later, in its Aztec formulation, was to become the rich source of twentieth century Mexican nationalism. In his own person, the author—as the son of a Spanish captain and an Indian princess of Inca lineage—embodied the process of racial admixture that produced, in later generations, a Creole aristocracy of *hidalgo* (gentleman or nobleman) caste composed of the mixed children of the two cultures. He wrote, then, as a new type of American person trapped in the often unbearable strain of a dual loyalty between the old order and the new. His main purpose, as he advised his readers, was not to dispute the Spanish accounts of the Conquest, but merely to offer a gloss, based on the fact that his command of the Inca tongue (which they did not possess) made it possible for him to describe Inca religion and government from, as it were, the inside. He did not write as a prophet of rebellion against the Spaniards; he was, rather, a court memorialist anxious at one and the same time to record, from personal memory and observation, the great tradition of the *Inca imperium*, both in its positive and negative aspects, and the benefits of the Christian religion brought by the Spaniards. The tone of the book is essentially aristocratic; it takes for granted the rule of Inca noble and priest, based on a remarkably efficient exploitation of defeated peoples; and it is written by a Catholic convert who, fully aware of the irreligiosity of Inca custom and belief from the Christian viewpoint, is at the same time unwilling to make any sort of judgment since, as he warns the readers, all comparisons are odious. Yet, notwithstanding all this, it is a proud celebration of the ancient republic before the Spaniards came. At the same time, it richly documents the slow amalgamation of the two cultures, despite the efforts of the Spanish to deliberately obliterate, by the destruction of Inca records, the memory of the Inca achievement. Merely to read the chapter in which the author describes, in rich and fascinating detail, the celebration of the Corpus Christi festival, with all the various dependent tribes of the old Inca empire participating alongside the Catholic priesthood in a variety of gold and silver costumes in the old Cuzco *plaza*, is to be made aware of how the pagan religion fused with the Christian to form a new syncretic ritual; and it is worth adding that the same chapter includes a spirited defense of one of the Inca chieftains of his participation in an earlier battle in the very same *plaza* in which he and his compatriots had put the Spanish soldiers of Gonzalo Pizarro to rout: it is one of the first declarations in Latin-American literature of the ideology of Indian power, notwithstanding the fact that Garcilaso did not mean to write it as such.[5]

That note of latent resentment against the new conquerors grew slowly but surely during the rest of the century. The Mexican historian Fernando Benítez, in his brilliantly executed book, *Los primeros mejicanos: La vida criolla en el siglo XVI*, has documented its development. Its social base was composed, first, of the mixed Creole group, like Garcilaso himself, suffering a double stigma, being regarded as traitors by the original native group and as bastards by their Spanish fathers; and, second, of the somewhat different group of Spanish Creoles, the soldiers and settlers of the original conquest, who resented the new authority of the salaried functionary representing the metropolitan interest. Benítez catalogs their growing restlessness in the early literature. There was the *Tratado* of the aristocrat Suárez de Peralta, who could insist that God had given the Indies to the Spaniards as recompense for the expulsion of the Jews and the establishment of the Inquisition, yet at the same time pen a spirited defense of the Indian herbalists; and could also, like some new American Don Quijote, write as if he were some Renaissance spirit still living in the archaic, enchanted world of West Indian chivalry. There was, again, the *Sumaria relación de las cosas de Nueva España* of the courtier Dorantes de Corranza, which in its fierce indignation constituted perhaps the first elaborate defense of the Creole descendants of the original *conquistadores* against all of those hated groups—the lower-class *manos blancas* (white laborers), the *arrivistes*, the newcomers, the royal civil servants—who were seen as having stolen his inheritance from the Creole and forced him to become a poor gentleman at court: the book transports to the New World the hatred and scorn which the poor feudal lord of medieval Europe reserved for the bourgeois possessors of great urban wealth. In both of those accounts, as in others, there are already present the basic ingredients of the new American spirit: a sort of spiritual *mestizaje*, a concern for the Indian, an emerging Creole assertiveness, a love for Mexico—not yet developed by any means into a full-blown anti-Spanish American nationalism, but clearly anticipating it. All this formed, as it were, a sort of Indo-Mediterranean humanism, searching in the new American world for a new identity and for a culture that would be distinct from, and unfettered to, the European original. As it strengthened its American roots, it created a common anti-European sentiment, irredentist, Creole, potentially nationalist, that has marked the Latin-American intellectual culture ever since.[6]

THE CARIBBEAN SPIRIT

That same American spirit also characterized the history of the Caribbean proper during the sixteenth and seventeenth centuries. It constituted, so to say, a Caribbean variant on the general process taking place in the new American world, Spanish to begin with, during the same period. Its embryonic form has already been noted in the discussion of Columbus. The first note of the Conquest, naturally enough, was one of military superiority to the encountered peoples in the service of the Castilian monarchy. "I could conquer the whole of them," wrote Columbus of the first encounter, "with fifty men and govern them as I pleased."[7] But the need to organize the new empire introduced new and more intransigent attitudes. Columbus was a typical man of the age in his loyalty to the Crown; he had none of the rebellious spirit which led other *conquistadores*, like the Pizarro brothers, into treasonable activities against the royal functionaries. At the same time, even so, loyalty to the King did not necessarily compel obedience to the new tribe of peninsular Spaniards who followed hard on the heels of the pioneers. So, just as in the case of Mexico and Peru, where a struggle for control took place between the ruthless, illiterate soldiers of fortune and the lawyers and financial experts representing the interests of the Crown, so in the islands proper the long struggle of the Columbus family to hold and extend their rights based on the original

royal grants against the slowly expanding authority of the overseas royal bureaucracy can be seen as an effort, albeit only half-consciously felt, to go
back in the New World to an older form of political feudalism that in Spain
itself had been destroyed by the centralizing Castilian state. The prolonged
quarrel between the Columbus family lawyers on the one hand and the protagonists of *regalismo* ("the doctrine of royal authority") on the other clearly
held within itself seeds of a separatist spirit—aggravated by the sheer distance
that divided the new tropical possessions from the Spanish center—which
some three centuries later was to lead to the wars of republican independence. Neither Columbus nor his son, let it be repeated, harbored dangerous
republican ideas. It was the case, rather, that the novel and unprecedented
exigencies of the Caribbean drove both of them deeper and deeper into serious differences with the Crown. The civil historian Zarate has described how
the civil war between the various factions of the Spanish soldiery in the Peruvian *sierra* gave rise to a so-called "Chilean party," with all that such a title
implied.[8] In similar fashion, the increasing demands of the Columbus family
claimants can be seen as forming, in the particular situation of Hispaniola at
the time, the threat of the emergence of an overseas feudal barony.[9] The
Crown lawyers, regalists as they were, saw the danger clearly; hence their
construction, during the post-Conquest period, of a new theory and practice
of empire embodied in the new institutions of the Supreme Council of the Indies, the *audiencia*, the *Capitanes Generales-Gobernadores* (office of the
Captain-General as Governor) and the *regio patronato indiano* (official policy
governing the Indians). Whether they knew it or not, they were building de-
fenses against an early Caribbean growth of the Americanizing spirit. They
thus anticipated the leading feature of Caribbean colonial politics for the
next three centuries or so: the embittered struggle between metropolitan-
appointed colonial governors and the various factions of locally elected colonial assemblies, councils, and town governments.

There is a general principle involved in all of this well known to all students of colonialism. The Creole settler, or the "old hand," feels an instinctive
jealousy of the bureaucratic official; the soldier on the spot resents what he
regards as the purely academic ideas of the "office wallah" at home; the resident official, frequently a scholar of no mean sort, identifies himself with an
oppressed subject-people as against the officials of the home office who seek
merely to enforce policies based on general theories of how "natives" should
be treated. In the British Empire, that has been the story of—to take more
modern examples only—Raffles in Singapore, Lawrence in Arabia, Olivier in
Jamaica, and Wingate in Palestine. Speaking still of the British case, they
have all been regarded by London as eccentrics, unreliable types, odd men
out. Raffles was a pioneer in the study of Oriental languages, to the conster-
nation of his East India Company employers; Lawrence upset his superiors
with a championship of the Arab peoples that went back to the studies of
Doughty; Olivier was a Fabian Socialist at a time when the Webbs were viewed

as dangerous revolutionaries in Edwardian London; and Wingate embarrassed London by being simply himself, that is, a Bible-reading guerilla-warfare leader who behaved as if he were, in the middle of the twentieth century, a captain of Cromwell's New Model Army. And, as a final example of this remarkable genre, so English in its magnificent eccentricity, there is the astonishing figure of Colonel F. M. Bailey, "Bailey of Tibet," who throughout a long lifetime of espionage and intelligence work, astonished his superiors by, variously, scrutinizing Central Asia during the Bolshevik Revolution, producing reports on the mountain peoples of the high Himalayas, mapping for the first time the Tsangpo gorges, and collecting Himalayan birds and plants never before known to natural history, not to mention his mastery of Asian dialect languages, learning Tibetan, in fact, from the Bengali agent who was the model for Kipling's Mokerjee in *Kim*.

In the early Caribbean, of course, these developments took on their own special character and form. The Americanizing process matured later there than in the mainland colonies, if only because the Europeans did not encounter anything comparable to the ancient civilizations of Peru and Mexico. They met, rather, less-developed Taino-Arawak-Carib tribal cultures. There was no literate priesthood to record the encounter with the new overlords; the aboriginal Indians played, as it were, little more than the role of Man Friday to the European colonizer's Robinson Crusoe. In one way, of course, both Indian aboriginal and, after him, African slave contributed to the American spirit by means of their resistance to their subjection, so that Indian caciques like Guarionex and Caguax and African slave leaders like Cuffy and Cudjoe have become heroic figures in the later martyrology of the nationalist movement. But in the very nature of things, neither Indian nor African (with some few exceptions later on) left any written or spoken record behind them in any way comparable to the written works of the Mexican Indian historians such as Ixtlitxochitl and Tezozomoc and the record of the Mayan myths and traditions in the books of Chilam Balam de Chumayel. The literary history of the Caribbean therefore begins with the various accounts written by the historians and travelers, Spanish, French, and English, during the first two centuries after the Discovery. Most of them held official positions in one way or another, whether secular or ecclesiastical. Some of them, like Oviedo, were official historians who took the view of the "home" government. Others, most famously Las Casas, made themselves controversial figures by adopting and defending the interests of the "natives." But they all instinctively recognized the intellectual and moral significance of the new world of the Caribbean.

A PRE-COLUMBIAN WORLD VIEW

But all that, let it be repeated, was the literary history. The absence of such a history in the pre-Columbian aboriginal cultures does not preclude a preliterate history on their part. So to assume would be to overlook the important truth that Caribbean ideology really begins with the ideology, the world view, implicit in the folklore and the mythology of the Indo-Antillean peoples— Siboney, Taino-Arawak, Carib—as they were described in the reports of the early explorers, historians, and missionaries. Anthropology, after all, as a modern scientific discipline, was born out of the prolonged discovery, between 1500 and 1800, of the peoples and cultures of the Americas and the Pacific region, between, say, the early report of the Jeronomite priest Ramon Pané, probably composed as early as 1498, on the customs and religion of the Indian inhabitants of Hispaniola, and the report of the young François Peron, the diarist of the French expedition to Tasmania in 1802, on the habits and life-style of the original Tasmanian native populace. Building on that foundation, the more recent modern work of archaeologists and anthropologists in the larger Caribbean area has established the general truth that the cultures met by the *conquistadores* in 1492 went back, directly or indirectly, to the older Igneri and Ostiones Indian cultures and therefore inherited a folklore tradition of no inestimable antiquity. It is true that their architectural survivals, like the ceremonial plaza-ballcourts of Puerto Rico and the Dominican Republic, do not match the mainland Aztec and Inca remains; there is no Caribbean island record to match the awestruck account that the young Spanish soldier Pedro de Cieza de León sent back to Spain in 1553 of the great golden temple and garden enclosures of Cuzco before it was destroyed by the conquerors. But it is also true that the pre-Columbian Indian groups possessed, in their general ideas about the world in which they lived, a cosmic outlook not very much less complex than the outlook that the European conquerors brought with them.

The essentials of that outlook were all described in Fray Ramón Pané's *Relación acerca de las antiguedades de los indios*. Written with a rare dispassionateness—for it avoids the trap, on the one hand, of assuming, as did a writer like Fray Domingo de Betanzos, that the Indians were cursed by a divine *maldición* so that nothing could save them, and, on the other, of assuming, as did early missionaries like Fray Juan de la Deule and Fray Francisco de San Román (anticipating the theme of Las Casas), that the Indians were "angels" endowed with intelligence and capacity to understand the Christian religion, thus in a way idealizing them—it succinctly describes the world vision of the Hispaniola Indians, a coherent mythology rooted firmly in the material conditions and necessities of an ordered subsistence economy. In that vision, human life is governed by the vaguely defined supreme being Yocahu, who is morally indifferent to the wishes and desires of his devotees; he must therefore be reached through the intermediary approaches of the characteristic three-pointed stone idol, the *cemi*, inhabited by the spirits of deceased *caciques*: the material embodiment, that is to say, of supernatural forces. Living an independent spirit life, the *cemis* themselves are capricious, requiring human ingenuity to manipulate them for purposes of human convenience; and the charming legends that Pané transcribes of the behavior of some of them indicate an erratic behavior corresponding to the behavior of the natural phenomena, the weather, for example, that they supposedly control. The natural universe that Taino-Arawak man inhabits, in turn, has been created by magical effects: the Sun itself was formed as a consequence of the failure of the subterranean cave-people of the Hispaniola mountains to properly guard their caverns; the same myth places the origin of species in the dark underground of those caverns. The oceans, in their turn, have their origin in the *higüera-agua-peces* (calabash-water-fish) legend, which tells, according to Pané, how the mythical father Yaya, killing his rebellious son, placed the bones in the branches of a calabaza or higüera tree, only to discover that they spawned a multitude of fish and the flood of the primeval oceanic waters.

Sexual nature, in its turn, springs from similar miraculous episodes, and there are few pages in Pané's brief account more fascinating than those in which he describes, actually, two different versions of the creation of women: the first, in which Taino men, driven desperate by sexual desire, capture certain sexless person-forms appearing out of trees and, strapping them to the ground, bring in the Antillean bird, the inriri, which then proceeds, in woodpecker style, to hammer out with its beak the female genitalia on the captive prisoners; the second, clearly related to the first, relates how one of the early Taino culture heroes carries away all the women of the tribe to seclusion on a remote island, thus offering some evidence for the later myth of the warrior Amazons as well as setting the scene for the act of sexual creation described in the first mythical story. Along with all that, finally, there goes the myth of the discovery of food products—the material base, that is to say, of Taino economic culture, symbolizing, as it does, the transition, at some point in the pre-Columbian cultures, from a nomadic pattern to a pattern of agricultural settlement.[10]

This account, of tantalizing brevity, written by a *pobre ermitaño*—as Pané calls himself—receives further documentation from the writings both of his fellow missionaries, including Las Casas, and of the early Spanish historians such as Oviedo. Its constituent elements, insofar as they differ from the European colonizing mythologies that overwhelmed them, merit special notice. For the European religions—Calvinist, Lutheran, Catholic—brought with them to the new tropical world their concepts, essentially antihumanist, of human shame, innate sin, and the subjection of man to a distant, vindictive, and ferocious Jehovah-God figure. The Indian religions, by contrast, showed a noticeable unconcern with the moral problem of good and evil, being content with only the necessary taboos against practices such as incest. Their gods, like the *loa* of the later Haitian vodun cult, are at best half-gods cut down to human size, responsive to human appeal since they share much of human frailty; and suggestively, there is nothing in their artistic portraiture matching the terrible ferocity of the Aztec and Maya gods. Man is much more the center of the universe, so much so that man himself appears as already created in the Taino mythology, and even the creation of woman—as the *pájaro-carpintero* (the bird-woodworker) story shows—is described as arising out of the sexual needs of men rather than as being, as in the biblical version, the end result of a divine concern. The myth of the flood, in turn, is portrayed, not as divine vengeance for human transgression, but as, at the most, the punishment inflicted upon sons for their revolt against their father. All in all, it is a cosmic vision that, in its gentle character, reflects a chieftain society halfway between a simple egalitarian society and an organized state system replete with lawmaking bodies and organized army systems. It knows little of brutality or degeneracy, although the story that Pané tells of the harsh vengeance, including physical mutilation, passed upon witchcraft doctors suspected of gross deception in their practices indicates at one and the same time the absence of a priestly caste strongly entrenched in power and the Indian capacity to be cruel when necessary.

Yet the final impression is one of a peaceful society at ease with its environment. The charge of cannibalism, beginning with Columbus's reports on his voyages, is certainly an empty one, almost certainly, indeed, an invention of the European conquerors, constituting what Lipshutz has termed an *antropologia física mitológica* (physical anthropology based on myth).[11] The peacefulness almost becomes docility, perhaps a morbid fatalism, expressed in the *cemi's* prophecy, which Pané cites, of an alien race which one day would overwhelm and conquer the island civilization. It is small wonder that the great work of the early Spanish religious humanists in the New World— Las Casas, Zumarraga, Sahagún, Vasco de Quiroga—created out of their admiration for the Indian cultures the dream of using the Indian peoples as an instrument for establishing the type of Sir Thomas More's *Utopia* in the Americas. The Puerto Rican scholar Mercedes López-Baralt justifiably concludes in her study of the Taino world, *El mito taino*:

> Without losing sight of Cassirer's warning that in primitive art "imagery never possesses an independent significance purely aesthetical" we can appreciate the beauty of the myth if we do not isolate it from its context. It is precisely the vivid articulated relationship between myth and reality, manifested in the symbolical genius and in the synthesizing power, or *totalización coherente*, of the Taino culture that permits us the aesthetical enjoyment of the mythology that is carried in Pané's text.[12]

An almost similar world picture emerges from the study of the Caribs. The ethnographic work of modern scholarship—Reichel-Dolmatoff, Torres Laborde, Chagnon, Roth, Willey, Rouse, and others—has demonstrated the truth that the Antillean and Amazonian Indian groups were part of a common culture area; and undoubtedly the Caribs formed a branch of that extended family. So, notwithstanding the fact that they have suffered from an evil reputation at the hands of hostile reporters—rather like the evil reputation of Mongol "hordes" and Barbary pirates and Comanche Indians in other areas—they, as much as the Tainos, personified an original Caribbean ideology, so contrastive to the European; for if the Europeans sought to conquer Nature, the Tainos sought to accommodate to Nature. So much so that their life-style even drew the reluctant admiration of the seventeenth and eighteenth century French travelers and writers who were their main chroniclers. The Sieur de la Borde's early description of 1674 emphasized the main points of the Carib religion. It accepts the doctrine of celestial descent: the first Carib man-god descended from the skies, to create the first men of earth. It even echoes the Christian myth of death and resurrection: for three days after his death that original being rose to heaven. There is, as with the Tainos, the same reverence for age: it is an aged woman who appears to early Carib man and teaches him the art of growing his staple foods like manioc. The heavens have always existed. But earth and ocean were created by the original man-god; indeed, it is that person, the Great Master of the *cemis*, who let loose the Flood as divine punishment for an ungrateful Carib people. De la Borde cites a slightly different version in the same account: the Europeans made heaven and earth, but not the Carib country itself; the belief suggests a defiant Carib patriotism. They wish the Europeans had never set foot in their country, De la Borde reports; and goes on to report the further Carib observation to the effect that they, the Caribs, have their own science and we, the Europeans, have ours. They esteem the Moon much more than the Sun, having, indeed, a crude calendar based on lunar changes.[13]

Père Du Tertre's account in the same century adds something to all this. De la Borde had insisted that the Caribs had no words to conceptualize abstract concepts such as virtue and justice. But Du Tertre's citation of Père Raymond's *Dictionnaire* of the Carib language suggests that this might have been an overhasty judgment. According to Du Tertre's version, the Carib world view envisages two kinds of gods: the one evil, the other good. Accompanying this Gnostic dualism there is a tradition of exorcist rites aimed against the evil forces which scandalizes him despite the fact that such rites were well-known in his own Catholic church.[14] Charlevoix, at much the same time, sees all this, typically, as pagan superstition, but nevertheless is sufficiently enchanted by the natural simplicity of the aboriginal way of life to excuse it all on the ground that the Indians are bereft of *raison naturelle*.[15]

In all of this literature there occur certain leading themes. There is a deep, instinctive pride in being Antillean: De la Borde reports the Indians as replying, when told that they live like animals, that the Europeans are more so because they do not live the Carib way. There is the absence of European sexual shame: all the chroniclers commented on the easy childbirth and the breast-feeding of the native women, and De la Borde noted that they had a horror of clothes equal to the Europeans' horror of nudity. There is the passionate love of the island home, which has always been the foundation rock of all Antillean nationalism; and Columbus reported in one of his letters how Taino Indian captives, rescued by him from their Carib captors in Guadeloupe, swam ashore at night in order to embrace the soil of their beloved Borinquén. There is, finally, a note of obdurate and stubborn resiliency, a refusal to be proselytized by the new conquering religion: De la Borde reports Indians as telling their compatriots that the cause of all the misfortunes and illnesses of the Christians stems from the fact that they do not live like Caribs.[16] That resistance, in fact, led to the massive failure of the missionary efforts in all early Antillean history, even lasting much later; and it is only necessary to read the pathetic account of the young Catholic missionary-priest William Stanton—who spent his whole life in a futile effort to Christianize the spiritually immovable Indian Mayan tribes of the interior riverine section of British Honduras at the turn of the nineteenth century—to appreciate the deep power of cultural resistance possessed by the Antillean native peoples.[17] They were overwhelmed by the material power of the European invaders. But they kept intact their religiocultural integrity, the memory of which, later on, was to become a major inspirational element in the *indigenista-romántico-costumbrista* novel of the Puerto Rican and Dominican literati of the nineteenth and twentieth centuries. Nor, when the full contribution of the first residents of the Caribbean region is being assessed, must we lose sight of the fact that they left behind a lasting influence in the realm of Caribbean language, as many of their words entered into and enriched the language of the European invaders: a contribution annotated in the later work of modern lexicographers.[18]

The general cosmic vision that all of this illustrates has been definitively stated, for the Taino Indian group of the Greater Antilles, by the Puerto Rican scholar Eugenio Fernández Méndez in his brilliantly rendered *Art and Anthropology of the Taino Indians of the Greater West Indies*. From the evidence of both extant native art and early European observation, it is eminently demonstrable that the vision was that of a larger continental mythology embracing both Maya and Mexican concepts of the origin, nature, and destiny of man. The striking similarity between the mythical stories is apparent in all of the elements of the total theogony and cosmology of the whole Mesoamerican pattern: the principal supernatural powers, the origin of the creator gods and goddesses in the myth of the cave, the emphasis of all art on the theme of fertility, the creator parents of the god of heaven and the goddess of the earth, and the rest—with the greatest similarity being the extraordinary importance of the female as source of creation, probably due to the matrilineal organization of the indigenous clans both in the Antillean and Mesoamerican social structures. A further similarity exists in the concept of death and in the symbolic ornamentation of art objects. Or, again, there is the similarity in the idea that collecting gold was a sacred occupation, so different from the Spanish attitude.

Fernández Méndez concludes:

> Everything seems to point to the fact that, in the Antillean religion, we find either an old formative version or as is also likely a somewhat late but still simplified version, of a religious pantheon which as it evolved into more complicated forms, produced the complicated calendar and rites of the Mexicans and Mayans.[19]

The Fernández Méndez book, admittedly, is a *parti pris* statement in favor of the Central American–Mexican genesis of the Antillean culture, as distinct from the more southern route of cultural diffusion. The important point to stress, however, is that all the evidence of art and mythology alike points to the existence of a highly developed and indeed sophisticated civilization, whatever route of origin is preferred. This, on any showing, is a needed and healthy antidote to the temper of absolute and seemingly ineradicable racism which the Europeans, of all persuasions, brought after 1500 or so to their own vision of the Caribbean, rooted in their assumption of innate and permanent Indian inferiority—so much so that the very idea of the Indian, just like the other idea of the Caribbean, was in fact a white European invention that ignored the fundamental truth that the so-called Indians of the so-called Caribbean belonged in truth to an extended cultural lineage of family stretching throughout the circum-Caribbean as a whole.[20]

THE SPANISH JURO-THEOLOGICAL CONTRIBUTION

The first chapter in the long history of the debate on the moral and intellectual significance of the Caribbean was written by those Spanish jurists, theologians, historians, and policymakers for whom the Discovery gave rise to serious and vexatious juridical problems. The central problem was that of the legitimacy of Spain's title to the Indies. What were the rights and wrongs, the purposes and the limits of the new imperial responsibility? From that enquiry flowed all the other questions of what constituted in effect a prolonged disputatious debate, by means of books, pamphlets, and official declarations, on Spanish rule in the Indies. Could it be justified by the right of conquest alone? What legal and political rights, whether founded on considerations of civil law or natural law, remained to the Indians as new subjects of the Spanish Crown? Did Papal grant or *raison d'état* (reason of state) confer moral authority upon Spanish rule? Since that rule, in turn, was also one of Catholic Christianity (which none of the many participants in the debate denied), should the Indian be converted by force or only by persuasion? And since, finally, all of these questions naturally related to the character of the new subject-peoples, what in fact was that character? For if they were to be regarded, like infidel or relapsed heretic, as beyond the pale of Christian charity, it followed that their complete servitude was justified; if, on the other hand, they were to be regarded as peoples potentially sharing the promise of the Christian revelation, it would follow that, at the least, they would have to be gently treated as some sort of innocent pagans who were legitimate candidates for successful evangelization. The answers proferred to all of these fundamental questions constituted, in sum, a body of literature on the *política indiana* of the period; that is to say, the official policy adopted for the treatment of the Indians.[21]

The orthodox answer to many of those questions appeared as early as 1540 in the form of the published lectures of the Dominican jurist Francisco de Vitoria's *Relectiones de Indis*. Anticipating the seminal argument of Grotius, he sought to place the Conquest within a framework of international law. The claim of neither Pope nor Emperor to exercise temporal jurisdiction over others seemed to Vitoria to be sufficient to legitimize war or conquest; only a law of nations, involving mutual rights and duties, could meet the problem. Just as Natural Law obligated individuals living in the state of nature, so the theory of international law bound states which, by virtue of their sovereignty, remained still in the natural state vis-à-vis each other. Applied to the New World, this doctrine meant that both Indian and Christian were bound by its dictates. The Indians must receive the Spaniards peacefully and hear the Gospel; the Spaniards must behave as Christians, present the Gospel fairly, and respect the secondary authority of Indian princes. There followed a long list of conditions which, if broken by the Indians, would justify the use of force: refusal to listen to the Gospel, attempts to force converted aborigines to return to "idolatry," the exercise of unnatural habits such as cannibalism, refusal to allow rights of travel and commerce to the Spanish, and so on.[22]

It is clear, as one reads all this, that one is in the presence of a highly academic juristic imagination. It assumed a relationship of juridical equality between Indians and Spaniards utterly at variance with the actual conditions of the relationships. The New World, after all, was conquered by the superior technology of European ship, gunpowder, armor, sword—not to mention the horse—against which the weapons of the Indians, as Las Casas noted, were children's toys. The Indians were presented with a choice which, in grim reality, was no choice at all. Vitoria painted a picture of international law; the reality was that even in Europe, and especially in the New World, the European colonizing powers, starting with the Spanish, operated within a framework of international anarchy. The theory never really explained how the Indian was supposed to have given his consent to a contractual relationship with the Spaniard. Worse than that, it assumed that somehow, again by a process never explained, the Spaniard would conduct himself in obedience to the norms laid down by the international moral code. In reality, of course, he behaved more in accordance with the code set out in Machiavelli's *Prince*. Other Spanish writers, indeed, saw the weakness of Vitoria's argument, if only because they chronicled the real behavior of their fellow countrymen in the Indies. As early as 1500 Columbus himself recognized them as a dissolute people, who feared neither God nor their King.[23] Some seventy years later, the historian López de Velasco added that it had been the general policy to send out as "settlers" men who hated work and were more anxious to get rich quickly than to settle permanently in the country. Forgetting their proper place, he added, they raise themselves to a higher level and go about the country, idle vagabonds, making pretensions of offices and allotments of Indians.[24] It was an indictment all the more credible because Velasco was no Las Casas, dedicated to the Indian cause. That general rabble of Spaniards, moreover, was only following the example of the early soldier-conquerors at a less dramatic level; for the treachery practiced by Cortes against Montezuma or by Pizarro against the Inca Huayna Capac rivaled anything practiced by the Tudors or the Medici at the same time in European state politics.

The importance of the sort of argument put forward by Vitoria, then, is of a somewhat different nature. Ignoring the facts—he was one of those theoreticians on the character of the Indies who never visited them—he brought to the debate on the New World an imaginary vision of the Spanish conquerors and settlers as actors in some sort of medieval chivalrous tale, just as the Inca Garcilaso de la Vega had written an idealized version of the old Inca state in order to prove Indian equality with the Spanish. Vitoria is almost the first thinker of the new age to develop, in embryonic form, that sort of apologetic literature for the new colonialism which, for the next three centuries or more came to constitute so important an element in the attitudes of the European mind toward the New World.

Yet however apologetic the literature, it is necessary to emphasize one aspect, since it illuminates so well the role that the Caribbean, albeit as a passive agent, played in the development of the European thought of the period. The need for a new, secular international law was made painfully clear by the new geographical discoveries. Papal authority for imperial enterprise in the Indies no longer sufficed, since it could not bind the Protestant powers like England and Holland. A body of doctrine had to be stated which rested upon different sanctions. The discoveries, more importantly, raised important issues of international trading and commercial rights involving a whole new science of international treaty-making. That science had to be formulated in such a way that it was binding upon, and willingly accepted by, men and nations of diverse faith, Protestant as well as Catholic; which meant, inevitably, that its sanctions would have to be secular and not religious. The original Spanish monopoly in the Indies, it is also important to remember, was attacked from the beginning by its rivals. As early as 1494 Portugal, although a Catholic nation, refused to accept the Papal Donation of 1493, and was rapidly followed by the Protestant maritime nations. The conflict raised all sorts of problems new to jurists and publicists: the desirability of arbitration, the exposition of the rights and duties of neutrals, the restraints suggested on pillage as incidents of war (dramatically illustrated by the new phenomenon of "privateers," who were nothing more than licensed pirates on behalf of different national states), the rights of new subject-peoples, and the rest. It is not too much to say that the growth of this new type of secular public international law received its initial impetus from the practical problems unleashed by the international struggle for the control of the Indies after 1492. Its theoretical formulation started with the treatise of Vitoria and ended with the definitive work of Grotius. Its practical end was to ensure a viable international peace with adequate institutional safeguards; and in the writings of both Vitoria at the beginning and Grotius at the end there can be perceived clearly the general idea that the final purpose of that peace was the legal protection, by means of appropriate institutions, of the new capitalist commerce of the age that had been opened up by the discoveries.

That last point is important. A whole body of European historical literature has mythologized the discoveries. They have been seen as the work of, on the one hand, greed and avarice, or "the lust for gold," on the part of a motley crew of adventurers, or, on the other hand, of superhuman heroic seamen and soldiers. So to see them is to misunderstand the crucial fact that they were, rather, the expression of the overseas thrust of the rising European commercial capitalism, symbolized in the new alliance between the commercial bourgeoisie and the emerging nation-state. In this sense, Columbus is not to be seen as a daring maritime adventurer, but as a person closely connected, in his own business affairs, with the slave trade and the early colonial sugar capitalism; similarly, the Catholic monarchs cannot be seen simply as persons solely interested in the spread of the faith in the new lands, but rather as personifications of the new political form of the nation-state, seeking, in alliance with the rising middle class and the impoverished lesser gentry, to overcome the old feudal baronies of the time. The movement of thought that started with Vitoria and ended with Grotius has to be seen within this socio-historical context. It sought to construct new rules of international relations to meet the new problems. Vitoria, of course, did so with an eye to the colonial rights of Spain; Grotius completed the work by incorporating in his more complete scheme the totality of the colonial rights of the other European states.

THE EUROPEAN CHRONICLERS

Vitoria wrote as a Salamanca professor and jurist; his interest in the newly colonized lands was academic. It is to the *cronistas mayores* (the major chroniclers)—Oviedo with his *Historia general y natural de las Indias* (1555-57), and Herrera with his *Historia general de los hechos de los Castellanos en las Islas y Tierra Firme del mar océano* (1601-15)—that the student must turn in order to understand how the more practical-minded of the Spanish imperialists viewed the new possessions. Oviedo spent twenty-four years of his life in the West Indies; Herrera, although lacking that firsthand experience, extensively used the libraries of original documents placed at his disposal by royal order. The influence of their writings is attested to by the fact that when the nineteenth-century Puerto Rican historian Alejandro Tapia y Rivera came to compose his *Biblioteca histórica de Puerto Rico* in 1854, substantial portions of that work were drawn from those two earlier official historians. The two works provide a vivid pen portrait of the Indies during their formative period. They illustrate, at the same time, how two different minds could draw more or less similar conclusions about the nature and character of the new possessions.

The discoveries, more than anything else, gave a fresh impetus to Spanish nationalism. The conquest of the Indies, as Francisco López de Gómara grandiloquently put it in the dedicatory preface to yet another chronicle, his own *Historia general de las Indias*, began providentially as the wars against the Moors ended, for the Spanish have always fought against infidels.[25] Oviedo is the leading ideologue of that spirit. He wrote as a royal official under instructions to fashion his history according to the wishes of the Council. His work, the first history of America to be printed in Spain, was thus imbued with the spirit of Spanish Manifest Destiny. There is, no doubt, much of interest to the culture-historian in his pages. He described, among a host of topics, tobacco cultivation among the aboriginal Indians of Hispaniola, the early rise of the sugar industry in the same colony, with its huge capital outlay already apparent; the nature and consequences of the policy of the *repartimiento*, of which he was not entirely uncritical; Indian ethnology, including descriptions of the Indian *batey* (small household backyard), the Indian canoe, and the Indian games such as *pelota* (tennis); and much else. In addition to all that, Oviedo was obviously a born naturalist, and he described the animal and vegetable life of the islands with a keen perception which must have given much pleasure to his European readers.[26] Even so, Oviedo has been remembered, by friend and critic alike, as the archetype of the insensitive European in the tropics. His huge work was infused throughout with a marked disdain and contempt for the aboriginal peoples, inspired not so much by racial animosity as such as by a combination of religious intolerance and cultural ethnocentrism. The Indians, according to him, were by nature idle and vicious, disinclined to work, cowardly and base, prone to evil, liars, forgetful, and inconstant. Even worse, they were sodomites, cannibals, and idolators; "they have many other vices," he added, "so ugly that many of them are too obscene to be listened to without loathing and shame, nor could I write about them because of their great number and filthiness." Being thus, their extermination by the Spaniards, he concluded, could be interpreted as divine punishment for their bestiality.[27]

Herrera's *magnum opus*, written half a century later, was equally apologetic. The author's purpose, as he stated in his dedicatory preface, was to answer those earlier writers, like Ramusio, who, according to him, had besmirched the good name of the Spanish in the Americas, not seeing that even their cruelty was justified by divine permission, as retribution for the enormous sins of the Indians. He seeks, as his title suggests, only to commemorate the great deeds of his countrymen. Whereas, then, Oviedo's method of justification had been to slander the indigenous inhabitants, Herrera's method was mainly to ignore them. For it is the astonishing thing about the voluminous collection of Herrera's work, that, apart from relying on the merely descriptive passages of Peter Martyr and repeating Oviedo's libelous observations, it hardly addresses itself in any serious way to a discussion of the original inhabitants of the islands. It is a sort of Homeric epic of the Spanish achievements, and little else. The temper of the work was, it is true, somewhat different, for whereas Oviedo had written as a highly opinionated and aggressively arrogant chronicler, Herrera wrote in the more cautious manner of the court scribe. But he was as much an apologist as his predecessor. He wrote approvingly of the work of the Inquisition. He praised the piety of the orders such as the Dominicans, but refrained from saying anything about the *crise de conscience* that drove many of their members, and not just Las Casas, into open disapproval of Spanish policies. He described the machinery of Spanish overseas government, including the provisions for administrative protection of Indian interests, but showed no interest in discussing whether the legislation was, in practical terms, a success or a failure. He noted how the Spanish evangelizing efforts had proved futile because of what he termed the "evil inclination" and the "defective memory" of the Indians, yet he could not see that the policy of forcible removal of Indian populations to places nearer the Spanish townships, in order to facilitate conversion by closer relations between master and serf, was equally doomed to failure if his own stereotyped understanding of the Indian character were true. The chief defect of Herrera's work, however, lies elsewhere. For centuries orthodox Spanish scholarship has praised Herrera, almost in the same breath as it has damned Las Casas for being the evil-minded author of the *leyenda negra*. The irony is that much of Herrera's text, including entire chapters, was copied verbatim from the unpublished manuscripts of Las Casas himself, only omitting the angry strictures on Spanish rule. The irony of that fact becomes more piquant still when it is remembered that Las Casas's manuscripts were denied publication for centuries, while the volumes of Herrera received the royal *imprimatur*.[28]

Looked at from the viewpoint of American freedom, the most important contribution of chronicles like those of Oviedo and Herrera, as well as a host of lesser imitators, was that they provided for the first time a plausible rationalization for Spanish oppression. Nor was that any accident. If Indian servitude—in effect, a revived form of slavery—was to be made palatable to public opinion, the old, traditional humanist view, inherited from the medieval teachings, and still in favor with the clerical and intellectual classes of sixteenth-century Spain, would have to be met and, if possible, destroyed. The new literature sought to do that by proving that the New World peoples were guilty of Natural Law offenses, such as tyranny, sodomy, bestiality, and human sacrifice, and therefore not to be regarded as members of Natural Society. That movement commenced, significantly enough, within a few years after Columbus's first voyage of 1492. The portrait of the Indians painted in the Columbus reports, as a timid and innocent people, was rapidly replaced with the Oviedo-Herrera stigmata. As early as 1512 Fray Tomás Ortiz could tell the Council of the Indies that the Indians were a drunken, worthless set of treacherous thieves and liars.[29] Four years later the report of the Jeronomite Commission to Cardinal Cisneros repeated the slander, adding that the cleverest among the Indians was more stupid than the humblest peasant in Spain.[30] Sepúlveda elaborated the same general attitude more systematically in his book of 1542, *Democrates Alter*, best known because it precipitated the famous official Valladolid enquiry of 1550-51.[31] How rapidly the attitude gained ground thereafter may be seen from the fact that, notwithstanding the comparatively mild temper of that book, written by a learned humanist who had counted Erasmus among his friends, its argument that Natural Law itself justified the government of the "lower" races by the "higher" raised such a storm of protest that it was denied permission for publication, while only a few years later Oviedo's volumes, with their quite different temper of scurrilous abuse of the Indian populations, were published with official blessing in his capacity as royal historian. Here, indeed, is the genesis, in its modern form, of the literature of ethnic stereotyping as intellectual justification for colonial rule: the process whereby gross and negative stereotypes are arbitrarily assigned to entire peoples. That certain elements of Spanish classical thought contributed to that process has been largely forgotten because, well before the end of the sixteenth century, the Indian had been replaced by the African slave as its leading victim, with the result that the Indian became resuscitated later on as the hero figure of the Creole *indianista* novel.

BARTOLOMÉ de LAS CASAS

It was, of course, the noble figure of Las Casas who helped, more than any other single person, to redeem that evil record. The supreme controversialist of his time, in his role as defender of the Indians, he provoked a lengthy and controversial literature that continues to the present day. His detractors, anxious to defend the good name of Spain, have portrayed him as being everything from an irresponsible forger to a certifiable madman. But their argument is so full of a reactionary Hispanophilism that it cannot be taken seriously. It is true that later scholarship has proved the inexactitude of his Indian statistics; but it has not been able to challenge the essential verisimilitude of his central thesis that the Conquest meant, in effect, a prolonged act of genocide against the aboriginal inhabitants of the islands. It has been argued, in turn, that, as a Dominican, he sought to erect a Catholic theocracy in the new possessions, as against both Crown and settlers. It is enough to read his severe strictures on the officialdom of both State and Church that helped to frustrate the application of the royal edicts on treatment of the Indians to realize that, on the contrary, he saw clearly that it was not Christianity, as such, but its corruption in the form of the organized church that had betrayed the Spanish mission in the transatlantic possessions. Going to the other extreme, his most recent champions, and especially the American historian Lewis Hanke, have been tempted to see him in individualistic terms, as a hero fighting singlehandedly for Indian justice against the entrenched political, military, and ecclesiastical interests of the period.[32] So to see him is to miss the point that, as the Cuban historian Juan Friede has pointed out, Las Casas was in fact only the most well-known spokesman of a party, or faction, within the conglomeration of the various interest groups of the sixteenth century that fought to have their particular outlook shape official policy in the New World.[33]

Hardly anybody, except the professional historian, reads Las Casas today. The sheer volume of his prodigious output, along with its character of earlier disputatious debate, is perhaps too formidable for the average reader. Yet to read the massive volumes even today is to feel everything that went into their composition: the pithy style, the irony, the rough eloquence, the enraged indignation against injustice, the Christian humanism, and not least of all the insatiable curiosity which enabled their author, by means of a lifelong questioning of the innumerable actors in the great drama he was describing and a veritable mania for the collecting of documents, to quote chapter and verse for every grim accusation that he made against his fellow countrymen. Underpinning all this there is an almost modern concept of historical science. It is the business of the historian, he tells the reader in his explicatory prologue, not to invent legends or seek to please kings, but to tell the truth about great events. Just as it was the aim of Josephus, he adds, to defend the Jews of the ancient world against their Roman detractors, so it is his purpose to defend the Indian peoples of the New World against their European detractors.[34] Every page of his various manuscript works bears the imprint of that modern insistence upon circumstantial evidence; and it was the absence of such evidence that made him so furious about what he called Oviedo's "gossip."[35] Las Casas, in brief, is at once the first American historian and the first Caribbean historian—the first American historian because he writes with a distinctively American flavor: the utilitarian temper, the importance of factual evidence, the marriage of theory and practice, the essential pragmatism of attitude; the first Caribbean historian because, if we mean by Caribbean history a recognition of the fact that the Caribbean peoples have been the most important actors (albeit not necessarily the most powerful) on the Caribbean stage, that note is first struck in the *obra lascasiana*. It is true that because the only force that could control the new colonial oligarchy was the enlightened absolutism of the Spanish Crown, Las Casas seems frequently to write as a defender of the royal cause. But, first and foremost, he regarded the Indian as the most important client, of whom he was the self-appointed attorney.

Despite their monumental size, the basic themes of the books—*Historia de las Indias, Brevísima relación de la destrucción de las Indias Occidentales, Apologética historia*—as well as the innumerable petitions, reports, and correspondence are simply stated. There was, of course, first and foremost, the unequivocal condemnation of the nature of Spanish rule in the Indies. It constituted, as Las Casas told Charles V, a "gigantically tyrannical system." The *Brevísima relación* cataloged the cruelties and abuses of the *encomienda* system, and especially the oppressive system of mine labor, in too much grim detail to be easily refuted[36]—so much so, that its critics had to resort to specious arguments in their effort to destroy its credibility: that it was used in French and English translations by Spain's hated rivals (a charge that overlooked the fact that Las Casas attacked not only the Spaniards but also the other Europeans, Germans, Italians, and Portuguese, who collaborated in the system), or that it was written in a rough, direct language scandalous to the mandarins of the purist Spanish learned academies (Las Casas had too much to relate to be concerned with the niceties of Castilian Spanish). He perceived clearly the economic consequences of the system. It reduced the Indians to a state of servitude, replacing their original subsistence economy with a dependent economy in which they played the role of a propertyless helotry.[37] They sweated in labor, wrote Las Casas, incomparably more onerous than that of miners in Castile. He noted the rise of a new social system based on that exploitation, poor whites who became the lords of native rulers, satisfying social ambitions denied to them at home; as Judge Hurtado of Hispaniola informed Charles V in 1550, all Spaniards who go to the Indies immediately become gentlemen, which makes it necessary for them to be able to purchase Negroes at reasonable prices.[38] Some of them climbed high enough to enter the new colonial seigneurial class; and Las Casas anticipated a theme that was to recur in Caribbean literature for the next four hundred years: the conspicuous waste of the life-style of the new white master class, with all of its greed, venality, corruption, and rascality. The pen portrait, in the *Historia*, of Rodrígo de Albuquerque, the first appointed *repartidor* (official in charge of land distribution) describes his record of financial malfeasance; and the description of the young spendthrift Santa Clara—made treasurer of the same young island colony, wasting the royal income on feasts of Lucullan prodigality in which favored guests were presented with salt cellars filled with gold dust—is even more damning.[39] Las Casas was also concerned with the cultural consequences of all this: his medieval sense of status and hierarchy was outraged at the fact that a common Spanish swordsman like Nuño de Guzmán should be granted ownership of a high-ranking *cacique* like Guaybona. The destruction of Indian village life; the breakup of Indian family life; the imposition of an iron discipline upon a frail and delicate people, the least capable—in Las Casas's phrase—"of enduring toil and the most susceptible to sickness": it is all there. Colonialism everywhere has witlessly destroyed native economies and cultures. Las Casas's account is the first detailed description of the process in the Caribbean area.

This led logically to the other theme of the *política indiana*. It enabled Las Casas to answer the thesis of the chroniclers that the Indians were idolatrous savages doomed inevitably to extinction. The answer, of course, did not take the form of a learned treatise on the matter, in the manner of Solórzano's *Política Indiana* or Padre Avendaño's *Tesoro Indico*. It took the form, rather, of a rich combination of narrative description and theoretical discourse spread throughout hundreds of pages written by an author with the inestimable advantage of having been a witness to the events that he described. To Oviedo's charges Las Casas answered at once in particular and general tones. In particular terms, the Indians, he argued, could not be regarded as naturally lazy, since their housework, fishing, and agricultural pursuits, in addition to their handicraft work, proved otherwise. The charge of sodomy has never been proved. That they were ungrateful was true, but the real cause was the original ingratitude of the Spaniards, who had betrayed the trust placed in them by the natives early on. That they had no virtues was patently untrue; and, adds Las Casas, the vice of marital infidelity is notoriously a Spanish, rather than an Indian one.[40] In general terms, the charge that the Indians live in a state of anarchic savagery was answered by Las Casas's fuller understanding of the anthropology of Indian life. It is true that there are passages in his writings which seem to suggest an Indian state of nature before the Europeans arrived. But the predominant note is more sophisticated. Rather than being a state of nature, in either the Christian or the Hobbistical sense, the Indian society as portrayed by Las Casas is an ordered society in the full Aristotelian sense, with its own structured hierarchy of priests, chieftains, and nobles and possessing its own handicrafts, its own cultural and religious character, and its own song and dance tradition. They are pagans, true. But that is no more than an offense of ignorance, not culpable sin. And even at that, they possessed their own pantheistic religious belief system; and Las Casas reported the harangue delivered to Columbus himself by an aged island chieftain who instructed the Admiral on the Indian concept of a heaven and a hell remarkably akin to the Christian belief in an afterlife.[41] The Indian way of life, in brief, was not the tropical anarchy portrayed by its enemies, but an ordered society based on convention rather than on nature. As such, it commanded respect.

The Indian moral character, continued Las Casas, was no less complex than the Indian social structure. For Oviedo, the Indian was little more than a beast that could talk. For Vitoria, he was an unfortunate creature who, although not unintelligent, was certainly primitive. Las Casas replied:

> The people with whom the New World is swarming, are not only capable of understanding the Christian religion, but amenable, by reason and persuasion, to the practice of good morals and the highest virtues. Nature made them free and they have their kings or rulers to regulate their political life. . . . Our holy religion adapts itself equally as well to all the nations of the world; it embraces them all and deprives no human being of his natural liberty under pretext or colour that he or she is *servus a natura*.[42]

The doctrine of Christian liberty thus harmonized with the rational character of the New World peoples. From this, Las Casas concludes, certain vital considerations flow.

1. Once again following Aristotle, there are only two forms of government in civil society—the one legitimate, the other despotic. The new Indian realms come within the former category, since they are composed of men capable of reason and therefore of comprehending the nature of their allegiance. Spanish authority, he concedes, flows from the Papal commission. But the sole reason for the Papal donation, he adds, was the conversion of the Indians. It is therefore made conditional upon the exercise of justice. The new system of overseas imperial government must consequently acknowledge the right of its new subject-peoples to claim the same guarantees of liberty provided by Castilian law to its own metropolitan subjects. So, the Indian subject cannot be asked to pay full tribute to the Crown, but only those gifts, limited in character, that are an acknowledgment of his allegiance. Just government must accommodate itself to the peculiar conditions and the disposition of the governed; the new possessions are not a *tabula rasa* upon which Spain may imprint its own religious and cultural character as it pleases. This, all in all, is a doctrine of Christian imperialism. It anticipates the concept of colonial trusteeship later developed by Edmund Burke in the case of the British colonial empire.

2. The free exercise of reason which all men, Christian or Indian, possess, requires that proselytization should be one of persuasion, not of coercion. Coercion of any kind, Las Casas remarks, is worthy only of Mahomet. The Indians would be the happiest people in the world, if only they knew God; but they must come to know Him by consent, not by intimidation or terror. At this point Las Casas appeals to the older tradition of religious toleration, before it was overwhelmed in his own day by the religious warfare of Catholic and Protestant and transported by them to the Caribbean. He saw, with simple clarity, that religious persecution, as much in the Americas as in Europe, meant the massacre of the innocents. If, he argues, the royal legislation protecting the Indians is honestly administered, they will arrive of their own accord at a willing reception of the Gospel. This, all in all, is the voice of the simple beauty of the original Gospel message before it was betrayed by the vested interests of the organized churches. It is the voice of the historical Jesus-figure himself, of the Johannine hymn to love, of Saint Francis of Assisi, transported to the New World.

3. If, however, Las Casas concludes, in defiance of all these precepts, justice is eluded, then the Indian peoples would be justified in undertaking rebellious activity. He wrote:

Since the laws and rules of nature and international law are common to all nations, Christians and Gentiles, whatever their sect, law, state, colour and condition, the inhabitants [of Cuba] had the same right to wage just war on the Admiral and his Christians in order to rescue their neighbors and compatriots.[43]

Oviedo had portrayed the Indians as barbarians whose very inability to resist the Spaniards was perversely interpreted as proof of their inferior status. Las Casas, on the contrary, at once wrote memorable passages on Indian revolts and uprisings that gave the lie to Oviedo's canard about Indian passivity and justified them in terms of the medieval doctrine of the just war. Vitoria and Sepúlveda had used that same doctrine to give legitimacy to the Conquest; Las Casas used it to justify Indian rebellion.

4. There is, finally, the argument in favor of a new political structure in the New World which, accepting the royal authority, would revive the authority of the Indian chiefs, the *señores naturales*, in a kind of Commonwealth arrangement of delegated rule. This structure would at once recognize the Indian capacity for self-rule and incorporate the Indian peoples into a political society founded on mutual duties and obligations, thus anticipating in a way the concept of a Commonwealth of Nations as it was instituted, centuries later, in the British colonial empire.[44]

Las Casas's contribution to the Caribbean debate—which, indeed, he may claim to have started—was, then, of inestimable value. He set it in terms of right, not of power. For his rival chroniclers, Spain had a general mandate to subjugate the Indians, by force if necessary. If the Indians proved intransigent, then that was viewed as proof that, like the heretic, they contentiously refused to embrace their own salvation. Las Casas countered that argument by denying its major premise, based on the sacred authority of Aristotle, that the native peoples were slaves by nature. Aristotle, he remarked with characteristic acerbity, was a pagan, now burning in hell, and only those of his doctrines should be accepted that do not contradict the Christian faith. More than that, Las Casas advanced a surprisingly modern theory of progress and cultural development—seeing all peoples as occupying different rungs on the evolutionary ladder, with all of them susceptible at once to cultural advance and moral elevation. Hanke writes:

> He did not automatically assume, that the Indians should be measured by a Spanish or even European yardstick, but on the contrary he tried to understand the importance of their customs and beliefs within the framework of their own culture. In so doing he developed an attitude toward change that was, in effect, one of the most interesting theories of progress of his day. Las Casas looked at all peoples, the ancient Greeks, the savage Tartars, and sixteenth-century Spaniards, as well as the New World natives, as human beings in different stages of development from rude beginnings to a higher stage of culture.[45]

Yet the major elements of his thought were fully traditionalist. He was no republican nor, indeed, a sceptic. As a devout Catholic, he accepted without question the right of the Spanish Crown and Church to exclusive evangelization in the Indies. Nor was he any friend to the new dogma of the time, the absolute monarchy. Indian freedom, for him, was, rather, the residuary legatee, as it were, of medieval kingship, with its panoply of duty and obligation. So, it is not surprising that his thought exhibits certain profound contradictions. He wanted a more positive royal control of the new colonial possessions, yet recognized, at the same time—as in his severe strictures on the Laws of Burgos (which laid down rules for the government of the Indies)— that such control was rendered ineffective by the fact that the royally appointed governors and judges themselves developed a vested interest in maintaining the abuses of the system. His ultimate ideal, as against that system, was the establishment of a new, popular colonization program by farmers "who would live by tilling the rich lands of the Indies, lands which the Indian owners would voluntarily grant to them," and whereby "the Spaniards would intermarry with the natives and make of both peoples one of the best Commonwealths in the world and perhaps one of the most Christian and peaceful." But he did not fully see that neither Crown nor Church could initiate such a program, since both had early on become too involved with the rewards of the latifundium system. He thought, finally, in terms of Catholic Christendom, without recognizing how the Reformation, in his own day, had forever shattered the edifice of medieval religious unity.[46]

The final comment on his work is that it testified to a persisting liberal-humanist tradition in Spanish thought that is often forgotten. A whole school of self-righteous English historians, for example, has propagated the legend of English primacy in the history of the libertarian movement in the Caribbean. Yet it was Las Casas, with his defense of the Indians, who was the pioneer in that field. His achievement was aptly summed up by the twentieth-century Puerto Rican leader Luis Muñoz Rivera, when he reminded the Americans that Las Casas had valiantly undertook to bring Christianity to the aboriginal inhabitants of America long before William Penn began his work with the North American Indians.[47] It is an interesting commentary on that Anglo-Saxon belief—that it was the Nonconformist conscience that first launched a frontal attack upon injustice in the islands—that when the English scholar J. W. Allen came to write his definitive *History of Political Thought in the Sixteenth Century* in 1928, he included chapters on England, France, and Italy, but none on Spain; thus cavalierly overlooking the prolonged Spanish debate on the implications of the discoveries for all of the leading issues of that political thought: the problem of authority, the limits of obedience, religious toleration, the rights of subjects, the rival claims of Papacy and nation-state, and the rest. It is therefore no accident that the new academic scholarship of revolutionary Cuba after 1959 has begun to rediscover Las Casas and his significance in the historic cause of Caribbean freedom.[48]

The general point about all this has been well made by the Argentinan scholar Alberto Salas in his balanced and sympathetic study on the three major chroniclers, Peter Martyr, Oviedo, and Las Casas. Peter Martyr, as he emphasizes, was the chronicler of the novelty of the New World as it appeared to the Renaissance scholars of the time—who were not particularly concerned with the moral and ethical problems raised by the conquest; Oviedo, in turn, wrote as the apologist of monarchical and Catholic Spain; while Las Casas is to be seen as the first critic of Spanish nationalism, concerned not so much with the purity of the ideal as with the complex reality of what really happened.[49] Nor is that all. For because the Spanish-shaped societies of the present-day Caribbean area—Puerto Rico and Santo Domingo in the north, Venezuela and Colombia in the south—still exhibit the deeply felt prejudices of being *hispanófilo* (hispanophile) and *blancófilo* (white-oriented), it is not surprising that their intelligentsia are still preoccupied with the debate that Las Casas started, and that it is still possible to find virulent traces of the xenophobic hatred for the Dominican priest, as well as continuing supportive argumentation for the reactionary thesis that both Indian and African must be considered subordinate strains in the national character—which is still seen as a New World testimonial to Spanish genius.[50]

THE SPANISH IMPERIAL SPIRIT

Yet the discussion of the total Spanish contribution to the formation of the New World cannot be left at this point. The *leyenda negra* fashioned by Las Casas and his school was substantially correct and justified. But at the same time it is possible to argue that their indictment was fatally prejudiced, since it looked almost exclusively at only one aspect of the contribution. Spain was far more than conquest and colonization. It is true that for the most part its representatives in the newly discovered lands were the soldier of fortune, the grasping merchant, the corrupt royal administrator, the poor gentleman out to save his fortunes. What they all represented was the Renaissance temper of Machiavellian power for power's sake. But there was more to the Renaissance than that; and the new empire felt much of it.

That is obvious in a number of ways. It is there in the fact that, as Maravall has pointed out, the Spaniard at his best, whether serving church or state, was a *renacentista* in the sense that he expressed all or many of the typical Renaissance qualities: a vigorous delight in the world of nature, as expressed in the new naturalism of Renaissance pictorial art; an almost morbid curiosity about new worlds and new peoples, so that the old medieval theme of *contemptu mundi* gives way to a new pleasure in the world of nature; the feeling that felt experience is more important than inherited tradition, so that the old fixed ideas about the flatness of the earth, inhabitable torrid zones, and the existence of the antipodes, are replaced by a new understanding of the physical world as it really is; and not least important, the idea that the New World offers to the Spaniards the opportunity to construct a new political world based on art and reason (so much as that idea was a typical Renaissance conceit).[51]

That large vision, moreover, is evident in the rich material of Spanish Renaissance political thought, as it has been documented most notably in J. A. Fernández-Santamaría's volume of 1977. In those parts of it that were devoted to the American controversy, much of the argument, as already noted, came down in favor of the Spanish right to subdue and rule the Indians. But it was never just anti-Indian prejudice, plain and simple. It was set within a serious attempt to justify the position within the framework of first principles, at once traditional and modern. It sought to construct the idea and the reality of a New World *república cristiana*—subject, of course, to Spanish kingly supremacy, but at the same time constituting within itself an ordered Commonwealth based on law and justice. Thus Vitoria argues that the Indian commonwealths of the new lands are juristically perfect states on the same footing with their European counterparts and that, once subject to Spain, they now merit consideration as such: alien government can only be justified if it recognizes the status of the Indians as rational subjects within the kingdom.[52] Covarrubias, in turn, argues that the Christian prince cannot justifiably wage war against the Indians simply because they are sinners or idolators, but only if they actively resist the preaching of the Gospel; *jus naturalis* requires that there be limits to the war-making power.[53] Even Sepúlveda, it can be argued, has been unfairly traduced because of his assult upon Indian rationality. For a full examination of his writings shows clearly that he was far more than the *bête noire* of the Las Casas school. In the same *Democratus Alter* where his almost cruel observations upon the Indians occur—including his denial, as opposed to both Covarrubias and Vitoria, of Indian rationality—he argues in favor of a well-ordered commonwealth in the Indies including both Spaniards and Indians. In such a regime there will exist a political compact of mixed nature. It will contain obligations binding on both sides. Its Spanish rulers will consist of the best to be recruited from the royal administrative service, possessed of the Ciceronian ideal of selfless public service. Its Indian subjects will be treated in the same way as European plebeians are treated in the Spanish hierarchical system, as inferiors possessing both rights and obligations. The Spanish rulers must at all costs avoid the fatal errors of the old Thessalians and Spartans, who, having treated their helots dishonorably, were rewarded with formidable rebellions.[54]

It is important to note, of course, that that ideal was more honored in the breach than in the observance. The actual record in the Indies was different. But it is also important to note that the ideal here postulated—that of a new world society forging a new alliance between American aborigine and Spanish administrator rooted in the nexus of Christian *caritas*—was not lightly held and was indeed shared even by Las Casas himself. The scholastics who fashioned it did so in a literature that was far wiser, far more humane, far more intellectually prepossessing, than anything that came out of the other European colonizing powers. Admittedly, much of its learned argumentation was put in the service of Spanish colonialism. But not always. When—to take one example only—in the 1930s and the 1940s (some four hundred years later) the Puerto Rican nationalist leader Albizu Campos undertook his struggle against American colonialism in the island, he took as his intellectual armory the traditional Spanish values of culture and language, of church and state, as a stick with which to beat the Americans.[55]

It is, indeed, only necessary to look at the beginnings of culture and thought in the island centers during this early period to realize how the Spanish spirit was carried, almost immediately, into the New World. Havana, Santo Domingo, and to a lesser degree San Juan, all became, so to speak, culture carriers. It is enough to look at the massive military fortifications of San Juan, or the early elegant houses of Santo Domingo, or the church buildings of Havana, to perceive that the Spaniards were determined to stay and settle, and to impregnate their new empire with the Spanish spirit at its best.

Early on, Spain planted its institutions of teaching and learning in the island townships. The history of the various foundations testifies to a real zeal for the spiritual and intellectual side of colonial life: the first bishoprics, under the jurisdiction of the Archbishopric of Seville (1511); the first schools, like those in Santo Domingo and La Vega of the Franciscan friars established by Governor Ovando after his arrival in 1503; the first schools planned specifically for boys and girls respectively, like the Colegio de San Ambrosio for boys founded in Havana in 1689 by Bishop Diego Evelino de Compostela and the Colegio de San Francisco de Sales founded a little later by the same patron; the first university, that of Santo Domingo, founded in 1538 out of the old college established earlier by the Dominican order.

Although documentation is scarce, there is little doubt that a real intellectual life, albeit constrained by Church and religious orders, developed early on, especially in Cuba and Hispaniola. As early as 1608 there appeared the very first specimen of what can be termed an indigenous Cuban literature, the poem *Espejo de paciencia* composed by Silvestre de Balboa Troya y Quesada. A series of adulatory sonnets written by friends of the author at much the same time suggests that there existed, even then, in Puerto Príncipe a tiny literary world concerned with poetry and letters. The flow of Cuban emigrants to Mexico and Peru in the following century, including jurisconsults, university rectors, teachers, doctors, and judges, as well as the flowering of Cuban letters in the later eighteenth century period, suggests, in addition, how important that early genesis of thought and interest in the arts must have been.[56] The contribution of Santo Domingo was perhaps even more significant. Bishops like Fray Francisco García de Padilla, Fray Pedro Suarez de Deza, and the learned doctor Alejandro Geraldini brought learning and even fame to their appointments. The new university taught the whole gamut of contemporary European thought from theology and philosophy to law and medicine; and there is evidence to suggest that in the field of medicine teaching, the texts, in typical Renaissance fashion, went back to the seminal ideas of Hippocrates rather than to the medieval scholastic prejudices. Captain Gonzalo Fernández de Oviedo wrote much of his work in the island capital, as did also the well-known Tirso de Moline; the Spanish poet Eugenio de Salazar recalled his experiences in the colony as judge in his unedited manuscript "Silva de Poesía"; and in the same work Salazar mentioned two local poets, Doña Elvira de Mendoza and Doña Leonor de Ovando, perhaps the first of their kind to be mentioned in the literary history of the New World.[57] Not least important of all, Spain exported her architecture to the colonies. By 1550 a firm architectural style and school had already been established in Santo Domingo. As early as 1510 officials had brought from Spain the plans of the leading Spanish architect Alonso Rodríguez for the construction of the great Cathedral; and local resident architects like Rodrígo de Liendo and Francisco de Garay carried on the tradition, not only in the field of ecclesiastical architecture but also in that of civilian housing, especially with their indigenization of the typical model of the Andalucian house.[58] In all of this, Spain contributed to the early cultural formation of the colonial world. It took out its treasure. But it also paid back its debt by sending its art and learning to the new possessions: constituting, in Max Henriquez Ureña's graphic figure of speech, the return of the galleons.

THE ENGLISH AND THE FRENCH CONTRIBUTION

The Spanish school, of course, wrote during the period of undisputed Spanish hegemony in the Caribbean. But by the time that Herrera came to publish his work, that hegemony had been successfully challenged by the rival powers of England, France, and Holland. The nascent capitalism of France (celebrated as early as 1664 by Colbert with the promulgation of his famous laws of commerce and navigation) as well as that of the emergent Protestant nations—which had become evident even earlier with the exploits of the English and Dutch seamen-adventurers against the Spanish New World strongholds —rapidly converted the West Indies into an international economy of European commercial capitalism. Hawkins's first daring slaver voyage of 1563 may be regarded as the starting point of the consequent international struggle for the Caribbean, which was only really brought to a close with the Seven Years War (1756-63), two hundred years later. But the intellectual and diplomatic attack upon the Spanish monopoly had begun even earlier, certainly as early as the frequently quoted remark by King Francis I of France in 1526 that he would be happy to see the clause in Adam's will which excluded him from his share when the world was being divided.

As the history and character of the Caribbean thus became international, so did its literature. The merchant-adventurers as well as the state planners of the rival colonizing powers required accurate information on the New World they sought to penetrate. This early period of the sixteenth and seventeenth centuries, then, is the classic period of the great work of research and translation by European scholarship. The *Orbe Novo* of Peter Martyr was translated into English, to become, in the form of the *Decades of Peter Martyr*, almost an English-language classic itself. Las Casas and Oviedo likewise were translated into English and French. Jean de Laet's famous Latin work, *Novus Orbis seu descriptiones Indiae Occidentalis*, was translated into Dutch. Rochefort's French book, *Histoire naturelle et morale des Antilles...*, became, in translation, John Davies's *History of the Caribby Islands*. Collected accounts of travels and voyages were immensely popular with the rising European reading public, as is testified to by the well-known English collections of Harris and the Churchills in the first years of the eighteenth century. It is important to emphasize the point that, idle curiosity apart, the main propelling force for all of this literary effort was essentially political. Peter Martyr was a member of the Spanish Council of the Indies. The prolific English translator Richard Eden was at one time employed in the English service of Philip of Spain. De Laet was himself one of the founders of the Dutch West India Company. And, of course, the English geographer and collector Richard Hakluyt was in his person and his great work nothing less than the voice of Elizabethan England, eager to stake England's claim against Spain as a serious maritime power. It is true that all literature, in one way or another, is socially conditioned. The plays of Shakespeare reflected Tudor nationalism; Sir Walter Scott's novels commemorated a half-forgotten Scottish nationalism in revolt against the forced amalgamation with England; Tennyson's poetry epitomized the agonized *crise de conscience* unleashed by the bitter struggle between Victorian religion and science. But Caribbean literature, whether it be, in its early stages, European literature on the Caribbean theme or, later, a Caribbean literature set on native grounds, has never been able to afford the posture of art for art's sake. In both of its manifestations, it has been the child of a philistine, brutalized society, literally struggling for survival in the wake of the social and economic forces unleashed by the tremendous revolution of the sixteenth century; and in one way or another always serving those forces.

The Spanish monopoly of the New World, then, in the age of Charles V and Philip II, was challenged by its European rivals. It generated its own justificatory literature. In the English case, its most notable expression was that of Hakluyt's *Principal Navigations, Voyages, Traffiques, and Discoveries of the English Nation*, written in 1589 and 1598–1600. The whole tone of the literature is raucous, defiant, full of the new nationalism of the age. It is violently anti-Catholic; but it is clear that the anti-Catholicism in many ways is simply a disguise for new forces eager to share in the new wealth of the Indies and not too scrupulous about the methods that they used. It seizes on any argument plausible enough to justify its denial of Spanish claims. There is the argument of a book like Robert Johnson's *Nova Britannia* of 1609 that New World colonization will provide employment for the swarms of idle persons who constitute a social pestilence.[59] There is the argument, summed up in the spirited and suggestively entitled *The English-American:*

A New Survey of the West Indies by the pamphleteer Thomas Gage (1648), that it is high time for the English to follow the Spanish and Dutch examples of successful colonization, if only because the English have already shown in their Barbados and St. Kitts ventures that they can weather the Caribbean climate.[60] There is the argument, so hypocritical in its Puritan self-righteousness, of Cromwell's instructions to the commanders of his Western Design of the 1650s, that England will rectify the cruelties wreaked upon the New World native peoples by the hated Spaniards.[61] It is sufficient commentary on the Cromwellian assertion to recall that, once entrenched in their new Jamaican possession, the English made no more humane colonizers than the Spanish; and it is enough to read the harrowing account penned by Henry Whistler of the sufferings experienced by the ordinary English sailor and soldier in the Jamaican campaign to be made aware of the terrible price paid by the English common people for the new imperial ambitions of their governing class.[62] Finally, and perhaps most important of all, there is the mercantilist argument that a strong state needs overseas colonies and plantations in order to achieve that economic and financial self-sufficiency it was the main purpose of mercantilist theory to ensure. That particular argument starts as early as Bacon, and is carried on until the end of the seventeenth century—when the new philosophy of economic liberalism begins to challenge it—by the political arithmeticians like North, Petty, Davenant, Sir William Temple, and Locke himself.

But it was Hakluyt, early on, who more than any other single propagandist helped to put the Caribbean on the British map and gave his countrymen a sense of its vital importance in the new age of the postmedieval nation-states. He makes short shrift of the religious argument: no Pope, he argues, has any authority to grant exclusive rights to the new worlds, as if there were not other Christian kings as great and zealous as the Spanish to advance God's glory. But it is the economic argument that he stresses most, thus reflecting the growing secular tone of the age. English colonization will replace dearly imported finished commodities with cheap and raw materials free from the burden of foreign taxation. It will help solve the chronic problem of domestic unemployment. Hakluyt acutely sees the relationship between mass idleness and the danger of social rebellion: "There are thousands of idle persons in the realm," he writes, who, "having no way to be set to work, to either mutinous and seek alteration in the state, or at least very burdensome to the commonwealth." The voice of the profit-seeking merchant can be heard, too, in the further observation that engagement in colonization schemes will rid the landed gentry of "those soft unprofitable pleasures wherein they now too much consume their time and patrimony." Religion, profit, and national regeneration—all go hand in hand for Hakluyt.

"If you touch him in the Indies," of the Spanish enemy he wrote, "you touch the apple of his eye; for take away his treasure which is *nervus belli,* and which he hath almost out of his West Indies, his old bands of soldiers will soon be dissolved, his purpose defeated, his power and strength diminished, his pride abated, and his tyranny utterly suppressed."[63]

Hakluyt must be seen, then, as the theoretician of the first British Empire, just as, three hundred years later, Mahan became the theoretician of the first American Empire after 1898. Hakluyt perceived with clarity the new importance of sea power, the use of the naval blockade, the necessity for a string of coastal bases, the need to add to mere exploration the less dramatic but equally important policy of planned colonization. It is true that he still retained the myths of Cipango, Cathay, Quivara, and Nova Albion; and he memorialized the court in favor of Raleigh's ill-fated dream of El Dorado. But essentially he was the hardheaded geographer, recognizing in the decline of Spain the supreme opportunity for English overseas expansion. Perhaps, indeed, his most important argument lay in his defense of the doctrine of the freedom of the seas, which Grotius later fashioned into a coherent theory of international maritime law. There are innumerable passages in the Hakluyt collection that advance the doctrine. But perhaps its most eloquent expression was contained in the reply of Elizabeth Tudor to the diplomatic protests of Spanish Ambassador Mendoza concerning the English privateer attacks upon the Spanish West Indian strongholds, as reported by the chronicler William Camden in his *Annales Rerum Anglicarum*.... The reply argued, speaking to the question of the controversial Papal Donation, the papal bull of 1493, that:

> This donation of alien property, which by essence of law is void, and this imaginary proprietorship, ought not to hinder other princes from carrying on commerce in these regions, and from establishing Colonies where Spaniards are not residing, without the least violation of the law of nations, since prescription without possession is of no avail; nor yet from freely navigating that vast ocean, since the use of the sea and the air is common to all men; further that no right to the ocean can inure to any people or individual since neither nature or any principle of public user admits occupancy of the ocean.[64]

The transformation of the Caribbean from a closed Spanish enclave into an open, cosmopolitan society, that took place with increasing momentum after the defeat of the Armada in 1588, was really nothing much more than the practical implementation of that doctrine.

The English interlopers were followed by the Dutch and the French, who, in their turn, laid the foundation of Dutch and French West Indian colonization. The Dutch and French West India companies had been formed by the end of the first quarter of the seventeenth century; and Colbert's policy of planned colonization had been copied early on by Danish business-statesmen like State Councillor von Plessen in their organization of the Danish West India Company, with its operations centered in the entrepôt of St. Thomas. The new French presence was commemorated in three notable books during this period: Rochefort's *Histoire naturelle et morale des Antilles de l'Ame-*

rique (1658), Du Tertre's *Histoire générale des Antilles habitées par les Français* (1667, 1671), and Père Labat's *Nouveau voyage aux Isles de l'Amérique* (1722). They documented a French expansionist drive that went back, of course, to the exploring voyages of Gonneville, Verrazano, Roberval, and Jacques Cartier during the first half of the sixteenth century. But despite the well-known influence of Cartier's *Brief Récit* (1545) on the writing of Rabelais's famous work, the French imagination during that earlier period had been more concerned with the Turks than with the Indians. A century later, however, the drive of the new mercantilist capitalism had turned to the Americas, and certainly by the time of the Anglo-French partition of St. Kitts in 1627, the foundations of French Canada and the French Antilles had already been laid. The volumes of Rochefort, Du Tertre, and Labat testify to their importance.[65]

All three books are distinctively different in their spirit. Rochefort, despite the fact that he almost certainly pirated much of Du Tertre's work, is, in a way, the comparative cultural historian, keenly aware of the concept of cultural diversity, and therefore able to see the life-style of the Caribs, for example, as an integral part of a cultural system. Du Tertre is the Catholic humanist, deeply religious, full of compassion for the plight of both the African slave and the Carib Indian in the manner of Las Casas, yet incapable in the final resort of openly challenging the system that oppressed them. Labat, finally, is the fully securalized priest, a natural diarist, obsessed with an insatiable curiosity about everything in the new world of the islands, much more interested in discussing, say, the relative merits of tea and coffee for the Creole table than in thinking about the meaning of Christianity for the new society he described: he reminds the reader of the figure of Chaucer's Pardoner in the *Canterbury Tales*. All three, of course, share a common conviction of the sanctity of the French colonizing mission, as is evident in the pride with which they all note that the institutional arrangements of the colonies in government, law, and justice are modeled, as they put it, after the custom of France. Yet they all at the same time have their own distinct opinion about the phenomena they describe, thus showing how in this earlier formative period, before slavery had become fully established, there was possible a liberal variety of opinion in colonial thought; before, that is to say—and the liberal attitude is especially evident in Rochefort and Du Tertre—it was obligatory upon every Frenchman, Creole or metropolitan, to support the slave institution unreservedly.

As one reads the voluminous detail of these curious accounts, at least four leading theses, approaching an ideological character, make themselves evident. There is, first, the theme of the Carib Indians, what Du Tertre called *les sauvages naturels*. Rochefort's attitude, first of all, is almost one of dispassionate anthropological interest. He sees the Caribs in terms of environment rather than nature. "It is possible," he writes, "that they may have different customs, according to the diversity of the island, though they all make up but one people."[66] The observation leads him to comment, further, that those Carib groups most touched by cultural contact with Europeans may be less "pure" than those, for example, of more isolated St. Vincent. Not surprisingly, then, he discussed in a long digression the problem of the geographical origin of the Caribs, concluding that they had migrated south from Florida: a theory generally frowned upon by later scholarship.[67] He noted, furthermore, by means of citing a complaint uttered by two elderly Caribs quoted in M. de Montel's *Rélation*, how the behavior of the Caribs was to be seen in terms of their cultural contact with the French and not in terms of innate character: "Our people are become in a manner like yours, since they came to be acquainted with you, and we find it some difficulty to know ourselves, so different are we grown from what we have been heretofore."[68] Du Tertre, in his turn, saw the Indians (as already noted) as reasonable men, only savage in name, living in a *petit Paradis* and possessed of at once great simplicity and natural naiveté. They do not buy or sell. They obtain all they want from Nature. "I can assert with truth," he observes, "that if our savages are more ignorant than we are, they are much less vicious." At the same time, Du Tertre, like Labat later, is too rigid a Christian not to notice what he views as the negative aspects of the Carib scene. The Caribs, as he says, will prefer to die of hunger than to live as slaves. But he also notes that they lack filial reverence, practice licentious marriage habits, ill-treat their womenfolk, consider drunkenness a pleasure rather than a crime, practice cannibalism, and indulge in religious practices and customs that are, as Du Tertre puts it, nothing more than deceptions practiced on them by the devil: fit to make you laugh, he observes, but really drive a Christian to tears.[69] In this more critical tone Du Tertre echoes the much more libelous and hostile account of the Sieur de la Borde written at much the same time (1674), which, despite its full account of Carib folktales, is full of horror at Carib ways: "God, I believe," De la Borde concluded, "has permitted all Europe to invade the lands of the Caribs because they are an affront to the Creator, because of their bestial way of life."[70]

What is evident from all of these accounts is a curious ambivalence, the schizoid character of early European attitudes toward native America, oscillating inconclusively between the utopian theme of the noble savage and the Christian view of the benighted pagan. There is at once fascination and repulsion. The official Spanish view, of course, set out in the royal *cedula* (edict) of 1508, was that the island Caribs were legitimate objects for slaving raids by the colonizers. Most of the accounts being discussed here reflect the hostility of that document to the Caribs. But there were exceptions; and to read, for instance, the manuscript on Grenada written sometimes in the mid-period of the seventeenth century by the so-called *l'anonyme de la Grenade* (who was probably the Dominican priest Benigne Bressen), is to appreciate how some of the Europeans could admire the Carib virtues. Describing how the small French military force sent in 1649 to subdue the island discharged their guns in order to intimidate the *sauvages*, it cites one of the Carib captains as retorting, not without some justice: "Nous ne voulons pas de votre terre et pourquoi prenez vous la notre?" (We do not covet your land, so why should you take ours?) It is a note of possessive island pride that the Caribs were never to lose.[71]

As a second theme, the French writers treat the matter of the African slave person. It is apparent enough that both Rochefort and Du Tertre were not insensitive men. Their Christian sensibility, indeed, was much perturbed by the temporary slavery of the black slave. It is true that Rochefort was obviously much more obsessed with the theme of the Indian than with that of the African. Yet even he perceived their tragic predicament. They are bought and sold, he remarks, in the same manner as cattle in other places. They have to be kept in order, of course. But they possess their own remarkable virtues, not least of all that of a sense of mutual aid in adversity: "They are passionate lovers one of another," he notes, "and though they are born in different countries, and sometimes, when at home, enemies one to another, yet when occasion requires they mutually support and assist one another, as if they were all brethren."[72] But it is to Du Tertre that one must turn for a more emphatic sympathy with the slave. For him, they are brothers, as it were, under the skin, human beings placed in a miserable predicament rather than an inferior sort of humankind. If work, as the Bible says, is punishment for man's rebellion against God, he writes, then the Negro slaves of the islands suffer the most rigorous pain of that punishment. The worst aggravation of that condition, he adds, is the slaves' knowledge that their work benefits only the masters; if they work for entire centuries, he comments, they will not get one iota of profit for their pains.[73] Yet that knowledge did not suppress their better traits. For Du Tertre, they were proud and brave, responsive to good treatment, resentful of cruelty, devoted to their families (he paints an almost idyllic picture of slave children growing up), amenable to conversion, unlike the intractable Indians, and loyal to their fellows. He even manages, in the utopian fashion, to contrast them with French people to the disadvantage of the latter: converted slaves, he states, live in a more Christian manner in their condition than do many Frenchmen, as their assiduous attendance to church meetings testifies; what would be unbelievable in France, he concludes, is the source of our admiration in America.[74] Underpinning all this, despite certain qualifications, is Du Tertre's conviction that the slave belongs to a common brotherhood. So, he is capable of repeating the comforting excuse of the planter class that if the thought of their oppression bothers the slaves one day, they do not think about it the next, but he can also assert that the sense of liberty is so natural to them that they are not so stupid or so ignorant as not to know the value of the good that they have lost.[75]

By contrast, Labat, as the last of these French compilers, is not so much the man of feeling as the man of pleasure. His massive work, written more as a diary than as a treatise, is an unending delight to the reader. He is everything: the gourmet, the raconteur, the garrulous conversationalist, the observer of the strange tropical scene possessed of an insatiable curiosity to know everything. Yet he reflects a pronounced insensitivity to the figure of the slave, who was, after all, the economic mainstay of the Antillean society. We see him arriving in colonial Martinique in 1693 and noting the marks of the whiplash on the bodies of the Negroes who boarded the ship, almost as if it were the most natural thing in the world.[76] He notes, with his keen eye for detail, the onerous working hours of the field slave, but without comment. He describes seeing freshly embarked blacks handsome enough to inspire an artist; but the aesthetic feeling did not lead him, as it did Du Tertre, to that sense of generous pity which almost makes the unfortunate appear to the reader in an illusive, almost ideal aspect. So, while Du Tertre prays masters, in the ameliorative fashion, to be merciful to their slaves, Labat suggests that slavery is a legitimate means of redeeming Negroes from superstition; indeed, Labat regards the Negro as a natural child of the devil, a born sorcerer, an evil spirit wielding occult power. He is remarkably free from religious bigotry, as his attitude to employing heretics on his ecclesiastical plantation shows. But he is the epitome of racial bigotry. If Du Tertre reflects the ameliorative element of the planter outlook, Labat reflects its absolutist element.

The third theme of this literature is implicit rather than explicit, but no less important. Caribbean thought, especially in this earlier period, was largely put together by writers and travelers from the mother countries who, through their love of the islands, became their ardent defenders against detractors at home. They developed a sense of island pride—later to become the sentimental foundation of separatism and nationalism. That creolizing element is already evident in these early writers. It is there in Rochefort's endless reiteration of the fact that a civilized society, and persons of reputable family, were to be found in the islands—intended to counteract European disdain and the European belief, as Rochefort put it, that the colonial settlements were only the "refuges and receptacles of bankrupts and debauched persons": This is a demand for recognition of the colonial social order as something worthy in itself.[77] The theme appears also in Du Tertre's anxiety to refute the calumnies against the island missionaries of the great religious orders contained in the earlier book of the Père Biet. He denies the charge of their deficiency in learning by asserting that in that respect they are no worse than the clergy in France itself. It is not true, he adds, that in their political sympathies they are more Roman than Gallican.[78] Nor, he adds further, are they the worldly types portrayed by their detractors (although, here, the reader is tempted to observe that if the worldly rationalism of Labat is taken as evidence, it would seem to support Biet's charge). The note of embryonic Antillean pride appears, finally, in the effort of Labat himself, in the preface to his own work, to answer the gross misrepresentation of tropical natural reality contained in the book of the Sieur Durret, *Voyage de Marseille à Lima*, published in 1720.[79] The tone of colonial indignation comes through clearly. Du Tertre compares his own long sojourn in the islands with the brief three weeks of Biet's visit; Labat notes caustically that Durret did not even visit the islands during his travels. It is, generally, the note of the longtime resident defending his beloved island home against the fly-by-night author from the metropole seeking local color for a best-seller. Labat refers to himself as a *naturel*, one who knows the islands through prolonged experience. The term sums up one whole element in the thought of colonial cultural nationalism.[80]

Fourth, and finally, the Antillean literature of the seventeenth century testifies, albeit indirectly, to the growth of the capitalist ethos in the islands, facilitated by a colonial entrepreneurial class which was a counterpart, in the Americas, of the rising European commercial bourgeoisie of the time; the only difference being, of course, that the new European capitalism was founded on the exploitation of the worker, while the new Caribbean capitalism was founded on the exploitation of the slave. In both cases, however, the capitalist doctrine identified wealth, rather than birth or rank, as the badge of social recognition. Rochefort notes how the ownership of slaves is the title to recognition: "As to the advantages accruing from the labours of these slaves," he writes, "he who is master of a dozen of them may be accounted a rich man." Du Tertre, going further, notes how such ownership becomes the exclusive title to recognition: "A man," he writes, "is only known by the number of slaves that he owns." "There is," he adds, "no point of difference among the inhabitants between noble and *roturier*, he who has the greatest amount of property is regarded the most highly; for only officers hold rank, so that wealth alone constitutes distinction among the others."[81]

An important corollary flowed from this principle of capitalist development. It facilitated the growth of rapid social mobility, again a hallmark of the new capitalist ethos. The evidence on this matter is indeed convincing. It goes back to the earlier Spanish period in the Greater Antilles. Oviedo, staunch royalist that he was, penned a eulogistic passage on the Spanish small farmers turned soldiers who distinguished themselves in the Indian wars; men such as Sebastian Alonso de Niebla and Juan de León, he wrote, came from a Spanish social background where, unlike in Italy and France, even common people were versed in the art of warfare; but being rough, unlettered men they did not get their fair reward, being cheated by royal appointees.[82] The account written by the Englishman Henry Whistler of the English expedition of 1654–55 against Spanish Jamaica makes the same point, although in a tone of social disgust rather than of admiration. "This island," he wrote disdainfully of Barbados, "is the dunghill whereon England doth cast forth its rubbish; rogues and whores and such like are those which are generally brought here. A rogue in England will hardly make a cheater here; a bawd brought over puts on a demure comportment, a whore if handsome makes a wife for some rich planter."[83] And, once again, the French writers reported a similar phenomenon in the French Antilles. Du Tertre, commenting on the high mortality rate in the system of *matelotage* (in which French indentured servants were worked by their masters as harshly as were the slaves), noted at the same time that most of the islands' prominent families had originated from that low social echelon—in much the same way, he added, as the sexual imbalance of the earlier settler period at the very beginning had meant that a poor French girl could be eagerly claimed as the bride of a planter as soon as she disembarked. It is true that he also noted that both phenomena had tended to disappear as wealth increasingly became a matter of family inheritance and as the growing body of eligible Creole girls displaced the arriving immigrants as a marriage reservoir. But for that early period at least, as his account makes clear, an enterprising indentured servant could aspire to planter status and a poor girl could give proof of the legend that, as Du Tertre put it, the Indies were a paradise for women.[84]

Our final informant, as always, is the irrepressible Labat. His description of planter neighbors like Monsieur Roy and Monsieur Verrier is that of men who came to the islands as engaged servants and rose to become, either through astute marriages or hard work, wealthy slave proprietors.[85] It is suggestive that his comments about the humble origins of these colonists considered high personages in their own small world were resented and in fact brought him an evil reputation in the old Creole communities, where any public mention of a family scandal is never forgiven or forgotten; for that sort of reaction, in turn, is yet another element of the capitalist ideology, in which the second and third generations seek to obliterate the memory of obscure social origins. Labat's reply to the complaints was, typically, that these families, in any case, constituted a new nobility, and that in any event it was better, as he phrased it, to found a family than to end one. All in all, men who would have been diminished as upstarts in Europe became persons of rank and respectability in the New World societies. Indeed, even Labat's rehabilitation of the debt-ridden ecclesiastical plantation of Fond Saint Jacques is, in itself, a remarkable example of the habits of work and business shrewdness, essentially bourgeois, that created the new class of wealthy Creoles.

It is easy, of course, to exaggerate all this. The phenomenon of easy social escalation did not last long. It was, at best, a mobility enjoyed mainly by the lower-class white groups and in any case soon disappeared as the small holdings gave way, after 1650 or so, to the large-scale capitalist plantation (an economic process of land consolidation described in Ligon's *History of Barbados* of 1659), with the result that those groups gradually degenerated to the status of poor whites.[86] Richard Sheridan's study of the rise of the colonial gentry in English Antigua in the middle period of the later eighteenth century shows how no entrepreneur could survive in a trader-dominated plantation system unless he was at the same time a planter-merchant.[87] Even so, it is clear that in the brief period of Caribbean social history before those processes took hold, the typically American dream of social advancement in an environment in some part free of the old European caste restrictions was a real element in early Caribbean norms and values. The very physical conditions of Caribbean life—in which protection by a metropole thousands of miles away was always slow, hazardous, and problematical—promoted a spirit of colonist independence; and the graphic description of the small pioneer township of St. Thomas in the Danish West Indies contained in Governor Iversen's edict of 1672, portraying a young colonial community struggling desperately to stay alive, huddled around the twin bastions of the church and the fort, battling incipient social anarchy with enforced Lutheran piety, and with each householder ready at a moment's notice to repel, with sword and gun, the ever-possible raiding party from outside demonstrates how the early colonists had to learn to look after themselves.[88]

THE EARLY SPIRIT OF COLONIAL ASSERTION

In such a situation, the spirit of self-help and independent effort inevitably spawned a nascent spirit of colonial liberty. The man on the spot develops his own initiatives, his own way of seeing things. The astonishing achievements of Labat, as engineer, architect, machinist, inventor, and religious administrator—his career, remarks his biographer, the Martiniquan historian E. Rufz, seems to more than realize the antique legend of the labors of Hercules—testify to that truth;[89] it is small wonder that his superiors, in the end, refused him leave to return to his beloved Antilles, for he was the kind of man a "home" government always finds it difficult to control.

The seeds of conflict, then, were already present. Especially so when it is remembered that certainly by 1700 the basic character of the Caribbean economy had already been firmly established: it was a plantation economy founded on the effective ownership of its resources by metropolitan-based corporate institutions adapted to the overriding purpose of exploiting imported labor and natural resources for metropolitan profit and rationalized in the economic literature of the time in terms of the theory of the mercantilist division of international labor. Within that system, it was the function of the overseas colony to provide the basic staples the metropolitan economy did not itself produce and at the same time develop itself as a purchaser of metropolitan products. European mercantilism, this is to say, was (as its foremost historian has pointed out) a system of national power that had as one of its economic functions the prevention of the development of the potentialities of the overseas colonies so that they would not be able to stand on their own feet and become politically independent.[90]

The subsequent history of the Caribbean was, as is well known, in large part the history of colonial revolution against that system. The ideology of that revolt did not take on a coherent form until the latter part of the eighteenth century, with the growing influence of the North American colonies, and their anti-English sentiment, upon the Creole groups of West Indian merchants, lawyers, and plantation owners. Even so, it is possible to see embryonic forms of that Creole nationalism during the earlier period. They had their roots, as already noted, in the inevitable conflicts of interest and opinion between the metropolitan bureaucrats and the colonial settlers and soldiers—in this case, those of the Spanish New World possessions. They were followed by a stream of complaints on the part of town councils and merchant bodies against the system of metropolitan monopoly. Herrera's account of how the Audiencia of Santo Domingo met to demand that their city be declared the exclusive port of entry for trade in the region, even though it might compromise the monopolistic power of the Seville merchant houses, is symptomatic of a new spirit of colonial assertiveness; and the reasons advanced for the change, accompanied by the argument that such a change would produce in no time a Caribbean city as important as Palermo in Sicily or London in England, evince a spirit of Creole pride keenly felt.[91] A similar spirit is evident in the letter of the Attorneys of New Spain who memorialized Charles V in 1545: obviously seeking to reply to the charges of the Las Casas school, they pointed out sharply that if the record of crimes committed in Spain itself were to be publicized, it would cause more scandal than any stories about cruelty done to the Indians of the New World. It is a note that would become more pronounced in later Caribbean thought: that of the New World apologist who compares the positive aspects of life in the colony with the negative aspects of life in the mother country, in favor of the former, and to the disparagement of the latter.[92] The complaints of the Spanish Caribbean colonists—the excessive costs of imports, the corruption of royal officials, the crying need for more effective defense against marauders like Drake—were the complaints of colonists everywhere placed in similar situations. But they were made more emphatic by the growing note of proud Creoledom: better, it was felt, to be a well-to-do planter in Hispaniola than a poor gentleman in Spain.

THE PUERTO RICAN CASE

The Puerto Rican documentary record of this period is especially illustrative. It consists of the so-called *Memoria Melgarejo* of 1582, the *Descripción de la Isla y Ciudad de Puerto Rico* of Diego de Torres Vargas of 1647, and the *Memoria Anónima* of, probably, 1679. As a later Puerto Rican historian has pointed out, their general tone is that of the traditional *relación*, that is, reports essentially made to the Crown, altogether pragmatic in their approach; there is, as yet, nothing of the tone of reform that will appear later in the eighteenth century in the work of Miyares, Abbad, and O'Reylly.[93] Even so, there are differences of emphasis and attitude between the three. The anonymous document of 1679, for example, although loyalist like the others, permits itself a note of strong civic protest against the gubernatorial regimes of the time, which are seen as fearsome and unbridled; the rule of one governor is even likened to the character of the hurricanes that occasionally assault the island. Yet all three documents, much more significantly, give expressions to a burgeoning spirit of *criollismo* (local island pride). It is already present in the *Memoria Melgarejo*, with its admiring description of the island fauna and flora, its clear rivers, its medicinal fruits, even the already famous Coamo springs (originally an Indian spa of sorts), as well as its complaints about French and Carib marauding expeditions and its plea to the Crown for permission to introduce Negro slaves in order to strengthen a labor force already much depleted by emigration of the more adventuresome resident Spaniards to the mainland colonies. Despite the objective tone of the document, which is, after all, a response by local officials to a royal questionnaire, it allows the reader to sense (reading between the lines) the psychological and social atmosphere of life in an overseas colony in which everything—strange climate, hostile enemies, scarcity of essential supplies—makes for a dangerous and precarious existence and which demands from the colonists almost superhuman qualities of courage and persistence.[94]

That note of an incipient pride in the new island life is even more emphatic in the two *memorias* of 1647 and 1679. The *memorial* of 1647, in its very opening passages, becomes a veritable hymn of praise to the island paradise. Surely, its author asserts, the Friar Luis de León must have been thinking of Puerto Rico when he described in his *Los Cantares* the foremost New World jewels of the Spanish Crown? Puerto Rico is foremost among the colonies, as the royal *cedula* of 1643 makes clear. The island is fertile beyond others; indeed, to live there is to enjoy a perpetual spring without excessive heat or excessive cold. Its ginger product is superior to that of Santo Domingo, although that of Brazil is admittedly the best. Its tobacco surpasses in quality that of Havana. It possesses excellent forest woods that would justify the establishment of a royal shipbuilding factory in the island. In the area of Cabo Rojo there are salt deposits that could supply a hundred galleons of the fleet. The native fruits are better than those of the other islands. Gold, glass, and copper deposits abound; all that is needed is labor to exploit them. The author goes on to add, almost as if he is engaged in fulsomely advertising his adopted island-home, that the homes of the Governors are oftentimes more luxurious than those of the Viceroys of Peru and Mexico; that in the figure of Alfonso Manso, the island was the first to be honored with episcopal appointment; and that the reputation of Puerto Rican women as beautiful, virtuous, and hardworking is so well known as to give rise to the saying that all prudent men in the Indies should marry in Puerto Rico. There are other laudatory themes as well. The Christian humility of the island ecclesiastics is praised, notably the Bishop Nicolás Ramos who felt so deeply for the doctrine of poverty that at one time he distributed the episcopal rent to the poor—testifying that he could not sleep until he had done so.

There is, naturally enough, the note of loyalty to Spanish values; it is recorded with pride that Puerto Rico was the first overseas colony to receive a royal visit in the form of the presence of the Duke of Escalona, who, passing through on his way to take up the viceroyalty of New Spain, occasioned an event which, in the words of the author, was the greatest ever to take place since the original Discovery. But there are also themes that strike a curious indigenous and proud Puerto Rican note: the list of residents who have been nominated to prestigious positions, in both church and state, in Spain and the Empire alike; the prodigal generosity of ecclesiastical donors to education; the moving story of the woman Gregoria Hernández who, grief-stricken at the capture of her sons by Turkish pirates, became so much a model of humility and patience as to be compared to the beatitude of the Saint María Raggi de Roma; and, not least of all, the first mention in Puerto Rican literature of the miracle of the dark-skinned Virgen de Monserrate, as well as a brief reference to the cult of spirit possession entertained by Negroes of the town and, no doubt, persecuted by the Inquisition, the presence of which the author also notes.[95]

All in all, there is present here, as well as in the anonymous *Memoria* of 1679, a spirit of exuberant *puertorriqueñidad*, the conviction of being indisputably Puerto Rican. It is taken for granted that Puerto Rico is important in and of itself; that it possesses its own unique life-style, half-Spanish, half-American; that it is worth writing about. The seeds of Antillean nationalism are present, albeit only in an embryonic stage, in such attitudes. The *Memorias* are even more significant in their tone when they are compared, say, with the account of the Bishop López de Haro, penned in 1644, which is simply a petulant record of the tribulations of his sea voyage out to Puerto Rico and the difficulties of life in San Juan, written from the viewpoint of a homesick Spaniard.[96]

THE BRITISH WEST INDIAN CASE

A similar note made itself evident in the British West Indies. A whole battery of later historians—Harlow, Parry, Williams, Sheridan—has shown how, during the last half of the seventeenth century, a new class of domiciled planters, merchant-attorneys, and town agents grew up in the developing colonies like Barbados and Jamaica, and how they felt increasingly restless under the punitive navigation and trade legislation of the imperial center. Their arguments were fully developed in the pamphlet literature that flourished as early as the 1680s and the 1690s, with the Barbados writers leading the West Indian attack. The *Groans of the Plantations*, a 1689 pamphlet by the Barbadian planter Edward Littleton, strenuously opposed the system of sugar duties on the ground that its cost was borne by the planter and not by the English consumer; the argument was answered on the English side by an anonymous pamphlet of 1695, *A Discourse on the Duties of Merchandise*, which argued that the abolition or reduction of duties could not possibly be to the advantage of the planters. Yet another anonymous tract, *The Interest of the Nation...* of 1691, advanced the planters' argument in favor of a local refining industry as opposed to the interests of the English refiners. The argument was driven further in the 1695 pamphlet *The State of the Case of the Sugar Plantations in America*, in which the author argued for the levying of additional duties on Brazilian sugar, as well as permission for enlarged trade between the planters and foreign countries. The argument was replied to in the same year, from London, in the anonymous *Case of the Refiners of Sugar in England Stated*.[97]

The importance of this pamphlet literature is that it reveals:

1. a growing, but by no means yet fatal, divergence between the economic interests of the English mercantilists and those of the West Indian planters, and

2. a developing sense on the part of the planter class that it performs an indispensable role in the total structure of English commerce and that it should be treated accordingly. There is, too, of course, as a reading of the literature shows, evidence of the fatal contradiction of the West Indian argument, although naturally it was not seen as such by its defenders: the insistence, at one and the same time, on an enlarged free trade with foreign nations, following the growing trade with the North American colonies (a trade already beginning even before 1700, as shown in Richard Pares's pioneer study *Yankees and Creoles*), and on a continuing privileged position within the British protectionist system.[98]

That sense of a separate West Indian interest received a somewhat more systematic expression in Dalby Thomas's book of 1690, *An Historical Account of the Rise and Growth of the West Indian Colonies*. One of the first publicists to present a pro–West Indian viewpoint, Thomas fully reflects the emergent sense of collective planter identity. Accepting the mercantilist argument of trade as the greatest source of the wealth of nations, he deploys it in favor of the West Indian planter class—which, he argues, is of paramount importance to England, since it at once produces and consumes more than it could have done in England itself. That being so, it is justified in its demands of reduction of duties on exports, local refining, and the rest, to which Thomas interestingly adds his own recommendations for centralization of sugar factories, credit facilities, and, in the political field, some mechanism for effective consultation when the imperial parliament considers legislation of mutual concern. This, altogether, is the voice of the planter mentality, with all of its prejudices. The produce of West Indian labor is seen as that of the slave owner, not of the slave. The plantation colonies are praised, the North American farming colonies put down. The planters are presented as creators of immense wealth, for which England should be grateful, despite the fact that, as Thomas's frank discussion of the relationship between the Royal African

Company and the planters shows, the author knew them to be irresponsible payers and deep in debt.[99] It is, in brief, a full-blown apologetic. It is instructive to compare it with Ligon's earlier volume, written some forty years earlier. Ligon wrote in the genuinely pioneer period of Barbadian settlement, and he drew with real sympathy a portrait of an infant colony of small planters and their white field-workers clearing the land. Thomas, writing after an interval of large estate formation in which the small planter was driven out, sees it all from the viewpoint of the large magnate; for him, the ruin of the smaller planters is merely seen as the consequence, not of the greed of a new landed gentry, but of the deficiencies of English policy. There is hardly anything of the spirit of common racial sympathy that might have been expected to make itself evident in such a situation; if the tone of Thomas's observations reflects anything at all, it is, rather, the contempt that the rich colonist felt for the poor white who had fallen to the social level of the Negro. The genesis of the planter ideology is here: but it is more concerned with the instinct of property than with the sentiment of race.

It would be misleading, of course, to read too much into the spirit of colonial antimetropolitan hostility. Anger with policies from London or Madrid or Paris did not necessarily mean revolutionary sentiment in Bridgetown or Havana or Fort-de-France. The Barbadian situation once again illustrates the point. Much has been made of the "Declaration of Independence" passed by the colonial General Assembly in 1651. Yet that document was not a declaration against England as such. Rather, it was a rejoinder by Lord Willoughby and his Royalist supporters to a discriminatory act on the part of the Cromwellian Commonwealth; and as such it is to be seen as nothing more than a colonial reaction to the changing fortunes of Crown and Parliament in the English Civil War period. Its tone, in fact, was one of loyalty to the English tradition and pride in the liberties and rights of Englishmen; "we will not alienate ourselves," its authors wrote, "from those old heroic virtues of true Englishmen, to prostitute our freedom and privileges, to which we are born, to the will and opinion of anyone."[100] The real subverters of the constitution, from this viewpoint, were not the protesting Barbadians but Cromwell and his Puritan Parliament. It was no accident, then, that when the later West Indian historian N. Darnell Davis came to reprint the Declaration in his book of 1887, *The Cavaliers and Roundheads of Barbados*, he should have interpreted it, correctly, as an expression of colonial patriotism, of the loyalty of "Little England" to the home country, having the ring about it, as he put it, of the old days of Rome.[101]

The most that can be said is that it was a patriotism with a difference. The first generation of Barbadian planters were political exiles, first from the Stuarts and then from the Puritans, and they brought their political animosities with them. But the colonial environment rapidly imposed conditions on the continuing exercise of those animosities, for the planter families were faced as early as the 1650s, as we know from passages in Ligon, with the ever-present danger of slave revolts. The danger required a united front on their part; and Davis has described in his book how the colonists, whether a Royalist like Walrond or a Parliamentarian like Drax, instituted a political truce among themselves, whereby any member guilty of calling another Cavalier or Roundhead was required as punishment to offer a dinner to all those in whose presence the epithet had been flung. They were Englishmen, true. But they already possessed the sense of being a colonial aristocracy: "Neither Creole nor Crab, but true Barbadian born." Interestingly, Du Tertre noted a not dissimilar episode in the so-called *petite révolution* of 1644-45 in the French Antilles, in which the French and English settlers of St. Kitts adopted resolutions determining that in the event of war between France and England the colonists would not be obliged to follow suit unless expressly commanded by their respective governments: a declaration that virtually amounted to a doctrine of colonial neutrality.[102] The accounts of other French writers of the time—Boyer in his book of 1654 and Clodore in 1671[103]—noted the significance of the affair, especially of the removal of the colonial governor by the French colonists. Undoubtedly there was at work a spirit of colonial liberty, seeing the old quarrels of Europe as irrelevant to the colonial situation.

Seen from the viewpoint of psychohistory, indeed, this early formative period of Caribbean society already showed signs of the well-known Caribbean disease, the deep and sometimes unbearable tension between the old metropolitan loyalty and the new colonial loyalty. The new social class of colonial settlers, planters, and entrepreneurs was at once, in the English settlements, Anglo-Saxon and anti-English, in the Spanish settlements pro-Hispanic and anti-Spanish, in the French settlements Gallic and anti-French. On the one hand, there was the natural loyalty to the "mother country" whose social and moral values the colonists had brought with them. Judge Littleton wrote, in his Barbados pamphlet:

> By a kind of magnetic force England draws to it all that is good in the Plantations. It is the center to which all things tend: nothing but England can we relish or fancy: our hearts are here, wherever our bodies be: if we get a little money, we remit it to England. When we are a little easy, we desire to live and spend what we have in England, and all that we can rap and rend is brought to England.[104]

On the other hand, there was the deeply felt colonial suspicion that the "mother country" failed to appreciate at once their strategic importance in wartime and their contribution to national prosperity in peacetime; and it is worth noting that when the English historian Oldmixon came to write his *British Empire in America* in 1708, he quoted extensively from both Littleton and Thomas in order to support his argument, which was also theirs, that English national policy should support the colonial interests within the framework of the mercantilist "balance of trade" theories, which, again, he defended as much as they did. It is true that he queried Thomas's extravagant population statistics; but at the same time he used both Thomas and Littleton to expose the anticolonial practices of the monopolistic African Company. To the argument that colonies drain the mother country of useful working people, there is opposed the argument that when those people remain at home, they become an idle body of parish poor, whereas in the colonies they became productive workers; and to that argument, aided by passages cited from Thomas, Oldmixon added his own argument that when the anticolonial writers urged the consideration that the colonies were graveyards for white people, they forgot that tropical sicknesses were not indigenous to the island, but rather had been imported by sick English soldiers and sailors not properly cared for by their commanders.[105]

All of these resentments, of course, were particular rather than general: that of the settler against the salaried functionary; that of the established resident against the metropole-appointed official; that of the colonial merchant against the metropolitan supplier. They did not amount in any way to a full-blown doctrine of colonial disobedience. The most that the French writer Biet could say against the French island missionaries of the time was they they were more Gallican than Papalist in their political sympathies; and even that was a charge vigorously denied by Du Tertre.[106] A century earlier, likewise—as already noted—even a chronicler as ardently royalist as Oviedo had defended the ordinary soldiers who had undertaken the real conquest of Puerto Rico as against the Crown Attorneys and agents who swindled them out of their just inheritance; but the complaint was against what were seen as dishonest servants of the Crown and not against the Crown itself. There is no evidence in the contemporary literature that the British West Indian colonists, many of whom were Scots, were ready to join the Jacobite movement after 1689 any more than there is any evidence that the *colons* of the French Antilles, many of whom were refugees from the revocation of the Edict of Nantes, were ready to support anything comparable to the republican revolutionary *Fronde* movement of the French civil upheavals of a century earlier. Indeed, the *revoltes blanches* (white uprisings) of Saint Domingue, first in 1670 and then later in 1722, were movements of discontented colonists more anxious to fight against the oppressive policies of the French West India Company than to show themselves either anti-French or antiroyalist. As Charlevoix noted, describing the *émeute* of 1722-23, the Saint Domingue rebels were loyal servants of the Crown, but wanted no part of the Company. The observation was repeated by Dubuisson somewhat later in his remark that the colonists had not abandoned the mother country but simply extended its boundaries, changing their province but not their nation.[107] It is not until the rebellious movement later in the eighteenth century that there emerges an openly seditious political thought, seeking to replace loyalty to France with the new *esprit américain*.

THE EARLY RELIGIOUS SPIRIT

A similar spirit prevailed in the religious life of the region. Admittedly, the Inquisition was present in the Spanish islands, albeit only by authority from the Cartagena tribunal. Admittedly, too, the entire planter class was hostile to the missionary enterprises in all of the islands, and the official churches were throughout the allies of the state power. Yet the Inquisition was never as omnipresent in the islands as it was in mainland centers such as Lima and Mexico City; and the story of Bishop Alonso Manso, who brought the office to the islands, being so horrified at the poverty of his primitive diocese that he immediately retreated to the comfort of his Salamanca canonry, shows how, early on, a habit of ecclesiastical absenteeism took the edge off religious persecution. So, it was that much easier for a multireligious Caribbean to grow up. The Quaker movement in the islands started with George Fox's visit of 1671, with that great stalwart admonishing the owners of slaves to treat them as human beings; and the account of island missionary work contained in the journal of the Irish Quaker William Edmundson, his fellow worker, vividly testifies to the work undertaken by these pioneers of the West Indian Nonconformist tradition.[108] The Jewish presence was even more noticeable. The Sephardic Jewish element came to the islands as refugees from both Europe and Portuguese Brazil, and they were in fact the carriers of the New World sugar industry from northern Brazil to the islands proper. Being cosmopolitan, multilingual, and more than generally literate, even learned, they brought a new element into the Caribbean mix. Both in Jamaica and Surinam they founded families, even dynasties, that have survived to the present day. They became the basis, early on, of the commercial wealth of Danish St. Thomas; the Danish Crown, indeed, became the first European power to pass legislation, in the form of the historic Royal Ordinance of 1814, for the protection of its Jewish citizens in the Caribbean, and the continuity of the Jewish presence in the Virgin Island group is attested to by the fact that the group's first Jewish Governor, Gabriel Milán, was appointed by Copenhagen in 1684 and its latest Jewish Governor, Ralph Paiewonsky, was appointed by Washington in 1961.[109]

In the island centers where these various groups concentrated, there developed, early on, a free *exercitium religionis*; and merely to read John Taylor's account, in his *Multum in Parvo* of 1688, of five different religious congregations worshiping in toleration of each other in the Jamaican town of Port Royal during the 1660s is to realize how early the spirit of religious toleration developed in those islands most receptive to the European nonconformist-dissenting tradition. That spirit, in its turn, no doubt helped encourage the growth of an Anglican altruism in the slave society. As early as 1680 the Reverend Morgan Godwyn's spirited pamphlet *The Negro's and Indian's Advocate* vigorously exposed the massive ill-treatment of overworked and underfed slaves on the Barbados plantations.[110] But it received its best expression in the famous Codrington bequest, whereby the Society for the Propagation of the Gospel in Foreign Parts was enabled to undertake its experiment in Negro Christianization within the framework of the slavery regime. Its original patron was, clearly, a remarkable man, as Professor Harlow's biography shows. A Creole West Indian proprietor educated in both England and France, he was that unique type, the cultured planter; and Père Labat's account of his dinner with the English governor in St. Kitts still fascinates the reader as it reveals two European men of the world, both knowledgable in West Indian affairs, playing the gentleman-courtier with each other. It is not too much to say that Codrington, educated as he had been at the Oxford of John Locke, brought to the British West Indies for the first time the energizing spirit of liberal Anglicanism. It was not, it goes without saying, an abolitionist spirit. But it anticipated that spirit with its insistence on the character of the slave as a moral being; and in its aggressive Anglican altruism, it anticipated, as it emerged a century later, the great work of men like Clarkson, Ramsay, and Wilberforce.[111]

Nor must the African contribution to the Caribbean religious life of this early period be overlooked. For it is in this period that there takes place the early formative stages in the growth of the Caribbean popular syncretic religions. That the mixture of Old World and New World religious and folkloristic traditions was already taking place is clear enough from Thomas G. Mathews's brief description of the Corpus Christi festival in the streets of San Juan, Puerto Rico, in the 1680s. The documents of that case portray an aged and strict Bishop of Puerto Rico writing reports home full of bitter and scandalized complaint about the way in which the San Juan mulattoes had introduced into the official religious ceremony the old Spanish *baile de espadas*, part fertility dance, part combat dance celebrating the Spanish-Moorish wars, and which almost certainly included the spectacle of female slaves nude from the waist up; so great is the scandal, complains the Bishop, that even the King of Angola, had he been head of the procession, would have been shocked by the indecency. The world, here in San Juan, he adds, is topsy-turvy, turned upside down. The complaint graphically indicates how the Catholic religion was already being compelled to adjust itself to the inroads of popular Creole traditions alien to its spirit.[112]

THE PIRATE COMMONWEALTH

Yet of all the institutions of the nascent Caribbean society during this period, the one that perhaps most dramatically expressed the open character of that society was that of organized piracy. The pirates, buccaneers, and freebooters, as they were variously called, have traditionally been seen through the eyes of romantic novelists and mythmakers. C. H. Haring's book of 1910,

The Buccaneers in the West Indies in the Seventeenth Century, was the first to see them differently from the viewpoint of a professional historian, as at once an economic institution and a social organism.[113] How a seventeenth century observer and participant like the Dutchman Esquemeling saw them in his firsthand account of 1674, *The Buccaneers and Marooners of America*, tells us much about the society of pirates and also about Caribbean values. That society, as Esquemeling described the infamous Tortuga island stronghold, was genuinely international: the leaders he wrote about included the Frenchman Lollinois, Bartholomew the Portuguese, and the Welshman Henry Morgan; while the marauding expedition led against Cuba by Morgan was a combined French-English force. Piracy, in this sense, was part and parcel of the international anarchy of the Caribbean, where there was frequently very little distinction between licensed privateering and piracy proper. The English author of the 1684 English translation saw this clearly. He wrote:

> We know that no peace could ever be established beyond the line, since the first possession of the West Indies by the Spaniards, till the burning of Panama.... Until that time the Spanish inhabitants of America being, as it were, in a perpetual war with Europe, certain it is that no coasts nor kingdoms in the world have been more frequently infested nor alarmed with the invasions of several nations than theirs. Thus from the very beginning of their conquests in America, both English, French, Dutch, Portuguese, Swedes, Danes, Courlanders, and all other nations that navigate the ocean, have frequented the West Indies, and filled them with their robberies and assaults.[114]

The Caribbean, in other words, was a seething cauldron of international rivalries that gave new opportunity and expression to all the passions that could no longer find an outlet in their native European soil. It provided room for an aggressive and violent individualism; and it is in that sense that the pirate of the seventeenth century was the logical successor to the Spanish soldier of fortune and the Tudor sea captain of the sixteenth century. All of them—maybe not consciously, but surely nonetheless—personified a revolt of Caribbean emergent values against the older European tradition.

The Esquemeling account makes that clear beyond a doubt. It shows how the pirate trade offered at once freedom and employment to the malcontent indentured servant escaping a hard master and the small planter ousted by the plantation economy (the author himself had been an indentured servant before joining the pirate fraternity). It describes the rough democracy of the pirate society, with contracts drawn up before each adventure, captains elected by free suffrage, and meticulous distribution of spoils after each success. "Among themselves," wrote Esquemeling, "these pirates are very liberal: if any one has lost all, they freely give him of what they have."[115] The attractive legend of the pirate leader as an autocratic despot is shattered by the description of men like Morgan participating in vigorous, democratic councils of war in which every member of the society engaged. Within that piratical commonwealth, each pirate ship constituted an entity unto itself, a self-governing and self-contained stock company, lasting only as long as the particular expedition itself lasted. It generated its own democratic ideology, which, with the English-born pirates, probably had its roots in the debate of the Cromwellian period. Other sources in addition to Esquemeling have documented that spirit; the Captain Bellamy who told his followers that organized society robs the poor under the cover of the law while they, the pirates, plundered the rich under the protection of their own pirates' courage,[116] or the unknown pirate, formerly an Oxford servitor and play actor, who told his fellow pirates that Rome itself had been peopled by runaway slaves and insolvent debtors and that they, in turn, could found a new empire in the Caribbean by recruiting Indians and the discontented and desperate people of the English and French colonies.[117] They were witness in their own way to the early democratic ideas of the period.

It is worth noting how, once again, as those ideas made their transatlantic passage, they gradually adjusted themselves to the Caribbean environment. That can be seen in the fact that the pirate commonwealths, in Tortuga or New Providence, were themselves slave-based, and Esquemeling notes without comment, as if it were entirely natural, how slaves, along with Spanish pieces of eight, were used as acceptable currency in pirate dealings.[118] Similarly, his view of the Indian allies of the Spanish colonists is typically that of the age, seeing them only as idolatrous savages. The pirate ideology, that is to say, was that of the small man, white and lower class, of the Caribbean society. As such, it was bound to fail, for it ran counter (in its Robin Hood manner of social justice) to the values of the dominant Caribbean social class. Esquemeling himself, indeed, shared those dominant values. It is clear that he has little sympathy for the pirate exploits, notwithstanding his ability to describe them with astonishing objectivity. The pirates, he observes, spend with huge prodigality what others have gained with no little labor and toil. The comment is that of the capitalist-burgher mentality, distressed at the profits of the capitalist accumulating process of Spanish settlers and merchants being wasted in a form of noncapitalist expenditure, in the gambling dens and stew houses of Caribbean ports. It was no accident, then, that as the capitalism of sugar and trade established itself, and as the need to use the system of nautical outlawry against the Spanish monopoly disappeared once that monopoly was ended after the Treaty of Utrecht, the Caribbean state-power moved to eliminate the system, a purpose substantially achieved with Woodes Rogers's suppression of the New Providence pirate stronghold and the conversion of the Bahamas into a royal colony, as well as by the reforms carried out by French West India Company agents like the energetic d'Ogeron against the Tortuga group. Like the system of white bondsmanship out of which it, in part, grew, it died of anachronism.

Inevitably, it was romanticized by later writers. In the French colonial case, local colonial champions like Moreau de Saint-Méry and Hilliard d'Auberteuil contributed to the pleasing myth that the filibusters and buccaneers were the founding fathers, as it were, of the Saint Domingue colony, fashioning a simple way of life that—according to those writers—was destroyed by the loose manners and luxury brought into the island by the Parisian riffraff and Versailles court favorites. A modern French writer—Gilles Lapouge in his book *Les piratas*—has attempted an even more pretentious thesis, arguing that there can be discerned a certain ideological typology in the pirate figures, so that some of them are anarchists, others *socialistas salvajes*, and yet others *nihilistas desesperados*. In this scenario a pirate leader like Misson anticipates the ideas of Fourier and Saint-Simon, Lewis anticipates the Marquis de Sade, Captain Bellamy anticipates Bakunin.[119] This, clearly, is romantic nonsense. The pirate attitudes—anger against the wealthy and the powerful of the world, compassion for the outcasts, even recognition that there exists a war in society between the rich and the poor—do not in themselves constitute a Socialist position. At best, they reflect a social indignation against injustice; at worst, a response that takes the form of robbing the rich. What the pirate commonwealths provided was a haven for the discontented: as Lapouge properly puts it, places where the pariahs discovered their promised land. But that is far from proving that they were consciously Socialist enterprises.

It is nearer the mark to say that they embodied a tradition of rough, quasi-democratic self-government characteristic of early Caribbean frontier conditions. Lipschutz has thus pointed out, in his 1974 *Casa de las Américas* essay, how all of the early Spanish and Italian chroniclers—Peter Martyr, Oviedo, Fernando Columbus—agreed in deploring the fact that the general body of early European immigrant crews came from the lower criminal classes of the time: more idiots than educated persons, in Oviedo's phrase: *más amigos de sediciones y novedades que de paz y tranquilidad* (more the friends of sedition and novelties than of peace and tranquillity), in Columbus's phrase.[120] As Lipschutz has no difficulty in showing, however, those sentiments reflected an upper-class sixteenth-century prejudice, which saw all lower classes as socially delinquent. Ideologically, these writers wanted American colonies filled with gentlemen and courtiers. What seemed to them criminal behavior on the part of the common people who in reality composed the main mass of the colonizers was, in fact, an expression, in ideological terms, of an unconscious revolt against a feudal Europe in favor of a democratic America. It is in this sense that the exaggerated legend of the pirate commonwealths has at least an element of truth in it. It would not be fanciful to employ as its epitaph the words of the anonymous eighteenth-century writer on the history of the notorious Captain Amery, who, along with his fellow pirates, established a sort of petty kingdom on the island of Madagascar:

One of these great princes had formerly been a waterman upon the Thames, where, having committed a murder, he fled to the West Indies, and was of the number of those who ran away with the sloops, the rest had all been foremast men, nor was there a man amongst them who could either read or write, and yet their Secretaries of State had no more learning than themselves.[121]

A fascinating footnote to the pirate-buccaneer-freebooter story is provided by the saga of the logwood cutters settled in the Campeachy and Honduras areas of the Yucatán peninsula. From the middle of the seventeenth century on, the logwooders created an essentially independent economy. Harassed by the Spanish and only ill-protected at best by the English, they formed their own independent communities, which lasted as long as the European demand for their product lasted. If, then, Frederick Jackson Turner's well-known claim that "since the days when the fleet of Columbus sailed into the waters of the New World, America has been another name for opportunity" has any validity at all, it surely has validity with reference to the Yucatán logwood settlements of the seventeenth and eighteenth centuries.[122]

That opportunity for the common man existed during the heyday of the logwood economy is evident enough from the pages of Dampier's definitive account, included as part of his *Voyages and Descriptions* published in the early eighteenth century. The logwood communities produced, of course, the usual buccaneer traits such as hard drinking. But they also produced rough democratic forms of government, just as in the more well-known pirate commonwealths: the democratic allotment of shares in the enterprise; the system of "consortship" in allocating rewards and obligations; rudimentary political structures—including regular public meetings which elected the settlements' magistrates, who in their turn were held accountable by a strict code of behavior. The title that they gave themselves—the Brethren of the Coast—was clearly not an empty one.[123] By the time of the later eighteenth century, the old social order based on those forms had practically disappeared. But the spirit of frontier independence died hard; and as late as the 1890s Olivier, as Colonial Secretary in British Honduras, could still be captivated by the life of the Belize descendants of the old logwooders, with its woodcutters' Christmas reveling, rowdy logwood camps, and the enchanting competitions of the white-sail fleets.[124] So long as the system lasted, it embodied all of the virtues, crude enough but real nonetheless, of the classical frontier life: primitive institutional organization; a violent distrust of authority, especially any authority to do with government; a masterful grasp of material things combined with acuteness and acquisitive instinct; a great disdain for anything philosophical; and a genius for ready action. It is enough to read the detail of a life like that of Captain John Coxon in the period of the later seventeenth century to appreciate how the logwood economy permitted an adventurous spirit to run the whole gamut of occupations between logwood cutter, buccaneer, and Indian raider, bargaining with both the Spanish and the Jamaican authorities with little regard for their eminence or power.

Once again, it is necessary to warn that all of this did not add up, during this early period, to any serious movement of colonial disobedience. These elements—of incipient political dissatisfaction, of a multireligious society, once the Spanish religious and political monopoly had been broken, and of the institution of pirate societies—were, at best, marginal elements only. They were overwhelmed by the repressive and authoritarian spirit of the dominant slave society. They were themselves infected by that spirit, so that, for example, if the pirate commonwealths accepted slavery, in similar fashion the Jamaican Maroon communities of the same period allowed themselves, through treaty agreement with the British Government, to become hunters of escaped slaves as a means of preserving their separate sovereignty. In the sphere of religion, the Spanish church failed to learn the lesson Las Casas sought to teach it, and it was the spirit of Labat, not that of Du Tertre, that prevailed in the French church—so much so that it became part of popular political belief in a later period of French Antillean life that Labat had been responsible for the introduction of slavery into the islands, notwithstanding the historical inaccuracy of the charge. Yet, having admitted all that, there is little doubt that these elements left behind them tiny seeds of freedom later to mature into full fruit.

THE CONTRIBUTION OF THE EUROPEAN UTOPIANS

There is one further topic of Caribbean-related thought during this period that merits consideration. It concerns the manner in which the islands became drawn into the movement of the European Utopians as those writers developed their critical literature on the shortcomings of their own societies—which utilized, for its raw material, the records of the discoveries and the reports of the Caribbean travelers. The movement has a long history. Geoffroy Atkinson's book *Les relations de voyages du XVIIe siècle et l'évolution des idées* has documented it for the period of the seventeenth century, and W. Stark's book *America: Ideal and Reality* has documented it for the period of the eighteenth century. It started with Sir Thomas More's *Republic* and Bacon's *New Atlantis*, on through Campanella's *City of the Sun* to terminate in the work of Fénelon in one century and the work of Rousseau in another. Its twin themes were that of the ideal commonwealth and that of the "noble savage." Its favorite literary device was that of the utopian romance, located in some imaginary land or island; a device, it is of interest to note, still utilized with success by modern English-speaking Caribbean novelists like John Hearne and George Lamming. Its practitioners used their fictional fantasies to criticize, directly or simply by the force of comparison, the absolutist societies of their own time. They are critical of private property, rank and dignity, orthodox religion and traditional theology, religious intolerance, and the sexual customs of the old world. They contrast the European obsession with war with the peaceful habits of their imaginary societies, the splendor of nature with the constraints of civil society, the "natural man" with the contemporary European. They laud political liberty, even social equality. They employ fictional figures—the Chinese philosopher, the Abyssinian sage, the Red Indian in the American forest, the missionary in the Christian republic —to deliver homilies on all of the social virtues that Europe does not possess. Under the guise, this is to say, of the exotic and the entertaining, they launch a philosophic attack upon the ills of their own contemporary society.[125]

The Caribbean, as a part of the New World, made its own contribution to this stream of liberal and radical thought. The note of Antillean paradisical innocence is first struck in the *Decades* of Peter Martyr, whose Renaissance humanism was profoundly attracted by the reports of the discoveries. Completely devoid of the polemical spirit, so that he neither condemned the Conquest, like Las Casas, nor applauded it, like Oviedo, his objective attitude made his estimate of Antillian native society all the more persuasive. These are people, he tells his readers, who are simple, peaceful, even intelligent. They live in ignorance of Christian religion, yet they are happy. If they know nothing of work, it is not because they are lazy but because the European concept of work has no meaning for them. They live in a golden age the ancients would have envied. The eulogy is all the more convincing because its author was by no means unaware of the fact that the New World Indians possessed their own habit of intertribal wars. The general picture he paints is that of a people who, notwithstanding such limitations, manage to live happily without laws, books, or money.[126] The theme of exotic paganism has thus already been struck, and it was a theme used by writers as diverse as Fontenelle and Vauban in their argument against the ancien régime. The note is not absent even in Las Casas, despite the fact that he sought to put the New World into the framework of some of the Aristotelian categories: Nearly one-fifth of his *Apologetica Historia* was devoted to the practices of the ancient Greeks, Romans, and Egyptians, in order to show that the customs and religions of the Indians were less corrupt than those of the ancients,[127] thereby demonstrating the utility of the method of comparative cultural analysis that was at the heart of the new rationalist investigations of the period, as can be seen from the way in which writers like Fontenelle, Fénelon, and Malebranche used analogies drawn from the travel literature to press home the rationalist argument.

If the Spanish West Indies were the catalyst, so to speak, for this stream of European thought in the sixteenth century, that role was taken over in the seventeenth century by the French West Indies. Both *libertin* and philosophe drew upon the travel accounts of the French colonizing process in the Americas, from Champlain's Canadian letters to the reports of the French missionaries in Brazil, as well as the Antillean *voyageurs*, to embroider upon the general theme. Men like Foigny and Denis Vairasse wrote their utopian romances on the basis of that literature, painting an imaginary commonwealth in pointed contrast to the France of the ancien régime. It is not at all difficult to see how the literature, even in its most casual observations about life as it was lived by Brazilian native, Canadian Red Indian, and Antillean Carib, stimulated their imagination. Père Claude d'Abbeville described, as early as 1614 in his account of the Brazilian mission of the Capuchin fathers, the communistic economy of the Brazilian natives; Père Biet spoke of the natives of Cayenne fifty years later in similar tones, asserting that they had no kings and all things were equally shared among them; while the same theme of social equality was emphasized by the Sieur de Boyer even more enthusiastically in his *Relation* of Bretigny's visit to the islands in 1654.[128] The persistent theme of all of these travelogues was that of political liberty—the idea, so astonishing to the European mind and at the same time so appealing, that men could be happy without government. It received its most eulogistic expression in the response of the French travelers to the phenomenon of the West Indian Caribs in the Lesser Antilles. Both Père Bouton, in his *Relation de la Martinique* of 1640, and de la Borde in his *Relation des Isles Antilles* of 1684, commented approvingly on the Carib life of ease. Du Tertre elaborated on the theme with characteristic enthusiasm, seeing the Caribs as all equal, none richer or poorer than another, and restricting their wants to only what was necessary. They naturally aroused Père Labat's ethnological curiosity. Not sharing Du Tertre's sentimental admiration, he saw clearly the Carib habits of idleness, revenge, and sloth; their incapacity for sustained interest in things; their inability to grasp alien ideas, even the simplest tenets of Christianity; and the fact that their vaunted life of tropical languor was in reality based on the hard work of their womenfolk, treated as an inferior caste. Even so, Labat's picture managed to capture the Carib violent sense of liberty, which made them unreliable servants and which fed their open contempt for, at once, the whites of the islands for their social hierarchy and their respect for rank, and the blacks for their servile status and betrayal of race pride. Each man does what pleases him, Labat wrote, and permits no one to give him orders. Labat's Catholicism, of course, was shocked by the Carib tendency to see all the sacraments as mere games. But his appreciation of the Carib sentiment of dignity and personal honor is evident, and he defended them against the charge of cannibalism, advanced earlier in Rochefort's account. Labat was no romanticizer. But his average European reader would have been excused for reading into his account many of the elements of the *rêve exotique*.

But the contribution of this literature was not restricted to the exotic theme. That theme, of course, was important and even perhaps the one that appealed most to European readers: it is well known how Du Tertre's history influenced Chateaubriand and the whole Romantic movement, culminating in the Parnassian poets and their sensous theme of *tristes tropiques* (sad and languorous tropics). But the other theme of social criticism was also present.

It perhaps received its fullest expression, on the Antillean side, in Rochefort's account of the Caribs. His surprisingly modern understanding of Carib culture has already been noted. But he went further in his description of the Carib economy as a form of primitive communalism. The Caribs, he writes, live without ambition and vexation, have no desire to acquire wealth or honors, are content with what Nature provides them with, and view work as recreation rather than penance. They are associated, he adds, in one common interest; their houses need no protection because theft is unknown to them. They reproach the Europeans for their avarice and their immoderate industry in the pursuit of wealth, for they themselves are completely free of the acquisitive instinct. Even more, they see clearly the relationship between the pursuit of wealth and unhappiness; this inordinate desire to possess property, they say, only breeds the fear of loss, the gnawing anxiety to get more, the sad knowledge that death will end it all. Why not, they ask, live like us in our natural simplicity, which you mistake for brutish stupidity? It is not really important that all this, in Rochefort's account, was stated in long imaginary harangues that no Carib could possibly have uttered. What is of interest is that it pokes gentle fun at the European bourgeois ideal as much as it satirizes the European Christian ideal, and that Rochefort should have used his Antillean experience toward that end. It constitutes one of the first statements, albeit visionary, of a neosocialist ideology in Caribbean-related literature. The Carib folkways are employed as a foil to European manners and beliefs, to the disadvantage of the latter. The Carib complaints, concludes Rochefort, may well exempt them from the opprobrious denomination *Sauvages*.[129]

And this, too, has had lasting effects. The literary device of the imaginary conversation, for example, just like the device of the imaginary island, has been used by later writers to underline the message. It can be seen in the philosophical work *Suite de voyage de l'Amerique* (usually attributed to Guedeville and actually composed by the Baron de la Houten in 1718), which is set within the framework of a series of imaginary discussions with the native philosopher Adario, and which discusses European philosophy, law, and religion from a comparative viewpoint.[130] Even Voltaire, whose attitude to the theme of the noble savage was usually one of derisory contempt, could not completely withstand the temptation of the theme and made his own contribution to it in the form of his *Conversations entre un sauvage et un gentilhomme*.[131] And how enduring the theme is can be seen from the fact that the modern twentieth-century Cuban writer Alejo Carpentier wrote his exotic opera *Concierto Barroco* centering around an imaginary conversation between the Renaissance Italian composer Vivaldi and an Indian personage.[132] In this way the Antillean reality became the raw material for the construction of the European radical dream.

It is of interest to note the relationship between this literary tradition and the work of Las Casas. There was, of course, no direct relationship because most of that work, with some exceptions, was not published during his lifetime. None of the early Utopians, then, could have read it. But there is a clear and unmistakable community of thought between his reformist ideas and their social and political criticism. For if it is true that one dominant theme of the Utopian literature was that of liberty as the state of nature, as exemplified in the treatment of the Carib theme, it is also true that another dominant theme was that of liberty as the end result of social planning. It is in that second sense that the Utopians paid serious attention to such issues as town planning, community organization of work, eugenics, the encouragement by the state of the arts and sciences, and state-directed education. Many of those themes were also those of the immense Las Casas output. Las Casas's instructions to the Jeronomite commission appointed by the Crown early on, as well as his memorial to Cardinal Ximénes in 1516—the same year as the publication of More's *Utopia*—shows him as at once a town planner and a social engineer. Although not a communistic scheme, it was an exercise in social planning whereby the freed Indians were to be relocated in new communities consisting of a Spanish town and a group of annexed Indian villages, and in which every detail of everyday life was regulated for the common good, including a work system of limited hours, food provisions, and ample vacation time.[133] Similarly, Las Casas's later scheme for planned Spanish peasant-emigration to the islands elaborated in great detail a state-planning system whereby the Crown would provide the rural settlers with land, animals, and farming tools, which they in turn would use to organize both private and collective production of tropical crops. Both native Indian and Spanish settler were thus to be converted into productive and tribute-paying vassals. Liberty did not mean that they could do as they pleased. It meant, rather, that their health, education, and working conditions were the proper concern of the state. These grand Utopian schemes were systematized, later on, in Las Casas's final, astonishing doctrine of universal restitution, whereby it was proposed that the Spaniards, quite literally, should return everything that they had stolen from the Indians since the Discovery itself.[134] As schemes, they clearly attempted to marry the Spanish feudal tradition in favor of centralized state administration to the novel social conditions of the islands. They thereby constituted some of the very first of the social experiments undertaken by the Spaniards in the New World. It is of interest, finally, to note that the bias in favor of bureaucratic state action found ready sympathy with an identical bias within the Inca political organization, which explains why the Inca state later on was cited by various European thinkers of the reformist-radical tradition—Voltaire, Humboldt, Marx and Engels, and Rosa Luxemburg—as supporting evidence for their particular theses.

This particular element of European liberal and radical thought, in which the Caribbean played the role of the land of *le bon sauvage* (the admirable native) is important in another sense. It enables the modern student to distinguish between the imaginary idea of Caribbean society during this early period and the actual, concrete reality of the society. The romanticizing tendency was part of European thought, although it should be noted that it became a real element in Caribbean thought itself later—as the *novela indianista* of the Cuban, Puerto Rican, and Dominican novelists of the nineteenth century period shows, not to mention the growth in certain business sectors of Caribbean society in the twentieth century of an "islands in the sun" attitude nurtured by modern tourism. It had the end result of blinding readers to the harsh and unpleasant realities of the Antillean situation. That has been noted recently by a modern French literary critic in a reference to the larger example of certain forms of Latin American writing. Speaking particularly to the Latin American *novela de la tierra* of the period of the 1920s, such as José Eustacio Rivera's *La vorágine* and Rómulo Gallegos's *Doña Bárbara*—which in a way belonged to the same genre as the earlier *voyage imaginaire* of the seventeenth century—he has noted its seductive effect. He observes:

> For some years, Latin American literature was just this: a literature of evasion...a literature that was of interest because it spoke of Indians, of marvellous journeys, of epic struggles of man against nature, against the jungle, against a grand and dangerous Nature; a literature that allowed the reader to wander dangerously through Peru, Ecuador, Brazil, and Colombia, while settled comfortably in an armchair with a glass of whisky or wine, near to a pleasing fireside, during the cold winter nights.[135]

There can be little doubt that many of the European readers of the earlier literature of the American voyage must have seen it in a similar fashion, more interested in the wonders it had to relate than in the social philosophy it sought to expound.

For, to tell the truth, the realities of Antillean society during these first two centuries of its development were far different. By the time that men like Du Tertre came to write, it was, in its main outlines, already a slave-based society. Its European ruling class of plantation owners and merchants, linked with each other in the sugar economy, had already taken shape. Its normative values, although not fashioned into a coherent philosophy, were already established. Even more than its European counterpart, it was a profit-oriented, acquisitive society, with little of the sense of community that the European societies still possessed from the precapitalist period. As contemporary observers noted, it produced a social climate far different from that of the New England colonies; in Oldmixon's phrase, speaking of seventeenth-century Barbados, persons went hither chiefly to raise their fortunes, not to enjoy the liberty of their consciences.[136] Puritanism itself, once it ventured into the Caribbean, absorbed those values, as is evident from A. P. Newton's account of the ill-fated effort of Puritan magnates to colonize the island of Old Providence off the Mosquito Coast during this period: the Puritan proprietary investor was not very different from the Royalist proprietory investor in that respect.[137] Even in Barbados itself, where a tradition of resident, as distinct from absentee, proprietorship established itself early on, the planter outlook was typically one of felt exile, summed up in the remark of Colonel Drax (as cited by Oldmixon) that he would not think of home, meaning England, till he was worth ten thousand pounds a year.[138] The emphasis on making a fortune was symptomatic (the next step being to found a family). Within that system, the slave was regarded, at best, as a nonperson; and it is suggestive that the romanticizing literature seized upon *le bon sauvage*, rather than *le bon nègre*, as its hero figure: it would have been difficult to have seen the detribalized and deculturated African slave as the repository of Antillean innocence; that was a task that would be left for the European abolitionist literature of the eighteenth century. The difference between Labat's partially sympathetic description of the Caribs and his unsympathetic comments on the Negro slaves speaks volumes for the distinction that was thus made by the Caribbean planter community (of which Labat, as ecclesiastical administrator of his order's Martiniquan sugar plantation, was a member) between enslaved African and independent Carib. All in all, it is the tragic irony of this early Caribbean society that the reports of the travelers were used by the European publicists to give detail to their attacks on organized religion or the divine rights of kings or class oppression when, in reality, it itself was a society founded on the gross exploitation, in the name of Christianity, of both Antillean Indian and African black.

That distinction between the Indian theme and the Negro theme reflected the fact that most of the new Caribbean societies did not become classic white master–black slave societies until the eighteenth century. Both Cuba and Puerto Rico remained small-plantation, mercantile economies with little demand for a large and expensive labor supply and, indeed, it was not until the first quarter of the nineteenth century that the black population surpassed the white in Cuba. The leading element of the classic planter ideology—the presence of a clearly defined Negrophobia—does not appear until the eighteenth century. Before, this is to say, the system of plantation servitude became entrenched, there existed, surprisingly, a relatively tolerant climate of opinion concerning the black person. That can be seen in a number of ways. It is there in the way in which the Spanish evangelical Catholic Church, notwithstanding the fact that it never challenged the institutive principle of slavery itself, took seriously its duty of protecting the religious and legal rights of its Negro communicants; the *sanctiones* (sanctions) passed by the first Caribbean church synod ever held—that of the Dominican provincial synod convened in Hispaniola in 1622—show (whatever their practical effect) a genuine concern for the spiritual welfare of the colored congregants of the church.[139] It is even there, in a paradoxical sort of way, in Labat's attitude toward the slave, for it is an attitude based more on a moral indifferentism to the barbaric cruelty of the system than on an openly racist conviction of the complete subhumanity of the slave person. It is there, finally, in the character of the celebrated judgment on the issue of the legitimacy of slavery rendered by the doctors of the Sorbonne in 1698. For—although finally passing in favor of the institution after much learned argumentation characteristic of the juro-theological mind—it did so on the basis of a series of considerations more practical than theoretical: that the slave gains the advantage of initiation into the Christian faith; that all Christian princes permit their subjects to engage in the trade; that the French and the Portuguese, who pride themselves on being the best Catholics of the world, permit it; that His French Catholic Majesty has no constraint about buying Turkish slaves, although few of them embrace Christianity; that the slave, in any case, is better cared for than in his own home country; and that the African chieftains themselves tolerate the trade. The absence of any argument based on the assumed natural inferiority or social degeneracy of the slave person is suggestive. For although the judgment clearly demonstrates the surrender of the orthodox churches, in the final resort, to the interest of planter property, it also shows how, at the end of this early period, the apologetic did not yet find it necessary to construct a pseudophilosophical or pseudotheological denigration of the slave person of an openly racist character.[140]

THE INCIPIENT INTELLECTUAL CLASS

A final note is pertinent on the sociology of the Caribbean-oriented historiography of this formative period. The Americas were discovered, and then populated, by a Europe that was still indubitably Christian, first Catholic and then Protestant. This, combined with the fact that the newly discovered lands were organized into overseas mission fields, explains why most of the travelers and writers came from the great religious orders. The rich Antillean bibliography, then, from the beginning, was the work of at once the court-appointed Catholic historians like Oviedo and Herrera and the monkish private chroniclers like Du Tertre and Labat. The Dominican and Franciscan orders also made their contribution, not to speak of the contribution of the famous Hieronymite mission to the Indies early on. There were other groups concerned with the discoveries: the Spanish Crown lawyers, the French state planners, the Erasmian humanists. But they remained at home; it was the religious, in the main, who did the fieldwork. Their funding, then, came from their priestly and episcopal salaries. Their books were religious rather than secular in tone, notwithstanding Labat's worldliness. It was only occasionally that an outsider invaded their monopoly: the curious figure, for example, of the eccentric Englishman Thomas Gage, whose book of 1648, *The English-American*, told an astonishing story of travels and escapades in Mexico, Guatemala, and Panama comparable to anything contained in the imaginary travel accounts—thus proving that truth is stranger than fiction. Yet even at that, Gage was a Dominican priest who, once relapsed, returned to England to join the Puritans and become adviser to Cromwell's Western Design. The exceptions to this general rule were few: Rochefort, for example, who wrote as a client of Poincy, albeit a Protestant minister, and Ligon, who wrote in order to refurbish his fortunes.

The settled intellectual class that existed in the island towns, then, was mainly that gathered in the convents of the various orders. Many of them were dedicated to the Indian emancipatory cause, sometimes even before Las Casas: Fray Antonio Montesino, for example, and the Fray Matías de Paz, whose Latin treatise *De dominio regum Hispaniae super Indos* early on anticipated much of the later argumentation of Las Casas. The best of them had all the intellectual curiosity of the educated priest, thus following not only the example of Las Casas but also that of Fernando Columbus, who accompanied his father on the fourth voyage and later enlisted scholars to help in his famous library in Seville. The first libraries to appear in the New World were brought by them. Bishop Balbuena, who wrote a New World epic poem in the old chivalric manner even after the genre had been laughed out of court by Cervantes's great satire, brought a substantial library to his Spanish Jamaican mission, only to have it destroyed later on in San Juan in the 1625 Dutch attack on that city. Others came after him in San Juan, like the *presbitero* Don Diego de Torres Vargas, who referred to his collection of books in his *Memoria* of 1647.[141] In the French Antilles, Labat had his collection of books, and Père Breton started the discipline of ethnolinguistic studies with his dictionary of the Carib language. In the English islands there was General Codrington, well-known in his lifetime as a famous bibliophile; and Labat noted in his visit to Barbados in 1700 that Codrington, then Governor of the Leeward Islands, possessed a large library of books on all kinds of subjects.[142] But Caribbean bibliography, it goes without saying, really started with Las Casas. All accounts indicate that his enormous library, collected throughout a lifetime, and which he finally arranged in his archive-cell in the Dominican College of San Gregorio, was in effect the first of the great West Indian collections, including, as it did, all the *relaciones* of conquests and expeditions published from the beginning, documents, particularly on Columbus; and innumerable and exhaustive reports from his disciples and correspondents in the islands, Mexico and Peru, covering literally every aspect of Indian life and society. It is not too much to say that, in the intellectual sense, he brought in the New World to redress the balance of the Old.[143]

These remarks have to be set within the context of the Caribbean colonial society of the time. Frontier colonists rarely take a metropolitan literary culture with them, at any time; and the Caribbean was no exception. That is evident enough from a book like that of the American scholar Irving Leonard, *Books of the Brave*, of 1949. Despite the fact that its purpose, actually, is to prove that peninsular Spain did not prevent the exportation of its literary culture to the New World colonies, thus refuting the "black legend" of an obscurantist colonialism, its analysis of the transatlantic book trade organized from Seville during the sixteenth century shows conclusively that the legend was at least true for the Caribbean colonial holdings. The main bulk of book consignments went to the mainland cities of Mexico and Lima. Caribbean ports like Nombre de Dios or Puerto Bello were transshipment points at best. Leonard catalogs a book consignment invoice sent out to Mexico in 1600 of some 678 titles, including many titles of Renaissance literature specifically condemned by the *Index Quiroga*, such as works by Cardan, Scaliger, Telesio, and Copernicus, all of them reflecting the new scientific and rationalist currents of the age. He also catalogs a 1583 list of a private library in Spanish Manila, much less eclectic but no less interesting, and presumably the property of a private gentleman or Spanish official. That he can provide no evidence of anything comparable in the Caribbean-island towns speaks for itself: what cultural life developed in colonial Spanish America belonged to the mainland rather than to the islands—which were regarded, once Mexico and Peru had been discovered, as merely stepping stones to more favored places.[144]

The convent and the church thus became, as best they could, oases of thought and meditation, sometimes of speculation, in the desert of the philistine island societies. Despite the exclusivist policies of the various colonizing powers, and especially Spanish exclusivism, the church and convent, more than any other burgeoning institution, reflected the character of sixteenth- and seventeenth-century Europe as a cosmopolitan society in which the common language of the learned was still Latin. That heritage of medieval universalism was immeasurably enlarged, as already noted, by the discoveries, for they precipitated a process of global reconstruction, seeing the world in a new and revolutionary light: the new geographical knowledge brought back by the discoverers made possible, for example, the development of the principle of the spherical projection method, the theoretical foundation of the modern atlas. The early literature on the Caribbean reflected that global sense. It was seen as part of a slowly developing conceptualization of the world, and more particularly of the American world, as a total whole. From the beginning, then, writers on the region exhibited the spirit of Renaissance catholicity, describing everything, so that their books touched on an enormous variety of subject matter: exploration, geology, geography, zoology, botany, history, and social organization. That can be seen (to take a few examples only) in Du Tertre; towards the end of the period it is there in Sir Hans Sloane's *Voyage to the Islands* of 1707; and the genre reached its classic culmination, of course, in the monumental work of Von Humboldt in the early nineteenth century, *Voyage aux régions equinoxiales du nouveau continent* (1805-34). Like Herodotus in Egypt, they had to cover everything because of the sheer novelty of things. As Elsa Goveia aptly puts it, it is the strangeness of the Caribbean society that accounts for the comprehensiveness of its history.[145]

The literature of the period thus possesses about it a sense of the Caribbean as an encompassing whole, a feeling for its grand sweep of history. Its most eloquent expression appears, perhaps, in Labat's 1722 book, *Nouveau voyage*. Barbadian novelist, George Lamming, puts in contemporary language Labat's conviction that there was a rhythm of history that held all of the islands together in a common destiny:

> I have travelled everywhere in your sea of the Caribbean...from Haiti to Barbados, to Martinique and Guadeloupe, and I know what I am speaking about....You are all together, in the same boat, sailing on the same uncertain sea...citizenship and race unimportant, feeble little labels compared to the message that my spirit brings to me: that of the position and predicament which History has imposed upon you ...I saw it first with the dance...the *merengue* in Haiti, the *beguine* in Martinique, and today I hear, *de mon oreille morte*, the echo of calypsoes from Trinidad, Jamaica, St. Lucía, Antigua, Dominica and the legendary Guiana....It is no accident that the sea which separates your lands makes no difference to the rhythm of your body.[146]

The prophetic vision of that passage has never been far from the conscious surface of the Caribbean imagination.

Chapter Three

The Eighteenth and Nineteenth Centuries: The Proslavery Ideology

THE GENERAL CHARACTER OF THE IDEOLOGY

The heyday of the slave-based sugar plantation economy was the period of the eighteenth and nineteenth centuries, only ending as late as the second half of the nineteenth century: 1834 in the British islands, 1848 in the French islands, 1873 in Spanish Puerto Rico, and 1886 in Spanish Cuba. Its very longevity is astonishing: The slave trade, with its various permutations, lasted for more than four hundred years. It was at once an economic institution and a political system; and it left its indelible mark, in varying degree, on the collective social psychology of all the Caribbean peoples. It reached its apogee at different times in different sugar islands: in Jamaica and Saint Domingue in the eighteenth century, in Cuba in the nineteenth century. Geographically, it extended in one vast district from the southern states of the American Union to northern Brazil, out of which developed the black under-class of the Americas. There was an enormous variety, of course, in the etiology of the slave plantation, from small estate to mammoth park. But the institutive principle of the slave regime was constant throughout: that (as Marx put it, quoting from the English economist Cairnes) in slave-importing countries the most effective economy is that which takes out of the human chattel in the shortest space of time the utmost amount of exertion it is capable of putting forth.[1] It constituted an integral part of the emerging Atlantic capitalist system; its main purpose, therefore, was the maximization of profit. That this has not always been fully appreciated is due to the fact that much of the vast literature on the institution, motivated by the philanthropic drive to abolish it, has been more concerned with its moral evil than with its economic function.

Slavery, this is to say, was originally an economic category rather than a racial category. That is evident enough, as the Dutch scholar Herman J. Niebohr showed in his early volume of ethnographical studies on slavery of 1900, from the fact that slavery is, historically, a worldwide phenomenon that has characterized most societies where there has been present a pattern of dominance and subordination between ruling and ruled groups, ranging from the Ottoman Empire to the pastoral tribes of the Pacific coast. Since, too, the classic definition of slavery is that, with variations, it constitutes a system of compulsory labor in perpetuity, in which the owner possesses not only the right of property in the person of the slave but also complete and arbitrary power over the will of the slave, the Roman *potestas dominica*, it follows that racial differentiation between owner and subject is not central or even necessary to the functional operation of the system. The social and political consequences of the system, correspondingly, are not of necessity racially oriented: as Niebohr points out, for example, a slave regime with many domestic slaves guarantees the freedom of women, since free women are no longer overtaxed with work, and slavery accelerates the social differentiation between rich and poor, since the poor man cannot purchase slaves as easily as the wealthy man. Slavery is thus functionally related to the growth of class society; although Niebohr, in a curious digression, hastens to assure his readers that this must not be taken as a supporting argument for the Socialist ideas of his own time, which he sees as a dangerous romanticism that underestimates the social function of the great manufacturer.[2]

Marx, as always, saw this clearly. "Direct slavery," he wrote in his important letter of 1846 to P. V. Annenkov, "is as much the pivot of our industrialism today as machinery, credit, etc. Without slavery no cotton; without cotton no modern industry. Slavery has given their value to the colonies; the colonies have created world trade; world trade is the necessary condition of large-scale machine industry."[3] Marx was referring to North American cotton-based slavery. But his observation applies equally, if not more so, to Caribbean sugar-based slavery. For the Caribbean was the perfected expression of the total Atlantic slave economy, with the cotton plantations of the American South being little more than a pale echo of the sophisticated sugar plantations of Jamaica, Saint Domingue, and Cuba. It was, then, only an accident of literature that the most famous of all popular novels on the system should have been Mrs. Stowe's *Uncle Tom's Cabin*, a crude and sanctimonious exposé that in no way matches the earlier works of the French eighteenth century novelists and playwrights of the *littérature négrophile*. The main function of the system, as Eric Williams has shown in his classic study *Capitalism and Slavery*, was to provide the accumulated capital for European capitalist expansion; and it is testimony to the essential correctness of that thesis that the attempt of later scholarship to impugn it has succeeded no more than the effort of subsequent investigators to disprove the thesis of the remarkable books of the Hammonds that the price the English village laborer had to pay for his forced transformation into the English town worker between 1760 and 1850 was a massive deterioration in the total quality of his life-style.[4]

These general principles, along with Niebohr's discussion of the land-population relationship in the development of comparative slavery systems, clearly apply to the Caribbean situation. The major problem of the Caribbean settler and planter, from the beginning, was a labor problem: it was essential to have at immediate command a large, regular, and plentiful supply of obedient labor. The problem was solved in the early period with, first, Indian labor and, second, white indentured servant labor. But it was only a temporary solution. The enslaved Indian was at once too physically weak and too psychologically negative to accept the hard labor of mine and *encomienda*, while the indentured servant was too expensive: as the governor of Barbados reported in 1676, the planters of that island had already discovered that the labor of three blacks was equal, in financial costs, to the labor of one white man.[5] The Indian labor force died out, without possibility of self-replacement; the white labor force, fleeing from the meshes of manorial serfdom in Europe, reemigrated north to the New England colonies, where land was plentiful and where they could more easily work for themselves. In the face of those difficulties, the Caribbean planter oligarchy turned to the African labor supply, not because it was black, but because it was cheaper. It possessed enormous economic advantages: as Cairnes pointed out, it admitted of the most complete organization; it could be combined on an extensive scale and directed by a controlling mind to a single end; and, notwithstanding its defects, its cost never rose above that which was necessary to maintain the slave in health and strength.[6] To all that was added the special considerations of tropical agriculture: in the northern temperate zone of cereal crops, the small proprietor could manage, whereas in the semitropical zone, to which tobacco, rice, cotton, and sugar were more adaptable, the advantage was with the large estate. Negro slavery was thus the end result of an economic revolution in the Caribbean economy, not the outcome of a race-based preference for black labor. As Eric Williams has succinctly put it, slavery was not born of racism, but racism was instead the consequence of slavery.

All this had important consequences for the general character of the Caribbean settler-planter ideology. It has been seen, too simplistically, as merely Negrophobic. On the contrary, there is much evidence to suggest that, in the beginnings, it was color-blind. The fact that the aboriginal Indian stock were fair-skinned, and perceived to be so by the discoverers, did not prevent the rapid emergence on the part of the Spanish settlers of a deep contempt for their Indian subjects; as early as 1517 the Hieronymite commissioners found in response to their enquiries that the Spanish settlers in Cuba vigorously upheld the doctrine of Indian depravity, denying that the Indians possessed any capacity for living in civilized fashion and even sustaining the curious thesis that their depravity and inconstancy were due to lunar influence on islanders.

In similar fashion, a typically European class hatred developed between the planter magnates of the early Barbadian colonial Assembly and the dispossessed lower-class whites, reflected in the contemptuous epithets conferred upon the latter group: *poor whites, mean whites, redlegs.* It was a hatred compounded by old ancestral hatreds, that of the English for the Irish, for example; and even a colonial gentleman as humane as Codrington could express his contempt for the Irish in terms so crude that Père Labat was driven to ponder on the vanity of the English. The Barbadian "poor white," in fact, was the equivalent of the "white trash" of the later American South; and merely to read the history of their attempts throughout the eighteenth century to be enrolled into the colonial militia is to understand how even the possession of a white complexion did not in any way guarantee them a role in island government.[7]

Racial prejudice, then, was mixed up with class prejudice in the planter mentality. It was also mixed up with religious prejudice. The religious toleration enjoyed by the Jewish communities in the English and Dutch colonies has already been noted. Yet the medieval temper of anti-Semitism still prevailed sufficiently to impose upon them civil disabilities that were not finally removed until the nineteenth century. That is evident enough, to take only one example, from the revealing *Essai historique sur la colonie de Surinam* that was published in 1788 by the *Regenten*, the governing body of the communal leaders of the Sephardic group in Dutch Guiana. Inspired by the earlier publication of the plea for Jewish emancipation made by the eminent German liberal publicist Von Dohm, which they had read with excitement, it was at once an expression of gratitude to the Dutch republic for the religious freedom enjoyed by the Jewish community in the colony—which, the authors say, would certainly form the happiness of the Jews of France and Germany—and a vigorous protest against a continuing tendency on the part of the Christian element to blame the Jews for everything that went wrong.[8] The irony of the document lies in the fact that although its authors were urban businessmen and estate owners who fully accepted without criticism the institution of slavery, even to the point of cataloging with immense pride the record of Jewish militia captains in hunting down runaway slaves in innumerable expeditions into the bush,[9] they nonetheless expressed a real bitterness about the failure of the Dutch Company, the colonial governors, and the local Christian governing group to fully appreciate that loyalist spirit. They pointed with pride to the social quality of the early Jewish settlers: "It was certainly not with vagabonds and with wretches drawn from the dungeons of England that the colony was founded, as several others in America were."[10] Yet the complaints of prejudice and ill-regard throughout the book indicate clearly that being of European lineage, white, and well-to-do did not in and of itself buy full acceptance even in a slave colony.

It was only in the eighteenth century that the plantation economy became wholly and exclusively identified with the Negro slave and that there took place the growth of a systematic racist ideology that identified the slave, in turn, with nonhuman and antinatural attributes. The system only needed an ideological rationalization once it had become fully established as an economic structure; and also, suggestively, when it came under attack from its religious and humanitarian critics sometime after the 1770s. Until then, slavery was not axiomatically identified with the white master–black servant axis. According to Rochefort, it existed among the Caribs, who believed that their bravest warriors after death would live in happy islands with their enemies, the Arawaks, as their slaves; Negro slaves captured as prisoners in the wars with the Spanish were kept as such; and captive women became slaves, their children given liberty if the mothers were taken as wives.[11] Up until the end of the seventeenth century, the French state recruited the bulk of its galley slaves in the royal navy from Moslem prisoners sold in the European slave marts and even compromised its Christian principles to enslave such nonconformist Christians as Russians and Greeks—so much so that the Marseilles merchants and shippers who effectively monopolized that trade openly opposed Colbert's plan to change to Negro slaves on the ground that they could not expect to break into an African trade already dominated by other companies.[12] It was not, all this is to say, until all of the earlier and alternative sources of labor supply—native Indian, indentured servant, peasant emigrant, transshipped prisoner and convict—had either dried up or proved unsatisfactory that the planter class moved to acceptance of the African trade. Like capitalism everywhere, Caribbean sugar capitalism was no respecter of persons.

It is only at that point, then—when the demand for labor coincided with the African supply—that the racist component began to emerge as the main property of the planter ideology. Or, rather, that the prejudices of social caste and of religious belief finally were joined together with the physiological prejudice to compose a more or less coherent view concerning black and white, which the planter class and its defenders promulgated in a growing literature after 1700. In that view the black person was condemned, and his slave status justified, from three different angles, now fused with each other: from the angle of social position because he was identified with menial labor; from the angle of religious belief because he was seen as pagan or heathen, beyond the reach of Christian compassion; from the angle, finally, of blackness itself, identified with evil bestiality. Irrevocably, after much loose terminology, the institution of slavery became equated with the Afro-American person in the imagination of Western society, and thereafter operated as a fixed article of faith.

The planter ideology has thus to be seen as the ideological superstructure of the revival of slavery as a mode of production in the post-Reformation period. It had its antecedents, as scholars like Winthrop Jordan have shown, in theological and pseudoscientific concepts that went back to the foundations of Judeo-Christian thought: the curse of Ham in popular biblical anthropology, the distinction between the children of light and the children of darkness, the Puritan obsession with sexuality so easily transferred to blacks, the concept of the non-Christian stranger.[13] But a theory of antecedents is ultimately unsatisfactory as an explanation for the rise of modern slavery and its accompanying theology. First, because it is tempted to exaggerate color prejudice to the exclusion of other, equally potent, prejudices. It is at least arguable that the medieval mind was more preoccupied with anti-Semitism than with Negrophobia. In the English literary tradition alone, the anti-Jewish note is strident from Chaucer to Shakespeare; and the marked difference between Shakespeare's portrayal of Shylock as the capitalist Jew (notwithstanding Portia's famous plea) and of Othello as the honorable Moor, is symptomatic. Second, although it is true that the racist creed goes back some two thousand years (the attribution of feelings of guilt and shame to color is at least as old as the Song of Solomon), the theory of antecedents still leaves unexplained why it lay dormant for so long, only to be revived in the eighteenth century—fomenting, among other things, new problems of legal definition of the status of the slave for the English common law. The answer lies in the sociology of ideas. Ideas realize themselves in the form of social institutions only when forms of production make it possible. Therefore, just as Plato's idea of sexual equality became capable of realization only when the nineteenth-century factory system replaced mere physical strength with manual dexterity—thus facilitating the entry of women into factory work—so the racist creed only became of practical utility once the system of modern Caribbean slavery created a new master class of slave owners who needed it for ideological justification.

The heart of the Caribbean planter ideology is, it goes without saying, the search for a rationalizing justification of Negro slavery. As such, it goes back to the very beginning of Caribbean history in its European phase. The motives were varied. In quantitative terms, the slave regime was of such enormous proportions that it could not be hidden from sight, like the longstanding Arab trade of North and East Africa; as such, it had to be defended from the beginning against its critics. Qualitatively, it violated at once Spanish medieval precepts and the English common law, both of which viewed slavery as a *status contra naturam*, only to be justified on the narrow ground of captivity in war; thus, it constituted a gross moral affront to all the principles on which Western Christianity, at its best, was founded.

The challenge of that contradiction between slavery and Christianity could not be avoided. No apologist for the system could adopt the attitude of Machiavellian amoralism that the Renaissance mind for a period made fashionable, summed up in Pope Leo X's remark, "now that we have the Papacy let us enjoy it." The early conquistadores, admittedly, shared much of that cynical outlook, as is evident from Fray Bernardino de Minaya's scandalized account of how, finally meeting with Pizarro in Peru and informing that soldier of fortune of the Emperor's instructions concerning humane treatment of the Indians, he was met with the Machiavellian retort that Pizarro had come from Mexico to take their gold away from the Indians and would do nothing else.[14] But no apologist for the slavery regime, European or Creole, putting pen to paper, could dismiss the problem in that contemptuous fashion. Being immersed in the value system of Western Christianity, he was forced to meet it more responsibly. That, as much as anything else, explains the sheer magnitude of the literature on the subject, which did not die until the slave system itself had died.

The debate on slavery, then, like the debate between feudalism and capitalism, or the debate between science and religion, became one of the great debates of the age and engaged the learned of both the old European societies and the new American societies. Its very longevity testifies to its importance, for it raged as incessantly in nineteenth-century Cuba as it had done in eighteenth-century Jamaica. Like other seminal issues—imperialism, for example, or women's rights—it was the sort of issue that cut across traditional ideological loyalties. Voltaire's attitude to the issue was equivocal; an aristocrat like Mirabeau was outspokenly antislavery. The socially conservative Methodist John Wesley fiercely attacked the system in his savage *Thoughts upon Slavery* of 1744; Gibbon, the great sceptic, could denounce it in the ancient world but could see nothing wrong about it in its modern form. Wilberforce, a reactionary in domestic politics, spearheaded the abolitionist drive; by comparison, Cobbett (the most famous of all Radicals), in his well-known letter to Wilberforce, properly condemned him for his indifference to the cause of the poor, yet went on to assert that Wilberforce's charges against the West Indian planter were completely false and misrepresentative of the true facts. Finally, Dr. Johnson, as a religious Tory of the old school, could propose a toast to "the next insurrection of the Negroes in the West Indies," which Bryan Edwards reported in tones of scandalized horror, while Jefferson, as a freethinking deist, could compose in his *Notes on Virginia* one of the most offensive passages in the literature of racial animosity.

THE DISCUSSION ON INDIAN AND NEGRO

The planter ideology starts, in effect, with the early movement to replace Indian labor with imported African labor. The continuous campaign of the Dominicans and Franciscans in defense of the Indians; the increasing requests from the settlers for Negro slaves; the profit to the Crown to be reaped from the slave trade: all of these factors facilitated the change. Even Oviedo, anti-Indian as he was, could argue that the rapid decimation of the Indians was due to their maltreatment at the hands of Spanish factors and overseers, acting on behalf of powerful court favorites who never visited the islands.[15] The enslavement of the African thus, through a cruel paradox, was justified in terms of the salvation of the Indian; the argument can be seen as the first expression of the general proslavery apologetic that African slavery, as an institution, worked for beneficent results. Even Las Casas petitioned the Crown in support of the trade.[16] But it would be historically inaccurate to accept the thesis, advanced by his enemies, that Las Casas was responsible for the change of policy. The thesis rested for a long time on the assumed veracity of Herrera's original accusation, on the basis of which eighteenth century writers as different as Robertson, Raynal, and Corneille de Pau repeated the charge. But the extracts of documents on the Negro trade put together in the great collection of Juan Bautista Muñoz, during the late eighteenth century, and on which Quintana in part based his corrective monograph on Las Casas of 1833, prove conclusively that the trade was already flourishing even before Las Casas's suggestion of 1518.[17] Las Casas's Sevillian background may have been responsible for his initial acceptance of Negro slavery. But the institution had its roots in collective interests and vague ideas present in the mental climate of the sixteenth century that could have had little to do with the outlook of one man, even although that man was as influential as Las Casas.

The theme of Indian emancipation thus became recruited into the slavery apologetic. The arguments were varied. The new African trade would bring profit to the Crown. Negroes were better than Indians since, as Judge Zuazo of Hispaniola told the regent of Spain in 1518, it was very rarely that a Negro died in the islands.[18] Negro slaves, as the bishop of San Juan advised in 1579, would revive the former prosperity of the Puerto Rican colony, since they could be made to work in the gold mines.[19] Or there was the argument that if the Spanish did not enter the slave trade, it would remain in the hands of the Portuguese, to the detriment of Spanish wealth and security. There was even the curious argument that slaves brought from overseas were much less likely to attempt escape than Indians enslaved locally; yet the argument had little ground in fact, for as early as 1574 the Havana *audiencia* was obliged to reprimand in stern tones those persons who helped runaway slaves—already by that time, obviously, a serious problem.[20] Underpinning all of these arguments there rested the general European ethnocentric tendency to place all non-European peoples in a sort of color continuum, with those more closely approximating white appearance being regarded as the more pleasing. Not even Las Casas himself was exempt from that prejudice; and in those chapters of the *Historia* in which he denounced the Portuguese slave raids in Africa, he innocently described the various gradations of the captives, "those who were reasonably white, handsome and elegant, others less white, who seemed to be *pardos* (gray or dusky), and others as black as Ethiopians, so malformed in their faces and bodies that they appeared to those who looked at them to be the image of another and lower hemisphere."[21] The prejudice helps to explain why African slavery failed to generate in the Spanish theologians and jurists of the time anything comparable to the great controversy on the Indian question.

The anti-African feeling finally matured, of course, into the proslavery ideology. Yet it is worth emphasizing the truth that it was neither an easy nor a rapid victory. The European mind was still dominated by the virtually universal assumption, dictated by both church and scripture, that all mankind stemmed from a single source and therefore enjoyed a common brotherhood. Notwithstanding their religious hatred of each other, the sentiment was voiced by both Spanish Catholic and English Protestant. As early as 1573 Bartolomé de Albornoz, in his *Arte de los Contratos*, answered the specious argument that slavery was justified because it saved men from an African paganism with the assertion that it would be better for an African to be king in his own country than a slave in Spanish America; in any case, the argument about the welfare of the slave did not justify, but rather aggravated, the reason for holding him in servitude. "I do not believe," added Albornoz finally, "those persons who will tell me that there is anything in Christ's law to the effect that freedom of the soul must be paid for by slavery of the body."[22] Fray Tomás Mercado described in grim detail the horrors of the Middle Passage in his *Suma de Tratos y Contratos* of 1587; his account makes it clear how the theory of the just war—half-plausible enough when used against Arab, Moor, and Mohammedan—had become dishonestly twisted into an excuse for the forcible capture of innocent African women and children.[23] Finally, Fray Alonso de Sandoval, in his treatise of 1627, invoked the authority of Plato, Philo Judaeus, and Euripides to deliver an impassioned condemnation of the slavery institution. "For if," he exclaimed, "the civil laws classify exile as a form of civil death, with how much more reason may we call abject slavery death? For it involves not only exile but also subjugation, and hunger, gloom, nakedness, outrage, imprisonment, perpetual persecution, and is, finally, a combination of all evils."[24] English writers echoed similar sentiments. The Reverend Samuel Purchas, who completed Hakluyt's work of compilation, expressed it in his elegantly worded declaration that "the tawney Moore, black Negro, duskie Libyan, ash-coloured Indian, olive-coloured American, should with the whiter European become one sheep-fold, under one great sheep-heard, till this mortalitie being swallowed up of Life, we may all be one... without any more distinction of Colour, Nation, Language, Sexe, Condition."[25]

Attitudes such as these, undoubtedly, were important. They came, especially in the Spanish case, from priests and officials who were often colonial residents, so that it could not be said of them that they were armchair critics who had never set foot in the islands (a frequent charge of the proslavery writers against their opponents). At the same time, they were clearly not much more than ideological survivals of the older medieval teachings. They lasted longer in Spain, where the influence of the priest maintained itself more effectively than in England or Holland. But outside of Spain the new forces of the age—mercantilism, capitalist acquisitiveness, the victory of the commercial bourgeoisie over the landed aristocracy, and the general secularizing tendency—combined to discredit the moralistic viewpoint. Slavery, when discussed at all, was seen in economic and not in religious terms, as is evident enough, in the English case, in the economic writings of men like Locke and Sir Josiah Child. By 1700, possibly even before, slavery had not only become an integral part of the new Atlantic industrial system but had also been accepted by the European mind, at all social levels, as a part of the natural order of things.

There is yet another sense in which the European-Indian confrontation constituted, as it were, a dress rehearsal for the later chattel-slavery regime. It gave a new impetus, in a new environment, to the values of the European master class. Those values, essentially, were two: that Europe possessed a natural right to arbitrary rule over non-European peoples, and that it was the obligation of the new subject-peoples, again by natural law, to work for their new masters. They are evident, from the very beginning, in the literature of the Conquest. After the first enraptured impressions, it is the common complaint of Columbus and his successors that the Indians do not like to work. Even Las Casas was not prepared to give the Indians complete liberty; his reform schemes envisaged that they would be organized in new communities along more rational lines in a regime of humanely controlled communal work. The Indians, it is charged against them, show no real appreciation of the value of gold and silver, which they use only for ornamental purposes (in a similar fashion, it was held against the Aztec and Inca Indians that they hoarded their wealth in palace treasure rooms instead of putting it to productive use). This is clearly the genesis of the later argument of the proslavery apologetic that if the slave is not forced to work, he will lie under a tree and live on mangoes and bananas. There is present here, first, the old Christian-medieval conviction that man must work by the sweat of his brow and, second, the new capitalist belief that natural resources must not be allowed to lie idle, but must be rationally exploited for the purpose of accumulating wealth.

THE SETTLER HISTORIANS

This general sense of Europe as a superior civilization with a manifest destiny to develop the New World was shared by all the colonizing powers. In the English case, it makes its appearance in the eighteenth century with the writings of the settler-historians and their like such as Atwood in Dominica, Poyer in Barbados, Dallas in Jamaica, and Sir William Young in St. Vincent. As early "local" historians, they wrote openly as apologists, mainly addressing British public opinion in defense of the West Indian social order. Their essentially paternalistic and favorable view of the planter society was complemented by their tendency to regard the stability of the slave system as a vital element in the continued viability of the political and social structure of the British colonial empire in the region as a whole. For Atwood, Dominica is an island healthier than St. Lucia and more capable of planned economic improve-

ment than Trinidad. A combination of English immigration and free grants
of the unappropriated Crown lands would soon put it ahead, in terms of commercial prosperity, of the old and exhausted sugar islands. In addition, the
island's strategic position, situated between the two main French colonies,
was inestimable. Atwood, again, writes almost as a tourist agent as he describes, in classic Arcadian style, the beauties of the island, not to mention
its importance as a watering spa for invalids; he even manages to claim that
lovers of astronomy would find in the island new opportunity to advance their
science. The only urgent problem that threatens the island's development is
the existence of the runaway-slave settlements. They must be crushed, if only
because the cost involved in pacification—which Atwood describes in detail
—places a tax burden so onerous on the planters that it threatens to put them
out of business. The note of jealous island particularism, so much a part of
the planter creed, is clearly struck in Atwood's book: Dominica is healthy
virgin territory awaiting the energetic settler, while St. Lucia is only the bury-
ing place of thousands of brave Englishmen.[26] The insularism was only overcome when planters needed help from other islands to repress a slave revolt,
for rebellion in one island encouraged rebellion in another. A sense of regional
identity was fragile at best, essentially narrow and selfish in its motives.

The Young book on St. Vincent was even more expansionist in its tone. It
is the voice of the white settler on the frontier, righteously indignant at the
continued existence of an aboriginal group—in this case, the Black Caribs of
St. Vincent—which by its endemic hostility to the settler presence places the
whole white European "civilizing" process in jeopardy. Young obviously felt
it necessary to construct some plausible thesis to justify the group's deportation since, unlike the Negro slaves, its members were keepers of an original
aboriginal heritage that rested on prior occupancy. He found the thesis in the
doctrine of the right by conquest. The English had conquered them, and
therefore, they possessed no rights beyond those granted by the Crown; correspondingly, those rights were forfeited by their rebellion and by their par-
tiality for the French. The thesis was completed by the typical method of
defamation of character: the Caribs were a barbarous and cruel set of savages beyond reason or persuasion and must therefore be eliminated.[27] It is
worth noting, comparing Atwood and Young, how the planter ideology singled
out for that defamatory process the group or groups that posed the greatest
danger to the planter interest. In Dominica, the real danger came from the
runaway slaves, not from the Caribs, who formed no more than twenty or
thirty families; in St. Vincent, by contrast, the Carib himself was the danger,
constituting as he did a strong and militant tribal enclave. So, Atwood saw
the Carib, in benign terms, as a "native Indian," while Young saw him as a
predominantly Negro person, with all of the Negro's negative traits. So again,
Atwood wanted to organize a political union with the Caribs, so that they
could become hunters of escaped slaves, following the Jamaica policy; Young
saw deportation as the only solution. Both apologists, with an unerring in-

stinct based on the sentiment of English moral paramountcy, identified their main enemy and then proceeded to vilify him, which in turn justified his extinction.

This theme of the white settler battling against a hostile internal enemy reached its fullest expression, however, in the Dallas account of the Jamaican Maroon wars. As an ex-liberal, Dallas felt compelled to embellish his defense of slavery as a civilizing force with pseudolearned observations. Like a lesser Burke, he saw the root cause of the Maroon revolt in the "mischievous effect" of the Enlightenment philosophy, although he provides no evidence that any Maroon leader had ever even heard about it. He also saw that philosophy as influencing planters to more humane treatment of their slave charges, again without supporting evidence. He even managed to defend the Maroons against the shrill invective of Bryan Edwards's portrait of them as a lawless banditti of cruel animals; their marriage customs, he acutely argues, ought not to be judged by alien European standards, and far from being animals they possessed most, if not all, of the senses in a superior degree.[28] He even gives the benefit of the doubt to the Maroons concerning the original cause of the war in his admission of the Maroon argument that they had been forced into hostilities out of self-preservation, being persuaded that the whites planned their destruction. He goes yet further, and admits that the technical violation of the treaty on the part of the whites—against which only General Walpole, to his credit, earnestly protested—and which was made the pretext by the local Assembly for their deportation, was probably due to the Maroons' suspicions of bad faith on the part of the colonial authorities.[29] Despite making all these concessions, Dallas arrived at substantially the same conclusions as the more reactionary Edwards. The Maroons had committed "horrid atrocities." They had rebelled against the legitimate authority of the Jamaica Assembly. Enslavement, after all, was not only God's will but also necessary in the light of the fact that the Negro "character" could never itself operate the sugar economy without the guidance of the whites.[30]

Three leading themes, characteristic of the planter outlook, infuse these writings of the settler-historians. First, there is the theme of the absolute monopoly of the slave-worked plantation system. It cannot tolerate any alternative system, nor indeed coexist with any alternative system. It must, therefore, crush any attempt at creating such an alternative, such as the elementary Maroon food-crop economy or the Carib self-sufficient economy; or such alternatives, as with the Carib regime, must at least be safely isolated by a policy of controlled reservations. Nor, of course, could any such alternative be allowed to become the economic basis for organized resistance to the plantation regime. "A cordial reconciliation between them [the Maroons] and the white people," Dallas concluded, "was hardly to be expected."[31] The white settler has taken that intransigent view of native peoples who stand in his way everywhere; and the treatment of the Maroons and Caribs in the West Indies anticipated the later treatment of the Maori tribes in Australasia and of the

Plains Indians in the American West—with the same perfidious record of military repression, governmental treachery, broken treaties, and forced evacuation from lands coveted by the whites.

Second, there is the theme of the "divide and rule" strategy, devised to prevent the emergence of a united front against the whites, pitting one set of native interests against another. Dallas saw that clearly. "Had the Maroons," he wrote, "shown that their rebellion was not a temporary struggle but a permanent and successful opposition to the government, it is highly probable that the example might in time have united all the turbulent spirits among the slaves in a similar experiment; if not in the same interest; or indeed such a decided triumph might have tempted numbers of the plantation negroes, unwilling before to change a state of peace for warfare, to join the Maroons. At all events, they would have been a rallying point for every discontented slave, and for all who dreading punishment were incited by their fears to escape." Such an event, he adds, would have meant total economic ruin for the island.[32] The danger was avoided by the policy of tolerating the Maroons so long as they faithfully served as hunters of runaway slaves and, indeed, of making that role a condition of their final surrender. Had there been such a body at Santo Domingo, General Walpole wrote to Lord Balcarres at the end of the war, the brigands would never have risen. The remark sums up a whole policy.

Third, there is the theme of Negro incapacity for freedom. For Atwood, there was, he wrote, "something so very unaccountable in the genius of all negroes, so very different from that of white people in general, that there is not to be produced an instance in the West Indies, of any of them ever arriving to any degree of perfection in the liberal arts or sciences, notwithstanding the greatest pains taken with them"; although, illogically, he conceded, as against that theme of natural inferiority, that second-generation Negroes, under the proper social influence, were capable of losing some of their "stupidity," thus allowing, inferentially, that their state was related to environment and not to inherent deficiency. For Dallas, as he put it in turn,"the notion of a free, active, negro republic, does not seem to have any reasonable foundation."[33] Such a republic, if it came to pass, would simply reveal a people without direction, union, or energy; he seems not to have realized that his own description of the Maroon social organization and fighting strategy belied the accusation. It was left to Edwards, in that section of his book that was originally written as an introduction to the published proceedings of the Jamaica Assembly on the Maroon affair, to develop the theme into an argument against slavery abolition. The "calm and unprejudiced reader," he wrote hopefully, will agree with him that the "wild and lawless freedom" of the Maroons proves that abolition would be nothing more than a state of things without control or restraint, neither benefiting society at large nor promoting the happiness of the slaves themselves.[34] The particular circumstance of a beleaguered racial minority engaged in a death struggle with a more complex and ruthless exploiting civilization was thus arbitrarily identified with the general circumstance of Negro freedom understood in its larger context.

These settler-historians, notably Atwood, Young, and Dallas, may properly be seen, as it were, as the Robinson Crusoe apologists of the slave regime; that is to say, they were all concerned with a crucial period when the colonial society was threatened, in Robinson Crusoe fashion, by a hostile force—runaway slaves in Dominica, Caribs in St. Vincent, the Maroons in Jamaica. The analogy is an apt one. For far from being the epic of primitive life, an idyll of tropical island life away from it all, that it has been popularly supposed to be, Defoe's famous book is better seen as a celebration of the heroic exploits of the *homo faber europeanus* in the New World, utilizing his European technology, in the form of goods and tools salvaged from his wrecked ship, to cultivate his island, once he had at hand a subordinate labor supply in the person of Man Friday; undertaking, that is to say, an economy of primitive capital accumulation. Along with that there went a sort of neo-evolutionary view in which the bands of *mauvais sauvages* (evil savages), the rescued native Friday, and Crusoe himself embodied perceived different stages, from lower to higher, in the growth of "civilization." Only the tropical setting of the story, facilely invoking the European dream of the idyllic island paradise, made it seem to the European reader to be something else, so that it was ironic that the book should have been seen by Rousseau's Emile as a picture of the ideal state of nature. It is closer to the truth to say that in its portraiture of Crusoe, incessantly working each day to build up his little empire against the threat of dark and unknown enemies, the book describes the European settler struggling to maintain his supremacy in the colonial world, just like the white groups of settler-historians. Nor was it incidental that Defoe should have made the foundation of Crusoe's success his earlier venture as a slave owner in Brazil, for it was from Brazil that many of the early Caribbean planters emigrated in order to establish the slave-based sugar economy in the islands.

The proslavery ideology reached its zenith in the period between the mid-eighteenth century and the latter part of the nineteenth century, when the slave economy entered into its golden age. It was centered primarily in English Jamaica, French Saint Domingue, and Spanish Cuba, with a distinct and recognizable literature of books and pamphlets written by the various schools of historians and publicists that developed in those three leading societies: the Jamaican planter historians; the publicists, both white colonist and "free coloreds," of Saint Domingue; the Cuban Creole writers and political leaders. To those sources must be added others, of course: colonial assembly debates, metropolitan state papers, the correspondence of governors, the vast literature of travelers' reports, not least of all the growing local press

—all of which enable the student to catch glimpses of the self-image of the plantocracy and the images that class entertained of the other actors in the dramatis personae of the colonial scene. For the essence of ideology is perceived self-image, how any societal group sees its function within the general matrix of the social structure, how it sees other groups, and what particular arguments it produces as a means of self-justification.

PARTICULAR CONSIDERATIONS

Concerning the proslavery ideology, certain particular considerations present themselves to the reader of the vast literature. In the first place, it is a defensive literature. Historically, every ruling class has been mainly concerned with power and the uses of power and has only attempted some sort of philosophic rationalization of its position when challenged by hostile forces. The Caribbean plantocracy was no exception. Its English echelon was responding to the abolitionist campaign mounted after the 1770s; its French echelon was reacting to the attack of the philosophes of the Enlightenment, given practical impetus by the assault on its position unleashed by the revolution of 1789; while its Cuban echelon, after the abolition of the slave trade in 1807, had to meet the hostile public opinion of nineteenth-century liberal Europe. It is enough to glance through the exhaustive compilation of the literature spawned by the English abolitionist campaign put together by the historian Lowell Joseph Ragatz—*A Guide for the Study of British Caribbean History, 1763-1834, Including the Abolition and Emancipation Movements*—to realize how the majority of pro-West Indian titles were improvised answers to the abolitionist writers.[35]

Second, it is noteworthy that, almost in the nature of things, the defensive literature was usually written not by planters themselves but by publicists who, sympathetic to the planter cause, were marginally placed in relationship to the slave institution. Although they were planters themselves, both of the Jamaican planter-historians, Long and Edwards, were educated Englishmen who had become creolized; men like Moreau de Saint-Méry in Saint Domingue were moderates distrusted by the *colon*; and the most ardent defender of Cuban slavery, for a while, was José Antonio Saco, not so much a planter as a leading member of the Cuban Creole intelligentsia. It is not surprising then that the proslavery movement in the Caribbean did not produce a Calhoun—who, in the North American case, fashioned a formidable and persuasive case for the Southern cause that was at once a brilliant defense of the plantation economy, an astute critique of the economic principle of the rival Northern industrial capitalist organization, and a presentation of the slave South as a civilization nobler and of finer texture than the coarse materialism of the North. Those particular arguments were also present in the Caribbean literature, of course, but they were never presented with the learning of a Calhoun. And that, probably, is due to the fact that the Caribbean plan-tocracy constituted the most crudely philistine of all dominant classes in the history of Western slavery. Even Labat, worldly realist that he was, lamented that everything had been imported into the Indies except books. One whole minor theme of Caribbean literature—Luffman's account of the Antigua planter class; Schomburgk's description of Guianese planter society with its ceremonial stiffness and affection; or the description of a decadent Cuban creole society penned by nineteenth century visitors such as Atkins, Turn-bull, Hazard, and others[36]—is almost unanimous in its general portrait of a planter way of life that is at once crassly materialist and spiritually empty. Anything even remotely approaching the intellectual was unlikely to make its appearance in such a milieu. Mental excitement, indeed, was provided by the outsider; reading Labat's diary or Lady Nugent's journal, for example, one is struck by the fact that in both cases intelligent conversation was provided by the resident and visiting-officer class present in the islands as a consequence of a wartime situation—the War of the Spanish Succession in Labat's case, the Napoleonic Wars in Lady Nugent's case. *Le luxe est grand dans les Isles* (Luxury is rampant in the islands), wrote Du Tertre early on. As much as anything else, the remark explains the intellectual paucity of the planter mind. It explains, equally, why the planter ideology cannot be seen in any way as constituting a serious philosophical system. It was, rather, little more than a series of rationalized prejudices and unexamined assumptions, trying to justify the vested interests of the dominant Caribbean groups.

EDWARD LONG AND BRYAN EDWARDS

The Jamaican contribution to the ideology is essentially that of Edward Long and Bryan Edwards in their respective histories, although there were lesser histories like those of Renny and Leslie and Browne. Long—to begin with—is concerned to argue the legitimacy of slavery against its critics. He argues the case within the framework of two general principles. In the first place, he posits an eternal struggle for power between warring factions in society. He declares:

> History evinces that, in all ages, there has been one set of persons uniting its efforts to enslave mankind; and another set, to oppose such attempts, and vindicate the cause of freedom. The accidental circumstances of men may, perhaps, occasion this difference: the rich are the natural enemies of the poor; and the poor, of the rich; like the ingredients of a boiling cauldron, they seem to be in perpetual war-fare, and struggle which shall be uppermost; yet, if both parties could compose themselves, the *faeces* would remain peaceably at the bottom; and all the other particles range themselves in different strata, according to their quality, the most refined floating always at top.[37]

Second, writing as a colonial Whig on the eve of the revolt of the North American colonies, Long advances the Whig concept of liberty. Much of his book, indeed, is an impassioned denunciation of the Crown for its abrogations of "British freedom" in its treatment of the colonies. There is, he argues, in the best Lockean manner, a contractual obligation that links government and citizen: "All societies of men, wherever constituted, can subsist together only by certain obligations and restrictions, to which all the individual members must necessarily yield obedience for the general good; or they can have no just claim to those rights, and that protection, which are held by all, under this common sanction."[38]

Long, hardheaded realist that he is, perceives, and admits readily, that slavery, on the face of it, cannot easily be reconciled with those principles. The first principle must meet the fact that, in colonial societies based on slavery, the war of rich and poor is made worse by the fact that the rich are white and the poor are black. The second principle is likewise embarrassing, for it is used by the enemies of the West Indian planters to point out the hypocrisy of claiming liberty for themselves while denying it to their slaves; indeed, Long himself admits at one point that slavery is repugnant to the spirit of the English laws. To make the difficulty even more pressing, Long also notes (with typical candor) how the spirit of liberty infects the slave population itself. The contagion of faction spreads; even our very Negroes, he laments, turn politicians.[39] That Long, indeed, was fully aware of the basic contradiction between the general principles that he espoused and the social order he sought to defend is evident from his citation of Montesquieu's argument that a large slave population is always dangerous in a moderate state, since the political liberty of the rulers only serves to accentuate in the slaves the keener awareness of their own lack of civil liberty, and the slaves, much more than in despotic states, consequently become the natural enemies of the society.

Faced with this fundamental problem—the tension between his English liberalism and his attachment to the moral validity of slavery—Long retreats into a farrago of inherited prejudices. He begins with a highly selective and prejudiced account of the African background of "Negro-land," drawn from the more negative sections of travelers' reports like those of Bosman, Snelgrove, Goguet, Le Maire, and others. It is a picture of unrelieved barbarity: all of these peoples—following, Long claims, a similar portrait painted by the ancient Greek and Roman authors—possess, "in abstract, every species of inherent turpitude that is to be found dispersed at large among the rest of the human creation." It follows, logically, that the slave trade must be seen, not through the perspective of British concepts of freedom, but through the perspective of African realities: the slave is transported from a condition of pure slavery in Africa into a condition of relative slavery in the Americas, where his servitude is tempered with lenity. Even the objection of the critics that many die in transportation to the colonies cannot be accepted, since the objection "does not bear against the trade itself, but against some defect or impropriety in the mode of conducting it."[40] Once settled in his new home, the slave enters into a "limited freedom" supervised by the white master who is his friend and father. "His authority," writes Long of the typical gentleman-proprietor it is his ultimate purpose to vindicate, "over them is like that of an ancient patriarch: conciliating affection by the mildness of its exertion, and claiming respect by the justice and propriety of its decisions and discipline, it attracts the love of the honest and good; while it awes the worthless into reformation."[41] That authority receives further legitimacy from the general character of the slave population. The Creole slaves are, in general, irascible, conceited, proud, indolent, lascivious, credulous, and artful; although the author is willing to admit that as far as the habit of drunkenness is concerned they are superior to the order of the lower-class white servants.[42] The "Guiney slaves," or newly imported Africans, are, if possible, even worse, which leads Long to conclude that any missionary effort among them is doomed to failure, since their "barbarous stupidity" and ignorance of the English language make them hopelessly intractable. Of these, the Coromantins, being warlike, are the worst, and the source of all slave conspiracies—so much so that the Jamaica planters should follow the example of the French islands and prohibit their further importation.[43]

If there is any scientific foundation for all this, Long claims to find it in a pre-Darwinite fixity-of-species theory, thus applying the popular "design of nature" argument to the problem, as he saw it, of the species of mankind. Within that scheme there are "gradations of the intellectual faculty," from the monkey at the bottom through the ape and the Negro man, on to pure white homo sapiens at the top: "Let us then not doubt, but that every member of the creation is wisely fitted and adapted to the certain uses, and confined within the certain bounds, to which it was ordained by the Divine Fabricator. The measure of the several orders and varieties of these Blacks may be as complete as that of any other race of mortals; filling up that space, or degree, beyond which they are not destined to pass; and discriminating them from the rest of men, not in kind, but in species."[44]

That position leads the author into some fairly severe strictures on the general plantation system, which, all in all, he has supported as the necessary order of things. Obsessed with racial purity, he inveighs bitterly against white miscegenative habits. White and black, he avers, are two tinctures that nature has dissociated, like oil and vinegar. Their unnatural mixture has produced, in Spanish America, a "vicious, brutal, and degenerate breed of mongrels." The solution, Long insists, is to strengthen the institution of marriage, in order to counteract illicit connections. That, in turn, requires incentives, among which should be the better education of the Creole white woman so as to render her a more agreeable wife. Even more than that, the law governing transmission of property should be revised, going back to the old feudal doctrine of nonalienation, in order to discourage the prevalent habit of white fathers willing their property to their colored children. The right to make wills and dispose of property is the creature of the civil law, and in slave societies it should be even more rigorously limited than in societies, like England, where "rational freedom" prevails. Nothing could illustrate better than this particular argument, in its proposal to circumscribe the right of private property, how far the racial apprehensions of the West Indian plantocracy could persuade them to subordinate economic to noneconomic considerations. The same consideration leads Long to advocate a policy of enfranchisement for all mulatto children, even at public cost; such a policy, he argues, will create a new class of trained lower-class artisans, who will become "orderly subjects, and faithful defenders of the country."[45]

All in all, Long is trapped in the inconsistencies between his eighteenth-century secular moralism and his proslavery stance. He claims that in charity, philanthropy, and clemency the Jamaican Creole gentlemen match at any time their English peers; yet he is appalled, as much as any missionary, by their reckless fornication. In that sense, he is the Puritan in Babylon. "To cast general reflections on any body of men," he writes in the best Burkean tradition, "is certainly illiberal"; he properly adheres to that principle in his discussion of the Jews and the Moravians in Jamaican society but throws it overboard in his discussion of the blacks. In his discussion, again, of the French *Code Noir* of 1685—which he reprints as an appendix—he can fully see the difference between the literary theory of slave-protective legislation and the actual reality of slave life: "It is not enough to make laws," he wisely observes, "it is also necessary to provide for their execution." Yet he seems incapable of applying the same pragmatic test to the slave laws of his own English islands. There is, finally, the glaring discrepancy between Long's view of the colonial-metropolitan relationship and his view, quite different, of the master-slave relationship. He perceives clearly the absence of any mutually beneficial contractual principle in the former, and unequivocally denounces it; yet he cannot see the absence of the same principle in the internal master-slave relationship. What, at best, he does is to attempt an unconvincing argument promulgating the curious thesis that, from the original point of purchase in Africa, there exists, so to speak, a "sort of compact" that buyer, seller, and bought slave all implicitly accept; and, once in the final point of destination in the islands, the compact is renewed between slave and master, in which a "reciprocal obligation" connects them, producing "protection and maintenance on the one hand, fidelity and service on the other." This, Long admits, is not a "voluntary banishment" on the part of the African. It is, however, he insists, an unwritten agreement, based on custom, to which all parties are tied.[46] The argument, ingenious enough, omits to note that the fulfillment of the compact depends exclusively on the will of the master. Long is capable of appreciating the weakness of such an arrangement when he discusses the British–West Indian system of colonial government. "We are not to expect," he opines, "that men, invested with power at discretion, will forbear, from an innate principle of goodness, to make an ill use of it, while they can abuse it with impunity and profit."[47] Yet the Jamaican social order that he describes, more or less approvingly, is made to rest upon the accidental possession of that very same "principle of goodness" on the part of the master class.

The final problem with which Long felt obliged to deal was that of the theme, so central to the discussion of slavery, of black capability. It was a problem that also preoccupied Jefferson at the same time. It is easy to see why. For once admit that the black, given access to education, could match the white, it would have been necessary to make a damaging exception to the racist assumption of a natural inequality of mental powers. So, Long felt it necessary to write a separate chapter, full of amused contempt, on the figure of Francis Williams, the Jamaican who was put through a course of English education by the Duke of Montagu in order to prove the intellectual capacities of the colored person. The best that Long can bring himself to say is that the Latinate compositions of Williams are no better than what might have been expected from a middling scholar at the seminaries of Eton or Winchester; the worst is to quote Hume's comment that a black scholar, thus educated, could become nothing more than a parrot who speaks a few words plainly. Long can even manage, unfairly, to laugh at Williams because of his habit of composing laudatory odes to successive Jamaican governors, despite the fact that the fulsome dedicatory preface to the aristocratic patron was the common practice of the eighteenth-century world of letters. He thus failed to see—as did Dr. Johnson in the case of the woman preacher—that the surprising thing about the black writer like Williams was not that the thing was well done but that it was done at all. The failure, no doubt, had its own psychological roots. For Long, no more than Jefferson, could not have endured, even temporarily, the continued existence of slavery had he thought that he was thereby maintaining in subjugation hundreds of mute, inglorious Miltons. In order to avoid that intolerable thought, it was necessary for him to rationalize the conviction that the Negro was by nature incapable of reasoning or of higher imagination.[48]

Edwards, by contrast with Long—whose help and friendship he acknowledged—is generally regarded as the "moderate" voice of the West Indian plantocracy. Humane and intelligent, he never lost his capacity to look at the slavery institution with some objectivity, despite the fact that he wrote at the time of the French Revolution and the Saint Domingue upheaval. He was that rare species, the educated planter—more at home, perhaps, in the study than on the plantation. Despite the fact, then, that his work was, in the final analysis, a reasoned defense of slavery, he was himself infected with the humanitarian temper of the age. He sought to reconcile the two outlooks and inevitably involved himself in irreconcilable contradictions. It was, of course, an impossible task. It was made even more impossible by the pressure of events; so that whereas in his earlier work on the British West Indies he managed to maintain the "moderate" pose, in his later work on Saint Domingue he reflected the mood of panic that engulfed the propertied classes and delayed abolition for a whole generation.

Edwards begins by establishing his humanitarian credentials. He is, he claims, no friend of slavery, for so degrading is its nature that "fortitude of mind is lost as free agency is restricted"; "cowardice and dissimulation," he adds, "have been the properties of slavery in all ages and will continue to be so, to the end of the world." He can even perceive that behavior patterns within the slavery institution may be shaped by culturally conditioning factors rather than being the expression of an assumed human nature, so, while he dismisses the popular theory about the impact of climate, he can observe that "it is no easy matter...to discriminate those circumstances which are the result of proximate causes, from those which are the effects of national customs and early habits in savage life."[49] He can even perceive, further, the interconnection of economic factors and group behavior; the notorious profligacy of the planter class, he notes perceptively, is traceable to the fact that (as he puts it), a West Indian property is a species of lottery, arising out of the fact that the island planter, unlike an English landed proprietor, cannot sublet to tenants and is obliged to become a practical farmer in an occupation full of uncertainty.

Yet, once having made those concessions, so damaging to the unconditional racism of Long, he proceeds to rob them of meaning by reverting, in the last resort, to moral absolutes unrelated to empirical reasoning. There is either the Hobbist argument that power makes right: "In countries where slavery is established, the leading principle on which the government is supported is fear; or a sense of that absolute coercive necessity, which leaving no choice of action, supersedes all questions of right." Or there is the Burkean argument of relapse into religious obscurantism: "Yet that the slavery of some part of the human species, in a very abject degree, has existed in all ages of the world, among the most civilized, as well as the most barbarous nations, no man who has consulted the records of history disputes. Perhaps, like pain, poverty, sickness, and sorrow and all the various other calamities of our condition, it may have been originally interwoven into the constitution of the world for purposes inscrutable to man."[50]

Having thus bypassed the dilemma posed by the simultaneous entertainment of the argument of nature and the argument of environment, Edwards passes on to a defense, point by point, of the slave-based social order. Admitting the many abuses connected with the slave trade, he invokes the popular argument that the slave is rescued from a barbarous Africa, although the evidence that he invokes—his own cross-examination of slaves concerning their original status in their homelands—is hardly credible when his earlier statements concerning the habitual mendacity of slaves are recalled. His account, in turn, of the slavers is hardly more convincing than the highly colored account of African society:[51] he makes the Middle Passage sound almost like a pleasant sea cruise. In any case, he adds, recent parliamentary legislation regulates the trade and makes it more humane; he neglects to note that that piece of legislation, like all ameliorative legislation, was vigorously opposed by the planter lobby. Even admitting, he goes on, that some slaves are originally free men, and not just war captives or domestic slaves, he insists that the West Indian planter, as the buyer, is completely innocent of the manner in which the trade is conducted, although we know from Labat's account that a century earlier the full details were already common knowledge in the islands. The trade, he concludes, should not be abolished but, at best, ameliorated.[52] Its sudden unilateral abolition by the British would merely benefit the other European powers involved in the traffic, and in any case an effective maritime blockade of the traffic, once it had been declared illegal, would be practically impossible. Any such attempt would be like chaining the winds or giving laws to the ocean.

Edwards's subsequent discussion of life on the West Indian plantation betrays a similar effort, almost desperate at times, to see things in terms of rosy optimism, playing down the dark side and exaggerating the bright aspects. The much-maligned West Indian planter, he insists, is a generous, proud, frank, hospitable person, possessed of a high degree of compassion and kindness towards his inferiors and dependents. He rules, it is true, a "miserable people...condemned to perpetual exile and servitude." But he rules them with paternal kindness. His interest concurs with his humanity, and a well-regulated plantation, as Edwards describes it, is a model of mild labor, decent housing, and adequate medical care. If there are abuses of this "plenitude of power"—and Edwards is sufficiently honest not to deny the charge—they are, he argues, the exception and not the rule. The difference between my view and that of the abolitionist critics, he writes, is that they claim that cruelty is the general rule, while I insist that it is only occasional; and he quotes Ramsay's remark that adventurers from Europe are universally more cruel towards the slave than are the Creoles or the native West Indians. The humane spirit of the age, he argues, notwithstanding the critics, is also present in the islands, and is felt where the law is a dead letter. Yet he admits at the same time that, granted the absolute discretion of the slave owner, the sense of decorum alone "affords but a feeble restraint against the corrupt passions and infirmities of our nature, the hardness of avarice, the pride of power, the sallies of anger, and the thirst of revenge."[53] Thus, in the last resort, he falls back on the argument, so typical of the eighteenth century, that however unjust a social order may be, the leading ills of mankind are traceable to a human nature that law cannot alter. His is, altogether, a generous moral nature unable to see the full evil of a way of life of which—so typical of West Indian estate ownership—he had become a member only by an accident of family relationship.

The histories of Long and Edwards were, of course, only two items in the

voluminous war of words—one of the first of the modern wars of literary propaganda—that took place between the friends and the opponents of the West
Indian slavocracy cause in the fifty years before Emancipation in the 1830s.
It addressed itself, both in England and France, to the rise to power of the
bourgeois public opinion of the age. The verdict of history has decided in
favor of the abolitionist argument, sustaining Wilberforce's remark—which
anticipated Lincoln's more famous dictum—that to unite slavery and freedom in one condition is impracticable. The English abolitionist groups tended
to emphasize the principle of Christian liberty; the French groups, the principle of the rights of man. There was, of course, wild exaggeration on the
part of both general protagonists in this great debate for and against slavery;
for if the one side was tempted to portray the West Indian scene as a heaven
of happy feudal relationships, the other was tempted to expose it as a veritable hell in which every plantation owner was a Simon Legree. The lines of
division, of course, were much more complicated than that, for there were
proslavery advocates, like Edwards himself, who could admit to the defects
of the slavery regime, just as the abolitionist leaders could decide, illogically,
to make a distinction between the slave trade and slavery itself for the purposes of parliamentary strategy. Even so, the long debate provides valuable
material for understanding the basic principles on which both arguments
were based.

THE WEST INDIAN PLANTER RESPONSE

The essentials of the planter outlook can be garnered from the colonial
responses, reluctant and indeed recalcitrant, to the various stages of the
increasingly critical metropolitan debate—the parliamentary debates on Wilberforce's various motions leading to the 1807 abolition of the trade, Wilberforce's Slave Registry Bill of 1815, Canning's Resolutions of 1823, and the
final emancipatory act of 1833. Eric Williams has extracted the leading contributions of the parliamentary debates for his volume *The British West Indies at Westminster.*[54] But what more particularly concerns our enquiry is the
character of the planter outlook as it appears in the titles published during
the period by those of its advocates who—sometimes as planters themselves,
sometimes as clergymen, sometimes as visitors—had resided in the islands
and had absorbed, through the famous West Indian hospitality, the planter
ideology. Very little of that literature was written by Creole planters themselves, for as one of their partisans—John Stewart in his 1823 volume *A View
of the Past and Present State of the Island of Jamaica*—himself confessed,
the arbitrary character of slavery was inimical to the improvement of mind
and manners: "Intellectual pleasures," he wrote, "are not so much suited to
the taste of the inhabitants as something that will create a bustle, and bring a
crowd of well-dressed persons in pursuit of amusements of a more tangible

nature—such, for instance, as the parish races, where, in one week, there is as much money spent as would establish a superb public library."[55] It was a rare West Indian-born planter who could write anything at all. It was even more rare for him to write an intelligent autobiography such as the anonymous *Memoirs of a West India Planter* edited by the Reverend John Riland in 1827; and even then the many improbable scenes described in that book, including the conversion of a planter to Christian retribution, cast some doubt on its authenticity.[56]

The pro-West Indian literature runs the entire gamut of planter pride and prejudice. There is the hackneyed theme of "barbarous" Africa, although it became an increasingly implausible argument as early nineteenth century African exploration revealed a more realistic picture of the African state systems. The slave trade, it is claimed, was a nursery of English seamanship—had not Nelson learned his apprenticeship in the West Indies?—so that if the battle of Waterloo was won on the playing fields of Eton it was equally true that the battle of Trafalgar had been won in the naval stations of the West Indies. There are the usual citations from Scripture—the laws of Leviticus or Saint Paul's letter to the slave owner Philemon—to justify slavery, although they became less frequent as the spirit of the age became more secular. There is the argument that the critics, in their detailed accounts of cruelty, are speaking of the island society as it was, say, twenty years ago; things are now much improved. It is instructive, with respect to that argument, to read the apologetic report of 1824 of a committee of the Barbados Council that proves, to its own satisfaction, that the slaves are "cheerful, happy, and contented," and cites as its "impartial" witnesses plantation owners and high-ranking officers of the local military establishment. There is the argument, again, that West Indian planters have to face problems unknown to English landlords; the garrulous Beckford, in his 1790 *Descriptive Account of the Island of Jamaica*, even managed to recruit his graphic description of the hurricane of 1780 into the service of the argument.[57] The planter, it is added, must deal with a labor force that is lazy, mendacious, contumacious, unreliable, and full of thievery; yet almost in the same breath, the author who makes those charges will regale his reader with sentimental stories of the slaves' childlike loyalty to their masters in times of distress, in order to disprove the abolitionist charge that they are unhappy and discontented wretches. That contradiction is even more pronounced in a more fundamental sense. For if, on the one hand, the proplanter literature portrays the West Indian society as almost idyllic—aptly illustrated in the hand-colored engravings of the artist James Hakewill in his 1825 book *A Picturesque Tour of the Island of Jamaica*, where classically composed tropical landscapes present, Watteau-like, pleasing prospects of plantation life[58]—on the other hand, it warns the would-be reformer that he is playing with fire, since slave discontent at any moment can explode into another Haitian *servile bellum* (servile war). The contradiction is even more painfully clear in the contrast between the optimistic account of amelioration by Edwards and the awful *Jamaican Slave Code*, which he printed as illustrative proof of his case.[59] To the modern reader there is an almost unbearable, indeed a tragic, tension between the need of the literature to show the slave as almost an animal in human form—for to admit his humanity would be to strike a mortal blow at the very basic principle of the system—and its need to defend the slave against the embrace of what the planters called the English "pseudo-philanthropists."

The leading argument in all this, however, was that based on the doctrine of legislative amelioration. The argument was persuasive, and was enthusiastically advanced by all of the writers who, although sometimes with serious reservations, could be regarded as defenders of the slave system, with knowledge based on their own experience in the islands: Edwards himself, Stewart, Collins, Williamson, Jordon, Barham, Barclay, and others. A gradual amelioration, it is argued, would be better than a precipitate abolition. In proportion, wrote Barclay, as moral improvement, religion, and habits of industry civilize the slave, "the arbitrary power of the master will become unnecessary, and slavery will gradually assimilate to the servitude of Europe." To the degree that we extract all its ingredients from the condition of slavery, added Barham, the "whole mass of slaves shall at once glide, as it were, into freedom."[60] The means to that end was to be colonial legislative enactment, for the doctrine of amelioration went hand in hand with the doctrine of local colonial jurisdiction—might be viewed, indeed, as a particular tactic under cover of which the larger doctrine could be advanced. It received a definitive expression in Jordan's 1816 *Examination of the Principles of the Slave Registry Bill*, composed in his capacity as Colonial Agent for Barbados. Barbados, he reminds his readers, flew the royal flag in the seventeenth century, when democracy and puritanism triumphed over the monarchy in England itself. But that does not give the Westminster Parliament the right to unilaterally legislate for the colonies. Extension of parliamentary power can only be effected by extension of parliamentary representation. Of such, there are two kinds: extended representation united and inclusive, as in the cases of Ireland and Wales, and representation separate and exclusive, which is the case of the West Indian colonies. The concept of sovereignty, as stated in Blackstone, belongs to metaphysical jurisprudence; what we appeal to is English statutory law, which, since Henry I, has always recognized the exclusive power of localities where, as in the West Indies, there exist duly established local parliaments based on the common rights of all English subjects. British commercial regulation excepted, then, London cannot legislate for Barbados in matters that concern the liberty and property of Barbadians.[61]

The argument notwithstanding, however, the amelioration doctrine was an empty one. Never seriously implemented by the colonial assemblies, as Goveia and Williams have shown, it was merely a desperate effort to save time; emancipation was accepted, but always at some safe, distant future date, never at the present moment.[62] It emphasized the need to improve the slave, through education and religion, in order to fit him for freedom; but at the same time it was openly hostile to the only force, that of the island sectarian missionaries, who took that task seriously, and the author of the 1824 Barbados committee report frankly conceded Wilberforce's charges on that matter.[63] Humane observers like Edwards could learn from events, and it is impossible to read the final paragraphs of his account of Santo Domingo, with its anguished appeal to the resident plantocracy to rise above "the foggy atmosphere of local prejudices" and accept the cessation of the trade before its intransigence leads it to the terrible fate of the French colony (which is the handwriting on the wall)[64] and then to compare it with the adamant refusal of the same plantocracy to listen to the warning without a realization of the completely Bourbonese, purblind, and reactionary character of the planter establishment. Even its friends recognized that aspect of it: "It would have reflected more honour upon those who live so much in the community of slaves," lamented Beckford, "if those alterations had been the spontaneous effects of their humanity, and had not originated in, and been enforced by the persevering compassion of England."[65] Every piece of circumstantial evidence (the Parliamentary returns, the reports of island correspondents, the dispatches of island governors, the reports of the Berbice Fiscal, or adjudicator) shows conclusively that every suggested reform of the ameliorative literature—the right of the slave to testify in court proceedings, the right to a free Sabbath, the elimination of the use of the cart whip—was frustrated by the fact that the administrative machinery of slave society was monopolized by the very class that stood to lose by their implementation. To use Burke's phrase in his letter of 1792 to Dundas, all of the ameliorative measures passed by the various colonial assemblies were good for nothing because, as Burke put it, they were totally destitute of an executory principle. It was, in sum, a losing battle. The moral climate of slavery itself made it so. "Doubtless, too," wrote Stewart, himself no friend to serious reform, "there is in the very nature of slavery, in its mildest form, something unfavourable to the cultivation of moral feeling. Men may be restrained...by very good and well-intentioned laws, from exercising acts of cruelty and oppression on the slaves, but still harsh ideas and arbitrary habits, which may find innumerable petty occasions of venting themselves, grow up, wherever slavery exists, in minds where principle has not taken a deep hold."[66]

That climate of opinion helps explain the other ingredients of the planter ideology. The planter mind lived in a world of self-sustaining myth. The mythology constituted the energizing principle of all colonial attitudes: the myth of African degeneracy, the myth of Negro happiness, the myth of King Sugar. When those myths were challenged, the plantocracy responded with yet another final exculpatory myth: that the challenge came from demonic, subversive forces ready to risk even slave rebellion for the purpose of destroying a social order they hated too much to understand. Those forces, of course, were seen as, first, the Baptist and Methodist missionaries and, second, the English and French philanthropists. The Nonconformist chapels were seen, in Bleby's words, as "dens of sedition, infamy, and blasphemy" deserving to be destroyed; and the account of white vigilante burnings, aided and abetted by conniving magistrates, perjured juries, and a venal press, in the Jamaica of the 1830s, which is described in Henry Bleby's firsthand account, *Death Struggles of Slavery*, testifies to the spirit of virulent hatred felt by the Creole white community for men who were no more socially radical than Wesley or Wilberforce. It is especially instructive to read the excerpts from the colonial press cited in that volume, for they tell us much more about the planter mentality than the books and pamphlets that, written for an English public, had to accommodate themselves to a quite different opinion. They show, indeed, a contemptuous disdain for English public opinion—as well as an open defiance of the British Parliament—that could more properly itself be described as seditious.[67] The hatred became even more splenetic in its attitude to the metropolitan humanitarians. Even Edwards, confronted with the horrors of the Saint Domingue civil war, came to write more with the zeal of a fanatic waging a holy war than in his usually moderate temper, exhorting Britain not to encourage "the pestilent doctrines of those hot-brained fanatics, and detestable incendiaries, who, under the vile pretence of philanthropy and zeal for the interests of suffering humanity, preach up rebellion and murder to the contented and orderly negroes in our own territories."[68]

The myth of the agitator thus provided the planter defendants with what was for them a half-plausible answer to the crucial question raised by the humanitarian criticism: if the Negroes were so contented, why then did they revolt—as they did so frequently? Like all conservative thought, the planter ideology thus failed to see that the "agitator" is not so much the cause as the consequence of discontent; he simply articulates the protest of general social forces against oppression too intolerable to be borne any longer. Equally, it failed to see that metaphysical systems do not subvert established orders but simply provide the intellectual justification for revolutions that would have taken place anyway. Therefore, in the wake of the 1831 rebellion, there were few members of the Jamaica colonial legislature like Beaumont—who could tell his fellow members that the sectarian ministers were no more guilty of that insurrection than were the advocates of reform in the British Parliament guilty of the conflagration of Bristol.[69] Nor were many legislators disposed to heed the observation, made indeed by one of their friends, that there are "those who can distinguish black from white in the colour of the human skin, but who cannot discriminate what is black from white in the integral conduct of man to man." They talked endlessly of the need for the moral reformation of the slave as a necessary prerequisite of freedom; they could not see, as the same friend insisted, that any meaningful reformation must begin with the white people themselves.[70] Their own gross irreligiosity, indeed, was a byword in the islands, as testified to by Lady Nugent in her Jane Austen–like journal, written in the early 1800s, and by "Monk" Lewis somewhat later in his own journal. They saw their adversaries as nothing more than self-seeking publicists looking for advancement; the Popish plot, wrote a group of their defenders, was never a better stalking horse than Negro slavery is at the present day.[71] They were, altogether, the champions of a dying social order. They were even wrong in their apocalyptic prophecies about the dire consequences that would follow its demise.

Yet it would be misleading to conclude that the West Indian planters always had the worse of the argument. They were, of course, doomed to lose the larger argument, for ever since Adam Smith's monumental demolition of protectionist mercantilism, they were on the defensive against the new vested interests of British industrial capitalism as a world economic system that demanded free trade as its instrument of expansion. But they were quick to point out the hypocrisy of that policy. The West Indian connection, their literature argued, was cherished by Britain so long as it was profitable in the regime of commercial capitalism, and was ruthlessly abandoned once it became unprofitable in the regime of industrial capitalism. Their exclusive possession of the home market, the argument continued, was their just reward for the restrictions imposed on them by the colonial system.[72] If Britain claimed the right to secure its supplies in the cheapest market, as in the case of East Indian sugar, then the West Indies ought to be granted the same right by means, for example, of an uninhibited trade with North America; that principle of reciprocal right was made as early as 1784 in Edwards's first published work.[73] The whole system, in brief, was "an implicit compact... for a mutual monopoly."[74] For one side to abrogate it unilaterally was a violation of trust.

The argument was carried even further. If, the West Indians claimed, slavery was in fact original sin, then who invented it in the first place? The English themselves. "Many persons," wrote Barham in his 1823 *Considerations on the Abolition of Negro Slavery*, "have been so used to charge all the odium of that system on those, who by accident happen to be the present owners of slaves, that they will be surprised to learn how much larger a share Great Britain has had, than the Colonies, in the formation, maintenance, and present extent of Slavery"; and he proceeds to prove his point by reference to the Elizabethan slave traders, the support of the trade by the Stuart and Hanoverian monarchies, the Asiento treaty with Spain of 1713, and the vast profits that the city of Liverpool gained from the enormities of the Middle Passage.[75] Barclay drove the point home four years later, in *A Practical View of the Present State of Slavery in the West Indies*, his answer to James Stephen's book. "Without stopping to enquire whether or not the condition of savages has been improved by the change," he wrote, "one thing is certain, that the merit or odium of it is due, not to the inhabitants of the colonies, but to the people of England. They reaped the advantages of establishing slavery in the West Indies; it was *their* ships and *their* capital that conveyed the negroes from their native land to these fertile islands, from the cultivation of which, the British people have derived much of the wealth they now possess; and if any of the existing interests are now to be broken up, these surely ought, in common justice, to be indemnified at the public expense."[76] The note of "perfidious Albion" is clear. The West Indians, true, were the most visible agents of the system. But they were not prepared to be made the scapegoats of its unpopularity. The argument is an embryonic form of colonial nationalism.

But the adroitness of the West Indian counterattack was best exhibited in its use of the vexed question, so prominent in the lengthy debate: which was the happier person, the West Indian slave or the English peasant and factory worker? It was the Achilles heel of the abolitionist-emancipationist assault, and the West Indians assailed it shrewdly. Edwards noted that the slave housing in the islands, allowing for the difference of climate, was superior to the cabins of the Scotch and Irish peasants described by Young and other travelers of the time. Beckford argued that the lot of the Negroes compared favorably with that of European peasants, soldiers and sailors, and imprisoned debtors—an argument not entirely of an abstract character since he wrote his *Remarks* of 1788, when he was himself a debt-ridden slave owner incarcerated in the Fleet Prison. Others echoed the argument, as good an example as any being an anonymous pamphlet of 1833, *The Condition of the West India Slave Contrasted with that of the Infant Slave in our English Factories*, embellished with pictures drawn by the celebrated cartoonist Cruikshank.[77] This, altogether, was the one argument that the humanitarians were never able satisfactorily to answer, for too many of them exemplified in their attitudes toward the struggle for factory legislation at home the hypocrisy that Dickens castigated in the figure of Mrs. Jellyby, the religious philanthropist speechifying in defense of the sufferings of the poor African yet oblivious to that of the new factory proletariat at home. The West Indians, indeed, might have carried their argument even further, for in one of their remarkable chapters the English historians, the Hammonds, have shown how the apologies for child labor in the new factory system were precisely the same as the earlier apologies for the slave trade—as the London workhouses of early Victorian England came to serve the purpose of the Lancashire cotton mills as surely as the Guinea coast had served that of the West Indian plantations.[78] The West Indians could not have been expected, naturally, to have appreciated the grim lesson of that fact: that, as in all imperialisms, the moral atmosphere of the colony becomes a breeding ground from whence retrogressive social ideas are imported into the metropolis.

Looked at in larger perspective, of course, the truth of the matter was that both West Indian slave and English factory operative were the exploited labor force of the modern industrial capitalism, the one in its earlier Atlantic phase, the other in its later world phase. The master class of the one was the West Indian plantocracy, of the other the rising English factory capitalist.

After the period of the Napoleonic Wars, their interests began to diverge, and they used the suffering of their respective slave populations as a stick with which to beat each other. Men like Edwards could clearly see the oppression of the English factory hand but seemed to develop a moral blind spot when it came to the question of the oppression of the West Indian slave; similarly, men like Wilberforce could indignantly admonish the planters about their treatment of the slave yet be silent on the issue of protective factory legislation in England itself. It was a struggle between two self-interested segments of a common ruling class similar to that between the territorial aristocracy and the capitalist industrialists in England itself: Lord Shaftesbury, the noble leader of the factory-legislation movement, could view the efforts of Joseph Arch to organize the laborers of the agricultural districts with hostility; John Bright, whose economic liberalism made him the enemy of all colonial enterprises, saw trade unions as a menace to industrial peace. Class interest, in each case, made it impossible for the protagonists to see that all of the exploited classes involved, English village laborer and factory hand as well as West Indian slave, were common victims of a system that had become truly global in its character. It was left to the socialist thinkers to perceive the real truth. In the eighteenth century it was the French philosophe like Mably; in the nineteenth century, the English Christian Socialist like Ludlow of the 1848 movement. Rather than simply reproach the American colonists for holding slaves, in the indignant manner of Raynal, Mably saw slavery as a variant of the wage-labor system of the bourgeois order. "I beg to remark," he wrote in his 1788 volume, *Recherches historiques et politiques sur les Etats-Unis de l'Amérique septentrionale*, "that the liberty which every European believes himself to enjoy is nothing but the possibility of breaking his chain in order to give himself up to a new master. Want here makes the slaves; and they are the more miserable, since no law provides for their subsistence." Ludlow, in his turn, saw the worldwide character of the new oppression. "You cannot do justice to India," he wrote, "without striking a blow at the fetters of the American slave; you cannot free the latter without giving an enormous impetus to the development of India." Everything was tied together, so that "the over-taxation of India and the exactions of London slop-sellers, the massacres of Ceylon or Cephalonia and the beating to death of parish-apprentices at home, are but pustules of the same plague."[79]

THE FRENCH ANTILLES

The historical evolution of French Saint Domingue was, of course, intrinsically different from that of the English colonies. It grew during the eighteenth century into the richest of all the sugar colonies; in 1776 it produced for France more wealth than did the whole of Spanish America for Spain. But the tremendous events of 1789–1804, which passed over the colony with all the destructive force of a tropical hurricane, transformed it, within a brief generation, into a new society that, politically, was the first independent black republic in the hemisphere and, economically, was a neofeudal system with the new Haitian peasant as its backbone. The change was swift and violent. There did not take place, then, the protracted controversy on the morality of slavery that took place between the West Indians and the English humanitarians. The philosophes, it is true, attacked slavery. But they did not constitute, as did the English humanitarians, a powerful political force with friends in government; the court at Versailles was not the House of Commons. The very nature of the cataclysmic changes after 1789, which were at once, in Saint Domingue, a generalized slave rebellion and a war for national liberation, necessarily precluded the growth of any sort of debate comparable to what took place in London.

Yet the Saint Domingue colonial society produced, in its manners, values, and attitudes, its own unique expression of the slavery theme. The older historical scholarship of Peytraud, Frossard, and Boissonade, as well as the later modern scholarship of Lepkowski, Pierre-Charles, Debien, Franco, and Hector and Moise, have together painted a graphic picture of its character. Historically, it had its origins in the early Tortuga island-stronghold of the filibusters and buccaneers, and although they soon disappeared, the colony retained much of their spirit of unbridled individualism and rapacity. Economically, it was a typically Caribbean hybrid economy, composed of the most advanced European elements of capital and technology mixed with the archaic (from the European viewpoint) element of slave labor, producing a tremendously complicated unit of organization in the form of the huge sugar plantations described by the contemporary observer Barré de Saint Venant. Politically, it was ruled with a strong hand by the centralized bureaucracy of the ancien régime, thus allowing little of the limited democracy of the assertive colonial assemblies of the English islands. Socially, all of those factors combined to shape a society of almost castelike distinctions, composed of *grands blancs, petits blancs*, mulattoes, blacks, governmental and military personnel, and impoverished French nobility; a pyramidal social structure in which the leading criterion of wealth and status was the ownership of slaves, *têtes de negres* in the telling parlance of the colony—bought and sold, and sometimes rented out, like so many head of cattle.

It was not without reason that the colony, in its brief heyday between the Treaty of Paris of 1763 and the French Revolution, was regarded as the Babylon of the Antilles. Its corruption, venality, brutality, and rascality would have taken the genius of a Molière or a Balzac fully to describe. The testimony of contemporaries, both Creole writers and European visitors, is overwhelming. Its descriptive detail helps to illuminate the principles on which the colonial life was conducted and how each group in the general concatenation of forces saw itself and saw the others. The general tone was one of ferocious cupidity and greed. The tone was set at the very top by the repressive administrative machine, led by the Governor and the Intendant—representing the monarchy and its ally, the rich maritime bourgeoisie of the French slave ports. "The Governor," wrote Pons, "exercises a monstrous power, the source of infinite vexations. At once head of justice and military chief, he holds in his hand the life and the fortune of everybody." "This office," added Baron de Wimpffen in his letter written on the eve of the French Revolution, "has ceased to be granted for merit, to become the prey of ignorance, irresponsibility, of the ability of some great person, impoverished when he arrives, to reappear later in France, after three years, and at the risk of seeming to be a bad citizen or even a fool, with a fortune equal to what it would have been difficult for three generations of wastrels to consume."[80] It was a rare governor, such as Bellecombe, who could spend his brief tenure translating the *Anabasis* of Xenophon, or a rare Intendant, such as Barbé-Marbois, who could use his retirement to publish his two definite works on Saint Domingue finances. The consequent nepotism, peculation, and bribery seeped down into every level of the system: the administration of justice, the regulation of trade and commerce, the licensing regime, the organization of public works, the award of land titles. And what was bad enough in France itself became doubly worse in the colony by reason of the vast geographical separation between metropolis and American dependency. A Choiseul or a Necker was possible in Paris but unthinkable in Saint Domingue. Even the parasitic sinecurism was worse, since every new governor added to the administrative chaos with his own mass of edicts, letters patent, and ordinances; the massive volumes of laws and administrative regulations that Moreau de Saint-Méry put together in his monumental *Loix et Constitutions des colonies françaises de l'Amérique sous le vent de 1550 à 1785* would have been sufficient to discourage any functionary with a taste for reforming codification.

In sum, the leading normative value of the society—and certainly of its warring and turbulent white groups—was that of the old pirate dream of easy plunder. Pons, Gel Chast, Girod-Chantrans, Moreau de Saint-Méry, Baron de Wimpffen, d'Auberteuil, all testify in one way or another to the chronic pervasiveness of the disease. To become rich and therefore socially respected; to rise into the local plutocracy; then to return to France with sufficient money to buy a title of nobility: it was the common aspiration of all. The means were legion: to connive at contraband trade; to exact exorbitant fees from clients; to swindle an absentee planter by mismanaging his property; to form a *mésalliance* with a rich and aged Negress. Even more than in the English colonies, it led to the even worse disease of absenteeism. In place of citizens, observed Wimpffen, in Saint Domingue there are only birds of passage. It is wrong to believe, added d'Auberteuil, that it is the climate that drives away the richest inhabitants, for here there are health and wealth, it is only a sense of security that is lacking. Everybody, concluded Moreau de Saint-Méry, says that he is leaving next year and considers himself merely a *voyageur* (transient) in a land where only too often he finds his final resting place.[81] Nor was this the aspiration only of the improvident and the rapacious. It infected all who came to the colony; and Victor Advielle's memoir of the architect Pierre Lefranc de Saint-Haulde shows how a prudent bourgeois, by means of speculating in the colonial stock-market of slaves, could amass a sufficiently tidy fortune to return to his native Normandy for a comfortable retirement.[82]

What shocked most of the observers, most of whom shared the new bourgeois philosophy of the age, was the sheer waste of the system. The wealth of the colony, they argue, is drained, by means of the infamous colonial pact, to France, to be spent by absentee planters and merchant princes. If it remains in the colony, it is drained from the countryside to the cities. The *corvée* system robs the plantations of their slave labor. The industrious planter, and especially the absentee owner, is swindled by the resident attorney-agent in charge of the estate. Agriculture, the most important resource of the colonial wealth, is the least protected. Its cultivators, writes Wimpffen, who owe in debt more than they possess, languish in misery and inertia; in the words of one resident planter quoted by Pons, agriculture is the slowest means of gaining a fortune, and often the quickest road to ruin.[83] The fabulous wealth of the country, in fact, is more apparent than real. Rather than being genuinely productive, it is wasted in habits of profligate consumption; and the French visitor Laujon described in tones of disgust the typical *soir de fête* held at the governor's palace—where fashionable society, richly dressed and bejeweled, danced to the steps of Vestris, listened to the latest *chanson* of Garat or of Blondel: the men splendidly arrogant, the women pursuing the only art known to them, that of Creole coquetry. Saint Domingue, exclaimed the comte d'Ennery, is a second Sodom, which the fire of heaven will destroy.[84] The habits of industry are thus sacrificed to a *luxe asiatique*; the whole society, in the phrase of the later historian Ardouin, confident in its delusive security, slept on the crater of a volcano ready at any moment to erupt and devour it.

Social morality and civic spirit alike withered in such a society. Wimpffen, noting the municipal squalor of Port-au-Prince, termed it a Tartar camp, and Moreau de Saint-Méry, while deprecating the sharpness of the expression, admitted that it was not entirely inapplicable.[85] The very paucity of architecture, both private and public, testified to a general disinterest in civic improvement; certainly, neither Port-au-Prince nor Cap Français produced anything to rival the cathedrals of Mexico or the churches of Havana, while no resident planter managed to build a "great house" in any way comparable, say, to Worthy Park in Jamaica or Sam Lord's Castle in Barbados. Moreau de Saint-Méry described at length the scandal of the sewage and drainage systems. Nor was the intellectual aspect of colonial life any more prepossessing. True, the local Philadelphian Circle discussed the latest books from Paris. But the generality of the society regarded such publications as little more than fancies indulged by a politically powerless elite of *beaux esprits* rather than warnings of the gathering storm. True, too, there was a handful of thoughtful and intelligent Creoles. Men like the merchant Delaire and the president of the colonial assembly, De Cadusch, provided Bryan Edwards with written narratives that he incorporated into his *Historical Survey of Santo Domingo*. The interest of the age in science, technology, and industry was also reflected in the colony in, variously, the work of Thierry de Menonville in tropical botany, of Trembley and de Saint-Ouen in hydraulic engineering, of Chastenet de Puysegur in maritime cartography, and of de Neufchateau in the general field of economic science.[86] But, even so, that had little impact upon a slave mode of production where the availability of plentiful servile labor, notwithstanding its high mortality rate, gave little incentive to the planter class to develop a practical interest in technological innovation along purely capitalist lines. The very hedonism of the society, the prevailing urge to make a rapid profit and decamp, precluded the growth of such an interest. The English observers of the society during the same period noted its anti-community spirit, notwithstanding the fact that they themselves were friends to the principle of slavery. Bryan Edwards, in his visit to Santo Domingo in 1791, was unimpressed by the majority of whites who were left after the first exodus, seeing them as a lower order of *noblesse* preoccupied solely with the restoration of their properties; and Lady Nugent, somewhat later, could find nothing charitable to say of the exiles she met in Jamaica.

Saint Domingue, in sum, was a bizarre exaggeration, a tropical carica-ture, of the ancien régime in France. The sole difference was that created by slavery: The only cement that held the society together, in, that is, its white groups, was unanimity on the issue of white supremacy. It all rested on a sim-ple catechism: The black was inferior both in cultural and biological terms; the white, however low on the social ladder, was a superior being; nothing must ever be countenanced that would seem—even in subtle ways that the eye of a European could not appreciate—to compromise the moral authority of the white master class.

The social history of Saint Domingue provided plentiful illustration of those imperatives. Adam Smith, in a frequently noted passage of his famous work, had argued that the condition of the slave was better under an arbi-trary government, as in the case of the French West Indian islands, than it was under a free government, as in the British islands, since in the latter case the power of the colonial state was in large part coincidental with the in-terests of the class of slave owners who were also the controlling force in the colonial legislative assemblies.[87] But the record of slave treatment in Saint Dominque does not bear out the accuracy of that assertion. The Lejeune case of 1788 proved that white Santo Domingo would not tolerate any inter-ference with white masters, even when they were proved guilty of the most barbarous methods of slave treatment.[88] The case of the Sieur Chapuzet in the 1770s, in its turn, proved that the privileges of white status would not be accorded to anyone possessing even the faintest traces of black ancestry, even if, as in that celebrated case, the plaintiff could prove that his forebears were not African imports but the free and noble Caribs that the old seventeenth-century French writers had celebrated.[89] To read, even today, the savage and punitive legislation passed by the local councils against the rising mulatto group is to realize, albeit faintly, how the paranoic obsession with racial purity was so intense that it even superseded consideration of class interest: the propertied mulatto group, in the white view, was dangerous not because it was bourgeois but because it was tainted with blackness.[90]

There is, indeed, almost a note of sexual guilt in the contemporary accounts of the attitude, as if the white mentality recognized in the figures of the *affranchis* (freedmen) and *gens de couleur* (people of color) the biological consequence of its own miscegenative habits. Originally, perhaps, an instinct of social preservation, the attitude became congealed into an institutionalized form of prejudice, so built into the very structure of social relations that, as events proved, only the destruction of the society itself could end it. The Swiss Girod-Chantrans noted that whiteness was a *titre de commandement* (sign of authority), blackness the *livrée du mépris* (badge of disdain). The prejudice of color, added Moreau de Saint-Méry, was the *ressort caché* (hidden spring) of the social machine.[91] Wimpffen noted, in his turn, that the prejudice took the place of *distinctions de rang, mérite de la naissance, honneurs et même de la fortune.* In such a way, he added graphically, that even if a black could prove his descent from the Negro king who came to adore Jesus Christ in the manger, even if he combined in his person the genius of a celestial intelligence with all the gold from the bowels of the earth, he would still be regarded as a vile slave, a *noir*, by the most cretinous, the most foolish, the poorest of whites.[92]

It is in this sense that colonial society differed, in its fundamentals, from metropolitan society. The French ancien régime was divided, horizontally, into the three estates of nobility, bourgeois, and peasantry. The Saint Domingue society was divided, vertically, into the three estates of whites, people of color, and blacks. There developed, in the colonial case, neither a discernible nobility based on title nor a distinctively clerical group. The rivalries that did exist—between large planter and small planter, between the civilian and the military arms of government, between town and country populations, between planters and merchants, and between the local petite bourgeoisie and the *petits blancs*—were real enough, as the insurrection of the 1760s on the part of the *petits blancs* shows. But they were overshadowed by the overriding sentiment of race solidarity, reinforced by the terrifying imbalance of sheer numbers between whites and nonwhites. That, as much as anything else, explains why the colonial historians, including Moreau de Saint-Méry, divided their material into sections and chapters subtitled in racial terms—the whites, the mulattoes, the blacks—to the practical exclusion of other differentiating criteria. It left behind a legacy of implacable race hatred that made impossible the continuance of a white presence in the new black republic after 1804; nicely summed up in the nineteenth-century anecdote of the encounter between the editor of the journal *Le Sauveteur*, Turpin de Sanzay, and President Salomon, in which the Frenchman's insulting remark, "Retirez-vous, vous occupez la proprieté de mes ancêtres, et je ne peux souffrir ici votre présence" (Go away, you occupy the property of my ancestors, and I cannot tolerate your presence here), was countered with the dignified retort that de Sanzay's own ancestor was a filibuster and that he, the President of the Republic, had no need to make an excuse for himself.[93]

MOREAU DE SAINT-MÉRY AND HILLIARD D'AUBERTEUIL

Just as Jamaica gave birth to its own school of local historians and writers, so did Saint Domingue. They were, most notably, Moreau de Saint-Méry himself and Hilliard d'Auberteuil, the first a Creole (his grandfather had been *sénéschal* of Martinique), the second a creolized *métropolitain*, and both of them eminent lawyers who held high office in the colony. In addition to the volumes on *Loix et Constitutions des colonies françaises de l'Amérique* (1784–90) already mentioned, Moreau de Saint-Méry also wrote *La Description de la partie française de Saint-Domingue* (1792). He was twice exiled by the Revolution—the first time from the colony and the second time from France itself—and the journal of his Philadelphia stay is a charming record of how his bookshop became the center of exile life; his friends included Volney, de Noailles, Talon, the duc d'Orléans (the future Louis Philippe) and the redoubtable Talleyrand himself, not to mention the English Radical Cobbett, who translated Moreau de Saint-Méry's other book on the Spanish part of Saint Domingue.[94] A historian and born researcher (he complained bitterly of the Spanish neglect of the riches of the Seville archives), he provides in his books a valuable commentary on all aspects of colonial life. In his turn, d'Auberteuil, of Rennes origin and domiciled in the colony, provided an equally valuable commentary in his volume of 1776–77, *Considérations sur l'état présent de la colonie française de Saint-Domingue*. Much more than Raynal, who used only secondary sources for his famous work, Moreau de Saint-Méry and d'Auberteuil constitute together an intimate and detailed description of colonial manners and values based on direct experience.

In the history of Caribbean political thought—as Charles Frostin has shown in his exhaustive study, *Les Révoltes blanches à Saint-Domingue aux XVIIᵉ-XVIIIᵉ siècles*—these two colonial writers are important because they gave eloquent expression to the ideology of *autonisme colon*, (local self-government), using what has aptly been termed "the American spirit" to attack the French colonial regime of oppressive royal administration and restrictive economic mercantilism. Just as in the case of the British West Indies

Long and Edwards fashioned a theory of colonial Whiggery against the English Crown and Parliament, so in the French West Indies Moreau de Saint-Méry and d'Auberteuil shaped arguments of an advanced politico-constitutional radicalism against a monarchy and a bureaucracy that they saw as the instruments of the vested interests of absentee planters, metropolitan merchants, and royal appointees. But because that movement of thought, in both cases, belongs more properly to the study of Caribbean colonial nationalism—despite the fact that it never flowered, as it did in the British North American colonies, into open rebellion—it is treated elsewhere in this volume. (See chapter 5.) What is more pertinent, at this point, is the manner in which these writers throw light on the planter collective mentality and how they came, despite their exposure to the ideas of the Enlightenment, to justify and rationalize its psychological assumptions.

Reading the three tomes of Moreau de Saint-Méry's *Description* compels admiration. A Freemason, vaguely deistical in his religious beliefs, an avowed disciple of Diderot and Rousseau, he evinces all the characteristics of the Enlightenment: its romantic sensibility, its intellectual curiosity, its belief in the goodness of man. If he is sufficiently a colonial snob to record with pride the brief visit to Saint Domingue in 1783 of the English royal heir-apparent Prince William Henry, he is also the *savant* who catalogs with equal pride the list of residents who adorned the colony with their learning: the Jesuit Père Boutin with his study of African languages, the medical doctor Desportes who almost single-handedly created the science of colonial pharmacology, the M. Dubourg who wrote on colonial botany, and the younger Weuves who sought, in his book of 1780, to refute the accusation that the colonies constituted an onerous burden for the metropolis.[95] His account makes it clear, too, that notwithstanding colonial philistinism, the exciting ferment of ideas taking place in France had its repercussions in the West Indies. For if there was an ideology of trade, institutionalized in the notorious *Exclusif* system, there was also a trade of ideology.

The influence of the French ideas comes through, loud and clear, in Moreau de Saint-Méry's incisive analysis of colonial habits and manners. He writes as an ethnologist would write. Seeing the colonial life as an eternal triangle, as it were, between whites, mulattoes, and blacks, he subjects each group to a rigorous examination. His bourgeois sense of business prudence is offended by the extravagance of colonial luxury, the passion for gambling (cockfighting for the slaves, card games for the white gentry), the obsession with expensive finery that penetrates every social level, including the slaves, the pervasive spirit of tropical hedonism. His spirit of *bon civisme* leads him to lament the general absence of public and private morality. Every group is indictable. Luxury, he observes, flourishes in the colony, and no profession is safe from its assault. Everywhere, he asserts, the military, who are the defenders of the country, are rarely the guardians of its morals; and Saint Domingue is no exception. The European residents imagine that a single day in the colony entitles them to ennoblement, so much so that they break off their family connections at home lest their low social origins be discovered.[96] The *creol blanc*, even although in his youth he may have received a French education, rapidly learns that his station in life predisposes him to cultivate his physical pleasures rather than his moral inclinations. The *creole blanche*, in her turn, is destined for a life of forced early marriage, obsession with sexual intrigue, and the torture of jealousy caused by the general practice of white male liaisons with mulatto mistresses.[97] The *affranchis*, likewise, are so devoted to the pursuit of pleasure that it becomes their despotic master; their three passions are dancing, horse riding, and *la volupté*.[98] As for the slaves, the transplanted African system of polygamy makes a happy family life even more impossible. Whether it is the langorous creole or the lascivious *mulâtre* or the lazy black, Moreau de Saint-Méry sees in all of them the dehumanizing influence of a laxity of sexual morals that, as he observes, takes the form, not of the scandalous public prostitution of the European cities, but of a total absence of any sense of morality. Nor is this the expression of an outraged puritan conscience in the English fashion. There are passages in both the Philadelphia journal and the Saint Domingue volumes that reveal the author as a sort of French-colonial Boswell, with a keen scientific curiosity, for example, about sexual aberrations. So, for him, colonial sexual license and marital infidelity are obnoxious not because they are sinful but because they are antisocial. It is the clear inference of the argument that in such an environment there can be neither moral happiness nor social utility.

In all of this Moreau de Saint-Méry speaks as a social critic after the manner of a Diderot or a Rousseau. Yet, interestingly enough, he refuses to draw the necessary radical conclusions from his critique. He recognizes the symptoms of the colonial social disease. But he stops short of indicting the system itself. He clearly perceives that the symptoms are related to the system. So, in his telling description of the upbringing of the white Creole child, he sees that its character of imperious arrogance is a consequence of being surrounded, from birth, by a fawning court of slaves—never was there a despot, he writes, that had adulation so assiduous; he is corrupted by being at once the object of parental indulgence and of slave idolatry.[99] Similarly, his portrait of the *mulâtresse*, half-admiring, half-censorious, condemns her indolence and her obsession with the sexual art, yet fails to insist upon its real cause in the sexual depredations of the white class; all the author will admit is that the general promiscuity is a necessary evil of the system, so much so that no legislation can touch it: the law remains silent, he comments, where nature speaks so imperiously.[100] He prints an exhaustive list of the 128 grades of color, officially enforced, of the resultant mélange, but he fails to recognize its comic absurdity. He even manages to imply that the slave trade, the origin of it all, was more the fault of the French than of the colonials.[101] But the most astonishing omission of the account is in its treatment of the slaves. It discusses, variously and with intense curiosity, the different tribal origins of the slave population, their distinctive characteristics, their intramural prejudices one against the other, their remarkable command of music, their passion for the dance, their bodily cleanliness, their religion of *vaudoux* or vodun, their sexual preferences, and much else. But it says hardly anything about their daily work, almost as if it did not exist.[102]

For all of his sensibility, Moreau de Saint-Méry was, in sum, an apologist for the planter cause. So part of the natural order of things did the system seem to him that he did not even attempt its defense in any serious fashion. The slave mind, he observed, was incapable of understanding religious ideas; he could not see that the real reason for the deficiency lay in the bitter resistance of the planters to any kind of religious instruction at all for their charges, although the evidence is overwhelming as much in Père Charlevoix's early account of 1730–31 as in the planter Malenfant's oddly sympathetic account published later, in 1814.[103] Many of the slaves, he wrote, were lazy, quarrelsome, liars, and thieves. Yet his own further account of their concern with cleanliness, their avoidance of drunkenness, the habit of breast-feeding their children on the part of slave mothers (which especially enthused him as a disciple of Rousseau), indicates an at least partial realization that nurture, as much as nature, shaped slave behavior patterns.[104] His reference to the Negroes as forming part of *les peuples non-civilisés*, suggests that, as with his English colonial counterpart, Edwards, his prejudice against them was cultural rather than racial. But prejudice of either kind could help buttress the same general conclusion that the slave order was sacrosanct. It is possible that he was even vaguely aware of the profound contradiction in which his argument placed him, for there is a curious passage in his book, omitted after the 1797 edition, that sought to excuse his failure to discuss the moral problem involved. "It is not pertinent," he wrote, "...to examine the question of slavery and to determine if such a state of things, over which humanity and philosophy can only heave a sigh, is to be made a matter of accusation against the colonies....A great nation has opened up a discussion on the subject which has attracted everybody...I very well know the interest it can inspire in the man of sensibility....But it is not by wishes alone that moral ills can be ended; for the deeper they are the more their cure requires genius, care, and time. Experience has unhappily shown that it would have been better for the man of sensibility that this cause, undoubtedly so appealing, had not been broached at all, that it would have been far better for him to have realized the impossibility of putting an end to slavery and to have considered only its amelioration, alleviating its rigors by means which would have gained, through self-interest, even the support of the slave owners."[105] The sentiment was in keeping with the main purpose of the book itself, which, as the author stated, was to remind Paris of the splendors of a colony created by the French genius and which, even after the events of the Revolution, could still be restored to its pristine prosperity. It was only logical, then, that in his role in those events after 1789 he should have acted as the spokesman of the planters and merchants as against the Parisian reformers; and his pamphlet of 1791, *Considérations présentées aux vrais amis du repos et du bonheur de la France*, was a characteristic attack on the Société des Amis des Noirs, the pro-Negro club of the French Revolution, assailing their effort (as Moreau de Saint-Méry saw it) to overthrow a social structure so nobly tested by history and experience in favor of fantastic theories presupposing an ideal human nature that had never really existed. The disciple of the philosophes thus ended as the supporter of the Napoleonic reaction.

Contemporary accounts testify to the sensation occasioned by the publication of Hilliard d'Auberteuil's book. It is easy to see why. It is a highly censorious account of French colonial administration written from the viewpoint of a bourgeois reformer (notwithstanding some sharp strictures passed on the philosophes). It has the spirit, in that respect, of Raynal; and it is suggestive that the author's plan to compose a more extensive work was dropped because the publication of Raynal's book forestalled it. Yet it was one thing to be a critic of Versailles, quite another to be a critic of the slave regime; and d'Auberteuil's section on that subject graphically reveals how, just as with Moreau de Saint-Méry, the prejudice of the colon effectively stifled the spirit of the reformer. It is almost as if a split intellectual personality is at work. Nothing could better illustrate how slavery suborned the critical instinct.

D'Auberteuil begins with the ritualistic obeisance to the spirit of liberty. The love of country, he says, is the first of the civic virtues. The best government is that in which no one shall find his interest in the misfortune of others. Law and administration should be accommodated to the peculiarities of the people, so that, in the case of Saint Domingue, many metropolitan laws are inapplicable because of the differences of climate and manners.[106] These truths, the argument continues, even apply to slavery. "The country where slavery rules," opines the author with candor, "is the anchorage of the man who possesses only the appearance of virtue. The habit of being obeyed makes the master proud, precipitate, harsh, angry, unjust, and cruel, and insensibly encourages an absence of all the moral virtues...he is alone in the midst of his enemies." He concedes even more when he argues that the vices usually attributed to the slave are not intrinsic to him but the direct consequence of his condition: "It is not surprising that the negroes, on becoming our slaves, contract an infinity of vices they do not possess in their natural state. They lose the sentiment of pity towards us, we, in our turn, because we are estranged from nature, have no sentimental feeling towards them."[107] The concession is all the more significant when it is remembered that even those French writers and travelers of the time who were critics of slavery— Lambert, Chanvalon, Pierre Poivre, Delacroix, Sonnerat—tended to accept the negative and unflattering portrait of the slave presented in the proslavery literature.

Yet, for all this, d'Auberteuil is no champion of emancipation. At best, he repeats the old amelioration recipe. Let the slaves have adequate medical care, rest periods, time to cultivate their own provision grounds. Let them be granted the right to lodge complaints against their masters. Above all, let them be governed by a revised civil law, in place of the present law of the master, which in reality confers the right of life and death upon the individual slave proprietor. If, he observes, we want to get the best from them, we must treat them humanely. We must accustom them gradually to an exact but unchanging discipline. It is urgent to make them happy; which, he adds, is not at all difficult, for they are content with little. If this is done, all will have a happy ending. Lighten the burden of your slaves, he admonishes the *créoles volupteaux* (indolent colonists), and you will find at home the happiness you vainly seek in France.[108] Having said all this, he assumes that the argument is closed. "I will not pause," he concludes disarmingly, "to examine the point as to whether this property of slavery is legitimate, it is at least profitable. If we treat the slaves with humanity, their condition will hardly seem to them to be unfortunate."[109]

The gross naiveté of the argument illuminates the fatal weakness of the proslavery thesis. With its tone of Panglossian optimism and sweet reasonableness, it refuses to face up to the two crucial contradictions of the situation. First, if the slave—as d'Auberteuil admits—is innately intelligent and capable of comprehending the nature of liberty, how could he be expected to accept the state of slavery? Second, if (as, again, d'Auberteuil honestly admits) the existing legislation of the 1685 *Code Noir* has turned out to be ineffective in its effort to protect the slave—so much so that, in his own phrase, any white in Saint Domingue can ill-treat blacks with impunity—then of what use is it to advocate even more legislative amelioration? Neither d'Auberteuil nor Moreau de Saint-Méry proferred a satisfactory answer to those questions. The truth is that both of them were men of colonial bourgeois prudence. Even when they seem to sympathize with the lot of the slave, it is more an exercise in elegance of diction than the expression of deeply felt compassion. It is suggestive that d'Auberteuil's criticism of the slave trade rests on utilitarian rather than moral argumentation; the trade must end, he argues, because of its economics of high mortality, so that it would be more advisable to adopt a public policy of encouraging the natural increase of the resident slave population, for the costs of natural reproduction are bound to be less than those of continued importation. Likewise, he is against the religious instruction of the slaves on the ground, again utilitarian, that the contemplation of a future life will make them inattentive to their work.

A final example of this general temper of prudent pragmatism is the manner in which both writers treat the question of colonial luxury. They write on this topic, not as old-fashioned clerical moralists but as hardheaded colonial gentleman-politicians. Luxury, they argue, bleeds the colony and benefits France, since it requires an unending stream of useless imported items. It leads to dissipation and downgrades the honor of work. Reading all this, it is instructive to compare it with the temper of the book written earlier, in the 1730s, by the Jesuit missionary Père Charlevoix, *Histoire de l'isle Espagnole ou de St. Domingue*. For the spirit that breathes through the pages of Charlevoix is that of a genuine Christianity, a note altogether absent in the two later writers. The grim picture that he painted of the slave population at that earlier date, in all of their misery, "despised of men and rejected by nature," is full of a compassionate pity his successors failed to repeat.[110] In this sense, the difference of tone between Charlevoix and d'Auberteuil is the same as the difference, in the previous century, between Du Tertre and Labat. As the slave regime solidified itself, its unconditional defense became more urgent.

Yet perhaps neither Moreau de Saint-Méry nor Hilliard d'Auberteuil may be viewed as the most representative voice of the French West Indian colonial ideology. They were both too much touched by the metropolitan currents of thought. A much more representative presentation of the planter outlook is that of the French resident Dubuisson who, in his *Nouvelles considérations sur Saint-Domingue* of 1780, attempted a rebuttal, point by point and page by page, of d'Auberteuil's work. All three writers are defenders of the slave regime. But if the first two are liberals, the third is unrepentingly conservative, even reactionary. At every point, he is incensed by each concession that his rival makes to the Enlightenment outlook. Where d'Auberteuil castigates colonial governors, Dubuisson eulogizes them. The idea that the colonists are alienated from the mother country, he insists, is as impossible as it is imaginary. The advocacy of free trade with foreign countries is misconceived. Even the criticism of absentee plantation owners is misguided, since the more they spend of their net income in France, the more they require that their colonial agents make the plantation operation more efficient and profitable.[111] As for the matter of slavery, Dubuisson becomes almost apoplectic. We whites, he answers d'Auberteuil, with our arts and science, do not need the pity of the slave; in fact, the pity that a slave might feel for a white is something *si peu natural* (so very unnatural) that the idea could only have entered the head of somebody like d'Auberteuil who has not been long enough in the colony to understand things. The qualities attributed to the Negro, such as intelligence, pity, and tenderness, are nonexistent. All they possess, in reality, is a sort of mechanical aptitude for music. Far from being obedient and affectionate, they are rebellious people, and d'Auberteuil's assertions about the state of security in the colony are belied by the prevalence of marauding Maroon Negro bands.[112] And how can we expect the sentiment of tenderness, he asks in a long harangue, from black women or even the *sangmêlees* (those of mixed blood), who are so much the carriers of a *debauche effrenée* (frightening debauchery) that they may inspire love but never the delicious emotions of a tender heart?[113] These people, he concludes, should in fact be grateful for slavery, for, *vainqueurs inhumains* (vengeful conquerers) or *captifs malheureux* (unhappy captives) in Africa, they have been brought to America to become beneficiaries of a new life. He finally admonishes those philanthropists who mourn over their condition to remember that the well-being of the slave lies safely in the care of masters whose self-interest alone guarantees the prevention of cruelty.[114]

Whereas Moreau de Saint-Méry and Hilliard d'Auberteuil are partial racists, Dubuisson is the complete racist. In an interesting passage, Moreau de Saint-Méry described how so many whites, coming to the colony, failed to recognize one Negro from another, seeing only a faceless black crowd, and how he himself had suffered from the embarrassment, but had managed to overcome it. For Dubuisson, however, the blacks remain forever a generic object of undistinguishable anatomic and physiological features. The slave, for him, is not a person. He is not even a nonperson. He becomes almost an antiperson. The term *l'homme sauvage*, he declares, applies only to the aboriginal Indians and not to the African slaves; he thus shows once again how the European mind could only idealize an American group that was no longer a threat to its hegemony. He is scandalized by the idea that blacks and whites could share human sentiments; the very thought is unthinkable. Merely to entertain it is to endanger the very existence of the colony.[115] There is, all in all, in all of these three writers, composing their work almost on the eve of the upheaval of 1789, a total absence of any awareness of the forces that, once that event took place, would put an end to their world.

THE CONTRIBUTION OF THE FRENCH REVOLUTION

These accounts, of course, were only one part of the rearguard action conducted by the French Antillean slavery vested interests against their enemies. They had to wage a war on three fronts: first, against the growing metropolitan antislavery opinion; second, against the free mulatto group on their own home ground; and, third, against the slave proletariat itself. The struggle was finally resolved with the abolition of slavery by the Paris revolutionary Convention in 1794, consolidated ten years later by the victory of the black war of liberation and the establishment of the new black republic. The war was accompanied by an extensive pamphlet literature, as well as the debates in the three successive revolutionary assemblies between 1789 and 1794 on the various issues that arose: the colonial grievances contained in the 1789 cahiers, the problem of colonial representation, the status of the free blacks, and the meaning of the Declaration of the Rights of Man for slavery and the slave trade. Both the literature and the debates throw additional light on the planter ideology as it was forced to come to grips with those issues.

The nature of the problem that confronted the colonial representatives—early on accepted by the States General as a legitimate delegation and organized in the form of the Massiac Club—is easily stated. They accepted the revolution because it promised the overthrow of Bourbon despotism in the islands and consideration of the grievances cataloged in their *cahiers de dolé-ances*; that is, the official reports of complaints: discontent with the trade laws, the discriminatory tax system, and the repressive colonial administration, in which they wanted a share. They even took the Tennis Court Oath. But they saw, correctly, that the universalistic principles of the Declaration of the Rights of Man logically threatened their slaveholding propertied interests, and so claimed that it did not apply to the colonies. They had to answer the argument of the Paris radicals and of the Société des Amis des Noirs that natural law and justice required the termination of slavery, or at least of the slave trade. They saw clearly that it was a fundamental conflict between the interests of property and the claim of principle, summed up in Moreau de Saint-Méry's defense of the May 1791 colonial constitution law: "You must renounce your wealth and your commerce," he told the National Assembly, "or declare frankly that the Declaration of Rights does not apply to the colonies."[116] That conflict, of course, had been fully publicized for some fifty years in the form of the French antislavery intellectual movement. But with 1789 it became, as the colonists clearly perceived, a clear and present danger with the radical parties in control of Paris. As Boissonade has put it, what had hitherto been dismissed as the paradoxes of an elite set of *beaux esprits* had become for the first time a practical threat both to metropolitan slave-based commerce and to the Saint Domingue colonists.[117] As Moreau de Saint-Méry put it in his apologetic pamphlet of 1791, the arrival at Cap-Français in 1788 of the issues of the *Mercure de France* that contained details of the discussion among the negrophiles of the problem created *une grande sensation.*[118] Faced with that challenge, the slave-owning interest—a combination of *grands planteurs*, metropolitan merchants, and high-ranking aristocrats possessed of lucrative properties in the colony, usually through marriage— was compelled to spell out some sort of reasoned defense.

The defense took the form of a virulent propaganda campaign effectively conducted by the colonial deputation and its friends, representing, as did the delegation, the colonial aristocracy *de fortune et de nom*; that is to say, the nobility both of wealth and title. It is worth noting that only two of its members, Jean-Baptiste Gérard and Bodkin Fitzgerald, dared to inscribe themselves as members of the Jacobin Club.[119] First and foremost, of course, there is the scurrilous libeling of the antitrade forces. They are seen as unrealistic philosophes, impractical dreamers, *enthousiastes*, and *frondeurs*. The fact that the highly respectable membership of the Amis des Noirs included the King of Poland and the Duc de Charost, and did not include either Mirabeau or Robespierre, does not prevent the charge that the Society seeks to destroy all religions, all empires, and all forms of government.[120] The admirable Abbé Gregoire was admired by all; but that does not deter the colon pamphleteers from spreading the calumny that he defends the *gens de couleur* because his brother is married to one of them; in a spirited reply, the abbé remarked that he would prefer such a sister-in-law to all the vaunted amiabil-

ity of the white colonial womenfolk.[121] Despite the moderate character of his
views, based on his American travels, Brissot is denounced by his colonial de-
tractor Louis-Marthe Gouy d'Aray as an irresponsible demagogue who would
be hanged a hundred feet in the air by the very Negroes he cherishes should
he ever set foot in Saint Domingue.[122] The double charge, even more serious, is
then made that the Society is responsible for the Saint Domingue civil war,
since its writings incite the slaves to revolt, and that some of its members are
even paid agents of the English cause: a charge formally presented to the National Assembly by the Martiniquan deputy Dillon.[123] The particular charge
of treason takes on piquant irony when it is remembered that the colonists
themselves were at this time in secret negotiations with the English and even
anticipated calling in North American aid, as the colonials' secret correspondence, published in Paris by the Society, makes clear; and Guy-Kersaint
noted correctly in his 1792 address to the National Assembly that the ultimate
aim of the colonists was independence. The abbé Gregoire warned his countrymen in his *Lettre aux Citoyens de Couleur* of 1791 of the same secessionist
temper, present in both white and mulatto elements of the colonial opposition.[124] To all of this there is added the occasionally quixotic note, such as the
charge that the abolitionists employ women publicists as a means of provoking the colonists; one of them, Olympe de Gouge, replied to the charge in a
vigorous polemic: without knowing anything of the history of America, she
writes, this odious traffic of Negroes has always excited my indignation.[125]
Our enemies, all in all, the colonists urge, are drunk with the language of liberty and must be stopped at all costs.

To this assault on abolitionist motives there were appended other theses.
There is the argument that the peculiar social structure of the colony absolves
it from the application of the social reforms mooted in Paris. "There is hardly
any Third Estate in Saint Domingue," writes the colonial committee to the
naval ministry in 1788, "since there are no free people, the slaves taking the
place of a working class; there are no clergy; there is only one order of citizens, that of the planter proprietors, who from this viewpoint are all equals,
all soldiers, and all officers, and all entitled as a result to enjoy the privileges
of nobility."[126] It was a shrewd point: the Revolution in France is geared to
the interests of the Third Estate; there is no Third Estate in the sugar colonies; therefore the colonies do not need the Revolution. The leading characteristic of the colonial society that from the liberal viewpoint demanded its
transformation—its racial polarization—was thus perversely invoked by its
defenders to nullify the demand. Or again, there is the argument that emphasizes the theme of the legendary colonial loyalty. If, as the colonists
charged, Mirabeau was in the pay of Pitt and Clarkson was a British spy, we,
they claimed, are the true defenders of French honor and interests. We are
loyal Frenchmen, the planters tell the king in their address of May 1788, and
the ocean cannot prevent us from being the first to approach the throne.[127]
Saint Domingue, reiterate the commissioners of the colonial deputation in

the same year, is the most precious province of France, and should indeed be considered a second kingdom.[128] That argument is logically tied to the further compelling argument of the economic importance of the colony. Interfere with either slavery or the trade, and the commerce of France, along with its prosperity, will be annihilated. Commerce, in turn, is the necessary agent of navigation, agriculture, and the arts; destroy commerce, and you destroy everything.[129]

Like overseas colonists everywhere, the Saint Domingue plantocracy thus grossly exaggerated their importance for the mother country. The argument of loyalty, in any case, was patently insincere, for its lyrical effusions were accompanied by a tone of haughty arrogance that at times bordered on sedition. Your Majesty, they told the king, cannot pass over us any more than we can pass over you. Yesterday, we were weak; today, we are strong and vigorous, and we have the strength of adolescence. You cannot regard us, they told the National Assembly, as you did before the American war of independence, as if we were destined merely to serve the interests of France. You should consider the example of the schism provoked by the English. England still permits the Jamaican planters only to approach it as suppliants; but we ourselves are not asking favors but rights founded on our wealth, industry, and loyalty.[130] The argument received its practical expression in the organization of the colonial provincial councils based on an openly racial suffrage, in clear defiance of the sovereignty of the National Assembly, effectively constituting an assertion of the constitutional principle, so fatal to that sovereignty, that the colonies alone should exercise the right to initiate legislation concerning slavery and the colored population.[131]

The final argument of the planter ideology, it goes without saying, was the racist one. Both the abbé Sibire, in his *L'Aristocracie negrière*, and Lecointe-Marsillac in his *Le More-Lack* noted the unexamined dogmas of the planter creed with respect to the slave: slavery is justified by customary law or by the right of captivity in war or by ecclesiastical and civil law; the Church condones it, as is evident in St. Paul's epistles, church council edicts, and even the Decalogue itself; the slave enters the system as an integral part of the necessary miseries of mankind; the slave is happier in America, where he gains physical safety and spiritual salvation through the ministrations of the Christian religion; the blacks are a race of men devoid of talent, reason, and intelligence; without slave labor it would be impossible to work the American plantations; the natural indolence of the African can only be overcome by harsh treatment; and the ever-present danger of servile revolt makes the harsh treatment even more obligatory.[132] The racist disdain extended even to the mulattoes, for to the "aristocrats of the skin" the people of mixed color were at once an affront to their racial pride and a reproach to their own miscegenative behavior. Malicious-minded genealogists, observed the abbé de Cournand scathingly, spend their time in odious investigations for the purpose of injuring innocent citizens.[133] The prejudice accounts for the fierce campaigns of the whites to deny the bastard-people of the mulattoes any sort of colonial representation in the prolonged struggle over the issue of the colonial suffrage after 1788, a campaign fought to the bitter end, even when the colony went up in flames after 1791.

All of the scholarly studies on the colonial question in the Revolution of 1789, albeit from different viewpoints—Dalmas, Boissonade, James, Deschamps, Garrett, Hardy—substantiate the general opinion of contemporary liberal observers like Brissot, Destuut de Tracy, Pétion de Villeneuve, and Condorcet that the Saint Domingue whites constituted a dominant, reactionary colonial ruling group of truly Bourbonese proportions. Their cast of mind was even more authoritarian than that of the governors and intendants they so much hated. They saw the slave population simply as *une canaille abominable* (an abominable scum of the earth). Both the chevalier de Laborie and the abbé Gregoire noted how the colonists' mode of argumentation, such as it was, was based not so much on reason as on blind prejudice and hatred.[134] They had no sense of compromise, because the habit of compromise was unknown to their experience. They sought to sabotage the conciliatory mission of the Commissioners sent out to the colony by the French government as surely as they refused to forge an alliance with the mulatto class with which, from the standpoint of economic interest, they had so much in common, and when they did finally bring themselves to countenance such an alliance, it was too late. For them, everything—in both racial and moral terms—was either black or white. The Amis des Noirs were evil-minded, misguided fools; the slave-generals of the revolution, who later became the black republic's slave-kings, were black monsters; and men of their own caste who showed even the slightest touch of the liberal disease were mercilessly destroyed: the abbé Gregoire recounted in one of his works how Hilliard d'Auberteuil, who was certainly no Jacobin, was arrested and imprisoned in Port-au-Prince on suspicion of preparing to write an advising brief in favor of the *sangmêlés* and was then released after two months to die.[135] Even Père Labat, uncritical loyalist to the slave regime that he was, had been able to write in bitter terms of the rapacity of the French Company of Senegal in its slave-raiding missions; and Lanthenas, who noted Labat's accusation in his rebuttal of the apologist Lamiral, added that you could expect not even that much from the present-day defenders of slavery who, as a class, knew only the routine of amassing wealth and lacked both taste and philosophy.[136] They knew only two slogans, Lanthenas went on to say, the "balance of commerce" and the "interest of the nation."[137]

THE CUBAN APOLOGETIC

After the English Antilles and French Hispaniola (Saint Domingue), the third case study of the planter mind is, of course, that of Spanish Cuba. With the disappearance of Saint Domingue as a rival sugar producer (which the Cuban sugarocracy welcomed, even at the terrible price of a successful slave uprising, thus demonstrating once again the absence of any genuine regional loyalty in the planter mentality), and with the English colonies hampered by the abolition of the trade and the subsequent efforts of the British navy to suppress the continuing illegal trade (those efforts being seen by the non-English Caribbean planter interests, perhaps justifiably, not as an exercise in British disinterested philanthropy, but as a sinister attempt to ruin their own Atlantic trade), Cuba moved into first place as the sugar bowl of the Caribbean and the last bastion of the slavery regime. A whole school of Cuban historians —Rivero Muñiz, Benito Celorio, Cepero Bonilla, Ramiro Guerra y Sánchez, Julio Le Riverend—has documented the century-long process whereby the island progressed from the status of a backward rural community in the eighteenth century, retarded by a restrictive Spanish colonial exclusivism, to that in the nineteenth century of an opulent slave-based capitalism dominated by sugar tycoons, cigar magnates, and wealthy landowners. Notwithstanding the fact that the island economy was far more diversified than the earlier English and French slave regimes—coffee and cattle raising held their own up until the very end—it was sugar, founded on eternally escalating illegal slave imports, that laid the foundations of the new fabulous wealth; so much so that all of the leading works of the Cuban socioeconomic literature—Saco's *Historia de la Esclavitud*, Guerra's *Azúcar y poblacíon en las Antillas*, Ortiz's *Contrapunteo cubano*, Fraginals's *El Ingenio*—have been concerned in one way or another with the creoledom of sugar and its massive distorting effects upon Cuban society.[138]

What strikes the reader of the Cuban proslavery apologetic, as it developed throughout the nineteenth century, is the fact that despite uniquely different conditions that theoretically should have encouraged more civilized attitudes than those of the earlier eighteenth-century English and French defenders of the cause, that apologetic, in its substantive elements, remained as fixed and obdurate as ever. The different conditions are well known. The white-black population ratio was far more in favor of the whites than it had been in English Jamaica or French Saint Domingue. Heavy miscegenation patterns, in turn, spawned a free mulatto class much larger, statistically speaking, than its counterpart elsewhere, thus taking the edge off the endemic hatred between white master and black slave, and facilitating the rise of at once a free mulatto professional class and a negro-mulatto intelligentsia. The slave regime, in its turn, was not necessarily exclusively identified with the sugar-plantation regime, for there were sizable elements of slaves both on the coffee plantations and in the urban centers; and contemporary accounts strongly suggest that they led a more tolerable life than the English factory operatives of the period. Added to all that was the fact that nineteenth-century Cuba existed within the framework of the era of victorious liberalism; internationally, in the form of a hostile world opinion spearheaded by the British naval power, and internally, in the form of a cosmopolitan, articulate, and well-educated Creole elite oriented toward the outside world. Internally, it was apparent by the 1860s that slavery was an inefficient mechanism for a continuing profitable sugar industry; externally, the defeat of the South in the American Civil War made it clear that slavery could not survive within the modernizing Atlantic state system.

It is chilling testimony to the habit of ideological persistency—the capacity, that is to say, of ideological systems to survive even when their social and economic infrastructures have been seriously weakened or have even disappeared —that all of these factors did not prevent a continuing defense of the slave system on the part of the Cuban plantocracy and its allies throughout the better part of the century. Despite the fact that Cuba never became, like Barbados or Jamaica, one vast, undifferentiated sugar plantation and that the investment, both economic and psychological, in the slave system was unequal in different strata of the Cuban top groups—making possible, for example, the well-known distinction between the Creole sugar oligarchs of the Occidente region and the more diversified Creole agriculturists of the Oriente region, which generated as it did a fundamental rift in political ideology as the irrepressible conflict with Spain sharpened—it was the psychopathology engendered by slavery that shaped the dominant values and attitudes of the society. Wealth replaced birth as the badge of social status, and the most fabulous wealth in the perennial "dance of the millions" came from sugar. The continuing vague stigma that attached to men who—like the Tomás Terry who became the Cuban Croesus of his time—dealt directly in the clandestine trade did not prevent either social recognition or political advancement. Every generation witnessed the same spectacle of yet another new group of sugar barons, often self-made men without a genuine claim to any aristocratic title, being received into the Havana *haut monde*: the O'Farrills and Arangos came to be accepted by the Montalvos and Calvos, just as, later, the Zuluetas were accepted by the O'Farrills. The sole, impregnable barrier to that social mobility was the inability to parade the *limpieza de sangre* (purification of blood). Whereas inbreeding was rampant, interracial marriage was the one unforgivable offense. The testimony of practically all of the travelers who reported on the society agrees in noting these twin characteristics, feeding on each other: its insensate profligacy and its paranoid racism.[139]

It was in those terms that white Cuba, including much of its educated intelligence, saw itself and perceived others. That self-image, and that image of others, expressed itself in a variety of ways. The Havana commercial and agricultural societies, reflecting the influence of Benthamite utilitarianism, undertook, early on, extensive statistical studies of trade, commerce, and industry; but the official indifference to and general distaste for the class of free Negroes carried over into census investigations, so much so that no real effort was made to ascertain their true numbers. It was left to visitors like

Humboldt in the early part of the century and De la Sagra in his *Historia económico-política y estadística* of 1831 to attempt any sort of reliable statistics in that field, while it was not until the 1860s, with the publication of Pezuela's extraordinary geographical dictionary, that another Spanish scholar completed the task.[140] Visitors were constantly startled to hear praise heaped on the *bozal*, the newly arrived, raw African, while little but contempt was expressed for the Creole-born black, whose claim to be Cuban was clearly regarded as an intolerable affront.[141] A veritable hierarchy of color prejudice offset the democracy of wealth; so, just as the resident Spanish *peninsulares* despised all Creoles as *mestizos* and defended their own often brown skin color evasively as proof of a manly "Moorish blood," and just as publicists like Cristóbal Madán in his *El trabajo libre* of 1864 dismissed the mulattoes as a lazy and vicious crowd,[142] so the mulattoes in turn took out their own frustrated feelings of racial identity in a brutal contempt for the blacks, so much so that there is evidence galore to show that in Cuba, as much as in Saint Domingue earlier, the worst planter-masters were often the mulatto rich and that the slaves feared them even more than they feared the whites. The ingrained obsession with heredity, so typically Spanish, was reinforced by an acute anxiety over racial purity, again so typically Spanish; and it is no accident that the most famous of all nineteenth-century Cuban novels, Villaverde's *Cecilia Valdés*, treated the theme of the *parda*, the colored woman, cruelly frustrated in her love for a scion of a Havana white family who, unbeknownst to her, is in fact her half brother, thus constituting in her figure at once a victim of white sexual exploitation and a casualty of a fiercely hierarchical system.

The key element in this set of attitudes was, of course, that of sex. Every ruling class has sought to use that element, through its marriage customs, as a means of collective self-defense. But in a racially divided society, the psychopathology of sexual anxiety is immeasurably intensified, for the fear of sexual pollution becomes not simply a matter of class integrity but one of racial purity. A racism of sex emerges. Martínez-Alier's study of racial attitudes and sexual values in nineteenth-century Cuba shows how that racism was perfected in the last of the Caribbean slave societies. Interracial marriage legislation, going back to the older edicts of the Council of the Indies, though often honored in the breach rather than in the observance, accurately reflected the ideological stance of upper-class white Cuba on the matter; inequality in color constituted a civil impediment to marriage that it was the business of both church and state to uphold. The civil legislation that controlled the marriage system was, in turn, accompanied by an obligatory ritual controlling seduction and elopement.

Two leading institutive principles lay at the heart of this discriminatory regime. There was, first, the Spanish concept of family honor, traditionally enforced by patterns of social class endogamy and, second, the metaphysical notion of pure blood. The Martínez-Alier study demonstrates clearly how the

Cuban slave regime gave both principles a new lease on life. Family honor, originally concerned with the dangers of lower-class penetration of aristocratic homes, became transmuted into a defense-mechanism against racial pollution on the part of socially aspiring colored adventurers. Similarly, the concept of purity of blood, originally used to distinguish old Christians from the new Christians in Spain itself, and largely discredited in the mother country by the end of the eighteenth century, gradually acquired the new meaning of distinction between people of African-slave origin and people of European-free origin. In the Cuban context, both of those principles became subtly transmuted to mean, more than anything else, protective shields against the ominous stain of slavery origin. It is true that the realities of the society—progressive miscegenation, the rise of a large free-colored group, the widespread practice of the policy of *adelantar la familia* (keeping intact the family whiteness), and the consequent ambiguity surrounding racial identity—all made nonsense of any effort to determine social stratification along strictly racial lines. The point to note is that the ideologues of the system persisted to the end in portraying a dreamworld in which only colored people should be slaves, and only free people white. The system contained its own seeds of destruction. But its dominant ideology, conceiving the system as it ought to have been rather than as it was, remained intact.[143]

Yet, however intact, the Cuban proslavery ideology was on the defensive throughout the century. If, in world opinion, Spain itself was regarded contemptuously as being nothing more than a geographical expression, its leading American colony was regarded as the immoral protagonist of the dying slave system. Internally, liberal movements of thought, from Varela's constitutionalist liberalism at the beginning of the period, through the autonomist ideas of the liberal reformers, on to the radical populism of Martí at the end of the period, compelled a critical reevaluation of slavery, although the reevaluation was by no means always in favor of abolition. Attitudes to slavery, indeed, were inextricably mixed with attitudes, variously, to the independence movement against Spain and the pro-American stance of the annexationist ideologues. The social question, the race question, and the national question were necessarily interwoven, making it difficult to impose any neat classification upon the competing intellectual positions.

ARANGO Y PARREÑO AND JOSÉ ANTONIO SACO

The two leading figures in the prolonged discussion on slavery were, it is generally agreed, Fransisco de Arango y Parreño and José Antonio Saco. Both sons of the Cuban social respectability, they have long been enshrined by orthodox Cuban scholarship in the national pantheon of patriots, statesmen, and shapers of the Cuban national destiny. Both of them, intellectually, were self-confessed disciples of the European liberal movement, from Adam

Smith to the Utilitarians, and employed their genius in a prolonged campaign to rid Cuba of an outmoded Spanish colonial mercantilism. They wanted to remake Cuba in the image of the England of triumphant technology, political liberty, and constitutional government that (as for so much of the Latin American intelligentsia of the period) was their model of the ideal society. But just as in Victorian England, liberalism, in practice, turned out to be an ideology working mainly for the interests of the rising industrial bourgeoisie, so in colonial Cuba it catered to the interests of the new wealth of sugar as against the interests of the masses; and since, furthermore, those masses were overwhelmingly black, it meant the perpetuation of Negrophobia. The writings of both Arango and Saco graphically illustrate the philosophical contradictions that arose, then, out of their effort, ultimately unsuccessful, to reconcile their liberalism with the slavery question.

Arango has been called "the colonial statesman" by the most uncritically admiring of his biographers.[144] The encomium is undoubtedly deserved. Appointed at a youthful age as *Apoderado General* of the Havana *ayuntamiento*, he devoted his intellectual gifts to a lifelong campaign in defense of the expansionist interests of the new, rising sugar wealth in the colony. On the one hand, it was a sort of Creole nationalist revolt against the old Spanish mercantilist closed system, a system rooted in the contemptuous observation by the Viceroy of Peru that "the American ought to know nothing more than how to read, write and pray"; on the other hand, it was a frank and completely unsentimental defense of the interests of the new Cuban bourgeois wealth, incarnated in the dictum of the Spanish minister of the time, Floridablanca, that "greed and interest are the main incentive for all human toil and they should only be checked in public matters when they are prejudicial to other persons or to the State."[145] Arango's work, it follows, was essentially that of the well-placed lobbyist who wrote important state papers seeking to influence the policymakers of Havana and Madrid. Despite his mastery of the problems of the Cuban economy, despite even his wide reading in, for example, the French encyclopedists, his vision was limited to the single purpose of transforming Cuba into an opulent sugar palace; so, although he could have written the first monumental history of Cuba had he so wished, it was left to the young Spanish scholar Pezuela to lament, on his arrival in Havana in the 1840s, that such a history did not exist and to prepare to undertake the task of composing it himself.

Accordingly, it is in Arango's state documents that we meet the first reasoned apologetic for the slave system in Cuban historiography. His very first memorial of 1789, significantly enough, was an extensive examination and defense of the Havana claim for a thoroughgoing liberalization of the restrictive Spanish legislation that inhibited the free entry of slaves into the colonial market. The old laws of the Indies—based on the traditional Spanish reluctance to allow an unrestricted import of Africans into the colonies—the argument went, have been rendered anachronistic by the vast contraband trade,

which benefits foreign nations and defrauds both Spain and Cuba. The crying need of Cuba was for a rapid and cheap supply of Negro labor; and if it
was impossible to give the trade entirely to Spanish ships, it should at least be
made free to all nationalities as the only way to avoid the evils of monopoly.[146]
Arango's famous *Discurso* of 1792 on the state of Cuban agriculture pressed
the argument further. It is the central theme of the *Discurso* to emphasize
the irony of the fact that with the most fertile soil of the Antilles, Cuba remains the most backward of the New World colonies. The reasons are clear:
the lower costs of slave importation in the rival islands; the equally lower
costs of slave maintenance, including the fact that the French and the English
slave owners permit fewer holidays to their slaves than do the Cubans; the
technological backwardness of the Cuban agriculturist, due in part, as Arango sees it, to the *indolencia criolla* (Creole indolence) of Latin Americans
in general; and the subjection of the Cuban planter to the merchant houses of
Spain and the usury-mongers of the Havana financial class, also mainly
Spanish. Only a free-trade system, ultimately giving the Cuban planter the
direct access to the African slave market hitherto denied him, can in the long
run override most of those disabilities.[147]

In all of this, Arango is the shrewd, hardheaded business ideologue ready
to employ any argument, however jesuitical, to foment a Cuban slave-based
capitalism. In that effort he had to meet the older conservative humanism of
the Council of the Indies, where the spirit of Las Casas was still very much
alive, and the new humanitarianism of the English and French abolitionists.
Both were met with the argument that theirs was a grossly misplaced concern, since the Negro was a piece of chattel property only, not a person with
rights; and in any case, he and his kind "were all becoming much happier
than they used to be." The Haitian revolt was due to the insidious propaganda
of the abolitionists, which the Saint Domingue planters had mistakenly imbibed, thus teaching their slaves the fatal lesson that they were deserving of
rights. In any case, the revolt is to be welcomed, since it annihilates a dangerous sugar rival: it was necessary to look at the French colony, "not only with
compassion, but with the eyes of hard political sense."[148] If slavery is unchris-
tian (as even Arango cannot deny), it is nonetheless necessary, for the tropical climate makes work by whites impossible (a myth later on vigorously
denied by Saco). In any case, continues Arango, the original sin is not
Cuban, but European (thus avoiding the question, surely pertinent, as to
whether it was not an equal sin to continue an offense launched by others).
"The inconsequential piety of Las Casas," Arango tells the Crown, "introduced negroes among us: a stupid policy has paralysed the progress of the
world and the vigor and number of the whites. We are just awakening with
all the lethargy of three centuries of exhaustion and neglect...we see that
without remedying our internal situation, without having any regard for it or
providing new aids for us, it is made a question of depriving us suddenly of
the means given us by the old laws and customs for our subsistence, or for

keeping up the culture which maintains our existence."[149] A policy originally misconceived thus becomes a policy absolutely necessary to a Cuban "culture" identified exclusively with the interests of its white men of property. Even as late as the prolonged controversy over the Spanish 1812 Constitution, the Council of the Indies still managed to see the issue in moral terms, summed up in its statement that "We ought, therefore, never to forget that the question is not one between Men and Brutes, but between Men and Men, lest our judgment should overlook the cause of humanity and lean towards that of Interests."[150] Arango's answer, in the strongly worded *Memorial* of 1811, was to reassert the paramountcy of the rights of Interests. Arango admonished the Crown:

> Think, Señor, about the political slavery of these regions before civil slavery, about the Spaniards before the Africans, about the rights and privileges of citizens here before determining the size and numbers of doors that should be opened or closed to people of color, about ways to breathe life into our inert police force, and all branches of our dead and decayed public administration, before increasing their risks and their burdens, define the role and powers of the Spanish and of the colonial government before undertaking to cure ills which are neither urgent nor paramount, fortify the old government's corrupted organs and adjust its defective spectacles before exposing the wounds and infections of remote sectors of our social body.[151]

The significance of all this, in the history of Cuban racism, is that it reveals Arango as the exponent of the slavery apologetic in its purest form. His arguments are those of a matured bourgeois consciousness. He sees the slave as the objectively necessary labor force of a new Cuba. If that end had been possible without slavery, he would have welcomed it. But Cuban conditions, including the aversion of white laborers to plantation work, made recourse to the African market inescapable. So while, on the one hand, his work is completely bereft of any of the romantic humanitarianism of the time, it is equally bereft of the Negrophobic racism of other Cuban ideologues like that of Lorenzo Allo in his *La esclavitud doméstica* and that of Betancourt Cisneros in his letters to Saco.[152] Or, to put it in another way, if on the one hand there is nothing in Arango's work of the doubts that assailed other slavery defenders like Edwards and Moreau de Saint-Méry, on the other hand there is very little of the Negrophobic hatred of writers like Delmonte and Echeverría—so little, in fact, that later on in his life he was capable of championing the idea of race admixture, whereby the black Cuban would eventually, by a process of genetic evolution, be obliterated by the white Cuban, thereby (in his own phrase) wiping out the memory of slavery.[153] For Arango, then, it is not a matter of slavery for slavery's sake. Rather, it is that since slavery will always exist where human nature exists, the statesman has no other choice than to put it to use for his own purposes. Brought up and educated in the age of Bonaparte and Metternich, Arango is the worldly-wise cynic for whom the only rationale is that of *raison d'état*. It is for that reason that his work constitutes, in Moreno Fraginals's phrase, the first great expression of the Cuban sugarcrat ideology, the most sincere, and hence, perhaps, the most significant, the most cynical, and the most pathetic.[154]

The importance of Arango's work, then, is that it confers intellectual letters of credit upon the rising native bourgeoisie and its incipient capitalism. Its gross and pathetic contradiction, of course, was that it sought, unsuccessfully, to marry the bourgeois ethic with the prebourgeois material base of slavery. For the essence of the bourgeois ethic was the concept of contract between capitalist and worker, a concept fatally compromised by the denial of contractual relationships in the master-slave system. That contradiction was reflected in the new ideology; Arango, as its chief intellectual protagonist, had (again in Moreno Fraginals's terms) one foot in the bourgeois future and the other in the remote slave past. That basic contradiction helps to explain all of the argumentative contradictions of Arango's work. The examples are numerous. There is the perpetuation of the legend (which Arango helped to create and which survives even into modern scholarship) that Cuban history starts with the English occupation of Havana in 1763—that is, with the first step in the realization of the paranoid dream of the Havana slavery group of a free and unrestricted importation of slaves, almost as if the previous two centuries of Cuban social development could be arbitrarily forgotten. For if that legend, as one American scholar has sharply put it, is yet another instance of Anglo-Saxon self-glorification,[155] it can also be seen as an instance of a self-congratulatory Cuban bourgeois historiography that only sees Cuban history as a real thing once its slave base becomes assured. Without slaves, Arango seems to be saying, we are nothing; with slaves, we are everything. Arango, in turn, defended the stability of the Cuban social order, founded as it was—unlike the English and French colonies—on a resident Creole proprietary class. Yet he was ready to weaken that stability with a heavy black influx, cavalierly ignoring the warnings—prolific in the official Spanish literature and reiterated, for example, in the objections of the directors of the Real Compañía in 1760—to the effect that an immoderate introduction of Negroes would jeopardize the security of the whole island.[156] The contrast, here, with the argument of an earlier Cuban economist like Arrate is instructive. For it was one of the theses of Arrate's work *Llave del Nuevo Mundo*, composed in the 1750s, that Cuban society would have been far better served if, instead of importing alien Africans who rapidly became an economic burden to their masters, it had nurtured its aboriginal Indians, who had shown themselves willing to work industriously for food and a modest wage return—by comparison with which slavery was wasteful and expensive.[157]

There emerged finally, then, the ultimate contradiction between Arango's real sense of Cuban nationalism and his obsession with the accumulation of riches. He shared with Arrate a real pride in Cuban identity. But whereas for Arrate that meant a *familia cubana* in which all shared full citizenship—as his appreciative observations on the positive role of Negroes and *pardos* in the eighteenth century civic militia clearly show[158]—for Arango it meant a socially exclusive club for the white respectability only. The club would only bend its rules to make way for the growth of the mulatto class, as a part of Arango's racial hygiene plan—which class, following the Haitian example (as Arango read it) would ally itself to the whites in a combined effort to keep the repressed black class in order.[159] Arango's concern with racial harmony, this is to say, was wholly that of the realpolitiker who thinks in terms of power-group alliances rather than in terms of social justice. If, then, the attempt throughout the century by the liberal party in Spain to instill its institutions into Cuba failed, the failure must be attributed in main part to the prevalence of Arango's ideology, which could see no way of saving the wealth of the island colony without slaves, nor of admitting democratic institutions without setting free a hazardously large number of Negroes. As a young colonial student of the work of the great Spanish agrarian reformer Jovellanos, Arango dreamed of a modernized Cuba. But the very institution of slavery that he had himself helped to create made its realization impossible. Its fulfillment was only made possible, later, by the growth of the *ideología mambisa* (ideology of the revolting slaves) and its acknowledgment of the truth that only the abolition of slavery could create the indispensable condition for a liberal Cuba. The social base of Arango's thought made that failure inevitable, for if Arrate was the expression of the old Havana town oligarchy, Arango was the expression of the new sugar aristocracy.

Next to Martí, Saco has been lauded as the greatest figure of the Cuban literary-political culture: the *gran profeta*, the *Oráculo cubano*, the exile (like Varela and Martí) devoting his polemical gifts to a sustained criticism of Spanish colonial rule, the powerful antagonist of the annexationists who would surrender Cuba to the United States, the leading intellect, all in all, of the liberal reforming element in Cuban political thought. Merely to read his collected work is to feel the justice of the claim; and few can read the moving autobiographical memoir that he composed toward the end of his life without readily recognizing that, as he put it, he had renounced the possibility of a brilliant law career that offered him riches, honors, and power in order to die poor in the service of Cuba.[160]

Yet even more than Arango, Saco delineated emphatically the contradictions inherent in the Cuban ideology. For, educated as a young man in the old Colegio de San Carlos, where the remarkable priest-educator Varela had attempted to replace the old scholastic regime with Cartesian science and metaphysics, he was an intellectual concerned with first principles—as distinct from Arango who never presumed to be anything more than a talented mind proselytizing in the defense of the Havana interests. Arango, as one of his later admirers put it, was a *cubano español*,[161] a position summed up in his own axiom that while commercial dependency mattered for Cuba, political dependency was, by comparison, of little importance. Saco, by comparison, believed ultimately in full independence, both commercial and political, although to the end he clung to the belief, mistakenly as events showed, that such independence would be the result of Spanish magnanimity. Yet, when that difference is acknowledged, Saco emancipated himself no more than Arango from the dilemma involved in his own ambivalent attitude towards slavery and the slave person.

Like Arango, Saco starts off with the conviction that the work structure of a new Cuba, in the best bourgeois fashion, must be based on the Protestant work ethic, adapted to a Catholic society. It is the main theme of his early essay *Memoria sobre la vagancia en la Isla de Cuba* that all social classes waste their time and energy in nonproductive pastimes so widespread that it constitutes a devouring cancer, an omnipotent sickness that destroys all proper social and moral values. Gambling infects everybody like a social disease. From the beginning, the child learns the habit as he sees his parents obsessed with card games at home. The father, as head of the Creole family, wastes his time and substance in the illegal houses where games of chance are the rage; he thinks they are innocent games, but in fact they lose him great quantities of money, not to speak of the neglect of his family and social duties.[162] For the populace at large there are the fairs and the *fiestas populares*, as well as the billiard parlors, where for a few pesos the gambling addiction can be easily picked up; and this in turn is exacerbated by the excessive number of holidays, both religious and otherwise, which occasion an economic loss to the society of incalculable proportions. It is scandalous, Saco implies, that literally one-quarter of the year should be devoted to such purposes.[163] All of this, in turn, is made worse by an educational system that teaches a civil and canonical law and ignores chemistry, mathematics, agriculture, commerce, and the arts and a social system that holds all of the useful occupations—shoemaker, carpenter, seamstress, manual laborer—in open disdain; as a result, if a well-to-do person, imbued from infancy with such antisocial prejudices, falls into poverty—as frequently happens—he is condemned to live in disgrace, since he regards as degrading all of those occupations in which he could earn a living. The whole ethic of work is vitiated. The "consequences of the gambling habit" are confused with the "results of prudential investment."[164] What Cuba needs, the argument concludes, is a veritable revolution in customs and moral ideas. It is right and proper, remarks Saco—for he is the Benthamite reformer rather than the puritan prohibitionist—that the people should sing and dance, promenade and enjoy good food. But those habits must be complemented by a vigorous state that sees education as the salvation of social ills. Unless we build up such a system our beloved country, he concludes in a graphic phrase, will only continue to take on the sad image of a man who, enclosed in an expensive overcoat, thereby hides the deep wounds that ravage his innermost recesses.[165]

All in all, Saco's *Memoria* is an incisive critique of a society based on the values of traditional Hispanic *hidalguia*. Indeed, as a later biographer of Saco has pointed out, its arguments were as valid, a century later, for the Cuba of 1940 as they were for the Cuba of 1840.[166] Even the revolutionary government of modern *fidelista* Cuba has found it useful to reprint it for school purposes. Yet the interesting thing about the *Memoria* is what it leaves out. It hardly touches on the issue of slavery, despite the well-known fact that, as in all slave societies, it is slavery, more than anything else, that denigrates the work ethic (as against the play ethic) by its ascriptive identification of unskilled manual labor with black skin-color. It is true that Saco sees something of that general truth. Thus, he notes, correctly, the correlation between race and occupations, so that agricultural work is the lot of the slaves; the arts, generally, are in the hands of the people of color; while the whites are concentrated in the religious, legal, and medical professions.[167] But when he attempts an explanation of that situation, he prefers to identify essentially secondary causes—the absence of an efficient road system to encourage a local marketing system, the calamitous state of a prison system that does not try to rehabilitate the prisoner, the lack of care for abandoned children, the gross defects of an antiquated educational system.[168] It is true, furthermore, that he shrewdly demolishes the argument of climate (going back as it does to Montesquieu) so often used to explain the absence of white workers in agriculture in the tropics, and a favorite thesis discussed in Saco's later *Supresión del tráfico de esclavos africanos en la isla de Cuba*. It is not climate, he argues, but socioeconomic conditions, that presently discourage white immigration. The dreaded yellow fever can be eliminated by a proper public-health program. A white peasant proprietary class only needs a radical agrarian reform program that will end the tyranny of the large *latifundia*.[169] And is it not true, speaking historically, that some of the world's most advanced civilizations have been located in the tropical and semitropical zones—the Assyrians, Arabs, and Phoenicians in the Old World and the Mexicans and the Peruvians in the New? It is time to stop fooling ourselves with the myth that all inhabitants of warm climates are weak and lazy and all inhabitants of cold climates are strong and virtuous.[170]

Yet when all this has been conceded, Saco cannot bring himself to condemn the primary cause of the Cuban social malaise, the institution of domestic slavery itself. And that, of course, is because of his own fundamentally ambivalent attitude toward the institution. As a liberal, he could not be entirely unaware of the contradiction in principle between liberalism and slavery, and he could reprint in his *Historia de la esclavitud* Varela's noble demand for slavery emancipation, with its assertion that such an act arose naturally out of liberal principles: "Let us not delude ourselves: Constitution, liberty, equality, are synonymous; and slavery and inequality of rights are in opposition to those terms. We pretend in vain to conciliate those opposites."[171] But his class and racial fears deterred him from arriving at Varela's abolitionist conclusion; and he found no contradiction in reprinting in the same work the *Exposición* of the Havana Junta de Fomento, which described in glowing terms the comfortable life of Cuban slaves, both urban and rural, in contrast to the conditions of hunger, cold, and sickness endured by the poor of even the most advanced European societies.[172]

His intellectual energy went mainly into his lifelong campaign for the cessation of the slave trade and a large-scale, planned white immigration into the island, with the end of terminating the "Africanization" of the society. To those twin ideas, linked to each other, he added the recommendation that all African persons found guilty of any crime, or even only of vagrancy, should be deported overseas to Spain or Fernando Po, while others not found so guilty should be encouraged to leave by schemes of voluntary emigration.[173] There should also take place a state-sponsored policy of racial admixture that, as he saw it, would gradually phase out the blacks in favor of the genetically superior whites. In any case, he continues, the ongoing illicit trade daily accelerates the flight of the whites from the land, a process that can only be brought to a halt by the abolition of the trade and a policy of planned white immigration, after the fashion of the United States. The furthest that Saco will go in the matter of emancipation is cautiously to approve the mode of emancipation embodied in the gradualist Columbian law of 1821. All in all, his position is clear: Cuban nationality is that created solely by the 400,000 Cubans who belong to the white race.[174]

Saco, to put it succinctly, was an educated intelligence who could not draw the full, logical conclusions of his liberalism because of his obsessive fears about the racially heterogeneous character of Cuban society. That is painfully evident, especially, in his treatment of the two major themes of nineteenth-century Cuban political thought: national independence from Spain and annexation to the United States. With reference to the annexationist ideology, he was undoubtedly sincere in his opposition on the basis of the argument that annexation would mean, following an inevitable mass immigration of Americans to the new state, complete cultural absorption and the disappearance of Cuban nationhood. But his greater fear, perhaps, was the probable impact of annexation upon the Cuban race question. Statehood in the Union would mean new power for the slave system and fresh imports of slaves into the island. Even more important, there was the vital consideration—as Saco elaborated it in his *Réplica* to Quiepo of 1847—that annexation could only come about by means of war. Spain is weak in Europe, but strong in Cuba; in Cuba, the Spaniards are more Spanish than the Spaniards at home; and Spain will never surrender the last of her empire without a struggle. In such a situation, both sides would inevitably seek an alliance with the Cuban black masses, after the fashion of the Haitian wars earlier. "There is no country in the world," Saco wrote gloomily, "where a revolutionary movement is more dangerous than in Cuba....In our actual circumstances, the political revolution must necessarily be accompanied by the social revolution; and the social revolution is the complete ruin of the Cuban race."[175] Unleash those forces and we will see the horrors of Santo Domingo repeated in Cuba; and an annexationist war would only result in the victory of 600,000 Negroes bathed in the blood of their masters, who would set a terrible example for their brothers in the Southern states of the confederation. That, Saco tells the annexationists, is too high a price for us to pay to be free from the Spanish yoke.[176]

The same race-based phobia made Saco, in turn, the reluctant *independentista*. He clearly perceived, granted Spanish reactionary intransigence, that independence could only come about by armed struggle; and events after 1868 proved him right. In such a struggle (as he analyzed the situation in his *La Esclavitud en Cuba y la revolución de España*), both sides must inevitably recruit the blacks to their standards; and the blacks, in his own phrase, are "our most formidable enemy." That would only end in racial civil war, a horrendous blood bath, and the final extermination of everything that Cuba stood for. Cuba would be lost, not for itself, but for the misguided abolitionists of Spanish liberalism who have never had to deal, as have the Cubans, with Negro insurrections.[177] That those fears were not, in fact, realized during the wars of independence after 1868 makes little difference to the obvious sincerity with which they were entertained. So, Saco could never bring himself to support the national rebellion. Until the end, indeed, he persisted in championing (as in his *Carta de un patriota* of 1872) the autonomist ideal of representative overseas provincial institutions, assuming a liberal attitude in Madrid that never really existed—and assuming, even more unrealistically, a theory of colonial representation in which (as he had outlined as early as 1837 in his *Examen analítico*) the Cuban coloreds would have the "right" to be represented by white propertied electors but not the right to represent themselves.[178] It is ironic, in the light of all that, that he should have had to defend himself, in his various polemical writings, against the gratuitous charge that he was an abolitionist.[179] He was, in fact, as he remarked of himself in the Carta, *un mensajero pacífico del siglo XIX*. He was trapped between his hatred of the colonial regime and his fear of black rebellion.

Saco is of particular interest in the evolution of the proslavery ideology because he represents its more intellectual and less racist character. Living most of his life in exile in the European liberal capitals, he absorbed the new European currents of thought that expressed Anglo-Saxon superiority less in openly racist terms and more in class and cultural terms. Bourgeois class elitism and a vulgar social Darwinism are the tone of his writings, less those of a philosopher than of a publicist. It would have been surprising, after all, if a Cuban liberal exile who had been exposed to the heady intellectual climate of the Parisian salons of the 1840s had expressed his bias in openly Negrophobic terms. His class fears were expressed in the dictum that "in all ages the servile classes have always been the most constant enemies of the tranquillity of peoples."[180] His cultural fears were expressed in his narrow Europocentrist view of Asians, speaking like some lesser Cuban Macaulay or Guizot: "I

agree," he wrote, "that the introduction of Asiatics into Cuba would be useful to her agriculture—but the nauseous corruption of their customs, the religious indifference of many of them, as with the Chinese, the anti-Christian
beliefs of almost all of them, as well as the additional complication they
would add to races so heterogeneous as already exist in that island, are evils
so large in the moral and political order, that they must be a cause of concern
to every good Cuban."[181] Granted those class and cultural prejudices, it
comes as a surprise to learn that the magnum opus to which Saco devoted his
learning was a large history of slavery from ancient times to the present, un-
completed at his death. Yet a reading of the four volumes of the *Historia de
la esclavitud* rapidly makes it evident that there is no cause for surprise at all.
They include some good things, of course; Saco is one of the first Cuban historians to give full weight to the consideration that it was the aboriginal Indians,
and not the Africans, who were the first victims of European colonization in
the Americas, thereby constituting the first chapter of the history of hemispheric slavery. But as a work of original historical scholarship, it is weak. It
is as much chronological narrative as anything else; it hardly addresses itself
to the important issue of the general cultural impact of slavery upon the arts
and customs of the Hispanic-American peoples; its source materials are limited—due in part to the fact that at that time the rich treasures of the European colonial archives were hardly available in any proper order for scholarly
use, but also, in part, due to the fact that (as the American critic Charles
Dana pointed out at the time) Saco had failed to use the work of scholars who
had already published in the field, such as Austin and Maine; and, finally (as
Ortiz has more lately pointed out) the sort of history Saco wrote made it impossible for him to see slavery as a socioeconomic phenomenon.[182] So, it is
difficult to accept the extravagant praise of the Cuban writer Silverio Jorrin,
who, in a moment of misguided zeal, compared Saco's work to Gibbon's
great book.[183] For when one remembers the elements of the *Decline and Fall*
—its massive erudition, its majestic style, its wit, its caustic irony, and its superb rationalism of temper—Saco's effort pales into insignificance. The Caribbean planter class never did, in fact, produce its Gibbon.

THE DEBATE IN THE CUBAN INDEPENDENCE WARS

Both Arango and Saco, of course, were merely the chief protagonists of a
white racist intellectualism that, with few exceptions, infected the entire Cuban intellectual class of the period. Luz y Caballero wrote finely on the theme
of philosophical moralism, but opposed abolition throughout.[184] Joaquín Suárez, of the liberal persuasion, claimed to have found justification for his theory of the natural inferiority of Negroes in his reading of De Tocqueville.[185]
Domingo Delmonte could compose, in his memorial on *La isla de Cuba tal
cual está*, a spirited denunciation of slavery, but only as the political slavery

of white Cubans and not the economic slavery of black Cubans; and we know from the story of Delmonte's patronage of the young Cuban writer Suárez, who wrote the antislavery novel *Fransisco*, that Delmonte sought to persuade the author to tone down the more "subversive" of the book's passages. Even more, we know that Delmonte supported the brutal repression of the uprising of *La Escalera* in 1844, even although it involved the execution of the mulatto poet Plácido whom he had once befriended.[186] Even Varela, who as early as 1822 had written, in his *Memoria*, a distinguished plea for slavery abolition, could object to the translation of Comte's treatise on legislation on the ground that it contained passages favorable to the idea of equality between the white and black races.[187] In this whole tradition—obsessed as it was, like Saco, with the morbid fear of racial contamination—it was a rare scholar and *pensador* like Bachiller y Morales who, in his pioneer work, *Los Negros*, could lay the foundations of the study, at once serious and sympathetic, of *afrocubanismo*. As a tradition, it saw the colored Cuban, in Varela's phrase, as a *signo de ignominia*, a shameful stain—like the blood on Lady Macbeth's hands—on the face of white Cuba. So, for all of the real patriotism of its leading literary figures—Saco, Luz y Caballero, Delmonte —theirs, as a later Cuban critic has put it in a lively polemic, was no more than a *falsa cubanidad*.[188] It is difficult to accept the thesis put out by the later schools of Cuban patriotic nationalism—Chacon y Calvo, Fernándo Ortiz, Ponte Domínguez, Vidal Morales, Figarola Caneda, Medardo Vitier, and others—that the literary intelligentsia of the period between 1820 and 1868, the year that marked the beginning of the First War of Independence, led a vigorous campaign against the slavery institution.

The questions of race and color, indeed, lay at the heart of all Cuban political thought. That can be seen, most demonstrably, in the way in which they shaped at once the movement for independence from Spain and the contrary movement in favor of annexation to the United States. Neither movement can be fully understood save by recognizing that both of them were efforts, in different ways, to contain the ever-present danger, as it was seen, of a Cuba dominated by the brown-black majority. The contemporary historian Pedro José Guiteras saw both ideologies as an unnecessary aberration fatally dividing the Cuban liberal forces;[189] but it is clear that his viewpoint failed to understand how both were inevitable once they were seen within the framework of the Cuban slave society. For the annexationists, completely opportunistic, the driving force was the ever-present fear that a weak Spain would yield to British pressure and general European liberal opinion and would promulgate slavery abolition—the most effective safeguard against that contingency being incorporation, as yet another slave state, in the American Union. For it was hardly imaginable that a Cuban *pensador* like Betancourt Cisneros, not to speak of a Cuban aristocrat like the Conde de Pozos Dulces, could have been enamored of either the vulgar materialism or the populist democracy of the United States. Yet, contrary to Saco's lifelong advocacy of the theme that annexation would mean, certainly, the cultural absorption of Cuba, they were prepared to take that risk simply because loss of sovereignty to the American power was preferable to loss of their slave property. The ties of Cuba with Europe, wrote Madan, present alternatives to the status of the slaves, and will surely mean emancipation.[190] "Domestic slavery," wrote Narciso López, "is not a primitive social phenomenon of Cuba alone, nor is it incompatible with the liberty of the citizen body. Ancient and modern history shows us that, and nearby you have the example of the United States, where three million slaves do not impede but rather reinforce the most liberal institutions of the world."[191] Annexationism, then, was trapped within its own contradictions: it wanted a revolt against Spain, yet its primary concern for the retention of slavery meant that it could not call upon the necessary help of the slave population in the endeavor—and Villaverde noted in his diary the remark of the wealthy planter José L. Alfonso that "if it was certain that they could count on the support of the people of color he would be the first to oppose the revolution with all his might."[192] That annexationism, in fact, was nothing more than an ideology crassly based on material interests can be seen from the fact that it flourished most vigorously after 1848, when Spain seemed likely to be engulfed in the general revolutionary conflagration of the continent, and died after the 1860s, when the American Civil War terminated slavery in the North American democracy itself.

Yet the antiannexationist wing of the liberal-reformist element was no less trapped in its own contradictions. As Cepero Bonilla has aptly pointed out, both annexationists and antiannexationists shared the same common ground of racism. The antiannexationists opposed union with the United States, not for any dislike of the American capitalist system—it is worth noting that in his long reply of 1849 to his critics, Saco emphasized the factors of language and nationality (both of which, he argued, are obliterated by the massive absorptive drive of the American system) rather than the factor, later so magisterially advanced by Martí, of the profit-making materialism of the American business civilization[193]—but because, quite simply, they believed that such a union would encourage the Cuban slaves to revolt in response to American democratic ideas. They would respond to the American Declaration of Independence as the Saint Domingue slaves earlier had responded to the Declaration of the Rights of Man. And in any case, union could only come about through a war between Spain and the United States, which again could only excite the slaves into rebellious activity. The antiannexationists hated Spain. But they hated and feared their own slave population even more. Their difference with their annexationist opponents, therefore, was one of strategy only, not of first principle. For both sides, the morbid memory of the "horrors of Haiti" stifled every movement towards reform. Both shared the conviction, summed up in the slogan of their North American friends, that "better Cuba were obliterated than 'Jamaicanized' by Negrophilism." Even Varela, humanist as he was, could not entirely escape the note of racial fear. "Let us not deceive ourselves," he wrote in his 1823 *Memoria*, "the island of Cuba is a colossus; but it is founded on sand." The only solution, he added, is a gradual emancipation that will eliminate the disaffection of the blacks. Otherwise, there will take place a general revolt that will reduce the island to an economy of poor fishermen. "As far as Bolívar is concerned," he concluded ominously, "it is well-known in Havana that he has said that with two thousand men under the banner of liberty he could take the island of Cuba, once he moved forward with his plans."[194]

In the end, then, all of these liberal groups resisted any kind of movement —practical reform, United States intervention, most of all an open war of liberation against Spain—that would shatter the fragile edifice of the slave-based society. They ended up in an ideological stance, therefore, not very different from, for example, the pragmatic conservatism of the historian Pezuela, whose *Historia de la isla de Cuba* furnished the historical background to his argument, presented in his *Necesidades de Cuba*, that reforms, however necessary, should seek to rehabilitate, rather than to weaken, the central Spanish power and that ill-considered reforms, like those propounded by the liberal Constitution of 1812, could only have the scandalous consequence of encouraging insurrections in which the title of general would be obtained by Indians, mulattoes, and even Negroes of Africa.[195]

The final example of the debilitating influence of racist fears on the Cuban liberal ideology was, of course, that of the first war of independence (1868–78). The fatal ambivalence of Saco in the face of that event has already been noted. Others showed similar attitudes. They had to decide, quite simply, whether they preferred a free Cuba without slaves or a colonial Cuba with slaves. Those who elected to join the revolution, like Morales Lemus, Mestre, Echevarría, and the so-called *aldamista* group (after the writer Domingo Aldama), did so with reservations, for throughout they sought alternatives— such as the grant of autonomy from Spain or even the old dream of annexation—that would prevent the one, single act they feared most, abolition of slavery. They sought to prove that the new republican constitution adopted by the revolutionary forces was a political rather than a social document, thus prohibiting, as they saw it, any move to rearrange what they called, euphemistically, the balance of races in the society. If, wrote Zambrana, the revolution is to keep the warm support of the comfortable classes, it is urgent that the prestige of the revolution not be compromised by any measures that stimulate their alarm and evoke their disaffection.[196] Their position had been made clear, even before the revolution, in the 1866 *Informe* on the possibilities of slavery abolition. They recognized, albeit reluctantly, the inevitability of abolition. But their nationalism, however sincere, could not stomach a new Cuba based on full equality of rights between all Cubans, irrespective of color. The condition of ignorance that characterizes the greater part of the free class of colored persons, wrote Morales Lemus, gives birth to a politics of prudence that requires that it is not granted a political participation equal to the white class. Echeverría was even more emphatic. "We recognize and acknowledge, finally," he wrote, "that humanity and progress alike demand that we break the chains of the slave, but in such a way that the more advanced race does not abdicate its preponderance, for no need at all, especially when confronted with the threat of uncivilized rabbles; to the end that civilization does not regress backwards to barbarous centuries, nor much less incautiously face the harsh alternative of being exterminated by, or having to exterminate, a semi-barbarous people."[197] That dogma of white supremacy made it impossible for the reformers wholly to embrace the revolutionary movement; as disciples of Saco, they could not forget his grim warning that revolution in Cuba necessarily entailed the liberty of the slaves. So, as Cepero Bonilla puts it, they entered into the revolution, but the revolution did not enter into them.[198] Their sense of nationalism was fatally compromised by their fear of racial upheaval. They remained to the end, then, in Martí's graphic phrase, the party of permanent equivocation.

The more *incondicionalista* (uncompromising) wing of the party accepted, more honestly, the full logic of their racist position: better Spain with slavery than Cuba without it. Men like Azcárate and Zayas placed their pens at the service of the colonial power, using language even more scabrous, if that were possible, than that of their more "liberal" coreligionists. Azcárate wrote in his *Votos de un Cubano*:

> I am not a separatist because I hold to the inner conviction that Cuba cannot be independent, nor is there any means of avoiding the fact that the war, if continued, will convert us into the expiatory victims of the slavery of the negroes; because the so much desired annexation of Cuba to the United States, evidence of our impotency to become independent, will increase the possibilities of the future predominance of the negro race...drowned in the horrendous abyss of a collision of races: the only consequence that a war of independence can have...we are the determined and sincere enemies of the independence of Cuba because, for us, that independence means either the abyss of a racial civil war or the surrender of nationality."

In his *Cuba: Su porvenir*, Zayas wrote in a similar vein:

> My hope for Cuba is, that cleansed of the leprosy of forced labor that today contaminates everything, it may educate its sons in the ethic of work, and fortify them in virtue and absolute respect for law, the immediate fruits of the extirpation of that cancer; I hope that the white population, under a regime productive and honoring work, will increase and acquire the preponderance that it ought to have, as much for reasons of its numbers as for its excellent and strong qualities, so that this land, so beautiful, will without question belong to the Caucasian family, and that the Latin race, which today is the foundation of its population, will not be obliged to cowardly surrender its convictions, thereby confessing its incapacity to form a nation, and dishonoring itself before the *familia sajona* [Anglo-Saxon family].

He ends by envisaging a new Cuba that could constitute a new power in the Gulf of Mexico, counteracting both the disgraceful republics to the south and the United States to the north. But it would have to be, he concludes, a Cuba that does not obtain its freedom to become simply another Haiti or Santo Domingo; better, if that were so, that it become absorbed, as the lesser of two evils, by the North American republic.[199]

Looked at in general terms, nineteenth century Cuban thought must be seen, of course, in terms of its international context. As is well known, all of the Latin American political and intellectual elites were Old World–oriented —influenced, both through education and travel, by the dominant European philosophies: liberalism, romanticism, positivism, and the rest. They saw themselves, in Sarmiento's famous phrase, as trapped between European civilization and American barbarism. That influence was strengthened in the case of Cuba by the fact that the Spanish colony throughout the century became an acrimonious international issue, involving at once Spain, Britain, and the United States. All of the European philosophies, in one way or another, were the ideological banner of the victorious European bourgeoisie; the emergent Cuban bourgeoisie, naturally, embraced them as the primordial arguments in defense of its own struggle. But because that struggle, internally, was not only a class struggle but a racial struggle, the Cuban ideologues found it necessary to add to the class bias of the European bourgeois ideology the further dimension of a racist bias.

The class element has been underscored, with disarming frankness, by the later conservative historian of Cuban ideology, Menocal y Cueto, in his *Origen y desarrollo del pensamiento cubano* of 1947. In tones of undisguised sympathy, he delineates clearly the class basis of the Cuban reform movement.

> It is undeniable that *evolucionismo*, propounded by the opulent Cuban classes in their distinct social groupings, was opposed with conviction to independence achieved through violence; so, if those classes were at odds with the Spanish privileged elements who ill-treated them so remorselessly, they no less feared the threat of the preponderance of the lower classes, composed in the main of social elements of a primitive mentality, which would tend not only to replace the colonial regime in the enjoyment of privileges and monopolies, but would also seek to appropriate the wealth created with so much sacrifice and privation....Cuban wealth once built up and established, it was not possible or conceivable that there should grow up a political situation that would place that wealth into the hands of an electoral majority which, in the first place, lacked anything of civilization and, in the second, had not contributed anything to the conception and the growth of that wealth; such a situation would have resulted in direct damage to the community as a whole. For that reason the manufacturers of the *conciencia cubana* [Cuban national conscience] and the wealth-creating classes in the period before 1868 had no choice but to fear the immediate or imminent establishment of a *regimen-democrático*; out of sheer necessity such a system would have to be watered down before it could be handed over to an ignorant population that did not know how to use rights.[200]

But this sort of rationalization was not enough. Granted the ethnic config-
uration of the Cuban social body, it was also necessary to denigrate the social
majority in its racial character. A typical expression of that exercise is to be
found in the report of the 1866 Cuban commissioners elected to advise Madrid
on constitutional reform. They state:

> The signatories (of the report) do not presume to resolve the controversial question
> as to whether one or the other of the different human races is organically superior,
> or whether the differences that they exhibit proceed only from local and transitory
> accidents, and can be susceptible to elimination by means of changing the context
> and the conditions in which they have been formed. It is sufficient for our thesis to
> note here that the one, the white or Caucasian race, today occupies the highest
> rung of the ladder of progress considered in its intellectual and moral manifesta-
> tions; that it is that class that has accumulated in its very fibre and assimilated into
> its person all of the talents of human perfectability; and has engineered the achieve-
> ment in substance of the most useful and splendid conquests, so that that record
> entrusts to that class the destiny, present and future, of the country, and thus as-
> sures that thereby it maintains its superior influence and retains its preponderance
> over the other races that compose the society. An element of order and stability, no
> other race but this can spread and perpetuate the culture of the spirit and the
> qualities of the moral universe.[201]

The theory of the master class thus becomes a theory of the master race.

Yet it would be erroneous to believe that Cuban racism was all that high-
minded. The 1866 commissioners, after all, were writing for European chan-
celleries, many of whose members, even in Spain, were liberals. To catch the
more raucous and vulgar spirit of the racism, it is necessary to look at the literature more specifically meant for home consumption. All of the pseudoscientific fads of the century—craniology, physiognomy, phrenology—were
invoked to prove the innate inferiority of the nonwhite races. The baron de
Vastey had noted, somewhat earlier, how that was so in the French and English cases. Anatomists like Barrère and Winslow considered that the bile of
Negroes was of a color *plus foncée* (thicker) than that of Europeans; authors
like Somering and Dr. Rush advanced the specious argument that black skin
color arose from a hereditary leprosy; and Jedediah Morse discovered the superiority of the white in cranial formation.[202] All of those arguments, and similar ones, reappeared in the Cuban case. The general prejudice even appears,
incongruously, in the antislavery titles of the Cuban liberal novelists of the
time. The writer and politician Morua Delgado thus protested, in his pamphlet of 1892, against the slanderous portrait of the mulatto type contained
even in a novel like Villaverde's *Cecila Valdés*, considered the most antislavery in tone of them all; and the animus lasted well into the later twentieth
century, evidenced in the curious story written by the novelist Hernández Cata
in 1917, in which the mulatto antihero—denied entry to the priesthood on
the ground that while black saints were possible in the Catholic Church black
priests were not—finally ends a frustrated life by being appointed, absurdly,
to the position of Cuban consul in the city of Birmingham, England.[203]

GENERAL CONCLUSION

What then, by way of conclusion, must be said about the proslavery ideology in its special New World locale of the Caribbean plantocratic order? Modern research in the disciplines of social and cultural anthropology has shown that it is possible to posit the existence of clearly defined structural-functional regularities in the plantation system of the region, as well as the existence of territorial diversities traceable to the differences among the socioeconomic-cultural mores brought in by the different European colonizing powers. A similar distinction between overall regularities and subtypical differentiations can be made in the analysis of the ideological superstructure that grew up, over the prolonged slavery period, between the English, Dutch, French, and Spanish Antillean systems.

The differentiae of the superstructure are readily identifiable. All of the colonizers brought with them the general values of Europe shaped by Renaissance, Reformation, and Counter-Reformation. But each motherland gave its particular impress to the general pattern: Catholic or Protestant, monarchical or republican. Linguistic colonialism, again, was a general feature, for all of the colonizer-planter groups conducted a process whereby the slave, forced to yield up his own language forms, was compelled to learn some vulgar variant of the master language in order to survive: it would have been unheard of for a planter to learn, say, Ibo or Ashanti, while for the middle "free colored" groups it became a symbol of respectability to speak the metropolitan language perfectly. Language thus became a value-symbol, a cultural mechanism to reinforce the general ideology of white superiority and black inferiority. It thus shaped, permanently, the linguistic map of the Caribbean. But again, each separate European power gave particular expression to the general practice. So, in the English Caribbean, it was the juxtaposition of "good" English and "bad" English; in the French islands, the rivalry between Parisian French and local patois; in the Dutch territories, the contest between Lowland Dutch and papiamento; and in the Hispanic Antilles the animosity between classical Spanish and the folk idioms of Boricuan Spanish and Afro-Cuban Spanish.

Or, yet again, there were the variations played on the general theme of the ideology of technology. All of the sugar islands joined in the adulation of the creoledom of King Sugar. As Ortiz has shown magisterially, sugar was not only a mode of economic production in the tropical capital-labor regime; it was also, in the imaginary world that the plantocracy constructed, a sort of divine, mystical cult.[204] But even here, at the very material base of the planter ideology, there were wheels within wheels. The attitude of the Jamaican planter of the 1760s was in many ways different from the attitude of the Cuban planter of the 1860s. Ragatz has described in a chapter of his classic study the ingrained technological conservatism of the English Caribbean planters and their opposition to innovations such as the plow and the steam engine in their tropical agriculture.[205] By contrast, Fraginals's classic work describes how successive generations of Cuban planters, including the self-made Spanish immigrant entrepreneurs and the plantation corporate managers who came to dominate the industry after the middle of the century, used every techno- logical innovation to direct the transition from the old *trapiche* (traditional grinding machine), with its more patriarchial form of slavery, to the more modern *ingenio* (sugar mill), based on a more systematic exploitation of a landless labor force.[206] The difference, of course, went back to the nature of the market system within which each group operated; for whereas the Jamai- cans operated within a closed and protective British market that only encour- aged their mercantilist prejudices, the Cubans, almost from the beginning, had to learn to survive in a world free-trade capitalist market far more com- petitive in its character. That difference, obviously, did not mean that Cuba, any more than Jamaica, could escape the basic contradiction of the slave pro- ductive regime, so that even in Cuba the modernization process never ran its full course, simply because too many planters preferred to rely on the twin factors of unparalleled soil fertility and a ready supply of cheap, unskilled slave labor rather than to risk capital in innovative methods that required skilled wage-labor. Even so, the difference was noticeable; and a work like Reynoso's classic manual of 1862, *Ensayo sobre el cultivo de la caña de azúcar* —which stands out, like the earlier work of Achard and Deresne, as a lead- ing item in the exhaustive bibliography on sugar put out by Ling Roth in 1890[207]—was received with enthusiasm in Havana, while, by contrast, the few individual planters in Jamaica who tried new experimental methods got prac- tically nowhere in the face of entrenched custom.

Yet in the last resort, the structural-functional regularities constituted the more important properties of the slave system. It was—from Cuba to the Guianas—a regional economic system, notwithstanding the fact that it never developed a regional political thought. Whatever the very real variations from sugar island to sugar island—in size of estate, white-mulatto-black popula- tion ratios, residency versus absenteeism in the planter group, conditions of work and the relative degrees of harshness, and so on—the system every- where was based on, as it were, a series of common propositions. (1) In spirit, it was a system geared exclusively to capital investment for continuing capital accumulation; (2) in form, it was an industrial-type discipline of African gang slavery, so that capitalist-type class distinctions became assimilated into non-capitalist-type racial caste lines; (3) its successful operation, therefore, depended upon the development, on the part of the master groups, of methods of control and coercion aimed not only at productive work discipline and maximum productivity on the part of the subject groups but also at habits of respect and obedience in a total master-slave relationship in which the usual distinctions of class were compounded by the more volatile distinctions of race and color.

Ideally, no doubt, the European and Creole master groups hoped to bring together all of those purposes into a single, harmonious whole. Their institutional ideal was probably of some such kind. "Though rarely voiced in any explicit detail," Mintz and Price opine, "it is clear that the European colonists hoped for the 'acculturation' of slave populations to a total acceptance of slave status—and surely many of them believed that proper methods, unrelenting discipline, and enough time would bring this about."[208] To some extent, it was the vision of the colonial gentleman class to become, so to speak, an European territorial baronage overseas: summed up in Bolingbroke's lyrical invitation to young British farmers, in his account of Guiana at the turn of the eighteenth century, *A Voyage to the Demerary, 1799–1806*, to emigrate to a society "where the superintendence of an agricultural concern, confers not merely the rank of a country gentleman, but that baron-like authority over the growing population of the vassals, which the ancestors of the country gentleman enjoyed in England during the feudal ages."[209] To some extent, it was the deluded belief, perhaps at times sincerely accepted by its protagonists, that the West Indian slaves were genuinely a happy and contented crowd: summed up in the ease with which "Monk" Lewis, in his *Journal* recording his visits to his Jamaican estates in the period after Waterloo, could persuade himself, in a spirit of Sternian whimsy, that his slaves were really black rustics enjoying a simple life of singing, dancing, and general jollity.[210] Or yet again, there was the religious gloss on all of this presented by the clerical apologists of the system: So, the cleric-historian Bridges advanced in his *Annals* the pleasing picture of a new multiracial community moving, under the wise guidance of the slaveowners, to a fuller civilization, while a little later Gardner's *History of Jamaica* treated the theme of a West Indian society becoming, once the distorting element of slavery had been removed, a sort of overseas English Victorian society tempered by the civilizing influence of Christianity.[211]

But this was little more, as it were, than the utopian element of the planter belief-system. That things were different, and known to be different, is evident from the nonutopian elements of the system. There were the slave laws revised regularly by the island assemblies and councils, with their mass of harsh and detailed punishment for every sort of slave misbehavior, from independent economic activity to traveling without a pass, on to attempted escape, insubordinate behavior to whites, and, of course, rebellion—and all of them resting on the planter recognition of the truth, that as Sir William Young (himself a West Indian) put it, "the authority of the few over the many rests everywhere on the resources for sustaining and enforcing it."[212] Goveia's study of the slave legislation in the case of the later eighteenth century British Leeward Islands is significant in this respect, for it shows that despite a noticeable relaxation of statutory punishments (the enactments of Antigua and St. Kitts prohibiting mutilation of slaves, for example) and furthermore, despite evidence of growing leniency in the administration of slave offenses (as in the case of the Montserrat Council), the underlying principle of all of the legislation was the strict subordination of the slave population. Even more than that: the subordination was seen not merely as a necessary device to maintain the sugar economy but as an indispensable mechanism for maintaining a whole social and moral order that, in the planter mentality, became almost an end in itself, even when its economic raison d'être had disappeared. "The slave system," concludes Goveia, "had become more than an economic enterprise which could be abandoned when it became unprofitable. It had become the very basis of organized society throughout the British West Indies, and therefore it was believed to be an indispensable element in maintaining the existing social structure and in preserving law and order in the community. The idea of a society in which Negroes were released from their subordination and allowed legal equality with whites was so antithetical to the principles on which the slave society rested that it seemed to threaten complete social dissolution and chaos."[213]

That general attitude—in which racial hostility superseded even economic self-interest—was, in turn, in itself part cause and part result of the overall climate of opinion that invested every New World plantation. For it was, in general, an isolated world of an island of whites surrounded by an ocean of blacks. In Goveia's words, the source of the whites' strength—their exclusive, oligarchical control over the blacks—was also the source of their weakness. The mental atmosphere of the white world was therefore dominated by the ever-present fear of black servile revolt, even when objective conditions made it highly unlikely. Miss Janet Schaw noted the fear among the Antiguan planters of the 1770s, especially during the dangerous Christmas holiday season.[214] Periods of war made the fear even more endemic, for it was yet another paranoic conviction of the planter mind that the planters of a rival island would even stoop to fomenting slave unrest in the general struggle of interisland economic competition. "I am sure," wrote Lady Nugent in Jamaica in 1805, "that the blacks are to be as much dreaded as the French."[215]

Granted this overriding fear, it was only natural that the Caribbean ruling class, like ruling classes everywhere, should construct, as one defense mechanism, a code of behavior every member was required to observe. The literature is full of anxious admonitions on that score. Not only was the massa-planter the symbol of white authority; he also lived, as Lewis noted, an open life in tropical housing conditions that allowed little room for privacy. The behavioral code, then, demanded of him that he not compromise his authority, and thereby the collective prestige of the white race, by behavior that could call it into question. The message ran from one extreme to the other. On the one hand, it admonished masters against barbaric treatment that could only be counterproductive; and the Huggins case of 1810 in Nevis and the Hodge case in the Virgin Islands a little later showed that even local-planter-controlled assemblies would at times move swiftly against individual masters who exercised needless brutality against their charges.[216] On the other hand, and far more frequently, it brought planter public opinion to bear against those, and especially newcomers, who "spoiled" the blacks by inconsiderate kindness: Lady Nugent was gently reprimanded by her Jamaican lady friends and told that dancing with Negroes at a plantation house party, as if it were nothing more than a servants' hall affair in England, could only have the effect of putting them on an equal footing with whites and might even produce a rebellion in the island;[217] while "Monk" Lewis found, to his astonishment, that the local magistracy considered him a threat to public order merely because he had advocated the "dangerous doctrine" that the evidence of Negroes should be permitted in court proceedings against whites.[218] In other slave colonies reprimand moved on to persecution. The missionary John Smith faced martyrdom in British Guiana; d'Auberteuil met imprisonment in Saint Domingue; and the antislavery voices in Cuba, like Varela and Martí, found it safer to live most of their lives in exile. In all of these cases the cardinal tenet of the planter creed was at stake, summed up in the protest of the West Indian planters and merchants in London to the British government that "opinion governs the world, and the moment the Negroes shall lose their opinion of the Superiority of White Men, the authority of the White Men will become precarious."[219]

The planter creed, in fact, was caught on the horns of a terrible dilemma. It needed slavery. At the same time, it feared slavery. If only, it seemed at times to be saying, we could have slavery without the slave, the institution without the person. It could not solve the problem with a policy of expulsion —following the original Spanish policy of the expulsion of the Jews and the Moors in the fifteenth and sixteenth centuries—nor with a policy of extermination—following the original English and French policy of the extermination of the Caribs in the seventeenth century—for its very existence depended upon the extracted surplus value of slave labor. Prudence itself dictated considerate treatment; after all, to kill or seriously maim a slave was to destroy a principal source of production, to risk a reduction of fixed capital. Conservation, therefore, became an important maxim of the planter's manual of estate management. Rochefort laid down the general rule early on in his book of the 1650s. "It is therefore requisite," he wrote, "that in the conduct of them (the slaves) there should be a mean observed between extreme severity and too much indulgence, by those who would keep them in awe, and make the best advantage of them."[220] The day's work, after all, had to be done. The estate had to show a profit at the end of the financial year or go into bankruptcy, to be taken over by a rapacious merchant or lawyer (and, indeed, the hatred of the town merchant-lawyer class was always a very real subsidiary element in the total planter ideology). Many a planter or overseer, then, must have found it more productive, in the long run, to cajole the slave-workman than to coerce him—making them amateur psychologists, as it were, of the slave character. That explains yet another note in the planter ideology, its indignation, not always insincere, at the temptation of its abolitionist critics to portray the plantation as a scenario of daily conflict between cruel masters and

suffering slaves. To the degree that this was so, the proslavery maxim that
the interest of the master guaranteed the welfare of the slave was an important half-truth: "Be assured, you philanthropists who are so alarmed by this
institution," declared Dubuisson in the Saint Domingue case, "that the lives
of our slaves are too costly to us for us to deal with them unreasonably."[221]

But it was a half-truth only, for a combination of other considerations—
the fear of "spoiling" the slave, the savage pressure to produce as rapidly as
possible with a high cost in lives, the planter's cherished belief that it was better to rely on a steady stream of new imported labor than to nurture the existing labor force and supplement it by planned natural increase—placed a real
and serious limit on the policy of prudence. The appalling work regime of the
plantation—and it is the defect of a document like Lewis's *Journal* that it
shows us the slave at play rather than at work—meant that the slave, literally, was worked to death. No human material would tolerate such a regime
except under the stimulus of steady and systematic pressure, mercilessly executed. It followed logically, as the planter mind saw it, that the only sure control lay, not in the policy of prudence, but in a policy of terror. The attitude
was summed up in the defiant defense of the Saint Domingue planter Lejeune
in his celebrated trial of 1788. He declared:

> My cause in this matter becomes the cause of every *colon* . . . . The unhappy condi-
> tion of the negro leads him naturally to detest us. It is only force and violence that
> restrains him; he is bound to harbor an implacable hatred in his heart, and if he
> does not visit upon us all the hurt of which he is capable it is only because his readi-
> ness to do so is chained down by terror; so, if we do not make his chains as heavy
> as, proportionately, to the dangers that we run with him, if we let loose his hatred
> from the present state in which it is stifled, what can prevent him from attempting
> to break the chains? The bird trapped in its cage will take advantage of the slight-
> est negligence to make its escape. I dare to assert that there is only wanting in the
> negroes sufficient courage and resolution to purchase their liberty by means of the
> blood of their masters. Just one single step is necessary to make them aware of
> what it is they have in their power to accomplish . . . it is only fear and the equity of
> the law that holds back the negro from stabbing his master in the back, only the
> sensation of the absolute power that we hold over his person. Take away that rein,
> and he will try everything.[222]

Grim, uncompromising, realistic, this is the language of naked power, stripped
of any pretense at apology or moralizing justification. It is the language of
Hobbes, not of Rousseau. Consent yields to fear. There is no room for the
social contract; everything is in the state of nature.

To read that kind of defense is to recognize the fundamental character of
the slavery institution: the difference between its essences and its accidents.
The policy of terror was its essence; the policy of prudence, only one of its accidents. As a modern Guyanese scholar has put it, placing the matter in the
context of a general principle:

The fundamental element of the terror process is the specific act or threat of violence which induces a general psychic state of extreme fear, which in turn produces typical patterns of reactive behavior. The system of violence may be a means of destruction, an instrument of punishment, or a method of control. One could construct a typology of power systems based on the use of violence. At one pole are systems that use violence as a last resort; at the other, those that use it as a first measure. Were we to fill out this skeleton with the flesh of historical experience, we could identify at one pole the systems blessed with concord, in which power is supported by minimal force, and in which violence is truly an *ultima ratio*. At the other extreme, we should find the terror systems, in which violence is *prima ratio potestatis*. Plantation despotism, which punished the smallest infractions with the severest violence, is to be placed nearer the latter pole.[223]

How empty was the policy of prudence, as distinct from the reality of that policy of terror, is evident enough from the record of amelioration in the sugar colonies, based as it was on the precepts of prudence. The record, as already noted, was almost wholly negative. No doubt there was a real spirit of pity for the lot of the nonwhites within the "moderate" elements; even a planter-historian as obdurate as Long could write a sympathetic account of the social tragedy of the light-skinned illegitimate sons and daughters of Jamaican white fathers who, educated as young ladies at finishing schools in Chelsea or as young men at Eton itself, returned to the island only to find themselves in a no-man's-land, accepted neither by the white parental society nor by the black slave society.[224] Yet that spirit of pity could never bring even the moderate voices—much more sympathetic than Long—to a wholesale denial of the system. That is why Edwards, in the Jamaican case, weighing his humanitarian spirit against what he termed the "absolute coercive necessity" of the system, came down finally in favor of the latter, and why even a plantocrat like Richard Barrett who, much more than Edwards, had so imbibed the Enlightenment spirit that he was generally regarded as an agnostic, perhaps even an atheist, could remain as a leader of his class in the 1820s and 1830s in its struggle to maintain slavery.[225] That is why, again, d'Auberteuil, in the Saint Domingue case, while readily conceding that liberty is what the slave wants most, deprived the concession of any real meaning by recommending that freedom should only be granted to those few slaves who in moments of crisis had demonstrated loyalty and respect to masters; for, he added, to give a slave freedom simply because he has cooked well for twenty years is as ridiculous as allowing membership in the Academy of Sciences to a man who can write the letters of the alphabet exactly.[226] That is why, finally, in the Cuban case, when Zarragoitia, as the voice of the nonsugar, cattle-raising economy of the eastern province, came to write his important report of 1805 to the *Real Consulado* (royal tribunal), he took issue on many counts with the sugar planters' viewpoint but could not bring himself, in the final instance, to impugn their sugar-obsessed capitalist ideology or to challenge its slave-labor base.[227] In all of these cases, certainly, there were "reformers" who did not accept the status quo in its entirety, for it would be idle to suppose that in the plantocratic membership, as in all ruling classes, there did not exist different factions espousing different views. Yet the differences were always about tactics, never about the leading principle of the slave system. The arguments of the reformers in favor of better treatment of the slaves—more protection, for example, in the courts—were in themselves proslavery, since better treatment was seen as weakening the case for early emancipation.

For all the accidents of the system—pity, prudence, amelioration, the nice legalistic distinctions between the various slave codes, the phenomenon of what Marvin Harris has called the "myth of the friendly master"[228]—were fragile plants bound to wither away under the gross pressures of the moral atmosphere that was at the heart of slavery and that constituted its essence. Any social order in which the exercise of authority by one group or class over another is not tempered by accountability to a neutral sovereignty or by internal moral constraint rapidly degenerates into unbridled absolutism. The ultimate moral criticism of New World slavery, then, was not that it produced individual cruel planter-masters but, rather, that it was governed, to its innermost recesses, by a general spirit of amoral caprice in which all human sentiment was eroded by the daily habit of irresponsible and untrammeled power. The Swiss traveler Girod-Chantrans acutely perceived how that general spirit was the result of the transition from Europe to America, illustrating, as it were, the Americanization of metropolitan European values. "Every day in this colony," he observed of Saint Domingue in 1782, "one sees young people newly arrived who show themselves to be at first human and sensible, and assert themselves with warmth against the tyranny (of the masters), and who end up by being almost as harsh as the oldest inhabitants....After a certain time, naturalized in some fashion in the New World, the European becomes a different man." Moreau de Saint-Méry commented on the same spirit of callousness in the white Creole youth, contracted indeed in childhood itself. Dr. Pinckard also noted it in the womenfolk of the Dutch planters in the Guiana of the 1790s: "The corporal punishment of slaves is so common," he wrote, "that instead of exciting the repugnant sensations, felt by Europeans on first witnessing it, scarcely does it produce, in the breasts of those accustomed to the West Indies, even the slightest glow of compassion."[229]

There is implicit in observations such as these the final justificatory argument of the proslavery creed. America, the argument goes, is not Europe. The truths, whether religious or philosophical, that Europe regards as universalist relate only, in fact, to European particular customs and experience. In America, where customs and experience are radically different, those truths are irrelevant. America must only be judged by American standards. Thus, the earlier idea of America, developed in the earlier literature of the European Utopians, as a new world of paradisiacal innocence and an ideal poetic landscape against which the ills of European society could be critically measured, was cleverly perverted by the Caribbean slavocracy into a thesis placed at the service of the slavery system. The Europeans had used it, so to say, in order to speak for Caliban. The Caribbeans used it in order to speak for Prospero.

A final observation is in order on the proslavery ideology. It would be naive to assume that, as slavery ended, it also ended. Ideological systems long survive the concrete economic conditions that originally give rise to them. In the Caribbean case a particular expression of that truth is to be found in the French Antilles. Slavery there was abolished finally in 1848. But the proslavery racism survived for the rest of the century and, indeed, into the twentieth-century proper. The white Creole descendants of the old sugarocracy never really surrendered the claim that by skin color alone they were the natural ruling class of the society. The claim received fresh impetus with the arrival, after 1870, of the Third Republic. For in the ideas of the new national status, the reactionary Antillean forces perceived all the evil and malignant forces hostile to their continuing hegemony: universal suffrage, secular schooling, republican egalitarianism, the primacy of the civil power, the rights of man as applied to the colonies, and anticlericalism. Like the colons of Saint Domingue in 1789, the Antillean ruling groups a century later proclaimed their loyalty to France. But the France they had in mind was the France of traditional yesterday, in which blacks and mulattoes knew their place as natural inferiors. It was an attitude, all in all, wholly reactionary; like their counterparts in Paris, these Antillean forces would substitute the Second Empire for the Third Republic at the slightest opportunity.

Nothing better illustrates the truth of all this than a study of the right-wing colonial press of the township of Saint Pierre in Martinique in the last two decades of the century before it was destroyed by the volcanic eruption of Mount Pelée in 1902. The contents of that press are full of all the vitriolic hatred of the Third Republic typical of the right-wing elements in France itself—the only difference being, of course, that the hatred is expressed in Antillean terms. It is an open and virulent racism, expressed in the most gross and vulgar terms. The anatomical characteristics of the Negro show him to be of small cranial size, with a brain so tiny that it explains why he is lazy, apathetic, untrustworthy, more given to idiocy than to mere folly. He has none of the sensibility or sensitivity of the European. He is an infant who has never grown up. The Koran of Muhammad tells us that all peoples have their prophets except the Negro. The present state of Haiti is proof that the Negro race is innately incapable of morality, self-government, and philosophy, thus proving at one and the same time its natural inferiority and the essential justice of slavery—a form natural to such inferior people. Slavery, indeed, is a natural state in which the Negro must accept the rule of the white master in the same way as the domesticated animal accepts the rule of his human owner. So, Toussaint L'Ouverture was a man certainly of high intelligence but mutilated by his antiwhite hatred, his crimes and his massacres—surely a lesson to all those misguided Antilleans who dream of separation from France. So, too, Schoelcher cannot be condemned too severely: He seeks to pollute the racial purity of his own race; he is indeed the vampire of his race; he dreams of a new mulatto domination in the Antilles while at the same time, as a Frenchman of Alsatian birth, he ignores the continuing subjection of Alsace and Lorraine to the German enemy. The Negro, to sum it all up, is more akin to the monkey than to other human races. That dictates all else. The mulatto politicians of the day, who are, in any case, only despicable renegade Africans, must be taught that lesson.[230] All in all, these journalistic extracts reveal an intractable white Creole racism of the crudest type. How it helped to destroy the happiness of all the groups involved in it in the Martiniquan society of the time comes out in the novel *Le Triomphe d'Eglantine*, published in the 1880s by the white Creole writer René Bonneville, in which everybody—the young white Creole scion, his colored mistress, his wife, and all the children, both legitimate and illegitimate, of the liaisons entered into —is made to suffer on the altar of color prejudice.[231]

Chapter Four

The Eighteenth
and Nineteenth Centuries:
The Antislavery Ideology

To the world that the slaveholders fashioned, and its ideology, there was opposed, of course, the world that the slaves themselves created, with, too, its own ideology. The indispensable starting point for any description of that ideology is, of course, recognition of the fact that the victim of the slavery system—whether in its earlier phase of Indian semibondage or its later stage of African total bondage—was throughout a lot more than the mere cipher, reacting passively to omnipresent oppressive forces and with a culture seen as deprived and a psyche seen as pathological, that has been portrayed in some of the traditional and myopically ethnocentric scholarship. That, it goes without saying, was the slaveholder view, which penetrated the older scholarship. Yet not even the more modern comparative slavery scholarship, presumably more sympathetic to the slave person, has done much better in understanding that the slave was not only a slave but also a man and a woman and a brother and a sister, with all of his and her myriad and complicated feelings and ideas. So, it is profoundly misleading to see him or her, in the manner of Fogel and Engerman, as a faceless statistic in the quantitative measurement of slavery; or, in the manner of Elkins, as the happy-go-lucky Sambo figure;[1] or, in the manner of Styron, as the black avenger in the sexual pursuit of white women.[2] Nor, yet again, is it in any way satisfactory to see the general problem, as do the comparative historians, as if slavery existed for some four hundred years or more in, as it were, a timeless universe, for it is clear that the plantation economy, and the various ideological patterns it engendered, was one thing in, say, the Barbados of 1660 and another thing in the Cuba of 1860. Just as it is necessary to see the slave, and not just slavery, so it is necessary to see the general system in terms of social dynamics and not in terms of social statics. Nor—to cite a final example of the distortions that arise out of misguided interpretative perspectives—is it enough to see slavery as a moral problem, in the manner of the successive books of scholars like Brion Davis, for so to see it is to imagine that slavery, as it were, had been specifically invented as a seismograph on which to record the nice responses of the conscience of Western civilization to the enormity of the peculiar institution.[3]

It is this institutionalist bias that accounts for the limited vision of the prevailing scholarship on the New World Antillean experience. We see slavery but not the slave—just as there is a type of scholarship in which we see imperialism but not the imperialist, or trade unionism but not the trade unionist. Ostensibly concerned with the Afro-American experience, it in fact tells us much more about the slaveholders' world than about the world of the slaves. Thereby, we see less than half of the real picture. For it is to the report of the slave experience itself that we must go if we are to understand the antislavery ideology in its fullest sense. Without that experience, there would have been no ideology at all, proslavery or antislavery. As Nash has acutely pointed out, Africans and Indians were not merely the members of a society standing on the lowest rung of the ladder; they were, rather, the basement dwellers in a house where the ladder leading to the first floor had been removed. Yet they were very much a part of the house, for without them the building could not have been constructed and could not have risen so high.[4] It follows from this, as Mintz has argued, that the great task of the serious student of Afro-Americana is to probe the conscious life of the slave masses as they sought to make comprehensible the destiny imposed on them by brute force; for the daily job of living did not end with enslavement, and the slaves created, over time, viable patterns of life and thought, for which their pasts were pools of available symbolic and material resources.[5]

There are two general considerations—by way of prelude—that ought to be remembered when those patterns are laid out for examination. In the first place, it is important to remember that not every behavior pattern that was in one way or another inimical to the planter interest was necessarily an antislavery stance. As has already been noted, many of the Maroon societies, notably the Jamaican, were ready to enter into treaty arrangements with the imperial power whereby they acted as hunters of escaped slaves in return for a guarantee of their own independence. The aboriginal Indian tribes, again, frequently allied themselves with the Europeans against the slave populations; and Hartsinck's account of the 1763 slave rebellion in Dutch Guiana makes it painfully plain how the Indians were used to prevent the escape of the defeated remnants of that uprising into the interior, and how, therefore, the imperialist plan of divide and rule found ready collaborators in New World native elements themselves.[6] The same was true, as is well known, of the Caribbean middle class of free blacks and free browns, who always sided, when they could, with the propertied class and against the laboring class in the general Caribbean class struggle; and Deschamps Chapeaux's account of them in nineteenth-century Havana shows them as ready as any white master to own slaves for household and rental purposes.[7] The general assumption, indeed, of the European mind that the slave, as a particular property, did not share the general sanctity of property as such, was not always that of the master class alone. Even the noble African Equiano, whose eighteenth-century *Travels* constituted a simplehearted Christian assault on the system, was not himself averse, as he disarmingly tells the reader, to himself undertaking a Mosquito Coast voyage with slaves bought in Jamaica for the purpose of becoming a successful planter.[8] The conclusion is clear: only the slave himself —who, in the values of the system, was the lowest of the low, the veritable scum of the earth—could be relied upon to challenge the system. Any analysis of the leadership of Caribbean servile rebellions bears testimony to that truth.

Second, it is almost axiomatic to say (as the eminent Caribbeanist Gabriel Debien has observed) that the report of the Caribbean slave experience comes to us only indirectly, it having been written in the main by others—and those frequently hostile to him.[9] The reasons are obvious. The antiintellectual character of the slavery regime; the oral, as distinct from written, tradition of the Caribbean slave culture-patterns; the natural anxiety to forget slavery as soon as it was over: all conspired to produce a situation in which the literary record of Caribbean slavery from the slave viewpoint is practically nonexistent. The comparison with the North American situation is instructive. The Federal Writers Project of the New Deal period accumulated more than 2,000 interviews made with ex-slaves, and in recent years these have been fully collected and annotated by scholars like Rawick, Yetman, and Botkin.[10] In addition to that, and much earlier, the massive accumulated files of the old Freedmen's Bureau—created by the U.S. Congress after the Civil War to help emancipated blacks—constituted in themselves dossiers on thousands of ex-slaves; and it is indeed only recently that scholars like Ira Berlin are beginning to put it altogether as a portrait of life in the antebellum South.[11] Other books, like Leslie Howard Owens's *This Species of Property* and Dorothy Sterling's *The Trouble They Seen*, have also used the slave narratives to tell their story.[12] In all of this literature, volume after volume, spoken and sometimes written by informants with little, if any formal education, we hear the voice—proud, defiant, angry, at times rising to cadences of simple beauty —of a slave population that had been robbed of its elemental dignity by slavery, and yet which at the same time puts in jeopardy the traditional notion of slavery, which has been advanced both by hostile white historians and radical black historians at different times, as an institution that brutalized its victim into a kind of nonintelligent, nonunderstanding person.

By comparison, the historian of Caribbean island slavery has little to go on. No European colonial government showed any interest, after Emancipation, in the life of the slavery period comparable to that of the progressive

and liberal scholars of the American New Deal period who concerned themselves passionately with the recording of the American past. The very time
periods involved—Emancipation took place in the English and French Caribbean a whole generation before it took place in the United States—made it
difficult to recapture the experience, say, of slavery in Jamaica before 1833 or
in Martinique before 1848; by 1900, certainly, most of the possible witnesses
would have been dead. Interestingly enough, it has been the same even with
the matter of East Indian indenture, which ended much later, in 1917; so
much so that when Trinidadian investigators decided in 1978 to do something about it, they had to settle for centering their account around an aged
Indian who had arrived in the island in the very last year, 1916, of the indenture period.[13] Nor have things been much better, say, in Cuba. The revolutionary government after 1959 might have been expected to have shown an
interest in the slave past, which ended, comparatively late, 1886. Yet even
there we have only the solitary example of the publication of Esteban Montejo's *Biografía de un cimarrón*.[14]

The general point being made here—that the antislavery ideology really
involves, of necessity, a systematic study of the totality of the slave life,
thought, and experience, all adding up to a special and idiosyncratic way of
looking at the complex relationships between man, society, and nature within
the framework of that experience—bears reiteration. Too much of Caribbean
scholarship (to employ a distinction made by Edward Brathwaite in a suggestive essay) has been concerned with the study of the "outer plantation" to the
neglect of the study of the "inner plantation." It has thus concentrated on
the economic, political, and constitutional relationship with the metropoles,
on the various institutions arising out of those relationships, and on the
norms and styles of the colonial master classes. It has been too much concerned only with what Brathwaite terms "Creole" versions of the imposed
plantation.[15]

The result has been a curious imbalance in Caribbean studies. To take
examples cited by Brathwaite, we know a great deal about the West Indian
territorial legislatures and their role in conflict or agreement with the metropolitan parliaments, but we know little about their roles as local instututions.
We probably know more about the established Christian churches, as voices
of the planter ideology, and less than we ought to know about the spectrum
of popular sectarian religious organizations from pentecostal and revivalist on
to shango and vodun. There is a traditional European scholarship that looks
at the record of early European settlement in terms of static political description, but we still await a more imaginative treatment that will see that record
as ancestral cultures adapting themselves to the peculiar Caribbean environment of land, ideology, and other peoples. Even the Caribbean family, and
its myriad forms, has suffered from the same kind of abstract-functionalist
treatment, seen through the limited vision of metropolitan social develop-

ment and welfare agencies, or even fertility concern agencies. What we need, concludes Brathwaite, is a new historiography rooted in the concept of process rather than in that of structure, and having as its base the whole, total experience of the inner plantation.[16]

CATEGORIES OF RESISTANCE

This line of argument has obvious implications for the study of the antislavery ideology. That ideology, denied any real literary expression, has to be located within the general parameters of the slave experience. That experience, in turn, may be divided, for the sake of convenience, into three general categories, notwithstanding that, in real life, they frequently overlapped. (1) The category of patterns of accommodation and of habits of learned survival in the daily experience of plantation life: this involved the whole gamut of slave response, short of escape and rebellion, to the general slavery situation, and included everything from feigned ignorance, malingering, sabotage, slowed-down work habits, suicide, and poisoning of masters, on to the endless invention of attitudes that reflected a general war of psychological tensions and stresses between both sides in the master-slave relationship. This was, generally, the category of covert protest. (2) The category of alternative life-style: this category includes the manifold ways whereby the slave populations nourished and developed their own autonomous world of culture —in the areas, variously, of family, religion, language, song and dance, and even economic organization. In part based on the remembrance of things past—of, that is to say, the remembered African tribal cultures—and in part a rich, creolized adaptation of that ancestral retention to the new conditions of Caribbean life, this general process produced, in the end, a distinct Afro-American culture within a pseudo-European environment that, in its own turn, became the foundation, once slavery was over, of the Caribbean popular folk cultures of the later nineteenth and twentieth centuries. This was, generally, the category of a rival social system whereby the slave masses, whether consciously or subconsciously, prepared themselves for the transition to freedom. (3) The category of escape and open revolt: this was the story of successive slave rebellions, culminating, of course, in the Homeric epic of the Haitian Revolution, but also constituting the saga of the Maroon societies and the "free villages" from Jamaica to the Guianas. This was, generally, the category of overt protest. It only remains to be added that in all of these areas, culture, in its widest sense, became the vehicle of ideology.

All of the evidence suggests that, as far as the first category of learned accommodation is concerned, the vast majority of the Caribbean slave populations came to realize, under the harsh pressures of the system, that a degree of acceptance was necessary for the sake of an easy life. Those who openly rebelled, after all, were always a minority, if only because the penalties for revolt—being broken on the wheel or literally roasted alive, as the many accounts of the judicial records of rebellions grimly testify—were in themselves sufficient to deter all but the most intransigent. Not every slave was a Spartacus, or even potentially one. Slavery, moreover, like every class-oppressive system in history, bred its own victim-collaborators, as is evident from the fact that practically every account of servile uprisings describes how many of the planned revolts were betrayed by slave informers, as well as by captured rebels who bought themselves pardon by turning against their comrades. Habit, as Plato insisted, is everything; and there must have been many slaves who preferred the devil they knew to the devil that they did not know. Many of them must have been like the Guiana Negroes George Pinckard reports having talked with, who were terrified of the very idea of freedom, since it would mean, as they saw it, lack of security in sickness and old age.[17] Granted that pleasing the master by telling him what he wanted to hear was a common Negro trait, the conversations surely indicate that many slaves became so acculturated to the plantation routine that they became, so to speak, long-term prisoners who feared release into an alien and unknown world. Psychologically, it is an understandable response; as Rousseau said, men run to meet their chains.

Yet having said all that, it would be a grievous misreading of the general situation to see it exclusively in terms of master authority and slave obedience. The very nature of the economic organization of plantation economy makes that thesis dubious, since rather than being a system based on undifferentiated slave labor, it was, in fact, as a prototype, a highly differentiated system employing an entire apparatus of skilled and semiskilled labor—wheelwrights, mechanics, carpenters, cooks, coachmen, not to mention gang drivers and supervisors—all of which assumed talent, reliability, mental dexterity, even at times decision-making power on the part of the slave person. Merely to read Debien's account of the division of labor in the eighteenth century French Antillean plantation sector, hardly the most technologically sophisticated of them all, is to be made aware of the fact that, with absentee masters and rascally overseers, many plantations must in real truth have been oftentimes in effect administered by the slave population.[18] All of this meant a crucial dependency upon a reliable slave labor force, often at the lower and middle administrative echelons. And that produced, in turn, a vital bargaining power, funneled through daily communication and delegation of command, which the slave was able to use to his advantage.

How he used that power sums up a separate chapter in the social history of the plantation economy. Granted the absence—in the very nature of things —of any permitted machinery for bargaining for improvements, the slave proletariat used the power to conduct what Hart has aptly termed a pattern of illicit bargaining.[19] Its most notable form was that of temporary absences from the plantation, termed, in the French islands, *le petit marronage*. Its frequent appearance in the literature of observers testifies to its widespread character, as well as the fact that it was accompanied by an elaborate ritual —temporary abscondment for private purposes, surrender to a neighboring landowner or overseer who then intercedes with the original master, and final adjudication of the case with the runaway's request for some marginal improvement in his lot being met[20]—which ritual in itself tends to lend support to the argument of those critics who have argued that, granted the gross inequity of power in the slavery regime, at the same time it was not a society divided into two hermetically sealed sectors (so much a part of the master's conception of the situation), but rather a mutually dependent society that out of sheer necessity had to allow the slave some kind of maneuverability, however tiny, within which he could express his separate humanity.

Yet even with that sort of give and take, *petit marronage*—even although undertaken for purely personal reasons—was clearly a form of protest. Other forms, equally attested to, were more radical. There was the relapse into a withdrawn psychological state on the part, usually, of newly arrived Africans still in traumatic shock. Beckford, commenting on the phenomenon in Jamaica, remarked on how the habit puzzled the masters; its victims, he observed, may be happy when silent or dangerous when sullen.[21] There was self-mutilation, as a morbid expression of revenge, along with self-inflicted illness or injury, much to the disgust of plantation doctors. There was the deliberate inducement of illness by the habit of dirt-eating, and a young Irish visitor to the Jamaica of the middle 1770s, William Hickey, attributed the habit to harsh treatment of slaves.[22] Many women, again, practiced crude abortion, much to "Monk" Lewis's curious interest, to avoid the enslavement at birth of their offspring. Or, yet again, there was the widespread practice of poisoning. But the evidence on this controversial matter is shaky. Debien concludes, after investigation of the French Antillean records, that more often than not the practice was used against plantation draft animals rather than against white masters or, alternatively, as the documented case of Fort-Dauphin of 1765 shows, as part of *une petite guerre civile* between the slaves of rival plantations. Yet the record of judicial convictions for poisoning—noted briefly by Schuler—suggests that poisoning white persons was at least not unknown.[23] If, however, it is impossible to measure the practice quantitatively, it is fairly certain that it played a not inconsiderable role in both slaveholder and slave attitudes. The very fact that island legislation, including the *Code Noir*, recognized the existence of poisoners and drew up punitive measures against them, as well as forbidding the manufacture of herbal medicines, points to white apprehension and might even perhaps justify Schoelcher's dramatic declaration that poison is the peculiar malady of slave territories. The judicial records, Debien concludes, say more about the morbid suspicion of the planter mind than about the actual proclivities of poisoners.[24] For the slave mind, on the other hand, the poisoner became a folk hero, and to read Moreau de Saint-Méry's description of the macabre execution of the famous Mackandal in Saint Domingue in 1758 is to be made vividly aware of how poison, especially if allied with intimations of witchcraft, could be seen by the blacks as purposeful revenge.[25] The activities of the Saint Domingue slave-poisoner Jeannit show how successful that revenge could be.[26] There is little doubt, too, that the success was due in part to popular slave support and protection of the poisoners. The visitor Daupion-Lavaysse recounted how, even although slaves might be aware that there was a poisoner in their midst bent on ruining their master by poisoning his most valuable slaves, they would guard his secret, even when tortured; and Schoelcher added his own assertion that as soon as the *Code Noir* recognized the existence of poisoners, the slaves formed secret organizations to make, distribute, and administer poison to both humans and animals.[27]

Poison, of course, could be self-inflicted, leading to slave suicide. Here again the evidence is fragmentary. There is documentation of the first appearance of suicide in jumping overboard from the slavers. Early on, Ligon warned the Barbadian planters not to use the threat of punishment without carrying it out immediately, otherwise the threatened slave will proceed to hang himself. Suicide seems to have occurred most usually during the first months of arrival in the islands; seems to have been somewhat limited to groups, like slaves from Benin and the Congo region, who suffered especially from homesickness, *du mal du pays*; and, as Labat noted, tended to disappear as slaves became Christianized.[28] Indeed, the available evidence supports the thesis, that both poisoning and suicide were resorted to by only a few slaves at any time; the matter of open slave revolt, of course, is a different matter, and deserves separate attention. Most slaves worked only as much as was necessary to escape punishment, alternating between sullen obduracy (far short of suicide) when worked hard, and manic cheerfulness when the load was lightened. As Craton has noted in his discussion of the case of the English islands, it is a psychological commonplace that such truculence is no more indicative per se of excessively harsh conditions than explosions of gaiety are of general contentment.[29] Rather, both were part of the mechanism of adjustment, designed to confuse and bewilder the master class.

It is, indeed, to that general area of mechanisms of adjustment—short of poisoning, suicide, permanent escape, and rebellion—that the social historian of slavery must look for the more characteristic and common of the exemplifications of slave protest. There was widespread malingering; "lazy" work habits; petty theft; sabotage of plantation machinery; mutilation of livestock; deliberate misunderstanding of orders; feigned stupidity; and ingenious ways of disguising low productivity. There was even feigned madness, and Lewis's amused description of the "mad" Negress Catalina and the "idle rogue" Nato makes it plain that the West Indian plantation as much as the English countryside had its "village idiot" who knew how to make life more tolerable by pretended lunacy. Others, again, survived the system by reenacting the slavocracy's "myth of the friendly master," "de good massa"—again well exemplified in Lewis's account of the sycophantic delight of his Jamaican slaves at his return to the plantation.[30] In thus treating the master as king or even God, Lewis's slaves were utilizing the mechanism of shameless flattery— playing on what they perceived to be the planter's self-image as seigneurial lord —as a means of alleviating their lot. The apparent acceptance of paternalism constitued, in effect, an astute recognition on the part of the slave that he had to make the best of a hostile and maleficent world if he were to survive. Even Lewis, who was no fool despite his whimsical naiveté, recognized that much. They love me well, he told himself, but they love themselves a great deal better. They are not ungrateful, just selfish. Ingratitude, he was told by one of his servants, is regarded in Jamaica as "bad manners";[31] just as one might say that honesty is only the best policy.

What Lewis is reporting here, in fact, is the slave usage of a remarkably astute, rich, imaginative, and evasive Jamaican creolized language to dazzle and confuse the figures of authority in a splendidly conducted linguistic game. Physical violence was out of the question; so, its place was taken by a verbal violence carefully disguised. Language, whether in ordinary day-to-day speech or in song and dance, thus became, in its Caribbean popular rhythmic and sensual forms, the classic mechanism used to provoke, tease, and satirize the white folk of the system, and was misinterpreted by the whites as Negro loquacity, duplicity, and deceit. "The most clever and intelligent Negro," observed the editors of the eighteenth century *Jamaica Journal*, "is usually the most deceitful and we have seen some with art enough to baffle the most expert lawyer that ever put question." Edwards, in turn, noted the speechifying habit as well as reluctantly admiring its capacity to produce, in his phrase, figurative expressions and pointed sentences as would have reflected no disgrace on poets and philosophers. "They are fond of exhibiting set speeches, as orators by profession," he wrote, "but it requires a considerable share of patience to hear them throughout; for they commonly make a long preface before they come to the point; beginning with a tedious enumeration of their past services and hardships."[32] The endless Negro chatter that so annoyed Lady Nugent had a point to it: the more you talked, the less you worked. Lewis speculated to himself, at the end of his stay, why he had never seen a full bosom (thus artlessly reflecting his own European concept of feminine beauty as against the Afro-American one). He might equally have wondered why he had never met a silent Negro.

The Caribbean slave person, in sum, had to learn to live by his wits in a system in which all the dice were loaded against him. So, with a fine detective instinct honed to perfection, he learned to play on and exploit the weaknesses and foibles of the white overlords. Long, who in his own turn was no fool despite his ingrained racism, saw this clearly in a passage noteworthy for its perception of the psychological roots of a Negro behavior pattern otherwise inexplicable:

> Their principal address is shown in finding out their master's temper, and playing upon it so artfully as to bend it with most convenience to their own purposes. They

are not less studious in sifting their master's representative, the overseer; if he is
not too cunning for them, which they soon discover after one or two experiments,
they will easily find means to overreach him on every occasion, and make his indolence, his weakness, or sottishness, a sure prognostic of some comfortable term of
idleness to them; but if they find him too intelligent, wary and active, they leave no
expedient untried, by thwarting his plans, misunderstanding his orders, and
reiterating complaints against him, to ferret him out of his post; if this will not succeed, they perplex and worry him, especially if he is of an impatient, fretful turn,
till he grows heartily sick of his charge, and voluntarily resigns it. An overseer
therefore, like a prime minister, must always expect to meet with a faction, ready
to oppose his administration, right or wrong; unless he will give the reins out of his
hands, and suffer the mob to have things their own way; which if he complies with,
they will extol him to his face, condemn him in their hearts, and very soon bring his
government to disgrace.[33]

The passage suggests at least three considerations pertinent to the evolution of a slave-based ideological system. It admits, implicitly, the presence in
the black person of ratiocinative and cognitive powers: the slave can perceive his own self-interest, identify friends and enemies, and shape strategies
of behavior and attitude to deal with them. It could be retorted that the passage, actually, only portrays the presence of learned habits of low cunning,
certainly not the capacity to write a learned treatise. But the answer to that,
of course, is that neither did the white Caribbean person at any time produce
such a treatise; certainly there was never at any time a Calhoun or a Fitz-
hugh, as in the American South, to write a reasoned defense of the slavery regime. Second, the passage shows how readily the slave person managed to
fashion a "divide and rule" strategy, pitting master against overseer, matching the whites' own "divide-and-rule" strategy. In the third place, it also
shows how, in response to the proslavery conceit that the masters "knew"
and "understood" their "niggers" in ways denied to meddling outsiders, the
slaves themselves could claim, and with much more justification, that they
themselves knew and understood the massa-figure and his like with equal
perspicacity. Long, unwittingly, here recognizes the existence, in however
limited a fashion, of intelligence. The point is basic; because without intelligence there can be no ideology.

The discussion of accommodation-adjustment patterns clearly broaches
the problem of self-image; and self-image, as well as sustained images of
others, constitutes a vital element of ideology. The particular Caribbean
discussion of the problem has centered around the stereotype of the lazy and
compliant Quashie figure (first introduced into the vocabulary of things Caribbean by Raynal), just as in the American South it has centered around the
childlike and improvident Sambo figure. Both stereotypes were obviously
fashioned and encouraged by the dominant white groups in order to assure
them of the willing acceptance of slavery by the slave mass; for it was urgent
that even the most hardened plantocrat should find some satisfying rationalization for the system. Both stereotypes, then, came to form a collection of

supposedly Negro traits that functionally fed the rationalization. As such, they formed an indispensable element of the plantocrat ideology.

But this, of course, is not to argue that the stereotypes played the same functional purpose for the slave himself. Indeed, the available evidence suggests the contrary: that the slave recognized the psychological need of the stereotype in the master mentality and cleverly exploited it for his own ends, thus undertaking the game of what Patterson has called "playing the stereotype." To deliberately feed the master's expectations of stupidity and laziness by appearing to be so; to delude the master into a false sense of security; to adopt an air of exaggerated deference before the white person, really a disguise for insolence; above all, to disguise one's own true feelings, since no one, least of all whites, could be trusted: all became part of the game, of putting on ole massa. At times it must have taken on the air of a melodramatic charade, for the more perceptive of the whites recognized its duplicity: Lewis was sceptical of the sincerity of the embarrassing adoration heaped upon him by his slaves, and Long recognized that many of the "digging songs" were satires at the expense of "Buckra." What were seen by the less perceptive whites as displays of the weaknesses of the Negro "character" were in fact mechanisms used by the Negro comedians to mock the very real weaknesses of the whites themselves.

This, of course, is not to argue that all black behavior was that sort of conscious role-playing. Many slaves must have successfully internalized master values, in the manner of many elements of every subjugate class in the history of class societies. It would have been surprising if the Caribbean black subclass had been an exception to that almost natural law of class-based civilization. At its worst, it generated a "false consciousness," as distinct from a genuine class consciousness, especially in house slaves and urban slaves, with the slave person aping the dress, the mannerisms, and even the speech of the whites, producing, that is to say, the fawning habit of the spoiled house slave, and reaching its perfected expression, at a higher class level, in the life-style of the middle group of free mulattoes. The observations of the young French apprentice Regnault de Beaumont on the haughty and arrogant house domestics in the Saint Domingue of the 1770s paint a characteristic picture of the type.[34] At its best, it gave rise, in individual instances, to the house slave who returned the genuine sense of noblesse oblige shown by the best kind of master with an equally genuine loyalty, notwithstanding the essential inequality of the relationship. It is impossible to read the story told by Long of the faithful Coromantine servant of Sir Charles Price, who was given manumission and was instrumental, through his powers of persuasion and voluntary intelligence work, in preventing the spread of the 1760 rebellion to his master's estate or the story of the female domestic Marie-Jeanne who belonged to the mistress of one of the Saint Domingue estates of the 1780s and who religiously sent small gifts to the Creole child she had helped raise without being made to feel that if on the one hand there were occasional

planters who retained the old paternalistic habits of the ancien régime, looking after faithful servitors into old age and death, there were on the other
hand slaves who, without hypocrisy, gave back a loyal regard. There were,
clearly, both masters and slaves who could manage to transcend the hatreds
and the fears of the system and to build bridges of mutual respect and even
affection.

Yet these latter, on any showing, were the exceptions rather than the rule.
Individual cases of mutual regard were possible; but the system itself made
impossible any form of collective mutual regard. The general atmosphere of
plantation life, then, was one of intractable and muted hostility, neither full
acceptance on the one hand nor open rebellion on the other. The characteristic mode of slave adjustment, therefore, was one, generally, of passive, muted
resistance, evinced in the various psychopathological forms already noted.
The forms, all added up, amounted to a complicated behavior pattern of posture. The typical master treated the slave as a fool; so, the slave responded by
acting the fool. The acting took place behind a cleverly constructed mask;
and, indeed, there is little doubt that the modern Fanonesque *peau noir,
masque blanc* syndrome received its origins during the slave period. Direct
aggression out of the question, the mask game became a form of indirect aggression. Its continuity is attested to by later, postslavery forms; thus, it has
been frequently pointed out how the modern Stepin Fetchit character is that
of a whining, vacillating, lower-class negro whose sullen, slow pace is in fact
that of a man forced to work for ends not his own and thereby subtly exhibiting
his resistance to white society. In the Caribbean slave society the resistance
showed itself, characteristically, in the folklore figure of the spider-trickster
Anansi, a weak creature who outwits oppressors and bullies by guile and
trickery and gets the better of them. In part based on West African folklore,
in part going back to the figure of the scheming servant in Elizabethan literature, Anansi is in some measure American con man, in some measure David
against Goliath, but always the seemingly dumb schemer who searches out
the weaknesses of his oppressors—their vanity, greed, and naiveté—and uses
them to stay alive and get ahead.[36] The Anansi figure thus embodies all of the
sharpness and keen apprehension of people and situations learned by the Negro in adversity; as Phillippo put it, writing immediately after Emancipation
in Jamaica, "so far from being more deficient in acuteness and discrimination
than other men, none can penetrate more deeply than the Negro into the character, or form an opinion of strangers with greater correctness and precision."[37]

If, then, there was a planter mind, there was also a slave mind. This has
not always been fully appreciated, even by authors sympathetic to the slave
cause. W. J. Cash's brilliantly executed book of 1941, *The Mind of the South*,
to take an example only, is concerned almost wholly with looking at the old
sentimental-romantic legend of the slavery South that was so much at the
heart of the South's slave owner apologetic, and says hardly anything about

the alternative life-style and alternative ideology constructed by the slave population. Later American progressive scholarship, of course, has made amends for that omission, and Eugene D. Genovese's *Roll, Jordan, Roll: The World the Slaves Made* stands as the definitive account of how the slave genius of the South, set within the framework of an objective social class, created, in slavery, a separate black national culture, fashioned by the church preacher, the sectarian evangelist, the songwriter, the musician, and not least of all by the common black person, man and woman, in his letters and narratives. This autonomous culture, born and nurtured in the valley of the shadow of death, constitutes, in truth, the real and lasting heritage of the South to the larger American civilization: it is the ancestral root of jazz, soul music, black religion, black nationalism, civil rights protest, and the rest within contemporary America. By comparison, the slaveholder ideology has left little of permanent value behind it. It has, as it were, gone with the wind; and Cash's book reads—as it was probably meant to be—like nothing so much as an eloquent obituary on its brief life.[38]

For the slaveholder ideology was, after all, a comparatively short-lived phenomenon, spanning the half century, more or less, that terminated with the Civil War. It has to be set within the larger and historically more extended hemispheric perspective, as Genovese himself perceives. That larger perspective was, in essence, that of Brazil, the Guianas, and the Caribbean island archipelago. It is there, more than anywhere else, that the historian has to record the genesis and fruition of Afro-America. Much more extensive, both in space and time, than the North American slave experience, it calls for the systematic study of the ways in which, through art, music, religion, family, and social organization, the slave masses shaped a new, separate life, a new self-identity, indeed, a new and syncretic world view. That study began, of course (to mention the seminal names only), with the scholarly work of Herskovits, Freyre, Ortiz, and Price-Mars; and the range of interests reflected in the 1977 conference on New World slavery organized by the New York Academy of Sciences reflects the shift from interest in slavery to interest in the slave—a recognition, as Brathwaite poetically puts it, of the face within the archive, although the bias of the old scholarship still remains.[39]

If this line of reasoning is correct—that there existed interstices within the socioeconomic fabric of the slave system that permitted the cultural expression of the slave personality—it follows that the argument, advanced most notably by Elkins, that the slave experience was analogous to that of the concentration camp of the Nazi holocaust of the twentieth century, is an overfacile historical analogy difficult to accept. In one way, of course, it is a tempting analogy, if only because the comparison with the historic experience of Jewry, with the New World black being seen, so to speak, as a black Jew suffering his own Babylonian captivity, has been a real part of the antislavery ideology, as the modern Rastafarian cult demonstrates. Yet the comparison ends at that point. Why that is so has been recently shown by the Brazilian scholar

Emilia Viotti da Costa, speaking particularly to the Brazilian case. The sole purpose of the German death camps (labor camps apart) was the physical destruction of the prisoner; by contrast, the slave played a working role in the production and profit system of the plantation economy. The mechanisms of repression and control, including psychological control, available to the German camp staff were of a terrifying sophisticated character unknown to the eighteenth and nineteenth centuries. Because of that, both the threat and the fear of insurrection were greater in the slave system. What this meant was that from sundown to sunup—to use Rawick's book title—the life of the slave was his own. As Drimmer puts it, if white men ruled the day, black men ruled the night. This was the physical setting for the creation of the alternative black community and culture. "Creating a black community in the slave quarters and holding onto traditions," concludes da Costa, "represented resistance to slavery because slavery implied not only the subordination and exploitation of one social group by another, but also the confrontation of two ethnic groups. The slave could resist in different ways: as a slave to his master, as a black man to the white man, and as an African to the Europeans. In this context cultural resistance could be interpreted as a form of social protest."[40]

THE SLAVE SUBCULTURE

All work and no play, as the English proverb has it, makes Jack a dull boy. Every working class in the history of civilization has responded to that warning with the creation, over time, of its own recreational patterns, almost invariably denigrated by other classes. The making of the English working class, in Thompson's phrase, was thus the creation by the English village and town laborer, between 1760 and 1850, of what the English social historians the Hammonds termed the "growth of common enjoyment." The Caribbean working class engineered a similar subterranean world of song, dance, and music. The two main attitudes that infused that world have passed into the Caribbean proverbial folk wisdom. The first recognized that the world of work and its usufruct belonged to the master, so that it was useless for the slave to concern himself with the canons of the Protestant ethic, summed up in the Haitian proverb *Bourrique travaille, choual galomne* (The donkey works, but the horse is promoted). The second recognized that the slave world of play had nothing to do with the masters' world of play, indeed had to be jealously guarded against it, summed up in the Jamaican proverb, "When cockroach give party, him no ax fowl."

The white attitude to all this, predictably, was one of misunderstanding founded on ignorance, oscillating between the fear that Negro dances were all wild, unnameable orgies and the self-congratulatory assurance that they proved the slaves were happy and contented (it was common practice for visitors to be taken to festive events on the plantation to prove that point). Early on, Las Casas had vigorously protested against the Spanish prohibition and destruction of the Indian *areitos* (playgrounds), and, later on, as the African cultural impulse replaced the Indian, scientific visitors like Sir Hans Sloane reported with keen interest in his 1707 journal on the instruments of West Indian Creole music,[41] while even Long admired the grace and drama of some of the African dances. And it was only one step more beyond that attitude to adopting the openly romanticizing attitude, given vent to in the picturesque 1764 poem by Dr. Johnson's friend James Grainger, *The Sugar Cane*, in which the depiction of slaves dancing was transformed into a sort of West Indian village Maypole dance.[42]

But the very cultural strangeness of an African musicological tradition that was oral rather than written made these tolerant attitudes increasingly difficult to maintain, and they were replaced by the typical missionary hostility to forms seen as heathen and idolatrous. It could be argued, of course, that the colonial plantation system could have copied the dyarchy policy that colonialism elsewhere evolved in Asia and Africa, delegating authority to native princes and tribal chieftains who then presided over more or less autonomous culture systems. But the very nature of slave-based plantation America, both geographical and political, made that impossible. Or, again, it could be argued that the system could have openly tolerated black amusements on the basis of the principle of Roman bread and circuses, following the maxim attributed to the Spanish colonial governor of Puerto Rico, Miguel de la Torre, *Pueblo que se divierte no conspira* (A people that amuses itself does not engage in conspiracy). But that maxim had in mind the Puerto Rican *fiestas populares*, always under the tight control of the colonial authority, rather than the ritual gatherings, frequently secret and illegal, of the slave congregations.[43]

Notwithstanding planter fears and official restrictions, however, it is plain enough that a rich and vigorous slave entertainment culture grew and flourished throughout plantation society. "On Sundaies in the afternoon," wrote Ligon of Barbados in the 1650s, "their musick plaies, and to dancing they go." The Cuban runaway slave Montejo reported the same thing in the Cuban slave society over two hundred years later: "The Barracoon," he recorded, speaking also of the Sunday activities, "came to life in a flash; it was like the end of the world."[44] During that historical time period the Antillean slave person managed, like the ancient Hebraic psalmist in an alien court, to console himself and herself with an improvised culture of song and dance. How they did it, against all the terrible pressures of slave life, still remains a mystery. As Montejo himself remarked, he didn't know where the slaves found the energy for it.

The full report of that process, of course, belongs to the anthropological subfield of ethnomusicology. But it had about it, in every island, two aspects of supreme importance. In the first place, it bore the hallmark of an emphatic *africanía* (africanness). However ethnocentric the European descriptions may be—whether one thinks of Père Labat's scandalized account of the Martinique slave *calenda*, the forbidden African dance, which he attributed in origin to the kingdom of Arada on the Guinea Coast; or Moreau de Saint-Méry's account of the Saint Domingue vodun dance, of Dahomean origin and at that time danced openly and witnessed by the whites as a sort of nocturnal diversion; or Pinckard's more precise description of body movement and facial expression in the West Indian dances of the English islands—they all infer the general truth, substantiated by later professional scholarship, that New World Negro music had its roots deep in the ancestral African background— understood, of course, regionally, as constituting, in effect, an Afro-American subsystem of the continental black African musical tradition, so profoundly different from the European. All of the distinctive characteristics of the tradition were carried over: the emphasis on rhythm and syncopation; the tendency to introduce polyrhythms; the antiphony between leader and chorus in singing; the choral circle; the usage of percussion; the crescendo that ends, especially in religious music, in frenetic climax; and the rest of the *música negro-africana*. This transatlantic passage, of course, just as with everything else, did not take place without the African and European dance forms interpenetrating each other. Just as the whites took over some slave dances—there is the astonishing vision that Père Labat reported of Catholic nuns dancing the *calenda* by themselves in the church chancels on Christmas night—so the blacks took over some white forms: Captain Marryat described the pleasing hymn-singing of the Barbadian black and colored Methodist congregations at the end of the slave period.[45] Notwithstanding that process, nonetheless, Africa and Europe were, in this area, two worlds apart. Africa retained its cultural integrity against the white European economic and political overlordship. It was the drum against the fiddle, the conga against the minuet, the barracoon yard against the ballroom.

Second, the black New World forms of song and dance were, in the social sense of the term, democratic. The white forms, like the white plantation world itself, were, by contrast, pseudoaristocratic and pseudobourgeois. There were survivals, of course, of the old African aristocratic forms in the figures of the vodun priest and the obeah man. But with such exceptions the leveling effects of slavery precluded the reestablishment of African hierarchy and caste in the new plantation society. It was in the upper-class white society that elitism survived. For that society, of course, it was the formal ball at Government House or the lavish entertainment of the private "great house," and if Leigh-Fermor's fictional account of the high Creole fiesta of aristocratic colonial French society, in his magnificently rendered *Violins of Saint Jacques*, seems dangerously romanticized, it is enough to read the account of foreign visitors, as late as the 1870s and 1880s, of the opulent hospitality of the more opulent Cuban planters to realize that it is, perhaps, not so wide of the mark after all.[46]

By contrast, the slave music was popular, democratic, participatory. Père Labat noted how it was joined in by all, men, women, and children, and Lewis noted, in turn, the spectator-participant character of the dancing events. The descriptions (again, provided by observers like Long, Renny, Moreton, Scott, Lewis, and Belisario) of the nascent forms of the Jamaican Creole carnival-tradition show vividly how many of the characteristic features of that splendid Caribbean bacchanal-fiesta—the advance and recoil of the carnival shuffle, part conga, part calypso step; the strident, apocalyptic beat of the drums; the mass participation of crowd and artists alike, with everybody in the "jump up," along with the mob theater of the streets—had their origin, for all of the later Euro-Creole accretions, in the slavery period.

Yet the significance of Afro-Antillean song and dance as forms of protest and assertion is even more fundamental than this. Just as Ortiz, in his *Contrapunto cubano*, could postulate the antiphony of sugar and tobacco—the one being seen as the economic expression of slavery, the other as the economic expression of freedom—so it is possible to look at the antiphony between European and African recreational modes in a similar fashion. African music spoke to the body, European music to the mind. The African mode celebrated the collective experience of the race, the European mode the griefs and pleasures of the private person. The essence of the African music was rhythm; that of European music, melody. African music was tribal, egalitarian, preliterate, and *sacro-mágica*; European music was individualistic, literate, hierarchical, divided artificially between its secular and religious expressions. Although there was specialism within the African system, there was little of the separation between artist and audience so characteristic of the European system. African music was outdoors, European music indoors; the one belonged to the concert chamber or the private salon, the other to the streets. Above all else, African music reflected the experience of the folk-people, while European music, far more elitist, reflected the more solipsistic, private, antisocial, and hedonistic experience of gentlefolk. All of those deep-rooted differences, arising out of historical civilizations profoundly different from each other, played themselves out in the Antillean scenario of work and pleasure.

Those differences, of course, deposited in the general Antillean experience, were gradually altered, through a process of social chemistry that Ortiz, with Malinowski's blessing, termed a process of transculturation, to become the foundation rock of post-Emancipation popular Antillean society. Not the least of its manifestations was its textual content, as it is known from the literal transcriptions that have been handed down. Many of the themes were familial and domestic, like the *Xango* cradle song that appears, in different renditions, in Brazil, Cuba, and the English-speaking Antilles.[47] Others were critical and humorous comments on current events, the best-known survival of that genre being, of course, the popular Trinidadian song type of the calypso. Others, again, concentrated on mordant social satire, commenting fatalistically or jibingly on the morals and manners, frequently in detrimental tone, of the blacks themselves, as well as the whites—illustrating how this kind of art helped make the intolerable burden of life tolerable by mordant self-mockery and savage commentary on the foibles of human nature and the vanity of human wishes; the widespread use of the proverb played much the same kind of therapeutic role in the popular life.[48] Others, finally, were pregnant (in the manner of the Negro spirituals of the American South) with an almost unbearable nostalgia for a half-forgotten African past, like the Jamaican "Guinea corn" song or the stanzas, also Jamaican, lamenting the fact that the white master could go back to England but the black slave could not return to the Guinea or the Congo.[49]

These were themes summing up the day-to-day slave experience, only covertly antisystem in the sense that they gave emotional sustenance to the slave as he faced the daily round of forced labor. But there were other, more overtly belligerent and rebellious, themes. They run the whole gamut of antiwhite feeling, from amused derision to open hatred. The white mistress cannot dance like the black girl, for the shay-shay and the "love dance" are echoes of African fertility-dance rites unknown to the European.[50] All of us must die; so, the "new-come buckra" will die of the fever and the foreign sailor will die of too much rum just as surely as the "neger" will die of hard work. Not only that, but all of us, black, white, brown, are all equal, "all de same." Black people may even rebel if that equality is not recognized; they will "take force by force."[51] That note of rebellion received its best-known expression, perhaps, in the apochryphal areito de Anacaona of the Saint Domingue slaves, with its defiant oath to destroy all the whites and everything that they possess; and whether it was, in fact, an old, innocuous Indian refrain or a genuine revolt song of the slaves or, as some have argued, an invention of the obsequious literati of the court of the Emperor Henri Christophe, does not detract from the message that it carried.[52]

THE IDEOLOGY OF SLAVE RELIGION

It goes without saying that all of this was functionally related to the world of slave religion. For if the European colonizer built his "new world," so did the colonized African. Preeminently, that new world—denied expression in either economic technology or political structures—found its classic, architectonic expression in the proliferating secret Negro religious cults of the Americas, Shango, vodun, bamboo-tamboo, camboulay, obeah, macumba, and the rest. In the manner of all religious systems in their historical stages before dogma and canon have hardened into orthodoxy, there took place a chemico-religious process in which, in both the area of ritual and of mythology, the imported African religions fused, over the centuries of culture encounter, with the imported European religions—with the end result of producing the characteristic Caribbean cults in all of their fantastic variety: Cuban *santería* (worship of the saints), Haitian vodun, Jamaican myalism, Trinidadian Shango, to name only the best known. The syncretizing process married the elaborate West African mythologies with the doctrines of the Catholic and Protestant variants of post-Renaissance Europe. It was, of course, a process common to the history of all of the great world religions; so, just as early Christianity in the Roman Empire derived much of its belief from the pre-Christian cults of the ancient world, including Mithraism, the Caribbean religious cults that have survived into the twentieth century (essentially now Afro-Christian) were the final consequence of a mixture of Africa and Europe. In Sylvia Wynter's succinct phrase—speaking to the Jamaican experience, but inferentially speaking for the Caribbean as a whole—Christianity, the religion of the invading civilization, had come into a relation of cultural continuity with the invaded culture. It is thus possible, as Wynter continues, to look at the Caribbean religions as constituting a continuum in which, in various sects and denominations, the African element predominates, then the European element predominates, with the middle portion being occupied by movements combining both elements in equal percentage.[53]

This, again, is a field of scholastic enquiry that belongs to the sociology of religion; and following the pioneering investigations of the two Herskovits, it has been mined exhaustively by subsequent scholarship, Caribbean, Luso-Brazilian, and North American: Ramos, Freyre, Simpson, Bascom, Bastide, Ribeiro, Bourguignon, Comhaire-Sylvain, Courlander, Dorsainvil, Métraux, Rigaud, Kerr, Carr, Crowley, Koss, Hogg, and others. As one reads that immense literature, there are two points worth remembering by way of preliminary statement. First, there were, obviously enough, important internal differences within the general picture. Vodun in Saint Domingue–Haiti contained a European Christian element that was Catholic; the mission churches and revivalist cults in Jamaica, an element that was Protestant. In similar fashion, the African element was varied; thus, the slave population of Saint Domingue, the French Antilles, and the English-speaking islands was, ethnologically speaking, overwhelmingly of Gold Coast–Angola–Congo origin, while that of Cuba, Puerto Rico, and Brazil, where the trade lasted longer, was Yoruba-Ibo in character; although, notwithstanding those differences, all slaves came from a common West African culture area with a communality of basic ideas and concepts secreted in ritual, myth, and folklore.[54] Second, the impact of that culture system was not just a matter of ancestral memory communicated by the oral tradition; on the contrary it was an influence continuously reinforced and strengthened by the constant infusions of new African blood. The historians of the Worthy Park sugar estate in Jamaica, with its more than three centuries of continuous history, have pointed out the significance of the fact, in this regard, that even after Emancipation, one-tenth of all of its slaves had been born in Africa.[55] Unlike the American South, where natural reproduction took the place of new and regular imports, the Caribbean slave society was never allowed to forget its African roots.

It is here, then, in the magico-religious field of Afro-American cultism that the slave populations developed and nurtured their own distinctive world view, their own distinctive ideology. It was, once again, a mortal struggle between Europe and Africa, waged as bitterly as any war of religion. European priest and African revivalist led opposing camps as hostile to each other as Catholic and Puritan. Seaga writes:

> At the root of the whole problem, lies the basic difference of religious thinking: on the one side, stands Christian Monotheism, exclusive, guarded by a jealous God who condemns the worshippers of the Golden Calf and other idols. On the other side there is African Polytheism, all-embracing and able to accommodate the Christian Trinity, the Angels and Saints, the Prophets and the Apostles, combining these, however, with the spirits including ancestral dead, and even with the diabolical host. Christianity, in particular Protestant Christianity, because of its exclusiveness and reliance on the truth of doctrine based usually on the Bible alone, has given rise to a multitude of interpretations of Scripture, and thus in turn has promoted the proliferation of a multitude of Christian denominations, none of which have really learnt in the final analysis to co-exist in doctrine. The Revivalist has no such problem. His Gods permit him free intercourse with the available pantheon of spirits.[56]

A European religious ideology, bibliolatrous, closed, monotheistic, intolerant, inquisitorial, was thus faced with the challenge of an Afro-American religious ideology open, congregationalist, ecumenical, pantheistic, and ultimately democratic, both fighting for the soul and spirit of the Caribbean masses.

The three seminal expressions of that Caribbean religious underworld are Saint Domingue–Haiti vodun, Cuban *santería*, and the widespread Myal cult in the English-speaking islands. Being damned as heretical by the white politico-ecclesiastical establishment, their origins are inevitably shrouded in mystery, so that the process, which evolved over generations, whereby their various elements of Islamic, African, and Christian sources finally meshed into a systemic theology-ideology is difficult to trace. The mystery was, in turn, deliberately compounded by the priestly practitioners of the occult arts, for to reveal their nature would be to encourage the loss of the prestige of the unknown. Yet it is certain that those arts came to the Caribbean early. The *Essai sur l'esclavage et observations sur l'état présent des colonies*, published anonymously about 1750, already described the embryonic form of vodun dance and ceremony in Saint Domingue.[57] African fetishism, the heart of *brujería* and *santería*, entered Cuba, as Ortiz remarks, with the first Negro. And John Taylor's account of Jamaican Negro life in the latter part of the seventeenth century makes it graphically clear how, early on, there were already present the African folk dances with their veneration for the Earth as the primordial life-giving force.[58]

The metaphysical structure of vodun—part imported African animism of the Dahomey-Guinea tribes, part sheer Creole invention born out of the melting pot of the slave barracoons—from its very beginnings in the "preparatory" period before 1790 constituted a totality of ideas and concepts as complex and abstruse as any ancient Greek or Christian cult religion. If, as one of its scholarly commentators has said, it is impatient of explanation, like all ancient religions,[59] that has not prevented the growth of a whole scholarly literature seeking to unravel its dark secrets. The variety of interpretations in itself testifies to the rich progeny of elements, African, Creole, French, and Latin, that have gone into the making of the religion. For Dorsainvil the element of spirit possession—the state of ecstatic trance that accompanies so much of the vodun ritual process—is seen, in psychological terms, as a form of deviant or pathological behavior, a sort of religious and racial psychoneurosis, essentially negative in character.[60] For Kiev, Bourguignon, Wittkower, and Douyon, it is seen still as pathological in character but in positive rather than in negative terms; as Kiev phrases it, spirit possession becomes an acceptable form of "going crazy" in a hostile world full of poverty, disease, and frustration. For others, following the thesis of Price-Mars in his epochal book of 1928, spirit possession is a normal cultural phenomenon; it has to be seen as a characteristically Haitian variant of the systems of medieval mysticism.[61] That argument has been pursued by the Haitian theologians of the post–Vatican II era; and in the analyses of commentators like Hurbon there can be seen a new appreciation of the fundamental truth that vodun must be perceived as a valid religious language of the Haitian popular cultural tradition, and whose gods should be seen, not as the embodiment of satanic evil, as their Catholic persecutors have seen them, but as gods of providential liberation.[62]

For, more than anything else, it is that spirit of liberation that speaks in the vodun religion. All of the three major rites—Rada, Congo, and Petro—address themselves, not to a lofty and remote Godhead, like the Hebraic Jehovah, but to the vast pantheons of the *loas* who, in themselves, attest in turn to the remarkable hospitality of the religion to all influences, thus producing its syncretic character; so if, on the one hand, there is the Catholic Saint James the Major who joins the vodun warlike Valhalla, on the other hand there is the dapper and courtly Baron Samedi, actually of native Haitian origin. All of them, along with their appropriate ritual paraphernalia and their complex hagiography, constitute for their devotees everything that is necessary to make daily life tolerable and enjoyable: they are guides, counsellors, judges, advocates, consolers, and friends. Through the rituals, they give divine sanction to human frailties and aspirations; they show their love for their followers by the miracle of incarnation; they give emotional release to troubled souls; they confer meaning, direction, and understanding on what otherwise would be the incomprehensible trauma of the daily tasks of life; above all, they form the bridge whereby the devotee establishes, at each ceremony, a familiar relationship with the ancestral African homeland. The descent of the gods, indeed, forms the tremendous climacteric of the vodun ceremonial event: summoned by drum and dance and sacrifice out of their remote African retreats, the divine horsemen of the *loa* make their celestial transatlantic trip in search of their exiled children and then confer upon them the final gift of apocalyptic visitation as represented in the purgative experience of the possession state. Vodun assures the *serviteur*, in sum, that all of nature and life is governed by a transcendental logic—an assurance that neither of the official institutions of his society, the Catholic Church and the secular political state, has been capable of making. It tells him that past, present, and future are all continuous and related moments in the passage of time, and that when the ancestors become *loa*—as they do all the time —the history of the race runs in his own blood as part of a unifying psychic heritage that is passed on from generation to succeeding generation.[63]

The same principle—that if life is to be made tolerable, you must be able to manipulate destiny, and you can only manipulate destiny if you are the devotee of gods who are at once your masters and your servants—infuses the comparable system of Cuban *brujería* and *santería*. Just like vodun in Saint Domingue-Haiti, both those forms were contemptuously dismissed, by white Spanish society and Creole respectability alike, as evil and satanic forces to be extirpated. It comes as a surprise, then, to note that the study of *brujería-santería* on the part of the Cuban intelligentsia goes back to the pioneering study of Bachiller y Morales, *Los negros*, published in 1887, almost simultaneous with the date of slavery abolition, and that, later, it inspired the trilogy of studies by Fernándo Ortiz on the general theme of Cuban Negro culture: *Los negros brujos, Los negros esclavos*, and *Los negros curros*.[64] It is true that Ortiz—who was, like the entire Caribbean and Latin American intelligentsia of the nineteenth century, a mind educated in the Western European intellectual tradition—saw his work as an effort to study, as he put it, the religious atavism that holds back the progress of the Negro population of Cuba. What matters, however, is that his anthropological curiosity proved, in the end, to be more powerful than his positivistic bias, so that his books still remain a testimony to his ardent nationalism embracing all Cubans, summed up in his assertion that *sin el negro, Cuba no sería Cuba* (without the Negro, Cuba would not be Cuba).[65]

Cuban *brujería* and *santería* share a similar metaphysics with vodun— without, of course, the vodun ritual of possession. Yoruban rather than Dahomeyan in origin, there is the same pantheon of intermediate gods and goddesses, beholden theoretically to the distant supreme god—Jupiter *optimus maximus*, the African Olorun—but playing the supreme role as interpreters of the universe as the *orishas*, they represent the three main branches of the religion (to be found, actually, all over the Caribbean) of Obatala, Shango, and Ifa. There is the same pleasing readiness to absorb the Catholic saints, so that they become, as it were, transfigured dual personalities: Shango-Santa Barbara, Babalu-Aye-Saint Lazare, Orunmila-Saint Francis of Assisi, Obatala-Virgin of Mercy, and the rest. Therefore, at once neo-African and neo-Catholic, as the ritual paraphernalia of the trade shows, the *santero* and the *brujo* play all three encompassing roles as priest, healer, and diviner. As priest, he consoles; as healer, he employs the traditional Caribbean "bush medicine"—of real medicinal power, as recent Western medical research is beginning to discover—to control and cure disease; as diviner, he helps the client to see the future, to control the course of love or fortune or plain daily living with all of its problems and to blame, if necessary, his problems on evil spirits, the loss of his soul, the anger of the gods, and other mystical reasons. In all of those roles, he symbolizes and expresses the ancestral African memory of things. Merely to read Montejo's affectionate account of the dark-skinned Negress *santera* Ma Lucia at the end of the slavery period—with her endless storytelling, her old African hairstyle, who was often received with derisive laughter by disrespectful boys—is to be made to feel how the *santero* and *brujo* acted not only as interpreters of the deities but also as the transmitters of customs, which are more important, Montejo remarks, than knowledge.[66]

It is important to note how these twin popular religions of the Catholic Antillean slave society contributed to the antislavery ideology. They did so in two ways: particular and general. Particularly, they became, first in Saint Domingue and then to some extent in Cuba, active protagonists in the war against the system. With freedom assured after 1804, it is true that the fundamentally conservative element of vodun, adapting itself to the needs of a conservative peasantry, asserted itself. But for the slavery period it was, on any showing, a conspiratorial cult opposed to slavery. Rebel leaders like Jean-François, Halaou, and Hyacinthe practised vodun rites as a means of imparting faith and courage to their followers; Makandal was able to convince the masses of his own immortality conferred by the gods; and Boukman used the same vodun ceremonies to help initiate the first act of the servile war in 1791. The evidence is scanty, as all commentators, including the post-1804 Haitian historians, admit. But there can be little doubt that during that formative period, vodun managed to achieve two large ends vital to the success of the revolution: (1) It helped to bring about a religious compromise that included the essentials of the various beliefs, and thereby to give some sort of unity to the operational ideology of the revolution, and (2) it laid the foundations of the assimilationist compromise with Catholicism; indeed, the syncretizing movement may be seen as a political strategy whereby the hostility of the Catholic power could at least be neutralized. In brief, much more than the new ideas from Europe that the plantocracy feared, it was the unifying force of vodun that nurtured the revolutionary drive. Its central ideas—the memory of Africa, unity against a cruel world, survival, the enthralling miracle of possession, the social warmth of the drum and the dance, the conviction of spiritual intercourse with the gods—provided the fanaticism of belief without which no revolutionary movement can succeed. So, it was no accident, but an integral element of the whole *schemata* of vodun, that the loas, like Castor and Pollux at Lake Regillus in the ancient Roman tradition, appeared on the battlefields and participated in the rout of the white enemy; just as, again, it is no accident, but completely fitting to the legend, that the hero-leaders of the war—Makandal, Boukman, Toussaint, Pétion, Rigaud, Dessalines— rapidly became triumphant denizens themselves of the vodun pantheon.

The Cuban case—as far as the contribution of black cultism to the black insurrectionist movement of the nineteenth century (in 1812, 1820, 1823, and, most importantly, 1844) is concerned—is much more complicated. The very ethnic heterogeneity of the national population meant that the slave element had to compete with others in leadership of the various movements. The leadership of the anti-Spanish revolutionary party, largely composed of free Negroes and "mixed bloods," itself suffered from its own racism, its mortal antipathy towards the slaves, as Colonel Flinter noted in his book of 1832,[67] and it is significant that the great colored military leader of the national independence war after 1868, Maceo, was a free mulatto not of slave origin and that the revolutionary government of Céspedes—like President Lincoln in the United States—only moved forward slowly and reluctantly toward embracing slavery abolition as an integral part of the anti-Spanish struggle. Insofar, then, as the Afro-Cuban contribution to the particular struggle for Cuban politial liberty is concerned, there were present too many domestic forces hostile to it for it to play a role as dramatic as that of its Saint Domingue-Haiti counterpart.

It is, then, in the general rather than in the particular contribution to the antislavery ideology that the Afro-Cuban religious elements, along with Haitian *vodun*, made their more important contribution. Whatever particular phenomenon one may think of—the transculturation of saints; the small temples devoted to separate religions; the Negro literary tournaments, described by Ortiz, in which candidates composed long literary improvisations on specific themes, directed perhaps against some institution or person who had committed an offense against the Negro way of life; the enchanting saga of the Abakua society enabling the souls of its members to rest permanently in limbo rather than to endlessly pursue the path of reincarnation,[68] the various vodun ceremonies (of degradation, transmission, renunciation, and dismissal) that catalog the successive stages of the relationship between the *serviteur* and the *loa-protecteur*[69]—all of them are infused with, and are vital expressions of, a whole world view, a cosmic vision, deeply rooted in traditional African religion and culture. In that vision, the human and the divine are encompassed together in holistic fashion. Man, nature, and society are seen as necessarily intermixed with each other. All of them compose the grand order of the universe; and in that order the gods are not so much awful celestial deities to be feared as they are sentient, almost human, beings who share with their devotees their own whims and caprices. Thus, the religious tradition dynamically reenacts and symbolically resolves the myriad problems of life. Man not only enters into a rich relationship with the invisible and supernatural world; he also is enabled to conclude, both in vodun and *santería*, an alliance of spirit with that world. He thus lives on intimate terms with the first cause of a philosophical belief system that, once its primary assumptions are accepted, is as logically consistent as any rival European belief system.

It was, once again—but this time in the far more fundamental terms of cosmological vision—Africa against Europe. Or rather, to be more historically correct, it was Africa against two Europes: first, against Catholic Europe, and second, against Cartesian Europe. For in the three centuries after 1500, just as Europe brought its ideological formations to the Caribbean, so Europe itself, or at least its educated elites, was going through the great process of secularization that involved an intellectual war between religion and science. That war, inescapably, was reflected in the historic formation, throughout the same period, of the Caribbean ideological systems. Caribbean Africa had to come to terms, in one way or another, with both of the constituent elements, religious and secularist, of that European chapter in intellectual history.

The religious element, as part of the proslavery ideology, was brought in, of course, by the official ecclesiastical forces. It encountered the stubborn resilience of the African force, and never really conquered it. Its greatest success came from the efforts of its more zealous missionaries: the Jesuits, for example, before their expulsion; Laborie, in his book of 1798 on *The Coffee Planter*, testified to the respect that the Jesuit priests evoked in their slave congregations.[70] But on the whole it was love's labor lost; and it is enough to read Malouet's depressing account of the fate that awaited the unfortunate monk who requested his superiors for an appointment to Saint Domingue—and was obliged to teach slaves in the simplest of fashions, for slaves, simple-minded children corrupted by their absurd belief in magic and their spirits, are completely immune to metaphysical or philosophical dissertations—to perceive that Catholic proselytization was a lost cause.[71] The Catholic religious saw it as a war against paganism and superstition, summed up in Père Labat's astonishing story of how he was driven to fury by discovering an obeahman secretly practising his rites and he himself mercilessly beat the offender.[72] Yet ironically, both of the protagonists in that struggle had much in common in their respective world views. There was, after all, sufficient magic, obscurantism, reaction, and supernatural miracle in Catholicism itself to match the vodun and *santería* forms. The later Haitian historian Cabon pointed out, shrewdly, that it is Christianity, not vodun, that is idolatrous.[73] But because colonial society did not produce its Voltaire or its Gibbon, there was nobody to shock the colonial Catholic mandarinate with that appalling analogy. The analogy helps, however, to explain why the colonial pagan cults could easily assimilate the Catholic sainthood into their own pantheons; and in that sense there was little to choose between the idolatrous gear of the native temple and that of the cathedral altar. The analogy, in turn, had its own special consequences in the area of the relationship between religion and politics. In Europe itself, the religious wars of the sixteenth and seventeenth centuries taught the state powers that only religious toleration could guarantee political peace. Similarly, in the Caribbean, the obdurate resistance of the Afro-Caribbean cults taught the colonial administrations that the only way to ensure political stability in the slavery regime was to adopt an attitude, so to say, of religious peaceful coexistence. So, just as in Europe—in J. N. Figgis's phrase, in his book on medieval political theory, *From Gerson to Grotius*—political liberty was the residuary legatee of ecclesiastical animosities, in the Caribbean, political liberty, in the long run, was the inheritor of an unofficial concordat between the Christianity of the slavocracy and the neo-African belief structures of the slave populations.

The conflict with Cartesian Europe took on, of course, a different shape. The typical planter, again, was no Locke or Descartes. But, as all the reports show, he shared the religious indifferentism that accrued from the rationalistic assault on religion. All of the Cartesian categories of thought, and their consequences in European behavior—economic individualism, the enthronement of private will, the radical separation of faith and reason, the general hubris of European man—were pitted against the African categories of thought. The differences were rooted firmly in different systems of phenomenology. For Cartesian man, knowledge springs from experimentally observed experience; for African man, it springs from faith in cosmologic principles not susceptible to experimentation. The one is a literary tradition; the other, an oral tradition contained in myth, legend, and folktale. The one perceives the universe in terms of scientific laws, the other sees it in terms of laws that can only be apprehended by means of therapeutic or redemptive episodes in ritual and ceremony that constitute, as it were, scenarios of the transformation, in essence magical, of personal states. For Cartesian man, life and experience are divided, artificially, into separate compartments: state and church, private will and public obligation, nature and convention, reason and desire. For African man, life and experience are unified in one total domain of knowledge and understanding in which past, present, and future fuse into the awful mystery of things. It is ritual against reason, mythology against science, dialect against the dialectic, and, set within the framework of the Caribbean slave society, people against property.

That general encounter constitutes the mortal struggle, in cultural terms, between the proslavery and the antislavery ideologies. How it developed, step by step, awaits the investigation of future Caribbean culture historians, building on what has already been done. They will find a rich field to mine. There is the way in which the cults established, as do all religions, permissible boundaries of behavior for their followers: Moreau de Saint-Méry mentions the taboo stipulating that all of those guilty of sexual intercourse in Holy Week would be transformed into frogs.[74] There is the growth of the Caribbean patois speech forms, starting with the imported African dialects: Drouin de Bercy, in his memoirs of 1814, *De Saint-Domingue, de ses guerres, de ses ressources*, remarked on the fact that in the beginning, the *loas* probably spoke in the original African languages, since people knew that they had not learned the Creole forms.[75] There is the whole problem of how to understand the psychodynamics of healing in practices like *santería*. There is, finally, the main, overarching difference between the two rival ideologies, summed up in the truth that the European ideology was thoroughly erastian in its assumptions about the nature of the relationship between the religious and the secular worlds, while the African, as well as being by its very nature antistate, was dedicated to the principle of spiritual paramountcy. The planter class, on the whole, possessed little interest in religion, either for themselves or for their slaves. Indeed, as one visitor to Saint Domingue noted, they could not even be called superstitious, or it was as if they believed in nothing at all; nor could they be termed unbelievers; rather, their general attitude, in this matter of religious belief, was more one of profligacy than of philosophy.[76] If, then, there was any real religion in the slave society, it belonged to the African cult priest, the *hougan*, of vodun and the practitioner of *brujería* and *santería*, who, albeit sometimes feared, was always respected. If, furthermore, there was any real religious democracy in the society, it also belonged to the African cults; as Courlander puts it, in vodun there is no supreme individual or group to instruct or give direction to the local cults, no Pope or Dalai Lama.[77]

The third example of this general process of syncretism is that of the British West Indies, where the process was made more precipitate by the more earnest and systematic character of the European nonconformist missionary efforts—Baptist, Methodist, and Moravian. It generated, in fact, two distinct streams of popular religious belief and practice: (1) the growth of Afro-Christian cults with the traditional African element predominating—out of which emerged, after Emancipation, sects like the Shango group in Trinidad and *pocomania* in Jamaica, as well as *Cumina* and the various Myalist groups, all of them, in one way or another, popular revivalist churches, and (2) the more distinctly Afro-Protestant chapels and churches, with the English element predominating but still distinctly marked with the African heritage, and out of which emerged later groups like Zion, Revival Zion, and the Afro-Baptist sects. There were differences between both types, as well as between both of them and their Cuban and Haitian counterparts. Thus, both Protestant revivalist and *pocomania* shepherd accept the multiple-soul concept of West African religion and the resultant invocation of spirits, but they differ from vodun in that they do not invoke the African gods so much as the Christian figures of the major and minor prophets of the Old Testament, and the four evangelists of the New. The African influence is pronounced in the *Cumina* sects, with their theology of sky gods, earthbound gods, and ancestral zombies, which is almost absent in the more thoroughly Jamaican revivalist cults. Yet notwithstanding those differences, they all possess the central conviction that the divine personages, whoever they are, exercise a constant and direct

intervention in human concerns and affairs and thus confer upon their devotees, however humble, a meaning to their lives they would otherwise not
possess.

The origin of the cults, including their West African elements, in the slavery period is well attested to. The evidence of literary form comes, of course,
from uncomprehending or even hostile reports by Europeans. But even at
that, they testify strongly to the *origines africanae* (African roots). The case
was most conspicuous in Jamaica. But it was also prominent even in Barbados, the most anglicized of the islands, and in Trinidad, where slavery only
existed for a brief half a century compared to the lengthy periods in Barbados
or Jamaica. The writers on eighteenth century Barbados—Oldmixon,
Hughes, Madin, and Porteous—described the elaborate mortuary rituals, essentially African, of the slaves, as well as the ritual of oath-taking by the eating
of dirt.[78] The writers on nineteenth century Trinidad of both the pre-Emanci-
pation and the post-Emancipation periods—Day, Underhill, Joseph, De
Verteuil, Mrs. Carmichael, Kingsley, and Collens—similarly described the
various elements of the Shango-Yoruba cult movement and the obeah movement, albeit in shocked, denunciatory terms, almost as if all of it was the evil
work of the West Indian embodiment of Macbeth's witches.[79] "Obi," wrote
Joseph in his account of 1838, "was the scapegoat of the West Indies; it covered a multitude of colonial sins."[80] What that remark failed to understand
was that the movement it referred to offered to its followers comfort and con-
solation in all of the major crises of their life experience, from the daily op-
pressions of slavery on to the nature of life itself and even to the nature of
death and the afterlife—granting them an importance in spiritual life denied
to them in the political and economic life of the societies in which they lived
out their daily lives as the despised and rejected.

But the cults never retained their pristine African forms intact. The inevitable process of accommodation with the European religions meant the growth
of the well-known New World syncretist religions. In the French and Spanish
islands that meant, of course, accommodation with Catholicism, rendered
more easy by the fact that the elements of Catholicism—an elaborate pantheon of saints, an annual calendar of religious festivals, and prolific sacred
insignia—seemed so similar to the African religious elements. In the English
islands, the marriage that took place was different, the European element
being evangelical Protestantism. It was another, quite different, element of
the Protestant sects—their evangelical fervor—that appealed, in this case, to
the African religious sensibility. The outcome of the fusion was to give the
British Caribbean its characteristic religious feature, which has lasted into
the present day, of being what Whitney Cross has called a "burned-over
district," that is, a region and a people scorched by the massive fervor of revivalist Protestantism.[81] Naturally, the African elements did not die, as their
reappearance in the Great Revival in the Jamaica of the early 1860s conclusively proves.[82] What took place, rather, was an intermingling of mutually

congenial elements: Myalist spirit-possession, for example, clearly had much in common with the New Testament pentecostalist tradition of "speaking with tongues," although the congruity was fiercely denied by the Protestant missionaries. The end result was the typical native Christianity of West Indian society—mixing, so to speak, African spirit with European form.

What all this has meant, in ideological terms, has come to constitute one of the serious controversies of modern Caribbean scholarship. Do the religious belief systems of the West Indian peoples—originating in slavery and flowering in the postslavery period—belong to the antislavery or the proslavery ideology? Is it true—as scholars like Goveia, Patterson, Green, Williams, Anstey, and others, have argued—that missionary Christianity simply served, by its socially quietist teachings, to buttress the slave-based social order, whether consciously or unconsciously?[83] Or can it be argued that, ideologically, the doctrine of Christian political liberty ultimately worked, as it was applied to the slave person, to undermine that order? The enquiry is crucial, because it goes to the heart of the Caribbean condition, in which religious modes of thought have helped shape the basic communal psychology of the society.

The answer to that enquiry is, no doubt, a complicated one. Partly, it lies in the nature of the general human condition itself, its temptation to identify particular facts of social constitution with general principles of universal life. Partly, it lies in the historical material; no social change however great (like slavery emancipation itself) can efface the traces of the behavior patterns conditioned by the situation—in that particular case, slavery itself—it is seeking to destroy. Partly, again, no new system of values is likely in every area in which it operates to possess the same validity; even in a comparatively small society like the emergent Methodist congregation of the eighteenth century, the different reactions like those of Wesley and Coke to the phenomenon of slavery make it clear that men sharing the same common moral principles may see those principles in a different perspective even when they are convinced that they share a common religious viewpoint. Partly, even yet again, since the general body of Christian teaching was in itself astonishingly catholic, bringing together, as it did, so many disparate elements of the thought and morals of the ancient world, there was always the fact that support could always be found for any one particular interpretation or argument; and the debate on slavery was no exception to that rule. All of these considerations, in sum, help to explain why it is so difficult to give one, definite, conclusive answer to the enquiry here raised: What was the nature of the contribution of Caribbean religious thought to the historic discussion on slavery?

That contribution, of course, is to be found in the body of literature—reports, memoirs, letters, diaries, and the rest—developed by the Christian forces in the Caribbean society, basically (1) of the resident English missionaries, and (2) of the body of local West Indian converts that they recruited and trained. That body of literature forms an integral part of the Caribbean

ideology. Altogether, it forms a corpus of social and moral thought that runs
the whole gamut from quietist to abolitionist, from complacency to humanitarian indignation. Its cumulative effect, as one reads the literature, is to testify to the remarkable capacity of the historic Christian message to provide
some sort of answer to every mind and tortured soul that seeks some explica-
tion of the nature of things in the human condition: in this particular instance, the character and meaning of modern slavery.

To begin with, there is no argument about the basically quietist character
of the general missionary enterprise. The resident missionaries, of all denominations, accepted the tactical and strategic norms of the metropolitan abolitionist movement in England itself: the artificial separation of abolition of
the trade from emancipation of the slave; the appeasement of the slaveholding interest by means of merely ameliorative proposals; the reliance on slow
parliamentary methods; above all else, the fear of independent slave activity
along Haitian lines. Instructions from London were always emphatic on the
question of the economic condition of the slave; as the 1816 instructions
given to the missionary John Smith in his British Guiana mission field put it,
he was sent out, not to relieve the slaves from their servile condition, but to
afford them the consolations of religion.[84] Most missionaries accepted the
general principle of their metropolitan instructions that their crusade was
moral rather than political, that their grand purpose was to save the West Indian "heathen" from the slavery of sin, not from the sin of slavery.[85] Missionary education was seen as, generally, an effort to encourage scripture reading
and attendance at religious services, as well as encouraging the slave congregation member to become a useful member of society in his humble station in
life. After all, the general body of missionaries shared the assumptions of
their own English society about the sanctity of social institutions and the general lesson that there was only a small part of life that kings or laws or parliaments might hope to cure. It was a deeply conservative spirit, convinced that
happiness was independent of birth or wealth, and that existing institutions,
however wrong in detail, were essentially right in general character.

That this was the prevailing prejudice of missionary enterprise is clear
enough from the definitive work of the Reverend Thomas Coke, published in
A History of the West Indies (1808-11), on the missionary enterprise in the
Caribbean. The work summarizes, like no other, the peculiar ambivalence of
the Protestant sectarian mind when confronted with slavery. Like Edwards
before him—whose work he sought to complete, since he saw it as deficient in
its treatment of the religious development of the islands—Coke sees the slave
as enmeshed in barbarism and ignorance, from which Christianization will
emancipate him. But it will not emancipate him, necessarily, from his servile
condition, since, although slavery is contrary to the spirit of Christianity, the
ultimate Christian virtues are those of obedience and subordination. Slavery
is a part of the divine ordinance of things. The ways of God are inscrutable,
but always, in the long run, good. Coke continues:

And yet, it is not an improbable case, that even this most abominable traffic (for the abolition of which every Christian will bless the God of love), and this condition in which human nature appears in one of its most degraded and unhappy forms, may be made subservient to those wise designs, which we shall not be able fully to unravel on this side an eternal world. We are not sufficiently acquainted with the extent of sin, nor with the vast designs of God, to pronounce these things absurd, or even improbable. Thus even the slavery of the human species, though so directly contrary to the spirit of Christianity, we plainly perceive, is now overruled by the unerring wisdom of God; and, strange as it may appear, myriads without all doubt will rejoice eternally that ever they were taken into the western world.[86]

It follows from all this, Coke concludes, that what the Christian mission seeks to do in the West Indian society is not abolish slavery but rather, by inculcating the general lesson of obedience to divine law, to help to stabilize it. Those who are held in bondage in that society, he declares in an almost Burkean sentence, are obliged to trust God where they cannot trace him, since they are called to walk by faith and not by sight. It is an argument in which, as Goveia properly remarks, there are more echoes of Saint Paul than of Raynal. Clearly enough, we are here in the presence of that general variant of Christianity that—showing no more interest in social problems than did its great original founder (as his sermons make evident enough)—emphasizes this present life only as the vestibule to eternity and places the chief importance of its dreams on the next world rather than upon this one. What that message meant, in reality, for the West Indian slave was that, in Coke's words, he could enjoy the liberty to praise God in the furnace of afflictions.[87]

Most of this, on any evidence, is accommodationalist, and therefore, at bottom, a proslavery outlook. But there are, as William James put it, varieties of religious experience. Coke's volumes are far from representing completely the Christian response to slavery. The social teaching of the Christian churches was far too complex and varied to be subsumed under a single rubric. There are at least two other major ideological strands in its message apart from the quietist strand emphasized by Coke. There is, in the first place, the radical note that is present in so many of the Christian themes: the compassion for the poor; the angry denunciation of the rich; the assurance that wealth is too corruptive to allow its owners to achieve salvation easily. All of the radical-mystic sects in the history of Christianity have gone back for their inspiration to the insistence—so implicit, for example, in the strong language of the Epistle of Saint James—that the wealth of the Church is, and always will be, the enemy of its divine purpose. There is, second, the humanitarian note of the Gospel literature. Even more than the socially radical note, it is the humanitarian element that creates the classic Christian doctrine of political liberty, founded as it is on the freedom and inviolability of the individual human soul, the freedom and dignity of the individual person, irrespective of power or status. The doctrine recognizes, as a principle that can never be compromised, the ultimate right of human personality—which offers to the individual believer the means of being significant in a world the very nature of which, as in the Caribbean slave world, tended to destroy his personality. In brief, it elevates the common man, a sentiment expressed in Tertullian's boast —at which Gibbon sneered—that a Christian mechanic could give an answer to problems that had puzzled the wisest heads of antiquity. Once he possessed that conviction, the black slave in Jamaica or Barbados or Guiana had a secret source of nourishment that made his inner life more real and far more happy than anything he endured at the hands of a slave master who exerted over him the power, literally, of life and death and who—if he had ever thought about the matter—would have echoed Gibbon's sneer rather than Tertullian's boast.

How these different elements of Christian doctrine worked out in practice in the Caribbean helps provide an answer to the question: did missionary Christianity belong to the proslavery or the antislavery camp? It is clear, to begin with, that the socially radical element had little impact on the West Indian society. Of necessity—for the Christian Socialist message did not appear in the English Anglican Church itself until the 1848 movement; although it is worth noting that Kingsley's book of 1869 on the West Indies, with its argument for a sort of socialism for the West Indian peasant, had its roots in his earlier concern, in 1848, for a Christian Socialist solution to the aftermath of the Chartist defeat of that year.[88] Any real doctrines of Caribbean socialism had to wait for the twentieth century for their appearance.

It is, then, the humanitarian note that forms the leading element of the Protestant missionary ideology, just as it did with the Catholic missionary element in Las Casas earlier on. The arguments in both cases are similar (with the additional argument in the Protestant case of the doctrine of individual free will), for they both respond to the historical body of Christian teaching. Clarkson traced the moral and intellectual genealogy of antislavery thought in the introductory chapters of his work. There was, to start with, he recalled, the antislavery language of princes of the church as different in their temperaments as Cardinal Ximenes and Pope Leo X, summed up in the latter's injunction that "not only the Christian religion, but that Nature herself cried out against a state of slavery." In England itself, there were, early on, the antislavery works of the Anglican priest Morgan Godwyn and Baxter's Nonconformist *Christian Directory*. Dr. Primatt's *Dissertation on the Duty of Mercy* argued that "whether a man be white or black, such he is by God's appointment, and, abstractly considered, is neither a subject for pride, nor an object of contempt." Bishop Warburton's sermon of 1766, in turn, insisted that "Nature created man free, and grace invites him to assert his freedom," combining in that brief sentence the doctrines of both natural law and Christian redemption, to which he added the argument, responding directly to the proslavery theme that slaves were happier in the West Indies than in the African homeland, that only God could determine grades of happiness: Let your slaves judge for themselves, he admonishes the slave owners, what it is that makes their own happiness. There was, again, Clarkson acknowledged, the special Quaker contribution, in both the English and North American congregations, based on the doctrine of the inner light that all men possess and reinforced by the pervasive principle of universal love, adumbrated in the 1754 declaration of the North American province that "the characteristic and badge of a true Christian is love and good works. Our Saviour's whole life on earth was one continual exercise of them....But how can we be said to love our brethren, who bring, or, for selfish ends, keep them [the slaves] in bondage?"[89] And, finally, of course, Clarkson adds his own special contribution to the debate, that of the sense of a stricken Christian conscience outraged by the sheer inhumanity of slavery, summed up in his moving description of how, as a senior bachelor at Cambridge in 1785, he undertook the composition of his prize-winning essay on the slave trade only to find that what started (in his words) as a trial for academical reputation became transmuted into the production of a work that might be useful to injured Africa.[90]

That, of course, was metropolitan Christianity. But it is impossible to read the record of the field missionaries in the islands without realizing how so many of them, seeing themselves, as it were, as Clarksons and Wilberforces on the front line of the struggle, brought the message to the West Indies and, having brought it, made it so much a part of Creole West Indian life and thought. They had a clear conceptualization of West Indian society. The record of how that conceptualization developed is set forth in Stir Jakobsson's exhaustive study of the missions, with its title borrowed from the famous abolitionist slogan, *Am I Not a Man and a Brother?*—which in itself says so much for the missionary attitudes.[91] Not all of them, of course, were out-and-out abolitionists as such, many of them going no further than presenting the case for strong ameliorist legislation. But even the most cautious of them saw the intrinsic evil of the system; it is impossible to read the accounts of the typical plantation workday by Buchner and Ramsay and feel otherwise.[92] All of them—Smith, Phillips, Knibb, Ramsay, Cernick, Lang, Dober, and many others—as they fought for amelioration, education, and, at times, abolition, became, in Ramsay's phrase, rebel convicts against the interest and majesty of plantership.[93] Not least of all, in training a whole generation of native West Indians in things like the bible-class leadership system, they laid the ground for the later development of the "black Christianity" movement.

Their general Christian ideology is finely summed up in the figure of Ramsay, who spent nearly twenty years of his life waging the struggle in Saint Kitts. His mature thoughts are contained in his work of 1784, *An Essay on the Treatment and Conversion of African Slaves in the British Sugar Colonies*. It is a mixture of Scottish moral philosophy learned from Thomas Reid and biblical humanism. As is usual with the antislavery literature, it takes a preliminary look at slavery in the ancient world. Exodus 21 is cited to prove the comparative humanity of the Hebrew law. Athenian law permitted slaves to purchase their freedom; but as luxury increased in ancient Rome, the slave condition worsened. The well-known story of Plutarch and his slave is recounted in order to show, however, that even the most philosophic of minds can be corrupted by ownership of slaves. As for the contemporary situation, the British Caribbean slave owners claim old British liberties for themselves but deny the same liberties to their slaves. It would be in their own interest if they accepted the economic truth that better-treated slaves, not to speak of legally free wage-laborers, would be more beneficial to their own interests than the present situation.

To Hume's gratuitous charge against the Negro race Ramsay replies, in turn, that there is nothing in Africa to match the vice of contemporary Europe. "Europe has not shown greater elevation of sentiment than has shone through the gloom of Africa." Both natural law and Christian teaching preclude the arbitrary rule of one race over another. Indeed, he continues, it is more honorable for the Negro to be a member of a free state than to be the most polished slave in America or Europe. It is true that, afraid of pushing his argument too far against prevalent public opinion, Ramsay concentrated on the abolition of the trade and amelioration of slavery rather than on outright abolition of slavery too. But the thrust of his argument is indubitably in favor of freedom, influencing not only English abolitionists but also devout planters like the Nevisian Richard Nisbet, whose 1789 pamphlet, *The Capacity of Negroes for Religious and Moral Improvements Considered*, was directly inspired by Ramsay.[94]

What conclusions are to be drawn from all of this argumentation with reference to the ultimate contribution of the Christian message to complete abolitionism? The important truth to emphasize, surely, is the nature of Christianity as a general civilizing idea. "A general idea," Whitehead has written, "is always a danger to the existing order."[95] The conception of the brotherhood of man, and of the intrinsic worth of the individual person, both of those ideas being at once half-Platonic and half-Christian, became, slowly, generation after generation, the final corrosive force that challenged the very basic assumptions of the slave-based order. Once that message presented to the slave, in however cautious a manner, the image of a Christ crucified by power and yet in the end resurrected, triumphant, and full of redeeming grace for the believer; once, in addition to that, it preached a view of life in which the individual slave master was accountable, like all persons, to a supreme Master weighing good and evil in His final balance of accounts, it inevitably dissolved the moral and ideological ground on which the very principle of slavery rested. Merely to insist upon slave intellectual capacity and spiritual equality became, in themselves, principles of social reformation. As Whitehead adds in his penetrating analysis, the whole bundle of the general idea at stake constitutes a program of reform. At any moment the smoldering unhappiness of mankind may seize on one such program and initiate a period of rapid change guided by the light of its doctrines.

That some such moral and intellectual process took place, under the guidance of the missionaries, is hardly beyond doubt when the West Indian example is looked at. The missionary ideology, it goes without saying, was not consciously revolutionary in any shape or form. As appropriate to their time, men like Knibb and Smith and Wray and Talboys, as well as Ramsay, were well aware of the nature of rank and station in society. They were no more Jacobinical than any Methodist or Wesleyan minister of their time. Yet their very teaching, even their very presence, put them into the role of critics of the slave order. "I look upon the question of slavery," wrote Knibb, "as one of religion and morality. All I ask is that my African brother may stand in the family of man."[96] Merely to echo the sentiment of the Christian hymn that anticipated that "Afric's sable sons" should become "Freedmen of the Lord" was to give voice to a potentially revolutionary feeling. Missionary evangelicism provided a communion of saints that gave new meaning and direction to ordinary lives. Merely to read Waddell's account of that new community life in Jamaica in the years before Emancipation—with its ritual of teaching, conversion, and baptism, with unlettered men and women becoming eager theologians as they discuss points of doctrine with the minister, and all of them imbued with a quite insatiable thirst for the new knowledge[97]—or to read the account in Caries's diary, dealing also with Jamaica but some eighty years earlier, of individual slaves who would walk some twenty miles, at the risk of being flogged by their master as punishment, in order to attend the mission services,[98] is to appreciate how the missions offered to their devotees a new and enriched life, both personal and collective.

The missionaries themselves may not have realized the ultimate implications of the doctrine of Christian liberty that they preached. But the planters, with the keen sense of interest threatened, perceived it clearly. "It is not a matter of surprise," wrote the Jamaican newspaper *The Colonist* in 1824, "that a negro slave who is taught that all men are equal in a religious point of view should wish to see the same principle prevail in politics."[99] The dynamic relationship between Nonconformist Christianity and liberty, rooted in the assurance of the inviolability of the human soul, was real and persistent. If, indeed, the message of Christianity was something else, offering an ideological justification for slavery, that is a charge more properly brought against the official Church of England mission in the slave colonies, as is readily admitted by its apologetic historian Caldecott in his *The Church in the West Indies*, published at the very end of the nineteenth-century period.[100]

THE ABOLITIONIST STRUGGLE: ENGLAND

It is clear enough, at this point, that West Indian black Christianity was an assimilated form of its European mentors. So, although the abolitionist movement between the 1770s and the 1830s was mainly a metropolitan movement, first of the English humanitarians and then of the French philosophes, it merits a separate notice, since it so deeply influenced Caribbean movements of thought and behavior. It is impossible to isolate the two areas one from the other, for they influenced each other; the outlook of a man like Ramsay, for example, was as much West Indian as it was English. The Caribbean colonial societies were not isolated and forgotten colonial outposts like, say, Australia or Timor or Raffles' Singapore. They were in constant communication with the mother countries. The ideas of the American and French revolutions were in the air and were widely known in the West Indies, and the particular influence of the American Revolution has been traced for Santo Domingo and Puerto Rico in the work of Santana, and for the Bahamas and the West Indies in the work of Siebert.[101] There took place, indeed, a continuous and rich intercourse of ideas between the metropolitan societies and the colonies, reaching even the slave populations, and about which the slave-owning class could do little, if anything. Long, in a candid passage of his book, noted the influence of the emancipating ideas in the case of his own Jamaican slave-laboring classes, tracing it to the relatively open character of the English island societies as compared to the French (before 1789):

> The Negroes in the foreign colonies are habituated to the sight of a despotic frame of government, which controls their masters from highest to lowest, and assimilates their condition nearer to that state of servility under which they live themselves. But, in our islands, the word *liberty* is in everyone's mouth; the assemblies resound with the clamour of "liberty and property"; and it is echoed back, by all ranks and degrees, in full chorus. The whites are nearly on a level; and the lowest can find the way of bringing the highest to public justice for any injury or oppression. The Negroes here grow habitually familiar with the term; and have that object ever obvious to their sight, which is wholly withheld from, or at least but dimly seen by, the French Blacks.[102]

Clarkson's citations from some of the English sources have already been noted. But the English debate, of course, was much more widespread than that. Wylie Sypher has annotated it, in all its rich variety, in his volume *Guinea's Captive Kings*. There developed an extensive literature in sympathy with the slave figure and his sufferings. All the poets of the age—Pope, Thomson, Savage, Cowper—wrote on the theme, culminating in Wordsworth's ode to Toussaint L'Ouverture. Chatterton wrote his *African Eclogues* based upon his firsthand knowledge of the slave trade as a resident of Bristol. Blake, taking a hint from the Song of Solomon, wrote his "Little Black Boy." Cowper's simple ballad stanzas on the theme of the remorseful sailor who had participated in the trade were done in the convincing manner of the "Ancient Mariner." In the realm of the theater there was the long life of the Oroonoko legend, starting with Aphra Behn's early novelette of 1688 and going through innumerable theatrical productions throughout the following century; Garrick is said by Davies to have made his first appearance, in Ipswich, in one of them. Plays like Bickerstaff's *The Padlock* brought in the new ingredient of the realistic Negro who attempts some of the earliest black English in the history of the English theater; while later plays like Colman's *Africans*, based in part upon the documentary evidence of the *Travels* of Mungo Park, introduced a new, serious sociological note, seeing the cultural realities of Africa as against the extravagant heroics of the earlier exotic efforts. In the sphere of the novel the contribution played on a whole gamut of themes. It began with novels like Defoe's *Captain Singleton*, which, although by no means an antislavery tract, managed to present perhaps the first account in English fiction of an attempted uprising on an African slaver. The genre continued in the various novels of Mrs. Scott, Henry Mackenzie, Charlotte Smith, and Mrs. Inchbald, all of them combining an antislavery stance with the sentimentalizing manner of Sternian whimsy. It ended with the type of novel (like Robert Bage's *Man as He Is* and William Godwin's *St. Leon*) in which an attempt is made, not always successfully, to marry the antislavery theme with Jacobinical egalitarianism. To all that was added the satiric portrait of the West-Indian-planter group in England penned by the picaresque novel of the day, as good an example as any being Smollett's picture in *Humphrey Clinker* of the arriviste West-Indian planter and overseer, as well as that of the East Indian clerk and factor—all of them devoid of breeding or taste, loaded with wealth they did not know how to use, currying favor with the highborn, and utterly intoxicated with pride, vanity, and presumption: even in the midst of Beau Nash's Bath, they stood out as a brutalized and corrupt set of men.[103]

All this, of course, reflected the new rising middle-class opinion of the period, freeing itself from the old aristocratic patronage and making possible the organized parliamentary lobbying campaign of the abolitionists. Few of the leading minds of the age joined it, both Hume and Gibbon being proslavery apologists. It was aided, however, by two main currents of thought, as distinct from the current of Christian humanitarian thought. The first was that of economic liberalism, summed up in the contribution of Adam Smith. The second was that of imperial trusteeship, summed up in the contribution of Burke. Smith's main achievement was to demonstrate the economic disutility of slavery rather than its moral evil, as well as to demolish once and for all the West Indian argument for protected status within the old closed mercantile regime. The argument was taken up from a somewhat different physiocratic viewpoint by publicists like William Spence in his once widely read *Britain Independent of Commerce* (1808). The so-called gains of commerce, argued Spence, are really only the profits made by importer and exporter. What little gain accrues to the nation is offset by the nonproductive expenditure on luxury goods that has helped accelerate the decline of morality in the national life. Both West Indian rum and American tobacco serve to debilitate the population. The expenditures of the East India Company outrun its profits, and by evidence of the West Indian planters themselves the profitability of the West Indian trade has declined catastrophically over the last twenty years. All this, Spence concludes, demolishes the argument of the economic importance of colonial possessions. The influence of Smith's utilitarian assault on the system is evident enough.[104]

The contribution of Burke was somewhat different. He did not so much launch a frontal attack upon slavery as undermine it indirectly by the force of his major hypotheses. He was, as has well been pointed out, the true founder of the third British Empire. He made its moral foundation the lesson that there existed, as it were, a compact within which the colonial subject has rights and the imperial master obligations. The lesson was set forth magisterially in his speeches during the Warren Hastings trial. "To this at least," he admonished the court, listing the duty of the English conqueror in India, "he is strictly bound—he ought to govern them as he governs his own subjects. But every wise conqueror has gone much further than he was bound to go. It has been his ambition and his policy to reconcile the vanquished to his fortune, to show that they have gained by the change, to convert their momentary suffering into a long benefit, and to draw from the humiliation of his enemies an accession to his own glory." With that he included the warning that all colonial rule should respect the inherited cultural forms of the colonial subjects. "If," he argued, "we undertake to govern the inhabitants of such a country [India] we must govern them upon their own principles and maxims, and not upon ours. We must not think to force them into the narrow circle of our own ideas; we must extend ours to take in their system of opinions and rites, and the necessities which result from both; all change on their part is absolutely impracticable. We have more versatility of character and manners, and it is we who must conform."[105] Burke, clearly, was the first English statesman to comprehend the moral import of the problem of subject races. It is true that he was not listened to in his own age, as the acquittal of Hastings shows. But it is also true that his doctrine of trusteeship became the operative ideal of the best of the English colonial administrative class that took over the government of the West Indies after 1838; and, even more, that it became the leading idea in all of the reforming West Indian forces themselves right up to the Second World War period of the twentieth century, claiming, as they did, that the British tradition they all admired required that Britain treat its colonial citizens with all of the sense of fair play and justice with which it treated its own domestic citizens.

THE ABOLITIONIST STRUGGLE: FRANCE

The French debate on slavery, summarized in Edward Seeber's book *Anti-Slavery Opinion in France During the Second Half of the Eighteenth Century*, was as widespread as the English, if not perhaps even more so, since in France it became involved with the larger intellectual assault upon the *ancien régime*, of which it was seen as an integral part; and with the further differ-

ence that whereas the English discussion tended to be romantic and sentimental, the French discussion tended to be more analytical and philosophical,
reflecting in a way the difference in the respective national modes of thought.

The French contribution has traditionally been seen as starting with Montesquieu's *Lettres persanes* of 1721, in which, without undertaking a demand
for the abolition of slavery, he argued strongly for at least a return to the old
Roman plan providing for humane regulation of the system. That, of course,
was an early critique. But after 1750 or so criticism begins to multiply. Writers as different in temperament as Voltaire and Raynal used the new popularity of the Indian theme, so evident in, for example, Mme. de Grafigny's
Lettres peruviennes, to castigate the atrocities of the Spanish conquerors,
while the accounts of Bougainville and Cook on the newly discovered Tahitian
islands were used to drive home the argument that the absence of slavery contributed to the happiness of their native inhabitants. The enormous popularity of the travelogue, in turn—as testified to by the influence of the abbé
Prevost's great *Histoire generale des voyages*—helped to rehabilitate the
African race in European eyes, with its various descriptions, by a myriad of
writers, of the customs, habits, and folklore of the African tradition. The
positive qualities of the Negro character were emphasized—following Buf-
fon's early encomium—in writers like Chambou, the abbé Proyart, and the
translator of Leslie's *New History of Jamaica*. Laplace's translation of Mrs.
Behn's *Oroonoko* inaugurated a veritable rage for the "noble savage" theme;
M. Mornet's study of the catalogs of 392 private libraries dating from 1760 to
1780 has noted the telling fact that *Oroonoko* was apparently among the nine
most widely read English novels in France during that period. The humanitarian writers took up that sentimental tone, attacking slavery for its essential cruelty and barbarity; the theme was conducted, with all of its appeal to
the *coeurs sensibles* of the reading public, by Saint-Pierre, the abbé Gérard,
Mailhol, the abbé Bardou, and Saint-Lambert, and was immeasurably reinforced by the French enthusiasm for the antislavery stance of the American
Quakers, from Voltaire on to Turgot. The theme flowered into the vast Negro-
phile literature that lasted well until the end of the Revolution of 1789 itself;
its various elements included, among others, the various antislavery articles
of both the original encyclopedia of the radical philosophes and Panckouke's
later *Encyclopedie méthodique*; Condorcet's remarkable *Réflexions sur l'esclavage des nègres*, which contained one of the most complete and thorough
plans of abolition in the whole literature; the satiric work of Delacroix and
Mercier; Bernardin de Saint-Pierre's sentimental novel *Paul et Virginie*, owing so much as it did, in its antislavery invective, to the author's personal observations of slavery in the Ile de France; and all culminating in the *Histoire
des Deux Indes*, written by the abbé Raynal and, as we know from recent
research, by a host of collaborators including Pechmeja and Diderot.[106]

The themes covered by this tremendous outpouring covered all aspects of
the slavery question. There is the description, by means of the sensational

anecdote, of the barbaric cruelty in the treatment of the slave, astutely used by Voltaire, relying on the work of Las Casas, and continued by Mailhol, Holbach, Saint-Lambert, and others. There is the condemnation of a Christianity that, in the name of salvation, justified slavery; if the non-Christian peoples, declaims the abbé Bardou, castigate us Christians for violating Christian precepts of liberty by enslaving Africans, are they not justified in the charge? The abbé Delaurens drove home the point in his animated dialogue between a Christian protagonist and a Negro philosopher in his *L'Aretin* of 1763, in which the Negro protagonist closes the argument by reminding his Christian antagonist that Christianity calls upon men to carry their cross but in colonial Martinique it is only the slave who really carries it. Voltaire, again, points out that there is nothing in the writings of the Apostles or in the teaching of the historical Jesus in the New Testament that condemns slavery, and agrees with Linguet that it is not Christian charity that has broken the chains of slavery; rather, Christianity has tightened the chains. The charge is all the more telling since Voltaire was not regarded in his own day as the most ardent antislavery writer and indeed was often accused of writing on the topic with unpardonable levity. The legal apology for slavery found similar critics; natural law, asserts Diderot, can no more make a slave the property of the master than it can make the citizen the property of the sovereign; and Raynal emphasized the same point. Nor is the contract theory of slavery any more plausible; Puffendorf has argued, says Voltaire, that slavery has been established by the mutual consent of the parties, but I shall believe him when he shows me the original contract. Rousseau added his own impressive opinion to the argument against self-sale in his criticism of Grotius on that important point.[107]

There is, finally, the economic argument against slavery. In part, it saw New World slavery as feeding the passion for luxury, including sugar products, that was corrupting European manners. There is not a barrel of sugar arriving in Europe, Helvetius comments, that is not tainted with human blood. I do not know, added Saint-Pierre, if coffee and sugar are necessary to the happiness of Europe, but I do know that they have been responsible for the unhappiness of two parts of the world (America and Africa). The physiocrat economists—notably Mirabeau, Du Pont de Nemours, and Turgot—went on to demonstrate, among other points, the uneconomically high costs of slave labor, the comparative economy of free labor, and the general opposition of the slave regime to all proper principles of agricultural science and population policy.[108]

This, then, was the metropolitan contribution, English and French, to the antislavery cause. Yet it is important to note its special characteristics, repeated as they were in the Caribbean elements that were influenced by it. For although it hated slavery, it was far from being an openly or fully revolutionary movement of thought. It was, in the main, the work of bourgeois publicists, constituting the literary wing of the rising middle-class public opinion of the age. It saw slavery as a moral excrescence or an economic aberration, not necessarily related, except by accident, to the bourgeois order of things. It thought of abolition in terms of metropolitan policy; it rarely considered the possibility, least of all the desirability, that the slave might emancipate himself by his own effort. It feared slave revolts as much as its adversaries; and, indeed, it shared with the more liberal of those adversaries a preference for a slow process of gradualist amelioration of the system rather than immediate abolition.

Thus, in the English case, the main note in the literature is not so much revolutionary indignation as sentimental pity, of what Sypher aptly terms the "delectable anti-slavery tear." For eighteenth-century England was the age of feeling. It cultivated its sentimental feelings by playing on all of the sublime themes that the figure of the slave provided: the primitivistic note that contrasts the pseudo-Africa of an idyllic life with the proslavery concept of Africa as a hell of cannibals and tigers from which the slave trade had rescued the slave; the Oroonoko legend of the regal African suffering in sublime dignity; the popular Inkle-Yarico story, telling the legend of unrequited love; the theme of the "dying Negro" who can expire nobly—much of it constituting, in sum, a dream picture of an imagined noble black existence that opposes to the Negrophobia of the proslavery ideology an ideology of its own, full of romantic effusions, enforcing (in Sypher's phrase) an ethical principle by an operatic gesture. It is frequently the cruelty of the planter to his slave charges, rather than slavery itself, that is lamented. All that, perhaps, helps to explain why the English abolitionist movement's leaders could persuade themselves that slavery and the slave trade were two separate evils and that it would be impossible to attempt to overthrow both at the same time. It also perhaps helps to explain why, once slavery was over, the same leadership wanted to see it replaced with a new social order requiring discipline and work habits almost as onerous as the slave system itself; that much is evident enough from the curious Christophe-Clarkson correspondence, in which the English reformer welcomed enthusiastically the efforts of the new black Haitian kingdom to organize a planned work regime placing severe demands upon the newly enfranchised peasantry.

The same note of social conservatism—that the abolition of the slave trade and slavery was not to be seen as any radical move to change the ranking system of the contemporary class societies—is present also in the French discussion on the matter, especially the debate on slavery that accompanied the successive phases of the revolution after 1789. Hardy's early study of 1919 on the question makes that painfully clear. On every critical matter—abolition of the trade, the right of the local white colonial assemblies to determine representation in Paris, the claims of the colonial mulatto delegations—the new leadership of Paris came down on the conservative side. Barnave accepted the peculiar doctrine, advanced by Du Pont de Nemours, of the legal fiction of the perpetual minority of the slaves, thus denying them representation according to their numbers.[109] The literary genius of the Revolution took much the same attitude, despite its very real hatred of slavery. Brissot strikes the typical note with his admonition, "Let us not be *enthousiastes* nor *frondeurs*."[110] Lanthenas writes that even Père Labat, in his *Nouvelle relation de l'Afrique Occidentale*, had been critical of the capacity of the old French slaving company of Senegal; but then, on a more cautious note, he defends the Amis des Noirs by pointing out that they realize that the time has not yet come for the liberty of the slaves and that they do not believe in slave rebellions.[111] The deputy Viefville des Essars, in turn, cites the *Social Contract* in support of the argument that no man can alienate his own liberty, but then goes on to assuage fears of slave revolt by advocating a gradual, annual release of slaves rather than a general and immediate emancipation.[112] The deputy Dorfeuille also recommends a similar plan of gradual freedom, and even includes a plan for the paid indemnity of the planters who will lose their slaves; the whole second part of his *Addresse*, indeed, is devoted to determining how it is possible to avert a general slave uprising in Saint Domingue, which can only be done, he adds, by an alliance between the colons, the people of color, and the Creole section of the slaves.[113] Bonnemain, again, is clear on the point that there is no excuse for slavery, for every man, he writes, who has had the misfortune to lose his liberty has the right to reclaim it. But he immediately hastens to add that this does not justify revolt, and goes on to warn the slaves not to abuse their new freedom, once they have it: "qu'une frénésie ne vous porte pas a des insurrections aussi dangereuses pour vous que pour vos maîtres" (that some madness does not encourage you in undertaking rebellions as dangerous to you as to your master).[114]

Except, then, for the more extremist and Jacobinical, the antislavery writers were as concerned as any colon with certain aspects of the problem going beyond an antislavery stance. They at times accepted the colon argument about the commercial value of the colonies to France, even a revolutionary France. One anonymous writer agrees that France cannot live without the colonies; so, let the colonists agree to a reasonable compromise; I wish, if it is possible, he asserts, to reconcile the prerogatives of man with the well-being of the state.[115] The chevalier de Laborie recommends, as the detail of such a compromise, the replacement of slave labor with free labor, whereby the slave will gain his liberty and the master will benefit from a work regime of increased productivity.[116] More generally, all of the writers agree on two basic principles of reform. The first is that of a gradual abolition. Abolition overnight can only have disastrous consequences. A sudden liberty of the Negroes, writes Lecointe-Marsillac in his widely read *Le More-Lack*, would be an act of arbitrary authority that would ruin the colonies and excite a dangerous revolution in the slave population; it is an admission all the more significant since it follows an exhaustive refutation of all of the leading elements of the proslavery ideology, including its myths about the Negro character.[117] The same fear of independent activity on the part of the slave masses informs the pamphlet by another anonymous author, in reply to the gratuitous charge of the colons that the Société des Amis des Noirs sought to foment subversive slave activities: They must be mad, writes the author, to think that a society with only fifteen members and only 800 livres in its treasury could instigate a global revolution, not to mention the fact that men as respectable as the King of Poland and the Duc de Charost are members, while men like Mirabeau and Robespierre are not members.[118]

The second principle involved is the precept that the New World slave, his slavery aside, remains still a child-person not eligible for full adult freedom. Mandar, in his pamphlet of 1790, could go so far as to argue that the slaves possessed a temper of natural indolence and that Europeans possess, as against them, *un ascendant légitime et naturel* (a legitimate and natural superiority).[119] The chevalier de Laborie added the argument that the chains of slavery must not be broken until the slaves are held by new ties of convenience and interest to a new regime of free labor.[120] Only Condorcet, perhaps, in his 1788 essay on slavery, managed to rise above that European ethnocentric temper in his assertion that "It is not climate, or geography, nor physical constitution, nor the national spirit to which can be attributed the seeming laziness of certain peoples; but the bad laws that govern them."[121]

Granted these attitudes, it is little wonder that the Convention only abolished slavery in 1795 under pressure from events in Saint Domingue itself, thereby making a virtue out of necessity. Its cautious temper on the colonial matter reflected its cautious temper in domestic matters. Property triumphed over principle. "The central abuse against which the Revolution reacted," concludes Hardy, "was the subordination of the interests of property to those of the nobility and clergy, and the same conservative impulse which led the bourgeoisie to protect the ballot from the *sans-culottes*... made them also very ready to weigh sugar heavy in the balance against slavery, and rotting ships against rattling chains."[122]

THE ABOLITIONIST STRUGGLE: SCHOELCHER

The final chapter in the history of antislavery struggle in the French Antilles relates, of course, to the Eastern Caribbean possessions. The reimposition of slavery by the Napoleonic regime prolonged the system until its abolition by the Second Republic in 1848. The leading spirit in the continuing struggle to end it was, of course, the noble figure of Victor Schoelcher. His lifelong struggle for slavery emancipation began when he observed the slave system at first hand in Havana and New Orleans during a trip made to Mexico in the interests of his family business as early as 1829–30. From then on he inherited the mantle of the abbé Gregoire. More than any other single figure, he made possible the 1848 abolition; and the savant Arago, who was named Minister of the Navy and Colonies in 1848, has described in his memoirs how it was the cogent argumentation of Schoelcher that persuaded him to replace a plan for gradual abolition with a decree ordering immediate emancipation.[123] Schoelcher helped to implement the plan in his capacity as elected deputy for Martinique, until forced to leave France as a result of the coup d'état of Louis Napoleon in 1851.

Disciple of de Tocqueville, Schoelcher emerges in his collected writings on the Caribbean as the liberal republican par excellence—anticlerical, antimonarchist, antiracist, convinced of the universal citizenship of all men. The principles of 1789, he is sure, apply to all men and all nations. Slavery is inadmissible not merely because it is cruel but because it violates those principles. Liberty, when its hour has come, he warns the Antillean slave owners, has its own indefinable force that will destroy everything that opposes it. The Negroes will appropriate their own liberty if the metropolis does not grant it. The experience of emancipation in the British islands shows that, if granted proper protective measures, the ex-slave will become a willing free laborer on the estates.[124] He notes that the planters of the Danish islands are more reasonable than those in the French islands, because they recognize the "irresistible necessity" of the times, that emancipation is inevitable; although, even then, he also notes their hatred of colonial administrators, like Governor von Scholten, who favor the move. In the same vein, he is critical of the ambivalent attitude of religious groups like the Moravian missionaries who, while championing religious liberty, at the same time retain their own slave system; they preach to their slaves twice daily, he observes bitterly, but they do not release them from their misery. The planter policy of amelioration— all this is to say, of a slow, gradual emancipation—will not work, because the planters themselves make little effort to implement it.[125]

In all of this it is urgent to note that Schoelcher is a man of his time. He is against slavery. But he is not necessarily against French colonialism as such. As much as any Gaullist a century later, he believes in the idea of the French colonizing mission, but in his case, of course, it is based on radical republican principles. For him, slavery is one thing, the colonial condition another. Or, to put it differently, slavery for him is a social question; it is not a national question. Its abolition concerns the relationship between master and slave, not the relationship between republic and colony. No more than Wilberforce in the English case, then, does he see that the two are related to each other, and that release from the one means, logically, release from the other.

Why that was so was related, ultimately, to the very character of the French political thought of the Left ever since 1789. It announced the great principles of universal brotherhood and the rights of man. But it always assumed that France remained as the supreme carrier of those principles, and the overriding assumption of Francophilia never left its leading protagonists. It is the France of Racine and Corneille, of Chateaubriand and Victor Hugo, of Voltaire and Rousseau, that is the embodiment of culture and civilization.

So, the Revolution of 1789 could declare its faith in universal fraternity but at the same time unleash wars of conquest that solidified the rule of the French bourgeoisie. Correspondingly, it was incapable, because of its Francophile obsession, of applying the doctrine of freedom to its colonial peoples; and neither the Second Empire nor the Third Republic was ever capable of any serious effort at such an application. That, then, explains why Schoelcher himself, as much as anybody else entrapped in that contradiction, could see slavery emancipation in 1848 as simply a grand method of retaining the loyalty of the Antilleans: the colonies, he wrote, have been saved by Emancipation.

The revolutionaries of 1848 saw it in the same manner, so that the ideology of *fraternalisme* (revolutionary brotherhood) really became an argument for denying any claims of independent nationalism that might have come out of the colonial empire. That assimilationist bias continued with the Socialists and Communists right through the next century or more, in both the metropole and the colony. It was strengthened by the Schoelcher legend that "Schoelcher freed the slaves," similar to the American legend that "Lincoln freed the slaves." Nothing illustrates better the deep power of the Francophile theme than the fact that, going on into the last quarter of the twentieth century, there are no openly nationalist-independence movements in the French Antilles comparable to those that have emerged in both the English-speaking and the Dutch Caribbean areas. Schoelcher himself admired the tradition of Toussaint and Dessalines, much admired the Haiti of his own day, and could insist that the "black republic" was not much less advanced than the much-touted "white republic" of Mexico. No more than most radicals, socialists, and communists in the history of the national republic, however, could he bring himself to recognize that all that logically involved the legitimacy of Antillean independence.[126]

Yet, when all that is admitted, Schoelcher's was perhaps the major single force in the shaping of French Antillean attitudes throughout the rest of the century, and indeed beyond. The France that he represented was at least France at its best. To read the journal of the Councillor Garnier—appointed to his Antillean judicial post in 1848 and surviving into the period of the Second Empire, who came from the lower provincial judicial circles of the metropolis—is to realize, by contrast, the full achievement of Schoelcher; for the journal is the diary record of an ordinary, cautious legal mind fully at ease in the humdrum daily life of the colony, not excited by large questions of social and political justice, welcoming the 1851 coup d'état as a triumph of the party of order, and content to accept all of the decadence and corruption of the Second Empire so long as his own interests and those of his family are secured.[127]

By contrast, with all of its ideological limitations, the lifework of Schoelcher illustrates at its best the French radical-republican tradition. More than anything else, he assailed the whole mythology of the planter ideology. The Negro is not irretrievably ignorant; he is the equal of us all. Climate in the tropics does not justify slavery, for the example of the hardworking white *jíbaro* class in Puerto Rico proves otherwise. There is little difference between Spain and the other slave powers in the treatment of the slave person; so, again in the Puerto Rican case, that particular myth, sustained even by many Puerto Rican liberal abolitionists of the time, is effectively challenged by Schoelcher's own personal observations: no nation, he writes caustically of the Spanish record, has treated its slaves better in terms of legislation and no nation has treated them worse in terms of actual colonial reality. Dogs in Paris, he added, are treated better than slaves in Puerto Rico.[128] That passionate concern for the Antillean peoples remained with him to the end, so that it is not altogether inappropriate that as late as 1882 he should have collaborated with his friend, the Puerto Rican nationalist Betances, in the preparation of a friendly introduction to a volume published by a group of Haitian students on the theme, once again, of the defense of Haiti against its European detractors.[129]

THE ABOLITIONIST STRUGGLE: THE FREE COLOREDS

It is at this point that the metropolitan antislavery ideology joins hands with the ideology of its natural allies in the colonial situation. The preeminent ally was, of course, the Caribbean mulatto "middle-class" group. The peculiar ambivalence of their location within the Caribbean society is, of course, well-known, and has been documented for particular societies—Jamaican, for example, by scholars like Dunker and Campbell. Phenotypic imprecision, their being neither white nor black, and social class insecurity—since they belonged neither to the black masses nor to the white elite—produced in them a crippling incertitude about identity. They were caught, quite simply, between the devil of white contempt and the deep blue sea of a black slave mass that did not want them either. Frequently slave owners themselves, they belonged, in class terms, to the white upper caste. Their final ambition, then, was to be accorded the legal status and social regard accorded to the whites, an aspiration met, at least in the case of the Danish West Indies, with the Danish royal order of 1830 that granted equality of status to approved ranks of the "free colored" elite; to which honor the colored group responded by proposing that a medal be struck, with royal approval, in recognition of the service done in their interest by the liberal governor Von Scholten.[130]

Not surprisingly, then—to come back to the French Antillean situation—the Saint Domingue mulatto representatives became the darlings of the Parisian salons of the revolutionary period. They saw themselves, so to speak, as the third estate of the colonial struggle; and the Parisian literature echoed their prejudice. Dorfeuille, dismissing the white colons as a people of barbarity and cruelty, repeats Barnave's idea of courting the people of color as an intermediary class. Lecointe-Marsillac uses the story of the African prince Job Ben-Solomon to underline the lesson that Africans have as much reason and intelligence as Europeans, and if they receive an European education, are as capable of absorbing knowledge as any European person.[131] The abbé Sibire vigorously assails the colonialist presumption that once a slave, always a slave: "The first juriconsult who gravely decided that the child of a slave is born a slave has determined in other words that a man is not born a man."[132] It was an important point; for presumption of free status at birth was the first point to be won if a slave child wished to become, in later life, a member of the free-colored group.

The mulatto *affranchis* were thus identified as the one group that could keep at bay both white colon and black slave—both seen as enemies of France. The Parisians waxed eloquent in their praise and admiration. In a fiercely anticlerical piece, Chaumette reminds his readers, citing Labat, how the priests argued Louis XIII into condoning the slave trade, and goes on to invoke the memory of the Saint Domingue mulatto leader Ogé as one type of ally who, if supported, could help to undo that great wrong.[133] The abbé de Cournand elaborates on the theme. Those who have preoccupied themselves with the slavery of the Negroes, he complains, have said nothing about the people of color; this is the real problem of the *injustice americaine*. They suffer from the prejudice of skin color: I imagine, he states, that the Jews have never suffered as many humiliations in any country of Europe. They must be defended against their detractors. After all, he continues, many of them have contracted honorable alliances with leading families in France; they have lost almost all of any African origin; and in their skin color they are hardly any different from many whites whose coloration has been darkened at once by the heat of our own provinces of the Midi and the heat of the tropics themselves. They are a class of men having the same interests as the colonial whites, linked by birth to the propertied class of Saint Domingue. It is to be hoped that reason and humanity will penetrate French America, and that we will begin to see the *sangmêlés* as a means of increasing the power and prosperity of the colony.[134] The admirable abbé Gregoire, finally, adds his own contribution to the defense. The *sangmêlés*, he reminds his fellow philosophes, suffer from gross civil disabilities: the Saint Domingue magistrate M. de Beauvois suggests, in his book *Idées sommaires*, that all of their nonmovable property should be taken away from them, in return for a modest pension; and the general temper of the whites can be gathered from the remark of the president of the Assembly of Saint Marc, which Gregoire quotes, that even to speak of the rights of *sangmêlés* is *un dérèglement d'idées* (to turn all accepted ideas upside down). This is all the more inexcusable, he tells the people of color themselves, when we remember that color prejudice does not exist in the East Indies and that the Academy of Sciences has a mulatto correspondent in the Ile de France.[135] "Cetto race croisée, partant robuste," he concludes, "est regardeé, depuis longtemps, comme le plus ferme appui de la colonie contre l'insurrection des Nègres et le marronage." (This race of mixed types, altogether robust, has been seen for a long time as the strongest bulwark of the colonies against Negro rebellion and escape from the plantations.)[136]

Much of all this reflects the self-image of the mulattoes themselves. Theirs was an ideological ambiguity. They were at once antislave and proslave: antislave because they shared the white hatred of the blacks; proslave because the refusal of the whites to join them in a common alliance drove them, under the pressure of events, into the proslave camp. That was so in both the Saint Domingue and the Jamaican cases. The Saint Domingue mulatto hated the blacks more than he hated the whites; the subtle ranking order, based on grades of color, read (in the phrase of C.L.R. James, the leading English-speaking historian of the revolution) like a cross between a nightmare and a bad joke. Both of the mulatto leaders, Raimond and Ogé, sought to persuade the National Assembly in Paris that civil liberty for the free colored population would not lead to slave rebellion, since the mulattoes—being themselves slave owners and forming the sole militia of the colony—were really the chief safeguard against such revolt.[137] As a group, the mulatto element invoked, like the white colons, the principles of the Declaration of the Rights of Man, but, again like the colons, they used them only as arguments to defend their own class interests. Their hatred of the black generals even lasted into the postindependence period, so that nineteenth-century mulatto Haitian scholarship, as in figures like Ardouin and Saint-Rémy, conspired to paint a derogatory portrait of Toussaint L'Ouverture, among others. It was, indeed, only a rare mulatto like the remarkable Baron De Vastey (who became the leading ideologue of the revolution) who was prepared to defend the revolution and all its works, from a *noiriste* viewpoint, in the period after 1804.[138]

Granted the different historical evolution of the society, it was much the same in slave Jamaica. One historian of the free colored has amply documented how their struggle for civil rights, as their numerous petitions show, deliberately excluded not only the slaves but also even the body of "free blacks"—only concerned with their own narrow interests, and pointedly avoiding any alliance with either group.[139] They were constitutionalists, but, again, only for their own cause. They kept away from the 1831 slave rebellion, just as they failed to join in any movement against the repressive behavior of Governor Eyre in the 1865 crisis. It is not surprising, then, that a man like Campbell should have stated the case for the disabilities of his class, early on, in terms of reverence for the British Crown; or that Jordon came to believe that pre-1865 Jamaica was not fit for self-government; or that Gordon's letter to his wife on the eve of his execution was a model of Christian resignation. Their historian, again, has noted how their general argumentation, in successive struggles with governors and assemblies, was in the manner of English empiricism, studiously avoiding any appeal to abstract ideas based on equality or the rights of man and going no further than to emphasize, pragmatically, the importance of the benefits that would accrue to society if they were granted equal rights.[140] Their struggle, essentially, was with the old aristocracy of Creole whites. It is not until that aristocracy came to change in its social composition that there emerges, later on, as in brown Jamaican leaders like Osborn, a new and more independent spirit of brown nationalism, based on a love for their native Jamaica and a conviction, absent in the earlier movement, that they were entitled to regard themselves as the natural successors, in the government of the society, to the white planter class: as, that is to say, an alternative ruling class.[141] But even then, their ideological baggage had little to do with seminal ideas or first principles. The contrast with the pervasive influence of such ideas and principles in the Saint Domingue–Haiti case, emanating from Paris and Philadelphia, is striking.

THE IDEOLOGY OF THE SLAVE REBELLIONS

In every movement of social change there has to be what H. G. Wells has called "a theory of the competent receiver." That is to say, there must be one group or class that by reason of experience and mood can put itself forward as the one group or class most competent to conduct the change. In the general area of the antislavery ideology in the old Caribbean slave society, that class, without doubt, was the slave class itself. It is, then, to the history of the great slave rebellions that the historian must go for the most revolutionary statement of the ideology—culminating, of course, in the great Saint Domingue servile war. It is, after all, no accident that the Convention's Abolition of Slavery in 1794 followed hard on the heels of the Saint Domingue 1791 uprising, or that the British parliamentary abolition of 1834 followed just three years after the Jamaica rebellion of 1831. The most oppressed victim of the system became its most intractable enemy.

Yet a preliminary note is in order on this matter. There has been a temptation, natural enough perhaps, on the part of modern Caribbean scholarship, both of the *négritude* and black power persuasions, to generate, so to speak, its own *leyenda negra*, eulogizing the Caribbean black slave person as the hero figure of antislavery resistance. That perspective, it has to be pointed out, ignores the vital fact that, historically, the resistance starts long before the introduction of African slavery, with the figure of the Antillean Indian, who was himself subjected to the earlier form of New World slavery, the Spanish *encomienda* system based on forced labor. The consequent distortion of the historical reality, it is only fair to add, has been compounded by the other school of Caribbean scholarship emanating from the Hispanic Caribbean area. Feeding on the various strands of the Latin American intellectual currents of the age—Sarmiento's adulation of European civilization, Rodó's *arielist* movement with its idealization of Latin aristocratic grace, Ortega's cultural pessimism: all of them imbued with racist assumptions—that scholarship has embraced the vision of a romantic and aristocratic Hispanophilism in which Antillean history begins, arbitrarily, with the arrival of the

conquistadores. The original Indian cultural component is thus either de-
leted or blandly ignored or, alternatively, converted into a romantic mystique
(which is, of course, only the logical reverse of the other attitude), as is evident enough in the history of the Antillean *indianista* novel. Both of these
schools of thought, the Africanist and the Hispanophilist, have, albeit from
radically different perspectives, managed to sustain an antiindigenous bias
about Antillean social history, relegating the original pre-Columbian tribal
cultures to the realm of the merely romantic picturesque or, even worse, of
the uncivilized cannibalistic.

The historical record speaks differently. Not only did the pre-Columbian
cultures provide an economic and social order alternative to the order imposed by the European supervening culture, they also wrote the first chapter
in the history of the American resistance. The Mexican scholar Josefina Oliva
de Coll has annotated that record in the early section of her book *La resistencia indígena ante la Conquista*, drawing heavily on Las Casas for the detail
of the matter.[142] As opposed to the myth of the fragile, docile Indian, there
was, in truth, the story of the chieftains, in Cuba, Hispaniola, and Puerto
Rico, who led their warriors into defiant resistance. Not to kill or rob Indians
here in the Indies, remarked Las Casas, is considered to be a crime. The Indians responded in kind. Confronted with a strange and terrifying European
weaponry—gunpowder, the armored horse, the horseriding soldier, the naval
galleon—they invented the methods of guerrilla warfare and scorched earth
to defend themselves. Leader chieftains like Guarocuya (Enriquillo) in Hispaniola and Guama in Cuba invented the strategic device of the mountain fast-
ness, insulating themselves effectively from the Spanish soldiery. They even
managed to master the art of taking over the Spanish warships and converting them to their own use, as testified to by an astonishing descriptive passage in Las Casas.[143] Even the collective hunger strike, a form of mass suicide,
was recruited as a method in the continuing struggle. The Spaniards had employed a sort of psychological warfare against their local enemies by promulgating the legend of their own immortality; the Borinquén leader Uroyoan
exposed the emptiness of the legend by having a group of his followers drown
a Spanish soldier: a story that later became immortalized in Puerto Rican literature.[144] The Indians even employed an early indigenous method of poison
gas against their enemies, as we know from an early account rendered by
Marcos de Aguilar, the Spanish senior mayor of Hispaniola, to the Jerónimo
order in 1517.[145]

Behind all of this physical resistance there also resided a psychological resistance. Albeit overawed by the sheer material force of the conquistadores,
the aboriginal peoples still had behind them a cosmological vision of things
that they did not lightly surrender. Caught within a collision between races at
different cultural levels that they could not fully comprehend, they returned
to that vision for sustenance. Guarocuya's vow that the gentlemen and kings
of this island will never recognize the king of Castille as overlord summed up

their spirit, as did also the well-known story of Hatuey's execution, in which that *cacique* refused the last rite of baptism on the ground that he did not wish to enter a heaven full of people such as the Christians[146]—an act of final defiance understandable enough in the light of Charlevoix's candid admission, in his book of 1730, that "the greater part of the infidels, judging the God of the Christians by the manner in which his followers have treated them, entertain no very strong conviction about his goodness or saintliness."[147] Du Tertre noted the same scepticism; the Indians, he observed, laugh and mock at the Christian religion, and the worst insult you can offer a savage is to call him a Christian.[148] The Sieur de la Borde, finally, commented on the same attitude in the Caribs—who conducted their own campaigns against the European intruders in the Lesser Antilles islands. They have, he wrote, the temperament of heretics in their religion; and those Caribs who have not changed tell the others that the cause of all of the misfortunes of the Christians, such as illness, stems from the fact that they do not live like Caribs.[149] The note of indigenous cultural loyalty is unmistakable; and in the case of the Hispaniola resistance it explains why a *cacique* like Guarocuya could pass through a Christianizing period under the wing of Las Casas himself and remain untouched by the experience.[150] It is clear from all of this that the portrait of the aboriginal cultures and people that has been painted by historians—of the clash between a European activism and an Antillean passivity—is a grievously mistaken one. What the Spanish viewed as an innate Indian incapacity for work was in truth a method of passive resistance; what they saw as insane suicide was, as Ortiz has noted, a biological act demanded by a nature the European mind did not understand; and the European-pragmatic syndrome of the spiritually alienated Indian is put to rest by Lévi-Strauss's tart remark that while the Spanish Crown was sending missionaries to the Indies to determine whether the Indians had a soul, the Indians were experimentally watching over dead bodies of Spanish soldiers to see if they would decompose.

Not least of all, the Indo-Antillean resistance left behind it an important element of Caribbean regional identity. The well-known political balkanization of the region was, in fact, another European import, reinforced by the inability of the proslavery ideology ever to give birth to a genuine sense of regional common purpose between the various sugar islands, English, French, Spanish, and Dutch. All of the historical evidence suggests that, apart from the conflicts introduced by the marauding Caribs, the Antilles encountered by Columbus were joined together, quite differently, by a common cultural bond. Its physical basis was the easy and rapid interisland traffic system of boat and canoe, described by Las Casas; its cultural expression lay in the bonds of consanguinity binding together the various tribal leaders of the different islands, and in the significant similarity of customs, such as games and religious ceremonies, as well as marriage forms, as remarked upon by Oviedo.[151] This cultural communality carried over into the resistance movement; so much so that Aguilar, in the report already referred to, described at length how the Cuban chieftains, having received news of the 1511 uprising in neighboring Borinquén, celebrated the event with a tremendous fiesta and then proceeded to conspire with the other leaders of the island to follow them in a similar uprising.[152] The leading contribution of the early native peoples to Caribbean cultural and political unity, in other words, was to embody, in themselves, an interisland patrimony, covering, as Las Casas hinted, the entire geographical area of the islands and the terra firma of the mainland, transcending the new and more limited political boundaries imposed by the European conquerors. It is a contribution that has often been forgotten even by the more radical voices of later Caribbean revolutionary thought, and of which they have had to be reminded by their colleagues who have dug into the primary sources.[153]

With the disappearance of the aboriginal races, the torch of the antislavery ideology passed from the Indian peon to the African slave. It is true that some philosophes did not hesitate themselves to uphold the right of slaves to revolt—including, most famously, Raynal's call for a "new Spartacus," in his famous book of the 1770s. But it is easy to exaggerate the importance of that element in the metropolitan antislavery assault. Raynal's forecast shocked even avowed enemies of the slavery system, Chenier for example. Nor was Raynal himself consistent in his argumentation, for much of his book was devoted to a gradual emancipation formula far different in tone from the call for immediate revolution. It was the same in the English case. Much of the antislavery outpouring was, at best, sentimental, as often as not concerned merely with the abuses of the slave system rather than with the system itself. If he weeps over a prisoner, remarked Sir Leslie Stephen of Sterne, he has no desire to destroy the Bastille. Poets like Hannah More and Thomson, even the urbane Addison, wept over the American slave in similar fashion.

So, it is to the record of the actual slave rebellions that one must turn for the understanding of the final, heroic expression of the antislavery theme. Of necessity, it is contained in the literature of the colonizer, whether local or metropolitan: court records, missionary accounts, official reports, parliamentary committee proceedings, and the rest. With the exception of Saint Domingue in 1791, of course, none of the uprisings succeeded; although it can be argued that the slave unrest in the Danish West Indies in 1848 precipitated the Act of Abolition during the same year. Most of the rebellions—and it is an uncomfortable truth to admit, since it shows that, as in every oppressive system, there were victims who were ready to become *collaborateurs* of the ruling class—were nipped in the bud by slave informers, rather than being apprehended by an alert master class. Other factors also contributed: the lack of arms and ammunition, the jealousies between rival bands and rival commanders, the ethnic exclusivism of the different tribal groups, the failure to organize a united front with other oppressed groups, like the Amerindian tribes in the Guianas, time wasted in fruitless negotiations with the white enemy, and the ability of that enemy, as a last resort, to bring in the naval and military power of the metropolitan center.

The questions raised by the history of the slave rebellions go, of course, to the very heart of the Caribbean problem. Why did the slave revolt? What were his motives, if any? Did he possess, singly or collectively, a coherent ideology? In answering these questions it is well, to begin with, to disabuse them of any false mystery. It is one of the defects of the modern social sciences that they are oftentimes tempted to offer complex interpretations of essentially simple phenomena; and even a cursory reading of contemporary scholarship on New World slavery will provide abundant evidence, depressingly, of that assertion. For the historians of slave revolt must start with the quite simple proposition that when the New World slave revolted, he did so because, as a person, he wanted his liberty. No doubt he hated the system. But he wanted, above all else, to get its individual instruments—master, overseer, driver— off his back.

That truth emerges with startling simplicity—if one may begin at the end of the story rather than at its beginnings—in the autobiographical account of the runaway slave Esteban Montejo, referring to the last period of the Cuban slave society in the latter half of the nineteenth century. Montejo is the supreme individualist. He runs away from his plantation on the spur of the moment, finally disgusted with being bullied and pushed around. He does not join a Maroon group or a slave rebellion; the most he does is to become a volunteer in the war of independence. He spends ten years in the forests as a lonely runaway; all that seems to have bothered him during that Robinson Crusoe adventure was the absence of sex. His experience of life has taught him to be suspicious of all men; you cannot put trust in people, he remarks, the truth is I don't even trust the Holy Ghost. He has learned to be cynical; everybody is out for himself. He is a rebel without a cause; even when he joins the independence force, it is not because he believes in the ideology, but because he sees, frankly, that the other side is worse. "I know myself," he opines, "that war destroys men's trust, your brothers die beside you, and there is nothing you can do about it. Then along come the smart guys and grab all the good jobs."[154] He welcomes the abolition of slavery, certainly. But he is not so sure whether the change has made things generally much better. He ends with the thought that perhaps only the ancestral wisdom of the African elders in the slavery barracoons, as he remembers it, can help a man in life: to be polite, not to meddle in other people's affairs, to speak softly, to be respectful and religious, and to work hard.[155]

There must have been many slaves, in the four centuries of the life of the system, whose experience and feelings are echoed in Montejo's account. It was preferable to be on your own on the loose, remarks Montejo, than locked up in all that dirt and rottenness. That is the *cri de coeur* of *marronage*. It is important. But it is also limited. It is with the organized slave rebellion that its dialectic becomes transformed into a new qualitative dimension, much more complex in its motives and aspirations. The act of individual evacuation, which leaves the system intact, is replaced with the act of collective resistance, which seeks to destroy the system. The one is apolitical; the other is fully political in the sense that it challenges the power of the regime. Above all else, slave insurrectionism—accompanied, of course, by the history of uprisings on slave ships, a subject yet to be fully documented[156]—confers upon Caribbean history two cardinal elements: one is that of historical magnitude, for the slave masses, in their successive revolts—starting, perhaps, with the slave insurrection in Santo Domingo of 1522—demonstrated that they could storm the heights of heaven in a way that not even Marx fully appreciated; and the other is that of historical continuity, in the sense that every revolt before 1791 in Saint Domingue led up to, and prepared the way for, that grand finale, while every revolt after 1791 was influenced by its tremendous success. Those two laws—of historical magnitude and historical continuity—constitute, in a way, the twin pillars of the slaves' contribution to the antislavery ideology.

If a composite portrait of the typical slave rebellion is drawn, it is clear that an impressive variety of elements—social, cultural, political, ethnic, geographical—went into its making. The existence of a strong and viable syncretic Afro-Caribbean culture—including slave family estates; town markets; dissenting churches; the role, both symbolic and practical, of religious cults; a semiautonomous economic structure of family agricultural plots and internal marketing: all of it almost constituting an internal black "political state"—provided the institutional base without which no rebellion, anywhere, can ever succeed.[157] That base, in turn, facilitated the emergence of effective and widespread systems of surreptitious communication; practically every extant account of revolts, including Long's account of the 1760 Jamaica revolt, describes how an interplantation system of verbal communication made possible simultaneous uprisings throughout a whole district, sometimes an entire island. There was the principle of mutual aid, heritage of the African communal tradition, generating a sense of felt comradeship in the new life of the exile; it is within the context of that tradition of cooperativism that the growth of the "shipmate" relationship must be set, starting, as it did, with bonds forged originally in the ordeal of the slave-ship passage and remaining to become a bond bringing together members of the same plantation, thus preserving the notion of fellow sufferers who have a special relationship with each other, and to be found all the way from Jamaica to the Guianas.[158] That sense of social cohesion, of course, did not in and of itself inspire revolt. But it was, undoubtedly, a sort of cement that held fellow conspirators together once revolt was underway; and it was reinforced by the imposition of the collective oath, again African in origin, holding the conspirators to secrecy and loyalty: a practice mentioned by all the extant accounts of the uprisings.

The experiental data of the various rebellions bear testimony to the contribution of these general phenomena. They also testify to how they gave rise to identifiable ideological components, forming not only a praxis but also a theory of revolution. There is, in the first place, and preeminently, the fusion of African cultural forms with revolutionary activity. The contribution of the vodun cult to the Saint Domingue uprising has already been noted. It has been documented in the modern *noiriste* school of Haitian historians, from the moderate Price-Mars to the more radical Lorimer Denis and François Duvalier, identifying the element of black consciousness and vodun African-rooted culture as the main driving force of both *marronage* and organized rebellion.[159] Yet the African imprint was prominent even in the English colonies. The local commissioners appointed to investigate the 1737 Antigua rebellion noted how leaders like Tacky and Tomboy claimed the title of African kings: "at the time of his execution," they noted of Tacky, "he endeavored to put on a port and mien suitable to his affecting the dignity of King."[160] Their description, likewise, of the oath taken by the conspirators, under the guise of an apparently harmless festival occasion, was clearly a rendition of the oath taken by African tribes on the eve of undertaking a warlike attack against a neighboring enemy. Nor must the significance be overlooked of the fact that what the commissioners regarded as, in terms of motivation, "hopes of lawless liberty" and "mere lust of power" encompassed, in reality, a well-organized plan to put fire to Government House at the time of a ball, rush the main town, seize the chief fort and arsenal, and requisition all shipping in the harbor: which bespeaks a capacity to organize on the part of the slave masses totally unimaginable in terms of the planter image of the slaves as mindless beings.[161] The reports on the Jamaica rebellion of 1831, both those by Christian missionaries like Clarke and Cornford, plus the court trials themselves, in turn testify to a rich mixture, in the form of the Afro-Baptist congregations, of Christian libertarian ideas and African religious ideas.[162] The black churches became secret societies plotting the detail of rebellion; and in a more general sense they were the carriers of a popular religious movement away from the written word of the white missionary churches into an emphasis, in the manner of an Afro-Creole *convince* and *Cumina* tradition of the Afro-American cults, on the central importance of spirit possession. It is in that sense that the rebellion became known as the Baptist war— to be distinguished from the other sense of that phrase whereby it was used by the planter press to condemn it as a consequence, deliberately plotted, of the white-led Baptist and Methodist mission enterprises.

There is, second, the note of black self-confidence. Psychologically, the mere act of rebellion required, on the part of the slave-person, the capacity to purge himself of the white bias, and its accompanying slavish deference to everything that the white system stood for; to perceive himself, in his self-image, as equal, or even superior, to the white master-person; to see himself, ultimately, as apocalyptic avenger and final nemesis. This general spirit is emphatic in the rough notes, written through an interpreter, that Cuffy, the leader of the 1763 Berbice rebellion, transmitted to the Dutch colonial governor. They are written, quite unselfconsciously, as one equal to another. "If Your Excellency makes war," writes Coffy, "the negroes are ready too.... The Governor Cuffy requests that Your Excellency come and speak with me, and Your Excellency must not be afraid, but if Your Excellency does not come, fighting shall last as long as there is a Christian in Berbice. The Governor Cuffy will give Your Excellency half of Berbice and his people will all go upriver, but you must not think that the negroes will be slaves again."[163] The imperial temper of the correspondence, as the Hartsinck manuscript reports it, reflected, in fact, the striking disparity—as another manuscript of the revolt quoted by Netscher described it—between the high morale of the rebels and the panic-stricken demoralization of the Dutch colonists, who were literally driven into the sea by the rebel strategy.[164] The slave-person, here, rises to a regal note of haughty magnanimity towards an enemy who, for the moment, is defeated. It engages the note of negotiated autonomy, offering to share the territory between both opposing sides, like some Caribbean version of the great papal schism that for a time divided the medieval Papacy between Avignon and Rome.

Third, there is the element of assertive black national consciousness, even going beyond the autonomist element. It congeals into an ideology of national independence, founded and rooted in a sense of ethnonationalism. It reaches its full maturity, of course, in the Saint Domingue case. The note is struck, however, as early as 1679 by the rebel Maroon leader Padre Jean, in his professed faith in a new state of black power. It is echoed, in turn, by Polydor in 1734 and by Médor in 1757, both clear on the point that the whites must be driven from the colony en masse as a prelude to setting up black rule, and, of course, in Makandal. It reaches its final embodiment in the period of struggle after 1791, when the slave rebellion becomes metamorphosed into the struggle for national independence.[165] In all of this, as the modern Haitian scholar Leslie Manigat has persuasively argued—following the analysis of other scholars like Fouchard—there ran a continuous dialectic making it impossible to separate *marronage* from revolution—both of them being composed at once of elements of racial struggle and elements of class struggle, with both of those elements, in turn, feeding the nationalistic impulse. Both *marronage* and revolution must be seen in the light of the "force of ideas" brought into the colony by Negroes who had been to France or America, metropolitan soldiers who had deserted to join rebel bands, book-reading slaves, and finally, educated Negroes, what Moreau de Saint-Méry and others termed "a superior quality of African." "A militant tradition," concludes Manigat, "plus exceptional human qualities of intelligence and moral energy met exceptional circumstances, internal and external, objective and subjective, to produce a critical threshold in the evolution of *marronage*, its mutation into revolution."[166]

It is of interest to note the somewhat different evolution of the matter in the English islands. The accounts of the earlier rebellions suggest that there had been present a sort of nationalistic element, in the sense that the slaves, in their image of the whites, perceived an undifferentiated mass, all of them enemies. That note was present even as late as the Barbados rebellion of 1816. "They maintained to me," the military commander wrote of the rebels he interrogated, "that the island belonged to them, and not to White men, whom they purposed to destroy, reserving the Females, whose lot in case of success, it is easy to conceive."[167] A similar note from the same episode portrays the militant figure of the woman leader Nanny Grigg, who told her fellow slaves, according to the official enquiry, "that they were all damn fools to work, for that she would not, as freedom they were sure to get. That about a fortnight after New Year's Day, she said the Negroes were to be freed on Easter Monday, and the only way to get it was to fight for it, otherwise they would not get it; and the way they were to do, was to set fire, as that was the way they did in Saint Domingo."[168]

By the time of the 1831 Jamaica rebellion, however, that radical perception had become blurred, in the sense that the abolitionist campaign in England itself had percolated through to the slave mind, persuading slaves that they had friends at court who desired their freedom, including the British government itself, and that its implementation was being sabotaged by the intransigent attitude of the local master class; Bleby's description of what is known about the motives of the rebel leader Sam Sharpe clearly shows that Sharpe believed from his reading of the English and colonial newspapers that the king had already issued a "free paper" announcing emancipation, and that the only obstacle impeding immediate freedom was the obstinacy of the planters.[169] The consequence, as Richard Hart has pointed out, was to blunt the nationalistic concept in the slave outlook, which was replaced by an ambivalent attitude that perceived both friends and enemies in the white camp. "Gone was the nationalistic concept," writes Hart, "which had been so decisive for the struggles of the slaves in the 17th and 18th centuries. The characteristic feature of the struggles of the 19th century was that they approximated more and more closely to struggles with the limited objective of achieving a readjustment of economic relations between the classes without disturbing the colonial relationship between peoples. Not only were they purged of any nationalistic objective, i.e., black self-determination; they were indeed accompanied by increasing loyalty to Britain, a legacy which lingered on to plague and hinder the agitational work of the pioneers of the new anti-imperialist movement over a century later."[170] Mary Reckord, the historian of the 1831 rebellion, corroborates that analysis: it was, basically, a protest movement rather than a crusade against the whites; and Sharpe regarded himself more as a political leader than as a prophet, aiming not to establish a new world but to accomplish specific and limited changes in Jamaican society. English metropolitan liberalism thus served to dilute local Jamaican radicalism.[171]

Fourth and finally, the literature of the Antillean rebellions reveals the ideal—never fully realized in practice, but nonetheless a felt aspiration—of the united front of all of the oppressed groups of the region against their common enemy. For united action depended on common loyalty to a common cause; and, as is well known, that common loyalty was frustrated in the slave masses by particular and fragmented loyalties and divisions of feeling: mulatto against black, Creole black against newly arrived African, tribe against tribe. But there are signs that the Antillean insurrectionist sought to overcome that divisiveness. Two examples will suffice. There is the impassioned outburst of the mulatto leader, Rigaud, defending himself against the charge that he was hostile to Toussaint on grounds of color prejudice: "indeed, if I had reached the stage where I would not wish to obey a black, if I had the stupid presumption to believe that I am above such obedience, on what grounds could I claim obedience from the whites?...Is it a tint of color, more or less dark, which instills principles of philosophy or gives merit to an individual?...I am too much a believer in the Rights of Man to think that there is one color superior to another."[172] The second instance comes from Long's account of a conversation between a Negro prisoner and a Jewish sentry at the time of the 1760 Jamaican affair, with the Negro attempting to persuade the Jew to come over to the Negro side: "You Jews," said he, "and our nation [meaning the Coromantins] ought to consider ourselves as one people. You differ from the rest of the whites, and they hate you. Surely then it is best for us to join in one common interest, drive them out of the country, and hold possession of it to ourselves."[173] The sentiment of common interest was, it goes without saying, an answer to the "divide-and-rule" strategy of the slave owners, succinctly summed up by Rigaud's friend, the mulatto Joseph Bonnet, in his later *Souvenirs historiques*; he thus described the grand plan of the Saint Domingue colons: "we will pit the mulattoes against the blacks, who then will ally with the whites; then we will pit the *Nègres creoles* against the Guinea Negroes, the latter of whom will then go over to the whites—so we shall rid ourselves of all of these *docteurs maroquins*—and then, finally, France will get so disgusted with all these crimes that it will reestablish slavery."[174]

There is one final footnote to all this. Like all movements in history, slave resistance gave rise to its own ideology of leadership. Individuals—sometimes acting alone, sometimes at the head of groups—became enshrined in the popular imagination. There is Makandal, endowed by the Haitian communal memory with miraculous powers.[175] In Jamaica, there is the figure of Three-Fingered Jack, a sort of folk hero–villain in the manner of Robin Hood, who used his Blue Mountain lair from which to maraud the country roads and plantations in the early 1780s.[176] There is, again in Jamaica, Sam Sharpe, leader of the 1831 rebellion; Bleby's conversations with him draw a half-sympathetic picture of a slave person well read in the Bible, constant reader of the London and local press, powerful speaker in the meetings of his small retinue, and convinced from his Bible reading that the slaves were entitled to freedom.[177] There is, to take a final example only, the figure of the

African Daaga, described in the last chapter of Joseph's *History of Trinidad*, who in 1837 led a brief and ill-prepared mutiny of the 1st West India Regiment in his determination to take his followers back to Guinea.[178] All of the extant accounts indicate that all of these leader figures were motivated at once by an ingrained hatred of the white man and a fierce resolve for revenge. There was also present, in some of them, a mixture of free will and fatalism. Thus, Joseph reports that in his conversations with Daaga on the eve of that individual's execution, it became evident that the seeds of the mutiny were sown on the passage from Africa, but that at the same time Daaga believed in some form of predestination, asserting that the Supreme Being of his African homeland had ordained that he, Daaga, should come to the country of the white man and be shot.[179]

Yet, obviously, the ideology of leadership received its most important and powerful expression in the leaders of the Saint Domingue rebellion, if only because those leaders were granted the historic opportunity to become directors of an independent black state power and thereby to give some sort of institutional form to their beliefs. At that point the antislavery ideology became married to the ideology of Caribbean state development. The revolutionary leadership had, of course, its differences; most notably, Toussaint and Henri Christophe and Dessalines have been put in the black camp, Pétion and Rigaud in the mulatto camp. Toussaint imagined a place for the whites in the new society, a misplaced faith that finally led to his fatal acceptance of Napoleon's good intentions and his death in the Jura mountain prison, while Dessalines, with his obdurate distrust of all whites, could never have made that mistake. Henri Christophe, again, had a complete grasp of the detail of statecraft, while Pétion was impatient with it.

Yet all of them shared a common passion for a new Haiti governed by the newly emancipated race. More particularly, they all believed deeply that reconstruction should be undertaken, first and foremost, by the new state authority. Economic liberalism, after all, was yet to make its way in Europe; still less could it have been expected that it would have appeared in Haiti. Nor was the Haitian peasant to be left to his own devices; he must be schooled into the new freedom. That was predictable as well, for popular democracy too had yet to make its way in societies even as liberal as England. So, the hallmark of the new regimes after 1804, both in the north and the south of the new reborn nation, is that of a benevolent despotism. At its worst, it became the new imperial court at Sans Souci, aping the Napoleonic aristocracy with its pretentious titles and absurd ceremony. At its best, it became a state-directed social and economic order, seeking, through new experimental legislation, to inculcate new agricultural methods, to foster the work ethic in the peasantry, to protect trade and commerce, to institute an attempt at national education, to reorganize the judicial system, and much else. Even more than that, both Toussaint and Henri Christophe turned to Christianity, especially the Protestant variant, as an aid in furthering those measures. Both sought to eliminate what they saw as the superstitious habits of the peasant; and Toussaint even sought, unsuccessfully, to introduce Christian patterns of marriage. Later twentieth-century writers like Fouchard and Dorsinville have noted the part played by that Christian element in the early formative years of the new nation. The end result was that of all the reigning orthodoxies of the republic after 1804, none of them included economic laissez-faire or liberal individualism.

THE MAROON COMMUNITIES

An additional chapter in the growth of the antislavery movement of thought belongs to the independent Maroon communities formed by runaway slaves over the centuries throughout the whole of Afro-America from Brazil, and the Guianas up through the islands, to the southern United States. Ranging from small bands with only a short survival span to powerful states surviving for generations, they were a monument to *marronage* on a grand scale, striking at the very heart of the slave system and constituting the final answer to the white myth of the Negro past. The end result of protracted guerilla wars with local and metropolitan military expeditions alike, their cultural tenacity, their sheer will to live, is attested to by the fact that, especially in Jamaica and Surinam, they have survived, although in varying degree, as vigorous semiautonomous groups within the state right up to the present day.

Their significance for the historian of the antislavery ideology lies in a number of vital points. They are summarized in the collection of articles and reports, *Maroon Societies*, edited by Richard Price. There is, first and foremost, the general consideration that—despite some of the romantic nonsense that has been written about them—far from being cultural isolates, like some sort of Shangri-La idyllic life hermetically sealed away from the outside world, the maroon communities constituted, in fact, one of the earliest forms of a living and vibrant syncretic Afro-American culture system. Their material culture mixed both African and Amerindian elements with elements borrowed from the white plantation economy. An ideological commitment to the remembered African background, evident in sorcery and divination (Maroon warriors underwent complex rites in order to persuade themselves that they were physically immune to Western guns and ammunition) went hand in hand with adaptive adjustments to the New World environment: the gradual change from the early African-chieftainship style of Maroon government to that of council government is a case in point. African methods of warfare, again, were widely used; but they were adapted to the local topographical environment—the riverine forest in the Guianas, the elevated "cockpit" mountain country in Jamaica—and the resultant mode of ingenious guerrilla warfare impressed both Dallas in the Jamaican case and Stedman in the Surinamese case.[180] Economic organization was also a mixture; the slave captive Louis's account of a rebel village in French Guiana describes a combination of African-style collective labor and shared possessions and Western-style personal property. In brief, the typical Maroon community was founded on what Price terms a homeland ideology: societies, he adds, that are uncannily "African" in feeling, even if devoid of any directly transplanted systems.[181]

That homeland ideology, reinforced by geographical isolationism, undoubtedly contributed to the other element of Maroon ideology—its ardent sense of moral superiority over both whites and coastal blacks. The sentiment comes through in the oral account rendered by the literate Bush Negro Johannes King in 1885 of the history of his Maroon ancestors. Its vivid description of the tribal celebrations marking the 1762 peace treaty with the Dutch colonial government makes it clear that the Maroons at that time saw the treaty as proof of the weakness of the whites and of their own military superiority—constituting, in effect, a humiliating capitulation on the part of the enemy. It was, as they saw it, the result of supplication on the part of the whites; not, as the whites saw it, the other way around. They gave thanks to Masra Gado, their supreme deity, in King's phrase, because he had given them strength in the forest to fight and win a major war against the whites.[182] This is a note of incipient nationalism. Nationalism, everywhere, is always made more fierce by the euphoric memory of a great victory against a hated enemy; and in the "Bush Negro" self-image, they had defeated the Dutch as surely as, later on, Sitting Bull would defeat the U.S. cavalry at Little Big Horn and the Zulus would defeat the British regiments at Isandhlwana. The nationalism was fed, again, by a devoted attachment to the Maroon mother country. Dallas describes how the Jamaican Maroon prisoners in 1796 feared deportation even more than death itself, because of their love for Jamaica; and there are few accounts more harrowing than those penned by Canadian historians describing the miseries endured by the hundreds of Maroon prisoners who were deported to the icy wastes of Nova Scotia.[183] With the passage of time, then, the nostalgia for Africa became transmuted, by subtle psychological processes, into a love for America.

The most lasting contribution of the Maroon phenomenon, perhaps, is its contribution, indirectly but surely, to Caribbean political thought. The political thought that the European colonizing powers brought to the Caribbean hinged on the sovereignty of the emerging European nation-state, beginning with the centralized bureaucracy of the Castilian monarchy, and formalized in the new machinery of government invented for the control and administration of the New World possessions. That sovereignty admitted of no challenge, not even from the Church; both the failure of the reformist faction identified with Las Casas in its effort to establish a sort of independent millenarian church in the Indies and the later expulsion of the Jesuits showed conclusively that the authority of the nation-state would brook no challenge and would tolerate no rival. That attitude reflected the central preoccupation of all European political thought in the sixteenth and seventeenth centuries: its preoccupation with the enshrinement of the national unitary state.

Within that framework of political thought, then, the success of the Maroon enterprises can be seen as a challenge to that ideal: The unitary state was challenged by the idea of the pluralist state. The pluralism is present, if not explicitly, in the terms of the various peace treaties terminating the Maroon wars, both in Jamaica and in the Guianas, but especially in the latter. All of them, considered together—Edwards printed the Jamaica Articles of Pacification of 1738—amounted to a devolution of authority on the part of the state. They recognize the territorial integrity of the Maroon communities, legitimize their system of government by chiefs, permit certain jurisdictions in the treatment of local crime, guarantee freedom from harassment by whites, and establish the principle of freedom of physical movement and freedom of trade between the communities of both parties. This, of course, was not independence. The state did not relinquish its ultimate authority; and the requirement that bound the Maroon side, contractually, to return escaped slaves was a condition that no free state would probably ever accept. Even so, it was a real concession of sovereignty within limited and defined areas. More, it implicitly recognized the existence of enclaves of people who, by reason of customs or religion or general way of life are entitled to special legislative and administrative treatment. In that sense, it anticipates the general problem of ethnic and cultural pluralism in the same Guianese and Surinamese independent societies of the later twentieth century, where, in Furnivall's phrase, differentiated groups mix but do not combine.[184]

THE ANTISLAVERY NOVEL

A separate and final note deserves to be written on the sexual dimension of antislavery feeling. In a very real sense, the history of the Caribbean slave regime is the history of the sexual exploitation of the black woman. Much of the proplanter ideology was rooted in racial fears; and racial fears, in their turn, are commonly rooted in sexual obsessions. In the Caribbean, of course, those obsessions had their own peculiar history. Quite differently from the situation in North American slavery, a number of factors facilitated interracial sex—the massive preponderance of blacks as compared to whites; the serious shortage of women, both black and white, in the total demographic picture; the failure of the West Indian colonists, unlike the New England colonists, to successfully transplant the values of the mother country to their local society. The resultant widespread practice of miscegenation, despite all legislative efforts to prohibit it, created the new group of mulatto Antillean people, a practice so widespread and so much an established feature of planter life that Long, always a realist, admitted that anyone who criticized it would be accounted a simple blockhead. Concubinage, as a modern scholar has put it, was such an integral part of Antillean island life that one might just as well have attempted to abolish the sugarcane itself.[185] The compulsive drive of sex thus operated as a racial solvent.

Caribbean novelists—De Lisser in Jamaica, Mittelhotzer in Guiana—have exploited this theme in its more melodramatic form, writing it up as lurid sex in the cane field and the "great house" boudoir. But there was, of course, much more to it than that. It generated in the proslavery ideology a particular venom against the mulatto groups, with all of its gross vulgarity: the plantocrat color feeling, here, was not the aristocratic hauteur with which a grand seigneur of the ancien regime would have treated a *roturier*, but a vulgar, low disdain for people regarded as the scum of the earth. The antislavery ideology responded in kind; and its most representative expression is to be found in the antislavery novel of the nineteenth-century period, noticeably in Cuba but in the other islands as well.

The novelistic literature, then, is in the main the apotheosis of the social tragedy of the mulatto group. Its leading theme is that of tainted blood. All the other themes flow from that: the unwritten laws that socially exclude the colored person; love crucified on the altar of racial purity; the fear of sudden exposure and social disgrace; families fatally divided. The genre starts with the early whimsical and ephemeral novels dealing with English Caribbean themes, written usually by outsiders but also written at times from direct West Indian experience. Not in and of themselves overtly antislavery tracts, they yet manage to describe how individual human lives are trapped within the constraints of the system. The figure of the attractive mulatto girl, sexually used by the white man, makes its appearance as early as *The Adventures of Jonathan Corncob* (1787). Orderson's later *Creoleana*, dealing with the Barbados of the 1830s, introduces the stock sentimental theme of the illegitimate mulatto girl, personal maid to her white half-sister, spurning her upright "free colored" suitor and allowing herself to be seduced by the flashy white Irish adventurer. By contrast, *Montgomery; or the West Indian Adventurer* (1812), set in Jamaica, while containing the usual passages of sentimental pity for the slave, deals with the minor theme of noble love between bookkeeper poor white and planter's daughter, typically resolved by the turn of fortune that helps break the barrier of social status. *Hamel, The Obeah Man* (1827), in its turn, deals with the problem of mistaken racial identity in the form of the quadroon domestic slave who, to her final embarrassment, falls in love with a mulatto who turns out to be a white man—although, as Brathwaite points out, it is redeemed by its sympathetic portrait of the obeah priest who, at the end, delivers what is probably the first black power speech in West Indian literature.[186] With the anonymously published *Marly* (1828), the mulatto theme reappears, having as its central figure the cultured Jamaican colored gentleman who, graduating from Edinburgh University, comes home to a "white gentleman" society that rejects him and his type.[187]

Thirty years later, the genre ends with Grant Allen's satirical romance *In*

All Shades, demonstrating, as it does, how color prejudice, even after slavery emancipation, still remained the prevailing standard of social position, accepted by all groups. For all of the figures in that novel repeat the well-known stereotypes of the West Indian multiple-character cast, all of them enmeshed in the tragicomedy of a colonial Vanity Fair from which they cannot escape: the educated mulatto son returning to vulgar family surroundings after being socially spoiled in England; the young English wife of the brown professional husband treated as a moral leper by the local whites; the affected and stupid "Hottentot Venus" of the brown middle-class daughter anxious to marry an English officer of good connections if only the shame of her racial ancestry can be hidden long enough; the visiting English aristocrat whose own identity as a "throwback" to unsuspected colored ancestors is readily exposed in a society that, unlike the English mother-society, has a fine detective instinct for the recognition of traces of miscegenation.[188]

The social and mental milieu out of which the Cuban nineteenth-century antislavery novel grew was, by contrast, far more sophisticated. Having its initial inspiration in the literary *tertulias* (salon conversations) sponsored by the liberal-minded philanthropist Domingo Delmonte, it was deeply influenced by the European literary fashions of the period: romanticism, Balzacian realism, neoclassicism, eclecticism, with the added Creole element of the exotic *costumbrista* tradition. Some of its authors have both North American and European experiences that shaped their outlook; and Zambrana, for example, was influenced both by Hugo's romanticism and by Renan's non-Christian idealism. All of its titles, then, in one way or another, play on the general theme of frustrated love in a racialist society. Preeminently, it is the tortured love, always forbidden any successful outcome, between the figure of the beautiful mulatto girl and the handsome young white scion of racially impeccable Havana society; and in both Suárez y Romero's *Francisco* and Zambrana's *El negro Francisco*, the girl, in the best manner of passionate melodrama, capitulates to the desires of the young white master in order to save her lover, a Negro slave, from torture, and her capitulation causes him to commit suicide. Set within this framework of the tension between the impure love of the master and the pure love of the slave, all of the characters of the novels are set types of pure romanticism: the degenerate Spanish-born slaver *don* Candido Camboa in *Cecilia Valdés*; the *mulata* Dorotea in *Francisco*, as well as the *mulata* Camila in *El negro Francisco*; the *mulato* tailor Uribe who teaches his friends how to dissimulate in the presence of whites; the central character in Avellaneda's *Sab* who, despite his rebellious temper, still persists in the impossible dream of marriage to a white woman; or, yet again in *Cecilia Valdés*, the white mistress Isabel whose compassion for her slaves is really based on the unexamined conviction that they are simple-minded children who must be humored.[189]

The attitude towards slavery that emerges from all this hardly constitutes a bold demand for abolition. In part because of a repressive Spanish censorship, in part because all of the authors themselves entertained a profoundly ambivalent attitude towards the slave, the novels, as a group, represent at best a mildly ameliorative position. They all accept Delmonte's admonition that "This is the recourse which is left open to us—to speak, to convince by talking about the subject, to circulate good works, to write, and to be prudent with regard to those who are suffering, in their interests and ours."[190] The economic side of slavery is hardly ever looked at. The plots, invariably, revolve around family domestic situations rather than general social-class or racial-caste situations. As Noel says of Zambrana—whose most radical criticism was that slavery made impossible the growth of the black Christian family based on free marriage—the antislavery novel is crying out for better treatment of slaves rather than making any rational argument for the abolition of slavery, with all of its radical implications of social upheaval.[191] As Schulman, in turn, notes, this attitude, translated into artistic terms, suggests the advisability of a mild rather than a bold or rebellious antislavery narrative, one in which the slave might draw tears from the reader rather than cries of fear or horror. Its ideal is the *negro racional* or the *criada de razón*—both of these terms meaning, generally, the rational, intelligent Negro —and the purpose of that idealized figure is not so much to foment sentiments in favor of abolition as to call forth a sympathetic reaction on the part of the more enlightened members of the community.[192] Even Villaverde—who perhaps comes nearest to a larger vision of the problem, seeing slavery as a moral cancer that invades all Cuban society and corrupts both black and white—never manages to rise above the position (as King puts it) that if he probes the mind of the slave owner, it is only to discover that Creole women are capable of compassion, and Spaniards, arriviste peninsular types, are not.[193] The final note, all in all, is one of lachrymose pity for the slave figure, who is worked into a rigid literary convention. As one reads the novels, they sound like nothing so much as a later Cuban copy of Richardson's *Clarissa Harlowe*, with the theme of slave martyrdom replacing the theme of feminine martyrdom; they exhaust practically every movement of the pathetic vocabulary of the time, prolonging the exquisite agony of the martyrdom until the sympathy of the reader becomes so involved and compromised that it is difficult to distinguish between delicious excitement and painful distress.

Yet it would be misleading to leave the Cuban antislavery novel at that point, as if it were nothing more. For all of its limitations of perspective and sympathy, it made a positive contribution to the antislavery cause. That cause, after all, is not to be identified exclusively with an ideology of open, Spartacus-like rebellion. It is possessed of a myriad of moods and nuances. The Cuban novelists had to work within the context of a society obsessed by demonic visions of racial fantasy. The fear of "Africanization," later to be termed, evasively, "Antilleanization," infested even the more liberal minds, summed up in the popular expression of the period—*Tiranizar o correr el riesgo de ser tiranizado* (you must play the tyrant or be yourself tyrannized).

Ortiz has reminded us that even after abolition and independence, well into the early twentieth century, to speak of the black man in Cuba was danger-ous and had to be done in whispers, as if one were speaking of syphilis or some nefarious skeleton in the cupboard.[194] By bringing both the black and the mulatto to the forefront as figures worthy of literary comment and analy-sis, the novelists of the nineteenth century managed to compose a morally in-spired social analysis critical of the slavery institution. To have asked them to have done more would be to assume on their part a supernatural ability to transcend the limitations of the time and the society in which they had to live and survive.

LAFCADIO HEARN

Yet if the Antillean mulatto class was a tragic class, the final comment on their role in the antislavery ideological movement has to be that—by their very physical and social existence, even if not in their social behavior patterns —they challenged the central premise of the slavery system; that is, that an impenetrable gulf existed between white and black, which no amount of ra-cial admixture or culture contact could hope to erode. They provided, albeit perhaps not consciously, a halfway house in which, albeit reluctantly, white master class and black subservient class could meet. Merely to read the Car-ibbean literature is to be made forcibly aware of the fact that every commen-tator, of whatever persuasion, had to come to grips with the existence of the mulatto class, to place it within the general Caribbean scheme of things.

The best example, perhaps, of that endeavor is to be found in the French Antilles, summed up in the observations of the strange wandering scholar Lafcadio Hearn in his 1889 volume of reminiscences, *Two Years in the French West Indies*. Hearn writes from a dual viewpoint: that of an educated nineteenth-century aesthete deeply influenced by the large speculative theo-ries of race and culture prevalent at the time, and that of a shrewd and keen psychologist, an acute observer of the manners and foibles of his adopted An-tillean island society. He uses the literary evidence, both past and present— from early chroniclers like Du Tertre and Labat to later social historians, both Creole and metropolitan French, such as Dauxion-Lavaysee, Dr. Rufz, Sou-quet-Basiege, Turiault, General de Brigade—and combines it with his own observations to pay tribute to the remarkable *femme de couleur* who emerged, after generations, out of the original intercrossing between early French peas-ant colonist and West African slave in the French Antilles. Hearn is fasci-nated with the long, slow biological process whereby, under the pressures of environment and customs in the tropics, the formation of a new and distin-guishable ethnic group, that of the mulatto, takes place. He sees it, overall, as a process of biological determinism whereby the power of sexual attraction overwhelmed every other consideration to create a new species of Antillean human nature.

Hearn quotes Dr. Rufz as saying:

> Under the sun of the tropics, the African race, as well as the European, becomes greatly modified in its reproduction. Either race gives birth to a totally new being. The Creole African came into existence as did the Creole white. And just as the offspring of Europeans who emigrated to the tropics from different parts of France displayed characteristics so identical that it was impossible to divine the original race-source, so likewise the Creole negro—whether brought into being by the heavy thick-set Congo, or the long slender black of Senegambia, or the suppler and more active Mandingo—appeared so remodelled, homogeneous, and adapted in such wise to his environment that it was utterly impossible to discern in his features anything of his parentage, his original kindred, his original source....The transformation is absolute.[195]

Proceeding from that point of departure, Hearn adds his own commentary to that long, drawn-out racial drama. Noting how the *Code Noir* sought to halt the mixing process, he annotates its failure.

> The slave race had begun to exercise an influence never anticipated by legislators. Scarcely a century had elapsed since the colonization of the island; but in that time climate and civilization had transfigured the black woman....Travellers of the eighteenth century were confounded by the luxury of dress and of jewelry displayed by swarthy beauties in St. Pierre. It was a public scandal to European eyes. But the creole negress or mulattress, beginning to understand her power, sought for higher favors and privileges than silken robes and necklaces of gold beads; she sought to obtain, not merely liberty for herself, but for her parents, brothers, sisters, even friends. What successes she achieved in this regard may be imagined from the serious statement of creole historians that if human nature had been left untrammelled to follow its better impulses, slavery would have ceased to exist a century before the actual period of emancipation....So omnipotent the charm of half-breed beauty that masters were becoming the slaves of their slaves. It was not only the creole *negress* who had appeared to play a part in this strange drama which was the triumph of nature over interest and judgment; her daughters, far more beautiful, had grown up to aid her, and to form a special class....They were results of a natural selection which could have taken place in no community otherwise constituted....But that which only slavery could have rendered possible began to endanger the integrity of slavery itself: the institutions upon which the whole social structure rested were being steadily sapped by the influence of half-breed girls.[196]

First the *belle affranchie*, then the *fille de couleur*, were the agents of this process. They embodied what, earlier on, the abbé de Cournand had termed "une conquête faite par la nature sur l'esclavage" (Nature's conquest over slavery). Neither official legislation nor the jealousy of the white mistress halted the process in any real way. General Romanet, who visited Martinique at the end of the eighteenth-century period, speaking of the tax on enfranchisement, noted its ineffectiveness because it went against the impulses of nature: "They know," he wrote of the brown women, "how to please; they have those rights and privileges which the whole world allows to their sex;

they know how to make even the fetters of slavery serve them for adornments. They may be seen placing upon their proud masters the same chains worn by themselves, and making them kiss the marks left thereby: the master becomes the slave, and purchases another's liberty only to lose his own."[197] The jealousy of the white woman was, perhaps, a more serious obstacle; and De Vastey described at much the same time, in his essay, *Le système colonial dévoilé*, how that jealousy had provoked dreadful punishments against offenders on the part of cruel mistresses like Madame Charette and Madame Larchevesque-Thibaud, easily matching the atrocities committed by planters like Cocherel, Vosanges, and Latoison-Labouille.[198] But, like King Canute, they were seeking to stem an irresistible tide; and the last chapter, fittingly enough, in the history of the antislavery movement was written not so much by the political ambitions of the *homme de couleur* as by the social ambitions of the *femme de couleur*.

Chapter Five

The Growth of
Nationalist Thought
to 1900

In the Caribbean, as elsewhere, the development of nationalism, and of nationalist sentiment, divides itself into two distinguishable elements, although they are of necessity interrelated. There is, in the first place, the growth of a cultural nationalism, of a congeries of feelings, beliefs, sentiments, in a given body of people that gives them a sense of distinctiveness, of being different from others, of being set apart. It feeds on religion, customs, geographical setting. It is immeasurably strengthened by exile or oppression, as the history of ancient Israel shows. The threat of war and war itself also give it new life, as can be seen in our own day in the reemergence of Russian nationalism in the Soviet Union after 1940. Nearly always, it flourishes as literary expression: it is there in the old Jewish Minor Prophets as it is in Shakespeare's historical plays. Undoubtedly, it responds, as history tells us, to deep emotive powers in human nature. There is, second, the process whereby cultural nationalism moves forward to political nationalism and whereby it becomes clothed with all of the paraphernalia of the independent nation-state, in which there is a government exercising the sovereign power—the authority, that is—to give orders to all and to receive orders from none, and requiring (sometimes with limits, sometimes without limits) the obedience of its subjects.

The history of the Caribbean up to 1900 is in large measure the history of those twin developments. Yet they were both made more complicated and more difficult by the manner in which they were interfered with by the twin epiphenomena of slavery and colonialism; so that there is little in their story of the straightforward, linear character of, say, European nationalism. Colonialism generated in the Caribbean mentality a divisive loyalty to the metropolitan culture that explains the historical tardiness of the final arrival of national independence, so that at the end of the period, only Haiti and Cuba and Santo Domingo had arrived at that terminal point; and even today, three-quarters of a century later, that perverse attachment to the governing colonial power explains why both Puerto Rico and the French Antilles remain politically tied to, respectively, the United States and France. That continuing dependency of thought and sentiment also explains why, ironically, the British West Indies were the first to join the British Empire and the last to leave it.

Slavery was also a powerful ideological deterrent, for it generated a scale of values in the top, dominant groups of the colonies, in which fear of the black masses stifled aspiration for national independence. At every turn in the story, those groups opted for selfish treason rather than for popular revolt. The Saint Domingue colons were ready to surrender to the national enemy, England, rather than accept a French Revolution moving towards abolition; the ruling Assembly forces in Jamaica, reacting in panic to the Morant Bay "rebellion" in 1865, supinely surrendered the old representative system of colonial government for the more authoritarian Crown Colony regime rather than accept a more democratic system; and the Cuban *incondicionalistas*, that is to say, the Cuban group most determined not to surrender any of its privileges, of the same period were willing to negotiate for annexation to the United States rather than continue allegiance to a Spanish government they feared might yield to British pressure and promulgate abolition. For all of them, the fulfillment of a truly nationalist policy would have necessitated—as Cuba showed—enlisting the active participation of the slave-masses; and that was a price they were not prepared to pay. The growth of nationalist thought, then, with few exceptions, was the work of other forces in the society.

CULTURAL NATIONALISM

The Caribbean nationalist ideology finds its most assertive expression, then, in the nineteenth century—leaving aside, of course, its later growth in the modern twentieth century after 1898. Its vehicle, naturally enough, was the Creole urban intelligentsia that developed from Havana to Port-of-Spain during that period: novelists, playwrights, historians, political leaders, educationists, and the rest. But, by way of preface, it is urgent to emphasize, once again, that its expression in the form of cultural nationalism predates the nineteenth-century period, being the autonomous, rival counterculture created by the slave masses, especially in its creative magico-religious forms, during the long night of the slavery period. Both Indian and African contributed to that tremendous phenomenon. It is no accident, then, that the early Indian resistance to the European colonial system became immortalized, in the later period, in the literature of the *indianista* novel in Puerto Rico and Santo Domingo, and that the leaders of the black slave rebellions became enshrined in the new national pantheon of heroes, first in Haiti and then, in the twentieth century, in Jamaica and Guiana. Nor, indeed, is it any accident, again—to take two examples, less well known, from the British Caribbean—that later local writers should have seen the mulatto leader Julien Fédon of the insurrection against the British in the Grenada of 1795–96 as one of the first national patriots rather than as what the British history texts call a brigand,[1] or that later nationalist forces in British Honduras should have acclaimed the celebrated battle of Saint George's Cay of 1798 in that mainland colony, not as an English victory over the Spanish enemy, but as the first historic event in the growth of a separate Honduran nationalism.[2]

The Caribbean culture forces matured during the same nineteenth-century period, a maturation made somewhat easier, but still by no means easy, by the new climate of opinion following abolition. The culture carriers, as always, were the despised lower classes. The popular amusements of the English islands alone provide rich material illustrative of the inventive and spontaneous creativity that went into them. There is the Jamaican Jonkonnu celebration of old Christmas mummery, with its finely costumed Set-Girls and Grand Masters, as portrayed in the 1830s in Belisario's colorful prints. There are the Island Maroon, the Dance of the Cakes, the Parents Plate of the wedding festival tradition of the Grenadines; there are the archaic African dances and the Old Creole dances of Carriacou, the former carrying the names of some of the "nations" of West Africa. There are the St. Lucian flower festivals, especially the Fête La Rose and the Fête La Marguerite of the rival Roses and Marguerites societies, invested, during the nineteenth century period of their life, with a political character; not to mention all of the splendid festivals of the Catholic calendar in which the St. Lucian populace accommodated their ancient West African patterns to the larger structure of traditional folk Catholicism that had its roots in the earlier character of the island as a French possession. There are, all over the region at this time, the *embarras de richesses* of the popular folk songs: the Shanto and Queh-Queh songs of Guiana, the Honduran "breakdowns," the prayer songs of the various cult-religions, the Jamaican market calypsos, the Barbadian hymnology.[3]

And of course, finally, there is the great Carnival fête in Trinidad. It is clear from the Hamilton Report of 1881, written from the official British viewpoint, that, already freed of its earlier French upper-class origins, the event had been taken over by the urban proletariat of Port-of-Spain, and already exhibited all of its well-known characteristics and features: the *Cannes Brulées* (burning of the sugar cane) opening feature, originally in slave days a thing of forced labor in order to put out estate cane fires and converted by the ex-slaves as "a kind of commemoration of the change in their condition"; the fighting street bands "carrying riot and disorder through-out the town"; the endemic state of mutual dislike between the Negro celebrants and the police, going back, again, to slave days when the town police, called *Aguazils*, were recruited from the hated free colored group "to mark their social inferiority";

the camaraderie existing, during the event, between the Trinidadian working class and the small-island immigrants; and, not least of all, a pronounced class consciousness expressed in "the vilest songs, in which the names of the ladies of the island are introduced to be sung on the streets," clearly anticipating the later development of the fully fashioned calypso, with all of its ribald irreverence for class and status.[4] Carnival, in brief, in this decisive and formative Camboulay period (1870-90), became the vehicle of the lower *jamette* class, a genuine people's festival, and a symbol of an emergent national sentiment. In its characteristic figure of the *kaisonen extraordinaire* (that is to say, the calypso singer par excellence), it embodied all of the lower-class subculture gifts—skill in fighting, sharpness of wit and repartee, talent in song and music, indifference to law and authority, immense sexual prowess, hard drinking, and the rest—that, for good or ill, and to the distress of Creole respectability, were to become, as time went by, the recognized insignia of the Trinidadian national character.[5]

All of this was the embodiment of the Afro-Caribbean forms of cultural identity. But there was also a not-less-important Indo-Caribbean tradition, arising out of the indenture system of contract labor that in the latter half of the century brought in the Asiatic person as the last major immigrant force in the region, concentrated mainly in Trinidad and the Guianas. Just as the Negro brought African life and thought to the Antilles, so the Asiatic brought the life and thought of India. As with the African contribution, it came from the lower social reaches, for if no captured slave could pretend, once in the Indies, to the status of a Dahomeyan or an Abyssinian prince, so no Indian indentured servant could pretend to be a highborn courtier in the retinue of Lord Rama, or even, for that matter, a high-caste Brahmin. The vast majority of the immigrants were agricultural laborers, both Muslim and Hindu, coming from the Bihar and Uttar Pradesh provinces of the continent and driven into emigration by the massive poverty of colonial India.

In one way, of course, it would seem perverse argumentation to claim that the East Indian, as he came to be called, contributed to the rise of Caribbean nationalism. That, in the beginning at least, must have been the last thing in his mind. All of the available evidence suggests strongly a fiercely held allegiance to the old ancestral homeland. The immigrant, following at least the legal theory of his contract, regarded his stay in Trinidad or Guiana as temporary, so that there was little attempt, at least in the first generation, to adapt to the new conditions of life. Other factors encouraged that unwillingness to adapt: the isolation of life on the sugar plantations, the persistent hostility of both colonial government and other ethnic groups, the reluctance to seek formal education since education in any case was perceived as a plot on the part of Western educators to convert the newcomers to the hated Christian religion. All of those factors encouraged strong cultural retentions, so that even Hindi survived as a functionally operating minority language, unlike, say, Yiddish in the United States. That, retention, in turn, encouraged the suspicion in the other groups that the East Indians, giving their loyalty to

Mother India rather than to Trinidad or Guiana or Surinam, were fatally divisive elements, standing in the way of the task of nation-building.

Yet such an argument was, and still is, surely debatable. In practical terms, a new loyalty to the receiving country gradually grows up, generation after generation, as the old ancestral memories recede, to be replaced by increasingly positive identification with the new home. Such a process certainly took place with the East Indian immigration as it lasted through its period of official encouragement (1838–1917). In theoretical terms, much historical evidence, including that of the Antilles themselves, shows that cultural diversity can live in peaceful coexistence with national unity. The sense of difference expresses itself at the lower levels of religion, marriage habits, family life, and friendship patterns; the sense of common interests in the society as a whole expresses itself at the higher levels of both economic and political life. That process, too, has been evident in the Antillean culturally pluralist societies in the later twentieth-century period, especially in the postindependence period after the 1960s.

Be this as it may, it is certain that the new East Indian presence brought a new, rich note of cultural differentiation to the nineteenth-century Caribbean. To be Caribbean not only meant Europe and Africa. It now also meant Asia. The despised "coolie" brought with him his own customs, most notably those pertaining to marriage and the extended-kin family, the latter based on the traditional rule of the patriarch as head. The successful survival within a hostile environment of both the ritual-marriage form and the extended family rooted in the consanguineal group is evident from the fact that the first—although not recognized by the colonial civil power until well into the twentieth century—maintained itself stubbornly intact, and from the fact that the second, although forced to change somewhat in the new environment, remained also basically intact, so much so that the twentieth-century East Indian novelist Vidia Naipaul was able to describe it as an ongoing reality, although by that time much enfeebled, in his novel of the post-1945 period, *A House for Mr. Biswas*. Much of that tradition was culturally admirable and added to the ethnic diversity of Antillean life. But much of it was also difficult to appreciate, especially the sexual brutalization of the Indian woman on which the whole system rested; and it is no libel to say that of all the Antillean groups, the East Indian was perhaps the most reluctant to accept the later modern idea of the equality of the sexes.

The detail of the East Indian contribution is well known and extensively documented. It was—as already noted—lower class; and Bronkhurst noted the absence of traditional Brahminical ritual in the life of the estates.[6] In an environment in which, almost by definition, there were no trained *pandits* (learned teachers), where caste could not sustain itself because of the enforced togetherness of the dismal barracks life, and where ritual purity was of necessity vulgarized by oral tradition, it was lower-class India that prevailed. Living a squalid and nasty life just above the poverty line, as Beaumont's sympathetic book *The New Slavery* and the Des Voeux *Enquiry* of 1870 exposed it,[7] the

East Indians managed to sustain their remembered song and dance, deeply spiritual in their character. There were the folk songs like the *hori*, the *rasiya*, the *bhangra*, and the *chowtal*. There were the work songs by the *kahars*, or water carriers, by the *kumhars*, or potters, by the *dhobiyas*, or washerwomen, as well as by the *bhaats*, or entertainers who rendered professional service at a wedding, at which time they would demand their fees from their client, shaming and coercing him into giving more. There was the large variety of songs that accompanied the grand ritual of the wedding ceremony and its different stages, with all the attendant ceremonies befitting the importance of the event in Hindu life. There were, again, the chanted verses from the great epic of Ramayan, telling of the marvelous episodes in the life of Lord Rama. Finally, there were the festivals—the Muslim Cid and the Hindu Phagwah— which were celebrated in, at best, rudimentary form early on, but which in the modern period of today have grown into mammoth events comparable to Carnival itself.[8]

This, naturally, was the Indian, as it were, at play. But he and she were also at work. They contributed signally to thought in both economic and political matters. In the economic field their dedication to agriculture sustained a vital productive sector when, in the post-Emancipation period, the ex-slaves vacated the estates. They became, in effect, the food bowl of the region. As one modern West Indian scholar has put it (being quoted by a Trinidadian fellow East Indian scholar): "For these Indian hands, whether in Guyana or Trinidad, have fed all of us. They are, perhaps, our only jewels of a true native thrift and industry. They have taught us, by example, the value of money; for they respect money, as only people with a high sense of communal responsibility can."[9] In the political field, likewise, the Indian brought with him the idea of the *panchayat*, the ruling council of elders, of the self-sufficient village community, acting as a tribunal for the settlement of disputes. This became a genuinely indigenous system of community government. So, just as in the economic sector the Indian contribution was to become the custodian of agriculture as against industry, in the political sector it defended the idea of local government as against the centralized governmental system of the colonial regime. Much of the cultural contribution—the traditional art forms, for example, of the dance dramas such as *Ramaleela*, *Krishnaleela*, and *Rasmandal*—was destined to disappear. But the economic and political legacies remained more or less intact; and in the later twentieth century they were to be referred to as inspirations for alternative models of economic and political organization, especially in the postindependence period.[10]

POLITICAL NATIONALISM

Beyond this contribution of lower-class Caribbean peoples to cultural nationalism, there were other threads in the general fabric, including a more precisely articulated literary nationalism, this time on the part of the rising colonial intelligentsia. Of necessity, both of the strands—cultural nationalism and literary nationalism—have been part and parcel of an anticolonial movement. But it is urgent to emphasize the complexity of that movement. Except in Saint Domingue after 1791, it was not simply a case of black insubordinate masses rising up against white European colonialism. It was a case, rather, in which the triangular slave trade gave birth to a triangular debate of ideas between the slaves, the colonists, and the metropolitan abolitionist forces. The political ideas of the humanitarians favored imperial interference: partly on the ground of Burkean trusteeship, partly on the grounds of a universal Christian liberty. Reliance on the colonial legislative institutions, as they saw it, for any policy of amelioration, not to speak of abolition, was meaningless, since those institutions were controlled by the slave-owner forces. The colonial proslavery forces, in response, developed political ideas fiercely critical of the metropolitan colonial administration, since, clearly, the defense of the slave regime called for resistance to imperial intervention. Paradoxically and ironically, the argument of political liberalism, with its traditional support for colonial liberties, became identified with the proslavery ideology, while the political ideas of the abolitionists became identified with continuing supervision from the metropolis, gradually enforcing, as Goveia points out, the identification of humanitarian reform with imperial paternalism.[11] Just as Las Casas, in the sixteenth century, had linked his argument for humanitarian treatment of the Indian with a political theory arguing for the enlargement of the authority of the Council of the Indies, so the later nineteenth-century abolitionists, in Madrid and Paris as well as in London, saw their only hope in the enforcement of policies from the metropolitan parliaments. Whereas, again—to give added emphasis to this point—the eighteenth-century critics of slavery, from Voltaire to Raynal, had argued as cosmopolites, linking the plea for slave freedom with criticism of arbitrary authority in the institutions of the ancien régime, their nineteenth-century successors, like Wilberforce in England and Schoelcher in France, argued, more narrowly, for the extension of the metropolitan parliamentary and republican institutions to the colonies. The upshot of all this was that, ironically, the defense of anything approximating a doctrine of Caribbean nationalism passed, for the time being, into the hands of the proslavery apologists themselves.

This is eminently clear from a study of the political ideas of the leading writers of the proslavery camp—Long and Edwards in the English Caribbean case, Moreau de Saint-Méry and d'Auberteuil in the French Caribbean case. All of them combine a defense of slavery (albeit at times with serious reservations), with a spirited criticism of colonial administration, the latter made more convincing by their detailed knowledge, especially with Long and Moreau de Saint-Méry, of the intricacies of constitutional law. The Jamaicans penned a theory of colonial Whiggism; the Saint Dominigue Creoles, a theory of *autonismo colon* (colonial autonomy). Neither of them was simply rationalizing efforts in defense of slavery, for both of them were founded in conviction and principle. Put together, they represent a political theory of a new American localism, a statement by the *indianos*—or people of New World residence, to use a Hispanic-American term—comparable, in a way, to the manner in which Ercillo's mid-sixteenth-century epic poem, *La Araucana*, constituted a poem of praise to the new America created by the *gesta conquistadora* (grand achievement of the Conquest) in Peru and Mexico.[12]

LONG AND EDWARDS

Long writes as the disciple of Lockeian contractualism. There is a "common sanction" that binds government and citizen together. The sovereign power of any government does not flow from itself, but from the delegated will of the citizen body; the government, at all levels, is their trustee, nothing more. There is a proper balance of power between the executive and legislative branches of government; and Long is even ready to accept the questionable doctrine of the separation of powers. The real danger is always the overween-ing ambition of the executive branch; and only a legislative body accountable to the people it represents can ever be the true guardian of liberty.[13] All this, of course, is straightforward Whig doctrine. What Long, writing as a self-conscious Jamaican, adds to it is to apply it to the colonial situation. His general distrust of the executive power became translated into his particular distrust of the Jamaican executive power, embodied in the governorship and the nominated Council; so his argument became a powerful criticism of the British imperial power itself, since both governors and members of the colo-nial upper house were the creatures of London. The abuses of an executive power become multiplied into the abuses of a colonial executive power, and Long's sustained and informed criticism of the abuses of fee'd office in Ja-maica constitutes one of the most bitter condemnations of official corruption to be found in West Indian literature.[14] Every office under the control of the Crown, Long documents, is one of perquisites and profits run by "Aegyptian task masters."[15] The criticism is no less pungent because it assumes, uncriti-cally, that native Jamaican appointees would somehow operate more honestly, for there is nothing in the subsequent history of the Jamaica Assembly to sus-tain that assumption. The charge almost reaches what must have seemed to English ears to be sedition. Governors override colonial liberties; the nomi-nated council interferes in matters, like finance, that constitutionally belong to the elected assembly; and, altogether, what Adam Smith called contemp-tuously the "paltry raffle of colony faction" becomes transmuted into a strug-gle of Jamaican-born Englishmen to assert their rights against an overweening expatriate crowd of rascals.

Long goes even further. He has read his Montesquieu as much as his Locke. So, following the French thinker, he argues that laws, governments, and customs are not truths absolute and universal, but relative to the time of their origin and the country from which they derive. Jamaican government can only be understood in Jamaican terms. Jamaica is a slave society, and you cannot apply English ideas of liberty uncritically to such a society. London is four thousand miles away, and you cannot properly govern an American colony from that distance. Jamaica and England are two separate communities, in which assimilation, to some degree, is desirable, but in which total identification is out of the question, because of the cultural differences involved. Jamaican political liberties are not derived from London, as if on the basis of some concession theory of power. They arise, fundamentally, from the Jamaican experience, and only a local "free and independent assembly" can ultimately assure those liberties.[16]

Edwards, like Long, is in the Whig tradition. Because he wrote after the American Revolution, while Long wrote before it, however, his position is in some ways more encompassing, since he criticizes not only the English Crown but also the English Parliament. His criticisms, in that respect, constitute the viewpoint, as it were, of some colonial Bentham who is justifiably dissatisfied with the admiring view of the English constitution promulgated by Blackstone. He will not accept the doctrine of parliamentary sovereignty, for any power that Parliament possesses is delegated by the people; and within the colonial context, that means that the general imperial power is a sort of unstructured federalism in which rights and areas of influence and interest are divided between the imperial government, whether Crown or Parliament, and the local parliaments representing colonial citizens.[17] It is true that Edwards does not follow Long all the way in the denouncement of the privileges, including the right to annul and amend legislation, of the nominated council, seeing those powers as so prescriptive that they almost constitute law. But he is more adamant in his view of the imperial legislative power, as his discussion of the various points at issue—taxation, freedom of trade with the American ports, the West Indian demand to refine their own sugar, financial support for British forces in the islands—makes clear. He readily accepts the principle that the original establishment of colonies by the European nations was for the purpose of enlarging their trading opportunities, but he adds that the protectionist system embodied in the old Navigation Acts has become an exploitative system of "monopoly for monopoly." Long severely criticized the protectionist doctrine; and Edwards, quoting Long, called it a "savage" doctrine.[18] It is true that the Jamaican critics advanced a contradictory argument, for they wanted free trade in the Americas for their imports and a closed, protected market for their exports in Britain. But the contradiction does not seriously diminish the force of their argument against the protectionist system.

Nor will Edwards accept the argument of imperial rule as being derived from the doctrine of conquest. Admittedly, he writes, Jamaica was conquered by the English. But that does not confer upon them continuing rights of conquest to the present day any more than the descendants of William the Conqueror could claim rights over present-day Englishmen, or any more than the Irish of the present time could be arbitrarily governed by the English because their ancestors were conquered by Henry II.[19] Jamaicans are not subjects, but fellow subjects of "one great empire" over which the legislative authority of Parliament is relative only. The original royal proclamations that set up the overseas colonies in the first place were based on a mutual understanding between the various parts of that empire; they were declaratory only of ancient rights and not creative of new privileges on the part of any of the contracting parties.[20] The retention, by parliamentary legislation and ministerial decree, of the policy of denying the North American trade to the West Indians, especially after the cessation of hostilities in 1783, Edwards clearly sees as the unfair creation of such new privilege; and he cannot forbear from commenting bitterly that it was impossible not to see in it "a lurking taint of resentment and malignity, the relics of former provocation against the Americans; and at least as ardent a desire to wound the new republic, through the sides of the West Indians." He ends with a spirited defense of the West Indian planters as a body of hardworking men who do not deserve the calumnies of their enemies—who paint an erroneous picture of "gigantic opulence"—and with a characteristic plea for moderation on both sides.[21]

MOREAU DE SAINT-MÉRY AND D'AUBERTEUIL

The background to the social and political thought of the Saint Domingue writers Moreau de Saint-Méry and d'Auberteuil has been fully described in Charles Frostin's fine book *Les Révoltes blanches à Saint-Domingue aux XVIIe et XVIIIe siècles*. Apart from the master-slave conflict, other conflicts, basically of a class nature, disrupted the society: the planter class against the administrative despotism of Paris; the *petit blanc* against the *grand blanc*; the resident planter against the absentee owner; the motley crowd of unemployed and discontented town proletariat, *les gens sans aveu* (the disreputable ones) against the propertied bourgeois; not least of all, the colonial groups, without distinction of separate interest, against the hated royal charter companies that monopolized the African trade. All of those conflicts, so characteristic of the socially explosive character of the colonial existence, gave rise to the well-known seditious uprisings of 1670, 1723, and 1769.

The ideological expression of those various discontents, all complaining in one way or another about *la peine de l'Amérique* (the sacrifices involved in living in America), found itself in the form of the *autonomisme colon* (idea of colonial autonomy). A variety of themes went into its formation, all of them responding to the grievances of the different colonial groups. There is the spirit of rough, almost communistic, independence of the buccaneers and filibusters, allied with the almost anarchical spirit of the island town crowd, both of which claim to be the original source of a burgeoning national spirit.

Seeking liberty rather than wealth, their adherents see themselves as constituting *la république des aventuriers*. There is the spirit of parliamentary
republicanism whereby the colonial councils emulate the attitudes of the seventeenth-century provincial councils in France itself, protesting loyalty to the
Crown but fiercely resisting the policies of the Crown's local officials: *Vive le
Roi, point de Compagnie*. There is the hatred of the colonial upper-class bourgeois for the restrictive *pacte colonial* that inhibits the vital "interloper"
trade with the North American colonies; and from that there flows the intensely felt Anglophilism of the colonists, their deep admiration for the British constitution and for what they saw as the British liberal treatment of the
Antillean colonies. "The inhabitants," observed the marquis d'Argenson,
"are rich, republican, and would turn themselves over to the English at any
moment." "Disgust for his own country," wrote the local colonial jurist Saintard, "and along with that a frivolous attachment to the laws of foreign countries, is what characterizes the [Saint Domingue] citizen."[22] All of this, it is
true, does not add up to an ideology of independence. What the colonists
wanted was a more liberal trade policy, especially with the North Americans,
on which their very economic survival depended. So, it is the *esprit américain*,
a sense of inter-American solidarity, that constitutes the leading element of
their position. It wants, essentially, not independence, but colonial autonomy. In Frostin's phrase, having ceased to be French, the Saint Domingue
colonial had not yet become fully American, and it is that absence of a fully
felt and clearly defined identity that explains, during this period, the sterility
of his political activity.[23]

Both Moreau de Saint-Méry and d'Auberteuil exemplify the ideology of
autonomisme colon (colonial autonomy). Moreau de Saint-Méry's American
diary reveals him as the great admirer of American institutions, although he
is still too much a Frenchman not to deplore what he sees as an absence of
polite manners in the American character.[24] In his massive collection of colonial laws, he notes the perennial complaints of the colonists against the metropolitan system.[25] He repeats Charlevoix's contemptuous dismissal of what
is seen as the colonial ragamuffin scum, including the women, who foment
the colonial uprisings. But at the same time he can perceive in a sympathetic
manner the nature of its grievances. He can even write passages in his work
on Saint Domingue that purvey the legend of the statesmanlike rule of earlier
governors like Larnage and Maillart as set against the rule of later governors,
who are seen as lesser men.[26] He is, all in all, the kind of Creole colonial
Frenchman who, educated in the spirit of the French philosophes, finds in
his American experience a new justification for their arguments. "There are
no quarrels over religion," he writes admiringly about the young American
republic, "and anyone is privileged to believe his own the best so long as he
does not try to force anyone else to adopt it. . . . This picture is admirable,
and should be brought home to all ministers of all religions throughout the
entire world—a sublime lesson from the Sovereign of Beings to all men to

show them that the most gratifying of gifts they can offer Him are tolerance and the love of one's neighbor."[27]

D'Auberteuil is, perhaps, a more radical spirit. He is a severe critic of the French colonial administration because he is, philosophically, a contractualist. Contract, he says, is the basis of the vaunted English liberty. The state contracts with its colonial subjects for mutual advantages. But in the French case the metropolitan merchants violate the contractual obligation with their maxim *Les colonies sont faites pour nous* (The colonies are made for us). Ideally, there should exist a theory and practice of *utilité réciproque* (mutually beneficial reciprocity). For the perfection of law is that nobody should find his interest in the misfortune of others. Each citizen, ideally, only seeks happiness in what he does within the context of the social virtues.[28] Based on these theoretical propositions, d'Auberteuil advances the argument that the colonies must be treated as equals because they cannot just be seen as overseas departments. There are differences between the metropolitan and colonial economies: Sugar and tobacco and indigo require large-scale enterprise, not like wheat and grapes in France. It follows that many metropolitan laws, when applied indiscriminately to the colony, do not make sense.[29] It is, of course, the protectionism of France that strangles the colonial commerce; and d'Auberteuil concludes that without the benefits of the illegal contraband traffic, the majority of the white population would starve and a large area of plantations would be abandoned by their owners.[30]

In more general terms, d'Auberteuil—fascinated like everyone else with the eighteenth-century debate on luxury—adds his own Creole thoughts to that vexed problem. He begins by noting, correctly, that luxury results from inequality of wealth; where there are rich men, there will always be luxury. It is therefore useless merely to rail against it, in the manner of the moralists of the age.[31] But, he goes on to say, luxury takes on more peculiar forms within the colonial situation. There is a *luxe de commodité*, which benefits not only the person but also the society as a whole; and both France and the colony benefit from it through the means of trade and commerce. There is also, however, a *luxe extérieur*, a sort of ostentatious spending concerned only with appearances in society. This becomes, in Saint Domingue, a *luxe* imported by the crowds of Frenchmen who have invaded the colony, and exacerbated by the Asiatic-type luxury imported by governors and their entourage—such as fancy uniforms that are emulated by the colonial militia, not to speak of horse carriages, resplendently dressed Negro servants, jewels, diamonds, and fashionable clothes—all of which benefit the French merchants but ruin the colony, because this sort of wealth produces nothing.[32] In Saint Domingue, in effect, there is no real *luxe de commodité*, whereby citizens spend for their own personal, intrinsic pleasure. Everything, rather, is for public ostentation. So, nobody spends his money, for instance, on improving private-home interiors, and there are no public gardens or town promenades. And the root cause of all this, d'Auberteuil concludes, is defective government. Everybody is in a state of continual alarm because of uncertain and unjust government; and distrust and vanity in social relationships are the consequences of that fact.[33]

The full measure of the contribution that Moreau de Saint-Méry and d'Auberteuil made to the cause of colonial autonomy can be better appreciated if their work is compared with another writer from the French Antilles of the same period. Emilien Petit was, in his own words, a *député des conseils superieurs des colonies françaises* (deputy of the higher Councils of the French colonies). In his two-volume work *Droit public, ou Gouvernement des colonies françaises*, published in 1771, he wrote an exhaustive account of public administration and administrative laws in the colonies. Like Moreau de Saint-Méry, he is the industrious compiler of laws and edicts. But he is hardly the severe critic of the system in the manner of his contemporary, not to speak of the autonomist vision of d'Auberteuil. At the most, he allows himself some brief passages cautiously advocating certain limited reforms. Most of them revolve around the American idea of the separation of powers, which Petit has obviously absorbed. Government by a single person, he advises, is dangerous; that is why the colonial governmental regime has two leading officers, the governor-general and the intendant. For two minds are better than one, and the division of powers protects the colonial inhabitants against arbitrary government. The success of the system depends upon the important proviso that the intendant not be of a lower social rank than the governor-general.[34] The same principle of divided authority requires that in the area of public order the lines of authority between the police and the army and navy units be carefully observed, as well as the demarcation between all of those and the civil magistrates. Neither must the officers of the regular troops interfere with the authority of the militia.[35]

Going beyond this, Petit takes a close look at the office of the governor-general. Since people in Paris do not appreciate local conditions, it is important, he argues, that the top post be filled with able nominees. At least one of the two appointees—governor and intendant—should know the islands, possessing an experience of the men and affairs of the colony that he cannot acquire in France. The three-year limit of gubernatorial appointees is also seen as defective; it would be better to introduce a regime of unlimited service, and the governor-general should only be removed at his own request or because of gross misconduct in the office.[36] The governor-general, in turn, should be assisted by new administrative councils, for the councils as they stand at the moment are too much preoccupied with financial and military matters, to the neglect of other problems. What is needed is a new system of advisory councils in the islands themselves, including in their membership at least four colonial inhabitants recommended to the Crown by colonial legislative assemblies. Such a reform would encourage the habit of public service, and its encouragement in the assemblies of the ethic of public service would be salutary.[37]

Yet these prescriptions do not add up to a doctrine of colonial autonomy. Petit is a cautious lawyer type. He accepts the colonial condition. All that he wants are procedural reforms within the system. His pages breathe nothing of the angry strictures characteristic of Moreau de Saint-Méry and d'Auberteuil. There is nothing of the kind of spirited defense of the colonies that another contemporary, Antonio Sánchez Valverde, advanced in his book of 1785, *Idea del valor de la isla Española*.[38] Petit is, in sum, the legal antiquary. He does not see that there is a world of difference between laws, on the one hand, and how they are actually put into practice. With all their deficiencies, Moreau de Saint-Méry and d'Auberteuil did not fall into that trap.

THE HAITIAN PAMPHLETEERS

Yet the most authentic note of French Antillean nationalism comes not from the colonial period but from the remarkable group of writers—many of them secretaries of state in the new Haitian government—who wrote a pamphlet literature defending the Haitian Revolution against its Parisian detractors after 1804. Their predecessors had written in terms of a theory of colonial self-government within the French system; they wrote, quite differently, in defense of a theory of independent black nationhood. The importance of their literature stems, to begin with, from the fact that they were proud, educated Haitians, theoreticians of a new black American republicanism. As Prince Sanders, the agent for the new Haitian government in London, urged in his own writings, they were not European hacks employed by the Haitian government, as charged by their enemies, but black Haitians of repute and learning; even Bryan Edwards, asserts Sanders, might change his mind about Santo Domingo if he could see the Haiti of today.[39] By the standards of the age in which they wrote, moreover, their ambience was almost democratic; visitors to the court of Henri Christophe, like Harvey, remarked on the spectacle of secretaries of state sitting down in a simple ordinary chair and conversing with workmen, and of how, to his own astonishment, domestic servants would casually intervene in dinner-table conversations to make their own contribution to the table talk, without embarrassment.[40]

For a whole generation after 1804, until French diplomatic recognition of the new regime finally came (1825), there was the ever-present danger of an attempt at French reconquest. So, the first note struck in the Haitian literature is that of national preparedness, of defiance of French intentions. One must remember, wrote Inginac in his later memoirs, that we were living in times when it seemed that every moment of the republic would be its last.[41] Replying to Charrault's prediction of a new victorious French invasion, Charlemagne reminds that ex-colon of the fighting qualities of the Haitians—including their art of guerrilla warfare—not to mention the tropical disease that the French call the "Siam sickness" awaiting the invaders. He answers Charrault's further charge that blacks only know how to be ordered about with the counterassertion that the Haitian of today is not the sort of person that the ex-colons knew twenty-five years ago. Any French expedition can only turn out to be a dangerous and impracticable adventure, ending in disaster like the earlier Le Clerc expedition.[42] You cannot cite one nation in history, adds the baron de Dupuy, that after twenty-five years of liberty would wish to subject itself voluntarily to the yoke of slavery; and he points with pride to the new Haitian army, with its weekly Sunday parades, as the means whereby that sentiment will be upheld.[43] The sense of danger leads, in turn, to insistence upon national unity and reconciliation in the face of the common enemy—our *guerres intestines* (fractured wars), argues the chevalier de Prézeau, only help the cause of the colons and the French: Black and yellow, we are all brothers, we belong to the same family.[44] De Prézeau presses home the lesson in another epistle, this time addressed to the head of a visiting French mission, General Lavaysse. Lavaysse had argued, in a public letter, that it was the usurper Napoleon and not royal France that had been responsible for the Le Clerc expedition; to which de Prézeau answers that both regimes had been guilty of perfidy and treason in their dealings with the Antilleans. We do not want French honors, *lettres de blancs*, de Prézeau adds, because we glory in the color that God has given us.[45] To Lavaysse's eulogy of French discipline as the best in the world, he retorts that the only discipline we in the Antilles cherish is Haitian discipline: talk with the remnants of Le Clerc's force, he adds, and see what your vaunted discipline was in reality. If you want peace with us, he concludes, then you must accept the fact of Haiti's independence. We will never proclaim Louis XVIII as king of France in Haiti.[46] Prévost, in turn, adds to all this the proud thought that the Haitian defeat of the crack French regiments recalls the fate of the armies of Xerxes after his famous expedition to Greece. It is, all in all, the note of a vibrant, insurgent, Creole nationalism. Prévost even gives it an Antillean historical dimension in his observation that it has its roots in the first Indian revolt against the Spaniards of 1517, led by the native Hispaniola chieftain Henry.[47]

Along with that theme there goes another: The new Haiti, like France itself after 1789, has become a new creative force constructing, through the art of constitution building, a new freedom for mankind. Each secretary of state, as he composes his piece, is anxious to reveal himself as the republican lawgiver shaping the administrative and constitutional structures of the new society, for new nations require new institutions. The baron de Dupuy contrasts the new *code de culture* with the old slavery regime. The mulatto administrative chief Bonnet describes, in his later memoirs, how it was his ambition to build up an efficient state machine on the ruins of the colony; and he tells his reader how, after 1809, with no records available, he was forced to go back to M. de Marbois's calculations of 1789 in order to prepare the first national budget. Likewise, Inginac describes his own administrative reforms under Dessalines and Pétion.[48] The eulogistic note does not disappear even when, as under Henri Christophe, the republican principles are sacrificed to the new black imperial regime. So, Prévost waxes eloquent about the construction of La Citadelle—like nothing so much as a courtier of the old French regime eulogizing the wonders of Versailles—and the largest section of his *Relation* is devoted to an enraptured description of the coronation of Henri Christophe, replete with loyal addresses, cantatas, and poems in the pastoral-romantic mode.[49] For the Haitian note of new freedom was, after all, a combination of social conservatism and political radicalism. The real victors of 1804 were the new ruling class of black generals and mulatto elite; there was no socialist left-wing element in the Haitian revolution to match the socialist movement of Babeuf in the last days of the French Revolution. This constitutional conservatism is reflected in the conversation that Bonnet reports, at the time, between the general Gerin and David Troy. "Your constitution," remarked Gerin, "is bad. You propose that the son of General Gerin be the equal of the son of a farmer." "Before the law, certainly," replied Troy, "but in society the son of General Gerin, by reason of his wealth and the education he has received, will occupy a position higher than the son of a farmer. The one will be no less equal to the other only in law."[50]

The final theme in this early Haitian literature is that of race and color. It portrays Haiti as a symbol of black dignity and power in a world dominated by the white European nations. Hitherto, the world has thought in terms of white civilization. Now Haiti reveals a black civilization. Colombel tells his fellow Haitians that they are the *régénérateurs de l'Afrique* and that their struggle holds out hope for two-thirds of the human race. Chanlatte dares to believe that the whole colonial edifice is now in ruins and that the nineteenth century will be witness to the liberation of the men of all races throughout the world. The Haitian revolution, comments the comte de Rosiers, marks the beginning of the redemption of Africa. Theories of racial inferiority are white inventions, and what has passed for black indolence and laziness are not innate characteristics but the results of slavery itself; as Darfour insists, such theories are simply rationalizations of economic interests. Milscent, finally, uses Montesquieu's climatological theories to advance his own peculiar argument that the origin of races resides in the divine decision to create different races appropriate to different climates so, since the Supreme Being has ordained that each race reside in that geographical zone that is suitable to it, it follows that European colonization in the Antilles is a violation of that geopolitical law.[51] In all of this, blacks are seen as co-equals with whites and others. Even more, there is presented a theory of citizenship in which all Haitians and Haitian residents are seen—as in the language of the first constitution— as *noirs*; so that in that sense, as Nicholls points out, the word *noir* is used for the first time in an ideological and not a racial sense.[52]

BARON DE VASTEY

Yet it is the intriguing figure of the baron De Vastey who is the most representative spokesman of the new Haiti. Son of a French father and a Creole mother, a young participant in the war, leading confidant of Henri Christophe, his writings reveal him not only as a polemicist but also as a scholar. It is important to realize that, all in all, he was responding to the new wave of European Negrophobia that followed the victory of 1804 or, indeed, that of 1791; as Chateaubriand himself noted, it was no longer fashionable, after those events, to talk about the noble black and the indignities that he suffered.[53] Two grand themes recur in De Vastey's pamphlets and books: first, the particular defense of the Haitian revolution and, second, the general defense of the black-Negro race in world history. In all of it, he reveals himself as a true child of the Enlightenment, with all of its wit and erudition, but this time married to the Antillean matter.

The defense of Haiti rests on both factual and interpretative grounds. The vast majority of those who have written on slave Saint Domingue, he notes in *Le système colonial dévoilé*, have been whites who have gone into great detail on matters of climate, production, agriculture, and so on, but have ignored the basic cruelty of the system; he then proceeds to describe the cruelty, not in general terms, but citing appalling individual examples of planter behavior.[54] The original cruelty, in slavery as also in the slave trade, was European, even going back beyond the period of African slavery to early Spanish colonization; and he cites Garcilaso de la Vega's *Memorias reales* to prove the point. Greece and Rome had colonies, he adds, but did not oppress them; in fact, they shared their commerce, learning, and the arts with their colonial subjects. Even Britain at the present time has shown in its Sierra Leone experiment how Africa can be helped to become a nation of arts and sciences:[55] The remark reflects De Vastey's deeply felt Anglophilism. The same regard for things English prompts his remark, in his reply to Malouet, that it is the French, not the Haitians, who have shown an irreconcilable hatred for the English. He adds a further argument in defense of the Haitian war in the same paper by pointing out all the atrocities of the French Revolution, for which no black is responsible; we no longer need to go back to the Neros and the Caligulas for evidence of barbarity, for it is there in France itself.[56] Added to all this there is the further argument, almost socialist in its character, that the Haitian Revolution is to be regarded as more transcendentally important in world history than the preceding American Revolution, since whereas the latter was only a political revolution the former was a social revolution, seriously reshaping property ownership and property relationships in the Haitian economic structure.[57]

The defense of the African race is equally spirited. Answering the slanders of De Mazeres, De Vastey sees that race as belonging to all humanity. He quotes Saint Pierre's *Etude de la nature* to prove that black skin color is only an accident of the species, being the effect of the sun. He further quotes contemporary writers like Knight to show that since black color is the attribute of the primitive race in all animals, then it is reasonable to believe that the Negro is the original type of the human race; and he quotes others like Hunter to underline the significance of the fact, so damning to the white-superiority thesis, that when the color of an animal whitens, it is taken as a sign of degeneration.[58] If, again, the white supremacists are correct, then it should follow that whites ought to flourish in tropical climates; but the evidence of writers like Demanet and Imlay on the degenerate character of the descendants of Portuguese settlers in Sierra Leone fails to support the argument. Standards of physical beauty are culturally conditioned, not absolute; thus, let us recall how the African traveler Bruce describes the horrified reaction of African women to his appearance as a white man.[59] It is true that slaves have always existed in Africa. But so have they always existed in Europe. Why reproach the Africans for their barbarity and ignorance when European races themselves have evinced similar characteristics, as the descriptions in Caesar and Tacitus of the barbarous customs of the old Gaul tribes sufficiently demonstrate?[60] If, again, Negroes are supposed to be naturally ordained for obedience, then have not the modern French people themselves been supine and obedient to all the Robespierres and Napoleons of the revolutionary period?[61] The investigations of scholars like Septante and Lesage have shown how, in fact, Africa has traditionally been the cradle of civilizations—Carthaginian, Ethiopian, Egyptian, Phoenician—predating the European forms by some 1500 years.[62]

In all of this, De Vastey uses his European learning in the cause of Africa. It was, indeed, a learning that would have done justice to the clubs of Dr. Johnson's London or the salons of Napoleon's Paris. He ends with a paean of praise to Africa as he sees it, taking the large imaginative view of the decline and fall of empires borrowed from Volney. Thebes, Memphis, Babylon, Athens—all have gone. Paris, presumptuous city, he declaims, do you think that you alone are exempt from this law of history? One day, perhaps, a traveler will search in vain along the banks of the Seine for a place where the city was supposed to have existed. The duration of empires, like the existence of man himself, is measured by the supreme arbiter of the universe, and at the end of their term, they will die and revive again like other productions of nature. Maybe one day it shall be the turn of Africa.[63]

THE HAITIAN HISTORIANS

After this early school of Haitian writers, the rest of the century witnessed the further development of Haitian political thought in the form of the historians of the second and later generations: Madiou, Ardouin, Joseph Saint-Rémy, Nau, and other publicists. They continue the international ideology of Haitian national independence with their defense of the revolution; but they add to it a new dimension in the form of, so to say, the domestic ideology of the revolution: that is, of the new interclass and intergroup relationships that slowly developed as the revolutionary regime became stabilized. There is, then, something old as well as something new in this later literature. In another way, it is different from the thought of the earlier writers in the sense that although the major themes remain unchanged, the treatment changes, so that the essay and the pamphlet are replaced by the extensive tomes of written history, using the accumulated archival material to present the great drama of the birth and development of a nation.

For these Haitian historians, then, history is not just a record. It is, much more, a celebration. Past and present are molded into one integral and continuous growth of the national spirit. It is true that there are important issues that divide them—the traumatic struggle, for instance, between the *noiriste* and the mulatto interpretations of the story that has always plagued Haitian historiography—but, taking the large overall view, they are united in their presentation of the drama that they unfold in their pages. The note is struck early on by the first of the historians, Madiou, in his *Histoire d'Haiti*. He portrays Haiti as a free homeland for African people, a repayment, as it were, to the peoples of Europe for the oppression that they had inflicted in the past and for their cruel destruction of the indigenous Indian peoples. The emergence of Haiti, furthermore, is a refutation of the view that certain parts of the globe should be restricted to particular races: the world belongs to the whole human race. In a long passage of his preface, suppressed by the Haitian Ministry of Education in the second edition, Madiou perceives the national history of his country as a logical outcome of the great principles of 1789; for Madiou, if anything, is the ardent liberal republican.[64] It is no accident that the great French historian Michelet should have congratulated him on his work in a warm personal letter.[65] Ardouin, in turn, in his voluminous series of *Etudes*, writes as a Haitian patriot whose sacred duty, as he says, is to record and hand on to future generations the story of past deeds. He uses earlier writers like Moreau de Saint-Méry and Hilliard d'Auberteuil, from whose writings he cites long passages *per verbatim*, to show how the colonial system inevitably bred revolt; those writers, he observes correctly and approvingly, wrote as critics of the colonial regime.[66] The subsequent transition from colonialism to freedom is thus seen by Ardouin not only as the achievement of men but also as a work of divine providence. Going beyond that, Saint-Rémy—who died, tragically, so young—wrote in his *Pétion et Haiti* not only a celebration of the national spirit but also a spirited defense of the black race against the pernicious ideas of once well-known writers like Mme. Marie de Fontenay. To all of this, other historians like Nau—in his *Histoire des cacaiques d'Haiti*—wrote of the early Spanish extermination of the Indians, and saw both Indian and African as the early progenitors of a truly indigenous Haitian culture mixing the Indian-African roots with the later European spirit, so that, ultimately, Haiti would produce its own literature of incontestable originality. Lespinasse, in his *Histoire des affranchis de Saint-Domingue*, urged likewise upon his readers the importance of the African roots of

Haitian culture.[67] In all of this, the historians agree on the common theme of
the seminal importance of the Saint Domingue–Haiti story: it demonstrates
that while each race possesses its own unique civilization, it also at the same
time belongs to the great family of humanity, so that there is no room for theories of racial inferiority.

Yet, like all schools of historical writing, the Haitian school has its own
share of flaws and defects. Within the context of nineteenth-century Haitian
realities, the flaws are two. The first is related to color, the second to class;
both of them are intermixed in the peculiar Haitian social structure in which
mulatto became identified with the ruling urban elite and black with the illiterate peasant mass. The varied mix of Haitian ideas and ideologies can only
properly be understood within that rigidified framework. The French observer
Lepelletier de Saint-Rémy summed it up in his sardonic observation of 1845:
"A hodge-podge of the most heterogeneous ideas, an alliance of the most
contrary principles, of American federalism with military control; the sovereignty of the people replaced by the sovereignty of a ruling clique; and finally,
all of the intellectual vainglory of a people young, inexperienced, and for a
long time denied the legitimate manifestation of their own wishes. Added to
all these inconsistencies is the antagonism of races."[68]

Since the intellectual class, by definition, belonged to the educated mulatto
element, they produced, as the first flaw of their writing, what Nicholls refers
to as the ideology of the mulatto legend. They celebrate the heroic record of
the Afro-Haitian people as all belonging to a single race. But they insist, at
the same time, and with fine illogicality, upon the preeminence of the free
mulatto group in the struggle, and thereby give credence to the ideas of color
prejudice. The story of the struggle becomes, as it were, a simplistic scenario
in which the black generals—Toussaint, Dessalines, Henri Christophe—are
the villains and the mulatto generals—Pétion, Rigaud, Boyer—the heroes.
So, Saint-Rémy talks of the revolutionary war as if it was conducted by an alliance of mulattoes and blacks. Lespinasse describes the moral sufferings of
the free coloreds under the ancien régime as if they are equal to the physical
sufferings of the slaves and claims that the mulatto force was the main inspiration of the revolt. Ardouin paints Pétion as a paragon of all the virtues while
Dessalines emerges as the embodiment of everything evil in Haiti and even
Toussaint, pictured more favorably, is portrayed as representing the unfortunate "aristocratic" tradition identified with the northern kingdom of the
country—so much so that, as later commentators put it, Ardouin writes his
account of the intramural struggle after 1804 as if he feels aggrieved that he
has to describe how the war of the South ended in the victory of Toussaint.[69]
All in all, the general picture is that of mulattoes and free coloreds as the true
patriots, the custodians of the ideas of the revolution: distrust of the whites,
constitutional government, the supremacy of the civil power over that of the
military, the purity of the presidential regime. What is present here is, in fact,
the Achilles heel of all Haitian political thought: the temptation of each

writer to interpret reality in terms of his own group in the Haitian caste structure. Baron De Vastey complained, in the very first sentence of his essay on the causes of the revolution, that Haiti had no general history written by a native of the country.[70] But those histories, when they came to be written, contained all the class and cultural bias of their authors, mulatto to begin with and then, later, the protagonists of the *noiriste* version. The varying and, at times, glaringly contradictory interpretations of the figure of Toussaint L'Ouverture are as good an example of the matter as any. For De Vastey himself, Toussaint, like Henri Christophe, is one of the great father figures of the new nation. For Ardouin, he is a tool of the whites in the struggle, because of his hatred for mulattoes. This irreconcilable difference of opinion was followed by other writers—both Haitian and foreign, and extends into the twentieth century itself. For James Stephen, Toussaint becomes the incarnation of the Oroonoko legend of the westernized, white black man, whose virtues are set off against the vices of the Emperor Napoleon. For Schoelcher he is essentially a good man corrupted by too much power—a view that naturally suggested itself to a disciple of Tocqueville. For Aimé Césaire—coming to the twentieth-century writers—he is the catalyst that turns a slave rebellion into a genuine social revolution. For the Haitians François Duvalier and Lorimer Denis, he is a noble spirit fighting against the greed of the whites and the prejudices of the mulattoes, almost as if Duvalier were thus presaging his own elevation to black power as the historic successor to Toussaint. For C.L.R. James, finally, Toussaint takes on the form of a great revolutionary leader who has lost contact with the masses and lacks an ideology, almost as if James were perceiving in Toussaint a historical anticipation of the failure of the Russian Revolution after 1917 in its Stalinist phase to create a genuinely classless society.[71] Not the least interesting aspect of this history of the permutations of interpretation is that it has lasted into the modern period itself, a fact explained by the unbroken continuity of Haitian political history itself, in which the political game has been played by a tiny urban professional elite, with black presidential regimes succeeding mulatto presidential regimes, and vice versa, so that the "revolution of 1843" is not very different, in its essential characteristics, from the "revolution of 1946."

The second flaw of the Haitian nineteenth-century nationalist writing relates to its class bias. Its authors were schooled in the tradition of French radical republicanism. The sovereignty of the people, wrote Ardouin, is a fecund and living principle for the nineteenth century, proclaimed by most civilized nations of the world. The national history of Haiti, wrote Madiou, is a logical outcome of the great principles of 1789.[72] But that was a rhetoric borrowed from the great French revolutionary periods. It is true that both Madiou and Ardouin were genuinely moved and excited by the events of 1830 and 1848 in Paris. But they saw the events through the eyes of Lamartine and Victor Hugo, not of Marx. They certainly did not envisage a Haiti in which the unlettered masses would be master. Even the French ideas could go too far; thus Ardouin could write disparagingly of the influence of the more revolutionary ideas on the Haitian *esprits*: it is the fate of France, he wrote, that every revolution in Paris agitates people in other countries against their governments, which amounts to *une imitation puerile*. Speaking of the 1830 upsurge in Paris, he noted that young educated Haitians circulate all of their revolutionary illusions. Yet even then Ardouin was certainly allowing his fears to run away with him, for he goes on to note that the European authors popular with the younger group included Adam Smith, Jean-Baptiste Say, Ricardo, and Sismondi—essentially, that is to say, the defendants of the new bourgeois industrial social order in Europe.[73] But he was even more critical, as was also Madiou, of the more socially radical extremist element that was a part of the 1843 movement against Boyer, an element led by the young Acaau that sought, according to Madiou, to end the political power of the mulattoes, to dispossess reputedly rich citizens, no matter of what color, and then to divide their property among the *prolétaires*. Madiou's reaction was almost philosophical; it was, according to him, simply an aspiration for the future. But Ardouin was more violent, horrified at what he saw as a pernicious communist doctrine.[74]

The Haitian writers, in effect, constructed their historical science upon an acceptance of the postrevolutionary social order. They were preoccupied with political and constitutional history to the almost complete exclusion of social and economic matters. Lespinasse perhaps apart, they were distrustful of the African elements in the popular culture, regarding vodun especially as barbaric and retrogressive. They discuss the political life of the capital, the endless parade of new constitutions, the perennial struggles between president and senate. They see Haiti in terms of its godlike or devillike figures; one is known as *christophien* or as a protagonist of *boyerisme*. Thus, when Joseph Saint-Rémy writes his *Pétion et Haiti*, he cannot seem to make up his mind whether he is writing about the man or the nation. Similarly, Justin Bouzon composes in his history of the regime of Faustin Soulouque a series of vividly drawn pen portraits of the main actors in the drama he is describing, but tells the reader little, if anything, about the larger national scene within which they conduct their play.[75] Later on in the century Louis-Joseph Janvier, writing as a parliamentary Anglophile, puts together all of the written constitutions of the century, as if they meant anything more than the obsession of their authors with the empty pastime of constitution-mongering.[76] The truth, of course, was that abstract constitutional principles had little to do with the real issues of Haitian experience. Their authors, educated in the history of the ancient world, thought of themselves as some Lycurgus who would confer the ideal constitution upon their people. The most appropriate comment on that delusion was written by yet another, later Haitian commentator: Haitian constitutions, observed Sannon sardonically, are generally put together on the morning after triumphant revolutions, even after a bloody battle, by men still covered with powder and smoke, and are far from being mature instruments of government and far from reflecting the aspirations and the real needs of the country.[77]

THE LATER HAITIAN PUBLICISTS

Yet for all of its political absolutism and caste hegemony—endlessly emphasized by its foreign critics—post-1804 Haiti had about it one attribute of singular importance: its own political sovereignty. Owing allegiance to no outside power, with no traditions to constrain it, it alone of all the Caribbean societies of the century possessed the opportunity to build a theory and praxis of nationhood. One element of that nationhood, as already noted, was that of citizenship. A further element was that of state planning, whereby the new state power undertook to initiate public policies with reference to education, industrial development, land usage, work habits, and the rest. Those policies, of course, were shaped to meet the interests of, alternatingly, the mulatto oligarchy and the black military caste. But at the same time they gave rise to forms of state-directed economic development and to a pioneering discussion on theories of development that the other Antillean societies, because of their continuing colonial dependency, were unable to undertake. It is in this sense that nineteenth-century Haiti anticipates the twentieth-century Antillean debate on the theory and practice of economic growth and development, the ideology, in brief, of economic nationalism.

The literature of that ideology was written, not by the historians, but by the publicists of the latter part of the century: Demesvar Delorme, Louis-Joseph Janvier, Edmond Paul, and Antenor Firmin. They were all concerned, of course, with the ever-present problem of *colorisme* (color pride or prejudice). But they attempted to put it into a larger perspective of the Haitian public good. They even managed to recognize the social function played by the two color ideologies, mulatto and black: summed up in Janvier's remark that the struggle for power in Haiti, conducted by those seemingly two irreconcilable camps, in fact disguises the existence of a dominant class that is a mixture of both elements, of a *"noire-mulâtre"* character.[78] As against that farcical struggle, these thinkers emphasized the social and economic conditions of the commonwealth. It is economic and financial considerations, writes Paul, that determine the course of political events; stocks and shares have won or stopped battles; they controlled the Eighteenth Brumaire in France.[79] Sincerely concerned with the plight of the peasant masses, even from their own class viewpoint, they wanted to use the state power as a means to undertaking vital reforms and as a means of stimulating and guiding some sort of planned economic growth, including industrialization. It may be noted, incidentally, that the *étatisme* (state sovereignty) they espoused had in some way been anticipated in the Saint Domingue slave society by the French Physiocratic thinker Le Mercier de la Rivière, who, as colonial administrator there, had worked out a grand scheme for building up an overseas "grain realm" aimed at obtaining, by state encouragement, increased food supplies and planned population growth.[80]

The general argument starts off with the assumption that a mercantilist-protectionist economy is necessary since, without it, the economy becomes victim to outside economic forces. The principle of free trade, observes Paul, while applicable to those states whose interests are tied up with it, is fatal for states, like Haiti, that are at the mercy of other states. The result, complains Janvier, is that the small Haitian entrepreneur is pushed out by foreign competition encouraged by the greed of the big merchants and the complicity of the governments they help fund. It leads, in another way, declares Delorme, to an absurd and ill-balanced economic development, for it is ridiculous to build railroads that people cannot afford to ride in; rather, we should think of improving roads and bridges, indispensable for real economic and commercial growth.[81] What, above all, is necessary is not, as others argued, the complete abolition of the famous law against white ownership, repeated in Article 7 of the 1846 Constitution, but a reasonable amendment of the prohibition in order to allow the entry of foreign capital, in alliance with local capital, in areas where the foreign capitalist and technician can provide skills not yet present in the local population.[82] For Firmin, that becomes a plea for allowing long-term leases on local property to the foreign investor, as well as a policy of carefully supervised white immigration. For Paul, it becomes a demand for state-directed technical and scientific education, for in the modern world a nation counts for more because of its industrialists than its writers. What Haiti needs are engineers, builders, industrialists, science teachers, not just more poets. It also needs a viable program of serious land and agricultural reform, including mechanization of agricultural methods and government loans to small farmers. Delorme saw such a reform in English terms. "What I wish for," he writes, "is to see my fellow-citizens of the towns address their intelligence and their capital that they presently use up fruitlessly in a commerce that has nothing to do with food; intelligent Haitians applying themselves to resuscitate the honorable existence of rural proprietors...and acquire the respect that the class of liberal-minded landowners enjoy in other countries...and in saying this I have in mind the England where the agricultural land-owners comprise the elevated classes of the society and are in control of the government."[83]

In terms of economic philosophy, all this constitutes an economic liberalism combined with moderate state direction. Some of its theoreticians, notably Firmin, claimed it to be socialist, in the Saint-Simonian rather than the Marxist fashion.[84] But the claim is certainly spurious. For none of the leading ideas of socialism—the collective ownership of the means of production, social equality, the organized working class as the proper vehicle of fundamental change, the class war—appear in the literature. The main note, on the contrary, is a Rousseauistic petty-bourgeois reformism. Delorme, in his major work, *Les théoriciens au pouvoir* (the title itself betrays its elitist prejudice), sees the state, in typical liberal fashion, as a neutral force to be used by the "enlightened" and "educated" class in the interests of all. The state, he writes, does not give property to its citizens. It merely gives them the right to acquire it, the right to work, to protection, to the aid of its institutions. In the state of nature, property is the right of the first and most powerful occupant; in the social state it cannot be anything but the right of work or of heredity that it represents.[85] Democracy, adds Delorme, is government for the people; government by the people is demagoguery. The best form of government for Haiti is a sort of Platonic aristocracy of the best talents drawn from all ranks, thus freeing it from the charge of being a caste or an oligarchy.[86] Janvier echoes the same prejudice in his *Affaires d'Haiti*: true democracy means a system in which the *majorités fermes* (established-majorities) are guided by the ruling group of *esprits scientifiques*.[87] These definitions, Delorme's argument proceeds, are to be distinguished from the socialist ideas of Morus, Campanella, Morelly, Babuef, Fourier, and Saint-Simon, for those ideas add up to a communism that destroys intelligence, property, and family.[88] So, despite the fact that Firmin manages to praise the struggle of the English Chartists against the territorial aristocracy and the new monied plutocracy, and that Janvier even praises the Paris Communards of 1871, they are far from feeling the same sentimental adoration for their own peasant masses. Indeed, when they come to mention the 1843 peasant uprising, their tone of excited indignation almost matches the fierce diatribes of the ultrareactionary writer Edouard. For if Edouard sees the masses as threatening barbarians at the gate, the liberal writers see them, in Delorme's words, as the lowest classes of the society whose insatiable appetites have taken property and wealth by force and have perpetuated terror and seduction.[89] The liberals, in brief, may have emancipated themselves, as they liked to believe, from race prejudice, but they had assuredly not released themselves from class fear.

This, of course, constitutes the ambiguity of the Haitian bourgeois nationalism. Ambiguities notwithstanding, however, the liberal body of thought possessed lasting value in at least the one important area of economic analysis. In their search for economic autarky, the liberal thinkers anticipated the later twentieth-century debate on neocolonialism. They saw that economic dependence effectively nullifies political independence. Unrestricted economic penetration by European and North American investors and businessmen could only lead to political interference, which in turn could lead to annexation. The apprehension is there in Paul's warning, from exile, that President Salomon's creation of the National Bank in 1880, depending mainly on foreign capital, could become a Trojan horse that would vomit into the midst of the country foreigners bent on annexation.[90] The theme is taken up by Janvier in his significantly titled *Haiti aux Haitiens*. In a veritable *cri de coeur*, he exclaims that "the earth of Haiti was not conquered and developed by our ancestors in order that we should now make a gift of it to future oppressors."[91] In the face of the threat of annexation by the United States, he recommends that the major European powers be requested to guarantee Haitian neutrality in some way similar to the statutes that protect the neutrality of Belgium and Switzerland. Delorme, in turn, denounces U.S. annexationist policies as being based on the exaggerated capitalist thirst for profits. Firmin, finally, for his own part, urges the creation of an Antillean confederation in order to offset the American threat. Whatever their differences—Janvier, for example, is an Anglophile, while Firmin is a Francophile—they are united in their intellectual defense of the integrity of the national patrimony.

After Haiti, the torch of Antillean nationalism passed to the Hispanic Antilles—Puerto Rico, Santo Domingo, and Cuba. Their political evolution, of course, was different, for whereas Santo Domingo obtained its independence by secession from the Haitian kingdom in 1844, both Puerto Rico and Cuba remained under Spanish suzerainty until the end of the century, being finally released by the Spanish-American War of 1898. But their cultural and intellectual evolution, based on a common Hispanic patrimony, had much in common. They constituted the last bastion of the old, historic Spanish empire in the Americas; so, not unnaturally, the Creole intelligentsia, both liberal and revolutionary, felt a common bond in their resistance to Spain. Cuba and Puerto Rico were seen, in the phrase of a later poet, as wings of the same dove. The Puerto Rican educator de Hostos spent much of his life in exile in Santo Domingo. The leading spirits—de Hostos, Betances, Martí, Duarte, Luperón—dreamed of a united Antillean confederation that would bind them all together. And, at the end, the Cuban Revolutionary party, founded by Martí in New York, had its own Puerto Rican section. It is only necessary to glance through the exhaustive inventory of the collected archives and correspondence to that party, put together by the Cuban National Archives from 1921 on, to appreciate how its membership ranged throughout the whole of the Spanish-speaking Caribbean, not to mention its numerous North American friends and correspondents.[92] Whereas, then, the British Caribbean islands like Jamaica and Barbados lapsed into comparative obscurity after slavery emancipation—there had been a time when British governments had regarded them as more important than Canada—the Spanish-speaking islands, and especially Cuba, moved into the limelight and, more than any others, kept alive the anticolonial ideology.

THE PUERTO RICAN LIBERAL MOVEMENT

That anticolonial ideology, in the Hispanic-Antillean case, offers a special example of how the ideology managed to state its case without at the same time following the North Americans into an armed struggle against the metropolitan power. The particular case of early nineteenth-century Puerto Rico exemplifies that truth. For Puerto Rico, like Cuba, was so much regarded as the most loyal colony, remaining faithful while the other mainland territories undertook their wars of national liberation, that Spain delayed for a century or more any meaningful reforms in the island.

Ultimately, of course, reforms came in the very last years of the century, with the Autonomy Charter of 1898: but too late and too little. The interest of the historian of ideas, however, centers on the fact that it is in early nineteenth-century Puerto Rico that a liberal-minded Creole intelligentsia spearheads the movement for reform. Their general outlook, undoubtedly, was shaped by the liberal economic and administrative reforms introduced by the enlightened and benevolent despotism of Charles III and his advisers in the later part of the eighteenth century. The spirit of those reforms, as far as Puerto Rico is concerned, is to be seen in the 1782 volume of Fray Iñigo Abbad y Lasierra, summarizing his impressions of Puerto Rico at the time of his residence. The *Historia geográfica, civil, y natural de Puerto Rico* breathes the spirit of the Bourbon reforms. Abbad writes like nothing so much as the energetic visiting colonial official eager to push the island economy into progress. Although he lauds the virtues of the Puerto Ricans—which later Puerto Rican writers will elevate into a myth of Puerto Rican "character"—he is impatient with the vices that impede change and development: avarice, laziness, indolence, and the rest. He is willing to admit, following Montesquieu's theory of climate, that those vices are in part the necessary consequence of tropical environment. But he is more generally ready to argue that they are also the result of inefficient colonial administration. The combination of military and political functions in the office of the governor means that the captains-general are more concerned with military than civilian matters; their rule is despotic and autocratic and prevents the growth of that sort of mild yet firm government that the island needs. Accustomed to commanding with energy and being obeyed without question, writes Abbad, they fail to evoke that affectionate loyalty of subjects that is so necessary to the well-regulated state.[93]

From all this emerges Abbad's blueprint for reform and reorganization. He wants a vigorous agricultural policy that will rationally exploit the fruits and trees of the island; a free-trade policy to replace the narrow mercantilist official policy that, among other things, only serves to encourage the prevalent contraband trade; a road-building program to enable farmers to bring their products to the urban markets; a better land-use policy that, among other things, will penalize landowners without proper title or who do not fully utilize their holdings and will facilitate rational redistribution. For, following his Physiocratic mentors, Abbad insists that agriculture is the first mainstay of any healthy economy and that without it, trade and commerce are, at best, precarious investments.[94] A proper population policy follows logically from that position, and Abbad recommends the establishment of at least thirty new townships to encourage the rehabilitation and expansion of the interior areas of the island.[95] Nor is there wanting in all this the spirit of eighteenth-century humanitarianism, so that, speaking of the various castes of the insular population, Abbad takes time to notice the brutal ill-treatment of the blacks: the worst affront in the society, he observes, was to be a Negro or the descendant of a Negro.[96] Indeed, the intellectual influence of Raynal is apparent throughout, and there are many passages in the work that parallel passages from the volumes of Raynal that are better known.[97]

Abbad, in brief, writes a critique, albeit only sometimes by inference, of Spanish colonial government. That he must have influenced contemporary Puerto Rican readers is evident enough from the fact that the instructions of 1810 given by the *ayuntamiento* of San Juan to Ramón Power, the first-ever locally elected deputy to the Spanish Cortes, reflect in their successive items many of the ideas advanced in the *Historia*. Broadly speaking, they cover the whole spectrum of liberal demands. Admittedly, there is here, of course, no declaration of independence, and they commence with the usual fulsome declaration of loyalty to Spain. But following that, the successive items register a firm, and indeed at times a bitter, complaint against colonial administration. They request, among other things: the establishment of hospitals and health centers; a school of mechanical arts aimed at the prevention of juvenile crime rather than the government simply meddling with punitive measures; a program of new roads and bridges in order to open up the interior; the opening up of Crown lands as a first measure in encouraging agriculture; the introduction of an experimental fifteen- or twenty-year period of free trade with neighboring islands as a means of encouraging commerce; taxation policies of a more liberal character; recognition of the right of qualified natives to occupy public offices; and, not least important of all, the establishment of a local university addressing itself to the education of the young in the humanities and the sciences.[98] A later Puerto Rican historian has seen the inspiration for those demands in the various works of the leading thinkers and reformers of the period like Voltaire and Rousseau, Adam Smith and Bentham, Locke and Beccaria, Turgot and Jovellanos.[99] This, obviously, does not mean that the Puerto Rican framers of the instructions had actually read all of those authors. It means, rather, that the general ideas of those authors had become part of the mental climate of the age, and were, so to speak, in the air, and that by 1810 they had made their presence felt in San Juan.

Both Abbad's work and *Las Instrucciones al Diputado Don Ramon Power Giral* of 1810 thus point to the existence of a gathering protonationalist feeling in the Puerto Rico of the time. Yet at the same time they were the sentiments of a small-town professional elite. They cannot in any way be seen as expressions of a wider popular movement. They were constrained by both class and race prejudices. No more than the bourgeois European reformers from whom they garnered their inspiration could they be regarded as harbingers of a genuinely democratic movement. That is evident enough, to take a single example, from the observations of the mayor of San Juan, Don Pedro Irizarri, written in 1809 as a sort of aide-memoire to the *Instrucciones*. They support the demands of the *Instrucciones*. But at the same time they supply them with a background of commentary that reveals an almost paranoid hatred of all of the lower-class types presumed to be responsible for the backwardness of the island economy. The native laborer, or *agregado*, Irizarri alleges, retreats into the mountains in order to work on a few acres of his own, paying no rents or taxes, growing a few ground provisions just to keep himself and his family alive, and refusing to grow the commercial crops like sugar and cotton and coffee that alone can make the country prosperous; he is, in truth, lazy, undependable, and antisocial. The Negro slave, in his turn, is even worse. Inhuman, irreligious, immoral, ungovernable, he will only do to Puerto Rico what he has already done to Santo Domingo if the Puerto Rican government continues its stupid policy of importing him as an answer to the labor-supply problem. There is, finally, the foreign immigrant who, despite strict governmental restrictions, invades the island. He comes in as a lamb, says Irizarri, and then behaves as a rapacious wolf to destroy us. He pretends to be a good Catholic, but in reality pays his dues to Bacchus and Venus, and thus foments infidelity and disorder.[100] There is apparent in all of this diatribe not only the class fear of all ruling groups against *los de abajo* (those from below) but also the antiforeigner prejudice so characteristic of all nascent nationalisms. The only cure for it all that Irizarri can recommend to the Spanish Crown is a new and vigorous immigration policy that will encourage workers from places like New Spain and the Canary Islands who, presumably, will be more pliable.[101]

Both the *Instrucciones* and the Irizarri memoir thus formulate a sort of embryonic political national consciousness. They want free trade, a more equitable tax system, a more amenable labor supply, more delegation of authority to local bodies, and continuing colonial representation in the national parliament. As such, they are little more than supplications for reforms in the spirit and practice of the colonial administration. They do not add up to a different spirit of cultural nationalism, reflecting a spirit of felt separate cultural identity in Puerto Ricans.

That quite different sense of social separatism has to be located elsewhere. In nineteenth-century Puerto Rico it was, in fact, the expression of the Puerto Rican insular rural and mountain working class, counterpart of the Cuban class, whose formation, in terms of historical sociology, went back to the later part of the eighteenth century; and was, in fact, the very class so thoroughly despised by Irizarri.

The formation of that class—essentially a unique preindustrial type—is to be found in the official and unofficial accounts of the period. To begin with, Marshal O'Reylly noted the origin of the type in his report made as early as 1785. Noting the preference of the highland people for smuggling over agriculture, he saw with some sympathy the roots of the preference: "The habits of indolence," he wrote, "were encouraged by a sweet climate that requires

very little clothing by way of protection, so that one could be content with an
ordinary striped shirt and a pair of loose trousers, and since everybody lived
thus there were no reasons for competing one against the other." Colonel
Flinter's report of 1833 noted the same features: "this individual [the *jíbaro*]
mounted on his emaciated horse, dressed in a broad-brimmed straw hat, cotton jacket, clean shirt and checkered pantaloons, sallies forth from his cabin
to mass, to a cockfight or to a dance, thinking himself the most independent
and happy being in existence."[102] The medical report of Drs. Bailey Ashford
and Gutiérrez Igaravidez of 1900 completed the picture:

> The *jíbaro*, mountain bred, avoids the town whenever possible, avoids the genteel
> life of a civilization higher than that of his own. He instinctively tucks his little hut
> away in the most inaccessible spots; he shrinks from the stranger and lapses into
> stolid silence when brought face to face with things that are foreign to his life. He
> does this because he has been made to feel that he must do all that he is told by es-
> tablished authority, and he knows that this authority never takes the trouble to
> look for him unless it expects to get something out of him; because he is suspicious
> of outsiders, having been too often led astray by false prophets and disappointed by
> broken promises; because he realizes that he is not a free agent anywhere save in
> the mountain fastnesses.[103]

There is contained, thus, in all of these reports the general portrait of a
lower-class mountain folk people, jealous of its independence, distrustful
both of Spain and of the *sanjuaneros*, the city people, and living a life of pastoral simplicity. It is an instinctively conservative group, clinging to the old
ways. It is not a revolutionary group; after all, the one single episode of Puerto
Rican revolt against Spain, the *Grito de Lares* (Lares revolt) of 1868, was undertaken not by this class but by the petty-bourgeois class of *hacendados*
(although it is still important to remember that that ill-fated rebellion also
took place in the mountain region). Yet at the same time there is inherent in
this general picture the social foundations of freedom: a sturdy independence
of spirit, an almost anarchical distrust of authority, a rustic simplicity of life
almost Rousseauistic in its character. Brought up in solitude, wrote Brau, we
don't do well in the bustle of the court.[104]

It is, then, no accident that the flowering of Puerto Rican letters in the
nineteenth century took the *jíbaro* class as one, though not the only one, of its
primordial inspirational themes. The record has been amply documented by
later Puerto Rican scholars: Concha Meléndez, Modesto Rivera, Margot
Arce, José Emilio González, Iris Zavala, José Luis González, to name only a
few. It begins with Manuel Alonso's essay of 1849, *El gíbaro*, although that
was preceded by the collection *Aguinaldo Puertorriqueño* of 1843 and the *Al-
bum Puertorriqueño* of 1844, not to mention the earlier *Coplas del jíbaro* of
Miguel Cabrera—all of them stimulating the collection and study of the
jíbaro songs and folklore.[105] This initial effort, however, lacks literary merit,
is unduly romanticist, and only serves to establish, as it were, a factual foun-

dation for later writers. It is followed, then, by a later movement of more na-turalistic romanticism, almost social realism, in which the *jíbaro* life-style, although still admired, is seen, nevertheless, as grossly deficient in its social and moral aspects. Fernández Juncos, in his *Costumbres y tradiciones* and his *Galería Puertorriqueña*, puts together gently satirical portraits of the so-cial types of the small-town and country life, but at the same time notes the poverty and ignorance of the same types that in turn generate prostitution, emigration, and distorted moral values.[106] Del Valle Atiles, in turn, looks with a detached sociological eye at the *jíbaro* popular music and dance forms —with all of their vulgarity, natural spontaneity, ingenious social satire, and ironic pessimism (especially in matters of love and passion)—and concludes that although the intellectual development of the *jíbaro* class may be defi-cient, it is more than compensated for by the capacity to produce an indige-nous musical tradition already giving way (in 1887) to modern dance forms. The *El campesino* volume, indeed, constitutes almost a pioneer effort in the area of rural sociology.[107]

It is followed by the more systematically organized work of Salvador Brau in his *La campesina* and *Las clases jornaleras*. Extending his view to take in not only the *jíbaro* but also the sugar-plantation slave and the newly emerg-ing agroproletariat of nonblack, wage-labor workers, Brau looks at the total working class in a way that combines dispassionate sociological observation with a real human sympathy for its plight characteristic of a humane mind trained, among other intellectual influences, in the world of John Stuart Mill, Henry George, and the French pre-Marxist socialists. He is a stern critic of what he sees as the cultural deficiencies of the popular life-style: the social docility of the *jíbaro*, the religious superstitions that have corrupted the origi-nal Christian message, the social disorder of the *fiestas populares*, the games of chance that only offer delusions of sudden fortune, the lack of respect for property, the casual attitude toward work and the responsibilities that go with it.[108]

Brau, altogether, is a particularly interesting figure. He is a sociologist, influenced at once by Robert Owen and Herbert Spencer. He thus conceives of society as a body of men whose activity unfolds gradually by virtue of the activities imposed upon them by the total experience of life. Those activities make up the book of history. Brau thus opposes to the traditional epic con-ception of history, inherited from classical Spanish scholarship, the more modern conception of history as composed of economic life, commerce, agri-culture, industry, and the rest. Yet at the same time Brau oscillates between different interpretations of the historical process. At times he is tempted to offer racial attributions to explain social phenomena, so that he can argue that the total Puerto Rican national charcter is the end result of a racial in-termingling that brings together Indian "indolence" and "taciturnity," Afri-can "sensuality" and "fatalism," and Spanish "austerity" and "gentlemanly sobriety of behavior."[109] At other times he recognizes the argument of environment: Puerto Rican habits are what they are because they are caused by a repressive colonial system. Based as that system is on force, it inhibits the growth of habits of thrift and industry. Quoting the Spanish writer Arenal, Brau argues that games of chance and the irresponsible philosophy of life that they encourage are as much the vice of the rich as they are of the poor.[110] He goes on to note the fine irony of the fact that the local Spanish governor could issue in 1825 a detailed edict on the rules to be observed in cockfighting events some forty years before the same Spanish government could bring itself to establish rural elementary schools in the island, thus reflecting a set of distorted social values typical of the colonial regime.[111] Brau, in sum, is the leading historian and the budding sociologist of Puerto Rican studies. He remains trapped in the ideology of biological determinism. But he still manages to identify the Puerto Rican worker and countryman as the most important actor in the social drama that he is describing.[112]

How influential Brau's work was can be appreciated from a brief look at the novelist Zeno Gandía, who wrote in *La Charca* (1894) perhaps the best-known title in nineteenth century Puerto Rican fiction. It is the outstanding example of what the critic José Luis González, in his book of 1980, *El país de cuarto pisos y otros ensayos*, has depicted as the literary tradition of the *realismo costumbrista* (realism of social custom) as distinct from the older tradition of *costumbrismo de origen romántico* (social custom literature of romanticist origin). That tradition describes, once again, the moral and physical debilitation of the Puerto Rican *campesino*. More interestingly, it shows the influence of Zola's earthy naturalism and Spencer's social Darwinism that had also influenced Brau. The author puts into the mouth of his main character rambling thoughts about the "morbid debility" of the peasant class; relates an agitated conversation between the small-town doctor and priest that shows how the tiny professional class thought about the same problem; and yet manages at the same time to present in the figure of the young peasant woman Silvina a complex personality that anticipates the new theme of feminism.[113]

In all of this the Puerto Rican countryman, unbeknown to himself, is celebrated as the symbolic figure of a patriotic creoledom. The protagonists of that ideology were the educated minds of the emergent Creole bourgeois group, marrying Puerto Rican themes to the European thought-currents of the day. Their writings reveal stricken consciences coming to grips with the "condition of the people" question. The old romantic evasiveness still continues, of course, so that it is possible for dramatists like María Bibiano Benítez to celebrate, like any loyal Spaniard, the theme of the English attack of 1625 on San Juan and for Corchado y Juarbe to write a play inspired by the theme of the maternal love of the wife of Louis XVI.[114] The conceptual framework is still European: a listing of the books on sale at the Gimbernat bookshop in San Juan in 1848 includes Ariosto, Santa Teresa, Cervantes, Schlegel, Shakespeare, Lamartine, Walter Scott, Balzac, Chateaubriand, Eugene Sue, and George

Sand.[115] There is, as yet, no large, encompassing theory that can be termed Antillean. The leading figures of the movement—Alonso, Brau, del Valle Atiles, Tapia y Rivera, De Hostos, Fernández Juncos—are, at best, liberals. So, as Iris Zavala has pointed out, they do not think in terms of class conflict; rather, their emphasis is on social happiness achieved by class collaboration.[116] They are, more than anything else, social moralists, deeply convinced that only education and the elevation of mental culture can solve the problems. So, Brau quotes the French bourgeois economist Bastiat to drive home the lesson that there is a common interest that binds capitalist and worker together, and ends by appealing to the respectable classes to support his favorite recipe of working-class cooperative associations after the English Rochdale model.[117] Fernández Juncos, in turn, retreats, after the classic manner of Larra and Calderón, into a literature of subtle irony and sharp caricature in order to express his disgust with colonial rule.[118]

EUGENIO MARÍA DE HOSTOS

Of all these figures, it is perhaps Eugenio María De Hostos who is the most intriguing. One of the first sociologists in Latin America, when the discipline was hardly known, he sought in his work, and especially in his *Moral Social*, to put together a grand theory, almost in the manner of Herbert Spencer, that would encompass at once the European origins of the discipline and the special Antillean conditions it would be obliged to explain.[119] So, inevitably, the sociologist could not escape the moralist. For De Hostos came to see that what could pass for an objective positivism in Victorian England, a society basically at ease with itself, was something different in the Antilles, where colonialism still reigned supreme. All of his work, then, reflects the dialectical tension between the objective and the subjective considerations of the situation within which he found himself. On the one hand, he advocates all of the moral imperatives of the liberal creed: duty, obligation, respect for parents, concern for the social order, the importance of education, the primacy of ethical principle in personal and social behavior. On the other hand, he sees that the colonial political backwardness of his region makes mere Positivism inadequate to solve the problem, creating a painful contrast between material progress and moral development. "Under every social skin," he writes in a graphic sentence, "there lurks some barbarism."[120] Faced with that contradiction, it is the obligation of the thinking human being to seek to apply the natural laws of the moral order to rectify such deficiencies. Sociology will thus become not simply an annotating science but a moral regenerative force. Patriotism and universalism go hand in hand; the cosmopolite, De Hostos writes, is not the man who fails in his duty to achieve the ends that his homeland imposes upon him, but rather he who, having struggled to achieve those ends, recognizes himself, beyond that, as the brother of all men and imposes upon himself the truth that he must extend the benefits of his efforts to any man in any space and time. It is in this awareness of the existence of universal duties and obligations that De Hostos goes beyond the historiographic regionalism of his fellow countrymen like Brau and Tapia y Rivera. As much as Martí, he is the conscience not merely of the Antilles but of Latin America as a whole.[121]

Yet, in the last resort, there is a curious dual personality in De Hostos. For he is at once the bourgeois humanist and the revolutionary American patriot. He is at once Dr. Jekyll and Mr. Hyde; and the tension between the two personalities explains much of his fascination for the annotator of Caribbean ideology. He is the bourgeois humanist, to begin with, as the disciple of Comte and Spencer. He repeats Comte's three stages of civilization theory. In his *Tratado de sociología* he sets out a highly abstract model of civilization, following Spencer. Civilization, he writes in the *Moral Social*, is reason as well as conscience, and, in addition, the capacity of mankind to harmonize both reason and conscience into a single *culto a la civilización*.[122] Following that dictum, De Hostos outlines in the *Tratado de sociología* the natural laws of society that, for him, alone make that harmonization possible: the laws of work, liberty, progress, and finally, what he terms the law of the ideal. This, in turn, leads him to argue that the law of harmony requires that all elements of the social and economic state involved in work—natural resources, the worker, and the capitalist—cooperate for the general good.[123] The real hero, then, for De Hostos, is—in the political realm—the leader like Garibaldi, who seeks a new national harmony against alien oppression; and—in the economic realm—it is the figure of the banker, who plays the indispensable role of mediator between the worker seeking employment and the capitalist seeking labor.[124] There is nothing here of the influence of the socialist schools. Indeed, when he comes to speak of the social and moral evils of modern society, De Hostos identifies among the worst the "collective madness" of the French Revolution, generated by the "nervous overexcitement of the masses"; in the same way, the popularity of ideas like anarchism is to be seen as the expression of a social illness comparable to epileptic diseases in medicine.[125] At the very end, then, De Hostos, as the disappointed idealist, is driven to the pessimistic conclusion that the laws of sociology that he announces play, in fact, a minor role indeed in the actual formation of modern states—being ignored by people and leaders alike. All in all, the most appropriate comment on his ethical theory of state and society is that of Herbert Spencer uttered in a different context: it is a beautiful theory murdered by a gang of brutal facts.

Yet because, on the other hand, De Hostos is (at his best) a citizen of the Latin American world, he is not altogether blind to those facts. Everything in human life, he observes, is work; the universe is never in a moment of repose.[126] But because men and societies violate the laws of civilization, work does not always mean progress. Examples abound. In too many countries the general good is sacrificed to selfish politics. The Indians of the New World remain as oppressed as ever. An irresponsible immigration policy in Peru permits the exploitation and degradation of the Chinese immigrant laborer.[127] In most of the world, and certainly in all Latin America, the woman suffers a comparable slavery; we have taught her to read, De Hostos observes sarcastically, so that she can read stupid novels, and we have taught her to play the piano so that she can just dance all her life.[128] The recent history of the United States with reference to its scandalous treatment of the native Indian tribes is yet another example of how the doctrine of biological competition is used to justify arrogant racism. That history, in turn, is typical of a North American nation that has lost its original Jeffersonian ideals, and regards the Latin American peoples of Hispanic origin with open contempt.[129] What the world needs, De Hostos proceeds to argue, is a genuine international state transcending narrow nationalistic sentiments, starting with an European federal state and possibly an Antillean federal or confederal state.[130] But no modern state, including the United States, is willing to take a lead in that direction. All in all, he concludes, Western civilization is certainly superior to all civilizations that have preceded it. But it still remains inferior to civilization as understood in its best sense.[131]

In all of this, De Hostos is the man of honor and conscience who becomes the angry social critic. Whether he is writing on the great figures of the Cuban war, or the Cuban exile workers of Key West, or the theme of international peace, or Puerto Rican national independence, or New World slavery, or the need for a new, rationalist education freed from the old religious prejudices, or the follies of narrow nationalist prejudice—he brings to every topic a keen sense of social justice and a passionate concern for the oppressed and the disinherited. As he himself wrote to his friend José Manuel Estrada in a letter of 1873, he devoted his life, "consecrated with my voice, my pen, and the example of a disinterested life, to the cause of the confraternity of all of these peoples, to the defense of all of these disinherited, whether they be Chinese or *quechuas* (Quechua Indians) in Perú, *rotos* (ragged ones) and *huasos* (herdsmen) and *araucanos* (Araucano Indians) in Chile, *gauchos* or Indians in Argentina."[132] The pursuit of that cause and that defense, even more importantly, was placed within the larger context of civilization seen as the march of intellect. The conviction was summed up in the short piece in which De Hostos recalled a conversation of Goethe in which that great figure, excited by the reports of the 1792 intellectual debate in revolutionary Paris between Lamarck and Cuvier on the seminal topic of evolutionary change in the history of mankind, insisted that the real revolutions in that history are, not the political revolutions, but the revolutions in thought engineered by the great thinkers like Bacon, Newton, Lamarck, and others. The political revolutions, agreed, are important. But they do little except sweep up the garbage of history. By contrast, the great thinker enables us to illuminate the road wherein truth leads us to the good society.[133]

It goes without saying that, Americanist as he was, de Hostos was first and foremost the patriot fighting for the independence of his homeland, first against Spain and then, after 1898, against the United States. He thus belongs to the Puerto Rican nationalist movement during the nineteenth century. Part liberal constitutionalism, part insurrectionary plotting, the main target of the movement was the Spanish colonial system, which, juridically rooted in the old *Leyes de Indias* (Laws of the Indies), was at once rigid and arbitrary. Its body of laws, in the words of Calixto Bernal, did not recognize political rights, the head and center of all other rights, and inculcated nothing but the habit of passive obedience and a philosophy knowing nothing save the omnipotent will of the monarch.[134] Kings who were constitutional in Spain, added Castelar, were absolute in the Antilles, and ministers who were responsible in Spain could proceed as they pleased in matters affecting the Antilles.[135] The history of nineteenth-century Puerto Rican political thought, as distinct from its social thought, is the story of how its protagonists, both reformers and revolutionists, came to grips with that situation.

The reformist impulse of the Creole liberals, to begin with, was concerned with extracting from Madrid the full measure of civic and political rights within the continuing framework of Spanish rule. The struggle begins with the early reforming measures of 1809 and is reaffirmed in the liberal constitution of 1812, which gave the island its first elected delegate to the Junta Suprema in Madrid, Dr. Ramón Power—with the local instructions given to Power expressing the liberal aspirations. They are followed by the Quiñones-Vorela project of 1823, the report of the Belvis-Quiñones-Acosta Commission of 1867, the Ponce Plan of 1886, the charter of autonomy of 1897. Each one of them presents various themes. There is the theme of loyalty: Puerto Rico deserves special consideration because, after the revolt of the mainland colonies, it remains loyal to Spain. There is the theme of utopian constitution-making, much of it supported by the Spanish constitutional experts: So, Pi y Margall recommends a close federal association between homeland and colonies on the North American model, while Rafael María de Labra advocates a loose confederal structure after the manner of the then emerging British Commonwealth. There is the theme of provincial autonomy, supported by the general argument that autonomy is implicit in the earlier effort of statesmen like Macanaz and Jovellanos to introduce the political and philosophical thought of the French Enlightenment into the governmental structure of Spain and her colonies in the period of Charles III.[136]

But Puerto Rican hopes foundered on the rock of Spanish reactionary intransigence. So, increasingly, the liberal outlook in San Juan became disillusioned, disappointed, bitter, and disgusted. The politicians of the various party permutations and groups, from Baldorioty de Castro to Muñoz Rivera, continued the strategy of courting friends within each political faction in Madrid as it came to power. But the finer spirits of the movement came to recognize that such a politics of appeasement only led to a dead end. It is a depressing record. They promised us special laws, writes Brau of the 1837 liberal moment, and then proceeded to wait in silence for thirty-one years.[137] What Fray Iñigo Abbad had said about the government of the island in his great history of 1788, observes Acosta, continues to apply, for the system remains substantially today as he then described it.[138] The plums of Puerto Rico, writes another liberal mind, are plucked in the island and eaten in Spain. The eminent historian Tapia y Rivera, in turn, describes how the publication of his pioneering work, the *Biblioteca histórica de Puerto Rico*, is delayed by the censors on the curious ground that it included, among other items, some lines extracted from the eulogy in verse written by the sixteenth-century soldier Juan de Castellanos and supposed by the censors to be injurious to the sacred reputation of the conquistadores.[139]

So, inevitably, faith in the willingness of Spain to grant real reform dwindled. The loss of faith is there in the semiautobiographical novel *La peregrinación de Bayoán*, composed hurriedly by the Young De Hostos while in Madrid and conceived, as he said, as at once a book on the aspirations of the Antilles and on the duties of Spain in the region.[140] It is there in the restrained scepticism of the 1867 commissioners who ask whether it is not meaningless to speak about reforms in a colonial system so utterly centralized that there are for all practical purposes no institutions to reform; as well as in the sharp observation of the same liberal commissioners that if indeed there is to be reform, it must be total and all-encompassing, not the sort of petty, gradual reform that only reflects *el sofisma de la prudencia reaccionaria* (the sophistry of reactionary prudence).[141] It is there in Tapia y Rivera's unfinished autobiography, in which there is drawn the portrait of a young and eager spirit, influenced by liberalism and Christian humanism, gradually learning how to survive in a colonial society full of routine, lethargy, and moral corruption, and governed by men, in the Puerto Rican's phrase, who deported themselves, not as mere officials, but as ancient viceroys living still in the period of the Conquest.[142] The loss of faith is there, finally, in Brau's lament on the general condition of the colonial life. "Without schools," he wrote, "without books, whose importation is banned by the Customs, without metropolitan newspapers whose circulation is suppressed, without political representation, without municipal self-government, lacking either thought or conscience, the physical and mental energies of our people are exclusively absorbed in the production of sugar to sell to England and the United States; Puerto Rico is simply a factory openly exploited."[143]

The outcome of all this was that the reformist ideology gave way to the openly revolutionary ideology. There is the gradual transformation of attitudes in De Hostos, so that, although he is the cultured man of letters who believes above all else in the life of the mind, he is finally persuaded that the only means for change is by armed struggle; all the verbiage of Spanish promises really mean nothing, he writes, and only a decisive separation from a "barbarous patriotism" in which the interests of Spain and the interests of humanity are conceived to be the same can satisfy the demands of freedom.[144] There is the rapid progression of ideas in Ruiz Belvis who, a respected liberal member of the 1866–67 commission, flees Puerto Rico surreptitiously to become a founding member in New York of the Republican Society of Cuba and Puerto Rico, which published about the same time its manifesto establishing once and for all the theoretical position of the armed struggle.[145] No one can read the impassioned *in memoriam* composed by De Hostos as he stood at the grave of Belvis on the hills of Valparaiso overlooking the Pacific years later in 1873 without realizing how the one deep fundamental element of the revolutionary nationalism of both De Hostos and the dear friend whom he described as *un vagabundo de la libertad* is their love for Puerto Rico, agonizingly aggravated by exile.[146]

BETANCES

And there is, not least of all, the noble figure of Betances. Betances's contributions to the nationalist ideology, indeed, are of some special significance because they strike notes not usually struck by others. There is his race pride: his unashamed assertion that he was born of an irregular relationship between his parents acquires its true significance when it is remembered that Puerto Rico was a society in which, in the words of the earlier historian Fray Iñigo Abbad, the worst affront was to be a Negro or the descendant of a Negro.[147] There is the insistence upon the basic civil liberties as the foundation of freedom, as set out in the manifesto of the *Diez mandamientos* that Betances published in 1870 from his St. Thomas exile home; and that manifesto, including all the usual liberal claims for freedom of speech, thought, and religion, full voting privileges, and national self-determination, shows once again how ideas that in the England of John Stuart Mill were acceptable became, as they crossed the Atlantic, revolutionary ideas.[148] There is the argument that Antillean freedom can only come from Antillean effort; so, in his letter to De Hostos of 1870, written this time from his Haitian exile, Betances insists that it is not England or the United States or even Spain that can bring independence to Puerto Rico, but only the struggle of the Puerto Ricans themselves.[149]

There is, finally, recognition of the signal truth that national independence, in and of itself, does not necessarily solve the complete problem of freedom; so, while Betances could translate the admiring piece of the North American abolitionist Wendell Phillips on the figure of Toussaint L'Ouverture, he could also at the same time recognize the elements of indigenous Antillean tyranny in his articles on the oppressive regime of, for example, Ulises Heureaux in

Santo Domingo, and could thus oppose the *ideología de heroísmo* that in Santo Domingo as in other Caribbean societies had done so much to justify the rule of the *caudillos*.[150] There is, finally, Betances's appraisal of the cultural foundations of political freedom. He is the declared opponent of reformers and annexationists alike because both of them assume that Puerto Rico can be spiritually free while politically related to an outside society. Both of them—as he put it caustically in his letter of 1892 to the director of the New York Spanish-language newspaper *El Porvenir*—dream of a future in which, so to speak, the apple tree would bear delicious fruit in Havana and the palm tree would bear coconuts in Washington, without seeing that in climates fatal to each fruit they would both be condemned to perish.[151] In all of this, Betances speaks, perhaps, as the most authentic voice of the Puerto Rican national conscience throughout the century as it has been summarized by later historians such as Bolívar Pagán and Antonio Rivera.

If, indeed, there is a single piece of the writings of Betances that sums up in one eloquent statement his Antillean spirit, it is the brief preface that he wrote in 1869 to his translation into French of the Wendell Phillips address on the subject of Toussaint. In it he recognized the significance of the fact that the address was given in 1861, before the Civil War led to slave emancipation. Chastising those Darwinian scholars and writers who justify Negro inferiority on supposed scientific grounds, he appeals to other European intellectual movements that recognize the equality of all races; and cites both John Stuart Mill's *Principles of Political Economy* and Buckle's *History of Civilization in England*. That certain races are superior, he goes on to point out, has always been a favorite thesis, even of educated persons: the ancients eulogized the Ethiopians in that way, and Voltaire the Chinese. Correspondingly, the Greeks looked at all other peoples as barbarians; and, today, it is the turn of the European Nordic race to advance the same error. Most important of all, perhaps, Betances correctly relates the struggle for slavery emancipation with the struggle of republican principles against the reactionary monarchical and aristocratic regimes of the Europe of his time. Unlike, say, the earlier English abolitionists, he perceives that the two struggles are necessarily related to each other. Where the republic has been established, albeit briefly, it has led to emancipation, as in France; and slavery still persists, significantly, under the two surviving monarchical regimes; Spain's Cuba and Portugal's Brazil. The struggle for freedom is indivisible.[152]

THE CONTRIBUTION OF SANTO DOMINGO

The contribution of Santo Domingo, in both political and literary terms, to Antillean nationalist thought, was special and unique in the sense that it was nurtured by a continuing struggle for independence in three separate stages: the early Saint Domingue revolt against France, the fight against the Haitian occupation, and the struggle against the reimposed Spanish rule. As each phase of the national struggle resolved itself, it fed the romantic idea of the *patria*. That feeling was reinforced, in turn, by the struggle of the intelligentsia as it saw its liberal constitutionalism overriden by the ideology of the heroic president-tyrant like Santana and Heureaux. It gave birth, all in all, to a romantic nationalism markedly Dominican in tone.

Its founder was the figure of Duarte, original member of the secret society Los Trinitarios and celebrated, like Martí in Cuba, as the father figure of the religion of the *patria*. The leading idea of his political thought was, in essence, quite simple: Santo Domingo should be allowed its full sovereignty, freed from the machinations of the great powers—Spain, France, the United States —seeking to use it for their own ends; and that insistence against foreign intervention Duarte wrote into his early constitutional blueprint. Only cowardice or perversity or ambition, he wrote, can persuade any Dominican to be neutral when outside powers are seeking to take over his country. He was not the ordinary politician on the make; like Luperón after him, he declined presidental ambitions. The portrait that his friend and fellow conspirator José María Serra has left of him, the whole face and body lighting up miraculously as he talks of his grand ideal, shows him to have been a man of remarkable character and integrity, with the power to inspire others to efforts that they would not have thought themselves capable of undertaking.[153]

As is usual with great leaders, a whole mythology has developed around Duarte, nurtured by overenthusiastic Dominican historians. The very title of Balaguer's book *El Cristo de la libertad* indicates the tone of exaggerated adulation. The adulation has been made possible, of course, because Duarte, unlike Martí, was not a prolific writer, so that his sister Rosa Duarte's *Apuntes* remains about the only authentic record of his early life and beginnings, allowing mythology to flourish. So, it is doubtful if the early travels of the young Duarte in the United States and Europe converted him, that early, into an eager and knowledgeable student of world affairs, as biographers like Troncoso Sánchez have ardently argued. It is equally doubtful whether Duarte, in his boyhood, lived in a political atmosphere, in his bourgeois home, of patriotism and virulent anti-Haitianism, as other biographers like Rodríguez Demorizi have sought to argue. Duarte, in brief, has become as much a victim of patriotic legend as George Washington has in the United States.[154]

What then, once the encrustations of the patriotic folklore are put aside, was Duarte's contribution? A more recent analyst, Jiménez Grullón, has identified the major European currents of thought that influenced the Dominican patriot: romanticism, liberalism, and nationalism. They led him to emphasize, among other things: the importance of municipal government in his constitution-making; the idea of racial equality, offsetting the hatred of the black Haitian that has so often persuaded even liberal writers that the Haitian, as another recent commentator has put it, is a monster coming out of the jungle; the necessity for constitutional guarantees of the rights of the individual citizen; and above all else, the ideal of a radical nationalism, which has to be obtained, if necessary, by armed force. The best government, Duarte insisted in a frequently quoted observation, is that which is popular in its origin, elective in its mode of organization, representative in its system, and accountable in its acts.

It is important to note the limitations of the Duartian outlook. It is politically radical and romantically nationalist, as can be seen from the fact that the favorite European literature of another of the Trinitarios group, Juan Isidro Pérez, was those plays that celebrated the proud heroism of peoples suffering under foreign domination: Eugenio de Ochoa's *Un día del año 1823*, Alfieri's *Bruto o Roma libre*, Martínez de la Rosa's *La viuda de Padilla*.[155] The ideology of the Duartian group takes the social structure of Santo Domingo, as it took shape in the 1830s and 1840s, for granted. It sees the people as a whole, not divided into social classes. It contains, in fact, little social content, and it has none of the socially revolutionary character of the ideological programs of the other leading Latin American figures like Bolívar, Morelos, and Artigas.[156] It is also profoundly orthodox in its views on religion. The very name of the group founded by Duarte has overtones of religious symbolism; Duarte gave the Catholic Church a special protected place in his ideal constitution, and it is well-known how the ultramontanist Peruvian priest Gaspar Hernández—whose book of 1853, *Derechos y prerogativas del Papa y de la iglesia*, took the most extreme Catholic position—helped to shape the young Duarte's thought in this matter.[157]

LUPERÓN

This curious combination of radical nationalism and social conservatism had, of course, its social roots. It was a typical ideological expression of the two leading groups in the emergent Dominican society—the territorial aristocracy and the urban Creole elite—who were not prepared to yield their power to any sort of mass radical movement; the pathological fear of what was known as the "Haitian horror" adequately expressed that position. And if Duarte personified that position in the first half of the nineteenth century, the other national hero, Luperón, expressed it in the second half. For if Duarte is the hero of the uprising against the Haitian occupation, Luperón is the hero of the period of the restoration. Neither of them, however, is the protagonist of a social revolution per se. That is clear enough from the three volumes of Luperón's personal memoirs, *Notas autobiográficas y apuntes históricos*. Himself a professional "revolutionary," protegé of President Espaillat, and perenially at the center of the complicated charade of the political rivalry, after 1865, between the "warlords" of the various regions that divided the country—Báez, González, Cabral, Santana, Guillermo, Heureaux, and the rest—Luperón writes as the annotator of the presidential wars. Apart from offering vivid pen portraits of the various protagonists, his history offers also a sort of apologetic for the characteristic figure of the *caudillo político*. Whether the aspirant for the presidential palace comes from the party of the reds or of the blues, he shares with all his rivals certain common features. He is fiercely patriotic. He is a seasoned practitioner of party intrigue. He is the complete pragmatist who manages his various alliances with strategic persons of all sorts, only permitting "elections" in order to legitimize his own power once he has arrived in office by armed force. He sees himself as a democrat; all his opponents are tyrants. Above all else, he is the champion of national order and discipline. He is the national hero. Set apart from him are the mass of the people, the *vulgos*, who know nothing of the art of government and are instinctively anarchistic; so, there must always exist a vast distance between the two, despite the fact that the hero-president may himself come from humble social origins. The hero shapes the national life much more than do abstract social and economic forces; so, naturally, Luperón, like others, compares the tragedy of Dominican life with the tragedy of ancient Greece and Rome, where great leaders, likewise, are sacrificed to the ignorant whims of the "mob." This attitude becomes, in effect, an open contempt for the vulgar: We fool ourselves, writes Luperón, when we speak of the *amor popular*, because the vulgar do not know how to love.[158]

If Luperón's account is to be regarded (as it almost certainly is), as a representative expression of the ideology of the Santo Domingo leading groups, it is proper to say that, far from being a radical nationalism, it is in fact a conservative nationalism. The patron-client tradition inhibits the growth of genuinely popular political movements in the same way that it breeds the habit of narcissism in its practitioners. It is true that Luperón, in his memoirs, can see the travesty of justice that the tradition ends in: the national life, he observes bitterly, is conducted with two constitutions, that of liberty enshrined in the written documents and that of tyranny based on unwritten custom. But he cannot see that the only solution for that contradiction is to resort to the vox populi. His virtues, admittedly, are real. He is the friend of De Hostos, and persuades that great educator to continue his work in Santo Domingo. He is the advocate of the pan-American idea long before it became official. He is almost the original creator of the policy of arbitration in the disputes between Latin American states, as seems evident from the story of his meeting with the El Salvador diplomat Torres Caicedo in Europe in 1882, when he persuaded him to agree to a treaty of permanent arbitration between Santo Domingo and El Salvador.[159] But for all that, he is still the politician with aristocratic prejudices, so that he will retire to his private *finca* or go into exile to St. Thomas in his moments of defeat rather than spearheading a popular movement based on popular discontents. He has no use for the more advanced European social doctrines, so that he can refer disparagingly to the Socialist ideology as a doctrine advocated by groups that preach demoralizing ideas and the concept of social war.[160] It is the "strong man," and not any organized social force, who is the electrifying stimulant of all historical change; Luperón would surely have endorsed the eulogizing verse addressed by Juan Isidro Pérez, one of the earlier Trinitarios group, to the memory of Napoleon.[161]

The real and lasting achievement of Luperón, in fact, lay in his role as the ardent defender of the national patrimony, of the integrity of the national sovereignty. More than any other single figure of his age, he was the authentic voice of the national spirit, recognized as such even by his enemies. The achievement has been recapitulated, albeit in a more radical Marxist spirit of interpretation, in Hugo Tolentino Dipp's volume *Gregorio Luperón: Biografía política*. Luperón fought against the Spanish annexation because he saw it as an insult to Dominican dignity; in that period, he wrote, the real oppression that both rich and poor suffered was not so much political as social, violating personal and domestic tranquillity, denying the basic freedom, natural to all men, of being able to come and go in daily life without the *impuesto del peonaje* (tax imposed upon the poor people) or the *incomodidad del pasaporte* (inconvenience of having to possess a passport).[162] With a similar passionate indignation, he fought against the successive attempts of Presidents Báez and Heureaux to lease the strategic Samaná Bay area to the North American government, seeing it, correctly, as presaging the new American imperialism of Manifest Destiny. The indignation comes through in Luperón's letter of protest written to President Grant in 1869. The American policy, he tells the president, is one of piracy, since it violates Dominican sovereignty, seeking Dominican territory through secret negotiations with Báez that bypass the Dominican legislative authority. We believe, he adds, that the Americas should belong to themselves, free of European influence, but that does not mean that they should be Yanqui. The North American government itself had notified the French in 1866 that the French presence in Mexico constituted a threat to America; in similar fashion, Luperón asks Grant, are not the usurping policies of your own government today also a threat to the Americas? That letter was followed by a letter of protest to the U.S. Congress itself in 1870, in which Luperón emphasizes the fact that all of the conditions of Dominican life—social structure, language, religion, social habits, and customs—are so different from those of the United States that they forbid annexation to the northern republic, not to mention that, in any case, a decision so to annex should be based upon a popular direct vote on the part of the island electorate.[163] Luperón, in sum, personified the best of Dominican liberal patriotism; so much so, that President Heureaux, whom he had fought for so long, was moved to visit him in his last dying days in his St. Thomas exile in 1896; the first time, as Heureaux himself put it, that a president had left the country to search out an enemy.

SANTO DOMINGO: THE LITERARY RECORD

The ever-present danger of invasion or annexation, including the omnipresent shadow of Haiti across the border, made every educated Dominican an ardent patriot. That perhaps explains the patriotic tone of the national literature, as distinct from the national politics. But both politics and literature, of course, were intertwined, if only because many of the young patriotic poets were also at the same time victims of political oppression, including imprisonment and death; and their memory provoked, in turn, a separate poetry of martyrology. Many of them, especially in the earlier period of the Haitian occupation, had been exiles in Cuba and had picked up the Cuban nationalistic spirit. That sense of fellowship with the Cuban struggle was echoed, in the later part of the century, by poets like Henríquez y Carvajal in his poem "Cuba Libre" and Billini in his eulogy "A Máximo Gómez." All of them, in any case, spoke the language of romantic nationalism. From Delmonte, considered the father of the literature of the national period after 1844, there is *Las vírgenes de Galindo*, with its anti-Haitian tone, and *El arpa del proscrito*, written in exile against the Santa dictatorship. The same defiant note is echoed in the verse of Rodríguez Obijo, Ortea, and, of course, Henríquez y Carvajal, whose long life spanned the nineteenth and twentieth centuries. A somewhat different note—emphasizing the themes of progress, peace, and civilization and exhorting the nation to unite rather than destroy itself in factional struggle—is heard in the work of José Joaquín Pérez and Salome Ureña; civil discord must give way to national unification, and fraternal love must replace selfish ambition. The two themes—indignation against the warrior-politicians and optimism for the future—come together in the well-known poem "Ololoi" by Deligne, in which the poet castigates the figure of President Heureaux without at the same time mentioning the president by name, since for the poet, the president is not just the president but something more: the symbol of an evil political system that has corrupted the whole social body.[164]

Much of all this, it must be admitted, is jejune, dilettantist, overly romanticist, and excessively exhortatory, with the poet frequently more concerned with his message than with the quality of art with which it is expressed. That is so much the case that when the Dominican writer Max Henríquez Ureña came to compose his standard work in 1945 on the theme *Panorama histórico de la literatura dominicana*, he avoided any serious literary criticism and simply concentrated on a narrative account of authors, dates, and themes. Joaquín Balaguer's later book of 1958, *Historia de la literatura dominicana*, was, if possible, even worse, devoid of any critical analysis of author or theme. Balaguer can describe with some feeling the tragedy of the leading Indian hero figures of the *Fantasías indígenas*; he can see how Salome Ureña becomes, in her poetry, the protagonist, early on, of the mental emancipation of the educated Dominican woman; he can even see that the European intellectual influence on a poet like Rodríguez Obijo is French while the intellectual influence on a poet like del Monte is Spanish simply because they lived at different historical periods in the evolution of Dominican nationhood. But these are almost casual asides in a work that reads more like a high school textbook than a serious examination of the relationship between Dominican literature and politics.[165]

For the sociologist, however, as distinct from the mere annotator of the raw facts of the story, the leading significant fact of the Dominican literary record, in poetry, novels, theater, and the rest, is that, in its patriotic thrust, it is far less Hispanophobic than the Cuban and Puerto Rican records of the same period. Understandably so, since Spain only ruled the island for two brief periods (1809-21 and 1861-65), whereas it was a continuous and daily colonial master presence throughout in both Cuba and Puerto Rico. It was that much easier to look at the Spanish tradition more benignly. That favorable attitude, in turn, was encouraged by the fact that the rival French literary tradition was identified, in the Dominican mind, with Haiti and was therefore suspect. So, the word *espagñol*, as Henríquez Ureña has pointed out, came to possess a special, subjective meaning in the Dominican literary lexicon, meaning that the people of Hispaniola were inheritors of a tradition, a culture, and a language set apart from others.[166]

This gave rise, curiously, to an almost schizoid attitude—not unlike the response, in the British West Indian islands at the same time, to the English tradition. Spain represents the heroic tradition of the *raza*; at the same time, claim must be made for Dominican independence and nationhood. The literature strikes both notes. José Joaquín Pérez celebrates the Indian aboriginal tradition, in the literary mode of the *indigenista*, in his *Fantasías indígenas*, but does not forget at the same time to celebrate the *gloria de Colón*. Galván, in his *Enriquillo*, writes the most famous of all of the novels on the Indian *caciques* and their struggles against the Spanish invaders, yet at the same time supports the annexation of 1861 as the best means of preserving the Dominican way of life against the Haitian threat. All of the *indigenista* poems, plays, and novels, indeed—such as, to take a further example, Angulo Guridi's *Iguaniona*—adopt the view that the Conquest is not to be seen in the manner of Las Casas, as a brutal assault against the Indians but rather as a Grecian tragedy in which two cultures, equally admirable in their respective virtues, are doomed to mortal confrontation because they cannot live with each other.[167] The same complex attitude—an unwillingness to condemn utterly or to condone utterly—is also present in the national historians. Thus, the early *Historia* (1853) of Del Monte y Tejeda is eminently fair to the Spanish record while at the same time regretting that official archival policy on the part of the Spanish authorities made it impossible for the author to consult the metropolitan primary sources: Unfortunately—the Dominican historian wrote with justifiable bitterness—the metropolitan government, through excessive caution, has covered its operation in the Americas with an impenetrable veil, making it difficult for even its own nationals to examine the archives of the Indies.[168] The later historian Emiliano Tejera, likewise, laid the foundations for the scholarly excavation of the origins of the Dominican society in the sixteenth and seventeenth centuries; but even then he devoted a large part of his talent to topics as esoteric and antiquarian as the authenticity of Columbus's remains and the nature and siting of the palace of Don Diego Colón.[169] His final comment on the Spanish civilization is summed up in his eloquent testimony to the memory of Duarte, contrasting it with the bestiality of the Haitian rule: "This Spanish race is at once the most virile and most noble of races, one of the most unique that exist in the world." It is this mixture of filial loyalty and independent critical judgment, seeing the worst of Spain yet not rejecting the best, that constitutes the special character of the Dominican contribution to Antillean nationalism.

That note of comparatively benign Hispanophilism was, of course, the reverse side of a coin that requires pro-Spanish sentiments as a means of offsetting the dreaded fear of black Haiti. It is necessary, then, to say something separately about the element of anti-Haitianism in the development of the Dominican national spirit. For the first stage in that development sprang out of the Haitian occupation, generating a paranoid fear in all classes of Dominican society and a cultural mythology about black and white not fundamentally different, in its psychological roots, from the old antislave ideology. That is why, in the crisis of the 1850s, Santana was ready to return the young republic back to Spain rather than to return it to Haiti. Nothing, after all, stimulates the nationalist sense so much as the presence, or near presence, of a hated enemy.

The anti-Haitian virus expressed itself in various ways. There is, as already noted, the growth in Dominican literature of the myth of the Indian, elaborated by the mulatto intelligentsia. To be a claimed descendant of the Indian *cacique* Henri bears more social prestige than to be a descendant of a black peon like Chomeur. There is, again, the systematic program of vilification of Haitian vodun, so that a Dominican journal in 1875 can propose the thesis that vodun, with all of its ugliness, terrorizes the Western world and that in the nineteenth century people still devour human flesh. Nor is that pathological fear restricted to popular prejudice: the Dominican popular poet José Antonio Alix manages to portray the same fear in his *Dialogue entre un dominicain et un haitien*. Bono alone among the educated class manages to rise above the psychotic miasma to declare in his letter of 1887 to Luperón, that the blacks and mulattoes have something to contribute to the cultural patrimony of the Americas; yet even a mind as liberal as Luperón seems not to have comprehended the full import of the declaration.[170] All in all, Dominican nationalism was rooted in the feeling, as a later Dominican writer has put it, that it was less compromising to breathe in the spirit of the Indians rather than the odor of the sweat of blacks working in the canefields. In this sense, altogether, Dominican nationalism was negative rather than positive in its root principles. It knew what it was against much more than it knew what it was for.[171]

Yet however divergent the Haitian and Dominican paths were, they had at least one thing in common. Being the only Antillean societies that achieved independent nationhood before the twentieth century, they perforce put together, in their innumerable constitutions of the period, a legal doctrine of nationality based on firm constitutional principles. The new architects of the state power were compelled to ask, and to answer, the questions: Who is a Haitian? Who is a Dominican? The answers provided helped forge a doctrine of national citizenship, something that the other Caribbean societies, still in colonial bondage, were not able to do until the later period of the twentieth century. A constitutional dress was thus fitted to the form of nationalist aspiration.

The new Haitian nationality grew out of the various constitutions and governmental edicts published by the various regimes of the early presidents and emperors: Christophe, Pétion, Dessalines, Boyer. To begin with, by declaring the generic name *noir*, or blacks, for all citizens of the new nation whatever their color, Dessalines's constitution of 1805 sought to forestall divisiveness among the Haitian family based on skin color. The same constitution formulated the famous prohibition of foreign ownership of land or property, as well as denying possible citizenship to white men. Those provisions, seeking to hold intact the national patrimony, were repeated in every succeeding constitution up to 1918. Citizenship was also offered to all outsiders who could claim African parentage. In the case of Santo Domingo, the first independence constitution of 1844 echoed the same urge to protect the new national patrimony in its invocation of the principle of *jus sanguinis*, granting nationality to all born of Dominican parents, including those born abroad. That exclusivity was somewhat relaxed by the acceptance, in the 1854 constitution, of the broader principle of *jus soli*, permitting children born of foreign parents to choose Dominican citizenship at the age of consent. The end result was a rather illogical combination of both principles. But the spirit of national autonomy, jealously held, was never seriously compromised; and the constitution of 1865 once again reaffirmed it with its prohibition of dual nationality: no Dominican citizen could acquire a foreign nationality and continue to reside in the republic.[172]

This noticeable difference between the Haitian and Dominican ideologies of national citizenship probably has its cause in the different larger ethnic ideologies of the two societies. In both cases the constitutional language paid ardent lip service to the ideal of race harmony. But the preferred race in Haiti was the black, and in Santo Domingo, the white. The Haitian preference was fed by various factors—hatred of whites, the ever-present fear of French counterrevolutionary intervention, the sense of being isolated in a hostile world: all of which conspired to persuade the new nation to become almost pathologically inward-turned and hermetic. The Dominican preference was fed by other factors: the very origin of the nation itself by means of the revolt of the mulatto South against the black North of Christophe, the closer links with Spain, the anti-Haitianism that was at once cause and consequence of the Dominican white bias. So, Dominican public policy actively encouraged immigration as a means of "whitening" the society, while Haiti remained throughout suspicious of the immigrant. Similarly, the Dominican ruling elite was capable in 1861 of the treason of returning the republic to the former metropolitan power; such an act, even when civil war might have made it feasible, would have been unthinkable in Haiti. Yet whatever the differences, both republics constructed their ideas of nationality and citizenship upon what a later twentieth century Haitian writer has called *la mystique d'indépendance*,[173] the conviction that nationality and citizenship can only properly be determined by leaders, constituent assemblies, and parliaments composed only of Haitians and Dominicans and responsible only to Haitian and Dominican citizen bodies.

THE CUBAN CONTRIBUTION

The growth of the nationalist spirit in Cuba revolves around the emergent spirit of *cubanidad* (the sense of being distinctively Cuban). It is, basically, the work of the Cuban liberal intelligentsia. As such, it divided itself into various and sometimes contradictory elements. Some of it, as with Saco and Andueza, was liberal about the slave trade and conservative about domestic slavery: in Andueza's phrase, nothing more just than the abolition of the trade, nothing more unjust than the emancipation of the slaves. Some of it was anti-Spanish and pro-American, as in the ideology of *anexionismo*; some of it was anti-Spanish and *autonomista*, seeking reforms within the system, as notably with Saco; some of it, again, was openly nationalist and insurrectionist, as with the growth of the *ideología mambisa* (ideology of the *mambisas*, or escaped slaves). But all of it, whatever its permutations and contradictions, was solidly Cuban, deeply rooted in Cuban national pride. Nineteenth century Cuba, in the words of a later commentator, had two lives, separate and mutually incompatible—that of Spanish Cuba and that of Cuban Cuba—and the result is, logically, that the society has two histories: one rooted in Spanish sources and values, the other rooted in Cuban sources and values.[174]

A variety of themes go into the pro-Cuban ideology. Saco writes against the pro-American forces because, in his words, their success will mean not simply annexation but, by means of an inevitable influx of North Americans, the absorption of Cuba by the United States.[175] Guiteras writes, from abroad, against Spanish colonial tyranny; examines the historical growth of Cuban nationality in his *Historia de la isla de Cuba*; and, stimulated by his meeting with Washington Irving in New York, celebrates the worth of Cuban poetry in his biographical *Vidas de poetas cubanos*: his nationalist sense is evident in his interesting decision to eliminate the world *isla* from the second edition of his historical work on the ground that the word only had geographical meaning and failed to convey the lesson that Cuba possessed its own intrinsic national personality.[176] The exiled Spanish liberal Andueza composes, in his *Isla de Cuba pintoresca*, at once a lyrical eulogy of the beauty of the island

and its people (especially the legendary attractiveness of its women) and a spirited liberal criticism of Spanish rule; that rule, he observes, is so endemic that Cuba cannot be properly called an overseas province of Spain, or even a colony, but, more correctly, a simple possession, for that, in effect, is what it is.[177] Later on, Bachiller y Morales undertakes, in his *Los negros*, the first systematic analysis and defense of the Cuban African past, as well as an attempt to look at, in an anthropological sense, the other component in the national culture of the obi, vodun, and myal religious cults.[178] He is followed by Sanguily, with his defense of the early Carib culture against those writers (like de Armas) who had sought to prove that the Caribs were nothing more than a fantastic legend existing in the mind of the conquistadores. Sanguily adds to that defense his *Los oradores de Cuba*, in which he celebrates the tradition of Cuban political oratory—an art form, as he sees it, discouraged but not eliminated by official Spanish hostility—and includes, among others, a eulogy of his beloved scholar-master Enrique Pineyre, whose own work did so much to lay the foundations of Cuban bibliography.[179]

It is, indeed, the impressive school of Cuban historians and historiographers who, in the nineteenth century, establish the scholarly foundations of Cuban nationalism. For nationalism everywhere feeds on the search for roots, the conscious discovery of the past. The Cubans took as their model the European history-writing of the time—Macaulay, Buckle, Taine, Guizet, Renan—and then used it to tell the Cuban story. History, observed Vidal Morales, is the photograph of a nation. Early on, of course, there had been the eighteenth-century writers like Arrate, Urrutia, and Valdéz; and Vidal Morales himself wrote a brief epitaph on them, seeing them as chroniclers in the old-fashioned style rather than historians in the modern style, but nonetheless as worthy precursors.[180] From that beginning, there followed the work of the historians of the nineteenth century proper. Despite his devout Hispanophilism, Pezuela manages, in his *Historia*, to present, for the first time, an ordered, chronological account of Cuban historical development; he undertook as well pioneer studies on Cuban topics as varied as the history of the *Real sociedad económica* of Havana and the general condition of Havana at the time of the English conquest of 1762, and, most notably, his *Diccionario* which, in the best manner of the French Enlightenment, gathered together so much informative detail of practically every aspect of Cuban life and society.[181] Bachiller y Morales puts together, in his *Apuntes*, a systematic history of Cuban education, theater, newspapers, pamphlet literature, and the rest. In addition, his *Cuba primitiva*, along with his better-known work, *Los negros*, lays the foundation of serious archaeological and anthropological study of Cuban origins.[182] Vidal Morales, in his turn, puts together in his learned articles (some published in the prestigious *Revista de Cuba*) documentation to support the thesis that Cuban self-government really begins with the effort of the old Council of the Indies to establish a decentralized Spanish regime in the government of the island, followed by the work of the Real Consulado (Crown tribunal of commerce) and the Sociedad Patriótica (Patriotic Society) in the early nineteenth century.[183] Alfredo Zayas advances the very same argument (also in articles in the *Revista de Cuba*) and adds the general thought that the principle of self-government is the *summum desideratum* of all colonial rule.[184] And to all this there must be added two further subgroups of Cuban literature: (1) those writers and critics, like Mestre, Mitjans, Cruz, and Ramírez, who treat more specific aspects of Cuban culture, such as philosophy, literary criticism, and the arts, and (2) the local historians, many of them amateurs, who compose the history of their local town or district, including, of course, the celebration of their beloved Havana—Cartas, La Torre, Rosain, Garay, Alfonso, González, Edo, Pérez Luna, Torres Lasqueti, Avila, and others.[185] Concerning that second category, it is, indeed, necessary to add the observation, that not only in Cuba but also in the other Antillean societies, the work of the local antiquary becomes a pronounced feature of Antillean literature during the nineteenth century. For love of country, everywhere, begins with love of native birthplace.

As elsewhere, not the least achievement of the nineteenth-century Cuban historical school was to put archival research and documentation on a proper footing. Its leading minds discovered the importance of the documentary record, without which no real history can be written. The more academic investigations of Pezuela included reports on the Muñoz collection in the Spanish Real Academia de la Historia as well as a systematic study of the other great Spanish collections, including that of the Archivo General de Indias. In the majestic silence of its galleries, he wrote of the latter, there lay dormant three centuries of the history of Cuba.[186] The journalist Joaquín José García used his own private collection to publish his *Protocolo de antigüedades*, for it would be an irreparable loss, he wrote, if all of this archival testimony should be buried in the night of time.[187] Piñeyro, likewise, worked in the Seville archives; if God, he wrote, had given me the gift to write history, my dream would be a table and a few months of entombment in that archive.[188] Vidal Morales, in his turn, after a lifetime of public service, was appointed director of the Cuban archives in the American military government at the end of the century—in which post he was instrumental in setting up the *Boletín de Archivo Nacional*.[189] The intensified awareness of the cultural patrimony thus became, for the educated class, the bedrock of Cuban patriotism.[190]

BACHILLER Y MORALES

This contribution by the Cuban group of historians, poets, publicists, and others, has tended to be overshadowed by the magisterial figure of Martí. For many outsiders—although not necessarily for Cubans, who know their own national cultural history better—Cuba has meant Martí. So it is worth elaborating upon the contribution of one of the most outstanding members of the group, Antonio Bachiller y Morales. Of well-to-do parentage, he was the archetypal man of letters, devoting a whole long lifetime to teaching and writing, a member of all of the prestigious Cuban societies as well as of the leading European and North American learned societies. No political activist as such, he was yet prepared to leave the comfort of his home to go into exile in the United States when circumstances and conscience demanded it. His prodigious output of articles and books earned him the title of *el patriarca de las letras cubanas*; and everybody else, including Martí, generously acknowledged their debt to his scholarship.

His major work, certainly, is the *Apuntes para la historia de las letras y de la instrucción pública en la isla de Cuba*. Going back to as many original sources as existed at the time, it sets out a narrative of Cuban letters, art, education, and music from the beginnings. It begins with a description of the growth of primary, secondary, and higher education in the society, having its early roots in the pioneering work of men like Francisco Paradas, the priest Juan Conyedo, and the Negro teacher Doroteo Barba, and becoming more institutionalized with the valiant work of the Real Sociedad Económica de la Habana (Royal Economic Society of Havana). Convinced as he is, however, that education, properly speaking, means the cultivation of the whole intellect of the child, Bachiller y Morales is bitterly critical of the system as it stands. The purpose of a free educational system, he observes, should be to create a nucleus of artisans, workers, and commercial entrepreneurs who, dedicating themselves to the exercise of the mechanical arts, the cultivation of the land, and market operations, will form an industrious and honest population; what we have instead is a system that has become a training ground of petty lawyers, small-time bureaucrats, and charlatans, who have risen to frightful numbers.[191] Higher education is not much better, for there has been both ecclesiastical opposition and governmental indifference to the successive struggles to establish faculties in the natural sciences as well as vocational schools, such as a nautical school.[192] The religious contribution to education is acknowledged. But the religious monopoly of the university is still seen as a limiting principle. Unfortunately, the governing rules of the university, established in 1728, were borrowed uncritically from those of the older university of Santo Domingo; the sixteenth century, observes Bachiller y Morales, triumphed in Havana over the eighteenth century.[193]

More than this, Bachiller y Morales is the cataloger of Cuban culture, in both its popular and its literary forms. He notes how the Cuban popular songs have been, from early on, a mixture of traditional Spanish airs and local native memories, and how song and dance went together, as in the *zarabanda*; and he goes on to quote from Hernando de la Parra how the sixteenth-century dances of Havana were, in that earlier observer's scandalized phrase, "vicious and grotesque," containing "the crude and low culture of the lower classes."[194] He is a convinced Anglophile in his political ideas; but at the same time he cannot refrain from printing some of the popular anti-English ballads that accompanied the English occupation of Havana in 1762. He is no snob, for he knows that the men of achievement have come from all walks of life. To that end, he quotes Arrate, noting how the official censorship suppressed the long passage in Arrate's work that insisted that every nation should not only recognize those of sublime rank and birth but also those who come from lower social ranks; there are those, says Arrate, who belong to the *mediana clase* (middle ranks) and those who are *los de superior jerarquía* (members of the higher social levels), but the first deserve honor as much as the second.[195] To all this, as a veritable pioneer in Cuban historiography, Bachiller y Morales provides an invaluable listing of newpapers published in Cuba, starting with the publication of the *Guía de Forasteros* in 1781, and a catalog of all books and pamphlets published since the introduction of printing in the island, starting in 1724 with the publication of the memoir penned by don Antonio de Sossa, *consultor* to the office of the Inquisition headquartered in Mexico.[196]

For, in truth, Bachiller y Morales is at once the culture historian and the liberal nationalist of Cuba. He is the first because he sees that everything Cuban is in and of itself important. That is the main lesson of the *Apuntes*. But it is also the lesson of his other work, *Los negros*, in which he celebrates the history of the movement of slavery abolition, and of his work *Cuba primitiva* as well, in which he establishes the worth of the original Indian contribution to the formation of the Cuban nation. He is also the liberal nationalist because he is at once the defender of liberalism and of nationalism. He notes with approval that the Real Sociedad published Say's *Compendio del tratado de economía política* in 1819, as well as Jovellanos's *Ley agraria*, both of them texts of the new economic liberalism.[197] At another point he notes the significance of the fact that the first edition of Varela's work on philosophy for students in 1812 was published in Latin, while the second edition of 1813 was published in Spanish.[198] Yet again, he reminds his readers that the censorship also cut out the word *criollo* as referring to native-born people in Arrate's volume.[199] Altogether, for Bachiller y Morales, education, language, even the sense of inhabiting the island, are the cornerstones of Cuban patriotism.

THE IDEOLOGY OF THE
CUBAN WAR FOR INDEPENDENCE

Cuban nationalist thought, of course, reached its apogee in the period after 1868, stimulated by the war against Spain. For war everywhere, but especially war against a hated enemy who also occupies the homeland, gives a tremendous impetus to nationalist feeling. That feeling, in the Cuban case, was naturally most intense and impassioned in the elements most active in the wars of independence, both the first and the second. It is in their political thought, known generally as the *ideología mambisa*, that the matured expression of Cuban nationhood is to be found.

The grand theme of the struggle, it has first to be noted, was celebrated by Cuban authors at the very time it was taking place. Figueredo, secretary to Céspedes, wrote his own eyewitness account of the events following the Grito de Yara.[200] Collazo, in turn, as *ayudante* to General Gómez, wrote of the later events, and made of his account a defense of the thesis that the revolution failed because it failed to produce a military dictator to lead it, yielding to the legislative group in the form of the Cámara de Representantes, and thus fatally compromising a strong and powerful leadership. Zambrana—writing, like many others, from exile—made of his own work, quite differently, a defense of the civilian power in the conduct of the war. Roa, former secretary to the Argentinan president Domingo Sarmiento, wrote his own account of the fighting. The young Manuel de la Cruz, likewise, wrote an account of the various permutations of the war as the voice of the younger generation celebrating the heroic exploits of the men of 1868.[201] In their turn, Varona, writing from New York, and Merchán, writing from Bogotá, presented a philosophical defense of the revolution, thus counterbalancing the pro-Spanish bias of the accounts by Zaragoza and Pirala. Valdés Domínguez wrote eloquently on the 1871 Spanish massacre of a small group of students, which constituted the most outrageous single atrocity of the war, while Trujillo described the life and work of the exiles in New York.[202] All of these writings, in different ways, sum up the themes of the *ideología mambisa*: hatred of Spain; love of the homeland, expressed, in typical Cuban form, in lyrical and almost sensuous terms; the legitimacy of armed struggle, stemming from the classical liberal argument that all peoples possess the ultimate right of revolution when all other means have failed: in Varona's phrase: *Cuba no ofende, se defiende* (Cuba does not seek to offend, only to defend herself). Not least of all, there is the theme of Cuban martyrology: as Giberga put it succinctly, the Ten Years War gave to Cuba what it had hitherto lacked, its own history, distinct and separate from the history of the metropolis.[203]

Much of all this is further illuminated by the contribution of the *caudillos* of the "thirty years war": Céspedes, Agramonte, Maceo, and Gómez. The contribution has been finely summarized in Jorge Ibarra's *Ideología mambisa*—written from the Marxist viewpoint of the post-1959 Cuban revolution, and locating it within the framework of the structures of class and race in nineteenth-century Cuba. It is the group of caudillos, along with the new group of black and mulatto intellectuals thrown up by the struggle, that enunciates for the first time the principles of ethnic fraternity, juridical equality, and national unity—thus making possible, in turn, a Cuban nation embracing all of its children, including the Afro-Cuban element, and thus offsetting the limited reform movement of the Junta de Información group of the 1860s, which still clung, despite its suggested reforms, to the ideology of white supremacy. Put together in the period between Céspedes's declaration of gradual slavery abolition of 1868 and the *Ley Moret* of 1882, it lays down the leading imperative of all Cuban nationalist thought ever since, reinforced by the official line of the *fidelista* revolution a century later: that Cuba is to be seen, not as a pluralist society in which the different ethnic groups nurture their own separate cultural sovereignties, but as a unitary society with all owing fealty to the national mainstream culture. Ethnic identity gives way to national patriotism. The group gives way to the nation.

That note is first struck by Céspedes. His signal contribution to the nationalist ideology is to have seen that national liberation and slavery abolition were indissolubly linked with each other; the one meant the other. His abolitionist decree of 1868 recognized the connection: "The people of Cuba," he announced, "cannot present themselves with dignity before the court of nations proclaiming their independence and liberty and yet sanction with an infamous silence the fate of their laboring poor." We recognize, the 1868 declaration of independence added, that all men are equal, that order and justice must be respected, that the life and property of all peaceful citizens, including even resident Spaniards, must be cared for, that the sovereignty of the people rests on universal suffrage, and that this requires the emancipation of slaves, gradual and with indemnification.[204]

It has been argued, notably by the later Cuban writer Cepero Bonilla, that Céspedes's gradualism throws into question his sincerity on the slavery issue. The charge has been answered both by Ibarra and by Le Riverend. The gradualism, they argue, was merely tactical: without the support of the slaveowning aristocracy of the Occidente province, the rebellion would have been doomed to failure; it was therefore necessary to wean them away gradually from their proslavery prejudice. That prejudice, as the correspondence of Villaurrutia, the revolutionary agent in Havana, with his compatriot Ponce de León in New York, makes clear, was real and deep-founded. Whereas, then, the gradualism of the 1866 liberal commissioners was grounded in their fear of slave liberty, that of Céspedes, quite differently, was grounded on the need for the vanguard of the rebellion to recruit the wealth of the moneyed groups in the search for arms.[205] That it was no more than that is evident enough from the hatred of the slavery institution that infuses Céspedes's well-known letter to U.S. Senator Sumner. He reminds his American correspondent that abolition was one of the main ends of the revolt; that as early as 1851, abolitionist sentiment had appeared in Cuba; that Spanish attempts at abolition, as in 1845, had been weak and futile; that Spain itself had connived at the continuing illegal trade; and that he, Céspedes, was also the determined enemy of the importation of Chinese laborers into the island, in itself a new slavery: *El culi era un animal valioso* (The coolie was viewed as a highly prized animal). Just as President Lincoln, in the north, was prepared to appease the borderline states on the slavery issue for the greater good of the Union, so Céspedes was ready to appease the Cuban slaveholding class in order to insure the national character of the rebellion. But once it became clear that the policy of appeasement would not work, and once, therefore, the radicalization of the rebellion accelerated in 1869-70, he did not hesitate to proclaim unconditional abolition and, as its logical sequence, the recruitment of the freed slave into the ranks of the revolutionary army.[206]

There followed from that the strategy of *la tea incendiaria*, the "scorched earth" policy. Sad, wrote Céspedes, but we cannot vacillate between our wealth and our liberty.[207] The strategy itself flowed naturally from the doctrine of the armed struggle, first enunciated clearly by Agramonte. More than anything else, Agramonte emerges as the revolutionary student, so typically Cuban, who moves from an excited reading of romantic literature—Lamartine's *History of the Girondins* and Victor Hugo's *Les Misérables*—to become the stern leader of the Jacobinical wing of the revolutionary assembly after 1868. Early on, his graduation address enunciated the philosophical basis of his brief insurrectionist career: the Spanish colonial state was founded solely on force, so force is the only answer to its tyranny. Whereas Céspedes came to that conclusion reluctantly, Agramonte embraced it readily, indeed almost happily. It followed, for him, that only an aggressively destructive campaign, following the "total war" strategy of Grant and Sherman against the South in the American Civil War, could finally destroy the Spanish power. Even before Martí, Agramonte personifies the classic mythology of the romantic revolutionist—half Byronic, half Bolívarian—that has made the Cuban political character seem so volatile in the eyes of the rest of the Caribbean.[208]

The contribution of Maceo to the *ideología mambisa* was that, merely because of his color, he personified its black component. In his person, and writings he compelled all of the actors in the drama to come to terms with the issues of race and color. Even more, Maceo—as mulatto, freemason, and rebel captain—symbolized the larger totality of elements in the revolutionary process: color, liberal thought, and revolutionary morality. All three elements come together in his thoughtful and critical commentary attached to the letter addressed by the Havana newspaper *El Yara* to the Spanish General Polavieja in 1889. The commentary, in effect, amounts to a testimonial declaration of Maceo's philosophy. It is no hyperbole to say, as Ibarra observes, that it puts into condensed form the entire moral and philosophical decalogue of nineteenth-century Cuban revolutionary thought. Much more than Gómez's *El viejo Edúa* or Piedra Martel's *Memorias de un mambi*, which are little more than campaign memoirs, it touches on all of the problems raised by war and peace in Cuba. Not an educated man in the traditional sense of the phrase—as Juan Marinello has pointed out—Maceo is nonetheless shown in the commentary to be a deeply reflective mind concerned with the underlying reasons for Cuban behavior.[209]

The commentary is, in fact, a statement on the theory and practice of revolution. Once it is granted that Spain will not compromise, it follows that Cuban freedom can only be reached by armed struggle; only by the machete, in Maceo's phrase. If that means the destruction of Cuban property, so be it: the right of property, which he respects, must not be allowed to become an

obstacle to higher moral principles. The policy of the *autonomista* (autonomist) party, seeking to wring concessions from Spain, is grievously mistaken.
It forms a sort of *maquiavelismo del bien* (well-intentioned Machiavellianism);
it prefers parliamentary oratory to armed struggle; it neglects to learn the vital lesson that independence can only come by means of unity among all the
anti-Spanish groups, from the Cuban soldiery at home to the exile groups in
New York. All intrigues, all tergiversations, all conflicts of personal ambition, must gave way to the imperative of unity: that is why, after all, Maceo
himself had been willing to give way to Gómez in the struggle for the leadership of the army. No true revolutionary, he goes on to say, can compromise
his ideals; and so he criticizes those who would use the same disgraceful
methods as the enemy, for such an attitude—claiming that the end justifies
the means—brings the Cuban patriot down to the same level as the hated
Spaniard. For independence is not an end in itself; it is, rather, a means
towards a new society in which freed Cuba will finally enter the modern
world, founded as that world is on the moral principles of a new national
citizenship. Both the modern democratic doctrine and the philosophy of
history, founded in reason, justify rebellion when justice has been denied, as
with Spain in Cuba. Rebellion even claims the approval of God; for, adds
Maceo, my God is the God of justice, not the God of those who buy their entry into Heaven with their contributions to the church, nor indeed the God of
those who announce the doctrine of papal infallibility.[210] It is his final duty,
concludes Maceo, to answer the slanderous charges of his enemies that he is
the advocate of a race war. He had already told Estrada Palma, in his letter
of 1885, that he was no champion of a Negro republic.[211] He now puts the
matter into philosophical perspective. I love all men, he asserts, because I
look at the essence of life and not its accidents; and so I place the interests of
Race, whatever that might mean, beneath the interests of Humanity. When
men allow their spirit to be taken over by prejudice, there is no longer any
room for reflective thought. Conscience becomes prisoner to the slavery of
the passions.[212] Thus, for Maceo, the revolutionary must be, above all else,
the man of honor and integrity. The message is all the more impressive
because it was couched, not in the flamboyant rhetoric so beloved of the
Latin literary temper (and from which not even Martí escaped), but in a terse
correspondence frequently composed on the very eve of battle.[213]

JOSÉ MARTÍ

But it is in the noble and attractive figure of Martí that Cuban, and indeed
Latin American, thought reaches its zenith. Like Lincoln in American life,
he became the supreme hero of the Cuban experience. As with Lincoln,
again, that elevation satisfied a vital and deep need in the mythopoesis of the
national tradition. More than any other single figure, he came to embody every-

thing sacrosanct about the Cuban psyche. As el Apóstol, he lived, wrote, and traveled throughout the Americas as much as Saint Paul proselytized the ancient Mediterranean, carrying his message of revolutionary nationalism. Even the very nature of his death, dying on the battlefield, like some other Byron in another Greece, helped to solidify the cult of his person. It is not surprising that ever since, every Cuban writer, of every generation, has felt that he must add his own quota of commentary on the life and work of Martí.

Simply because the accumulated commentary is so lyrically adulatory, it is difficult to obtain a critically objective view of Martí's contribution to American thought and letters. His own prodigious output, writing incessantly for newspapers and journals all over the continent, including Charles Dana's *New York Sun*, adds to the difficulty. What strikes the modern reader of the *Obras completas*, once he manages to get away from the effusively idolatrous tone of every later admirer, is the sheer intellectual curiosity of Martí. He is at once journalist, politician, aesthete, philosopher, essayist, poet, and orator. The catholic bent of his mind makes him receptive to all of the various currents of nineteenth-century thought, both European and American: historicism, mysticism, transcendentalism, social Darwinism, democratic populism, liberalism, romanticism, and the rest. He seems to have read something of everybody: Fichte, Goethe, Emerson, Kant, Carlyle, Tolstoy, Balzac, Shakespeare, Dante, as well as the ancient classics. He knows as much of the Bible as he does of Cervantes. He writes, with equal ease, on literally dozens of themes: the aesthetics of literature, the nature of the self, the idea of God in religion, the problem of death, the nature of genius, the topic of egotism and altruism in philosophical discourse, ethics and conduct, the nature of the ideal society, democracy, the liberal concept of free thought, and much else. So omnivorous is the mind that takes in all of this, that the Cuban scholar Roberto Agramonte, one of Martí's most recent biographers, requires almost a thousand pages in which merely to outline the master's general view of the universe.[214]

It is, indeed, this very catholicity of temper, the eager readiness to embrace and discuss every new idea, that is at once the strength and the weakness of Martí's thought. The strength lies in the fact that practically every philosophical system of the century is introduced by Martí to the Latin American reading public. The weakness lies in the inability to weld all of the multitudinous material into a single and coherent viewpoint that can be called his own. That is why it has been possible for later commentators to extract sentences and passages from the collected work to prove almost any point of view. For Martí, in fact, is more the *litterateur* than the original thinker. There are too many contradictory elements in his work to make him, like Hobbes or Rousseau or Marx, the philosopher who analyses the universe from one leading, seminal principle of interpretation. Examples proliferate. As the disciple of Luz y Caballero (who translated Volney's rationalistic *Ruins of Empires*), Martí seems sceptical of traditional religion; at the same time, much of his poetry is lyrically religious, and his lasting faith was not so much the radical Christianity revealed in the work of Strauss and Feuerbach as a sort of vague, optimistic pantheism. He is the admirer at one and the same time of Emerson and Whitman, without seeming to perceive that they spoke to quite different elements in the American experience: the one of New England transcendentalist unitarianism, the other of frontier democratic populism. He celebrates the ideal life of Cartesian reason, and almost in the same breath celebrates the intuitive and the mystical. He is, in his more overtly political thought, the modern revolutionary; yet at the same time he is capable of defending the implicitly reactionary idea of medieval *hidalguía*, the knightly creed of the gentleman. He is for the equality of all humanity: but when he writes about love, women, and the family, he becomes, at best, a romantic bourgeois who believes that woman's place is in the home as mother to her children and helpmeet to her husband, almost as if George Sand and George Eliot had never written. He writes with fierce indignation against injustice everywhere, yet manages to suggest in his most famous poem, *La rosa blanca*, that the best ethical code is that of Christian meekness and forgiveness, almost of Christian resignation.[215]

The same fatal imprecision appears in Martí's social ideas. Certainly his essays and reports on the United States describe his hatred of the new industrial capitalism and its Robber Barons with their "cult of wealth." But his own favorite alternative principle of social organization seems to have been the ideal of a propertied democracy of small farmers. He saw the struggle between capital and labor more as a contest between rich and poor than as a historically inevitable clash between truly antagonistic classes rooted in property relationships. There is no evidence that he ever read Marx or was influenced by Marxist thought; nor does he seem to have responded to the anarcho-syndicalist ideas of the Cuban workers he came to know in the Tampa and Key West districts of the Florida area. In sum: like his hero Emerson, he was too much the mystic and the poet ever to shape an internally consistent social and political philosophy. Like Emerson again, he believed, perhaps, more in the free individual than in the free society, more in moral improvement than in social action. The *doctrinal martiense*, the major principle underlying Martí's work, shows all the weaknesses that flow from those preferences. It is shaped by the mystic seer, not by the clinical analyst. "The greatest pleasure," he once wrote, "the only absolutely pure pleasure that I have enjoyed was that afternoon in which, from my half empty room, I saw the city lying prostrate before me, and looked into the future, thinking of Emerson."[216] That is—as with Coleridge and Carlyle, both of whom also influenced the impressionable Martí—the genius of the visionary. It is not the genius of the trained philosopher who creates a coherent map of the universe.

Even so, there is originality in Martí. But it lies elsewhere. The first thing to be noticed is the contribution he made, in a lifetime of reporting and analysis, to a greater mutual understanding between North and South America.

His reportage on the realities of North American life in particular—based on prolonged residence and factual observation, and getting away from his metaphysical preoccupations—educated Latin Americans about the North American democracy, helping to demolish many of the insubstantial myths surrounding the matter. The second thing, related to the first, is the contribution that Martí made to the Pan-American ideology. Going back beyond Bolívar to Las Casas himself, he, more than any other single Latin American, resurrected the idea of America as a new regenerative force in world affairs. He wrote, not as the provincial Cuban, but as the complete Americanist, taking the whole of the Americas, both North and South, as his province of enquiry.[217]

Because of both the geographical proximity of North America and its economic and technological development, Latin and Caribbean thinkers and leaders have had to come to some sort of terms with the North American power. It is the supreme achievement of Martí that he was almost the very first to do this and that he undertook the task seriously. He saw, from the very first visit, that there was much to love and much to hate in the American experience. "In our America," he wrote at the very beginning, "it is vital to know the truth about the United States. We should not exaggerate its faults purposely, out of a desire to deny it all virtue, nor should these faults be concealed or proclaimed as virtues."[218] What followed from that was a stream of brilliant and perceptive commentary on an enormous variety of aspects of the American way of life; they have been collected in English translation, many of them for the first time, in Philip Foner's excellent three-volume project.[219]

Like the American writings of Marx himself, much of the Martí commentary is, of course, journalism. But, as also with Marx, it is journalism imbued with moral passion and a fine historical sense. The astonishingly varied topics —whether it is Roscoe Conkling as the typical political boss, or New York in winter, or mob violence in New Orleans, or the tragic plight of the Chinese immigrant, or woman suffrage, or his sympathetic and admiring portraits of Mark Twain, Wendell Phillips, Henry Ward Beecher, and the famous Negro orator Henry Garnet, or even the momentous prize fight of 1882 between John L. Sullivan and Paddy Ryan—testify to the visitor's absorbing curiosity about this new land. Like all visitors, he perceives that the energizing principle of American life is the aggressive drive for self-improvement, open to all, free from the social caste and the artificial inequalities of the Old World. It is the bold optimism; the experimentation; the openness to new ideas so long as they work; the impatience with form and the passion for success, however it comes; that makes the new American species of mankind. "Here," observes Martí, "a good idea always finds welcoming, soft, and fertile ground. One must be intelligent, that is all. Do something useful, and you will have everything you want. Doors are shut for those who are dull and lazy; life is secure for those who obey the law of work."[220] Merely to read his piece on Coney Island is to see how all of the contradictory and confusing elements of American life—vast technological achievement, rapid growth, carefree optimism, unbridled excess, racial and cultural intermingling, the very bustle of life itself —appealed to him as the evidence of a dynamic society, so different from the static society of his own Havana, the stifling temper of which he was never able to tolerate even when permitted residence by the Spanish authorities.

More than anything else, perhaps, he sees the tremendous and exciting variety of American life. "Between the shanties of Dakota and the virile and barbaric nation in process of growth there, and the cities of the East—sprawling, privileged, well-bred, sensual, and unjust—lies an entire world," he tells his readers. "From the stone houses and the majestic freedom north of Schenectady, to the dismal resort on stilts south of St. Petersburg, lies another entire world. The clean and concerned people of the North are worlds apart from the choleric, poverty-stricken, broken, bitter, lackluster, loafing Southern shopkeepers sitting on their cracker barrels."[221] The only mistake Martí made there was to assume that all of that colorful diversity of elements was not held together by a common Americanism, a common bond of values and norms. Like most Latin Americans, whose success with federal unions has been dismally unsuccessful, he was tempted to underestimate the power of the unifying elements in the American experience as opposed to the centrifugal elements.

Martí, then, was wrong in his pessimistic estimate concerning the weakness of the federal principle of American life. Where, by contrast, he was eminently right was in his growing awareness of the truth—as his early enthusiasm became tempered by larger knowledge—that democratic America was increasingly becoming capitalist America. For it is important to remember that Martí was writing in that period, between Appomattox and the Spanish-American War, when American capitalism began to pass into its first stage of monopoly and when, in turn, a nefarious alliance of big business and big government organized the rule of a new governing class of politicians and business adventurers exploiting the sovereign power of the republic for their own ends of profit and power. They fulfilled the earlier prophecy of Tocqueville when he warned the United States against the rise of an "aristocracy of manufacturers," which, as he said, would be the one serious threat to the survival of democratic institutions in the life of the nation. The "promise of American life," which Martí had so lyrically celebrated, became transmuted into the "degradation of the democratic dogma." Not even Henry Adams or Mark Twain, both of whom annotated the change from their different viewpoints, could have matched Martí in his eloquent denunciation of the transformation. His fine indignation knows no bounds. There has grown up a new class of vulgar rich: soon it will be an elegant thing, he observes of the typical business tycoon, to paper one's walls with bank notes. He describes how Grant, soldier turned president, hands over the public wealth of the nation to the new business establishment: it is Grant, he remarks, who wears his campaign boots in the White House, and does wrong.[222] "These new Tartars," he writes of the businessmen and the politicians of the Gilded Age, "sack and pillage in the modern manner, riding in locomotives.... These birds of prey form syndicates, offer dividends, buy eloquence and influence, encircle Congress with invisible snares, hold legislation fast by the reins as if it were a newly broken horse, and, colossal robbers all, hoard and divide their gains in secret. They are always the same, sordid, puffed up with pride, coarse, their shirt fronts covered with diamonds. Senators visit them by back doors, cabinet members visit them in the quiet hours after the working day is over; millions of dollars pass through their hands; they are private bankers."[223] It is a brilliantly painted indictment of what America had come to. Its descriptive power is not really diminished by the fact that its half-realized ideological assumption is more the neo-Socialist indignation of, say, Rousseau against social injustice and less the fully Socialist recognition, as in Marx, that these behavior patterns of a ruling class spring, necessarily, from property relationships and class struggle and cannot merely be seen as exercises in social psychology.

Yet Martí's more lasting contribution is his defense of Pan-Americanism. He does that in two ways, related to each other: (1) his assault upon the emerging imperialism of the United States, and (2) his elaboration of the idea of the Latin and Caribbean heritage of the Americas. The first is based on his perception of the fact that the changing face of American society—the increasing stratification of social classes, the rise of a militant workers' movement, the transformation of competitive capitalism into monopoly capitalism, the new protectionism—intensified the drive towards imperialist expansionism overseas. The second flows from the first: for this new U.S. system is not interested in continental partnership, but only in its own hegemony throughout the continent—making it thus more imperative on the part of the Latin American ideologues to sound a warning against the danger. Among those who did—Saco, Sarmiento, Rodó, Rubén Darío—Martí was clearly the leading figure. What Darío called Martí's *patriótica locura* (patriotic madness) became expanded into a larger, continental vision of *nuestra América*.

It is important to note that the critique of the United States did not become, as some of Martí's later Marxist-Leninist champions have argued, a total rejection of the U.S. system. Martí still retained his admiration for its democratic and populist elements. That is why his frequently quoted phrase (taken from one of his letters)—living in the heart of the monster—can give a misleading idea of his complete attitude. Rather, it is the case that he comes to see that the new imperialism begins to threaten not only democracy internally in the U.S. but also democracy throughout the western hemisphere as a whole. There exists in the northern republic, he warns his readers, all of the violence, discord, immorality, and disorder blamed upon the peoples of Spanish America. He resents the economic ambition, the cultural arrogance, and the moral egocentricity that all went into the ideology of American Manifest Destiny, and writes with biting sarcasm of North American attitudes: "They study and chronicle us," he observes, "with merely a hasty glance and with obvious ill-humor, like an impoverished nobleman in the predicament of asking a favor of someone he does not regard as his equal." He deplores the increasing intolerance, frequently racist, of the *yanqui* attitude toward the other Americans: "They believe in need, in the barbarous right as the only right: 'this will be ours because we need it.' They believe in the invincible superiority of the 'Anglo-Saxon race over the Latin.' They believe in the inferiority of the Negroes whom they enslaved yesterday and are criticizing today, and of the Indians whom they are exterminating. They believe that the Spanish American nations are formed principally of Indians and Negroes."[224] Martí properly insists—writing at the time of the Pan-American Congress of 1889—that any kind of continental federation or confederation must be undesirable if it means that the Latin nations would be bound to:

> A nation [like the U.S.] of different interests, hybrid composition, and frightful problems, a nation resolved, before putting its own house in order, to engage in an arrogant and perhaps childish rivalry with the world. It will have to be determined whether [the Latin American] nations that have learned how to establish themselves independently—and the farther away, the more efficiently—should surrender their sovereignty to the nation which, although under greater obligation to help them, never once came to their aid, or whether it is right to set forth in full view of the world the determination to live in the health of truth, without unnecessary ties to an aggressive nation of another composition and purpose, before the demand for a forced alliance can rankle and bow to vanity and a national point of honor.[225]

Moving on from this position—in which reside the seeds of an independent Latin American foreign policy—Martí declares the ideology of Americanism in his essay "Nuestra América." Even its style, combining Castillian Spanish with New World vocabulary, is uniquely American, uniquely Cuban, what the later Latin American critic Gabriel Mistral terms *la tropicalidad de Martí* (Martí's tropicality). It is, essentially, an impassioned plea for cultural independence. It does for Latin America what Emerson's essay "The American Scholar" did for the young United States: argues the brief for an indigenous literature on native grounds, responsive to the unique character and experience of the New World. Just as Emerson with North America, so Martí with Latin America: both are convinced that the societies they defend have about them an autochthonic quality that they owe, not to a decadent Europe, but to their own uniqueness.

"Nuestra América," quite simply, is a vigorously argued polemic against the intractable provincialism of the colonial mentality. If we want to be anything at all, we must seize upon the idea of our Creole personality, and be ourselves; we must not copy others. We cannot rest in our own little pueblo; we must shake the world with our own idiosyncratic power. If we do that, we shall become giants with seven-league boots; if we fail to do it, we will remain as weak as infants who are born prematurely in the seventh month of pregnancy. Foreign models are irrelevant: you cannot undo the tax on the pony of the pampas cowboy with an edict of Hamilton or give new life to the congealed blood of the Indian race with a phrase of Sieyes. When a problem emerges in Cojimar, we do not have to seek its solution in Danzig. Our frock coats may still be French; but our ideas must begin to be those of America. Neither the European nor the *yanqui* book offers the key to the Hispano-American enigma. For the literature they represent reflects all of the useless hatreds of the Old World, all of its sterile conflicts: reason against power, the city against the countryside, urban social castes against national unity. The ideal form of government is not French or German, but government composed of institutions born and created out of the local American experience itself. So, the hierarchical forms of government imposed by Spanish repressive rule must give way to native republican forms whose growth, so far, has been retarded by the alien force. Above all else, America must rediscover the natural reason of its children, as against the artificial reason of the decrepit European conquerors. For the problem of independence is more than a question of changing constitutional forms; it is a question of changing the basic spirit of things. All forms of government must accommodate themselves to the natural elements of the society they represent.[226]

Much of this, of course, is not new. It is, indeed, Aristotelian—not to mention the echo of Rousseau and the European Romanticist tradition. What Martí adds is a romantic vision of the new America, going back, indeed, to the European utopian literature of the sixteenth and seventeenth centuries on the American theme. Here, in the American soil, he declares, "the imported book has been conquered by the natural man. The men of nature have conquered the artificial men of letters. The *mestizo autoctono* (autochthonous half-caste) has conquered the *criollo exótico* (exotic Creole). There is no conflict between civilization and barbarism, but only between false erudition and nature."[227] It is the victory, altogether, of the American indigenous elements against the alien, foreign elements. The political tyrants of the Latin American republics have come to power when they have utilized those indigenous elements; and they have fallen from power when they have betrayed them. It is the business of our universities, Martí adds, to teach that seminal lesson. To know your country and people, and to govern according to that knowledge, is the only way to free yourself from those political tyrannies. "The European university must give way to the American university. The history of America, from the Incas on, has to be taught to the fingertips, even if we do not teach that of the argonauts of Greece. Our Greece is to be preferred to the Greece that is not ours. Ours is more necessary."[228] Latin America is a rich, mixed society of Indians, Negroes, Creoles; they all seek a new world of harmony: there can be no race hatred, because there are no races. It is now high time to use those rich gifts in the service of a new American civilization.

Martí is important for a number of reasons. It is true (as already noted) that he had his defects. He is the Latin exuberant declaimer, and with him, as with others, the flow of oratory at times disturbs the power of objective analysis. His frame of reference, ideologically speaking, is the nation rather than the social class, so that he is a revolutionary in the sense of Mazzini rather than of Marx. He is not even above the temptation of writing about the North American Indians and the Chinese in the United States in terms that suggest, as Philip Foner admits, elements of a racist stereotype: that is to say, attributing to a national type behaviorial characteristics related to their socio-economic situation. His attitude toward the United States oscillates between admiration and fear: the materialism of the system is counterpoised against its liberal tradition, so that the figure of Emerson comes to embody American idealism, just as later, in the Darian ideological system, the figure of Poe is seen as the idealized antithesis to the *yanqui* monsters of electricity, whiskey, dollars, and the Bible—without any sustained effort being made to bring the materialist and the idealist visions into an internally consistent, connected whole.

Yet, with all that admitted, Martí remains the most attractive figure in the history of Cuban-Antillean-American nationalism. All of the intellectual currents of the age that influenced him—liberalism, romanticism, modernism—were used in the service of a generously conceived concept of human freedom. He did not allow himself to be tempted by the romantic dream of the lonely genius or by the modernist portraiture of the gifted artist escaping the abominable reality of the world by retreating into the sanctuary of his own inner world of fantastic images and linguistic innovation. It is true that, as much as Baudelaire or Wilde, he experiences the fin-de-siècle affirmation of artistic independence against bourgeois conformity; as much as they do—as his *Poemas del Niagara* show—he can feel the dreaded existentialist loneliness of the human soul. As much as Becquer or Campoamor, he can almost masochistically enjoy the melancholy of escapism into the exotic or even the agony of cultivated suffering: can resurrect in his own remembered experience, that is to say, the tragic figure, so preeminent in classical Spanish literature, of the man of honor pitted against fate and injustice, summed up eloquently in De Hostos's *Decálogo* and Martí's own *Testamento*.

But he was too much the Cuban patriot to believe that the freedom of the individual could be separated from the freedom of the society as a whole; and he was also too much the humanist to believe, as with Nietzsche, that the antagonism between bourgeois society and the marginalized intellectual could be resolved by elitism and Caesarism. As much as any French Parnassian poet of the time he can feel the sentiment of *tristes tropiques*; but he also knows that that condition is not so much a permanent condition of Antillean nature as a condition that arises out of the concrete sociohistorical fact that the Americas, both islands and mainland, have been ruled by the reactionary forces of both Spanish church and monarchy. There is, again, little in his collected writings of the sort of aesthetic Hispanophilism that marked the work of Darío and Rodó. More than anything else, he is the *pensador*-actor who perceives, with audacious clarity, that only the hidden forces of life and nature in the Americas themselves can operate as the propulsive mechanisms for the total renewal of their own cultural background. That conviction drove him to the very last: summed up finely in his approving quotation of the remark of his fellow Cuban spirit Socorro Rodríguez: "If the Romans did not learn Greek, then why is it necessary that the students of the Spanish tongue should have to learn Latin?"[229]

Martí, in sum, is the social and political conscience of the Americas. On the domestic American scene, he is almost the first to insist upon the positive value of the American societies as racially and ethnically mixed societies. It is this *mestizo* character of America, claims Martí, that sets the New World apart from the Old; and in the Manifesto de Montecristi his demand for the full incorporation of the Cuban negro into the national life expresses his feeling for all of the despised races of the continent. It is an element of Martí's thought that later critics like Rétamar have justly emphasized.[230] Martí, again, is almost the first American thinker to give new meaning to the concept of Americanism. The German critic Hans-Otto Dill has pointed out how this was so. With the earlier architects of the concept such as Bolívar, it was mainly a spiritual, almost religious concept. But with Martí it became a more concrete concept. His North American residency and travels had made it possible for him to understand much more fully than, say, Bolívar or Sarmiento the socioeconomic realities of North American life. He could see, therefore, that the real difference between North America and the rest of the continent was that North America was a capitalist society, with businessman and industrial worker playing the major roles in the social war, whereas, by contrast, Latin American societies were composed of landowners on the one hand and peasants on the other. Americanism, then, was bound to mean different things to societies so different in their material base. For the early strugglers for liberty it had meant, of necessity, freedom from the Spanish yoke. For Martí, sixty years later, it meant, again of necessity, freedom from the North American yoke. It meant, not just a political freedom, but a larger freedom, at once social, cultural, and economic.[231] *El pueblo que compra, manda* (the people that buy, command), he wrote, looking at the new commercial expansionism of the North American capitalism. The phrase anticipates, prophetically, the unequal relationships that were to develop between the United States and the rest of the American republics for the next century or so.

THE HISPANIC-ANTILLEAN CONTRIBUTION: CONCLUSION

It is evident enough that the contribution of the Spanish-speaking Antilles to the evolution of nationalist thought was a lasting one. More than the other Antilles—British, French, and Dutch—they were in the vanguard of the movements seeking the discovery, or the rediscovery, of the regional cultural patrimony. The main reason for that difference, perhaps, was that intellectual activity, especially in Cuba and Santo Domingo, was electrified by political revolution and anticolonial insurrection. But there was another reason: that of the intimate contact existing between the island centers and the leading mainland centers of the Latin republics. The contact had its basis in a common Hispanic culture and was fed immeasurably by the continued residence of Antillean refugees in Mexico City, Caracas, Bogotá, Buenos Aires, and the rest. It is, then, no accident that the history of Antillean nationalism is the history of the exile: Varona, Heredia, Martí, Betances, De Hostos, to name only a few. The nationalist ideology is forged in the trauma of the lonely exile. As much as the history of Russian thought in the same period, with liberals like Herzen, for example, in their Paris refuge, the history of nineteenth-century Antillean thought is the history of the romantic exiles. Whether it is the Dominican writer Manuel de Jesús Galván conceiving the idea of his famous *indianista* novel *Enriquillo* while witnessing the ceremony of the reading of the proclamation of slavery abolition in San Juan, Puerto Rico; or Betances managing, surprisingly, to obtain an audience with the prime minister himself, Mr. Gladstone, during his London visit; or Martí, as we see him through the fascinated eyes of a friend like Vargas Vilá, holding audiences in Bogotá spellbound with his oratorical power combined with deep humility of spirit; or Heredia making an almost religious pilgrimage to the Niagara Falls region where the French romantic Chateaubriand had set his novel *Atala*, almost the pioneer work of the romantic obsession with the American theme; or de Hostos fashioning his rationalistic theories of education in Santo Domingo—in all of them we see the presence of a burgeoning American patriotism, immeasurably and indeed almost unbearably intensified by the homesickness that comes with all exile.

It is important to remember that the new spirit did not win its victory overnight. The old colonial mentality—taking everything from Europe as gospel truth—did not die easily. Everywhere—in the novel, the theater, poetry—even if the themes were American, the stylistic forms tended to remain European. In some ways, of course, that was natural and inevitable, indeed admirable, for it reflected the global character of intellectual effort, transcending geographical and political boundaries. But in the Caribbean additional negative factors conspired to exaggerate the dependency on European currents: general economic backwardness, political immaturity, the almost total absence of general popular education, and, therefore, the absence of a large reading public. Thus in Haiti, where all of those conditions were the worst of all, the Haitian writer, living in a cultural desert, was perforce obliged to write for the metropolitan audience, and therefore of course in French rather than in the Creole patois: so even well into the twentieth century, Jean Price-Mars noted the consequence in his observation that *la rêve du chaque écrivain haitien, c'est la conquête de la France* (the dream of every Haitian writer is the conquest of France). The sociology of Dominican literature led, in turn, (as Harry Hoetink has noted) to an almost morbid preoccupation with literature, and especially poetry, on the part of the tiny educated class denied the expression of its talent in politics and public service. Hence, the characteristic note of that literature: humanistic-aristocratic, and an exaggerated adulation of European culture. The journalist Eulogia Horta's self-portrait, published in 1896 and noting his preferences in practically everything, might almost be seen as characteristic: Voltaire, Renan, Paul Bourget as favorite authors; Byron, Musset, Lamartine as favorite poets; Chopin, Schubert, Bellini as favorite composers; Hamlet as favorite fictional personage, Paris as favorite city; and Marcus Aurelius as favorite ideal model of what a man should be.[232] Similar preferences are reported in the catalog of the library of the Ateneo Puertorriqueño in neighboring San Juan in 1897, with the list including the works of Lamartine, Renan, Edgar Quinet, Victor Hugo, Zola, and Pérez Galdós.[233] All this went hand in hand with the habit of literary *preciocismo* (charming exquisiteness), a sort of literary gentility in which it became the fashion to publish a slim volume of jejune romantic verse. Fernández Juncos satirized the habit in his little piece *Yo quiero ser Poeta* in the Puerto Rican case. Pedro Bono, in turn, deplored it in the Dominican case. "In my country," wrote Bono, "much more attention has been given to the letter than to the spirit; form counts for all, people pursue the ideal of *bien decir*, they flog style, they magnify it, there develops an exaggerated cult of things empty of feeling, the detail of trivia and infantile fantasies. There are newspaper editorials and discourses whose phrases and periods sound and look like the Olympian Jupiter in the midst of thunder and lightning, and which when squeezed out do not yield one drop of sense."[234]

Within the whole complex relationship between the European tradition and the theme of Americanism, including its Antillean elements, it would be dangerous to underestimate this particular expression of European escapism. In its Antillean embodiment it took the well-known form of cultural colonialism in which the colonial subject-person became more metropolitan than the metropolis, more royal than the king. It lasted well into the twentieth century, giving rise, variously, to the Haitian who has seen himself as the *boulevardier parisien*; the West Indian who has seen himself as the "black Englishman"; the Hispanic Antillean who has seen himself, in Santo Domingo, as the *caballero madrileño* or, in Puerto Rico, as the *piti-yanqui*. Political independence, in and of itself—already achieved by the end of the century in Cuba, Santo Domingo, and Haiti—did not necessarily terminate that more pervasive sense of cultural inferiority. It is no accident, then, that so much of Caribbean political thought in the twentieth century was to concern itself with the whole problem of psychological decolonization.

Yet by 1900 it is true to say that the Hispanic Antillean intellectual force, following that of Latin America, had come, more or less, to a final decision in favor of continental America as against Europe. That is apparent enough if a brief glance is taken at the stage at which the well-known Europe-Prospero versus America-Caliban debate had arrived by the end of the century. The original terms of that debate, of course, had been set by Sarmiento in his *Facundo*: barbarism was represented by the "barbarian *caudillos*" like Rosas and the crude life of the pampas; civilization was represented by everything that "white" European civilization stood for, even including its North American offshoot. Yet by the turn of the century, other voices in the Latin American literary renaissance had managed to put the argument into reverse gear, engineering a sort of Jekyll-and-Hyde transfiguration. Instead of being perceived (as in the Shakespeare play) as the symbol of noncivilization, the Caliban-cannibal figure became eulogized as the symbolic representative of American vitality and genius. The change began in Sarmiento's own day with José Hernández's monumental *Martín Fierro*, celebrating the almost anarchistical freedom of the Argentinan gaucho who, aided only by his horse and his knife, battles for his life in the open as against the decadent European style of the cities. It continued with Da Cunha's equally monumental *Os Sertoes*, sympathetically memorializing the struggle of the wretched peasantry of the Brazilian northeast backlands against the military power of the republic.

Other related movements fed the general current: the revived interest in the pre-Columbian past, as in Heredia's defiant eulogy of the Aztec warriors; the *indianista* novel, also celebrating the Indian presence, as well as the *romántico-costumbrista* movement trying to revive the disappearing folklore of the common people; and a separate poetic tradition in which the great lyrical poets of the continent—Acuna, Florez, San Martín, Almafuerte, Díaz Mirón—paid homage to the luxuriant, pantheistic prodigality of American nature, unleashing the hidden forces of that nature in a manner that made the European romantic genre seem pallid by comparison.

It all ended—for the nineteenth century at least—with the work of the Nicaraguan Rubén Darío and the Uruguayan José Enrique Rodó, with both of them giving a new twist to the Prospero-Caliban theme. Rodó's significantly titled *Ariel*, published in the first year of the new twentieth century, was initially inspired by Martí's term *nuestra América*, and Darío's poetry was in turn inspired by Rodó's lively polemic. In the Rodó-Darío vision, the contrast painted between the two life-styles, Latin and Anglo-Saxon, is continued, but the villain of the piece—reflecting the changing balance of power in the region—is now the United States. Taking its cue from the premises of pure Bergsonian spiritualism—contrasting technology and soul, machine and man, collective and individual interest—Latin America is seen, ideally, as Catholic, spiritual, poetic, and the United States is seen as gross, materialistic, money-mad. North America is utilitarian, lacks kindness and heart, and believes, in Rodó's phrase, that it can rewrite Genesis to the formula of "Washington plus Edison." Its sole god is the "almighty dollar." Its touted "American way of life" is, in reality, little more than mass standardization and uniformity inherent in mass production based on the money-making motive, and so lacks the profundity and creativeness of Latin life.

This was the note on which the nineteenth century ended, with the Rodó-Darío literary anti-U.S. theme becoming the ardent message of the literary intelligentsia. Yet much of it was empty of any real lasting content. It was politically reactionary in its "art for art's sake" bias, dreaming of democracy ruled by the artist, with his supposed superiority of feeling. Darío chose the term *modernism* to label his movement; it is curious that the movement, then, had nothing whatever to do with the contemporary modernist movement in the European Catholic Church, in which scholars like the abbé Loisy sought, unsuccessfully, to persuade the hierarchy to accept the findings of the new biblical criticism. Rodó idealized England as much as Darío idealized France; neither of them appears able to have understood that it was English and French commercial capitalism, as much as North American capitalism, that had undertaken to introduce slavery to the Americas. They commemorated the early struggles in which idealized Indian heroes fought the conquistadores; but they had nothing to say about the oppressed Indian descendants of those same heroes in their own day in Central and Latin America. There was, in fact, a noticeable absence of social protest in their writings. They accepted Renan as their great French mentor. But they could not see that Renan's famous *Vie de Jesus* was an appeal, in one way, to the more wholesome democratic elements of early Christianity. Finally, they were so obsessed with their polemical hatred of North American materialism that they failed utterly to see how, as their own Latin American civilization developed, it also gave birth to great industrial cities like Mexico City, Caracas, Buenos Aires, and Montevideo, which evinced the same characteristics and the same stratifications as New York and Chicago. They all became metropolitan centers of worldwide capitalist culture, as indeed Havana also did in the Caribbean proper. It was thus left to the later, more radical scholarship of the twentieth century, especially the scholarship of post-1959 Cuba, to write yet another version of the Prospero-Caliban theme with deeper attention paid to its racial and social-class aspects.[235]

THE BRITISH WEST INDIES

It is evidence of the multifaceted character of the Caribbean that no nationalist movement comparable to that of Haiti or Cuba developed in the British West Indies in the long post-Emancipation period (1834–1900). As in the similar case of the French Antilles after 1848, social and political energy went into the formidable task of structural readjustment to a free society with slavery gone, and the early accounts of outside observers like Sewell and Bigelow, as well as others like Sturge and Harvey, show how preeminent was that problem of readjustment. The framework of imperial control was taken for granted; it was assumed by all that the really important problem, that of slavery, having been ended, it was now a matter of slow and patient reconstruction; there existed no large professional class of people, as, say, in Havana, who could have led an anticolonial struggle; and, in any case, the kind of group that came nearest to being such a class, the independent free coloreds, who were so much the immediate beneficiaries of abolition, mainly occupied themselves with a limited struggle for the retention and expansion of their civil rights within the colonial relationship. There were, admittedly, rebellious episodes like the Jamaican Morant Bay rebellion of 1865. But even those protests were more against the abuses of the colonial system than against the system as such.

What protonationalist thought develops in the English-speaking region during this period, then, is mainly that of individual voices rather than of mass movements. They are accompanied by the visiting, sometimes resident, outsiders, mostly European and English, most of them historians in one way or another: Breen on St. Lucia, Schomburgk on Barbados, Gardner on Jamaica, Fraser on Trinidad, as well as the more general accounts of Sewell, Martin, Southey, Lucas, Caldecott, and Davy; their special contribution, in particular their meticulous work in the resuscitation and compilation of documents, has been fully described in Elsa Goveia's study. Their Creole counterparts took over, for the most part, their pro-English bias and their assumption —which was the theme of Gardner's *History of Jamaica*—that the old slave society must yield to a Victorian-like class society tempered by the civilizing influence of Christianity. The positivist bias in favor of history as fact gathering is evident in most of the works produced; there is certainly little of the temper of the contemporary Haitian history-writing, in which history became the patriotic reconstruction of the past. What there is, rather, is a general conviction that a new era in West Indian freedom has emerged with slavery abolition. The old planter oligarchy is gone, and must be replaced with a new and wider set of social relations. Most of these historian-writers would have agreed with the general comment of Sewell, speaking of the old planting interest before 1834, that "Theirs was not the broad, grasping selfishness of a powerful oligarchy wise enough to combine their own aggrandizement with that of the nation at large; but it has been from first to last a narrow-minded selfishness that pursued crooked paths to accumulate gain at the expense of the public weal, and to the infinite detriment of the colonial credit."[237]

What emerges during this period, then, is not a Creole demand for political independence but a variety of voices that emphasize all of the social and cultural values that constitute, as it were, the indispensable prelude to independence, the prior conditions and attitudes that, later on, will make independence possible. There is the insistence in Dalton's history of British Guiana that slavery had been an "abominable traffic" and that "like to the barons of former Europe, the lordly planters of America enacted in the New World scenes similar to those which had nearly been abolished in the civilized parts of Europe." To which is added a plea in favor of race mixture as a means of obliterating the race hatred of the old regime.[238] The same argument—that abolition now requires the termination of all of the rigid inequalities of race and color that had accompanied slavery—is echoed in Hill's brief sketch of Jamaican history; and to that argument, based on Hill's personal experience, there is added the political argument that the old Whig thesis of legislative freedom had been nothing much more than the effort of a narrow Jamaican assembly to "be oppressive without accountability."[239] To this line of argument, Woodcock, in his history of Tobago, adds a plea for further self-government, buttressed by a hearty dislike of arbitrary powers in government. Woodcock, of course, does not convert his dislike of the old representative system into a demand for full independence; rather, following Gardner, he uses it for welcoming the new Crown Colony system—within the framework of which, he appears to assume, local self-government could the more readily flourish. Following Gardner again, he is convinced that the rising free-colored class, if granted the franchise, is fully capable of meeting the demands and obligations of self-government.[240]

Borde's history of Spanish Trinidad, in turn, documents the rise of the polyglot Trinidadian society of Spanish planters, French immigrants, and African slaves, for the formative period 1498-1797. A French Creole, Borde celebrates the cosmopolitan nature of the resultant mixture. He is proud of the contribution made by both Spanish and French (his history, significantly, is composed in French, not English); at the same time, he identifies himself as a Trinidadian rather than as a French Creole, and he clearly hopes that all of the diverse heritages of the island society will fuse into a common whole, shared by all. He is, of course, a white Trinidadian. But he can speak with real sympathy of the plight of the free coloreds under the old slavery regime; and although he appreciates the special quality of Trinidad Carnival in its early period as a French, upper-class fête, he refrains from condemning the event in its later period as what his fellow-historian, the Scotsman Fraser, was prepared to deride as "a noisy and disorderly amusement for the lower classes."[241]

Borde, in fact, represents a very special Trinidadian source of British West Indian patriotic ideology. Unlike Jamaica or Barbados, Trinidad had received a noticeable Franco-Hispanic stamp before the English takeover of 1797, with the result that, again unlike the other British possessions, it developed as an ethnically pluralist society. Whereas, then, Barbados evolved as an overseas colonial copy of Victorian England, Trinidad evolved as a cosmopolitan society both in the religious sense (Catholicism as well as Protestantism) and in the linguistic sense (sizable minorities speaking French and Spanish). As, then, the sense of being a Trinidadian slowly grew up, it required the formulation of an all-embracing civic creed granting hospitality to all of the component groups of the national family.

No one person, perhaps, in both his writings and his life of public service, did so much to foment that creed as Sir Louis De Verteuil. Coming from a lineage that had been not only French Royalist but also legitimist in its political predilections, he was intensely loyal to the old French tradition, as well as staunchly Catholic, enabling him to take a cool and detached view of the colonial English. At the same time, he was no extremist of the anti-English party, and in all his reformist activities, like the struggle for lifting civil disabilities against the Catholics, he remained a loyal supporter of the British Crown, a loyalty rewarded by his final inclusion in the Honours List.

It is in his book *Trinidad*, published in 1856, that he presents his case for a cultural nationalism quite distinct from an anticolonialism based on any kind of hatred for the mother country. It is, to start with, a plea for radical electoral reform, argued against an officialdom that regarded the claimants as French foreigners and adherents of the Romish religion and therefore inherently traitorous. It is, beyond that, a plea for radical educational reform: "Our best schoolboys," he wrote, "are able to give the names of the principal towns in Great Britain and even in Russia and China, but they are ignorant perhaps of the names of the Guataro and Oropouche. They know that San Fernando exists but may not be able to say whether it is on the eastern or western side of the island; can enumerate the chief productions of England, but they do not know what are the agricultural products of their own country."[242] Not only did he want a free education for all, a radical enough sentiment in his day; he also wanted an education geared meaningfully to the West Indian experience. Above all else, De Verteuil is the champion of racial equality and tolerance. He perceives that if the Creole Negro exhibited characteristics of indolence and improvidence, they were in large part "the consequence of a protracted state of debasing bondage rather than the effects of a wicked and perverse nature." He takes an equally understanding attitude in his comments on the Indian and Chinese immigrant groups. "In a colony like Trinidad," he concludes, "diversity of races will probably continue to exist for many years, a contingency which some may deplore but which should not disturb their equanimity. In fact it would be a most suicidal policy on the part of the Government to allow, much less to encourage, any one class of colonist to arrogate to itself a superiority over the rest. Mere difference of origin, or religion, or of social habits should not be permitted to raise barriers between different sections of the community; still less should they form an excuse for hedging in a few as a superior caste."[243] It is a measure of De Verteuil's perspicacity and wisdom that many of those observations ring as true, over a century later, in the postindependence period as they did at the time they were penned.

It would be misleading, however, to read Borde and De Verteuil and conclude that racial feelings had disappeared in the Antilles. Both the work of the Guianese Rodway, *History of British Guiana*, and the book of the English historian Froude, *The English in the West Indies*, with its meretricious fame, are evidence enough that even in the liberal nineteenth century such feelings were so deeply imbedded that they could enjoy a revival. Both of those writers repeated all of the prejudices of the older planter histories. Rodway sympathized with the planters, saw the slave masses as irresponsible, lazy, and immune to educational effort, and came near to implying that slavery was justifiable. Froude, in turn, turned his own fine disgust with the decadent Antilles, as he saw them, into a plea for the adoption of the authoritarian rule of the British Raj in India as the only means of their salvation.[244]

Yet because both Rodway and Froude were throwbacks, as it were, to the old racist bias, they are not really representative of the new varieties of racial prejudice that developed during the second half of the nineteenth century. Those new forms, more sophisticated but in the long run equally prejudicial, were the outcome of the new science that developed the first anthropological theories of race and, likewise, the half plausible arguments that came out of the ideological current of social Darwinism. Writers like Rodway and Froude could be easily answered; it was much more difficult to answer the new pseudoscientific argumentation. The older and cruder ideas—the supposed innate inferiority of the nonwhite races, for example, or the arguments based on biblical exegesis—were abandoned, to be replaced by ideas founded in the new science of evolution, as Darwin's seminal concept of the evolution of the natural species was taken over, often uncritically, to apply to the evolution of the human species in their cultural-historical environment. It was that new mode of argument, seemingly more learned but nonetheless equally racist, that the emerging Antillean nationalist spirit was now required to answer.

No one single book exemplifies the matter better than the volume published by the English publicist W. P. Livingstone in the very last year of the century entitled *Black Jamaica*. The argument throughout takes for granted the assumptions of the prevailing popular ideas of evolution and eugenics. In one sense, that makes it superior to the simplistic moralizing of a Froude, for it recognizes that all "races" are subject to laws that shape their behavior. So, slavery and the slave trade are seen as barbaric; the old white planter class was almost as degenerate as the simple blacks they ruled; the discussion on the Morant Bay rebellion of 1865 places the blame squarely on the obtuse ignorance of Governor Eyre and his advisors; and the colonial neglect of Jamaica after 1834 is properly censured. But all of these seemingly liberal concessions to historical fact are more than negated by a larger argument that assumes the growth of "civilization" as made by "higher races" and "lower races." The key differentiating factor in that evolutionary ladder, argues Livingstone, is climate. The march of civilization has taken place in the temperate zone, whose peoples, reacting to challenge, have organized the masculine part of world nature, while, by contrast, the equatorial areas, where fecundity and not progress predominate, are the feminine part of the earth's surface. It follows that the Negro can only advance under the tutelage of the white race; "Alone and voluntarily it is impossible for him to develop; not from any inherent inability—for he started from the same point as the other member of the family, and is fundamentally equal to him in character —but simply because his environment has been too much for him. . . . The advancement of the Negro is contingent on his association with the white race, and on the character of that race. Without the stimulus of this factor he cannot better himself."[245] Everything of African origin is dark, vicious, retrograde. Only its better elements—the mixed mulatto class—can bring up the race out of its barbaric morass, and that because those elements are a compound of both white and black, amalgamating the "intelligence" of the first with the "animalism" of the second.

Livingstone, reflecting the new protectionist imperialism of the British politics of his time, ends with a plea for a rejuvenated colonial policy that will bring the Negroes, as racial children, into the wider, broad life of the empire. Unlike Froude, Livingstone does not despise the Negro as subhuman. But he arrives at the same conclusion as Froude about Negro incapacity for self-rule on the basis of his own different unproved assumption that, as he puts it, "there is...no certain prospect of Creole rule of any kind being able to induce the uninterrupted social progress of tropical communities. Their advancement is conditioned on the amount and quality of the ethical force introduced from the temperate zone. If the Negro is to attain to the highest degree of efficiency it is possible for him to reach in the special circumstances of his existence, he must submit to be controlled and guided by the white."[246]

The Livingstone volume has been worth quoting at some length because it indicates the continuing capacity of racist feelings and attitudes to absorb "modern" systems of thought and recruit them into their service—pouring, as it were, new wine into old bottles. The process showed itself both in the more progressive elements like Fabian socialism in Britain and in the emerging discipline of sociology in the United States; indeed, with reference to the latter, Livingstone observed in his introductory preface that his argument agreed with that of Benjamin Kidd's *Control of the Tropics*, published in 1898, which book sought an ideological justification for the newly acquired American tropical possessions. These, altogether, were attitudes and assumptions shared by many of the liberal and progressive elements of nineteenth-century European thought. They were polygenist, asserting that blacks and whites belonged to separate species. Polygenism, in fact, became the received wisdom, giving rise, for example, to the new pseudoscience of eugenics, in which it was believed possible to undertake public population policies of selective breeding that would eliminate the pernicious influence of the "lower breeds" in favor of a "higher" race. It was no accident, then, that when the French scholar Pierre Larousse brought out his *Grand dictionnaire universel* in 1866, which was to summarize all known human knowledge, he should have uncritically embraced the polygenist thesis, and that popular French fictional writing of the period should have accepted the same ideology of biological racism as it was filtered down to its authors from the academic intelligentsia. That whole body of prejudicial thought, disguised as scientific knowledge, received its most notorious expression in Gobineau's *The Inequality of the Human Races* (1853), with its insistence on the permanent inferiority of the nonwhite races stemming from the argument of the absolute biological separation and differentiation of the races.[247]

J. J. THOMAS

Both the Froude and the Gobineau types of argument stimulated a Caribbean response in the latter part of the century, and from three different points of the Caribbean compass. The first, from Trinidad, was J. J. Thomas's spirited answer to the Froude volume, aptly entitled *Froudacity* (1889); the second, from the Danish West Indies, was the collected work of the savant Edward Wilmot Blyden in the general field of comparative religion and culture, and notably his major book, *Christianity, Islam, and the Negro Race* (1887); and the third was composed of the series of essays and books put out by a trio of Haitian writers at much the same time: Louis Joseph Janvier's *L'égalité des races* (1884), Antenor Firmin's *De l'égalité des races humaines* (1885), and Hannibal Price's *De la réhabilitation de la race noire par la république d'Haiti* (1900).

Thomas's book, to begin with, was the work of a schoolmaster in colonial Trinidad who, by sheer perseverance and self-education, had made his way in the educational system introduced by the liberal-minded colonial governor Lord Harris and proved, by his own remarkable achievement, that given proper encouragement, the "mute inglorious Miltons" of colonial society could pass all the tests imposed upon the men and women of Creole talent by the colonial system. He wrote the first systematic analysis of the Trinidadian Creole grammar; and only his early death prevented him from writing the history of Emancipation that was to have been his lifework. His critique of Froude therefore remains as the chief testimony of his unfulfilled talent.

Thomas has little difficulty in demolishing the racist Froude argument. The argument that a popularly elected black government would result in a new "Haitian horror" is "perversity gone wild in the manufacture of analogies," since it cavalierly ignores the fact that general conditions in the British West Indies are utterly different, notably a blending of the race producing a solid mixed mulatto class that makes nonsense of the claim to see things in polarized terms of merely black and white. There are differences of skin color, it is true. But there are other differences that preclude using skin color as the sole criterion for judgment. "In speech, character, and deportment, a coloured native of Trinidad differs as much from one of Barbados as a North American black does from either, in all the above respects."[248] The movement for constitutional reform in Trinidad cannot be dismissed, as Froude dismisses it, as an evil design to enthrone "negro domination"; rather, it is led by responsible gentlemen none of whom are "Negroes." The West Indies, indeed, are a "free mixed community" of racial harmony, quite unlike the portrait of mutual race hatred painted by Froude. There are rich blacks as well as poor whites in its social structure. The success story of a colored man like Sir Conrad Reeves in Barbados is not an isolated case but representative of a whole class of eminent colored persons in the professions. Almost every West Indian island can offer examples of Negro voters who will elect representatives solely in terms of competency for office and not skin color, as well as white Creoles who will support any black candidate seen as a fitting representative of their interests. "No one can deserve to govern simply because he is white, and no one is bound to be subject simply because he is black."[249] Froude, full of his Anglo-Saxon racism, portrays the islands as full of half-barbarian ignorant Negroes of African descent; but he can only do that because (1) he ignores the social realities of the situation, and (2) he has uncritically accepted the prejudices of the narrow class of white planter hosts whose hospitality blinded him to the truth. His report, therefore, is based on hearsay rather than on personal investigation. Any topic that he touches upon —the alleged incurable idleness of the Negro worker, for example—is colored by that fact.

It is worth noting that, despite the admiring introduction of C.L.R. James to the edition of 1969, Thomas is no revolutionary. He takes the English connection for granted; he is no nationalist, like the Cuban and Puerto Rican separatists of his day, seeking West Indian independence. His quarrel with Froude is a matter of degree rather than of kind; Froude exemplifies, as he sees it, the worst of the English tradition, whereas he himself appeals to the best of that tradition. His greatest praise in the colonial life itself is for the "coloured elements." He appears to accept Froude's assumption that obeah, cannibalism, and devil-worship characterize Haitian life, only arguing that Froude is wrong to assume that they will be adopted by blacks in the West Indies. He continues to accept the conventional view, destroyed by later scholarship, that slavery emancipation was an act of English beneficence. His view of the North American situation at the time is marred by his temptation to believe that the Reconstruction period has ushered in a new age where educated blacks have been incorporated fully into American government and the social system. Nor is he any advocate of popular rule anywhere: "No one in the West Indies," he assures the reader, "has ever done so silly a thing as to ask for the Negroes as a body that which has not, as everybody knows, and never will be, conceded to the people of Great Britain as a body."[250] All in all, this is to say, Thomas was the educated colonial who, like everybody else in the long *Pax Britannica* of the Victorian age, almost seemed to believe that the British Empire, unlike previous empires, was an empire on which the sun would never set.

Yet, having admitted all that, at the same time he saw, prophetically, that the time was coming when the black race would come into its own in the developing course of human history. He concluded:

> The years of civilized development have dawned in turn on many sections of the human family, and the Anglo-Saxons, who now enjoy pre-eminence, got their turn

only after Egypt, Assyria, Babylon, Greece, Rome and others had successively held the palm of supremacy. And since these mighty empires have all passed away may we not then, if the past teaches aught, confidently expect that other racial hegemonies will arise in the future to keep up the ceaseless progression of temporal existence towards the existence that is eternal? What is it in the nature of things that will oust the African race from the right to participate, in times to come, in the high destinies that have been assigned in times past to the many races that have not been in anywise superior to us in the qualifications, physical, moral, and intellectual, that mark out a race for prominence amongst other races?[251]

EDWARD WILMOT BLYDEN

With Blyden, of course, we are in a different universe of discourse. Unlike Thomas and the Haitian writers, he was West Indian only by birth. Early removed from Saint Thomas, denied because of prejudice the education he sought in the United States, he emigrated to Africa, where, in a lifetime of public service in Liberia and Sierra Leone, he became the classic expatriate. His intellectual formation was overwhelmingly African, and it is from his African experience that he derived his leading ideas. He starts off by accepting the premise of the European racial theories that the primordial secret of all life is race and that, furthermore, mankind is divided into separate races whose mixture becomes dangerous contamination. But in that global relationship, the Negro race is only different; it is not inferior. It possesses its own noble history, especially on the African continent, where pre-European civilizations, partly indigenous, partly Arab, have created a distinctively African culture and personality. In Africa, its main progenitor has been Islam, far more generous and persuasive than European Christianity. For whereas Christianity came to the African in his form as a slave, Islam came to him as an independent being in his own habitat:

> Wherever the Negro is found in Christian hands, his leading trait is not docility, as has often been alleged, but servility. Individuals here and there may be found of extraordinary intelligence, enterprise, and energy, but there is no Christian community of Negroes anywhere which is self-reliant and independent. Haiti and Liberia, so-called Negro Republics, are merely struggling for existence, and hold their own by the tolerance of the civilized powers. On the other hand, there are numerous Negro Mohammedan communities and states in Africa which are self-reliant, productive, independent and dominant, supporting, without the countenance or patronage of the parent country, Arabia, whence they derived them, their political, literary and ecclesiastical institutions.[252]

Under Christian proselytization, whether in North America or the Antilles, the Negro has encountered repression and unnatural absorption; only under Islam, with its more open view of race, has he met healthy amalgamation. In the white European countries, he is the victim of an anti-Negro literary tradition; under Islam, he has felt nothing of that withering power of caste.

It follows from all this, Blyden argues, that a whole new philosophical revolution in the study of race is necessary. Race prejudice makes it impossible for the white man—occasional rare exceptions like the explorer Livingstone apart—to understand the genius of Africa and the African. The European world is, as yet, only in the infancy of its studies in African psychology. It may discover the source of the Nile, but it cannot comprehend the intellectual character of the Negro. That task belongs to the new African scholarship of the future: "only the Negro will be able to explain the Negro to the rest of mankind." What is now needed is a new syncretizing movement that will marry the best of the Christian message with that of Islam and thereby finally crush the worst elements of tribal paganism. The instrument for that regeneration lies in the millions of the African diaspora who, as they return to the ancestral home, will bring their race-vitality to that great task—especially the Negro in exile in America, for his residence there has predisposed him in favor of progress and civilization. It is in that sense, adds Blyden, that the slave trade can be seen as a beneficent process, not the first time that wicked hands were suffered to execute a Divine purpose. Racial intermingling is bad; cultural intercourse is admirable. It is now time for the Negro to make his own contribution, untrammeled by colonialism, to that process.

> The African must advance by methods of his own. He must possess a power distinct from that of the European. It has been proved that he knows how to take advantage of European culture, and that he can be benefitted by it. This proof was perhaps necessary, but it is not sufficient. We must show that we are able to go alone, to carve out our own way. We must not be satisfied that, in this nation, European influence shapes our policy, makes our laws, rules in our tribunals, and impregnates our social atmosphere. We must not suppose that the Anglo-Saxon methods are final, that there is nothing for us to find for our own guidance, and that we have nothing to teach the world. There is inspiration for us also.[253]

THE HAITIAN SCHOOL

A similar note—albeit set, naturally, within the framework of their own national experience—is struck by the Haitian writers. Janvier's contribution is contained in his essay—along with essays by others—in the 1882 volume *Les détracteurs de la race noire*. It is a spirited answer to the anti-Haitian article of the savant Leo Quesnel, with its charge that Haiti has regressed to savagery and that hostility to the white race is the permanent disease of all Haitians. It is true, Janvier replies, that hereditary psychological factors explain why Haitians do not yet possess the civic sense of, say, the English since their 1688 revolution. But Haiti at the same time is on the road to civilization. There is Haitian bravery, as in the war of liberation; the Haitian facility for learning languages; the standing affection for *la gentille France*; the physical beauty stemming from the race admixture of African and European; not least of all, the fusion of ideas characteristic of the educated class, so that in all the areas of modern learning— medicine, science, jurisprudence, the natural sciences—the ideas of Paris circulate in Haiti. Haiti, in brief, is not the closed society it is supposed to be; nor should it be so. Indeed, it constitutes a laboratory of "sociological experimentation" insofar as its people, in their physical, moral, and intellectual characteristics, are a unique race progressing toward civilization along evolutionary lines.[254]

Price's argument takes up the same theme, only more systematically, since it is a book, not just an article. With Sir Spencer St. John's scurrilous book in mind, he notes that vilifying Haiti has become a sort of article of faith with certain sections of European writers. The burden of his reply is to argue that race prejudice, like religious intolerance, is irrelevant. The only real question worthy of discussion is: Is the Negro race capable of civilization? Yes, answers Price, for, a priori, civilization, being the common patrimony of mankind, is not built up by any one people or race, but by all of them in a process of mutual assimilation of thought and deed. There are, certainly, superior cultures, but not superior races. What is more, the superior culture exists not because of inherent superiority but because of fortunate circumstances. It is circumstance, not nature, that conditions the position of each race on that scale; thus, Price cites from Moreau de Saint-Méry to show that the character of all groups involved in the old slave society arose from the system in which they lived.[255] Grant the black race the education hitherto denied it, and it will make its own great contribution to the world civilization. There must be open hospitality to all thought; the progress of China was halted because it set up barriers against other peoples. In that evolutionary process, Haiti will not be led to its fullfilment, but will seek it by its own efforts. If it is difficult to do that at the moment, it is because the inherited legacy of slavery still frustrates; after all, Price notes acidly, everybody knows that the white colon of Saint Domingue did not look at the slaves through the eyes of the *contrat social* or *l'ésprit des Lois*, anymore than the Jamaican sugar proprietor looked at his slaves through the eyes of Burke's discourses.[256] So Haiti, now possessed of its own national responsibility, has its own special destiny to fullfil: the instrument to prove the reality of the Christian doctrine of the equality of races.[257]

Yet it is Firmin's book that is the most substantial of all. Unlike the others, he does not write in response to a particular critic but sets out to construct a whole apologetic in its own terms. He is the Haitian anthropologist par excellence. Widely read in that new discipline, he composes a systematic study, not just a polemic. The breadth of the discussion and the wide variety of scholarly sources referred to testify to the fact that he has mastered all of the existing literature in the field of anthropology, both physical and cultural. The study of anthropology, he observes—that is to say, the scientific study of mankind as a human species, from all perspectives, physical, intellectual, and moral—started with Kant's *Anthropologie pragmatique*, published in 1798. The chief argument presented by Firmin is that the only scientifically valid first principle of the discipline is the monogenist principle, as against the polygenist principle: that is to say, the principle of the unitary oneness of the human species. Admitting that there is confusion among anthropologists themselves about the proper definition of "race," he is at least certain that the concept of color cannot be used as a criterion. It is, of course, one obvious criterion. But in and of itself it is not enough. Terms such as Aryan and Indo-European to denote race are misleading, for they are used to attribute inferior or superior characteristics to particular groups or "races."[258] Nor is a pseudoscience like craniology (taken seriously at the time) any more reliable, if only because there is too much disagreement among its practitioners. Nor can the morphology of language be recruited into the service of racist feeling; for example, there is no evidence to prove that the so-called Indo-European languages have a common root.[259]

Firmin takes the larger view. All cultures and civilizations belong to the common tradition of mankind. They each are born, grow, and decline. Their nature is set by the material conditions within which they flourish. No characteristic is innate; monotheism, for example, is no more natural to Oriental than it is to Western peoples; and Pouchet's argument that certain "races" are apt to adopt certain religious ideas is misinformed. So to argue, observes Firmin, is to confuse the moral aptitudes of peoples with their religious systems.[260] There is no one pure "race," as the history of eugenic crossing demonstrates. So, again, it is absurd to argue that mixed "hybrid" peoples cannot produce offspring; and the point is emphasized by reference to the mulatto group in Santo Domingo, which, certainly, has met the test of fecundity.[261] By the same token, it is absurd to assume that there exist absolute standards of beauty, as do Gobineau and Broca. The evidence of geographers like Reclus and travelers like Hartman sufficiently shows that there exists a great variety of physionomic features even among the African peoples; and recent archaeological findings show that the white European "race" itself has evolved through different stages with different physiological features. You will find men and women of remarkable beauty in modern-day Haiti. They may not be the Venus de Milo or the Olympian Jupiter. But then, those pieces of art are themselves idealized versions of beauty, not necessarily reflecting the anthropological reality.[262]

The evolutionary process, of course, is unequal. Different groups pass through different stages at different times. It is unscientific reasoning to compare one group at a lower stage with another at a higher stage. Any comparison, if made at all, should be made between comparable stages. The white race did not invent the science of numbers or mathematics, and only the difficulties of deciphering the ancient Egyptian hieroglyphics has prevented us from acknowledging that the Egyptians discovered geometry.[263] It is the difference in the historical time span of social evolution that alone accounts for differences between different civilizations. Every group is endowed with the capacity for moral and intellectual development; all depends on the particular environmental conditions that happen to accelerate or retard that development.[264] The world, concludes Firmin in an almost lyrical passage, is not stationary. All peoples and nations pass by on the theater-stage of history, each playing a different role. But within the grand harmony of the human destiny, none of the roles they play is without use. The actors are all equal in dignity; in a perpetual transformation, each assumes and then vacates the leading role. This will continue until the time when all of them will fade away into a general whole, of which the capital function will be to uphold the *flambeau intellectuel* that illuminates the moral world as much as the sun illuminates the material world.[265]

Some later writers have seen in this Haitian literature anticipations of the later twentieth-century ideology of *négritude*. Yet that is a mistaken analysis. For the two leading themes of *négritude* have been (1) criticism, sometimes of almost obsessive violence, of the European civilization, partly rooted in Marx, partly in Spengler, and (2) belief in the mystique of an African soul different from and superior to the Western spirit. Neither of these themes appears in the earlier writings. Just as the post-1804 writers, such as Milscent and Darfour, had been ambivalent in their attitude toward Africa and Africans, so the group of later writers perceived Africa as a culturally backward continent. Thus Janvier notes approvingly that all Haitian rulers after Toussaint had tried to extirpate African "superstitions" in the new nation. Price, in turn, devotes a separate chapter to the same "superstitions." He does not deny their existence, but excuses them on the ground that Haiti has lacked popular education. The Haitian dances, for example, are a heritage of the old colonial system based on the cynical white-colon maxim that *plus les négres dansent, plus ils sont tranquilles* (the more the Negroes dance, the more docile they will be).[266] All of them agree that as soon as the light of civilization, which for them is European in its best aspects, comes to Africa then the "dark continent" will make its own contribution to world culture. Ideologically, all this is to say, the Haitian literati are located within the humanist tradition of the Western civilization; all that they ask is that the black race be admitted into its membership on full and equal terms. There is nothing here of the telluric mysticism and the revolt against European materialism and technomania typical of the later *négritude* movement. What are present, rather, are the basic themes: the revindication of Africa as a center of great pre-European civilizations, the insistence on the place of the Negro in the world as a cultural equal, the denunciation of color prejudice as a cunning white trick to perpetuate inequalities, and the rest. It all constitutes what a later Haitian writer has properly termed a pre-*négritude* movement.[267]

All of these later nineteenth-century writers, especially from the non-Hispanic Caribbean region, are thus ideologues who attempt to marry the best of the traditional European tradition, as they perceive it, with their own emphasis upon the need for a new scholarship and philosophy that will finally accept the African race as a legitimate newcomer in the world community. Naturally they do not write as a school, for they lived and wrote in a region intellectually as well as politically fragmented. So, again, naturally there are differences in their views. That can be seen, for example, in their markedly different views on the issue of religion. For Firmin, the ever-ready influence of Renan persuades him to take a humanist understanding of the best of Christianity. One day, he writes, the universal alliance of all peoples and races will make itself felt, based on the *douceur évangélique* of the Prophet of Nazareth.[268] Blyden, in his turn, is less charitable to Christianity. For him, the Christian religion has become too much of an "Aryan" religion, falsely encouraging Negroes to forget their African heritage and overlooking its origin in the "grand Semitic idea" of the conversion to Divine truth of all the races of mankind.[269] For Thomas, yet again, the Anglicized Christianity that Blyden so much disliked is the greatest of all teachings, so much so that Thomas, as much as any Victorian rector out of Trollope's novels, is hostile to the new biblical scholarship of the time that pitted science against religion; there are echoes here in colonial Trinidad of the great Victorian debate between blind faith and rationalist doubt.[270]

Yet despite those differences, all of these writers have at least one theme in common. They are champions of the Negro-African race seen, not in local, but in global terms. They see the peoples of Africa not just as Africans but as members of a dispersed race inhabiting both sides of the Atlantic. Both parts of the race—those of the African homeland and those of the New World Diaspora—are brought together into a single whole, giving them a new and larger vision of themselves. The American Negro is now enabled to see himself as related to the old ancestral home. The African Negro is given an opportunity to see his New World counterparts as brothers and sisters. Thus these Antillean-born writers can properly be appreciated as forerunners of the later twentieth-century Pan-African movement.

Chapter Six

Conclusion

The Caribbean entered the twentieth century carrying with it all of the inherited baggage of the various ideologies that had gone to make up its history since the Discovery itself. It still remained, in large part, a regional society characterized by continuing colonial subjection, inequalities of race and class, poverty, and general economic backwardness. Even when formal political independence occurred, as with Cuba in 1900 and the British colonies in the period after the Second World War, the political sovereignty was rendered null and void, in large part, by the economic sovereignty exercised by the metropolitan business forces, so that the history of the region became pretty much the history of Manifest Destiny and Dollar Diplomacy. Those forces were immeasurably increased by the entry of the American empire into the region, for it is clear that after World War I, and certainly after World War II, both the British and the French nations were imperialisms in decline, while, by contrast, the United States was an expanding imperialism. The general scenario of the Caribbean as slums of empire remained the same; only the cast of actors changed.

The Caribbean societies thus continued to be societies markedly lacking effective forms of community consciousness based on unifying norms and values. Recent historians—such as Edward Brathwaite in his book *The Development of Creole Society in Jamaica, 1770-1820*—have attempted to show that the Jamaican slave society constituted a valid and substantial historic body, bound together by a sense of common creoledom; a culture neither wholly European nor wholly African, but possessed of a feeling of being distinctly Jamaican. Yet the evidence advanced for that thesis is hardly persuasive. It is difficult to believe that slave and master shared any common values, let alone any sort of social contract holding them together. There were intimations of such a community feeling, but they hardly add up to a distinct culture shared by all. Slave Jamaica, rather, was an accidental society composed of different groups alienated from each other, each understanding Jamaica in different terms; so much so that Brathwaite's very system of classification—dealing separately with European, Euro-Creole, Afro-Creole and West Indian segments—implicitly recognizes the sharp and oftentimes mutually irreconcilable character of the groups. Certainly the Jamaican-planter ruling group appealed to the sense of being distinctively Jamaican in their struggle with England. But it was in many ways an opportunistic rather than a real Creole patriotism; and the real ideology of the group was better summed up in the remark offered to Lady Nugent by old Simon Taylor: his life's ambition was to make his nephew "the richest commoner in Europe." The Jamaican sense never really matured into an independent national sense encompassing all Jamaican society. It remained throughout—as indeed in all of the slave societies—an ideology of narrow interest.[1] That is why, at a crucial moment, it failed to join the revolution of the North American colonies, with which it sympathized. The opportunity to make a creative decision in favor of national freedom yielded to timidity and self-interest. It thereby merited English contempt: "The North Americans were indeed too much for us," an English visitor noted in 1825, "the West Indians can be crushed by a wave of Mr. Canning's hand."[2]

The proslavery ideology, then, simply because it saw the slavery institution as the linchpin of its culture, never became a creative force based on positive institutional principles. That task was left to the other ideologies of Caribbean history, including the multi-faceted antislavery ideology. The antislavery current of thought began as early as the dream of Las Casas, rooted in late medieval humanism, to found a Christian *respublica* in the New World; received fresh impetus from Renaissance and Reformation sources; became a part of the philosophy of the Enlightenment; and then, in its African sources, reached out to religious and philosophical forms alien to the European tradition. It is important to note the sheer diversity of the elements that went into its making. Much of it came from European learned thought. But much of it also came from the humanitarian movement, sometimes linked to the current of Christian teachings. So it is worth noting that support for both proslavery and antislavery ideologies came at times from unexpected sources. Two examples will suffice. In the proslavery case, the Surinam Jewish group could cite, with apparent approval, the critical investigations of the seventeenth-century scholar Richard Simon in the field of biblical textual studies as part of the free-thought tradition to which it appealed in 1788 in support of its claim for better treatment within the colony, without appreciating the fact that the same tradition, if applied to slavery, would almost certainly have condemned it.[3] In the antislavery case, there is no finer statement of what it meant, in its largest perspective, than the compassionate thoughts that Captain Cook, thinking of his beloved Tahitian islanders, put down in his journal in the 1770s. "We debauch their morals already too prone to vice," he wrote, "and we introduce among them wants and perhaps diseases which they never before knew and which serve only to disturb that happy tranquillity they and their forefathers had enjoyed. If anyone denies the truth of this assertion let him tell me what the natives of the whole extent of America have gained by the commerce they have had with Europeans."[4] It is a note of European guilt for having destroyed the innocence of America that goes back to Las Casas. That it should have been repeated by Captain Cook shows that it was possible for that note to be heard even in the eighteenth-century British fleet, hardly known as a hotbed of humanitarian feeling.

It goes without saying, of course, that when these twin ideologies are examined, it is apparent and evident that in the history of the Caribbean, they played different and indeed antithetic roles. The proslavery ideology was essentially procapitalist and proimperialist; the antislavery ideology, by definition, was, in part at least, anticapitalist and antiimperialist. The first had life only as a rationalization of white supremacy and its implicit correlate, non-white inferiority. The second was intrinsically revolutionary to the degree that it was essentially an ideology of protest on the part of the Caribbean masses—Indian, African, and even at times European—against an exploitative economic and political system seeking to justify itself in terms of a pseudoscientific doctrine of race. Within that framework, of course, the antislavery ideology possessed its own internal variations, ranging from covert protest and civil disobedience to outright rebellion: covering, that is to say, the whole spectrum of violent and nonviolent resistance. Violent resistance expressed itself in the history of slave revolts, with their accompanying varying ideological concepts. Recent investigation on the 1763 Berbice rebellion, for example, suggests that the very real tribal rifts among the rebels of that event were only neutralized by the presence, in the figure of the Negro leader Cuffy, of a Creole ambience able to take a larger, colony-wide view of the struggle.[5] The classic case of armed resistance was, as always, Saint Domingue–Haiti, which obtained not only independence but also the genesis of black pride in the Americas; and the Haitian poets and novelists, as well as the publicists and historians, celebrated it in a literature of patriotic self-exaltation. Nonviolent resistance, in its turn, made its own important contribution. Typically, it was expressed in slave Christianity, as in Equiano's *Travels*. A predestinarian, as he called himself, Equiano had read Fox's *Martyrology* with its fierce anti-Catholic bias and believed that only the English "gentlemen in power" could give freedom to the slaves. But he saw clearly enough the moral evil of the system. "When you make men slaves," he wrote, "you deprive them of half their virtue, you set them in your own conduct an example of fraud, rapine, and cruelty, and compel them to live with you in a state of war, and yet you complain that they are not honest or faithful."[6]

The other leading Caribbean ideological expression was, of course, that of nationalism, mainly a nineteenth-century product. It was not always a straight-forward anticolonialist system, for it possessed its own internal doctrinal contradictions. For just as the antislavery ideology was not always necessarily

Creole and nationalist—there were many British West Indian strugglers against slavery who placed their main hope for emancipation in the metropolitan forces, thus forging a momentous and well-known alliance between liberal white English official and politically conscious West Indian Negro that was to last well into the twentieth century—so, in a somewhat similar fashion, the nationalist ideology was not always necessarily against slavery, as the political thought of Cuban liberals like Saco in the nineteenth century shows. Yet a further contradiction of the nationalist creed lay in the fact that although anti-European by its very nature, it had not managed by 1900 to divest itself entirely of the colonial admiration for the European model. Much of it was still tied to the apron strings of the Old World. As a later twentieth-century Latin American intellectual has phrased it, New World thought at that point was still immersed in a receptive rather than a critical period. What the same critic has termed "the cultural emancipation of America" would have to wait upon the more indigenous New World patterns of the twentieth century.[7]

Yet even with those limitations, the nationalist movement of the nineteenth century in the Antilles achieved much. It propounded the message, quite simply, that the Caribbean was important simply because it was the Caribbean. It was against European cultural disdain; against racism just as before it had been against institutionalized slavery; against North American economic penetration and political expansionism. The general note is there in the Haitian and Cuban historians. It is there in the literature of the romantic novel. It is there in the figure of Martí as he moves forward from simply treating Cuba in relationship to Spain and begins to fashion, after Bolívar, the idea of an Americanism that will possess its own special flavor; so much so that even although he admires a European revolutionary liberal like Heine, he can see that the problems with which Heine was concerned are not necessarily the same problems with which the Latin American intellectual must be concerned.[8] It is there, again, in the Haitian ideologues who critically studied the new European forms of racism, not because they were enamored of those forms, but because, as a later French Antillean scholar has put it, it was important to study them in much the same way as it has been important for European scholarship to study the ideology of Nazism.[9] It is there, finally, in the political thought of the nineteenth-century regional thinkers—Martí himself, Betances, De Hostos, and others—who argued for a unified Caribbean system, federal or confederationist, that would help the region to throw off the artificial boundaries and irrational loyalist psychologies imposed by colonialism. Such a system, as they saw it, rested on a sort of New World geographical determinism, in which the Caribbean was perceived as the appropriate heart and center of the Americas, expressed in Bolívar's observation that "If the world were to select a spot for its capital, it would seem that the isthmus of Panama must needs be chosen for this august destiny, situated as it is at the center of the world, looking in one direction towards Africa and Europe, and equidistant from America's two extremities."[10] Only continuing allegiance to insular nationalism has made that regional concept seem like a romantic dream, so that as late as today (1983) it is still possible for Caribbean thinkers to argue that there exists little of a positive Caribbean consciousness to convert the dream into reality.[11]

The nationalist ideology, naturally, meant the popularity of the concepts of nationhood and nationality. They were legitimate and self-validating concepts. But in the Caribbean, as elsewhere, they were sometimes accompanied by less plausible concepts. Such a concept was the idea of national character, assuming that every particular national group is possessed of certain idiosyncratic and peculiarly characteristic features marking it off from others. The Caribbean literature had its own examples: that Cubans are one thing, and Puerto Ricans another; that Barbados is this and Trinidad that. It was, as with much else, a concept borrowed from the nationalistic writings of nineteenth-century Europe itself. It evolved into crass and set conceits: The Dutch were thrifty; the English polite; the French sexy; the Americans hard-boiled; the Spanish chivalrous; the Latins great lovers; and so on. But on examination it is clear that the theories could not hold water. The "national character" invoked was, in fact, little less than a series of stereotypes arising, not out of national cultures as a whole, but out of the selected mini-cultures of the ruling groups and top classes of the different societies: the Dutch Puritan burgher, the English public-school gentleman, the French Parisian elite, the American businessman, the Spanish aristocrat. For it is always the character type of the dominant class segment that presents itself to the outside world and thus sets the yardstick of analysis. How far this mistaken mode of seeing national character has persisted even in the modern Caribbean can be seen from a reading of the 1969 publication of the lectures entitled *Teoría de la frontera* that the Cuban scholar Jorge Mañach had proposed to give at the University of Puerto Rico before his death, in which it is argued, following Madariaga, that what is proper and distinctive for the English is action; for the French, rational thought; and for the Spanish, emotion. Whole peoples are thus arbitrarily placed into a straitjacket of assumed psychological traits.[12]

Yet even so, this process of falsely identifying ruling group with national character did not go unchallenged as it was copied in the Caribbean. Even a cursory glance at Caribbean history provides the reason why: quite simply, the ruling groups of the region never matured to a general life style that could compel admiration. Henry James could admire the English gentleman; Proust could adore the French aristocrat; even Burke, when he came to write of their predecessors, the old English territorial aristocracy and the old French monarchy, could seem as if he were composing on his knees. Not even the most ardent protagonists of the Caribbean sugar plantocracy could rise to such heights of adulation. The record was too bleak. Even in those Caribbean centers—like the bustling commercial entrepôt of St. Thomas in the Danish Virgin islands—where some kind of lively mental activity might have been expected to develop, there was little to show. The resident American Charles Edwin Taylor noted in his memoir of life in the town during the 1880s, *Leaflets from the Danish West Indies*, that its social tedium was only occasionally relieved by the *soirée* or the "fiddle dance" or by the visiting circus or dramatic company; and a newspaper account at the same time noted of the average Saint Thomian businessman that he was a shopkeeper with little sense of humor but possessed of a certain dry sharpness of his own, not much interested in poetry, music, or literature and infinitely preferring to converse about the latest speculations in sugar or to go home satisfied after a good day's transactions with his Santo Domingo purchasers. There was little in such a life-style to provoke the admiration of any local Burke or Proust.[13]

Consequently, the growth of any national-character mythology came to settle upon the Caribbean common man as its representative type. Earlier on, it had been different. Eighteenth-century England, for example, had seen the affluent West Indian planter in that role. But that was soon challenged by the abolitionist literature, helping to make the figure of the slave the embodiment of the soul and spirit of the West Indies. After abolition, in turn, it was the slave turned independent peasant proprietor who, with his thrift and energy, was seen as the salvation of the new economy; and that particular theme was the message of both Sewell's book of 1859, *The Ordeal of Free Labor in the British West Indies*, and Kingsley's book of 1869, *At Last: A Christmas in the West Indies*.[14] In similar fashion, it was the lower class in colonial Trinidad that became identified with the carnival fête; and to compare Day's account of carnival in 1847 with that of Hamilton over thirty years later is to appreciate how the imported European elements of the event were replaced during that period with the typically native elements.[15] In a somewhat different way the nineteenth-century literature composed by European visitors, to the degree that it was tempted to write melodramatically about vodun, unwittingly made the vodun priest the centerpiece of the national persona; notwithstanding the fact that the portrait was invariably painted in hostile terms, as in Sir Spencer St. John's book of 1889, *Hayti, or the Black Republic*.[16] In such various ways the protagonist of the spirit of Caribbean cultural nationalism came to be the man, and the woman, of the Caribbean street.

As the nineteenth century turned into the twentieth century, of course, new ideas and ideologies began to emerge within the region, anticipating many of the different themes that would dominate the Caribbean debate for the best part of the new period after 1900. In particular, as a distinctive artisan-craftsman class grew up in the expanding urban centers of the region, it produced the characteristic type of the self-educated proletariat widely read in the new European theories of social cooperativism, socialism, anarchism, and communism, thus evincing a social-class consciousness hitherto known in the island societies only in vague and ill-defined forms. The last quarter of the century was the formative period of Antillean labor organization, with the growth of labor unions, workers' study circles, working-class journals, and the rest. In Cuba it produced a new literature of working-class group manifestos.[17] In Puerto Rico it expressed itself, to begin with, in the formation of the first cooperative society in San Juan by the humble carpenter Santiago Andrade in 1873.[18] After that, it expressed itself, around the turn of the century, in a new literature of radical social protest, mainly inspired by Spanish anarcho-syndicalist ideas, discussing the social question, the woman question, the "condition of the people" question. The sense of an international working-class brotherhood replacing, ideally, the narrow feelings of skin color prejudice and craft jealousy so evident in the artisan guilds appeared as early as 1874. It was followed, a generation later, by a vigorously written pamphlet literature that, as in Ramón Romero Rosa's *The Social Question and Puerto Rico* (1904), exposed the new capitalist industrial system as an exploitative machine replacing the old aristocracy of blood with its new aristocracy of money and, by means of its international character, rendering anachronistic the old patriotic obsessions such as Puerto Rican national independence; or, as in the memorandum defending the sugar workers' strike of 1905 (also written by Romero Rosa), it poked fun at all of the various groups—journalists, politicians, jobholders, the police—that could only see workers' strike action as an invitation, spurred on by irresponsible Socialist agitators, to chaos and disorder; or, as in the various books written by the early feminist advocate Luis a Capetillo, it attacked with fierce indignation the new slavery of wage labor that theoretically frees the will of the worker but in practice deprives him of the means to use it.[19] All in all, it was a new literature emphasizing new themes—class war, wage exploitation, the need for the social revolution—quite different from the themes that had characterized the Caribbean literature of the previous century.

In retrospect, the historian of the Caribbean, and certainly of Caribbean ideologies, has to recognize the existence of at least two general considerations of paramount importance. In the first place, the general Caribbean society formed during the four centuries after the Discovery was marked throughout by a spirit of cultural philistinism probably unmatched in the history of European colonialism. It has been argued by some writers that the European emigrants brought with them four centuries of European culture. That romantic claim has been answered sharply by the French historian Lucien Febvre, who asks:

> How many of those who left Europe for the West Indies, compelled or uncompelled, during the sixteenth, seventeenth and eighteenth centuries were in fact the bearers of a civilization with whose true significance, and intellectual, spiritual and moral refinements, they were really familiar? How many of the crowd of adventurers, desperadoes, or failures hoping to make good or start a new life overseas, how

many of all those sisters of Manon Lescaut purged from Paris or elsewhere, were capable of finding at their own level of civilization the strength to resist the impulses which their sudden elevation from the status of "inferior whites" in Europe to that of privileged overlords in America would inevitably arouse? How many of them would be able, by adherence to a highly developed European code of morals, to find the force to resist the excesses, the violence and the depravity which their carnal appetites were likely to engender under a burning tropical sun? And lastly, how many of them could resist the temptation to grow rich again by any and every means, and to subordinate all else in their new life to that end?[20]

The second general consideration is that, notwithstanding all that, Caribbean society managed, over the centuries, to give birth to its own ideological expressions, even to an indigenous moral and intellectual culture. Basically, it was rooted, as the Brazilian scholar Alceu Amoroso Lima has noted, in the growth over the centuries of an independent American spirit, spilling over into the Caribbean, especially in the nineteenth century.

While the impulse might have come from the centre to the periphery, from the top to the bottom, from the leaders to the masses, or vice versa, the same aspiration to a culture of their own took shape in all regions and led in turn to the beginnings of a new continental spirit. . . . The anti-European complex brought with it as a natural consequence another concomitant tendency, which took the shape no longer of a merely negative disposition to hostility but of a positive inclination towards the non-European cultures as substitutes. This was not only the acute phase of anti-Europeanism, but also remained a permanent tendency deeply rooted in the American mentality as a sign of its independence. The other cultures which now began to influence American humanism secured acceptance primarily through this natural inclination, reinforced still further by the reaction against colonialism. The Amerindian, the African and the non-European were the currents which began to contribute to American humanism and fuse or clash with those elements drawn from European intellectual culture.[21]

The passage summarizes in a nutshell the main sources that went into the formation, slowly but surely, of Caribbean thought, values, attitudes, and belief systems. It was a process involving the interpenetration of civilizations; and in that sense it constituted one of the latest examples of a process that goes back to the record of the earliest riverine civilizations of India, Egypt, and the Middle East as they became the precursors of the ancient Graeco-Roman world. Obviously, it did not take place overnight; and even by the end of the period in 1900, it was in many ways still in the process of development. It helped to create, as well as being the expression of, the Caribbean society as it flowered in the twentieth century: a society at once multiracial, multicultural, multireligious, multilinguistic. Not even its most ardent admirers would claim that it is—as it enters the final decades of the twentieth century—the utopia that Las Casas, in the very beginning, thought it might become. It is still plagued by all of the evils that make it a part of the Third World: widespread poverty, gross inequities of wealth and income, serious structural unemployment, educational backwardness, a monoculture too heavily dependent on world market forces over which it has little control, political instabilities that give rise to ugly Creole fascist systems like Batista's Cuba, Trujillo's Santo Domingo, Duvalier's Haiti.

Yet at the same time it possesses features that might well make it the envy of so-called more advanced societies. Its various groups, whether identified in racial, ethnic, or religious definitional terms, live, if not in complete harmony, at least in a peaceful coexistence that other Third World areas ravaged by communalism and tribalism might envy. Its peoples and cultures, indeed, being so much a rich mixture of America, Europe, Africa, and Asia, have shaped out of their experience some of the leading ideas of the modern world especially relevant to Third World problems: *négritude*, black power, black nationalism, Creole Marxism, Cuban socialism, and the rest. Indeed, relative to its size, the region has produced a disproportionate number of artists, thinkers, and scholar-politicians, many of them with an international fame: Ortiz, Price-Mars, Eric Williams, C.L.R. James, Fanon, Garvey, Aimé Césaire, Muñoz-Marín, Fidel Castro; and many of them, in addition, combining political leadership and intellectual culture in a way that has almost disappeared in the political life of countries like Britain and the United States. All of these things have added up to constitute the never-ending fascination felt by travelers and visitors to the region. They are the elements of the promise of Caribbean life. The future of the Caribbean lies within the capacity and the willingness of those elements to fulfill and indeed enlarge that promise.

Notes

CHAPTER ONE

1. Harold Mitchell, *Caribbean Patterns: A Political and Economic Study of the Contemporary Caribbean* (New York: John Wiley and Sons, 1967), ch. 19.

2. As only one example of the Afro-American emphasis, see Richard Frucht, ed., *Black Society in the New World* (New York: Random House, 1971).

3. For general histories of the region see Bartolomé de las Casas, *Historia de las Indias*, 3 vols. (Mexico City: Fondo de Cultura Economica, 1951); Eric Williams, *From Columbus to Castro: The History of the Caribbean, 1492–1969* (London: André Deutsch, 1970); Juan Bosch, *De Cristobal Colon a Fidel Castro: El Caribe Frontera Imperial* (Madrid: Ediciones Alfaguera, 1970); J. H. Parry and P. M. Sherlock, *A Short History of the West Indies* (London, Macmillan, 1956).

4. Sidney W. Mintz, "The Caribbean as a Socio-Cultural Area," in *Peoples and Cultures of the Caribbean: An Anthropological Reader*, ed. Michael M. Horowitz (New York: Natural History Press for the American Museum of Natural History, 1971), p. 36.

5. R.A.J. van Lier, *Frontier Society: A Social Analysis of the History of Surinam* (The Hague: Martinus Nijhoff, 1971).

6. Philip Curtin, *The Atlantic Slave Trade: A Census* (Madison: University of Wisconsin Press, 1969).

7. *Lady Nugent's Journal* (Kingston, Jamaica: Institute of Jamaica, 1966); Bryan Edwards, *History, Civil and Commercial, of the British Colonies in the West Indies*, 5 vols. (London, 1793), vol. 3, p. 36; Edmund Burke, *The Works of Edmund Burke*, 6 vols. (London: George Bell and Sons, 1901), vol. 3, p. 517, vol. 5, pp. 521, 524.

8. Médéric-Louis-Elie Moreau de Saint-Méry, *Description topographique, physique, civile, politique, et historique de la partie française de l'Isle Saint-Domingue*, 3 vols. (Philadelphia, 1779). English version in *Slaves, Free Men, Citizens: West Indian Perspectives*, ed. Lambros Comitas and David Lowenthal (Garden City, N.Y.: Doubleday, Anchor Books, 1973), pp. 53–54.

9. François-Jean de Chastellux, *Voyages dans l'Amérique septentrionale dans les années 1780, 1781, et 1782*, 2 vols. (Paris, 1786); English version in *Travels in North America* (London, 1787). Citation from French edition, vol. 2, pp. 193 et seq.; my translation.

10. Edward Long, *History of Jamaica*, 3 vols. (London, 1774); Bryan Edwards, *History, Civil and Commercial, of the British Colonies in the West Indies*, 5 vols. (London, 1793).

11. Baron Alexandre de Wimpffen, *Voyage à St-Domingue*, cited in Placide David, *L'Héritage colonial en Haiti* (Madrid, 1959), p. 85.

12. Père Labat, *Nouveau voyage aux Îles de l'Amérique* (Paris, 1722); *Lady Nugent's Jour-*

nal; Edwards, *History. Civil and Commercial*; Père Du Tertre, *Histoire générale des Antilles Habitées par les Français* (Paris, 1667-71); Friedrich H. A. von Humboldt, *The Island of Cuba* (Havana, 1831); M. G. Lewis, *Journal of a West Indian Proprietor. Kept during a Residence in the Island of Jamaica* (London, 1834); Sir Robert Hermann Schomburgk, *The History of Barbados* (London, 1848).

13. Long, *History of Jamaica*; Edwards, *History. Civil and Commercial*.

14. "Racial Mixture in Colonial American Painting," *San Juan Star*, October 31, 1976.

15. Luis Palés Matos, *Poesia, 1915-1956* (San Juan: Ediciones de la Universidad de Puerto Rico, 1968).

16. Patrick Leigh-Fermor, *The Violins of Saint-Jacques* (New York: St. Martin's Press, 1977 edition).

17. René Marqués, "El puertorriqueño dócil," in *Ensayos, 1953-1966* (Río Piedras, Puerto Rico: Editorial Antillana, 1966).

18. David Lowenthal, "The Range and Variation of Caribbean Societies," in *Social and Cultural Pluralism in the Caribbean*, ed. Vera Rubin (New York: New York Academy of Sciences, 1960), p. 789.

19. See Frank Moya-Pons, "Is There a Caribbean Consciousness?" *Americas* 31, no. 8 (August 1979).

20. Agustin de Zarate, *The Discovery and Conquest of Peru*, trans. J. M. Cohen (London: Penguin Books, 1968).

21. Hans Koning, *Columbus: His Enterprise* (New York: Monthly Review Press, 1976).

22. Samuel Eliot Morison, *The European Discovery of America: The Southern Voyages, A.D. 1492-1616* (New York: Oxford University Press, 1972). See also Daniel J. Boorstin's review of that book in *New York Times Book Review*, October 13, 1974.

23. Bernardin de Saint-Pierre, *Voyage à l'île de France* (Paris, 1818), letter xii.

24. Paul Morand, *Hiver Caraïbe* (Paris, 1928).

25. C.L.R. James, *A History of Negro Revolt* (London: FACT, 1938), pp. 84-85.

26. For Caribbean and Mediterranean underwater archaeology, see Alexander McKee, *History under the Sea* (New York: E. P. Dutton, 1968).

27. Fray Bartolomé de Las Casas, *Historia de las Indias*, 3 vols. (Mexico City and Buenos Aires: Edición Biblioteca Americana, Fondo de Cultura Economica, 1951), bk. 2, pp. 252-53, 465-66.

28. Père Du Tertre, *Histoire générale des Antilles habitées par les français* (Paris, 1667-71); Père Labat, *Voyage aux Îles d'Amerique* (Paris, 1722).

29. Las Casas, *Historia de las Indias*, bk. 3, ch. 79, pp. 92-93.

30. See, generally, Morton Scott Enslin, *Christian Beginnings* (New York and London: Harper and Brothers, 1938), and Charles Norris Cochrane, *Christianity and Classical Culture* (New York and London: Oxford University Press, 1944).

31. Ernst Troeltsch, *The Social Teaching of the Christian Churches*, trans. Olive Wyon (London: 1930; paperback ed., New York: Harper and Row, 1971).

32. Carnival.

33. Pedro C. Escabí and Elsa M. Escabí, *La Décima: Estudio etnografico de la cultura popular de Puerto Rico* (Río Piedras, Puerto Rico: Editorial Universitaria, 1976), section on "Implicaciones sociológicas," pp. 120-46.

34. Marcelino Canino Salgado, *La copla y el romance populares en la tradición oral de Puerto Rico* (San Juan: Instituto de Cultura Puertorriqueña, 1968).

35. Antonio S. Pedreira, *Insularismo* (Río Piedras, Puerto Rico: Editorial Edil, 1973). For a critical appraisal see Juan Flores, *The Insular Vision: Pedreira's Interpretation of Puerto Rican Culture* (New York: Research Foundation of the City University of New York, 1978); René Marqués, "El Puertorriqueño dócil," *Cuadernos Americanos*, January-February 1962, pp. 86-93; Vidia Naipaul, *The Middle Passage: The Caribbean Revisited* (London: André Deutsch, 1963). For a critical appraisal see Gerald Guinness, "Naipaul's Four Early Trinidad Novels," *Revista-Review Interamericana* 6, no. 4 (winter 1976-77); and essays by Karl Miller and David Omerod

in *Critics on Caribbean Literature*, ed. Edward Baugh (London: George Allen and Unwin, 1978).

36. Eric Williams, *Inward Hunger: The Education of a Prime Minister* (London: André Deutsch, 1969), p. 49.

37. Margaret Olivier, *Sydney Olivier: Letters and Selected Writings* (London: Allen and Unwin, 1948), pp. 12-13.

38. Maurice Collis, *The Journey Up: Reminiscences, 1934-68* (London: Faber and Faber, 1970).

39. Melville J. Herskovits, *The New World Negro: Selected Papers in Afroamerican Studies*, edited by Frances S. Herskovits (Bloomington: Indiana University Press, 1966); L. J. Ragatz, *Fall of the Planter Class in the British Caribbean, 1763-1833* (New York: Octagon, 1963).

40. Philip D. Curtin, *Two Jamaicas: The Role of Ideas in a Tropical Colony, 1830-1865* (Cambridge: Harvard University Press, 1955), p. xi.

41. Roland T. Ely, *Cuando reinaba su majestad el azúcar* (Buenos Aires: Editorial Sudamericana, 1963), chs. 27-30.

42. Elsa V. Goveia, *A Study on the Historiography of the British West Indies to the End of the Nineteenth Century* (Mexico City: Instituto Panamericano de Geografía e Historia, 1956), p. 167.

CHAPTER TWO

1. Henri Baudet, *Paradise on Earth: Some Thoughts on European Images of Non-European Man* (New Haven: Yale University Press, 1965), p. 6.

2. Baron Charles de Montesquieu, *L'Esprit des lois*, ch. 5, cited in Voltaire, *Dictionnaire philosophique*, s.v. "Esclaves," in Voltaire, ed. Moland (Paris, 1877-83), 18:604.

3. *The Log of Christopher Columbus' First Voyage to America in the Year 1492*, ed. J. O'H. Cosgrave (London: W. H. Allen, n.d.).

4. *The Letter of Columbus on the Discovery of America* (New York: Trustees of the Lenox Library, 1892). In Las Casas.

5. Garcilaso de la Vega, El Inca, *Comentarios reales de las Incas* (Lima: Editorial Horacio M. Urteaga, 1920).

6. Fernando Benítez, *Los primeros mejicanos: La vida criolla en el siglo XVI* (1962); English ed., *The Century after Cortes*, trans. Joan Maclean (Chicago: University of Chicago Press, 1965).

7. See *The Log of Columbus' First Voyage to America in the Year 1492* (London: W. H. Allen and Co., n.d.), p. 75.

8. Agustin de Zarate, *The Discovery and Conquest of Peru*, trans. J. M. Cohen (London: Penguin Books, 1968), p. 236.

9. Troy S. Floyd, *The Columbus Dynasty in the Caribbean, 1492-1526* (Albuquerque: University of New Mexico Press, 1973).

10. Fray Ramón Pané, *Relación acerca de las antiguedades de los indios*, ed. José Juan Arrom (Mexico City: Ediciones Siglo XXI, 1974).

11. Ibid., Las Casas and Oviedo.

12. Mercedes López-Baralt, *El mito taino: raíz y proyecciones en la amazonia continental* (Río Piedras, Puerto Rico: Ediciones Huracán, 1978), pp. 84-85. See also Jalil Sued Badillo, "Ideology and History: The Indian," in *Culture and the Puerto Ricans: Critique and Debate* (New York: Centro de Estudios Puertorriqueños, 1974), pp. 1-26.

13. Sieur de la Borde, *Relación des Caraibes* (Paris: Colección Billaine, 1694); Spanish trans. Manuel Cárdenas Ruiz, in *Revista de la Cultura Puertorriqueña*, no. 62 (January-March 1974): 117.

14. Père Du Tertre, *Histoire générale des Antilles Habitées par les Français*, (Paris, 1667-71), ch. 7, "Les Sauvages Naturels," p. 372.

15. Pierre François Xavier de Charlevoix, *Histoire de l'Île Espagnole ou de Saint Domingue* (Paris, 1730), p. 53.

16. De la Borde, *Relación des Caraïbes*, Spanish trans., pp. 14, 16, 19.

17. Martin Carrabine, S.J., *William Stanton of Belize* (New York: Jesuit Mission Press, 1932).

18. Juan Clemente Zamora Munné, *Indigenismo en la lengua de las Conquistadores*, Colección Uprex no. 51 (Río Piedras: Editorial Universitaria, Universidad de Puerto Rico, 1956). See also Manuel Alvarez Nazario, *El Influyo indígena en el español de Puerto Rico* (Río Piedras: Editorial Universitaria, Universidad de Puerto Rico, 1977).

19. Eugenio Fernández Méndez, *Art and Mythology of the Taino Indians of the Greater West Indies* (San Juan: Ediciones "El Cemi," 1972), pp. 47–48. See also Sven Loren, *Origins of the Tainian Culture, West Indies* (Gothenburg, 1935); and José Juan Arrom, *Mitología y artes prehispánicos de las Antillas* (Mexico City: Ediciones Siglo XXI, 1974).

20. For this see Robert F. Berkhofer, Jr., *The White Man's Indian: Images of the American Indian from Columbus to the Present* (New York: Alfred A. Knopf, 1978).

21. J. A. Fernández-Santamaría, *The State, War, and Peace: Spanish Political Thought in the Renaissance* (Cambridge: At the University Press, 1977).

22. For Vitoria, see Camilo Barcia Trelles, *Francisco de Vitoria: Fundador de derecho internacional moderno* (Valladolid, Spain: Sección de Estudios Americanistas, Universidad de Valladolid, 1954). Also by the same author, *Internacionalistas españoles del siglo XVI: Francisco Suarez* (Valladolid, Spain: Sección de Estudios Americanistas, Universidad de Valladolid, 1956).

23. "Letter of Columbus to the Nurse of the Prince Don John," in Eric Williams, ed., *Documents of West Indian History, 1492–1655* (Port-of-Spain, Trinidad: People's National Movement Publishing Co., 1963), p. 36.

24. López de Velasco, *Geografía y descripción natural de las Indias* (Madrid, 1571–74), cited in Williams, *Documents of West Indian History*. p. 41.

25. Francisco López de Gómara, *Historia general de las Indias* (Madrid: Editorial Calpe, 1922), p. ix.

26. Fernando de Oviedo y Valdés, *Historia general y natural de las Indias, islas y Tierra Firme del mar océano* (Madrid, 1555–57). See also Edición Amador de los Ríos, 8 vols. (Madrid: Spanish Royal Academy of History, 1851–55).

27. Ibid., 1851–55 edition, bk, 3, ch. 6, vol. 1, pp. 142–46.

28. Antonio de Herrera, *Historia general de los hechos de los Castellanos en los Islas y Tierra Firme del mar océano* (Madrid, 1601–15).

29. Speech of Fray Tomás Ortiz to Council of the Indies, 1512, cited ibid., decada 3, bk. 8, ch. 10, vol. 5, pp. 31–32.

30. Report of the Jerónomite Commission to Cardinal Cisneros, 1516, cited in Alejandro Tapia y Rivera, *Biblioteca histórica de Puerto Rico* (San Juan: Instituto de Literatura Puertorriqueña, 1945), pp. 216–19.

31. Juan Gines de Sepúlveda, *Democrates Alter* (Madrid, 1542), cited in Lewis Hanke, *La lucha española por la justicia en la conquista de América* (Madrid: Editorial Aguilar, 1949) p. 335.

32. Lewis Hanke, *La lucha española*. See also his *Bartolomé de Las Casas, Historian* (Gainesville: University of Florida Press, 1952).

33. Juan Friede, *Bartolomé de Las Casas: Precursor del anticolonialismo* (Mexico City: Ediciones Siglo XXI, 1974) pp. 11–12.

34. Prologue to Fray Bartolomé de Las Casas, *Historia de las Indias*, 3 vols. (Mexico City: Fondo de Cultura Economica, 1951).

35. Ibid., bk. 3, chs. 142–46, vol. 3.

36. Bartolomé de Las Casas, *Brevísima relación de la destrucción de las Indias Occidentales* (Philadelphia, 1821), introduction by Gervando Teresa de Mier Noriega y Guerra.

37. Las Casas, *Historia de las Indias*, bk. 2, chs. 13–14, vol. 2, pp. 240–57.

38. Cited in Williams, *Documents of West Indian History*, p. 144.

39. Las Casas, *Historia de las Indias*, vol. 2, pp. 554–56; ibid., bk. 2, ch. 42, vol. 2, pp. 344–45.

40. Ibid., bk. 3, chs. 142–46, vol. 3, pp. 320–36, and vol. 2, pp. 326–30.

41. Ibid., vol. 1, pp. 391-92.

42. Ibid., bk. 3, ch. 149, vol. 3, pp. 342-44; my translation.

43. Ibid., bk. 1, ch. 46, vol. 1, pp. 232-33.

44. Friede, *Bartolomé de Las Casas*, ch. 6.

45. Hanke, *Bartolomé de Las Casas, Historian*, p. 6.

46. Agustin Cueva, "Historia, ideología, y lucha de clases: A propositio del 'asunto' Las Casas," mimeographed (Mexico City: n.p., n.d.).

47. Luis Muñoz Rivera, *La Democracia* (San Juan) October 28, 1911, cited in Gordon K. Lewis, *Puerto Rico: Freedom and Power in the Caribbean* (New York: Monthly Review Press, 1963), p. 547.

48. Friede, *Bartolomé de Las Casas*. See also, for the accumulated work on Las Casas, Julio Le Riverend, "Problemas históricas de la Conquista de America: Las Casas y su tiempo," mimeographed (Havana, n.d.); Alejandro Lipschutz, "La vision profética de Fray Bartolomé de Las Casas y los rumbos étnicos de nuestro tiempo," ch. 7 in his *Marx y Lenin en la América Latina y los problemas indigenistas* (Havana: Casa de las Américas, 1974); *Bartolomé de Las Casas (1474-1974) e historia de la iglesia en América Latina* (Mexico City: Comisión de Estudios de Historia de la Iglesia in Latinoamerica, 1976); Marcel Bataillon, *Estudios sobre Bartolomé de Las Casas* (Barcelona: Editorial Península, 1976); Marcel Bataillon and André Saint-Lu, *Las Casas et la défense des Indiens* (Paris: Julliard, 1971).

49. Alberto M. Salas, *Tres cronistas de Indias* (Mexico City: Fondo de Cultura Economica, 1959).

50. Eladio Rodriguez Otero, "Tainos, negros y españoles," *El Mundo* (San Juan), July 26, 1975. For the growth of the anti-Las Casas *leyenda negra* see Rómulo Carbia, *Historia de la leyenda-negra hispanoamericana* (Madrid: Consejo de Hispanidad, 1944), and Ramón Menéndez Pidal, *El Padre Las Casas: Su doble personalidad* (Madrid: España-Calpe, 1963).

51. José Antonio Maravall, "El descubrimiento de América en la historia del pensamiento político," *Revista de Estudios Politicos* 43, no. 63 (1952): 229-48.

52. Fernández-Santamaría, *The State*, pp. 75-80.

53. Ibid., pp. 87-92.

54. See ibid., pp. 196-236.

55. Partido Independentista Puertorriqueño, *Pedro Albizu Campos: Vida y pensamiento*, Editorial de Educación Política, vol. 1, no. 1 (San Juan: n.d.); and Federico Ribes Tovar, *Albizu Campos: el revolucionario* (New York: Plus Ultra Educational Publishers, 1971).

56. Max Henriquez Ureña, "Desarrollo histórico de la cultura en la América Española durante la epoca colonial," in his *El Retorno de los galeones* (Madrid: Compañía Ibero-Americana de Publicaciones, 1930), pp. 97-114.

57. Ibid., pp. 87-96.

58. Erwin Walter Palm, *Arquitectura y arte colonial en Santo Domingo* (Santo Domingo: Editora de la Universidad Autónoma de Santo Domingo, 1974).

59. Robert Johnson, *Nova Britannia* (London, 1609), cited in K. E. Knorr, *British Colonial Theories, 1570-1850* (Toronto: Ashton, 1944), p. 43.

60. Thomas Gage, *The English-American: A New Survey of the West Indies*, ed. Arthur Percival Newton (London: George Routledge, 1928).

61. Oliver Cromwell, Commission of the Commissioners for the West Indian Expedition, December 9, 1654, cited in C. H. Firth, ed., *The Narrative of General Venables* (London: Royal Historical Society, 1900), pp. 112-14.

62. Henry Whistler, "A Journal of Admiral Penn's Expedition to the West Indies, 1654-1655," Sloane ms. 3926 (London), reprinted in *Journal of the Institute of Jamaica*, vol. 2 (Kingston, Jamaica, 1899).

63. Richard Hakluyt, *The Principal Navigations, Voyages, Traffiques, and Discoveries of the English Nation* (London, 1599; reprint ed., London, 1927) pp. 303-4.

64. William Camden, *Annales Rerum Anglicarum et Hibernicarum regante Elizabetha* (London, 1615), cited in Williams, *Documents of West Indian History*, p. 208.

65. Charles de Rochefort, *Histoire naturelle et morale des Antilles de l'Amérique* (Rotter-

dam, 1658)—translated into English by John Davies as *History of the Caribby Islands* (London, 1666); Du Tertre, *Histoire Générale des Antilles*; Père Labat, *Nouveau voyage aux Isles de l'Amérique* (Paris, 1722).

66. De Rochefort, *History of the Caribby Islands*, p. 250.
67. Ibid., pp. 225–40.
68. Ibid., p. 250.
69. Du Tertre, *Histoire générale des Antilles*, pp. 358, 372.
70. De la Borde, *Relación des Caraïbes*, p. 15.
71. Jacques Petitjean-Roget, ed., "Un manuscrit sur la Grenade," *Archives Antillaises*, 1973, p. 12.
72. Rochefort, *History of the Caribby Islands*, p. 202.
73. Du Tertre, *Histoire générale des Antilles*, pp. 520–25.
74. Ibid., pp. 501–2.
75. Ibid., pp. 534–35.
76. Labat, *Nouveau voyage*, p. 66.
77. Preface to Rochefort, *History of the Caribby Islands*.
78. Du Tertre, *Histoire générale des Antilles*, p. 456.
79. Labat, *Nouveau voyage*, preface.
80. Ibid., pp. ix–xxx.
81. Rochefort, *History of the Caribby Islands*, p. 202; Du Tertre, *Histoire générale des Antilles*, pp. 504, 474.
82. Oviedo, *Historia general*, bk. 33, vol. 3.
83. Henry Whistler, "An Account of Barbados in 1654," in N. C. Connell, "An Extract from Henry Whistler's Journal of West Indian Expedition under the Date 1654," *Journal of the Barbados Historical Society* (1938): 5.
84. Du Tertre, *Histoire générale des Antilles*, pp. 382, 472–76.
85. Labat, *Nouveau voyage*, pp. 116–25, 172, 227–29.
86. Richard Ligon, *A True and Exact History of the Island of Barbados* (London, 1657, 1673; reprint ed., London: Frank Cass, 1970). See also Jill Sheppard, *The 'Redlegs' of Barbados* (Millwood, N.Y.: KTO Press, 1977).
87. Richard B. Sheridan, "The Rise of a Colonial Gentry: A Case Study of Antigua, 1730–1775." *Economic History Review* 20, no. 3 (April 1961):342–57.
88. Royal Edict 1672 by Governor Iversen, cited in J. Antonio Jarvis, *Brief History of the Virgin Islands* (St. Thomas: Art Shop, 1938), pp. 33–35.
89. Dr. E. Rufz, *Etudes historiques et statistiques sur la population de Martinique* (St. Pierre, Martinique: 1850), cited in Lafcadio Hearn, *Two Years in the French West Indies* (New York and London: Harper and Brothers, 1900), p. 163.
90. Eli F. Heckscher, *Mercantilism*, trans. Mendel Shapiro, 2 vols., ed. (London: Allen and Unwin, 1955), 41.
91. Herrera, *Historia general*, 4, bk. 6, ch. 13, vol. 5, pp. 323–27, cited in Williams, *Documents of West Indian History*, pp. 169–71.
92. "Memorial of the Attorneys of New Spain to Charles V...June 1545," cited in Hanke, *La lucha por la justicia en la conquista española de América*, pp. 233–34.
93. Isabel Gutierrez de Arroyo, *Historiografía Puertorriqueña* (San Juan: Instituto de Cultura Puertorriqueña, 1956), pp. 1–4.
94. *Memoria Melgarejo* (1582), in Eugenio Fernández-Méndez, *Crónicas de Puerto Rico* (San Juan: Editorial Universidad de Puerto Rico, 1976), pp. 107–34.
95. Diego de Torres Vargas, *Descripción de la Isla y Ciudad de Puerto Rico* (1647) in Fernández Méndez, *Crónicas*, pp. 171–217.
96. *Carta del Obispo Fray Damián López de Haro, 1644*, in Fernández Méndez, *Crónicas*, pp. 157–69.
97. *The Groans of the Plantations...*(London, 1689), noted in H. Ling Roth, *A Guide to the Literature of Sugar* (London: Kegan Paul, Trench, Trubner and Co., 1890), p. 118; *A Discourse*

on the Duties on Merchandise...(London, 1695), noted ibid., p. 101; *The Interest of the Nation*...(London, 1691), noted ibid., p. 119; *The State of the Case of the Sugar Plantations in America*...(London, 1691), noted ibid., p. 120; *Case of the Refiners of Sugar in England Stated* (London, 1695), noted ibid., p. 117.

98. Richard Pares, *Yankees and Creoles: The Trade between North America and the West Indies before the American Revolution* (New York: Longmans, Green, 1956).

99. Dalby Thomas, *An Historical Account of the Rise and Growth of the West Indian Colonies* (London, 1690).

100. "A Declaration of Lord Willoughby and the Legislature of the Island of Barbados against the British Parliament," cited in R. H. Schomburgh, *The History of Barbados* (London, 1848), pp. 706–8.

101. N. Darnell Davis, *The Cavaliers and Roundheads of Barbados, 1650–1652* (Georgetown, British Guiana: Argosy Press, 1887), ch. 11, "A Declaration of Independence."

102. Du Tertre, *Histoire générale des Antilles*, 1:18–20, 270–71, 295.

103. Paul Boyer, *Veritable Relation de tout ce qui s'est fait et passé au voyage que Monsieur de Bretigny fit à l'Amérique Occidentale* (Paris, 1654); J. de Clodore, *Relation de ce qui c'est passé dans les Îles et Terre Ferme de l'Amérique*...(Paris, 1671).

104. Judge Littleton, cited in John Oldmixon, *The British Empire in America* (1741), 2 vols., Reprints of Economic Classics (New York: Augustus M. Kelley, Publishers, 1969), 1:xxii–xxiii.

105. Ibid., *The British Empire*, 1:xvi–xix.

106. Du Tertre, *Histoire générale des Antilles*, pp. 456–58.

107. Pierre François Xavier de Charlevoix, cited in Charles Frostin, *Les révoltes blanches à Saint-Domingue aux XVIIe et XVIIIe siècles* (Paris: L'Ecole, 1975), pp. 195–96; V. B. Dubuisson, *Nouveaux considérations sur l'état présent de Saint-Domingue*, 2 vols. (Paris, 1779), 1:7.

108. George Fox, *Gospel Family Order, being a short discourse covering the Order of Families, both of whites, Blacks, and Indians*, Barbados meeting house 1671 (London, 1676), pp. 7, 13, 14, 22; *A Journal of the Life, Travels, Sufferings, and Labour of Love in Work of the Ministry of William Edmundson* (London, 1829).

109. Jacob P. M. Andrade, *A Record of the Jews in Jamaica from the English Conquest to the Present Time* (Kingston: *Jamaica Times*, 1941); and Isaac S. Emmanuel and Susan A. Emmanuel, *History of the Jews of the Netherlands Antilles*, 2 vols. (Cincinnati: American Jewish Archives, 1970).

110. John Taylor, *Multum in Parvo* (1688), vol. 2, Ms. 105, Taylor Mss., Institute of Jamaica, Kingston; Morgan Godwyn, *The Negro's and Indian's Advocate, Suing for Their Admission into the Church*...(London, 1680).

111. Vincent T. Harlow, *Christopher Codrington, 1668–1710* (London: Oxford University Press, 1928); and Frank J. Klingberg, ed., *Codrington Chronicle: An Experiment in Anglican Altruism on a Barbados Plantation, 1710–1834* (Berkeley and Los Angeles: University of California Press, 1949).

112. Thomas G. Mathews, "African Presence in Seventeenth Century Puerto Rican Religious Ceremonies," mimeographed (San Juan, n.d.).

113. C. H. Haring, *The Buccaneers in the West Indies in the Seventeenth Century* (New York: E. P. Dutton, 1910).

114. Esquemeling, *The Buccaneers and Marooners of America*, ed. Howard Pyle (London: T. Fisher Unwin, 1892), translator's preface, p. 45.

115. Ibid., p. 90.

116. Cited in Gilles Lapouge, *Los piratas* (Barcelona: Editorial Estela, 1971), pp. 76–77.

117. Cited in George Woodbury, *The Great Days of Piracy in the West Indies* (New York: W. W. Norton and Company, 1951), pp. 77–80.

118. Esquemeling, *Buccaneers and Marooners*, pp. 197–98.

119. Lapouge, *Los Piratas*, p. 96.

120. Lipschutz, *Marx y Lenin*, pp. 144–48.

121. Quoted in Esquemeling, *Buccaneers and Marooners*, p. 402.

122. Frederick Jackson Turner, "The Frontier in American History," reprinted in *American Issues* (New York: J. B. Lippincott, 1944), p. 674.

123. William Dampier, "Two Voyages to Campeachy," in *Voyages and Descriptions*, 2d ed. (London, 1726), vol. 2, pt. 2. See also O. Nigel Bolland, *The Formation of a Colonial Society: Belize, from Conquest to Crown Colony* (Baltimore: Johns Hopkins University Press, 1977), ch. 3.

124. Margaret Olivier, *Sydney Olivier, Letters and Selected Writings* (London: Allen and Unwin, 1948), ch. 4.

125. Geoffroy Atkinson, *Les relations de voyages du XVIIe siècle et l'évolution des idées* (Paris: Librairie Edouard Champion, n.d.); W. Stark, *America: Ideal and Reality* (London: Kegan Paul, Trench, Trubner and Co., 1947); and Hugh Honour, *The New Golden Land: European Images of America from the Discoveries to the Present Time* (New York: Pantheon, 1975).

126. Pedro Mártir de Anglería, *Décadas del Nuevo Mundo* (1539; reprint ed., Buenos Aires: Ed. Baziel, 1944).

127. Introduction by Edmundo O'Gorman and Miguel Leon Portilla to Bartolomé de Las Casas, *Apologetica Historia Sumaria* (Mexico City, 1967).

128. Atkinson, *Les Relations*, ch. 3.

129. Rochefort, *History of the Caribby Islands*, ch. 9.

130. Baron de La Houten, *Suite de voyage de l'Amérique en Dialogues de M. de Baron La Houten et d'un sauvage de l'Amérique* (Amsterdam: Boeteman, 1718).

131. German Arciniegas, "Voltaire y America Salvaje," *El Mundo* (San Juan), November 25, 1978.

132. Partido Socialista Puertorriqueño, *Claridad* (San Juan), March 30, 1976.

133. Bartolomé de Las Casas, *Historia de las Indias*, bk. 3, ch. 88, vol. 3, pp. 123-30.

134. Friede, *Bartolomé de Las Casa*, pp. 155-56, 182-88.

135. Claude Couffon, "La Literatura hispanoamericana vista desde Francia," in *Panorama de la Actual Literatura Lationoamericana* (Havana: Casa de las Americas, 1969), pp. 224-25.

136. Oldmixon, *The British Empire*, 1:27.

137. A. P. Newton, *The Colonizing Activities of the English Puritans: The Last Phase of the Elizabethan Struggle with Spain* (New York: Kennikat Press, 1966).

138. Oldmixon, *The British Empire*, 2:124-25.

139. Cited in Herbert S. Klein, *Slavery in the Americas: A Comparative Study of Cuba and Virginia* (Chicago: University of Chicago Press, 1967), pp. 91-94.

140. Cited in Antoine Gisler, C.S.S.P., *L'Esclavage aux Antilles Françaises (XVIIe-XIXe siècle)* (Fribourg: Editions Universitaires, 1965), pp. 152-57.

141. Sylvia Wynter, "Bernardo de Balbuena, Epic Poet and Abbot of Jamaica, 1568-1627," *Jamaica Journal* 3, nos. 3, 4; 4, nos. 1, 3 (1969, 1970); Diego de Torres Vargas, *Descripción de la Isla*, pp. 174-75.

142. *The Memoirs of Père Labat, 1693-1705* (1722), trans. and abridged English version by John Eaden (London: Frank Cass, 1970), p. 122.

143. Lewis Hanke, Prologue to Las Casas, *Historia de las Indias*.

144. Irving Leonard, *Books of the Brave* (New York: Gordian, 1949).

145. Elsa V. Goveia, *A Study on the Historiography of the British West Indies to the End of the Nineteenth Century* (Mexico City: Instituto Panamericano de Geografia e Historia, 1956), p. 171.

146. Père Labat, cited in George Lamming, "The New World of the Caribbean," radio script, program 4, mimeographed (Georgetown, British Guiana: Public Library Archives, 1957).

CHAPTER THREE

1. J. E. Cairnes, cited in Karl Marx, *Capital* (London: George Allen and Unwin, 1938), 1:251-52.

2. Herman J. Niebohr, *Slavery as an Industrial System: Ethnological Researches*, B. Franklin Research and Source Works Series, no. 770 (London, 1971).

3. Karl Marx, in *Correspondence of Marx and Engels* (London: Marxist-Leninist Library, Lawrence and Wishart, 1941), p. 14.

4. Eric Williams, *Capitalism and Slavery* (Chapel Hill: University of North Carolina Press, 1944). See also Roger Anstey, *The Atlantic Slave Trade and British Abolition, 1760–1810* (Atlantic Highlands, N.J.: Humanities Press, 1975).

5. Cited in Williams, *Capitalism and Slavery*, p. 19.

6. Cairnes cited in Niebohr, *Slavery as an Industrial System*, p. 303.

7. Jill Sheppard, *The "Redlegs" of Barbados: Their Origins and History* (Millwood, N.Y.: KTO Press, 1977), ch. 5.

8. Preface to *Historical Essay on the Colony of Surinam, 1788*, ed. Jacob R. Marcus and Stanley F. Chyet (Cincinnati: American Jewish Archives, 1974).

9. Ibid., pp. 66–73.

10. Ibid., p. 36.

11. Charles de Rochefort, *Histoire naturelle et morale des Antilles de l'Amérique* (Rotterdam, 1658)—translated into English by John Davies as *History of the Caribby Islands* (London, 1666).

12. Henry Raup Wagner, *The Life and Writings of Bartolomé de Las Casas* (Albuquerque: University of New Mexico Press, 1967), p. 221.

13. Winthrop D. Jordan, *White over Black: American Attitudes Toward the Negro, 1550–1812* (Baltimore: Penguin Books, 1969), chs. 1, 2.

14. Fray Bernardino de Minaya, *Memorial to Charles V* (n.d.), cited in Eric Williams, ed., *Documents of West Indian History, 1492–1655* (Port-of-Spain, Trinidad: People's National Movement Publishing Co., 1963), p. 136.

15. Fernando de Oviedo y Valdés, *Historia general y natural de las Indias* (Madrid, 1535–1556), cited ibid., pp. 111–13.

16. Bartolomé de Las Casas, *Historia de las Indias* (Mexico City: Fondo de Cultura Económico, 1951), cited ibid., p. 141.

17. Cited in Wagner, *Life and Writings of Las Casas*, p. 11.

18. Alonzo Zuazo, Judge of Hispaniola, to Cardinal Ximenes, Regent of Spain, January 22, 1518, cited in Williams, *Documents of West Indian History*, pp. 144–45.

19. Diego de Salamanca, Bishop of San Juan, to Philip II, King of Spain, April 6, 1579, cited ibid., p. 144.

20. *Ordenanzas para el cabildo y regimiento de la villa de la Habana y las demás villas y lugares de esta isla que hizo y ordeno el ilustre Sr. Dr. Alonso de Caceres, oidor de la dicha Audiencia real de la ciudad...*, January 14, 1574, cited ibid., pp. 153–54.

21. Quoted in Wagner, *The Life and Writings of Las Casas*, p. 247.

22. Bartolomé de Albornoz, *Arte de los Contratos* (Valencia, 1573), quoted in Williams, *Documents of West Indian History*, p. 161.

23. Fray Tomás Mercado, *Suma de Tratos y Contratos* (Seville, 1587), cited ibid., pp. 158–60.

24. Fray Alonso de Sandoval, *De Instauranda Aethiopum Salute* (Seville, 1627), quoted ibid., p. 163.

25. Samuel Purchas, *Purchas his Pilgrimage. Or Relations of the World and the Religions Observed in all Ages and Places Discovered, from the Creation unto This present* (London, 1614), cited in Jordan, *White over Black*, pp. 12–13.

26. Thomas Atwood, *The History of the Island of Dominica* (London, 1791, reprint ed., London: Frank Cass and Co., 1971).

27. Sir William Young, *An Account of the Black Charaibs in the Island of St. Vincent's* (London, 1795).

28. R. C. Dallas, *History of the Maroons*, 2 vols. (London, 1803). 1:viii, 87–95.

29. Ibid., 1:148.

30. Ibid., 1:45.

31. Ibid., 1:180–81.

32. Ibid., 2:2–3.

33. Atwood, *History of the Island*, p. 267; Dallas, *History of the Maroons*, 2:453–54.

34. Bryan Edwards, *The History, Civil and Commercial, of the British West Indies*, 5 vols. (London, 1819), 1:522–79.

35. Lowell Joseph Ragatz, *A Guide for the Study of British Caribbean History, 1763–1834, Including the Abolition and Emancipation Movements* (Washington, D.C.: U.S. Government Printing Office, 1932).

36. John Luffman, *A Brief Account of the Island of Antigua, 1786–1788* (London, 1789), reprinted in Vere Langford Oliver, *History of the Island of Antigua*, 3 vols. (London: Mitchell and Hughes, 1894), pp. cxxviii–cxxxviii; Richard Schomburgk, *Travels in British Guiana, 1840–1844*, ed. Vincent Roth (Georgetown, British Guiana: Guiana edition, *Daily Chronicle*, 1953), 1:47; noted in Roland T. Ely, *Cuando reinaba su majestad el azúcar* (Buenos Aires: Editorial Sudamericana, 1963), ch. 28.

37. Edward Long, *History of Jamaica*, 3 vols. (London, 1774, reprint ed., London: Frank Cass and Co., 1970), 1:25.

38. Ibid., 2:324.

39. Ibid., 1:25.

40. Ibid., 2:354, 398.

41. Ibid., 2:271.

42. Ibid., 2:407.

43. Ibid., 2:429–30.

44. Ibid., 2:375.

45. Ibid., 2:326–27, 332–33.

46. Ibid., 2:393–94, 400–404.

47. Ibid., 1:4.

48. Ibid., vol. 2, ch. 4.

49. Edwards, *History of the British West Indies*, 2:93–94.

50. Ibid., 3:13, 2:179.

51. Ibid., 2:124–28, 140–44.

52. Ibid., 2:148–49.

53. Ibid., 2:169–70.

54. Eric Williams, ed., *The British West Indies at Westminster*. Part 1:*1789–1823* (Port-of-Spain, Trinidad: Historical Society of Trinidad and Tobago, Government Printing Office, 1954).

55. John Stewart, *A View of the Past and Present State of the Island of Jamaica* (1823; reprint ed., Westport, Conn.: Negro Universities Press, 1969), p. 205.

56. Rev. John Riland, ed., *Memoirs of a West Indian Planter* (London, 1827); and note in Ragatz, *Guide for the Study of British Caribbean History*, pp. 232–33.

57. *A report of a committee of the Council of Barbados, appointed to inquire into the actual conditions of the slaves in this island…*(1824), in *West Indian Slavery: Selected Pamphlets* (Westport, Conn.: Negro Universities Press, 1970), pp. 6–9; Wm. Beckford, *A Descriptive Account of the Island of Jamaica*, 2 vols. (London, 1790).

58. James Hakewell, *A picturesque tour of the Island of Jamaica…*(London, 1825).

59. Edwards, *History of the British West Indies*, vol. 2, app. 1, bk. 4, pp. 187–225.

60. Alexander Barclay, *A Practical View of the Present State of Slavery in the West Indies*, 2d ed. (London, 1827), p. 42; J. F. Barham, *Considerations on the Abolition of Negro Slavery and the Means of Practically Effecting It* (1823), in *West Indian Slavery: Selected Pamphlets*, p. 9.

61. G. W. Jordan, *An Examination of the Principles of the Slave Registry Bill and of the Means of Emancipation* (1816), in *West Indian Slavery: Selected Pamphlets*, pp. 43–46, 61–66, 68–70, 75–84.

62. Elsa Goveia, *Slave Society in the British Leeward Islands at the End of the Eighteenth Century* (New Haven: Yale University Press, 1965; reprint ed., Río Piedras: Institute of Caribbean Studies, University of Puerto Rico, 1969), p. 330; Eric Williams, *Capitalism and Slavery* (Chapel Hill: University of North Carolina Press, 1944), pp. 184–85.

63. *A Report of a Committee* (1824), pp. 30–31.

64. Edwards, *An Historical Survey of the French Colony of St. Domingo*, vol. 3 in *History of the British West Indies*, pp. 208–10.

65. Beckford, *Descriptive Account of Jamaica*, p. 6.

66. Stewart, *View of Jamaica*, pp. 181–82.

67. Henry Bleby, *Death Struggles of Slavery*, 3d ed. (London, 1868), ch. 11, "Pernicious Influence of a Licentious Press."

68. Edwards, *History of the British West Indies*, 3:208–9.

69. Beaumont, cited in Bleby, *Death Struggles*, p. 27.

70. Beckford, *Descriptive Account of Jamaica*, pp. 117, 48.

71. *A report of a committee* (1824), p. 40.

72. Williams, *Documents of West Indian History*, p. 244.

73. G. W. Jordan, *The Claims of the West India Colonists to the Right of Obtaining Necessary Supplies from America*...(1804), noted in Ragatz, *A Guide*, pp. 301–2; and Bryan Edwards, *Thoughts on the Late Proceedings of Government, Respecting the Trade of the West India Islands with the United States of America* (1784), noted ibid., p. 292.

74. Edwards, *History of the British West Indies* 2:281.

75. Barham, *Considerations*, p. 27.

76. Barclay, *A Practical View*, p. 15.

77. Edwards, *History of the British West Indies* 2:163–64; Wm. Beckford, *Remarks upon the Situation of the Negroes in Jamaica*, noted in Ragatz, *A Guide*, p. 479; *The Condition of the West Indian Slave Contrasted with That of the Infant Slave in Our English Factories* (London, c. 1833), noted ibid., p. 420.

78. J. L. Hammond and Barbara Hammond, *The Rise of Modern Industry* (London: Methuen and Co., 1944), ch. 12.

79. Abbé de Mably, *Recherches historiques et politiques sur les Etats-Unis de l'Amérique septentrionale* (1788), cited in W. Stark, *America: Ideal and Reality* (London: Kegan Paul, Trench, Trubner and Co., 1947), p. 48; John Ludlow, *Progress of the Working Class* (London, 1867), cited in Gordon K. Lewis, *Slavery, Imperialism, and Freedom: Essays in English Radical Thought* (New York and London: Monthly Review Press, 1978), p. 184.

80. A. Pons, *Observations sur la situation politique de St-Domingue*, cited in Placide David, *L'Heritage colonial en Haité* (Madrid, 1959), p. 279; Baron Alexandre de Wimpffen, *A Voyage to Santo Domingo in the Years 1788, 1789, and 1790*, English edition, cited ibid., p. 279.

81. Baron Alexandre de Wimpffen, *Voyage à St-Domingue*, letter 22, p. 277; Hilliard d'Auberteuil, *Considérations sur l'état présent de la colonie française de Saint-Domingue*, 2 vols. (Paris, 1776–77), vol. 1, Discours preliminaire; Médéric-Louis-Elie Moreau de Saint-Méry, *Description topographique, physique, civil, politique, et historique de la partie française de l'île Saint-Domingue*, 3 vols. (Philadelphia, 1797), 1:2.

82. Victor Advielle, *L'Odyssée d'un Normand à St-Domingue au dix-huitième siècle* (Paris: Librarie Chaltanel, 1901).

83. Wimpffen, *Voyage à St-Domingue*, letter 10, p. 103; Pons, *Observations*, p. 3.

84. A. De Lauzon, *Souvenirs de trente années de voyage à Saint-Domingue*, cited in David, *L'Héritage colonial*, pp. 48–50; Comte d'Ennery, cited in d'Auberteuil, *Considérations*, vol. 2, Discours preliminaire.

85. Wimpffen, *Voyage à St-Domingue*, letter 22; Moreau de Saint-Méry, *Description*, 3: 227–31.

86. Moreau de Saint-Méry, *Description*, pp. 227–31.

87. Adam Smith, *The Wealth of Nations* (London: Everyman's Library, 1917), bk. 4, pt. 2, pp. 84–85.

88. Cited in Antoine Gisler, *L'esclavage aux Antilles Françaises, XVII–XVIII siècle* (Fribourg: Editions Universitaires, 1965), pp. 117–21.

89. Noted in C.L.R. James, *The Black Jacobins* (London: Secker and Warburg, 1938), p. 30.

90. Noted in P. Boissonade, *Saint Domingue à la veille de la Révolution* (Paris and New York: Librarie G. E. Stechert and Co., 1906), pp. 33–34. See also James G. Leyburn, *The Haitian People* (New Haven: Yale University Press, 1942), pp. 17–20.

91. Girod-Chantrans, *Voyage d'un Suisse dans differentes colonies d'Amérique* (Neufchatel, 1785), cited in David, *L'Héritage colonial*, p. 87; Moreau de Saint-Méry, *Description*, cited ibid., p. 87.

92. Wimpffen, *Voyage à St-Domingue*, pp. 54–55.

93. Cited in Adveille, *L'odyssée*, p. 142.

94. *Moreau de Saint-Méry: American Journey, 1793–1798*, trans. and ed. Kenneth Roberts and Anna M. Roberts (Garden City, N.Y.: Doubleday and Co., 1947).

95. Moreau de Saint-Méry, *Description*, 3 vols. (Paris: Theodore Morgand, Librarie-Dépositaire, 1875), 3:216–18.

96. Ibid., 1:7–8, 11–12.

97. Ibid., 1:17–18, 20–27.

98. Ibid., 1:79–82.

99. Ibid., 1:15–16.

100. Ibid., 1:82.

101. Ibid., 1:83–89, 82.

102. Ibid., 1:27–46.

103. Pierre de Charlevoix, *Histoire de l'île Espagnoleou de St-Domingue* (Paris, 1730–31); Malenfant, *Des Colonies et particuliérement de cette de Saint-Domingue* (Paris, 1814).

104. Moreau de Saint-Méry, *Description*, 1:51.

105. Ibid., vol. 1, Discours preliminaire.

106. D'Auberteuil, *Considérations*, 1:4–5.

107. Ibid., 1:136–37, 130–33.

108. Ibid., 1:143, 133, 135.

109. Ibid., 1:132.

110. Charlevoix, *Histoire de l'île espagnole*, 1:496–97.

111. Paul Ulric Dubuisson, *Nouvelles considérations sur Saint-Domingue* (Paris, 1790), 1:6, 146–47, 154–56.

112. Ibid., 1:69, 72–73, 77–78.

113. Ibid., 1:80–81.

114. Ibid., 1:83–84.

115. Ibid., 1:67–68, 69.

116. Moreau de Saint-Méry, debate of May 7, 1791, *Moniteur Universel* (Paris), edition of 1853–63, pp. viii, 333–36, cited in Charles Oscar Hardy, *The Negro Question in the French Revolution* (Menasha, Wis.: George Banta Publishing Company, 1919), p. 45.

117. Pierre Boissonade, *Saint-Domingue à la veille de la Révolution et la question de la représentation coloniale aux Etats Generaux* (Paris: Paul Geuthner, 1906), p. 36.

118. Moreau de Saint-Méry, *Considérations présentées aux vrais amis du repos et du bonheur de la France* (1791), cited in Boissonade, *Saint-Domingue*, p. 42.

119. Boissonade, *Saint-Domingue*, pp. 166–67.

120. *Il est encore des Aristocrates, ou Réponse a l'infame auteur d'un Ecrit institué: Decouverte d'un conspiration contre les intérêts de la France* (Paris, 1790), pp. 3–4; reprinted in Ediciones d'Histoire Sociales (EDHIS), *La Révolution française et l'abolition de l'esclavage*, 12 vols. (Paris: EDHIS, 1968), vol. 4.

121. M. Gregoire, *Lettre aux citoyens de couleur et Nègres libres de Saint-Domingue* (Paris, 1791), p. 19; reprinted in EDHIS, *La Révolution Française*, vol. 4.

122. Louis-Marthe Gouy d'Aray, *Première et dernière lettre à Jean Pierre Brissot* (Paris, 1791), p. 11.

123. Armand Guy-Kersaint, *Moyens proposés à l'Assemblée Nationale pour rétablir la paix et l'ordre dans les colonies* (Paris, 1792); reprinted in EDHIS, *La Révolution française*, vol. 5; Gregoire, *Lettre*, pp. 14–15.

124. Cited in Hardy, *The Negro Question*, pp. 38–40.

125. Olympe de Gouge, *Réponse au champion américain ou colon très-aisé à connaître* (Paris, 1790), p. 5; reprinted in EDHIS, *La Révolution française*, vol. 4.

126. *Mémoire instructif à consulter et consultation* (1788), cited in Boissonade, *Saint-Domingue*, pp. 115–16.

127. "Lettre des colons résident *à Saint-Domingue au Roi*" (May 1788), Bibliothèque Nationale, Paris, bk. 12, vol. 23.

128. *Lettre des commissaires de la colonie de Saint-Domingue aux présidents des Bureaux de l'Association des Notables* (November 1788), cited in Boissonade, *Saint-Domingue*, pp. 123–24.

129. Boissonade, *Saint-Domingue*, pp. 95–97.

130. Ibid., pp. 95–96, 118–19.

131. Hardy, *The Negro Question*, pp. 34–35; Boissonade, *Saint-Domingue*, pp. 74–76.

132. Abbé Sibire, *L'Aristocracie négriere* (Paris, 1789), reprinted in EDHIS, *La Révolution française*, vol. 2; and Lecointe-Marsillac, *Le More-Lack* (Paris, 1789), reprinted (ibid.,) vol. 3.

133. Abbé Antoine de Cournand, *Requête présentée à Nos Seigneurs de l'Assemblée Nationale, en faveur des gens de couleur de l'île de Saint-Domingue* (Paris, 1790), p. 5, reprinted in EDHIS, *La Révolution Française*, vol. 4.

134. Chevalier de Laborie, *Propositions soumises à l'éxamen du Comité de Marine de l'Assemblée Nationale* (Paris, 1790), pp. 11–12, reprinted in EDHIS, *La Révolution Française*, vol. 4; Gregoire, *Lettre*, p. 20.

135. Gregoire, *Lettre*, pp. 9–10.

136. François-Xavier Lanthenas, *M. Lamiral Réfuté par lui-même* (Paris, 1790), pp. 58–59, reprinted in EDHIS, *La Révolution française*, vol. 7.

137. Ibid., p. 69.

138. José Antonio Saco, *Historia de la esclavitud de la raza africana en el Nuevo Mundo y en especial en los paises américohispanos*, 6 vols. (Barcelona, 1879); Ramiro Guerra, *Azúcar y población en las Antillas* (Havana: Instituto del Libro, Ciencias Sociales, 1970); Fernando Ortiz, *Contrapunteo cubano del tobaco y el azúcar* (Havana: Casa Montero, 1940)—translated into English by Cedric Belfrage as *Cuban Counterpoint, Tobacco and Sugar* (New York: Knopf, 1947); Manuel Moreno Fraginals, *El Ingenio: El complejo económico—social cubano del azúcar* (Havana: Casa Montero, 1964)—translated into English by Cedric Belfrage as *The Sugar Mill: The Socioeconomic Complex of Sugar in Cuba, 1760–1860* (New York: Monthly Review Press, 1976).

139. Ramiro Guerra et al., eds., *Historia de la Nación Cubana*, 10 vols. (Havana: Editorial Nacional, 1952); Willis Fletcher Johnson, *The History of Cuba*, 5 vols. (New York, 1920).

140. Friedrich H. A. von Humboldt, *The Island of Cuba* (New York, 1856); Ramón de la Sagra, *Historia económica-política y estadística de la Isla de Cuba* (Havana, 1831); Jacobo de la Pezuela, *Diccionario geográfico, estadístico, histórico, de la isla de Cuba*, 4 vols. (Madrid, 1859).

141. Kenneth F. Kiple, *Blacks in Colonial Cuba, 1174–1899* (Gainesville: Center for Latin American Studies, University of Florida, 1976), pp. 42–43.

142. Cristóbal F. Madán, *El trabajo libre* (1864), cited in Franklin W. Knight, *Slave Society in Cuba during the Nineteenth Century* (Madison: University of Wisconsin Press, 1970), p. 97.

143. Verena Martínez-Alier, *Marriage, Class, and Colour in Nineteenth-Century Cuba: A Study of Racial Attitudes and Sexual Values in a Slave Society*, Cambridge Latin American Studies (Cambridge: At the University Press, 1974).

144. Francisco J. Ponte Domínguez, *Arango Parreño: El estadista colonial* (Havana: Editorial Trópico, 1937).

145. Viceroy of Peru and Floridablanca, cited in Manuel Colmeiro, *Historia de la economía política en España*, 2 vols. (Madrid, 1863) 2:243.

146. Ibid., pp. 28–30.

147. Fransisco de Arango y Parreño, *Discurso sobre la agricultura de la Habana y medios de fomentarlo*, in *De la factoria á la colonia* (Havana: Cuadernos de Cultura, 1936), pp. 1–113, and especially "Proyecto," pp. 94–112.

148. Arango y Parreño, *Memorial* (1791), in *Obras del Excmo. Señor D. Francisco de Arango y Parreño* (Havana, 1888), 1:49–52, 93.

149. Arango y Parreño, *Memorial* (1811), cited in Hubert H. S. Aimes, *A History of Slavery in Cuba, 1511 to 1868* (New York and London: G. P. Putnam's Sons, 1907), p. 66.

150. Aimes, *History of Slavery,* p. 77.

151. Arango y Parreño, *Memorial* (1811), in *Obras,* 2:208.

152. Lorenzo Allo, *La esclavitud doméstica en sus relaciones con la riqueza,* cited in Raul Cepero Bonilla, *Azúcar y abolición: Apuntes para una historia crítica del abolicionismo* (Havana, 1948), p. 24; ibid., p. 43.

153. Ibid., pp. 94–96.

154. Moreno Fraginals, *The Sugar Mill,* p. 60.

155. Aimes, *History of Slavery,* p. 33.

156. Ibid., pp. 30–31.

157. José Martin Félix de Arrate, *Llave del Mundo Nuevo, antemural de las Indias Occidentales* (Mexico City: Biblioteca Americana, 1949), ch. 6. See also José Manuel Pérez Cabrera, *Historiografía de Cuba* (Mexico City: Instituto Panamericano de Geografía e Historia, 1962), pp. 93–102.

158. Arrate, *Llave del Mundo Nuevo,* ch. 19.

159. Cepero Bonilla, *Azúcar y Abolicíon,* p. 96.

160. Miguel de Villa, ed., *Colección póstuma de papeles científicos, históricos, políticos, y de otros ramos sobre la Isla de Cuba, por Don José Antonio Saco* (Havana, 1881), pp. 130–31.

161. Raul Maestri, Introduction to Fransisco de Arango y Parreño, *De la Factoria,* pp. 15–16.

162. José Antonio Saco, *Memoria sobre la Vagancia en la Isla de Cuba* (Havana: Instituto Cubano del Libro, 1973), p. 17–18.

163. Ibid., pp. 21–22.

164. Ibid., pp. 24–28.

165. Ibid., pp. 19, 34.

166. Raúl Lorenzo, *Sentido nacionalista de pensamiento de Saco* (Havana: Editorial Trópico, 1942) pt. 3, ch. 4, pp. 169–79.

167. Saco, *Memoria,* pp. 28–30.

168. Ibid., pp. 22–23, 25–26.

169. Cited in Lorenzo, *Sentido nacionalista,* pt. 3, ch. 4, pp. 171–73.

170. Saco, *Memoria,* pp. 31–32. See also Saco, *La Supresión del tráfico de esclavos africanos en la isla de Cuba,* in Domingo del Monte, ed., *Obra de José Antonio Saco* (Havana, 1845).

171. *Memoria de Varela* (1822), in José Antonio Saco, *Historia de la esclavitud de la raza africana en el Nuevo Mundo* (Havana, 1938), 4:6.

172. Junta de Fomento, *Exposición,* pp. 48–60.

173. De Villa, *Colección,* p. 149.

174. José Antonio Saco, *Contra la anexión* (Havana: Libreria Cervantes, 1928), 1:224.

175. José Antonio Saco, *Ideas sobre la incorporación de Cuba en los Estados Unidos: Replica á Vazquez Quiepo* (1848), in *Contra la anexión,* pp. 46–47.

176. Ibid., pp. 45–46.

177. Saco, *La Esclavitud,* cited in Lorenzo, *Sentido nacionalista,* p. 181.

178. José Antonio Saco, *Carta de un patriota,* in *Ideario reformista* (Havana: 1935), pp. 24–30.

179. José Antonio Saco, *Carta á J. L. Alonso,* in *Contra la Anexión,* p. lxxv. Prologue.

180. Cited in Lorenzo, *Sentido nacionalista,* p. 181.

181. José Antonio Saco, *Colección,* edition of Nación de Cuba (Havana, n.d.), 3:570.

182. Criticisms of Charles Dana and Fernando Ortiz, noted in Pérez Cabrera, *Historiografia de Cuba,* pp. 200–202.

183. Silverio Jorrin cited ibid., p. 199. For more on Saco, see Leopoldo Zea, *Dos etapas del pensamiento en Hispanoamérica, del romanticismo al positivismo* (Mexico City: El Colegio de Mexico, 1949); Domingo Figarola Caneda, *José Antonio Saco: Documentos para su vida* (Havana: 1921); Manuel Moreno Fraginals, "Nación o plantación, el dilema político cubano visto á

travès de José Antonio Saco," in *Estudios Históricos Americanos* (Mexico City: Colegio de Mexico, 1953), pp. 241–72.

184. Manuel Sanguilly, *José de la Luz y Caballero, estudio crítico* (Havana, 1890); and José R. Fernández, "José de la Luz y Caballero" in *El Caiman Barbudo*, August 1975, pp. 29–31.

185. Cited in Cepero Bonilla, *Azúcar y abolición*, pp. 98–99.

186. Lloyd King, "Some Cuban Literary Intellectuals and Slavery," mimeographed (St. Augustine, Trinidad: University of the West Indies, n.d.), pp. 2–6.

187. Cited in Cepero Bonilla, *Azúcar y abolición*, p. 11.

188. Rafael Soto Paz, *La falsa cubanidad de Saco, Luz, y Del Monte* (Havana: Editorial Alfa, 1941).

189. Pedro José Guiteras, *Historia de Cuba*, cited in Pérez Cabrera, *Historiografia de Cuba*, pp. 234–35.

190. Cited in Cepero Bonilla, *Azúcar y abolición*, p. 39.

191. Ibid., p. 48.

192. Narcisco López, ibid., p. 50.

193. José Antonio Saco, *Contra la Anexión*, pp. 69–239.

194. *Memoria de Varela*, p. 17, 13.

195. Jacobo de la Pezuela, *Necesidades de Cuba*, cited in Pérez Cabrera, *Historiografia de Cuba*, pp. 217–18.

196. Cited in Cepero Bonilla, *Azúcar y abolición*, p. 120.

197. José Morales Lemus, *Informe sobre la Question Política*, cited ibid., p. 103; José A. Echeverria, *Información sobre Reformas en Cuba y Puerto Rico*, cited ibid., pp. 102–3.

198. Cepero Bonilla, *Azúcar y abolición*, p. 163.

199. Nicolás Azcárate, "Votos de un Cubano," cited in Cepero Bonilla, *Azúcar y abolición*, José M. Zayas, "Cuba: Su Porvenir," cited ibid.; pp. 159–60.

200. Raimundo Menocal y Cueto, *Origen y Desarrollo del Pensamiento Cubano* (Havana: Editorial Lex, 1947), 2:101–3.

201. Ibid., pp. 184–85.

202. Baron de Vastey, *Le Système Colonial Dévoilé* (Cap. Henry, Haiti, 1914), pp. 32–33.

203. King, *Some Cuban Literary Intellectuals*, pp. 16–17.

204. Fernando Ortiz, *Contrapunto Cubano*.

205. Ragatz, *A Guide*, ch. 2.

206. Manuel Moreno Fraginals, *El Ingenio*, pt. 4.

207. Note on Reynoso in H. Ling Roth, *Literature of Sugar*, p. 74.

208. Sidney W. Mintz and Richard Price, *An Anthropological Approach to the Afro-American Past: A Caribbean Perspective* (Philadelphia: Institute for the Study of Human Issues, 1976), p. 3.

209. Henry Bolingbroke, *A Voyage to the Demerary, 1799–1806* (Georgetown, British Guiana: *Daily Chronicle*, 1947), p. 150.

210. M. G. Lewis, *Journal of a West India Proprietor, 1815–1817* (London: George Routledge and Sons, 1929).

211. G. W. Bridges, *Annals of Jamaica*, 2 vols. (London: Frank Cass, 1968); W. J. Gardner, *A History of Jamaica from Its Discovery by Christopher Columbus to the Year 1872* (London: Frank Cass, 1971).

212. Sir William Young, *An Account of the Black Charaibs in the Island of St. Vincent*, cited in Elsa Goveia, *Slave Society in the British Leeward Islands at the End of the Eighteenth Century*, Yale University Caribbean Series 8 (New Haven: Yale University Press, 1965), p. 155.

213. Goveia, *Slave Society*, p. 329.

214. Evangeline and Charles M. Andrews, eds., *Journal of a Lady of Quality* (New Haven: Yale University Press, 1921), pp. 108–9, 112.

215. *Lady Nugent's Journal* (Kingston: Institute of Jamaica, 1966), p. 237.

216. Richard Pares, *A West India Fortune* (London: Longmans, 1958), pp. 150–58.

217. *Lady Nugent's Journal*, p. 156.

218. M. G. Lewis, *Journal*, pp. 181–82.

219. Quoted in Goveia, *Slave Society*, p. 253.

220. John Davies, *History of the Caribby Islands* (London, 1666), p. 202.

221. Dubuisson, *Nouvelles considérations sur Saint-Domingue*, 1:83–84.

222. Cited in Gisler, *L'Esclavage aux Antilles Françaises*, pp. 119–20.

223. Paul Singh, *Political Thought in Guyana: An Historical Sketch* (Georgetown: University of Guyana, 1972), p. 9.

224. Long, *History of Jamaica*, 2:328–29.

225. H. P. Jacobs, *Sixty Years of Change, 1806–1866* (Kingston: Institute of Jamaica, 1973), pp. 46–47.

226. D'Auberteuil, *Considérations*, 1:86–97.

227. Fraginals, *The Sugar Mill*, p. 69.

228. Marvin Harris, *Patterns of Race in the Americas* (New York: W. W. Norton, 1974).

229. Girod-Chantrans, cited in Gisler, *L'Esclavage aux Antilles Françaises*, p. 70; Moreau de Saint-Méry, cited ibid., p. 70; Dr. George Pinckard, *Letters from Guiana* (Georgetown, British Guiana: *Daily Chronicle*, 1942), pp. 18–19.

230. René Acheen, "Les blancs créoles de Saint-Pierre au début de la troisième République," *Colloque de Saint-Pierre* (Martinique: Centre Universitaire Antilles-Guyane, 1973), pp. 57–67.

231. René Bonneville, "Vision de la Société Pierrotine dans *Le Triomphe d'Eglantine*," pp. 71–75.

CHAPTER FOUR

1. Robert W. Fogel and Stanley L. Engerman, *Time on the Cross*, 2 vols. (Boston: Little Brown, 1974); Stanley Elkins, *Slavery: A Problem in American Institutional and Intellectual Life* (Chicago: University of Chicago Press, 1959).

2. For the Nat Turner controversy, see Eric Foner, *Nat Turner* (Englewood Cliffs, N.J.: Prentice-Hall, 1971), and William Styron, *The Confessions of Nat Turner* (New York: Random House, 1967).

3. David Brion Davis, *The Problem of Slavery in Western Culture* (Ithaca, N.Y.: Cornell University Press, 1970).

4. Garry B. Nash, *Red, White, and Black: The Peoples of Early America* (Englewood Cliffs, N.J.: Prentice-Hall, 1974), p. 237.

5. Sidney W. Mintz, Foreword to N. Whitten and J. Szwed, eds., *Afro-American Anthropology: Contemporary Perspectives* (New York: Free Press, 1969), p. 15.

6. J. J. Hartsinck, "The Story of the Slave Rebellion in Berbice," *Journal of the British Guiana Museum and Zoo*, no. 20 (1958): 21–48.

7. Pedro Dechamps Chapeaux, *El negro en la economía habanera del siglo XIX* (Havana: Unión de Escritores y Artistas de Cuba, 1971).

8. *Equiano's Travels*, abridged and ed. Paul Edwards (London: Heinemann Educational Books, 1967), p. 142.

9. Gabriel Debien, *Les esclaves aux Antilles Françaises* (Basse-Terre and Fort-de-France: Société d'Histoire de la Guadeloupe, Société d'Histoire de la Martinique, 1974), p. 8.

10. George P. Rawick, *The American Slave: A Composite Autobiography*, 8 vols. (New York: Negro Universities Press, 1970); Norman Yetman, *Life under the Peculiar Institution: Selections from the Slave Narrative Collection* (New York: Holt and Co., 1970); Benjamin A. Botkin, *Lay My Burden Down: A Folk History of Slavery* (Chicago: University of Chicago Press, 1945).

11. Ira Berlin, "From Slave to Freedman: A Documentary Record," *Miami Herald*, February 26, 1978, sec. B.

12. Leslie Howard Owens, *This Species of Property: Slave Life and Culture in the Old South* (New York: Oxford University Press, 1976); Dorothy Sterling, *The Trouble They Seen: Black People Tell the Story of Reconstruction* (Garden City, N.Y.: Doubleday and Co., 1976).

13. "The Saga of 'Kaniah,' " *Express* (Port-of-Spain, Trinidad), August 9, 1980, p. 1.

14. Esteban Montejo, *Biografía de un cimarrón*, ed. Miguel Barnet—translated into English by Jocasta Innesas, *Autobiography of a Runaway Slave* (New York: Vintage Books, 1968).

15. Edward Brathwaite, "Caribbean Man in Space and Time," *Savacou* 11/12 (September 1975):1–11.

16. Ibid., p. 11.

17. Dr. George Pinckard, *Letters from Guiana* (Georgetown, British Guiana: *Daily Chronicle* edition, 1942), pp. 260–62.

18. Debien, *Les esclaves*, chs. 5, 60.

19. Richard Hart, "Formation of a Caribbean Working Class," extract, offset copy (London, n.d.), p. 135.

20. Debien, *Les esclaves*, ch. 19.

21. William Beckford, *A Descriptive Account of the Island of Jamaica*, 2 vols. (London, 1790), 1:89.

22. William Hickey, cited in Monica Schuler, "Day to Day Resistance to Slavery in the Caribbean during the Eighteenth Century," *African Studies Association of the West Indies Bulletin*, no. 6 (December 1973): 59. See also Jerome Handler, *Plantation Slavery in Barbados* (Cambridge: Harvard University Press, 1978), pp. 208–9.

23. Debien, *Les esclaves*, pp. 399–410; Schuler, "Day to Day Resistance," pp. 69–70.

24. Victor Schoelcher cited in L. Peytraud, *L'esclavage aux Antilles françaises avant 1789, d'après des documents inédits des archives coloniales* (Paris: Hachette, 1897), pp. 317–18. Debien, *Les Esclaves*, p. 410. See also E. Brutus, *Révolution dans St. Domingue*, 2 vols. (Brussels: Les Editions du Pantheon, n.d.).

25. Médéric-Louis-Elie Moreau de Saint-Méry, *Description topografique, physique, civile, politique, et historique de la partie française de l'îsle Saint-Domingue*, 3 vols. (Paris: Edition de la Société de l'Histoire des Colonies Françaises et Librarie La Rose, 1958), pp. 629–30.

26. Debien, *Les esclaves*, pp. 405–6.

27. Jean François Daupion-Lavaysse, *A Statistical, Commercial, and Political Description of Venezuela, Trinidad, Margarita, and Tobago...*, ed. Edward Blaquiere, (London: G. and W. B. Whittaker, 1820), pp. 385–86; Schoelcher cited in Peytraud, *L'esclavage* pp. 318–19. See also Y. Debbash, "Opinion et droit: Le crime d'empoisonnement aux îles pendant la période esclavagiste," *Revue française d'histoire d'outre-mer* (1963), pp. 137–38.

28. Richard Ligon, *A True and Exact History of the Island of Barbados* (London: P. Parker and T. Guy, 1673), p. 50; Père J. A. Labat, *Nouveau voyage aux îles de l'Amérique*, 8 vols. (Paris, 1742), 2:405.

29. Michael Craton, *Sinews of Empire: A Short History of British Slavery* (London: Temple Smith, 1974), p. 235.

30. M. G. Lewis, *Journal of a West India Proprietor, 1815–1817* (London: George Routledge and Sons, 1929), pp. 280–81, 288–89, 59–61, 269–70.

31. Ibid., p. 120.

32. *Jamaica Journal* 13 (1777): 122; Bryan Edwards, *The History, Civil and Commercial, of the British West Indies*, 5 vols. (London, 1819), 2:100.

33. Edward Long, *History of Jamaica*, 3 vols. (London: T. Lowndes, 1774), 2:405.

34. Regnault de Beaumont, letters of November 8 and 29, 1776, cited in G. Debien, "A Saint-Domingue avec deux jeunes économes de plantation, 1774–1788," *Revue de la Société Haitienne d'Histoire*, July 1945.

35. Edward Long, *History of Jamaica*, 3 vols. (1774; reprint ed., London: Frank Cass and Co., 1970), pp. 473–74; Debien, *Les esclaves*, p. 89.

36. Philip Sherlock, *Anansi the Spider Man: Jamaica Folk Tales* (London: Macmillan, 1956); *Anancy Stories, Retold by Una Wilson* (Kingston, Jamaica: *Jamaica Times*, 1947).

37. James M. Phillippo, *Jamaica: Its Past and Present State* (London: Dawsons of Pall Mall, 1843), p. 121.

38. W. J. Cash, *The Mind of the South* (Garden City, N.Y.: Doubleday Anchor, 1954); Eugene D. Genovese, *Roll, Jordan, Roll: The World the Slaves Made* (New York: Vintage Books, 1976).

39. Edward Kamua Braithwaite, "Caliban, Ariel, and UnProspero in the Conflict of Creolization: A Study of the Slave Revolt in Jamaica in 1831–32," in *Comparative Perspectives on Slavery in New World Plantation Societies*, Annals of the New York Academy of Sciences, vol. 292 (New York, 1977), pp. 41–60.

40. Emilia Viotti da Costa, "Slave Images and Realities," ibid., p. 301.

41. Sir Hans Sloane, *A Voyage to the Islands Madera, Barbados, Nieves, S. Christophers, and Jamaica* (London, 1707), p. xlix.

42. James Grainger, "The Sugar Cane: Advice to the Planters of St. Christopher," in *Writings, Past and Present, about the Leeward Islands*, ed. John Brown (Kingston, Jamaica: Department of Extra-Mural Studies, University College of the West Indies, 1961), pp. 40–43.

43. Federico Asenjo, *Las Fiestas de San Juan* (1868; reprint ed., San Juan: Editorial Coqui, 1971).

44. Ligon, *A True and Exact History*, p. 50; Montejo, *Autobiography of a Runaway Slave*, p. 29.

45. Père Labat, *Nouveau voyage*, 5:116; F. Marryat, *Peter Simple* (London, 1834), pp. 452–53.

46. See Roland T. Ely, *Cuando reinaba su majestad el azúcar* (Buenos Aires: Editorial Sudamericana, 1963), chs. 26–28.

47. Fernando Ortiz, *La africanía de la música folklórica de Cuba* (Havana: Ediciones Cardenas y. Cia, 1950), Introduction, pp. 322–25.

48. Izett Anderson and Frank Cundall, Comps., *Jamaica Proverbs and Sayings* (Shannon: Irish University Press, 1972); B. David and J. P. Jardel, *Les proverbes créoles de la Martinique* (Fort-de-France, Martinique: CERAG, 1969).

49. Edward Brathwaite, *The Development of Creole Society in Jamaica, 1770–1820* (Oxford: Clarendon Press, 1971), pp. 220–25.

50. Sylvia Wynter, "Jonkonnu in Jamaica," *Jamaica Journal* 4, no. 2 (June 1970):44.

51. Brathwaite, *Development of Creole Society*, pp. 223–24, 211.

52. Ortiz, *La Africanía*, pp. 61–79.

53. Wynter, "Jonkonnu in Jamaica," pp. 45, 41–42.

54. Ortiz, *La Africanía*, p. 287.

55. Michael Craton and Garry Greenland, *Searching for the Invisible Man: Slaves and Plantation Life in Jamaica* (Cambridge: Harvard University Press, 1978), p. 148.

56. Edward Seaga, "Revival Cults in Jamaica," *Jamaica Journal* 3, no. 2 (June 1969):4.

57. Cited in Jean Price-Mars, *Ainsi parle l'oncle* (Paris: Imprimerie de Compiègne, 1928), p. 113.

58. Fernando Ortiz, *Los negros brujos* (Miami: Ediciones Universal, 1973); p. 24; Taylor cited in Wynter, "Jonkonnu in Jamaica," p. 37.

59. Remy Bastien, "Vodun and Politics in Haiti," in *Religion and Politics in Haiti* (Washington, D.C.: Institute for Cross-Cultural Research, 1966), p. 39.

60. Justin Chrysostome Dorsainvil, *Vodou et névrose* (Port-au-Prince: Impr. la Presse, 1931), p. 3.

61. Ari Kiev, "Spirit Possession in Haiti," *American Journal of Psychiatry* 118 (1961):137; Price-Mars, *Ainsi parle l'oncle*, p. 193.

62. Laennec Hurbon, *Dieu dans le Vaudou Haitien* (Paris: Livres Partisans, 1972).

63. Maya Deren, *Divine Horsemen: The Living Gods of Haiti* (London and New York: Thames and Hudson, 1953).

64. Ortiz, *Los negros brujos*. See also Ortiz, *Los negros esclavos* (Havana, 1916), and *Los negros curros* (Havana, 1911). For chronology of Ortiz's work, see *Los negros brujos*, pp. xx–xxiii.

65. Ortiz, *Los negros brujos*, p. xv.

66. Montejo, *Autobiography of a Runaway Slave*, pp. 161-65. See also Migene González-Wippler, *Santería: African Magic in Latin America* (Garden City, N.Y.: Anchor Books, 1975).

67. J. D. Flinter, *Examen del estado actual de los negros de la isla de Puerto Rico* (New York, 1832), pp. 31-32.

68. Cited in Hugh Thomas, *Cuba: The Pursuit of Freedom* (New York: Harper and Row, 1971), pp. 521-22.

69. George Eaton Simpson, *The Religious Cults of the Caribbean: Trinidad, Jamaica, and Haiti* (Río Piedras: Institute of Caribbean Studies, University of Puerto Rico, 1970), pp. 273-86.

70. P. J. Laborie, *The Coffee Planter of Saint-Domingue* (London: Cadel and Davies, 1798), appendix, p. 98.

71. P. Malouet, *Collection de mémoires et correspondances officiales sur l'administration des colonies*, 5 vols. (Paris, 1799), 4:340.

72. Père Labat, *Nouveau voyage*, 1:166-67.

73. Adolphe Cabon, *Histoire d'Haite* (Port-au-Prince: La Petite Revue, n.d.), pp. 150, 544.

74. Moreau de Saint-Méry, *Description*, cited in Patrick Leigh-Fermor, *The Traveller's Tree* (London: John Murray, 1950), p. 315.

75. Drouin de Bercy, *De Saint-Domingue, de ses guerres, de ses ressources* (Paris: Hocquet, 1814), p. 178.

76. Gabriel-François Brueys d'Aigalliers, *Oeuvres choisies*, cited in Debien, *Les esclaves*, p. 271.

77. Harold Courlander, "Vodoun in Haitian Culture," in *Religion and Politics in Haiti* (Washington, D.C.: Institute for Cross-Cultural Research, 1966), p. 13.

78. Quoted in Handler, *Plantation Slavery in Barbados*, pp. 208-9.

79. Simpson, *Religious Cults*, pp. 13-16.

80. Edward Lanzer Joseph, *History of Trinidad*, ed. H. J. Mills (1838; reprint ed., London: Frank Cass and Co., 1970), p. 213.

81. Whitney Cross, *The Burned Over District* (Ithaca, N. Y.: Cornell University Press, 1950).

82. Philip D. Curtin, *Two Jamaicas: The Role of Ideas in a Tropical Colony, 1830-1865* (Cambridge: Harvard University Press, 1955), pp. 170-72. See also Monica Schuler, "Myalism and the African Religious Tradition in Jamaica," in *Africa and the Caribbean: The Legacies of a Link*, ed. Margaret E. Crahan and Franklin W. Knight (Baltimore: Johns Hopkins University Press, 1979).

83. Elsa Goveia, *Slave Society in the British Leeward Islands at the End of the Eighteenth Century* (New Haven: Yale University Press, 1965); Orlando Patterson, *The Sociology of Slavery: An Analysis of the Origins, Development, and Structure of Negro Slave Society in Jamaica* (Rutherford, N.J.: Fairleigh Dickinson University Press, 1967); Wiliam A. Green, *British Slave Emancipation: The Sugar Colonies and the Great Experiment, 1830-1865* (Oxford: Clarendon Press, 1964); Eric Williams, *Capitalism and Slavery* (London: André Deutsch, 1964); Roger Anstey, *The Atlantic Slave Trade and British Abolition, 1760-1810* (Atlantic Highlands, N. J.: Humanities Press, 1975).

84. Cited in Gordon K. Lewis, *The Growth of the Modern West Indies* (New York: Monthly Review Press, 1968), p. 62.

85. Patricia T. Rooke, "'The World They Made': The Politics of Missionary Education to British West Indian Slaves (1800-33)," mimeographed draft (Edmonton: University of Alberta, n.d.), p. 9.

86. Thomas Coke, *A History of the West Indies, containing the natural, civil, and ecclesiastical history of each island*, 3 vols. (1808-11; reprint ed., London: Frank Cass and Co., 1971), 1:38.

87. Ibid., p. 28.

88. Charles Kingsley, *At Last: A Christmas in the West Indies* (London: Macmillan, 1887). For Kingsley's earlier Christian Socialist period, see Gordon K. Lewis, *Slavery, Imperialism, and Freedom: Essays in English Radical Thought.* (New York: Monthly Review Press, 1978), ch. 4.

89. Thomas Clarkson, *The History of the Rise, Progress, and Accomplishment of the Abolition of the Slave Trade by the British Parliament*, 2 vols. (1808; reprint ed., London: Frank Cass and Co., 1968), 1:140.

90. Ibid., 1:209.

91. Stir Jakobsson, *Am I Not a Man and a Brother? British Missions and the Abolition of the Salve Trade and Slavery in West Africa and the West Indies, 1786–1838*. Studia Missionalia Upsaliensia 17 (Uppsala: Gleerup, Sweden, 1972).

92. Rev. J. H. Buchner, *The Moravians in Jamaica* (1854), cited in Fred Linyard, "The Moravians in Jamaica," *Jamaica Journal* 3, no. 1 (March 1969):8; Folarin Shyllon, *James Ramsay: The Unknown Abolitionist* (Edinburgh: Canongate, 1977), pp. 24–26.

93. Ramsey quoted in Shyllon, *James Ramsey*, p. 5.

94. Ibid., pp. 18–38.

95. Alfred North Whitehead, *Adventures of Ideas* (New York: Macmillan, 1943), p. 17.

96. Knibb quoted in Rooke, "The World They Made," p. 5.

97. The Reverend Hope Masterton Waddell, *Twenty-Nine Years in the West Indies and Central Africa* (1863; reprint ed., London: Frank Cass and Co., 1970), pp. 35–36.

98. Caries cited in Fred Linyard, "The Moravians in Jamaica," in *Jamaica Journal* (Kingston), March 1969, p. 9.

99. *The Colonist* quoted in Rooke, "The World They Made," p. 11.

100. Alfred Caldecott, *The Church in the West Indies* (1898; reprint ed., London: Frank Cass and Co., 1970), ch. 3 and p. 97. See, more generally, Allan Nanton-Marie, *Toward a Selected Bibliography of Missionary Sources in the Caribbean* (1977), copies located at the Missionary Reserve Library of Union Theological Seminary Library and at Yale University Divinity Library.

101. Arturo Santana, *Puerto Rico y los Estados Unidos en el periodo revolucionario de Europa y América, 1789–1825* (San Juan: Instituto de Cultura Puertorriqueña, 1957); Wilbur H. Siebert, *The Legacy of the American Revolution to the British West Indies and Bahamas*, Ohio State University Bulletin no. 113 (Columbus, Oh., April 1913). See also W. Kerr, *Bermuda and the American Revolution, 1760–1783* (London: Oxford University Press, 1936).

102. Long, *History of Jamaica*, 2:430–31.

103. Wylie Sypher, *Guinea's Captive Kings: British Anti-Slavery Literature of the Eighteenth Century* (Chapel Hill: University of North Carolina Press, 1942).

104. William Spence, *Britain Independent of Commerce* (London, 1808).

105. *The Collected Works of Edmund Burke* (London: G. Bell and Sons, 1914), 7:100, 44.

106. Introduction to Edward Derbyshire Seeber, *Anti-Slavery Opinion in France during the Second Half of the Eighteenth Century* (Baltimore: Johns Hopkins University Press, 1937).

107. Ibid., ch. 4.

108. Ibid., ch. 5.

109. Charles Oscar Hardy, *The Negro Question in the French Revolution* (Menasha, Wis.: The Collegiate Press, George Banta Publishing Company, 1919), pp. 51–52, 57–58.

110. Jean-Pierre Brissot, *Mémoire sur les noirs de L'Amérique Septentrionale* (Paris, 1789), reprinted in EDHIS (Editions d'Histoire Sociales), *La révolution française et l'abolition de l'esclavage*. 12 vols. (Paris: EDHIS, 1968), 7:35–57.

111. François-Xavier Lanthenas, *M. Laminal réfuté par lui-même* (Paris, 1790), pp. 58–59, 63, reprinted in EDHIS, *La révolution française*, vol. 7.

112. Viefville des Essars, *Discours et projet de loi pour l'affranchissement des nègres* (Paris, 1790), pp. 12–13, 15–18, 27–28, reprinted ibid.

113. Antoine Dorfeuille, *Adresse…* (Paris, 1793), reprinted ibid., vol. 5.

114. Antoine-Jean-Thomas Bonnemain, *Régénération des colonies…* (Paris, 1792), pp. 15, 82, reprinted ibid.

115. *Réflexions sur l'abolition de la traité et la liberté des Noirs* (Paris, 1789), pp. 2, 6–7, reprinted ibid., vol. 4.

116. Chevalier de Laborie, *Propositions soumises à l'examen de Comité de Marine de l'Assemblée Nationale* (Paris, 1790), pp. 6–8, reprinted ibid.

117. Charles Lecointe-Marsillac, *Le More-Lack* (Paris, 1789), p. xi, and ch. 22, reprinted ibid., vol. 3.

118. *Il est encore des Aristocrates, ou réponse à l'infame auteur d'un écrit intitulé: Decouverte d'un conspiration contre les intérêts de la France* (Paris, 1790), pp. 5-6, reprinted ibid., 4:74.

119. M. Théophile Mandar, *Observations sur l'esclavage et le commerce des Nègres* (Paris, 1790), pp. 7-9, reprinted ibid., vol. 4.

120. Chevalier de Laborie, *Propositions*, pp. 9-10.

121. Antoine-Nicholas Marquis de Condorcet, *Refléxions sur l'esclavage des Nègres* (Paris, 1788), p. 18, reprinted in EDHIS, *La Révolution française*, vol. 6.

122. Hardy, *The Negro Question*, pp. 59-60.

123. Arago cited in Liliane Chauleau, "Idealisme et realisme dans l'oeuvre de Victor Schoelcher" (Fort-de-France, Martinique: Archives Departamentales, 1971), p. 7.

124. Victor Schoelcher, *Esclavage et colonization* (Paris: PUF, n.d.), pp. 137, 156.

125. Victor Schoelcher, "Colonies danoises," in his *Colonies étrangères* (Paris: Pagnerre Editeur, 1843), pp. 19, 25-26.

126. Edouard Lépine, "Pour une nouvelle critique du Schoelcherisme," in his *Questions sur l'histoire antillaise* (Fort-de-France, Martinique: Desormeaux, 1978), pp. 11-124.

127. *Journal du Conseiller Garnier à la Martinique et à la Guadeloupe, 1848-1855* (Fort-de-France, Martinique: Société d'Historie de la Martinique, 1969).

128. Victor Schoelcher, *Des colonies françaises: Abolition immediate de l'esclavage* (Paris: Pagnerre Editeur, 1872), p. 7; Victor Schoelcher, *Colonies étrangères*, p. 331.

129. Jules Auguste et al., *Les Détracteurs de la race noire et de la République d'Haiti* (Paris: Marpon et Flammarion, 1882). See also Thomas G. Mathews, "La visita de Victor Schoelcher a Puerto Rico," *Revista del Instituto de Cultura*, no. 50 (January-February, 1971); and André Midas, "Victor Schoelcher and Emancipation in the French West Indies," *Caribbean Historical Review*, no. 1 (December 1950):110-23.

130. Isidor Paiewonsky, "History Corner," *Daily News* (St. Thomas), April 12, 1976. See also Neville Hall, "The 1816 Freedom Petition in the Danish West Indies: Its Background and Consequences," *Boletín de Estudios Latinoamericanos y del Caribe*, no. 29 (December 1980).

131. Antoine Dorfeuille, *Adresse*, pp. 15-16; Lecointe-Marsillac, *Le More-Lack*, ch. 17.

132. Abbé Sibire, *L'Aristocratie négrière* (Paris, 1789), p. 64, reprinted in EDHIS, *La Révolution française*, vol. 2.

133. Anaxagoras Chaumette, *Discours...*(Paris, 1793), reprinted ibid., vol. 5.

134. Abbé Antoine de Cournand, *Requête présentée à nos seigneurs de l'Assemblée Nationale en faveur des gens de couleur de l'île de Saint-Domingue* (Paris, 1790), pp. 1-3; reprinted in EDHIS, *La Révolution française*, vol. 4.

135. Abbé M. Gregoire, *Lettre aux philanthropes* (Paris, 1790), pp. 4, 10, reprinted ibid., and Gregoire, *Lettre aux citoyens de couleur et Nègres libres de Saint-Domingue*, p. 8, reprinted ibid., vol. 4.

136. Abbé M. Gregoire, *Lettre aux philanthropes*, p. 4. On Gregoire see Hippolyte Carnot, *Notice historique sur Henri Gregoire* (Paris: Baudouin, 1837), and Ruth F. Necheles, *Abbé Gregoire, 1787-1831: The Odyssey of an Egalitarian* (Chicago: Negro Universities Press, 1971).

137. On Raimond, see Julien Raimond, *Observations sur l'origine et les progrès du préjugé des colons blancs contre les hommes de couleur* (1804), noted in B. Ardouin, *Etudes sur l'histoire d'Haiti*, 6 vols. (Paris, 1853), 1:18; and Mercer Cook, *Five French Negro Authors* (Washington, D.C.: Associated Publishers, 1943).

138. A. Lebeau, *De la condition des gens de couleur libres sous l'ancien régime* (Poitiers: n.p., 1903).

139. Mavis C. Campbell, *The Dynamics of Change in a Slave Society* (London: Associated University Presses, 1976), pp. 191-92, 239-40.

140. Ibid., p. 101.

141. Gad J. Heuman, "Robert Osborn—Brown Power Leader," *Jamaica Journal*, 2, nos. 1, 2 (1968). On the free coloreds in general, see Campbell, *Dynamics of Change*; Eva Lawaetz, *Free*

Coloured in St. Croix, 1744–1816 (St. Thomas: Virgin Islands Bureau of Libraries, Museums, and Archaeological Services, 1978); Yvan Debbasch, *Couleur et liberté: Le jeu de critère ethnique dans un ordre juridique esclavagiste,* vol. 1, *L'Affranchi dans les possessions françaises de la Caraïbe, 1635–1833* (Paris, 1967); Sheila Duncker, "The Free Coloured and Their Fight for Civil Rights in Jamaica, 1800–1830," M.A. thesis, University of London, 1960; and Jerome S. Handler, *The Unappropriated People: Freedmen in the Slave Society of Barbados* (Baltimore: Johns Hopkins University Press, 1974).

142. Josefina Oliva de Coll, "La primera oposición: Las islas," ch. 2 in *La resistencia indígena ante la Conquista* (Mexico City: 1974), Siglo Veintiuno Editores.

143. Bartolomé de Las Casas, *Historia de las Indias,* 3 vols. (Mexico City: Edición Biblioteca Americana, Fondo de Cultura Económica, 1951), bk. 3, ch. 93.

144. René Marqués, "Tres hombres junto al río," in his *En una Ciudad llamada San Juan* (Río Piedras, Puerto Rico: Editorial Cultural, 1970).

145. *Archivo general de Indias: Legislación Independiente General, 1624,* cited in Emilio Rodríguez Demorizi, *Los domínicos y las encomiendas de indios de la Isla Española* (Santo Domingo: Editorial Nacional, 1973).

146. Las Casas, *Historia,* bk. 3, ch. 125, and bk. 3, ch. 25.

147. Père Pierre-François-Xavier de Charlevoix, *Histoire de l'Île Espagnole ou de St-Domingue,* 2 vols. (Paris, 1730), 1:329.

148. Père Du Tertre, *Histoire générale des Antilles habitées par les Français* (Paris, 1664), pp. 413–19.

149. Sieur de la Borde, *Relation... des Caraïbes,* Collection Billaine (Paris, 1674); Spanish trans. by Manuel Cárdenas Ruiz in *Revista del Instituto de Cultura Puertorriqueño,* no. 62 (January–March 1974): 26.

150. Olivia de Coll, *La resistencia,* pp. 32–37.

151. Las Casas, *Historia,* bk. 2, ch. 4; Fernando de Oviedo y Valdés, *Historia general de las Indias* (Madrid, 1851), bk. 16, ch. 1.

152. *Archivo general de Indias,* cited in Demorizi, *Los domínicos.*

153. Mercedes López-Baralt, "Carta a José Luis González," *Claridad* (San Juan), vol. 3, no. 113 (1977): 14–17.

154. Barnet, *Biografía de un cimarrón,* p. 167.

155. Ibid., p. 165.

156. Lorenzo Greene, "Mutiny on the Slave Ships," *Phylon Magazine* 5 (1944):346–55.

157. Michael Mullin, "Slave Obeahmen and Slaveowning Patriarchs in an Era of War and Revolution, 1776–1807," in *Comparative Perspectives on Slavery in New World Plantation Societies,* pp. 481–89.

158. Bryan Edwards, *History of the British West Indies,* 2:94.

159. Jean Price-Mars, *Une étape de l'évolution haitienne* (Port-au-Prince, Haiti, Imprimerie La Prense, 1929); Denis Lorimer and François Duvalier, *L'évolution studiale du vodu: Bulletin du Bureau d'Ethnologie* (Port-au-Prince, Haiti: Bureau d'Ethnologie, Port-au-Prince, 1955).

160. *A Genuine Narrative of the Intended Conspiracy of the Negroes at Antigua* (Dublin, 1737; reprint ed., New York: Arno Press, 1972), p. 4.

161. Ibid., pp. 13–14.

162. Henry Bleby, *Death Struggles of Slavery* (London, 1868); Curtin, *Two Jamaicas,* ch. 5; Brathwaite, "Caliban, Ariel, and UnProspero in the Conflict of Creolization."

163. Cited in J. J. Hartsinck, *Vooreden,* English trans. in "The Story of the Slave Rebellion in Berbice," *Journal of the British Guiana Museum and Zoo,* no. 20 (1958), sec. 3, pp. 7–8.

164. P. M. Netscher, *History of the Colonies Essequebo, Demerary, and Berbice from the Dutch Establishment to the Present Day,* trans. W. E. Roth (Georgetown, British Guiana: *Daily Chronicle,* 1929). See also Governor Wolfert Simon van Hoogenheim, "Journal," trans. Barbara Blair, manuscript (Georgetown: Caribbean Research Library, University of Guyana, 1972).

165. Leslie Manigat, "The Relationship between Marronage and Slave Revolts and Revolution in St.-Domingue-Haiti," in *Comparative Perspectives on Slavery,* pp. 420–36.

166. Ibid., p. 435.

167. Cited in Michael Craton, "The Passion to Exist: Slave Rebellions in the British West Indies 1650–1832," *The Journal of Caribbean History* 13 (1980):13.

168. Ibid., p. 16.

169. Bleby, *Death Struggles*, p. 123.

170. Hart, "Formation of a Caribbean Working Class," p. 142.

171. Mary Reckord, "The Slave Rebellion of 1831," *Jamaica Journal* 3, no. 2 (June 1969):31.

172. Rigaud quoted in C.L.R. James, *The Black Jacobins* (London: Secker and Warburg, 1938), pp. 190–91.

173. Long, *History of Jamaica*, 2:460.

174. Guy Joseph Bonnet, *Souvenirs historiques* (Paris: Auguste Durand, Libraire, 1864), p. 108.

175. Among many references to the Makandal legend see, for example, E. Brutus, *La révolution dans St. Domingue*, 2 vols. (Belgium: Les Editions du Pantheon, n.d.), 1:124.

176. L. Alan Eyre, "Jack Mansong, Bloodshed or Brotherhood," *Jamaica Journal* 7, no. 4 (December 1973): 44–49.

177. Bleby, *Death Struggles*, p. 116.

178. E. L. Joseph, *History of Trinidad* (1838; reprint ed., London: Frank Cass and Co., 1970), ch. 19.

179. Ibid., pp. 260–62. For further examples of black talent and capability see *Francis Egan, The Negro Vocalist* (London, 1834); *History of Mary Prince, a West Indian Slave* (London: T. Pringle, 1831); Richard Price, "Kwasimukamba's Gambit," *Bijdragen* (Leiden, Netherlands: Koninklijk Instituut voor Taal, Land en Volkenkunde, 1979); John A. Aarons, "The Story of Archibald Monteith," *Jamaica Historical Society Bulletin* 7, no. 5 (March 1978); Beverly Brown, "George Liele: Black Baptist and Pan-Africanist 1750–1826," *Savacou* 11 / 12 (September 1975); Locksley Lindo, "Francis Williams—A Free Negro in a Slave World," *Savacou* 1, no. 1 (June 1970).

180. R. C. Dallas, *The History of the Maroons from Their Origin to the Establishment of Their Chief Tribe at Sierra Leone*, 2 vols. (London: Frank Cass and Co., 1968); John Gabriel Stedman, *Narrative of a Five Years' Expedition against the Revolted Negroes of Surinam in Guiana on the Wild Coast of South America from the Years 1772–1777* (1782), 2 vols. (Barre, Mass.: Imprint Society 1971).

181. Richard Price, ed., *Maroon Societies: Rebel Slave Communities in the Americas* (Garden City, N.Y.: Doubleday Anchor, 1973), ch. 18 and p. 28.

182. Ibid., ch. 16.

183. M. Lawson, *History of Dartmouth, Preston, and Laurencetown, 1750–1898* (Halifax, Nova Scotia, n.d.), especially chs. 1, 2, "History of Township of Preston."

184. Price, *Maroon Societies*. See also *Cimarrons* (Point-à-Pitre, Guadeloupe: Institut Caraïbe de Recherches Historiques, 1980); and Alex Gradussov, *Jamaica Maroons*, trans. A. D. Dridzo (Moscow: Nanka Publishing House, 1971).

185. Winthrop Jordan cited in Eugene D. Genovese and Laura Foner, eds., *Slavery in the New World: A Reader in Comparative History* (New York: Doubleday, 1969), p. 118.

186. Edward Brathwaite, "Creative Literature of the British West Indies during the Period of Slavery," *Savacou* 1, no. 1 (June 1970):112–37.

187. *Marly* (1828), described in Ansell Hart, *Monthly Comments* 1, nos. 6 and 7 (August and September 1954).

188. Ibid., vol. 1, nos. 10, 11, 12.

189. José Z. González del Valle, *La vida literaria en Cuba, 1836–1840* (Havana: Dirección de Cultura, 1938); Pedro Barreda, *The Black Protagonist in the Cuban Novel* (Amherst: University of Massachussetts Press, 1979); and Robert L. Jackson, *The Black Image in Latin American Literature* (Albuquerque: University of New Mexico Press, 1976).

190. Domingo Delmonte, quoted in Lloyd King, "Some Cuban Literary Intellectuals and Slavery," mimeographed (St. Augustine, Trinidad: University of the West Indies, n.d.), p. 3.

191. Jesse Noel, "Race, Politics, and the Literary Art of Antonio Zambrana y Vasquez," mimeographed (St. Augustine, Trinidad: University of the West Indies, October 1976), p. 9.

192. Ivan A. Schulman, "The Portrait of the Slave Ideology and Aesthetics in the Cuban Anti-Slavery Novel," in *Comparative Perspectives on Slavery*, p. 359. See, in general, Samuel Feijoo, *El Negro en la literatura folklorica Cubana* (Havana: Biblioteca Básica de Literatura Cubana, 1980).

193. King, "Some Cuban Literary Intellectuals," p. 13.

194. Ortiz, *Los negros brujos*, p. xvii.

195. Dr. E. Rufz, *Etudes historiques et statistiques sur la population de la Martinique* (St. Pierre, Martinique, 1850), 1:148–50, quoted in Lafcadio Hearn, *Two Years in the French West Indies* (New York and London: Harper and Brothers Publishers, 1900), pp. 320–21.

196. Hearn, *Two Years*, pp. 323–24.

197. Général de Brigade, *Voyage à la Martinique* (Paris, 1804), cited in Hearn, *Two Years*, pp. 332–33.

198. Baron de Vastey, *Le système colonial dévoilé*, pp. 35–61, 84–85.

CHAPTER FIVE

1. Alistair Hughes, "Adventures in History," *The West Indian* (St. Georges, Grenada), January 14, 1964.

2. Monrad Sigfrid Metzgen, comp. *Shoulder to Shoulder; or the Battle of St. George's Cay* (Belize, British Honduras: Belize Literary and Debating Society, 1928).

3. For all this, see Gordon K. Lewis, *The Growth of the Modern West Indies* (New York: Monthly Review Press, 1968), pp. 418–19, fn. 14.

4. "The History of Camboulay, the Hamilton Report," *Vanguard* (Port-of-Spain, Trinidad), February 8, 1969, pp. 5–8.

5. Andrew Pearse, "Carnival in Nineteenth Century Trinidad," *Caribbean Quarterly* 4, nos. 3 and 4 (1956): 192.

6. Bronkhurst cited in Peter Ruhomon, *Centenary History of the East Indians in British Guiana, 1838–1938* (Georgetown, British Guiana: *Daily Chronicle*, 1938), p. 250.

7. Joseph Beaumont, *The New Slavery* (London, 1871); Sir G. William des Voeux, *Experiences of a Demerara Magistrate, 1865–1870* (1872) (Georgetown, British Guiana: *Daily Chronicle*, 1948), no. 11.

8. Ruhomon, *Centenary History*, chs. 9, 18, 19; Nasaloo Ramaya, "Songs of Tears and Laughter," *Trinidad Guardian* (Port-of-Spain), July 25, 1973.

9. George Lamming, cited in Balgobin Ramdeen, Citizens Forum, *Express* (Port-of-Spain), August 29, 1980.

10. Tapia House Group, *Memorandum to the Constitution Commission of Trinidad and Tobago* (Port-of-Spain, Trinidad: Tapia Publishing House, 1973); and *Report of the Constitution Commission* (Port-of-Spain, Trinidad: Government Printing Office, 1974), pp. 76–77.

11. Elsa V. Goveia, *A Study on the Historiography of the British West Indies to the End of the Nineteenth Century* (Mexico City: Instituto Panamericano, 1956), p. 89.

12. Agustin Cueva, "El espejismo heroico de la Conquista: Ensayo de interpretación de *La Araucana*," *Casa de las Americas* (Havana), no. 110 (September–October 1978), pp. 117–39.

13. Edward Long, *History of Jamaica*, 3 vols. (London, 1774), 1:56.

14. Ibid., vol. 1, bk. 1, chs. 1–9.

15. Ibid., 1:82.

16. Ibid., vol. 1, bk. 1, ch. 1.

17. Bryan Edwards, *History, Civil and Commercial, of the British Colonies in the West Indies*, 5 vols. (London, 1819), 2:434–42.

18. Ibid., 2:414.

19. Ibid., 2:414–15.

20. Ibid., 2:416.

21. Ibid., 2:498, 586–91.

22. D'Argenson and Saintard quoted in Charles Frostin, *Les révoltes blanches à Saint-Domingue aux XVIIe et XVIIIe siècles* (Paris: L'Ecole, 1975), pp. 289, 295.

23. Charles Frostin, "L'autonomisme colon de la partie française de Saint-Domingue," *Archives Antillaises* (Guadeloupe, 1974): 2:21.

24. *Moreau de St-Méry's American Journey, 1793–1798,* trans. and ed. Kenneth Roberts and Anna M. Roberts (Garden City, N.Y.: Doubleday and Company, 1947).

25. Médéric-Louis-Elie Moreau de Saint-Méry, *Loix et constitutions des colonies françaises de l'Amérique sous le vent,* 6 vols. (Paris, 1784–90).

26. Médéric-Louis-Elie Moreau de Saint-Méry, *Description topographique, physique, civile, politique, et historique de la partie française de l'Île Saint-Domingue,* 3 vols. (Philadelphia, 1779), 2:865–67, 3:334.

27. *Moreau de St. Méry's American Journey, 1793–1798,* p. 338.

28. Hilliard d'Auberteuil, *Considérations sur l'état présent de la colonie française de Saint-Domingue,* 2 vols. (Paris, 1776–77), 1:10–12, 19–20.

29. Ibid., 1:5, 13–14.

30. Ibid., 1:63–64, 285.

31. Ibid., 2:97–98.

32. Ibid., 2:100–103.

33. Ibid., 2:105–8.

34. Emilien Petit, *Droit public, ou gouvernment des colonies françaises,* in Delalain Librarie, 2 vols. (Paris, 1771), 1:457–58, 461–62.

35. Ibid., 2:270–76.

36. Ibid., 1:473–74, 2:471–72.

37. Ibid., 1:463–71.

38. Antonio Sánchez Valverde, *Idea del valor de la Isla Española* (Ciudad Trujillo, Santo Domingo: Biblioteca Dominicana: 1947), ser. 1, vol. 1.

39. Prince Sanders, *Haytian Papers* (London: W. Reed, Bookseller, 1816), pp. iii–v.

40. W. W. Harvey, *Sketches of Haiti* (London, 1827), p. 282.

41. *Mémoires de Joseph Balthazar Inginac, ex-Sécrétaire-General d'Haiti* (Kingston, Jamaica, 1843), p. 26.

42. Philémon Charlemagne, *Réfutation d'un écrit de Charrault, ex-colon, intitulé: Coup d'oeil sur St. Domingue* (Cap Henry, Haiti, n.d.), pp. 3, 5–8.

43. *Deuxième lettre du Baron de Dupuy à M. H. Henry* (Cap-Haitien, 1814), pp. 2–3.

44. *Lettre du Chevalier de Prézeau á ses Concitoyens de parties de l'Ouest et du Sud* (Palais Royal de Sans-Souci, 1815), p. 3.

45. Chevalier de Prézeau, *Réfutation de la lettre de Général François Dauxion Lavaysse* (Cap Henry, Haiti, 1814), pp. 7–10, 21.

46. Ibid., pp. 18, 21–22.

47. Julien Prévost, Comte de Limonade, *Rélation des glorieux événements que ont porté Leurs Majestés Royales sur le Trône d'Hayti* (Cap Henry, Haiti, 1811), pp. xii, xv–xx.

48. *Deuxième lettre du Baron de Dupuy,* pp. 5–9; Guy Joseph Bonnet, *Souvenirs historiques* (Paris: Auguste Durand, Libraire, 1864), pp. 209–11, 214–15; *Mémoires de Inginac,* pp. 28–44, 105–11.

49. Prévost, *Rélation,* pp. 17, 112–97.

50. Bonnet, *Souvenirs historiques,* pp. 154–55.

51. Colombel, cited in Joseph Saint-Rémy, *Pétion et Haiti* (Port-au-Prince and Paris: Durand, 1956), 4:81; F. D. Chanlatte, *Appel aux Haytiens* (Port-au-Prince, 1817), p. 4; Comte de Rosiers, *Hayti reconnaissante* (1819), p. 5; Félix Darfour, *L'Eclaireur Haytien ou le parfait patriote,* August 5, 1818, cited in David Nicholls, *From Dessalines to Duvalier: Race, Colour, and National Independence in Haiti* (Cambridge: At the University Press, 1979), p. 42; J. S.

Milscent, *L'Abeille haytienne*, August 1, 1817, cited in Nicholls, *From Dessalines to Duvalier*, p. 42.

52. Nicholls, *From Dessalines to Duvalier*, pp. 35–36.

53. René Chateaubriand, "Genie de Christianisme," in *Oeuvres Complètes* (Paris, 1827), 14:61.

54. Baron de Vastey, *Le système colonial dévoilé* (Cap Henry, Haiti, 1814), pp. 38–39, 35–61.

55. Ibid., pp. 1, 19, 18.

56. Baron de Vastey, *Notes à M. le Baron de V. P. Malouet* (Cap Henry, Haiti, 1814), pp. 8– 13, 14–15.

57. Baron de Vastey, *Essai sur les causes de la révolution et des guerres civiles d'Hayti* (Sans-Souci, 1819).

58. Baron de Vastey, *Réflexions sur une lettre de Mazères...sur les noirs et les blancs, la civilization de l'Afrique, le Royaume d'Hayti* (Cap Henry, Haiti, 1816), pp. 11, 19.

59. Ibid., pp. 21–33.

60. Ibid., pp. 43–45.

61. Baron de Vastey, *Notes*, pp. 20–21.

62. Baron de Vastey, *Réflexions*, pp. 33–37.

63. Ibid., pp. 77–78.

64. Thomas Madiou, *Histoire d'Haiti*, 3 vols. (Port-au-Prince, 1847, 1848), vol. 1, preface.

65. Michelet cited in Gatts Pressoir, Ernest Trouillet, and Henock Trouillet, *Historiographie d'Haiti* (Mexico City, Instituto Panamericano de Geografía e Historia, 1953), p. 141.

66. Beaubrun Ardouin, *Etudes sur l'histoire d'Haiti suivies de la vie du général J-M Borgella*, 3 vols. (Paris, 1853–60), 1:10.

67. Joseph Saint-Rémy, *Pétion et Haiti*; Emile Nau, cited in Nicholls, *From Dessalines to Duvalier*, pp. 74, 92; Beauvais Lespinasse, cited ibid, p. 75.

68. Lepelletier de Saint-Rémy, "La Republique d'Haiti: Ses dernières révolutions; sa situation actuelle," *Revue des Deux Mondes* 15, no. 4 (November 1845): 681–82.

69. Pressoir et al., *Historiographie d'Haiti*, p. 182.

70. Baron de Vastey, *Essai*, p. 15.

71. George F. Tyson, Jr., ed., *Toussaint L'Ouverture* (Englewood Cliffs, N.J.: Prentice-Hall, 1973).

72. Ardouin, *Etudes*, 1:5; Madiou, *Histoire d'Haiti*, 1:141.

73. Ardouin, *Etudes*, 10:26.

74. Madiou, *Histoire d'Haiti*, 4:48; Ardouin, *Etudes*, 10:26.

75. Justin Bouzon, *Etudes historiques sur la Présidence de Faustin Soulouque* (Paris and Port-au-Prince: Bibliothèque Haitienne et Gustave Guérin et Cie., 1894).

76. Louis-Joseph Janvier, *Les Constitutions d'Haiti* (Paris, 1886).

77. H. Paulens Sannon cited in Pressoir et al., *Historiographie d'Haiti*, p. 215.

78. Louis-Joseph Janvier, cited in Benoit B. Joachim, "Sur l'esprit de couleur en Haiti," *Nouvelle Optique*, no. 9 (January–March 1973): 156.

79. Edmond Paul, *Questions politique-économiques*, vol. 2, *Formation de la richesse nationale* (Paris, 1863).

80. Louis-Philippe May, *Le Mercier de la Rivière, 1719-1801* (Paris: Editions du Centre National de la Recherche Scientifique, 1975), especially ch. 1, "Le Mercier de la Rivière, l'homme et sa formation administrative: le gouvernment économique des Antilles, 1759-1764."

81. Paul, *Questions*, 2:103–4; Louis-Joseph Janvier, *Les anti-nationaux* (Paris, 1884), p. 60; Demesvar Delorme, *La misère au sein des richesses: Réflexions divers sur Haiti* (Paris, 1873), pp. 103–4.

82. Paul, *Questions*, 2:74, 118; Louis-Joseph Janvier, *La république d'Haiti et ses visiteurs, 1840-1882* (Paris, 1883), p. 78.

83. Anténor Firmin, *Lettres de Saint Thomas* (Paris, 1910), pp. 2–85; Paul, *Questions*, 1:32; Delorme, *La misère*, pp. 108, 111.

84. Firmin, *Lettres*, pp. 345, 369, 372, 379.

85. Demesvar Delorme, *Les theoriciens au pouvoir* (Paris, 1870), p. 220.

86. Ibid., pp. 19, 21, 24, 29.

87. Louis-Joseph Janvier, *Les affaires d'Haiti, 1883–1884* (Paris, 1885), p. 141.

88. Delorme, *La misère*, pp. 223–27.

89. Demesvar Delorme, *Les paisibles* (1874), p. 4.

90. Paul cited in Nicholls, *From Dessalines to Duvalier*, p. 105.

91. Louis-Joseph Janvier, "Haiti aux Haitiens," in *Les affaires d'Haiti*, pp. 260–61. See, in general, Pradel Pompilus et al., *Manuel illustré de l'histoire de la littérature haitienne* (n.p.: Impr. Henri Deschamps, 1962); and A. Viatte, *Histoire littéraire de l'Amérique française, des origines à 1950* (Quebec and Paris: Gallimard, 1954).

92. *Inventario General del Archivo de la Delegación del Partido Revolucionario Cubano en Neuva York, 1892–1898*, 20 vols. (Havana: Publicaciones del Archivo Nacional de Cuba, 1955), vol. 1.

93. Fray Iñigo Abbad y Lasierra, *Historia geográfica, civil, y natural de la isla de San Juan Bautista de Puerto Rico* (1782; reprint ed., Río Piedras: Ediciones de la Universidad de Puerto Rico, 1959), p. 149.

94. Ibid., chs. 26–28.

95. Ibid., pp. 152–53.

96. Ibid., pp. 182–83.

97. Ibid., B. pp. lxxxvii–cii.

98. Lidio Cruz Monclova, *Historia de Puerto Rico, Siglo XIX*, vol. 1, *1808–1868* (Río Piedras: Editorial Universitaria, Universidad de Puerto Rico, 1958), pp. 33–35. See also Rafael W. Ramirez, *Instrucciones al Diputado Don Ramón Power Giral: Boletín de la Universidad de Puerto Rico* 14 (June–July 1936): 9–31.

99. Cruz Monclova, *Historia de Puerto Rico*, pp. 36–38.

100. *Informe de don Pedro Irizarri, Alcalde ordinario de San Juan sobre las Instrucciones que debian darse à don Ramón Power*...(1809), in Eugenio Fernández Méndez, *Crónicas de Puerto Rico* (Río Piedras: Editorial, Universidad de Puerto Rico, 1976), pp. 351–55, 364–65.

101. Ibid., pp. 355–56.

102. Marshal O'Reylly, *Memoria sobre la isla de Puerto Rico* (Madrid, 1785), in Alejandro Tapia y Rivera, *Biblioteca Histórica de Puerto Rico* (1854, reprint ed., San Juan, Puerto Rico: Instituto de Literatura Puertorriqueña, 1945), p. 528; Col. George Flinter, *An Account of the Present State of the Island of Porto Rico* (London: Longman, 1834), p. 118.

103. Drs. Ashford and Igaravídez, cited in Dean Fleagle, *Social Problems of Porto Rico* (Boston: Heath, 1917), pp. 10–15.

104. Salvador Brau, *Las clases Jornaleras*, cited in Iris Zavala and Rafael Rodríguez, eds., *The Intellectual Roots of Independence* (New York: Monthly Review Press, 1980), p. 81.

105. Manuel Alonso, *El gíbaro, cuadro de costumbres de la isla de Puerto Rico* (1849), in Fernández Méndez, *Crónicas*, pp. 443–77.

106. Manuel Fernández Juncos, *Costumbres y tradiciones* and *La Galería Puertorriqueña* (San Juan: Instituto de Cultura Puertorriqueña, 1958).

107. *El campesino puertorriqueño, de la memoria de D. Fransisco del Valle Atiles*, in Fernández-Méndez, *Cronicas*, pp. 505–40.

108. Salvador Brau, *Las clases jornaleras de Puerto Rico*, in Eugenio Fernández Méndez, ed., *Salvador Brau: Disquisiciones sociológicas* (Río Piedras: Ediciones del Instituto de Literatura, Universidad de Puerto Rico, 1956), pp. 123–88.

109. Ibid., p. 128.

110. Ibid., p. 153.

111. Ibid., p. 150.

112. See, in general, Arturo Córdova Landrón, *Salvador Brau: Su vida, su obra, su época* (Río Piedras: Editorial de la Universidad de Puerto Rico, 1949).

113. Marta Aponte Alsina, "Notas para un estudio ideológico de las novelas de Manuel Zeno Gandía," in *Revista Sin Nombre* 10, no. 1 (April–June 1979): 56–61.

114. Angélica Luiña de Palés, "El Romanticismo en nuestra literatura," *El Mundo* (San Juan), Saturday supplement, October 31, 1959.
115. Iris M. Zavala, "Puerto Rico, Siglo XIX: Literatura y sociedad," *El Mundo* (San Juan), October 2, 1977.
116. Zavala and Rodríguez, eds., *Intellectual Roots of Independence*, p. 20.
117. Brau, *Las clases jornaleras*, pp. 174, 181-87.
118. Manuel Fernández Juncos, *La galería Puertorriqueña*. See, in general, José Luis González, *Literatura y sociedad en Puerto Rico* (Mexico City: Ediciones Tierra Firme, Fondo de la Cultura Económica de Mexico, 1976).
119. Eugenio María de Hostos, *Obras completas*, 20 vols. (San Juan: Instituto de Cultura Puertorriqueña, 1969), vol. 16, *Moral Social*.
120. Ibid., 16:98.
121. José Luis Méndez, "The Emergence of Sociology in Puerto Rico," *Caliban* 3, no. 1 (1976): 11.
122. De Hostos, *Obras*, 16:99, 232-34.
123. Ibid., 17:46-47.
124. Ibid., 14:33-37, 139-42.
125. Ibid., 17:190-91.
126. Ibid., 17:55.
127. Ibid., 14:77-88.
128. Ibid., 12:52.
129. Ibid., 16:102-3, and 17:173.
130. Ibid., 17:168-75.
131. Ibid., 16:96.
132. Ibid., 4:44.
133. Ibid., 15:432-35. See, in general, Juan Bosch, *Hostos, el Sembrador* (Havana: Ed. Trópico, 1939); Francisco Elías de Tejada, *Las doctrinas políticas de Eugenio María de Hostos* (Madrid: Ediciones Cultura Hispánica, 1949); and Carlos Méndez Santos, *Eugenio María de Hostos, sociólogo* (Ponce: Universidad Católica de Puerto Rico, 1969).
134. Calixto Bernal, cited in Cruz Monclova, *Historia de Puerto Rico*, p. 302.
135. José Castelar cited in Gordon K. Lewis, *Puerto Rico: Freedom and Power in the Caribbean* (New York: Monthly Review Press, 1963), p. 51.
136. See, in general, Cruz Monclova, *Historia de Puerto Rico*, vols. 1-3.
137. Salvador Brau, "Lo que dice la historia," in Fernández Méndez, *Salvador Brau*, p. 288.
138. Julián Acosta, cited in Cruz Monclova, *Historia de Puerto Rico*, 1:613.
139. Alejandro Tapia y Rivera, *Mis memorias, o Puerto Rico como lo encontré y como lo dejó* (New York: De Laisne and Rossboro, 1928), pp. 88-89.
140. Eugenio María de Hostos, Prologue to *La peregrinación de Bayoán* (Madrid: Imprenta del Comercio, 1863).
141. *Junta informativa de ultramar* (Madrid, 1867), cited in Cruz Monclova, *Historia de Puerto Rico*, 1:542-44.
142. Tapia y Rivera, *Mis memorias*.
143. Brau, "Al Señor Ministro de ultramar," p. 289.
144. De Hostos, cited in Cruz Monclova, *Historia de Puerto Rico*, 2:10 n. 15.
145. *Acta de Constitución de la Sociedad Republicana de Cuba y Puerto Rico*, cited in Cruz Monclova, *Historia de Puerto Rico*, 1:566-67 n. 200. See also Vicente Geigel Polanco, "Trajectoria civica de Segundo Ruiz Belvis," *Puerto Rico Ilustrado* 28, no. 1482 (August 6, 1938); and Segundo Ruiz Belvis, José Julián Acosta, and Francisco Mariano Quiñones, *Proyecto para la abolición de la esclavitud en Puerto Rico* (1867; reprint ed., San Juan: Editorial Edil, 1978).
146. "En la tumba de Segundo Ruiz Belvis," reprinted in Manuel Maldonado-Denis, *Eugenio María de Hostos—America: La lucha por la libertad* (Mexico City: Siglo Veintiuno Editores, 1980), pp. 51-53.
147. Luis Bonafoux, *Betances* (San Juan: Instituto de Cultura Puertorriqueña, 1970), p. ix.

148. Cited in *Betances: Puerto Rico Will Be Free*, flysheet distributed at the University of Puerto Rico, April 1977.

149. "Carta de Betances à Hostos," *Claridad* (San Juan), September 20, 1980. See also Betances, "Souvenirs d'un Révolutionnaire," *La Revue Diplomatique* (Paris), October 10, 1897, reprinted in Paul Estrade, *La Colonia Cubana de Paris, 1895–1898* (Havana: Editorial de Ciencias Sociales, 1980).

150. Ramón Emeterio de Betances, *Las Antillas para los antillanos*, ed. Carlos M. Rama (San Juan: Biblioteca Popular, 1975).

151. Ibid., pp. 150–56.

152. Ramón Emeterio de Betances, Preface to Wendell Phillips, *Discours sur Toussaint L'Ouverture*, trans. Betances (Paris, December 1879). See also Emilio Godinez, "En el centenario de un trabajo betancino," *Claridad* (San Juan), December 7–13, 1979. See also Bonafoux, *Betances*, and Ada Suárez Díaz, *El doctor Ramón Emeterio Betances: Su vida y su obra* (San Juan: Ateneo Puertorriqueño, 1968). See, in general, Bolívar Pagán, *Procerato Puertorriqueños, desde sus origenes hasta 1898* (San Juan: Editorial Campos, 1961).

153. José María Serra, *Apuntes para la historia de los Trinitarios* (Santo Domingo: Colección Enriquillo, 1974), p. 12.

154. Joaquín Balaguer, *El Cristo de la libertad* (Santo Domingo: Edición especial Fundación de Crédito Educativo, 1970); *Apuntes de Rosa Duarte: Archivo y versos de Juan Pablo Duarte* (Santo Domingo: Instituto Duartiano, Editora del Caribe, 1970); Pedro Troncoso Sánchez, *Vida de Juan Pablo Duarte* (Santo Domingo, 1967); E. Rodríguez Demorizi, *Duarte romàntico* (Santo Domingo: Editora el Caribe, 1969); and Juan Isidro Jiménez Grullón, "La ideología revolucionaria de Juan Pablo Duarte," in *Duarte y la independencia nacional* (Santo Domingo: Ediciones Intec, 1976), pp. 141–68.

155. Max Henríquez Ureña, *Panorama histórico de la literatura dominicana*, 2 vols. (Santo Domingo: Librería Dominicana, 1965), 1:163.

156. Juan Isidro Jiménez Grullón, "La Ideolgía de Duarte," p. 168.

157. Ibid., pp. 160–61. See also Leonidas García Lluberes, *Critica Històrica—Influencia de la Iglesia Católica en formación de la Nacionalidad Dominicana y en la creación de la República Dominicana* (Santo Domingo: Editora Montalvo, 1964).

158. H. Hoetink, *El Pueblo Dominicano 1850–1900* (Santiago, Dominican Republic: Universidad Católica Madre y Maestra, 1971), pp. 206–8.

159. Henríquez Ureña, *Panorama histórico*, 2:419.

160. Hoetink, *El Pueblo Dominicano*, p. 201.

161. Juan Isidro Pérez, cited in Henríquez Ureña, *Panorama histórico*, 1:164.

162. Gregorio Luperón, *Notas autobiográficas y apuntes históricos*, cited in Hugo Tolentino Dipp, *Gregorio Luperón: Biografía política* (Santo Domingo, Dominican Republic: Editora Alfa y Omega, 1977), p. 88.

163. Ibid., pp. 455–56.

164. For all this, see Henríquez Ureña, *Panorama histórico*.

165. Ibid., and Joaquín Balaguer, *Historia de la literatura dominicana* (Ciudad Trujillo, Dominican Republic: Ed. Librería Dominicana, 1972).

166. Henríquez Ureña, *Panorama histórico*, 1:177.

167. See, in general, ibid.

168. Del Monte y Tejeda, ibid., 1:92.

169. Ibid., 2:411, 413.

170. Cited in Lil Despradel, "Les étapes de l'anti-haitienisme en Republique Dominicaine: Le rôle des historiens," in *Nouvelle Optique*, no. 8 (October–December 1972): 78–79. See also Franklin J. Franco, *Cultura, política, e ideología* (Santo Domingo: Editorial Nacional, 1974), pp. 47–54.

171. Gérard Pierre-Charles, "Genèse des nations haitienne et dominicaine," *Nouvelle Optique*, no. 8 (October–December 1972), pp. 17–44; and Francisco A. Avalino, *Las ideas políticas en Santo Domingo* (Santo Domingo, Dominican Republic: Editorial Arte y Cine, 1966).

172. Juan Jorge García, "Enfoque histórico de la legislación sobre la Nacionalidad Dominicana," *EME. Estudios Dominicanos*, no. 2 (August–September 1972): 121-30.

173. Jean-Baptiste Saint-Victor, *Haiti: Sa lutte pour l'émancipation* (Paris: La Nef de Paris Editions, 1957).

174. Domingo Méndez Capote, *Trabajos*, 3 vols. (Havana: Molina y Companía, 1929-30), 1:204. See also Cintio Vitier, *Lo cubano en la poesía* (Las Villas, Mexico: Universidad Central de las Villas, 1958).

175. José Antonio Saco, cited in Rául Lorenzo, *Sentido nacionalista del pensamiento de Saco* (Havana: Editorial Trópico, 1942), p. 110.

176. Introduction to Pedro José Guiteras, *Cuba y su Gobierno*, Coleccíon de Libros Cubanos, vol. 31 (Havana, 1932), cited in José Manuel Pérez Cabrera, *Historiografía de Cuba* (Mexico City, Instituto Panamericano de Geografía e Historia, 1962), p. 230.

177. José María de Andueza, *Isla de Cuba pintoresca* (Madrid, 1841), cited ibid., p. 170.

178. Antonio Bachiller y Morales, *Los negros* (Barcelona, 1887), cited ibid., p. 301.

179. Manuel Sanguily, "Los Caribes de las islas," in *Revista de Cuba* (1884), vol. 16, and "Los oradores de Cuba," in *Revista Cubana* (1886), vol. 3, cited ibid., pp. 321-23.

180. Vidal Morales, "Tres historiadores cubanos," *Revista de Cuba* (1877), 1:9-16, cited ibid., p. 311.

181. Jacobo de la Pezuela, *Historia de la isla de Cuba*, 4 vols. (Madrid, 1868, 1878), and *Diccionario geográfico, estadístico, histórico de la Isla de Cuba*, 4 vols. (Madrid, 1863, 1866), cited ibid., pp. 206-12.

182. Antonio Bachiller y Morales, *Apuntes para la historia de las letras y de la instrucción pública en la Isla de Cuba*, 3 vols. (Madrid, 1859, 1860, and 1861), and *Cuba primitiva* (Havana, 1883), cited ibid., pp. 298-302.

183. Vidal Morales, "Los precursores de la autonomía," *El Fígaro*, nos. 2, 3, 4 (1898), cited ibid., p. 312.

184. Alfredo Zayas, *Cuba autonómica* (Havana, 1889), cited ibid., pp. 313-14.

185. Pérez Cabrera, *Historiografia de Cuba*, chs. 5, 6.

186. Pezuela, cited ibid., pp. 214-15.

187. Joaquín José García, *Protocolo de antiguedades. literatura, agricultura, industria, comercio* (Havana, 1845, 1846), cited ibid., p. 303.

188. Enrique Piñeyro, cited ibid., p. 319.

189. Pérez Cabrera, *Historiografia de Cuba*, pp. 310-11.

190. For all this, see, in addition, Carlos M. Trelles, *Biblioteca histórica cubana*, 3 vols. (Matanzas-Havana, 1922-26); Hortensis Pichardo, *Documentos para la historia de Cuba*, vol. 1 (Havana: Ediciones de Ciencias Sociales, 1977); and Salvador Bueno, *Figuras Cubanas del Siglo XIX* (Havana: Unión de Escritores y Artistas de Cuba, 1980).

191. Antonio Bachiller y Morales, *Apuntes*...3 vols. (Havana: Ed. Colección de Libros Cubanos, Cultural S.A., 1936), 1:28-29, 102-4.

192. Ibid., 1:146-47, 189-200.

193. Ibid., 1:259-75.

194. Ibid., 3:83-84.

195. Ibid., 3:125-32.

196. Ibid., 3:207-66.

197. Ibid., 1:146-47.

198. Ibid., 3:139-40.

199. Ibid., 3:125.

200. Fernando Figueredo, *La Revolución de Yara. 1868-1878: Conferencias históricas* (Havana: M. Pulido y Compañia, 1902).

201. Enrique Collazo, *Desde Yara haste el Zanjón. apuntaciones históricas* (Havana: Tipografía de "La Lucha," 1893); Antonio Zambrana, *La República de Cuba* (New York: Librería y Imprenta de N. Ponce de León, 1873); Ramón Roa, *Con la pluma y el machete*, 3 vols. (Havana:

Publicaciones de la Academia de la Historia de Cuba, 1950); Manuel de la Cruz, *Episodios de la Revolución Cubana* (Havana: Establicimiento Tipográfico, 1890).

202. Enrique José Varona, *Cuba contra España*, edited in *De la Colonia a la República* (Havana: Sociedad Editorial Cuba Contemporáneo, 1919); Rafael María Merchán, *Cuba: Justificación de su guerra de independencia* (Bogotá: Imprenta de "La Luz," 1896); Fermin Valdés Domínguez, *El 27 de noviembre de 1871* (Havana: Imprenta y Papeleria de Rambla y Bouza, 1909); Enrique Trujillo, *Apuntes históricos* (New York: Tipografía de "El Porvenir," 1896).

203. Giberga, cited in Pérez Cabrera, *Historiografia de Cuba*, p. 273.

204. Céspedes, cited in Raimundo Menocal, *Origen y desarrollo del pensamiento Cubano* (Havana: Editorial Lex, 1947), pp. 422–23.

205. Jorge Ibarra, *Ideología Mambisa* (Havana: Instituto del Libro, 1967), pp. 86–89.

206. Carlos M. Céspedes, "Carta al Honorable Sr. C. Sumner," cited in "Céspedes Abolicionista," *Bohemia* 66, no. 13 (March 29, 1974): 28–35.

207. Céspedes, cited in Ibarra, *Ideología Mambisa*, p. 90.

208. Agramonte cited ibid., pp. 83–86. See also "El rescate de un héroe" in Manuel de la Cruz, *Episodios.*

209. Ibid., pp. 147–48. See also Juan Marinello, "Maceo," in Leonardo Griñan Peralta, *Antonio Maceo* (Havana: Editorial Trópico, 1936), pp. 241–42.

210. Ibarra, *Ideología Mambisa*, pp. 147–55.

211. Maximo Maceo cited in Hugh Thomas, *Cuba: The Pursuit of Freedom, 1762–1969* (New York: Harper and Row, 1971), p. 265.

212. Ibarra, *Ideología Mambisa*, pp. 155–58.

213. See also Maximo Gomez, "Odisea del general José Maceo," in his *El Viejo Edúa* (Havana: Instituto Cubano del Libro, 1972), pp. 55–74. See, in general, Philip S. Foner, *Antonio Maceo: The "Bronze Titan" of Cuba's Struggle for Independence* (New York: Monthly Review Press, 1977). See also José L. Franco, *Antonio Maceo: Apuntes para una historia de su vida* (Havana: Ediciones de Ciencias Sociales, 1975).

214. Roberto Agramonte, *Martí y su concepción del mundo* (Río Piedras: Editorial Universitaria, Universidad de Puerto Rico, 1971)

215. See in general, José Martí, *Obras completas* (Havana, 1963–65). For the traditional liberal view of Martí see, for example, Jorge Mañach, *Martí, El Apóstol* (Madrid: España-Calpe, 1946). For the later, Marxist view see, for example, Leonardo Acosta, *José Martí, La América Precolombina y la Conquista Española* (Havana: Casa de las Américas, 1974).

216. Martí, cited in Agramonte, *Martí*, pp. 707–8.

217. Salvador Morales, "José Martí: Ideas anticoloniales," in *Claridad* (San Juan), April 14, 1975; and Gaspar J. García Gallo, "Martí: La formación multilateral del hombre," in *El Caiman Barbudo* (Havana), May 1974.

218. Cited in José Martí, *Inside the Monster: Writings on the United States and American Imperialism*, ed. Philip Foner, trans. Elinor Randall (New York: Monthly Review Press, 1975), p. 49.

219. Ibid., and José Martí, *Our America—Writings on Latin America and the Cuban Struggle for Independence*, ed. Philip Foner, trans. Elinor Randall (New York: Monthly Review Press, 1978).

220. Martí, *Inside the Monster*, pp. 31–32.

221. Ibid., pp. 50–51.

222. Ibid., p. 107.

223. Ibid., p. 204.

224. Ibid., pp. 329, 372.

225. Ibid., p. 351.

226. José Martí, "Nuestra América," in *José Martí: En los Estados Unidos*, ed. Andrés Sorel (Madrid: Alianza Editorial, 1968), pp. 299–309.

227. Ibid., p. 302.

228. Ibid., p. 303.

229. Socorro Rodríguez, cited in Agramonte, *Martí*, p. 754.

230. Roberto Fernández Retamar, *José Martí: Páginas escogidas* (Havana: Editora Universitaria, 1965), p. 31.

231. Hans-Otto Dill, *El ideario literario y estético de José Martí* (Havana: Casa de las Américas, 1975), pp. 25-31. See, in general, V. Juan Marinello, *Martí, escritor americano* (Havana: Imprenta Nacional de Cuba, 1962). See also Jorge Ibarra, *José Martí: Dirigente político e ideólogo revolucionario* (Havana: Editorial de Ciencias Sociales, 1980), especially ch. 5.

232. Eulogia Horta, cited in Hoetink, *El Pueblo Dominicano*, pp. 265-66.

233. Ateneo Puertorriqueño, *Catálogo...de las obras existentes en la Biblioteca del Ateneo Puertorriqueño* (San Juan: Tipografía de "El País," 1897).

234. Pedro F. Bonó, *El Moutero*, cited in Hoetink, *El Pueblo Dominicano*, p. 265.

235. For the traditional view of all this see, for example, Diego Manuel Sequeira, *Rubén Darío, Criollo* (Buenos Aires: Editorial Guillermo Kraft Ltda., 1945). For a later, more critical, view see, for example, Keith Ellis, *Critical Approaches to Rubén Darío* (Toronto: University of Toronto Press, 1974).

236. Goveia, *Historiography*, pp. 107-65; W. J. Gardner, *A History of Jamaica* (1873; reprint ed., London: Frank Cass and Co., 1971).

237. Wm. G. Sewell, *The Ordeal of Free Labor in the British West Indies* (New York: Harper and Brothers, 1861), p. 38.

238. Dalton quoted in Goveia, *Historiography*, pp. 113-16.

239. Hill quoted ibid., pp. 116-18.

240. Ibid., pp. 119-21.

241. Fraser quoted ibid., pp. 125-27.

242. Anthony de Verteuil, *Sir Louis de Verteuil: His Life and Times, Trinidad, 1800-1900* (Port-of-Spain, Trinidad: Columbus Publishers, 1973), p. 123.

243. Ibid., pp. 172-73.

244. J. Rodway, *History of British Guiana*, 3 vols. (Georgetown, British Guiana, 1891, 1893, 1894); and J. A. Froude, *The English in the West Indies* (London, 1888).

245. W. P. Livingstone, *Black Jamaica* (London: Sampson Low, Marston and Company, 1899), pp. 10, 15.

246. Ibid., pp. 288-89.

247. William B. Cohen, "Literature and Race: Nineteenth Century French Fiction, Blacks, and Africa, 1800-1900," *Race and Class* 16, no. 2 (October 1974): 56-76.

248. J. J. Thomas, *Froudacity* (1889; reprint ed., Port-of-Spain and London: New Beacon Books, 1969), p. 74.

249. Ibid., p. 154.

250. Ibid., p. 131.

251. Ibid., pp. 180-81. See also Carl Campbell, "John Jacob Thomas of Trinidad," in African Studies Association of the West Indies (Kingston, Jamaica), *Bulletin*, no. 8 (1965): 26-42; and Bridget Brereton, "John Jacob Thomas: An Estimate," *Journal of Caribbean History* 9 (1977):18-43.

252. Edward W. Blyden, *Christianity, Islam, and the Negro Race* (Edinburgh: Edinburgh University Press, 1967), p. 10.

253. Ibid., p. 77.

254. Louis Joseph Janvier, *Les détracteurs de la race noire* (Paris: Marpon et Flammarion, 1882), pp. 33-76.

255. Hannibal Price, *De la réhabilitation de la race noire par la république d'Haiti* (Port-au-Prince, Haiti: Imprimerie J. Verrollot, 1900), pp. 117-18.

256. Ibid., p. 382.

257. Ibid., pp. 144-45.

258. Anténor Firmin, *De l'égalité des races humaines* (Paris: Levaine Cotillon, 1885), pp. 115–16, 126–28, 169–75.

259. Ibid., pp. 191–93.

260. Ibid., pp. 63–64.

261. Ibid., pp. 94–102.

262. Ibid., pp. 275–92.

263. Ibid., pp. 250–52.

264. Ibid., pp. 650–52.

265. Ibid., p. 653.

266. Janvier, *Les détracteurs*, pp. 43–44; Price, *Réhabilitation*, pp. 404–10, 425–26.

267. René Depestre, "Problems of Identity for the Black Man in the Caribbean," *Caribbean Quarterly*, no. 3 (September 1973): 55.

268. Firmin, *De l'égalité des races*, pp. 658–62.

269. Blyden, *Christianity*, pp. 14–15.

270. Thomas, *Froudacity*, pp. 164–76.

CHAPTER SIX

1. Edward Brathwaite, *The Development of Creole Society in Jamaica, 1770–1820* (Oxford: Clarendon Press, 1971), and review by John Hearne, *Caribbean Quarterly* 19, no. 2 (June 1973): 81–84.

2. Henry Nelson Coleridge, *Six Months in the West Indies in 1825* (London: John Murray, 1832), p. 281.

3. *Historical Essay on the Colony of Surinam, 1788* (Cincinnati: American Jewish Archives, 1974), p. 17.

4. Capt. James Cook, *Voyages of Discovery* (New York: Everyman's Library, E. P. Dutton and Co., 1906), p. 227.

5. A. J. Mc.R. Benjamin, "Some Notes on the Origins of 1763," *Release* 1 (1979).

6. *Equiano's Travels*, trans. and ed. Paul Edwards (London: Heinemann Educational Books, 1967), p. 73.

7. Eugenio Pereira Salas, "The Cultural Emancipation of America," in *The Old and the New World: Their Cultural and Moral Relations* (Basle: UNESCO, 1956), p. 105.

8. Hans-Otto Dill, *El ideario literario y estético de José Martí* (Havana: Casa de las Américas, 1975), pp. 25–31.

9. René Acheen in *Compte-rendu des travaux du Colloque de Saint-Pierre* (Fort-de-France, Martinique: Centre Universitaire Antilles Guyane, 1973), p. 67.

10. Simon Bolívar, quoted in Adolphe Roberts, *The Caribbean: The Story of Our Sea of Destiny* (Philadelphia: Bobbs-Merrill, 1940), p. 263. See also Carlos Rama, *La idea de la federación antillana en los independentistas puertorriqueños del siglo XIX* (Río Piedras, Puerto Rico: Ediciones Librería Internacional, 1971).

11. Frank Moya Pons, "Is There a Caribbean Consciousness?" *Américas* 31, no. 8 (August 1979): 72–76.

12. Jorge Mañach, *Frontiers in the Americas: A Global Perspective*, trans. Philip H. Phenix from *Teoría de la frontera* (New York: Teachers College Press, Columbia University, 1976), p. 48.

13. Charles Edwin Taylor, *Leaflets from the Danish West Indies* (London: Wm. Dawson and Sons, 1888), ch. 26.

14. Wm. G. Sewell, *The Ordeal of Free Labor in the British West Indies* (1859; reprint ed., London: Frank Cass and Co., 1968), and Charles Kingsley, *At Last: A Christmas in the West Indies* (1869; reprint ed., London: Macmillan, 1900).

15. Charles Day, *Five Years Residence in the West Indies*, cited in Andrew Pearse, "Carnival in Nineteenth Century Trinidad," *Caribbean Quarterly* 4, nos. 3 and 4 (March, June 1956); and *The Hamilton Report, 1881*, reprinted in *Vanguard* (Port-of-Spain, Trinidad), February 8, 1969, pp. 31–45.

16. Sir Spencer St. John, *Hayti, or the Black Republic* (London, 1889).

17. *El Movimiento Obrero Cubano, documentos y artículos*, vol. 1, *1865–1925* (Havana: Instituto de historia del movimiento comunista y la Revolución Social de Cuba, 1975).

18. "Don Santiago Andrade, visionario del cooperativismo," *Puerto Rico Ilustrado* (San Juan), December 14, 1973.

19. Angel Quintero Rivera, *Workers' Struggle in Puerto Rico: A Documentary History* (New York and London: Monthly Review Press, 1976).

20. Lucien Febvre, "The Counsels of Clio," in *The Old and the New World*, pp. 160–61.

21. Alceu Amoroso Lima, "Europe's Past and Potential Contribution to American Culture," in *The Old and the New World*, pp. 80–81.

Index

Abbad y Lasierra, Iñigo, 70, 265-66
d'Abbeville, Claude, 85
Abolitionism: and colonialism, 245; in England, 205-8; English planter response to, 116-23; in France, 208-16; and mulattoes, 216-19; and national character, 11-12
Acosta, José Julián, 275
Advielle, Victor, 126
Agramonte, 291, 293
Agramonte, Roberto, 295
Aguilar, Marcos de, 220, 221
Albornoz, Bartolomé de, 102
Aldamista, 157
Allen, Grant, 233-34
Allo, Lorenzo, 147
Alonso, Manuel, 22, 268, 271
Amelioration, 118-20
American Revolution, 206
Andueza, José M., 286-87
Anstey, Roger, 199
Antigua, 1737 rebellion, 225
Anti-Semitism, 97-99
Antislavery arguments, early, 102
Antislavery novel, 232-36. *See also* Abolitionism
Arago, 213-14
Arango y Parreño, Fransisco de, 144-50
Arce, Margot, 268
Ardouin, 126, 218, 256-60
Arrate, 287, 290; and Arango, 148-49
Atkins, Edwin F., 109
Atkinson, Geoffroy, 83
Atwood, Thomas, 103-7
d'Auberteuil, Hilliard, 125, 129, 245; in Ardouin, 257; on emancipation, 167; background of, 248-49; persecution of, 140, 165; on pirates, 80-81; political ideas of, 249-52; racism of, 136; as representative, 135; on slavery, 133-36
Avellaneda, 234
Avendaño, 52
Azcárate, 158

Bachiller y Morales, 155, 287-90; on slave religion, 192
Bailey, F. M., 37
Balaguer, Joaquín, 278, 282
Balbuena, Bishop, 91
Bamboo-tamboo, 19, 188
Barbados: Declaration of Independence of 1651, 74; 1816 rebellion, 227; nationalism in, 264
Barbé-Marbois, 125
Barclay, Alexander, 118, 121
Bardou, Abbé, 210
Barham, Henry, 118, 121
Barnave, Antoine, 211, 216
Barrett, Richard, 167
Baudet, Henri, 30-31
Beaumont, 120
Beaumont, Joseph, 243
Beaumont, Regnault de, 181
Beavois, M. de, 217
Beckford, William, 117, 119
Bellecombe, 125
Benítez, Fernando, 34
Benítez, María Bibiano, 270
Berbice, 1763 rebellion, 226, 323
Bercy, Drouin de, 196

Bernal, Calixto, 274
Betances, 264, 276-77, 304; and Schoelcher, 216
Betanzos, Comingo de, 38
Biet, Père, 66, 76, 85
Bigelow, A., 307
Black nationalism, 2, 227
Blacks: compared to Jews, 183-84; as custodians of culture, 19-20; early attitude toward, 89-90. *See also* Racism; Slaves
Bleby, Henry, 120, 227, 228
Blyden, Edward Wilmot, 313, 315-16, 320
Boissonade, Jean F., 124, 137, 140
Bolingbroke, Henry, 163
Bonilla, Cepero, 156, 158, 292
Bonnemain, 212
Bonnett, Joseph, 228, 253-54
Bonneville, René, 170
Bono, Pedro, 305
Borde, Sieur de la, 221, 309; on Caribs, 41-42, 64, 85
Bougainville, Louis-Antoine de, 209
Boukman, 193-94
Bourguignon, M., 191
Boutin, Père, 130
Bouton, 85
Bouzon, Justin, 260
Boyer, Sieur de, 75, 85
Brathwaite, Edward, 183, 233, 321; on historiography, 174-75
Brau, Salvador, 268-72, 275
Brazil, origin of slaves in, 189
Breen, H. H., 308
Bressen, Benigne, 64
Breton, Père, 91
Bridges, 163
Brissot, Jacques, 138, 140, 212
British West Indies: black nationalism in, 227; creole nationalism in, 72-75; nationalism in, 307-15; origin of slaves in, 189; religion and emancipation, 20; slave religion in, 197-205
Bronkhurst, H.V.P., 243
Browne, 109
Brujería, 192-97
Buchner, 203
Buckle, Henry, 277
Burke, Edmund, 207-8; on amelioration, 119; in Edwards, 114; on slaves, 6

Cabon, F., 195
Cabrera, Miguel, 268

Cadusch, De, 127
Caguax, 37
Cairnes, John E., 94, 96
Caldecott, Rev. A., 205, 308
Camboulay, 19, 188
Camden, William, 62
Campbell, John, 218
Campos, Pedro Albizu, 58
Caneda, Figarola, 155
Canina Salgado, Marcelino, 22
Cannibalism, 40, 85
Capetillo, Luis a, 327
Capitalism: Arango on, 148; development of, 67; and exploration, 46; industrial, 121-23; and pirates, 80; and planters, 121; and slavery, 97
Caribs: cannibalism of, 85; culture of, 40-42; French impression of, 63-64; in planter ideology, 104; slavery among, 98; Spanish impression of, 64; as utopian ideal, 85-87
Caries, Rev. M., 205
Carmichael, Mrs., 198
Carnival, 241-42
Cartesianism, 195-96
Cash, W. J., 182-83
Catholicism: as antislavery, 202; early attitude of, toward blacks, 89-90; and Indians, 43-46; in Santo Domingo, 279; against slave religion, 195; in slave religion, 189, 192-93, 198
Catholic theocracy, Las Casas on, 49
Cernik, L., 203
Césaire, Aimé, 259
Céspedes, 194, 291-92
Chacon y Calvo, 155
Chanlatte, 254
Chanvalon, 133
Charlemagne, 252
Charlevoix, 132; on Indians, 41, 221; in Moreau de St.-Méry, 249
Charrault, 252
Chaumette, 217
Chinese workers, 5; in Cuba, 292
Christian imperialism, 53
Christianity: ideological contributions of, 199-208; and Indians, 221; and slavery, 99-100, 210. *See also* Catholicism; Protestantism
Christophe, Henri, 229; Clarkson correspondence, 211; government of, 252-54
Cisneros, Betancourt, 147, 155
Clarkson, Thomas, 202-3, 211
Class consciousness, 327

Class prejudice: and racism, 97; and Haitian nationalism, 259-61
Climate and white labor, 151
Clodore, J. de, 75
Code Noir, 177-78, 237
Codrington, 78; library of, 91
Coke, Thomas, 199-201
Collazo, 291
Collens, J. H., 198
Collins, W. E., 118, 198
Colombel, 254
Colonialism: and abolitionism, 245; compared to other colonial areas, 23; creation of, 3-4; effect of religion on, 10-11; ethnic justification for, 49
Colonial mentality, 24-25
Columbus, Christopher, 31, 32; on early colonizers, 44; family claims of, 35-36; first reports of, 35; historical image of, 13, 30; on Indians, 32, 41, 48, 103
Columbus, Fernando, 81, 91
Condorcet, 140, 209, 213
Conquistadores, image of, 13
Cook, James, 209; on slavery, 322-23
Corchado y Juarbe, 270
Cortes, 32
Cosmology, early modern, 29-30
Costa, Emilia Viotti da, 184
Cournand, Abbé de, 139, 217
Covarrubias, 57
Craton, Michael, 178
Creole nationalism: in British West Indies, 72-75; in Puerto Rico, 70-72; roots of, 70, 75-76
Cromwell, Oliver, 61
Cross, Whitney, 198
Cruz, Manuel de la, 291
Cuba: abolition in, 292; agricultural diversity of, 141-42; annexation of, 149, 152-53, 155-56; antislavery novel in, 234-36; class consciousness in, 327; class ideology in, 159; ethnic heterogeneity in, 194; first war of independence, 157; international context, 159-60; origin of slaves on, 189; planter ideology in, 107, 108, 140-44; racism in, 154-60; technology in, 161-62
Cuban literature, early, 58
Cuban nationalism, 264, 286-303; and Santo Domingo, 282; wartime ideology, 290-94
Cudjoe, 37
Cuffy, 37, 225-26, 323
Cumina, 197

Cunha, Euclicles De, 306
Curtin, Philip, 5, 26

Daaga, 229
Dallas, R. C., 103, 230-31; on Maroons, 105-6
Dalmas, P., 140
Dalton, H., 308
Dampier, William, 82
Danish West Indies: miscegenation in, 8; mulattoes in, 216; slave rebellion in, 222
Darfour, Felix, 254, 319
Darió, Rubén, 302, 303, 306-7
Daupion-Lavaysse, 178
Davies, John, 60
Davis, Brion, 172
Davis, N. Darnell, 74-75
Davy, John, 308
Day, Thomas, 198
Debien, Gabriel, 124, 173; on division of labor, 176; on poisoning by slave, 177
Declaration of the Rights of Man, 137, 218
Defoe, Daniel, 1, 107
Delacroix, Jacques-Vincent, 133
Delaire, R., 127
Delaurens, Abbé, 210
Deligne, C., 282
Delmonte, Domingo, 147, 154-55, 234-35, 282-83
Del Monte y Tejeda, N., 283
Delorme, Demesvar, 261-64
Demorizi, Rodrígues, 278
Denis, Lorimer, 225, 259
Deschamps, A., 140
Deschamps Chapeaux, Pedro, 173
Desportes, W., 130
Dessalines, 194, 229, 253
Destuut de Tracy, 140
Des Voeux Enquiry of 1870, 243
Deule, Juan de la, 38
Deza, Pedro Suarez de, 58
Diderot, 209, 210
Dill, Hans-Otto, 303
Dober, Rev. L., 203
Dollar Diplomacy, 4, 321
Dorantes de Corranza, Baltazar, 35
Dorfeuille, Antoine, 212, 216
Dorsainvil, Justin Chrysostome, 191
Douyon, G., 191
Drimmer, Carl, 184
Duarte, Juan Pablo, 264, 278-79
Duarte, Rosa, 278
Dubourg, M., 130

Dubuisson, M., 7, 135-36, 166
DuPont de Nemours, 210, 211
Dupuy, Baron de, 253
Durret, Sieur, 66-67
Du Tertre, 90, 92; on capitalist ethos, 67; on Caribs, 41, 63-64, 85, 221; on creole nationalism, 75, 76; creolization in, 66-67; on ethnicity, 18; on planters, 8; on slaves, 65-66; on social mobility, 67-68
Duvalier, François, 225, 259

East Indians, 11, 242-44
Echevarría, José Antonio, 147, 157-58
Economic determinism, 13-14
Eden, Richard, 60
Edouard, 263
Education; earliest, 58; Saco on, 150; of slaves, 119
Edwards, Bryan, 108, 130, 245; on amelioration, 118-20; and Arango, 147; on factory workers, 123; on French colonials, 127; ideology of, 113-16; on Maroons, 105-6; on planter lifestyle, 8; political ideas of, 247-48; racism in, 7; on Saint Domingue revolution, 120; on slave language, 179; on slaves, 167
Elizabethan explorers, image of, 13
Elkins, Stanley M., 171
Ely, Roland, 26
Engerman, Stanley L., 171
England: abolitionism in, 205-8, 211, 222, 227; early planter ideology, 103-7; humanitarianism, 27
English literature, 60-62; and slavery, 206-7
Enlightenment, 27; in Moreau de Saint-Méry, 130-31; in de Vastey, 255
d'Ennery, Comte, 126
Enriquillo, 220
Equiano, 173, 323
Escabí, Elsa, 22
Escabí, Pedro, 22
Esquemeling, 79
Exploration, effects of, on Europe, 29-32
Eyre, Governor, trial of, 24

Febvre, Lucien, 327
Fédon, Julien, 241
Fernández Juncos, Manuel, 269, 271
Fernández Méndez, Eugenio, 42
Fernández-Santamaria, J. A., 57
Figgis, J. N., 196
Figueredo, 291

Firmin, Antenor, 261-64, 313, 317-20
Flinter, Colonel, 194
Fogel, Robert W., 171
Foner, Philip, 297, 302
Fouchard, 226
Fraginals, Moreno, 141; on Arango, 148; on technology, 161-62
France: abolitionism in, 124, 208-16; slavery in, 98; utopian literature of, 84-86
Franco, Franklin, 124
Fraser, L. M., 308, 309
Free blacks, as proslavery, 172-73
Free coloreds. See Mulattoes
Free trade: and planters, 121; in Puerto Rico, 265, 266
French colonies, origin of slaves in, 189
French Revolution, 206; Francophilia of, 214-15; and planter ideology, 136-40; and slavery, 212-13
Freyre, Gilberto, 183
Friede, Juan, 50
Frontier thesis, 4, 82
Frossard, 124
Frostin, Charles, 129
Froude, James A., 26, 310-14

Gage, Thomas, 61, 90
Galván, Manuel de Jesús, 283, 304
Gandia, Zeno, 270
Garay, Francisco de, 59
García, Joaquín José, 288
Gardner, W. J., 163, 308-9
Garnier, A., 215
Garrett, Mitchell B., 140
Garvey, Marcus, 20
Gel Chast, 125
Genovese, Eugene D., 183
Geographical determinism, 16-17
Geraldini, Alejandro, 58
Gibbon, Edward, 202, 207
Giberga, 291
Girod-Chantrans, 125, 128
Gobineau, 312-13, 318
Godwyn Morgan, 77, 202
Gómez, Máximo, 194, 291, 293
González, José Emilio, 268
González, José Luis, 268, 270
Gordon, George William, 218
Gouy d'Arày, Louis-Marthe, 138
Goveia, Elsa, 27, 92; on amelioration, 118; on Coke, 201; on early nationalism, 308; on humanitarian reform, 245; on mission-

ary Christianity, 199; on slave legislation, 163-64

Grafigny, Mme. de, 209

Grainger, James, 185

Green, William A., 199

Gregoire, Abbé, 137-38, 140, 217

Grigg, Nanny, 227

Grotius, 45-46, 62

Guama, 220

Guarionex, 37

Guarocuya, 220, 221

Guerra y Sánchez, Ramiro, 141

Guiridi, Angulo, 283

Guiteras, Pedro José, 286

Guy-Kersaint, Armand, 138

Haiti: Dominican fear of, 278-79, 282, 284-85; economic theory in, 261-64; racism in, 285-86; religion and emancipation, 20; socialism in, 262-63

Haitian nationalism, 252-54, 256-64, 316-20; literature of, 304-5

Haitian Revolution, Negrophobic response to, 255

Hakluyt, Richard, 60-62

Halaou, 193

Hamilton Report of 1881, 241

Hanke, Lewis, 50, 54

Hardy, 140, 211, 213

Haring, C. H., 78-79

Harlow, Vincent, 72

Harris, Marvin, 168

Hart, Richard, 176, 227

Hartsinck, J. J., 172, 226

Harvey, Thomas, 307

Hastings, Warren, Trial of, 24

Hatuey, 221

Havana Junta de Fomento, 152

Hazard, Samuel, 109

Healing in slave religion, 193, 197

Hearn, Lafcadio, 236-37

Hector, M., 124

Henríquez y Carvajal, 282

Heredia, 304, 306

Hernández, Gaspar, 279

Hernández, José, 306

Herrera y Tordesillas, Antonio de, 59, 90; on Indians, 46-48; on Las Casas, 101

Herskovits, 2, 25, 183; on slave religion, 189

Hickey, William, 177

Hill, Richard, 309

Hobbes, Thomas, 114

Horta, Eulogia, 305

Hostos, Eugenio María De, 264, 271-76, 304

Hughes, Rev. W., 198

Hurbon, Laennec, 191

Huizinga, Johan, 31

Humanism, 27

Humboldt, Alexander von: catholicity of, 92; in Cuba, 143; on planter lifestyle, 8

Hume, David, 204, 207

Hyacinthe, 193

Ibarra, Jorge, 291, 292

Ideología mambisa, 290-94

Incas, 33-34; in reform literature, 87

Indentured servants, 96

India. *See* East Indians

Indianista novel, 49, 88, 306

Indians: and Christianity, 221; cultural unity of, 221-22; Herrera on, 46-48; as labor, 96, 103; Oviedo on, 46-49; in proslavery ideology, 100; resistance by, 219-21; Sepúlveda on, 57; against slaves, 172; Spanish attitude toward, 96

Inginac, 252-53

Inquisition, 32, 77; in Puerto Rico, 72

Insularity, 12-13, 104

International law, 44-46

Irizarri, Don Pedro, 267

Jakobsson, Stir, 203

Jamaica: as a coherent culture, 321-22; 1831 rebellion, 225, 227; Jews in, 77; Maroons in, 230-32; Morant Bay rebellion of 1865, 308; mulattoes in, 218; nationalism in, 264; planter ideology in, 107-16; technology in, 161-62

James, C.L.R., 140, 218, 314; on slave resistance, 14; on Toussaint, 259

Janvier, Louis Joseph, 260-63, 313, 316-17, 319

Jean-François, 193

Jeannit, 178

Jernomite Commission, 49

Jews, 77; compared to blacks, 183-84; in Surinam, 322; toleration of, 97

Jibaros, 5, 216, 268-69

Jiménez Grullón, Juan Isidrio, 278

Joaquín Suárez, 154

Johnson, Robert, 60

Jordon, Edward, 118, 218

Joseph, E. L., 198, 229

Kidd, Benjamin, 312
Kiev, Ari, 191
King, Johannes, 231
Kingsley, Charles, 198, 326
Knibb, Rev. William, 203, 205
Koning, Hans, 13

Labat, Jean Baptiste, 26, 63, 90, 93, 212;
    career of, 69; on Caribs, 85, 89; creoliza-
    tion in, 67; on ethnicity, 18; library of, 91;
    on planter lifestyle, 8; on slave dance, 186;
    on slave religion, 195; on slaves, 65-66,
    89; on slave trade, 140; on social mobility,
    68
Laborie, Chevalier de, 140, 195, 212-13
Labor organization, 327
Labra, Rafael María de, 274
Laet, Jean de, 60
Lambert, Abbé Claude-François, 133
Lang, W., 203
Language: and ideology, 161; slave, 179
Language barriers, 12
Lanthenas, 140, 212
Lapouge, Gilles, 81
Las Casas, Bartolomé de, 3, 37, 49-57; Aris-
    totelianism of, 84; on Catholic theocracy,
    49; on Columbus, 30; and Columbus's re-
    ports, 32; community ideal in, 6; contra-
    dictions in, 55; creole reaction to, 70; in
    Herrera, 48; as historian, 50; historical
    image of, 49-50; as humanitarian, 202; on
    Indians, 39, 52, 103, 185, 220-22; library
    of, 91; in Martí, 297; modern reputation
    of, 56; as St. Paul, 18-19; Salas on, 56;
    and slavery, 17, 101; social concerns of,
    51; translation of, 60; and utopians, 86-
    87; in Voltaire, 210
Laujon, D., 126
Lawrence, T. E., 36
Lecointe-Marsillac, 139, 212, 216
Leigh-Fermor, Patrick, 11, 186
Lejeune case, 127, 166
León, Pedro de Cieza de, 38
León, Ponce de, 32
Leonard, Irving, 91
Lepkowski, P., 124
Leslie, Charles, 109
Lespinasse, Beavais, 257-58, 260
Levaysse, General, 253
Lévi-Strauss, Claude, 23-24
Lewis, Matthew G. ("Monk"), 165; on plant-
    ers, 8, 120; on slave behavior, 177-79,
    181; on slaves, 163, 166

Libraries, first, 91-92
Liendo, Rodrígo de, 59
Lier, R.A.J. van, 4
Ligon, Richard, 68, 74, 91, 185; on slave pun-
    ishment, 178
Lima, Alceu Amoroso, 328
Lipschutz, Alejandro, 81
Lisser, Herbert De, 233
Littleton, Edward, 72, 75
Livingstone, W. P., 311-12
Locke, John, 246
Logwooders, 82
Long, Edward, 108, 130, 228; ideology of,
    109-13; on mulattoes, 9, 167; political
    ideas of, 245-47; racism in, 7; on slave be-
    havior, 179-81; on slave dance, 185
López-Baralt, Mercedes, 40
López de Gómara, Francisco, 47
Lopez, Narciso, 156
Lowenthal, David, 12
Lucas, C. P., 308
Ludlow, John, 123
Luffman, John, 109
Luperón, 264, 278-81
Luz y Caballero, 154, 155, 295

Mably, Gabriel, 123
Maceo, 194, 291, 293-94
Macumba, 188
Madán, Cristóbal, 143, 156
Madin, B., 198
Madiou, Thomas, 256, 257, 259-60
Makandal, 193-94, 226, 228
Malenfant, 132
Malouet, 195
Mañach, Jorge, 325
Mandar, M. Théophile, 213
Manifest Destiny, 4, 321
Manigat, Leslie, 226
Mannheim, Karl, 24
Manso, Bishop Alonso, 32
Maravall, José Antonio, 56
Marinello, Juan, 293
Maroon Wars, 105-6
Maroons, 230-32; as slave hunters, 83, 106,
    172
Marqués, René, 25
Martel, Piedra, 293
Martí, 144, 149, 264, 272, 278, 288, 294-304;
    eclecticism of, 295-96; persecution of,
    165; on reformers, 158; in Rodó, 306; on
    the United States, 297-300
Martin, R. Montgomery, 308

Martínez-Alier, 143
Martyr, Peter: on early immigrants, 81; in
    Herrera, 48; Salas on, 55-56; translation
    of, 59-60; utopian images in, 84
Marx, Karl, 24, 94-95
Marxist historians and racism, 7
Mathers, Thomas G., 78
Mazeres, Monsieur De, 255
Mediterranean, comparison to, 16-20
Médor, 226
Meléndez, Concha, 268
Memoria Anónima, 70
Memoria Melgarejo, 70-71
Mendoza, Doña Elvira de, 59
Menocal y Cueto, 159
Mercado, Tomás, 102
Mercantilism, 207; and colonial power, 69;
    English, 61
Merchán, Rafael, 291
Mesoamerican culture, 42-43
Mestre, José Manuel, 157
Mexican nationalism, 33-35
Middle Passage, 5, 102
Mill, John Stuart, 277
Milscent, J. S., 254, 319
Mintz, Sidney, 4, 163, 172
Mirabeau, 210
Miscegenation, 8-9, 232-33; Arango on, 147;
    in Cuba, 141, 143-44, 155; Long on, 111-
    12. *See also* Mulattoes
Missionaries, 200-204; and slave education,
    119
Mitchell, Sir Harold, 2
Mittelhotzer, Edgar, 233
Miyares, 70
Modernism, of Darío, 307
Moise, 124
Moline, Tirso de, 59
Motejo, Esteban, 174, 185; on rebellion, 223;
    on slave culture, 193
Montesino, Antonio, 91
Montesquieu: in Abbad, 265; and abolition,
    209; in Haitian nationalism, 254; in Long,
    110, 246; on slavery, 31
Morales Lemus, 157
Morales, Vidal, 155, 287-88
Morand, Paul, 14
Moreau de Saint-Méry, 108, 129-36, 177,
    245; and Arango, 147; in Ardouin, 257;
    background of, 129, 248-49; on colonial
    morality, 130-31, 168; on community and
    slavery, 6; on the Declaration of the Rights
    of Man, 137; on pirates, 80-81; as planter

apologist, 131-33; political ideas of, 249-
    52; in Price, 317; racism in, 7, 128, 136; as
    representative, 135; on Saint Domingue
    society, 125-26; on slave dance, 186; on
    slave religion, 196
Morison, Samuel Eliot, 13
Mulattoes: abolitionism among, 216-19; in
    antislavery novel, 233-36; in British West
    Indies, 308; in Cuba, 141; in Danish West
    Indies, 216; and Haitian nationalism, 258-
    59; Hearn on, 236-37; Livingstone on,
    312; as police, 241; as proslavery, 172-73,
    218; in Saint Domingue, 128; social role
    of, 9; sociosexual origins of, 232-33;
    Thomas on, 313; women, social role of,
    236-38
Muñoz, Juan Bautista, 101
Muñoz Rivera, Luis, 55
Music: African compared to European, 187;
    slave, 185-88
Myalism, 189, 190, 197

Naipaul, Vidia, 25
Nash, A., 172
National character, 325-26; and abolition,
    11-12; and religion, 10-11; and slavery, 11
Nationalism: cultural, 239-44; and ethnicity,
    18; political, 244-46. *See also under indi-
    vidual countries*
Nau, Emile, 256, 257
Négritude, 22, 319
Negrophobia: and Haitian Revolution, 255; in
    planter ideology, 89
Netscher, P. M., 226
Neufchateau, L. de, 127
Nicholls, David, 254, 258
Niebohr, Herman J., 95, 96
Nisbet, Richard, 204
Nonconformists, 120, 202
Nugent, Lady, 5-6, 165; fear of blacks, 164;
    on French colonials, 127; on planters, 8,
    120

Obeah, 188
Ogé, 218
Oldmixon, J., 198; on creole nationalism, 75-
    76
Oliva de Coll, Josefina, 220
Olivier, Lord Sydney, 25, 36-37; on logwood-
    ers, 82
Orderson, C., 233
O'Reylly, Marshal, 70, 267-68
Oroonoko, 206, 209

Ortea, J., 282
Ortega y Gasset, José, 219
Ortiz, Fernándo, 141, 155, 183; on black culture, 192; on Cuban racism, 235-36; on Indians, 221; on Saco, 154; on slave culture, 187; on sugar, 161
Ortiz, Tomás, 48-49
Osborn, Robert, 219
Ovando, Doña Leonor de, 59
Oviedo, Gonzalo Fernández de, 37, 58, 76, 90; on early immigrants, 81; on Indians, 39, 46-49, 52, 54; Las Casas on, 52; Salas on, 56; on social mobility, 67; translation of, 60

Padilla, Francisco García de, 58
Padre Jean, 226
Pagan, Bolívar, 277
Pales Matos, Luis, 9
Pané, Ramón, 38-40
Papal Donation of 1493: English reaction to, 62; Portugal refusal of, 45
Pares, Richard, 73
Paris Revolutionary Convention, 136
Parry, J. H., 72
Patterson, Orlando, 199
Pau, Corneille de, 101
Paul, Edmond, 261-63
Paz, Matias de, 91
Pedreira, Antonio S., 25
Pérez, José Joaquín, 282-83
Pérez, Juan Isidro, 279
Pétion, 194, 229, 253
Pétion de Villeneuve, 140
Petit, Emilien, 251-52
Petit marronage, 176-77
Peytraud, Lucien, 124
Pezuela y Lobo, Jacobo de la, 143, 287-88
Phillippo, George, 182
Phillips, Wendell, 203, 276
Pierre-Charles, Jean, 124
Pinckard, George, 168, 176; on slave dance, 186
Pineyre, Enrique, 287
Pirala, Antonio, 291
Pirates, 78-83
Pi y Margall, 274
Plácido, 155
Planter ideology, 117-22; impermanence of, 183; main themes, 105-7; and nationalism, 245-46; Negrophobia in, 89; and political liberalism, 245; roots of, 74; and slave legislation, 163-64; utopian elements, 163; weakness of, 108-9
Planters: code of behavior, 164-65; philistinism of, 25, 109, 327; policy toward slaves, 165-68; religion of, 197
Pocomania, 19
Poivre, Pierre, 133
Politica indiana, 43
Polydor, 226
Pons, A., 125-26
Ponte Domínguez, A., 155
Porteus, Beilby, 198
Pouchet, D., 318
Power, Ramón, 266, 274
Poyer, J., 103
Pozos Dulces, Conde de, 155
Pre-Columbian culture, 37-43. *See also* Caribs; Indians
Prevost, Abbé, 209, 253
Prézeau, Chevalier de, 253
Price, Hannibal, 313, 317, 319
Price, Richard, 163, 230
Price-Mars, Jean, 183, 191, 304-5; on slave rebellion, 225
Primatt, Dr., 202
Proslavery ideology. *See* Planter ideology
Protestantism in slave religion, 189, 197-98
Puerto Rican nationalism, 264-77; literature of, 305
Puerto Rico: class consciousness in, 327; creole nationalism in, 70-72; origin of slaves on, 189; revolt of 1868, 268; revolutionary ideology in, 275-77
Purchas, Samuel, 102
Puritanism, 88
Puysegur, Chastenet de, 127

Quakers, 77; and antislavery, 203; French enthusiasm for, 209
"Quashie," 7, 180
Quesnel, Leo, 316
Quintana, 101

Racial purity, 8-10. *See also* Miscegenation; Mulattoes
Racism: in British West Indies, 310-11; and class prejudice, 97; in Cuba, 142-44, 154-58; effects of, 6-8; French colonial, 139-40; and Haitian nationalism, 258-59; and Marxist historians, 7; origins of, 96-98; persistence of, 169-70; in Saint Domingue, 127-29; scientific arguments for, 160, 311-12; and slavery, 96

Raffles, Thomas S., 36, 206
Ragatz, Lowell J., 25, 108; on technology, 161
Raimond, 218
Raleigh, Sir Walter, 32
Ramos, Nicolás, 71
Ramsay, James, 203-4, 206
Rastafarians, 19, 183
Rawick, George P., 184
Raynal, Gillaume, 129, 209; in Abbad, 266; on abolition, 245; and d'Auberteuil, 133; on Las Casas, 101; on slave rebellion, 222
Reckford, Mary, 227
Religion: African, 78; and colonialism, 10-11; and emancipation, 20; master and slave, 19; and national character, 10-11; pre-Columbian, 39-40; and race relations, 10. *See also* Catholicism; Christianity; Protestanism
Religious prejudice and racism, 97
Religious toleration, early, 77-78
Renny, R., 109
Republican Society of Cuba and Puerto Rico, 276
Retamar, Roberto Fernández, 303
Reynoso, Alvaro, 162
Ricardo, David, 260
Richardson, Jonathan, 235
Rigaud, André, 194, 228, 229
Rivera, Antonio, 277
Rivera, Modesto, 268
Riverend, Julio Le, 292
Rivière, Le Mercier de la, 261-62
Robertson, William, 101
Rochefort, 62, 91; on capitalist ethos, 67; on Caribs, 63-64, 98; creolization in, 66; on slaves, 65, 165; as social critic, 86; translation of, 60
Rodó, José Enrique, 219, 303, 306-7
Rodriguez, Socorro, 303
Rodriguez Obijo, 282
Rodway, J., 310-11
Romanet, General, 237-38
Romero Rosa, Ramón, 327
Rosiers, Comte de, 254
Roth, H. Ling, 162
Rousseau, 210
Rufz, Dr., 236-37
Ruiz Belvis, Segundo, 276

Saco, José Antonio, 108, 141, 144-47, 149-54, 158, 286; background of, 149; on Cuban annexation, 152-53, 155-56; on Cuban independence, 153; racism in, 7

Sagra, de la, 143
Saint Domingue: mulattoes in, 216-18; planter ideology in, 107, 108, 123-40; postrevolutionary ideology, 229-30; *revoltes blanches*, 76; 1791 rebellion, 222, 224-26; society of, 124-27
St. John, Sir Spencer, 317, 326
Saint-Ouen, de, 127
Saint-Pierre, Bernardin de, 13, 209
Saint-Rémy, Joseph, 218, 256-58, 260
Saint-Rémy, Lepelletier de, 258
Salas, Alberto, 55-56
Salazar, Eugenio de, 59
"Sambo," 7
Sánchez, Troncoso, 278
Sánchez Valverde, Antonio, 252
Sanders, Prince, 252
Sandoval, Alonso de, 102
Sangmêlés. See Mulattoes
Sanguily, 287
Sannon, H. Paulens, 260
San Román, Francisco de, 38
Santana, Arturo, 206
Santería, 19, 190, 192-97
Santiago Andrade, 327
Santo Domingo: early intellectual life on, 58-59; fear of Haiti, 278-79, 282, 284-85; 1522 insurrection, 224; literature of, 281-84, 305; nationalism in, 264, 277-86, 305; racism in, 285-86
Sarmiento, 159, 219, 306
Say, Jean-Baptiste, 260, 290
Schaw, Janet, 164
Schoelcher, Victor, 213-16, 245; on poisoning, 177, 178; on Toussaint, 259
Scholten, Governor von, 8, 214, 216
Schomburgk, Robert H., 308; on planters, 8, 109
Schuler, Monica, 177
Schulman, Ivan A., 235
Seaga, Edward, 190
Seeber, Edward, 208
Sepúlveda, Juan Ginés de, 54, 57
Sewell, W. G., 307, 308, 326
Sex and antislavery ideology, 232-34
Sexuality and slavery, 8-9
Shango, 19, 188, 189, 197, 198
Sharpe, Sam, 227, 228
Sheridan, Richard, 68, 72
Sibire, Abbé, 139, 217
Siebert, William Henry, 206
Sieur Chapuzet case, 127
Sismondi, 260

Slave, historical images of, 171-72

Slave legislation, 163-64

Slave rebellion: African culture and, 225; black nationalism in, 226-27; deterrents to, 175-76; ideology of, 219-30; in music, 188; planter fear of, 5-6, 164; in planter ideology, 119-20; and popular religion, 21; and vodun, 193-94

Slave religion: in British West Indies, 197; Catholicism against, 195; and cultural nationalism, 240; evolution of, 188-90; healing in, 193, 197

Slavery: accommodation to, 175-84; and Christianity, 99-100, 210; compared to factory work, 122-23, 152; in Cuba, 141-42; dynamic nature of, 171; economic role of, 5, 94-97; effect on French thought, 63-64; ideological antecedents, 98-99; Long on, 110-11; and national character, 11; necessity of terror in, 166; among pirates, 80; and racism, 96; as regional economic system, 162; Saco on, 151-52, 154; on Saint Domingue, 127-28; and sexuality, 8-9; social effect of, 168; and traditional ideologies, 100; and the work ethic, 151

Slaves: abortion by, 177; as administrators, 176; Christianization of, 178; culture of, 14, 182-88; education of, 119; "false consciousness" in, 181; French impression of, 65-66; initial shock of, 177; language, 179; literary record of, 173-74; loyalty of, 181-82; music of, 185-88; origins of, 189; poisoning by, 177-78; resistance of, 14-15; self-image, 180-82; self-mutilation by, 177; suicide of, 178

Slave trade mortality, 5

Sloane, Sir Hans: catholicity of, 92; on Indian music, 185

Smith, Adam, 23, 207-8; and Haitian nationalism, 260; on slavery, 127

Smith, John, 165, 203, 205

Smollett, Tobias, 14

Socialism, 27, 202; in Haiti, 262-63

Social mobility, early, 67-69

Société de Amis de Noirs, 137-38, 140, 212-13; Moreau de Saint-Méry on, 133

Solorzano, A., 52

Sonnerat, 133

Southey, Robert, 308

Spain: early challenge to, 59-62; export of culture, 58-59; and Inca culture, 33-34

Spanish Antillean nationalism, 303-7. *See also under individual countries*

Spanish conquest, early justification of, 43-45

Spanish humanism, 55

Spanish nationalism and discovery, 47-49

Spanish Renaissance thought, 56-59

Spence, William, 107-8

Stanton, William, 42

Stark, W., 83

Stedman, Captain John Gabriel, 230-31

Stephen, James, 259

Sterne, Laurence, 14

Steward, 118, 119

Stowe, Harriet Beecher, 95

Sturge, Joseph, 307

Styron, William, 171

Suárez de Peralta, Juan, 34-35

Suárez y Romero, Anselmo, 155, 234

Sugar: in Cuba, 141-42; and ideology, 161; primacy of, 13-14

Surinam, Jews in, 77

Sypher, Wylie, 206, 211

Tacky, 225

Talboys, 205

Taino-Arawak culture, 38-40

Tapia y Rivera, Alejandro, 46, 271, 272, 275

Taylor, Charles Edwin, 326

Taylor, John, 77

Technology: and conquest, 44; and exploration, 30; and market systems, 161-62; and slavery, 127

Tejera, Emiliano, 283-84

Thierry de Menonville, 127

Thomas, Dalby, 73-76

Thomas, J. J., 313-15, 320

Three-Fingered Jack, 228

Toussaint L'Overture, 194, 218, 229; historical images of, 258, 259; and Wordsworth, 206

Trembly, J., 127

Trinidad Peoples' National Movement, 15

Troeltsch, Ernst, 20

Troya y Quesada, Silvestre de, 58

Trujillo, 291

Turgot, 209, 210

Turnbull, David, 109

Underhill, Dr. B., 198

United States in Hispanic Antillean literature, 305-7

Ureña, Max Henriquez, 59, 282

Ureña, Salome, 282

Uroyoan, 220

Urrutia y Montoya, Ignacio José de, 287
Utopianism, use by planters, 168-69
Utopian literature, 83-87

Valdes Dominguez, 291
Valdéz, Antonio José, 287
Valle Atiles, del, 269, 271
Varela, 144, 149, 290; persecution of, 165; on race, 155; racism in, 156
Vargas, Diego de Torres, 70, 91
Varona, Enrique José, 291
Vastey, Baron De, 218, 254-56, 259
Vega, Garcilaso de la, 33-34, 45, 255
Velasco, López de, 44
Verteuil, Sir Louis De, 198, 309-10
Viefville de Essars, 212
Villaurrutia, 292
Villaverde, Juan de 156, 235
Virgin Islands, Jews in, 77
Vitier, Medardo, 155
Vitoria, Francisco de, 44-46; on Indians, 52, 54
Vodun, 19, 188-97; Catholicism in, 189; in Haitian national character, 326; and Haitian nationalism, 260-61; in Santo Domingo, 284; and slave rebellion, 225
Voltaire, 209-10, 245

Waddell, Rev. Hope Masterton, 205
Warburton, Bishop, 202
Wesley, John, 199
Weuves, P., 130
Whistler, Henry, 61, 67
Wilberforce, William, 116, 119, 245; on factory workers, 123
Williams, Eric, 3, 25, 72, 95-96, 199; on amelioration, 118; on slave legislation, 116
Williamson, H., 118
Wimpffen, Baron de, 7; on racism, 128; on Saint Domingue society, 125-26
Wingate, Orde, 36-37
Wittkower, R., 191
Woodcock, H. J., 309
Wray, Rev. W., 205
Wynter, Sylvia, 189

Young, Sir William, 103-5, 107, 163

Zambrana, 157, 234-35, 291
Zaragoza, Justo, 291
Zarate, Agustin de, 36
Zarragoitia y Jáuregui, Ignacio, 167
Zavala, Iris, 268, 271
Zayas, Alfredo, 158, 288